This false-colour composite image was recorded in June. Glasgow and Edinburgh and other settlements in the Forth–Clyde Valley are clearly visible in blue. The bright red areas are fields of healthy crops. Imagery such as this is used to police EU agricultural subsidies. *(EROS)*

Beatrice Johnston

Beatrice Johnston

MODERN SCHOOL ATLAS

95TH EDITION

IN ASSOCIATION WITH
THE ROYAL GEOGRAPHICAL SOCIETY
WITH THE INSTITUTE OF BRITISH GEOGRAPHERS

CONTENTS

SUBJECT LIST AND MAP SYMBOLS 3
SCALE, LATITUDE AND LONGITUDE 4
MAP PROJECTIONS 5

REMOTE SENSING 6–16

SATELLITE IMAGERY AND REMOTE SENSING
  INTRODUCTION 6–7
COLOUR COMPOSITES 8
VEGETATION AND LANDFORMS 9
GLOBAL MONITORING 10–11
ENVIRONMENTAL MONITORING 12–13
GEOLOGICAL INTERPRETATION 14
SYNTHETIC APERTURE RADAR 15
DIGITAL ELEVATION MODELS AND LAND USE 16

BRITISH ISLES 17–48

NORTHERN SCOTLAND 18–19
SOUTHERN SCOTLAND 20–21
NORTHERN ENGLAND 22–23
SOUTH AND SOUTH-EAST ENGLAND 24–25
WALES AND SOUTH-WEST ENGLAND 26–27
IRELAND – NORTH 28–29
IRELAND – SOUTH 30–31
BRITISH ISLES GEOLOGY 32
BRITISH ISLES RELIEF OF LAND 33
BRITISH ISLES CLIMATE 34–35
BRITISH ISLES WATER RESOURCES 36
BRITISH ISLES ENVIRONMENT, CONSERVATION AND POLLUTION 37
BRITISH ISLES AGRICULTURE AND FISHING 38–39
BRITISH ISLES INDUSTRY AND EMPLOYMENT 40
BRITISH ISLES ENERGY 41
BRITISH ISLES TRANSPORT 42
BRITISH ISLES TRADE AND TOURISM 43
BRITISH ISLES COUNTIES AND REGIONS 44–45
BRITISH ISLES POPULATION TRENDS 46–47
BRITISH ISLES STANDARDS OF LIVING 48

THE WORLD 49–122

THE WORLD RELIEF OF LAND 50–51
THE WORLD COUNTRIES 52–53
ARCTIC OCEAN AND ANTARCTICA 54–55
EUROPE RELIEF OF LAND 56
EUROPE COUNTRIES 57
EUROPE POPULATION 58
EUROPE ECONOMIC 59
EUROPEAN UNION 60–61
EUROPE CLIMATE AND NATURAL VEGETATION 62
SCANDINAVIA AND THE BALTIC LANDS 63
BRITISH ISLES 64
BENELUX AND THE RUHR 65
CENTRAL EUROPE 66–67
FRANCE 68
SPAIN AND PORTUGAL 69
ITALY AND THE BALKAN STATES 70–71
EASTERN EUROPE AND TURKEY 72–73
ASIA RELIEF OF LAND 74
ASIA COUNTRIES 75

ASIA POPULATION AND WEALTH 76
ASIA ECONOMIC 77
ASIA CLIMATE AND NATURAL VEGETATION 78
RUSSIA AND CENTRAL ASIA 79
CHINA AND THE FAR EAST 80–81
JAPAN 82
SOUTH-EAST ASIA 83
SOUTH ASIA 84–85
THE MIDDLE EAST 86–87
ARABIA AND THE HORN OF AFRICA 88
AFRICA CLIMATE AND NATURAL VEGETATION 89
AFRICA RELIEF OF LAND 90
AFRICA COUNTRIES 91
AFRICA POPULATION AND WEALTH 92
AFRICA ECONOMIC 93
NORTHERN AFRICA 94–95
CENTRAL AND SOUTHERN AFRICA 96–97
AUSTRALIA AND OCEANIA 98–99
OCEANIA CLIMATE AND NATURAL VEGETATION 100
OCEANIA POPULATION AND ECONOMIC 101
PACIFIC OCEAN 102–103
NORTH AMERICA RELIEF OF LAND AND CLIMATE 104
NORTH AMERICA COUNTRIES, CLIMATE AND NATURAL VEGETATION 105
NORTH AMERICA POPULATION AND WEALTH 106
NORTH AMERICA ECONOMIC 107
CANADA 108–109
UNITED STATES 110–111
NORTH-EAST UNITED STATES AND THE ST LAWRENCE 112–113
MEXICO, CENTRAL AMERICA AND THE CARIBBEAN 114–115
SOUTH AMERICA RELIEF OF LAND 116
SOUTH AMERICA CLIMATE AND NATURAL VEGETATION 117
SOUTH AMERICA POPULATION AND WEALTH 118
SOUTH AMERICA ECONOMIC 119
SOUTH AMERICA 120–121
SOUTH-EASTERN BRAZIL 122

WORLD THEMES 123–160

THE WORLD GEOLOGY, VOLCANOES AND EARTHQUAKES 124–125
THE WORLD TEMPERATURE AND OCEAN CURRENTS 126
THE WORLD PRESSURE, WINDS AND PRECIPITATION 127
THE WORLD CLIMATE 128–129
THE WORLD CLIMATE STATISTICS 130–131
THE WORLD NATURAL VEGETATION 132–133
THE WORLD ENVIRONMENTAL CONCERNS 134–135
THE WORLD AGRICULTURE 136–137
THE WORLD ENERGY AND MINERALS 138–139
THE WORLD INDUSTRY AND TRADE 140–141
THE WORLD TRAVEL AND TOURISM 142–143
THE WORLD STANDARDS OF LIVING 144–145
THE WORLD POPULATION DISTRIBUTION 146–147
THE WORLD POPULATION TRENDS 148–149
THE WORLD LANGUAGES AND RELIGIONS 150
THE WORLD INTERNATIONAL ORGANIZATIONS 151
THE WORLD HUMAN CONCERNS 152–153
THE WORLD SOCIAL AND ECONOMIC STATISTICS 154–159
THE WORLD PHYSICAL DIMENSIONS 160

INDEX 161–184

Published in Great Britain in 2006 by Philip's, a division of Octopus Publishing Group Limited, 2–4 Heron Quays, London E14 4JP

Cartography by Philip's
Ninety-fifth edition

Copyright © 2006 Philip's
Reprinted 2007

PAPERBACK EDITION
ISBN-13 978–0–540–08746–4
ISBN-10 0–540–08746–7

HARDBACK EDITION
ISBN-13 978–0–540–08745–7
ISBN-10 0–540–08745–9

Details of other Philip's titles and services can be found on our website at:
www.philips-maps.co.uk

Printed in Hong Kong

Philip's World Atlases are published in association with The Royal Geographical Society (with The Institute of British Geographers).

  The Society was founded in 1830 and given a Royal Charter in 1859 for 'the advancement of geographical science'. Today it is a leading world centre for geographical learning – supporting education, teaching, research and expeditions, and promoting public understanding of the subject.

  Further information about the Society and how to join may be found on its website at: **www.rgs.org**

PHOTOGRAPHIC ACKNOWLEDGEMENTS
All satellite images in the atlas are courtesy of NPA Group, Edenbridge, Kent (www.satmaps.com), with the exception of the following: p. 17 M-SAT Ltd/Science Photo Library; p. 49 PLI/Science Photo Library; p. 134 NASA/GSFC.

SUBJECT LIST

Acid rain	37
Agriculture	38–9, 136–7, 140
Aid (international)	92, 152
AIDS and HIV	153
Air travel	42, 61, 142
Alternative energy	139
Assisted areas	40
Carbon dioxide emissions	37, 134
Child mortality	149
Climate regions	128
Climate statistics	35, 130–1
Coal/oil/gas	138
Conservation	37
Continental drift	124
Conflicts	153
Debt	92, 152
Deforestation	135
Desertification	135
Drugs	153
Earthquakes	125
Education	48, 61, 145
Electricity	41, 139
El Niño	129
Employment	39, 40, 140
Energy	41, 138
Ethnic groups	47
European Union	60–1
Exports	141
Family size	149
Famine	135
Fishing	39, 136–7
Flood risk	36
Food production	38, 136–7
Foot-and-mouth disease	38
Forestry	37, 39, 137
Fuel	41, 138
Gender development index (GDI)	145
Geology	32, 124
Global warming	134–135
Greenhouse effect	37, 134
Gross domestic product (GDP)	144
Health care	48, 61, 145
Human development index (HDI)	144
Hydroelectricity	139
Illiteracy	145
Industry	40, 61, 140
Internet	141
Languages	58, 150
Latitude and longitude	4
Life expectancy	149
Literacy	145
Manufacturing	40, 140–1
Map projections	5
Migration	47, 152
Monsoon	128
Multinational corporations	141
National parks	37
Natural vegetation	37, 132–3
North Sea fishing	137
Nuclear power	139
Ocean currents	126
Ozone layer	37, 134
Plate tectonics	124–5
Population change	47, 146, 148
Population density	46, 146–8
Population pyramids	47, 146
Precipitation	34, 127
Rainfall	35, 130–1, 135
Refugees	152
Religions	150
Remote sensing	6–16
Renewable energy	41, 139
Research and development	140
Satellite imagery	6–16
Scale	4
Sea-level changes	134
Services	40, 140
Soils	132–3
Standards of living	48, 144
Telecommunications	141
Temperature	35, 126, 135
Time zones	142
Tourism	43, 113, 143
Trade	43, 141
Transport	42, 61
Travel	42–3, 142
Unemployment	40, 61
United Nations	151
Urban population	148
Volcanoes	125
Water pollution	36
Water supply	36, 144
Wealth	48, 61, 144
Wind power	139
Windchill effect	129
World Heritage Sites	37, 143

MAP SYMBOLS

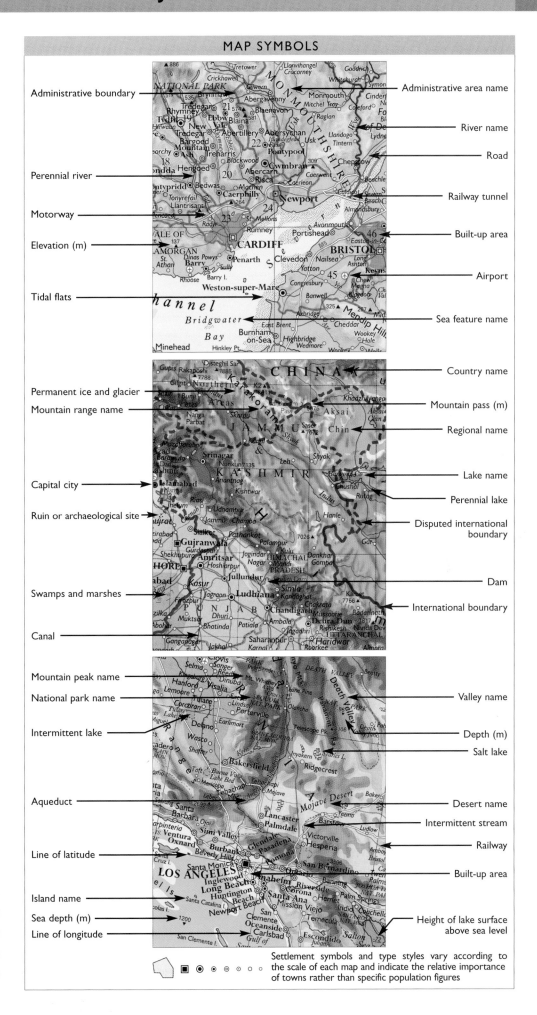

Administrative boundary — Administrative area name
— River name
— Road
Perennial river — — Railway tunnel
Motorway — — Built-up area
Elevation (m) — — Airport
Tidal flats — — Sea feature name

Permanent ice and glacier — — Country name
Mountain range name — — Mountain pass (m)
— Regional name
Capital city — — Lake name
— Perennial lake
Ruin or archaeological site — — Disputed international boundary
Swamps and marshes — — Dam
Canal — — International boundary

Mountain peak name —
National park name — — Valley name
Intermittent lake — — Depth (m)
— Salt lake
Aqueduct — — Desert name
— Intermittent stream
— Railway
Line of latitude —
— Built-up area
Island name —
Sea depth (m) — — Height of lake surface above sea level
Line of longitude —

Settlement symbols and type styles vary according to the scale of each map and indicate the relative importance of towns rather than specific population figures

SCALE

The scale of a map is the relationship of the distance between two points shown on the map and the distance between the same two points on the Earth's surface. For instance, 1 inch on the map represents 1 mile on the ground, or 10 kilometres on the ground is represented by 1 centimetre on the map.

Instead of saying 1 centimetre represents 10 kilometres, we could say that 1 centimetre represents 1 000 000 centimetres on the map. If the scale is stated so that the same unit of measurement is used on both the map and the ground, then the proportion will hold for any unit of measurement. Therefore, the scale is usually written 1:1 000 000. This is called a 'representative fraction' and usually appears at the top of the map page, above the scale bar.

Calculations can easily be made in centimetres and kilometres by dividing the second figure in the representative fraction by 100 000 (i.e. by deleting the last five zeros). Thus at a scale of 1:5 000 000, 1 cm on the map represents 50 km on the ground. This is called a 'scale statement'. The calculation for inches and miles is more laborious, but 1 000 000 divided by 63 360 (the number of inches in a mile) shows that 1:1 000 000 can be stated as 1 inch on the map represents approximately 16 miles on the ground.

Many of the maps in this atlas feature a scale bar. This is a bar divided into the units of the map – miles and kilometres – so that a map distance can be measured with a ruler, dividers or a piece of paper, then placed along the scale bar, and the distance read off. To the left of the zero on the scale bar there are usually more divisions. By placing the ruler or dividers on the nearest rounded figure to the right of the zero, the smaller units can be counted off to the left.

The map extracts to the right show Los Angeles and its surrounding area at six different scales. The representative fraction, scale statement and scale bar are positioned above each map. Map 1 is at 1:27 000 and is the largest scale extract shown. Many of the individual buildings are identified and most of the streets are named, but at this scale only part of central Los Angeles can be shown within the given area. Map 2 is much smaller in scale at 1:250 000. Only a few important buildings and streets can be named, but the whole of central Los Angeles is shown. Maps 3, 4 and 5 show how greater areas can be depicted as the map scale decreases, down to Map 6 at 1:35 000 000. At this small scale, the entire Los Angeles conurbation is depicted by a single town symbol and a large part of the south-western USA and part of Mexico is shown.

The scales of maps must be used with care since large distances on small-scale maps can be represented by one or two centimetres. On certain projections scale is only correct along certain lines, parallels or meridians. As a general rule, the larger the map scale, the more accurate and reliable will be the distance measured.

LATITUDE AND LONGITUDE

Accurate positioning of individual points on the Earth's surface is made possible by reference to the geometric system of latitude and longitude.

Latitude is the distance of a point north or south of the Equator measured at an angle with the centre of the Earth, whereby the Equator is latitude 0 degrees,

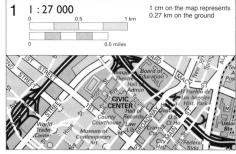

1 | 1 : 27 000 — 1 cm on the map represents 0.27 km on the ground

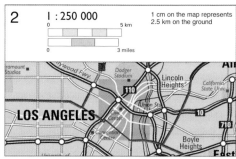

2 | 1 : 250 000 — 1 cm on the map represents 2.5 km on the ground

LOS ANGELES

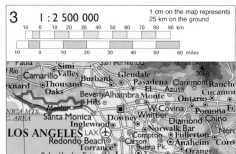

3 | 1 : 2 500 000 — 1 cm on the map represents 25 km on the ground

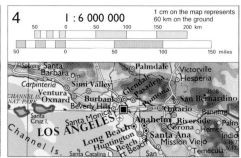

4 | 1 : 6 000 000 — 1 cm on the map represents 60 km on the ground

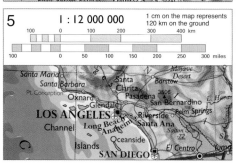

5 | 1 : 12 000 000 — 1 cm on the map represents 120 km on the ground

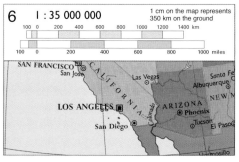

6 | 1 : 35 000 000 — 1 cm on the map represents 350 km on the ground

the North Pole is 90 degrees north and the South Pole 90 degrees south. Latitude parallels are drawn west–east around the Earth, parallel to the Equator, decreasing in diameter from the Equator until they become a point at the poles. On the maps in this atlas the lines of latitude are represented by blue lines running across the map in smooth curves, with the degree figures in blue at the sides of the maps. The degree interval depends on the scale of the map.

Lines of longitude are meridians drawn north–south, cutting the lines of latitude at right angles on the Earth's surface and intersecting with one another at the poles. Longitude is measured by an angle at the centre of the Earth from the prime meridian (0 degrees), which passes through Greenwich in London. It is given as a measurement east or west of the Greenwich Meridian from 0 to 180 degrees. The meridians are normally drawn north–south vertically down the map, with the degree figures

in blue in the top and bottom margins of the map.

In the index each place name is followed by its latitude and longitude, and then its map page number and letter-figure grid reference. The unit of measurement is the degree, which is subdivided into 60 minutes. An index entry states the position of a place in degrees and minutes. The latitude is followed by N(orth) or S(outh) and the longitude E(ast) or W(est).

For example:
Helston, U.K.　　　　50°7N 5°17W　　**27** G3
Helston is 50 degrees 7 minutes north of the Equator and 5 degrees 17 minutes west of Greenwich, and is on map page 27, in grid square G3.

McKinley, Mt., U.S.A.　　63°4N 151°0W　**108** C4
Mount McKinley is 63 degrees 4 minutes north of the Equator and 151 degrees west of Greenwich, and is on map page 108, in grid square C4.

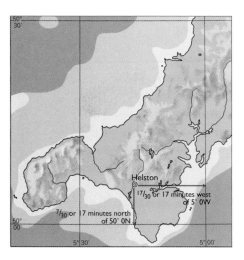

Helston
17/30 or 17 minutes west of 5° 0W
7/30 or 17 minutes north of 50° 0N

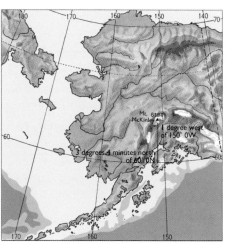

Mt. McKinley
1 degree west of 150° 0W
3 degrees 4 minutes north of 60° 0N

How to locate a place or feature
The two diagrams (*left*) show how to estimate the required distance from the nearest line of latitude or longitude on the map page, in order to locate a place or feature listed in the index (such as Helston in the UK and Mount McKinley in the USA, as detailed in the above example).

In the left-hand diagram there are 30 minutes between the lines and so to find the position of Helston an estimate has to be made: 7 parts of the 30 degrees north of the 50 0N latitude line, and 17 parts of the 30 degrees west of the 5 0W longitude line.

In the right-hand diagram it is more difficult to estimate because there is an interval of 10 degrees between the lines. In the example of Mount McKinley, the reader has to estimate 3 degrees 4 minutes north of 60 0N and 1 degree west of 150 0W.

MAP PROJECTIONS

A map projection is the systematic depiction of the imaginary grid of lines of latitude and longitude from a globe on to a flat surface. The grid of lines is called the 'graticule' and it can be constructed either by graphical means or by mathematical formulae to form the basis of a map. As a globe is three dimensional, it is not possible to depict its surface on a flat map without some form of distortion. Preservation of one of the basic properties listed below can only be secured at the expense of the others and thus the choice of projection is often a compromise solution.

Correct area

In these projections the areas from the globe are to scale on the map. This is particularly useful in the mapping of densities and distributions. Projections with this property are termed 'equal area', 'equivalent' or 'homolographic'.

Correct distance

In these projections the scale is correct along the meridians, or, in the case of the 'azimuthal equidistant', scale is true along any line drawn from the centre of the projection. They are called 'equidistant'.

Correct shape

This property can only be true within small areas as it is achieved only by having a uniform scale distortion along both the 'x' and 'y' axes of the projection. The projections are called 'conformal' or 'orthomorphic'.

Map projections can be divided into three broad categories – **'azimuthal'**, **'conic'** and **'cylindrical'**. Cartographers use different projections from these categories depending on the map scale, the size of the area to be mapped, and what they want the map to show.

AZIMUTHAL OR ZENITHAL PROJECTIONS

These are constructed by the projection of part of the graticule from the globe on to a plane tangential to any single point on it. This plane may be tangential to the equator (equatorial case), the poles (polar case) or any other point (oblique case). Any straight line drawn from the point at which the plane touches the globe is the shortest distance from that point and is known as a 'great circle'. In its 'gnomonic' construction any straight line on the map is a great circle, but there is great exaggeration towards the edges and this reduces its general uses. There are five different ways of transferring the graticule on to the plane and these are shown below. The diagrams below also show how the graticules vary, using the polar case as the example.

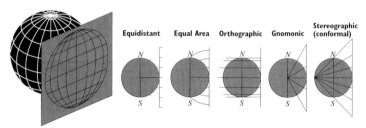

| Equidistant | Equal Area | Orthographic | Gnomonic | Stereographic (conformal) |

Polar case

The polar case is the simplest to construct and the diagram on the right shows the differing effects of all five methods of construction, comparing their coverage, distortion, etc, using North America as the example.

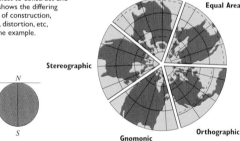

Equidistant, Equal Area, Stereographic, Gnomonic, Orthographic

Oblique case

The plane touches the globe at any point between the Equator and poles. The oblique orthographic uses the distortion in azimuthal projections away from the centre to give a graphic depiction of the Earth as seen from any desired point in space.

Equatorial case

The example shown here is Lambert's Equivalent Azimuthal. It is the only projection which is both equal area and where bearing is true from the centre.

CONICAL PROJECTIONS

These use the projection of the graticule from the globe on to a cone which is tangential to a line of latitude (termed the 'standard parallel'). This line is always an arc and scale is always true along it. Because of its method of construction, it is used mainly for depicting the temperate latitudes around the standard parallel, i.e. where there is least distortion. To reduce the distortion and include a larger range of latitudes, the projection may be constructed with the cone bisecting the surface of the globe so that there are two standard parallels, each of which is true to scale. The distortion is thus spread more evenly between the two chosen parallels.

Simple Conical with one standard parallel

Bonne

This is a modification of the simple conic, whereby the true scale along the meridians is sacrificed to enable the accurate representation of areas. However, scale is true along each parallel but shapes are distorted at the edges.

Albers Conical Equal Area

This projection uses two standard parallels. The selection of these relative to the land area to be mapped is very important. It is equal area and is especially useful for large land masses oriented east–west, such as the USA.

CYLINDRICAL AND OTHER WORLD PROJECTIONS

This group of projections are those which permit the whole of the Earth's surface to be depicted on one map. They are a very large group of projections and the following are only a few of them. Cylindrical projections are constructed by the projection of the graticule from the globe on to a cylinder tangential to the globe. Although cylindrical projections can depict all the main land masses, there is considerable distortion of shape and area towards the poles. One cylindrical projection, Mercator, overcomes this shortcoming by possessing the unique navigational property that any straight line drawn on it is a line of constant bearing ('loxodrome'). It is used for maps and charts between 15° either side of the Equator. Beyond this, enlargement of area is a serious drawback, although it is used for navigational charts at all latitudes.

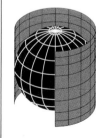

Mercator

Simple Cylindrical

Eckert IV (pseudo-cylindrical equal area)

Cylindrical with two standard parallels

Hammer (polyconic equal area)

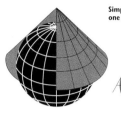

The first satellite to monitor our environment systematically was launched as long ago as April 1961. It was called TIROS-1 and was designed specifically to record atmospheric change. The first of the generation of Earth resources satellites was Landsat-1, launched in July 1972.

The succeeding decades have seen a revolution in our ability to survey and map our global environment. Digital sensors mounted on satellites now scan vast areas of the Earth's surface day and night. They collect and relay back to Earth huge volumes of geographical data which is processed and stored by computers.

Satellite imagery and remote sensing

Continuous development and refinement, and freedom from national access restrictions, have meant that sensors on these satellite platforms are increasingly replacing surface and airborne data-gathering techniques. Twenty-four hours a day, satellites are scanning and measuring the Earth's surface and atmosphere, adding to an ever-expanding range of geographic and geophysical data available to help us identify and manage the problems of our human and physical environments. Remote sensing is the science of extracting information from such images.

Satellite orbits

Most Earth-observation satellites (such as the Landsat, SPOT and IRS series) are in a near-polar, Sun-synchronous orbit (*see diagram opposite*). At altitudes of around 700–900 km the satellites revolve around the Earth approximately every 100 minutes and on each orbit cross a particular line of latitude at the same local (solar) time. This ensures that the satellite can obtain coverage of most of the globe, replicating the coverage typically within 2–3 weeks. In more recent satellites, sensors can be pointed sideways from the orbital path, and 'revisit' times with high-resolution frames can thus be reduced to a few days.

Exceptions to these Sun-synchronous orbits include the geostationary meteorological satellites, such as Meteosat. These have a 36,000 km high orbit and rotate around the Earth every 24 hours, thus remaining above the same point on the Equator.

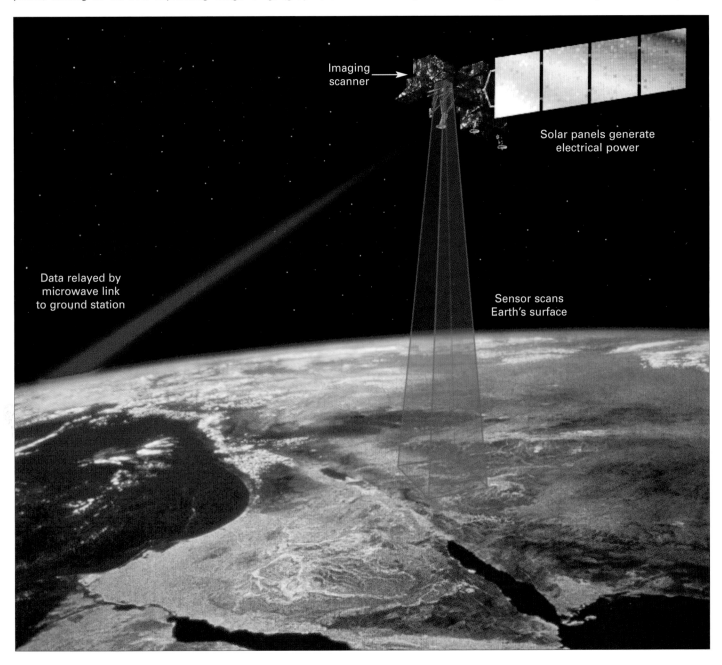

Imaging scanner

Solar panels generate electrical power

Data relayed by microwave link to ground station

Sensor scans Earth's surface

Landsat-7
This is the latest addition to the Landsat Earth-observation satellite programme, orbiting at 705 km above the Earth. With onboard recorders, the satellite can store data until it passes within range of a ground station. Basic geometric and radiometric corrections are then applied before distribution of the imagery to users.

These satellites acquire frequent images showing cloud and atmospheric moisture movements for almost a full hemisphere.

In addition, there is the Global Positioning System (GPS) satellite 'constellation', which orbits at a height of 20,200 km, consisting of 24 satellites. These circle the Earth in six different orbital planes, enabling us to fix our position on the Earth's surface to an accuracy of a few centimetres. Although developed for military use, this system is now available to individuals through hand-held receivers and in-car navigation systems. The other principal commercial uses are for surveying and air and sea navigation.

Digital sensors

Early satellite designs involved images being exposed to photographic film and returned to Earth by capsule for processing, a technique still sometimes used today. However, even the first commercial satellite imagery, from Landsat-1, used digital imaging sensors and transmitted the data back to ground stations (*see diagram opposite*).

Passive, or optical, sensors record the radiation reflected from the Earth for specific wavebands. Active sensors transmit their own microwave radiation, which is reflected from the Earth's surface back to the satellite and recorded. The SAR (Synthetic Aperture Radar) Radarsat images on page 15 are examples of the latter.

Whichever scanning method is used, each satellite records image data of constant width but potentially several thousand kilometres in length. Once the data has been received on Earth, it is usually split into approximately square sections or 'scenes' for distribution.

Spectral resolution, wavebands and false-colour composites

Satellites can record data from many sections of the electromagnetic spectrum (wavebands) simultaneously. Since we can only see images made from the three primary colours (red, green and blue), a selection of any three wavebands needs to be made in order to form a picture that will enable visual interpretation of the scene to be made. When any combination other than the visible bands are used, such as near or middle infrared, the resulting image is termed a 'false-colour composite'. An example of this is shown on page 8.

The selection of these wavebands depends on the purpose of the final image – geology, hydrology, agronomy and environmental requirements each have their own optimum waveband combinations.

GEOGRAPHIC INFORMATION SYSTEMS

A Geographic Information System (GIS) enables any available geospatial data to be compiled, presented and analysed using specialized computer software.

Many aspects of our lives now benefit from the use of GIS – from the management and maintenance of the networks of pipelines and cables that supply our homes, to the exploitation or protection of the natural resources that we use. Much of this is at a regional or national scale and the data collected from satellites form an important part of our interpretation and understanding of the world around us.

GIS systems are used for many aspects of central planning and modern life, such as defence, land use, reclamation, telecommunications and the deployment of emergency services. Commercial companies can use demographic and infrastructure data within a GIS to plan marketing strategies, identifying where their services would be most needed, and thus decide where best to locate their businesses. Insurance companies use GIS to determine premiums based on population distribution, crime figures and the likelihood of natural disasters, such as flooding or subsidence.

Whatever the application, all the geographically related information that is available can be input and prepared in a GIS, so that a user can display the specific information of interest, or combine data to produce further information which might answer or help resolve a specific problem. From analysis of the data that has been acquired, it is often possible to use a GIS to generate a 'model' of possible future situations and to see what impact might result from decisions and actions taken. A GIS can also monitor change over time, to aid the observation and interpretation of long-term change.

A GIS can utilize a satellite image to extract useful information and map large areas, which would otherwise take many man-years of labour to achieve on the ground. For industrial applications, including hydrocarbon and mineral exploration, forestry, agriculture, environmental monitoring and urban development, such dramatic and beneficial increases in efficiency have made it possible to evaluate and undertake projects and studies in parts of the world that were previously considered inaccessible, and on a scale that would not have been possible before.

SELECTED REMOTE SENSING SATELLITES			
Year Launched	**Satellite**	**Country**	**Pixel Size (Resolution)**
Passive Sensors (Optical)			
1972	Landsat-1 MSS	USA	80 m
1975	Landsat-2 MSS	USA	80 m
1978	Landsat-3 MSS	USA	80 m
1978	NOAA AVHRR	USA	1.1 km
1981	Cosmos TK-350	Russia	10 m
1982	Landsat-4 TM	USA	30 m
1984	Landsat-5 TM	USA	30 m
1986	SPOT-1	France	10 / 20 m
1988	IRS-1A	India	36 / 72 m
1988	SPOT-2	France	10 / 20 m
1989	Cosmos KVR-1000	Russia	2 m
1991	IRS-1B	India	36 / 72 m
1992	SPOT-3	France	10 / 20 m
1995	IRS-1C	India	5.8 / 23.5 m
1997	IRS-1D	India	5.8 / 23.5 m
1998	SPOT-4	France	10 / 20 m
1999	Landsat-7 ETM	USA	15 / 30 m
1999	UoSAT-12	UK	10 / 32 m
1999	IKONOS-2	USA	1.0 / 4 m
1999	ASTER	USA	15 m
2000	Hyperion	USA	30 m
2000	EROS-A1	International	1.8 m
2001	Quickbird	USA	0.61 / 2.4 m
2002	SPOT-5	France	2.5 / 5 / 10 m
2002	DMC AlSat-1	Algeria (UK)	32 m
2003	DMC UK	UK	32 m
2003	DMC NigeriaSat-1	Nigeria (UK)	32 m
2003	DMC BilSat	Turkey (UK)	32 m
2003	OrbView-3	USA	1.0 / 4 m
2004	Formosat-2	Taiwan	2.0 / 8 m
2004	KOMPSAT-2	South Korea	1.0 / 4 m
Active Sensors (Synthetic Aperture Radar)			
1991	ERS-1	Europe	25 m
1992	JERS-1	Japan	18 m
1995	ERS-2	Europe	25 m
1995	Radarsat	Canada	8–100 m
2002	ENVISAT	Europe	25 m

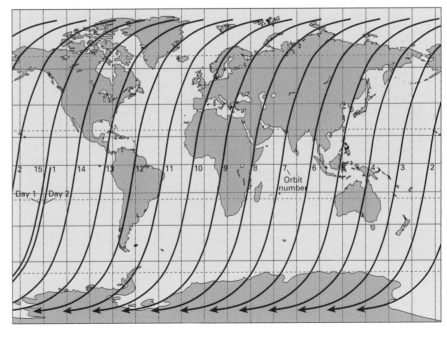

Satellite orbits
Landsat-7 makes over 14 orbits per day in its Sun-synchronous orbit. During the full 16 days of a repeat cycle, coverage of the areas between those shown is achieved.

Natural-colour and false-colour composites
These images show the salt ponds at the southern end of San Francisco Bay, which now form the San Francisco Bay National Wildlife Refuge. They demonstrate the difference between 'natural colour' (*top*) and 'false colour' (*bottom*) composites.

The top image is made from visible red, green and blue wavelengths. The colours correspond closely to those one would observe from an aircraft. The salt ponds appear green or orange-red due to the colour of the sediments they contain. The urban areas appear grey and vegetation is either dark green (trees) or light brown (dry grass).

The bottom image is made up of near-infrared, visible red and visible green wavelengths. These wavebands are represented here in red, green and blue, respectively. Since chlorophyll in healthy vegetation strongly reflects near-infrared light, this is clearly visible as red in the image.

False-colour composite imagery is therefore very sensitive to the presence of healthy vegetation. The bottom image thus shows better discrimination between the 'leafy' residential urban areas, such as Palo Alto (south-west of the Bay) from other urban areas by the 'redness' of the trees. The high chlorophyll content of watered urban grass areas shows as bright red, contrasting with the dark red of trees and the brown of natural, dry grass. *(EROS)*

Western Grand Canyon, Arizona, USA

This false-colour image shows in bright red the sparse vegetation on the limestone plateau, including sage, mesquite and grasses. Imagery such as this is used to monitor this and similar fragile environments. The sediment-laden river, shown as blue-green, can be seen dispersing into Lake Mead to the north-west. Side canyons cross the main canyon in straight lines, showing where erosion along weakened fault lines has occurred. *(EROS)*

Ayers Rock and Mt Olga, Northern Territory, Australia

These two huge outliers are the remnants of Precambrian mountain ranges created some 500 million years ago and then eroded away. Ayers Rock *(seen at right)* rises 345 m above the surrounding land and has been a part of Aboriginal life for over 10,000 years. Their dramatic coloration, caused by oxidized iron in the sandstone, attracts visitors from around the world. *(EROS)*

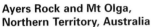

Mount St Helens, Washington, USA

A massive volcanic eruption on 18 May 1980 killed 60 people and devastated around 400 sq km of forest within minutes. The blast reduced the mountain peak by 400 m to its current height of 2,550 m, and volcanic ash rose some 25 km into the atmosphere. The image shows Mount St Helens eight years after the eruption in 1988. The characteristic volcanic cone has collapsed in the north, resulting in the devastating 'liquid' flow of mud and rock. *(EROS)*

Niger Delta, West Africa

The River Niger is the third longest river in Africa after the Nile and Congo. Deltas are by nature constantly evolving sedimentary features and often contain many ecosystems within them. In the case of the Niger Delta, there are also vast hydrocarbon reserves beneath it with associated wells and pipelines. Satellite imagery helps to plan activity and monitor this fragile and changing environment. *(EROS)*

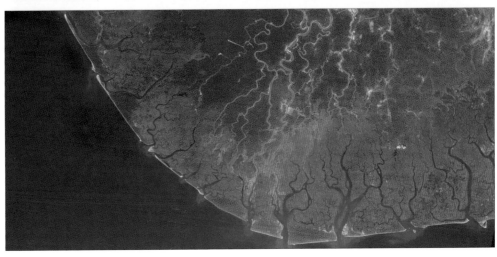

Europe at night

This image was derived as part of the Defense Meteorological Satellite Program. The sensor recorded all the emissions of near-infrared radiation at night, mainly the lights from cities, towns and villages. Note also the 'lights' in the North Sea from the flares of the oil production platforms. This project was the first systematic attempt to record human settlement on a global scale using remote sensing. *(NOAA)*

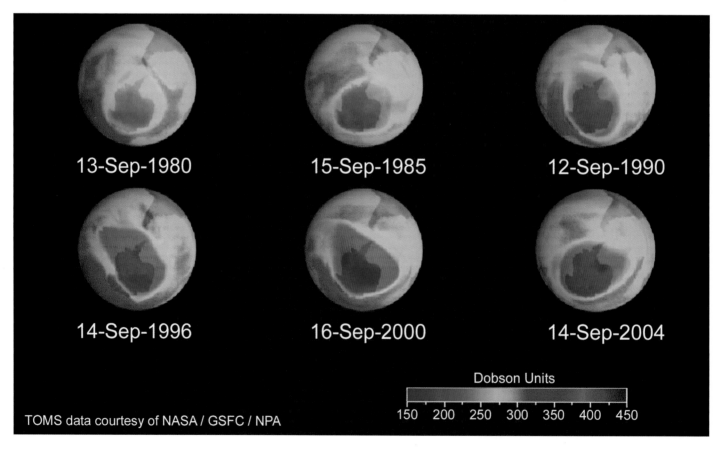

13-Sep-1980   15-Sep-1985   12-Sep-1990

14-Sep-1996   16-Sep-2000   14-Sep-2004

Dobson Units

150 200 250 300 350 400 450

TOMS data courtesy of NASA / GSFC / NPA

Antarctic ozone depletion

The Total Ozone Mapping Spectrometer (TOMS) instruments, first launched in 1978, can measure a range of atmospheric trace constituents, in particular global ozone distributions. Environmental and public health authorities need this up-to-date information to alert people to health risks. For example, low ozone levels result in increased UV-B radiation, which is harmful and can cause cancers, cataracts and impact the human immune system. 'Dobson Units' indicate the level of ozone depletion (normal levels are around 280DU).

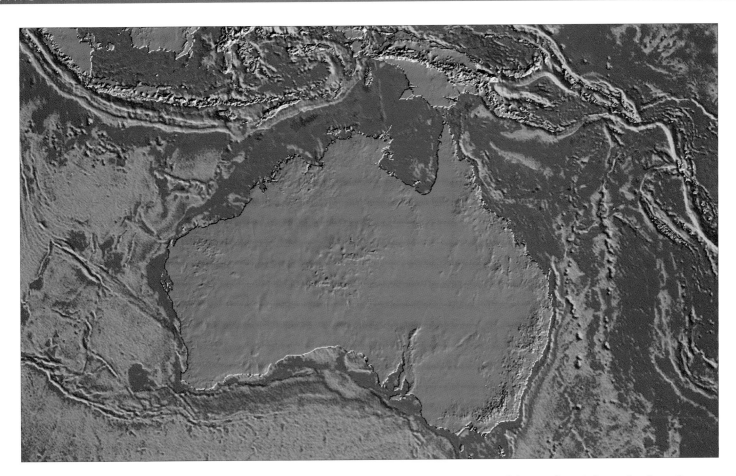

Gravitational fields

The strength of the Earth's gravitational field at its surface varies according to the ocean depth and the density of local rocks. This causes local variations in the sea level. Satellites orbiting in precisely determined orbits are able to measure the sea level to an accuracy of a few centimetres. These variations give us a better understanding of the geological structure of the sea floor. Information from these sensors can also be used to determine ocean wave heights, which relate to surface wind speed, and are therefore useful in meteorological forecasting. *(NPA)*

Weather monitoring

Geostationary and polar orbiting satellites monitor the Earth's cloud and atmospheric moisture movements, giving us an insight into the global workings of the atmosphere and permitting us to predict weather change.

Hurricane Katrina

Making landfall along the US Gulf coast on 29 August 2005, Hurricane Katrina became the most expensive natural disaster ever to strike the USA. Its path was tracked by images such as this. *(NASA/J. Schmaltz, MODIS Land Rapid Response Team)*

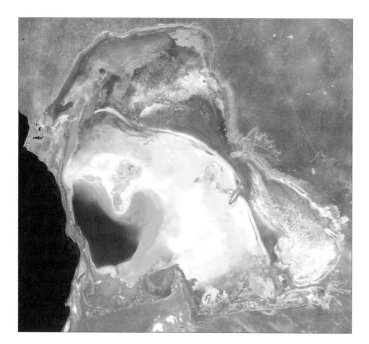

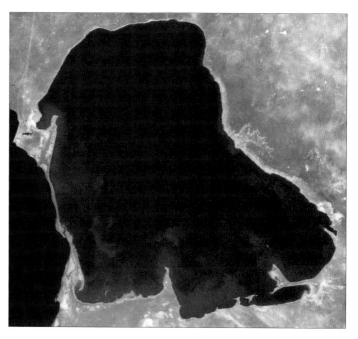

Kara-Bogaz-Gol, Turkmenistan

The Kara-Bogaz-Gol (*above, left and right*) is a large, shallow lagoon joined by a narrow, steep-sided strait to the Caspian Sea. Evaporation makes it one of the most saline bodies of water in the world. Believing the Caspian sea level was falling, the strait was dammed by the Soviet Union in 1980 with the intention of conserving the water to sustain the salt industry. However, by 1983 it had dried up completely (*above left*), leading to widespread wind-blown salt, soil poisoning and health problems downwind to the east. In 1992 the Turkmenistan government began to demolish the dam to re-establish the flow of water from the Caspian Sea (*above right*). Satellite imagery has helped to monitor and map the Kara-Bogaz-Gol as it has fluctuated in size. *(EROS)*

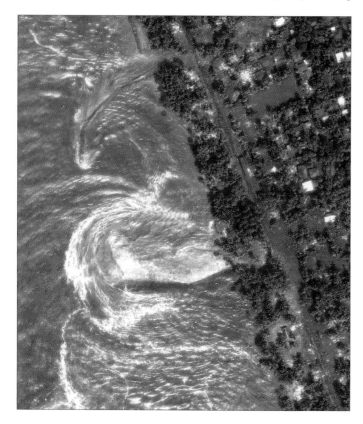

Southern Asia tsunami, Sri Lanka

The turbulent receding waters of the Southern Asia tsunami on 26 December 2004 can clearly be seen in this high-resolution imagery collected by the QuickBird satellite. The area shown here is the holiday resort of Kalutara on the west coast of Sri Lanka, to the south of Colombo. Such imagery enabled rescuers to assess the worst affected areas and direct the overstretched emergency services where most needed. *(DigitalGlobe)*

Lake Amadeus, Northern Territory, Australia

This saline lake system is an important wetland environment situated at the heart of one of the most arid areas in Australia. It supports a wide range of complex habitats and owes its existence to seepage from the central groundwater system. Changes in its extent in an otherwise remote site can be monitored using satellite imagery such as this Landsat ETM scene. *(EROS)*

New Orleans, Louisiana, USA
These two images show the area around the New Orleans Superdome before *(top)* and after *(below)* Hurricane Katrina struck in August 2005. In the lower image, damage to the dome roof can be clearly seen, and the darker areas surrounding the buildings are streets inundated by floodwaters. In the aftermath of the hurricane, satellite imagery played a key role in the assessment of the damage caused and the deployment of emergency services. *(DigitalGlobe)*

Larsen B ice shelf, Antarctica
Between January and March 2002, the 3,250 km^2 Larsen B ice shelf on the Antarctic Peninsula collapsed. The upper right-hand image shows its area in December 2001 before the collapse, while the lower image shows the area in December 2002 after the collapse. The 200 m thick ice sheet had been retreating before this date, but over 500 billion tonnes of ice collapsed in under a month. This was due to rising temperatures of 0.5°C per year in this part of Antarctica. Satellite imagery is the only way for scientists to monitor fragile environments, such as this, in inaccessible areas of the world.

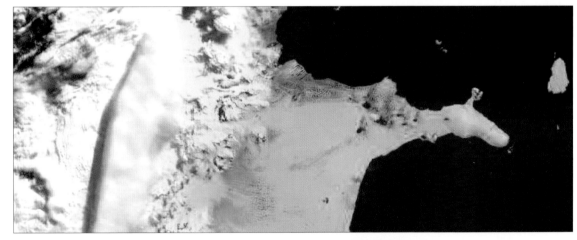

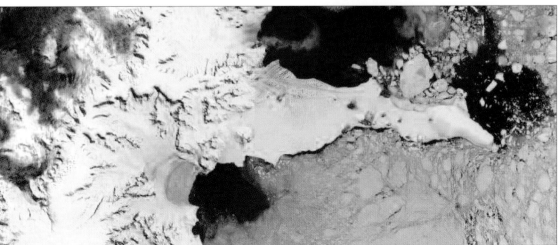

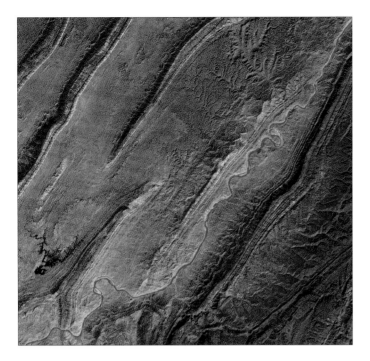

Sichuan Basin, China
The north-east/south-west trending ridges in this image are anticlinal folds developed in the Earth's crust as a result of plate collision and compression. Geologists map these folds and the lowlands between them formed by synclinal folds, as they are often the areas where oil or gas are found in commercial quantities. The river shown in this image is the Yangtze, near Chongqing. *(China RSGS)*

North Anatolian Fault, Turkey
The east–west trending valley running through the centre of this image is formed by the North Anatolian wrench fault. It is the result of Arabia colliding with southern Eurasia, forcing most of Turkey westwards towards Greece. The valley was created by the Kelkit river removing the loosened rock formed by the two tectonic plates grinding together. This active fault has also caused considerable damage further east in the Gulf of Izmit. *(EROS)*

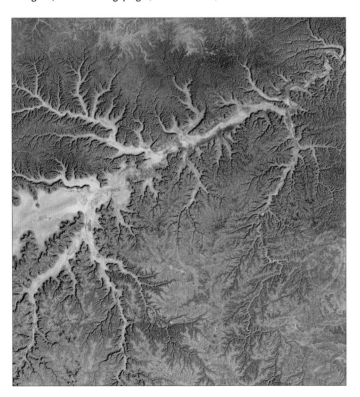

Wadi Hadhramaut, Yemen
Yemen is extremely arid – however, in the past it was more humid and wet, enabling large river systems to carve out the deep and spectacular gorges and dried-out river beds (*wadis*) seen in this image. The erosion has revealed many contrasting rock types. The image has been processed to exaggerate this effect, producing many shades of red, pink and purple, which make geological mapping easier and more cost-effective. *(EROS)*

Zagros Mountains, Iran
These mountains were formed as Arabia collided with Southern Eurasia. The upper half of this colour-enhanced image shows an anticline that runs east–west. The dark grey features are called *diapirs*, which are bodies of viscous rock salt that are very buoyant and sometimes rise to the surface, spilling and spreading out like a glacier. The presence of salt in the region is important as it stops oil escaping to the surface. *(EROS)*

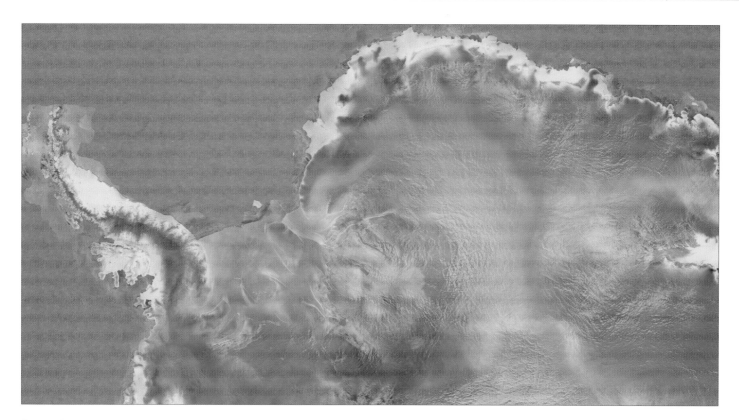

Antarctic Peninsula
Synthetic Aperture Radar (SAR) image brightness is dependent on surface texture. This image of part of Antarctica clearly shows the ice tongues projecting from the Wilkins and George VI Ice Shelves at the south-west end of the peninsula, as well as other coastal ice features. Images can be received, even during the winter 'night', and over a period of time form a valuable resource in our ability to monitor the recession of the ice. *(Radarsat)*

Montserrat, Caribbean Sea
SAR sensors send out a microwave signal and create an image from the radiation reflected back. The signal penetrates cloud cover and does not need any solar illumination. This image of Montserrat shows how the island can still be seen, despite clouds and the continuing eruption of the Soufrière volcano in the south. The delta visible in the sea to the east is being formed by lava flows pouring down the Tar River Valley. *(Radarsat)*

Las Vegas, Nevada, USA

Two satellite images viewing the same area of ground from different orbits can be used to compile a Digital Elevation Model (DEM) of the Earth's surface. A computer compares the images and calculates the ground surface elevation to a vertical precision of 8–15 m, preparing this for thousands of square kilometres in just a few minutes. Overlaying a colour satellite image on to a DEM produced the picture of Las Vegas shown here. (NPA)

London, United Kingdom

Lasers based on aircraft or satellites can be used to scan surface elevations to an accuracy of a few centimetres. This extract from a survey of the whole of London shows the City of London (from St Paul's Cathedral in the north-west to the Tower of London and Tower Bridge in the south-east. The very narrow and deep urban canyons and atriums in this area clearly demonstrate the advantages of airborne laser scanning (Lidar), which only requires a single line-of-sight to obtain precise measurements. A basic variant of this technology has been used for several years from satellites to acquire elevation profiles of the surface of Mars. Sensors capable of more detailed scanning are currently under development for Earth-orbiting satellites. (Precision Terrain Surveys Ltd – www.precisionterrain.com)

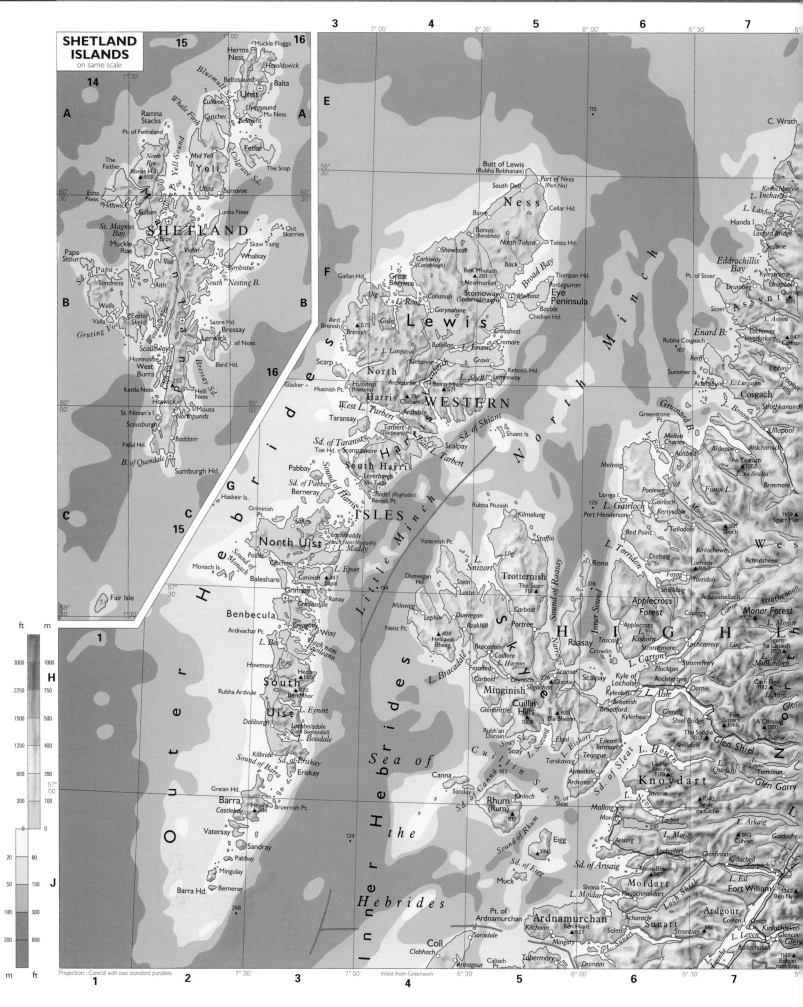

SHETLAND ISLANDS
on same scale

Projection : Conical with two standard parallels

West from Greenwich

ORKNEY ISLANDS on same scale

1: 1 000 000

COPYRIGHT PHILIP'S

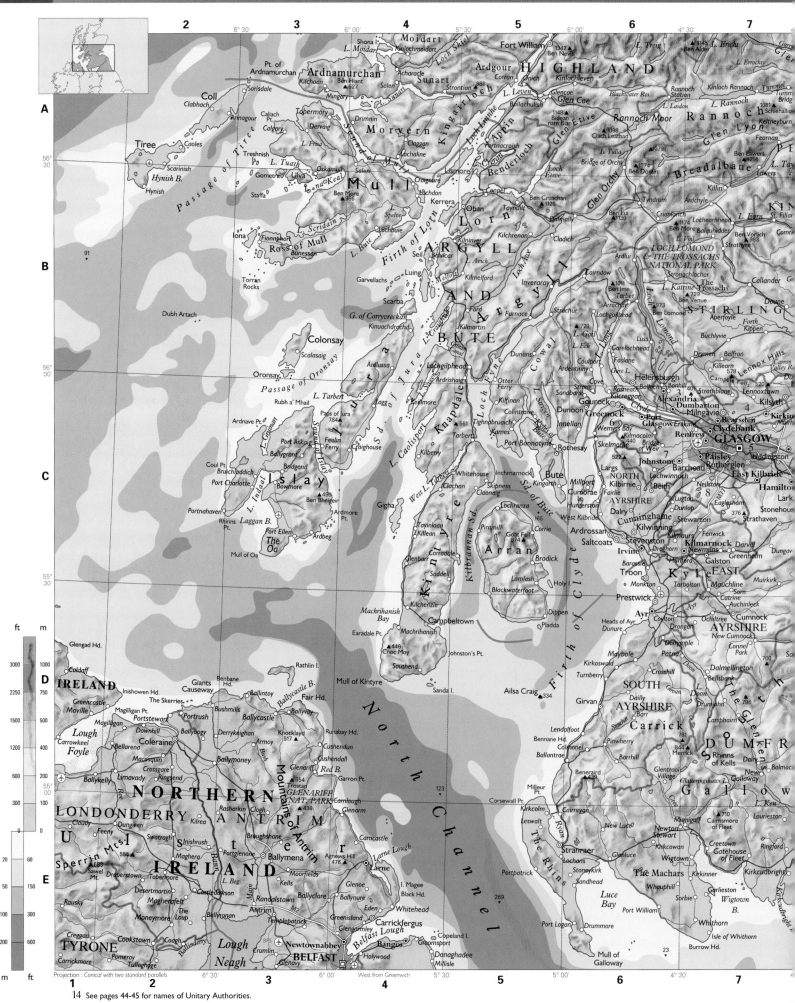

1:1 000 000

Projection : Conical with two standard parallels
West from Greenwich

20 See pages 44-45 for names of Unitary Authorities.

ft m

NOTTINGHAM
DERBY
LEICESTER
BIRMINGHAM
WEST MIDLANDS
WOLVERHAMPTON
COVENTRY
STAFFORDSHIRE
SHROPSHIRE
WORCESTERSHIRE
WARWICKSHIRE
HEREFORDSHIRE
POWYS
CARMARTHENSHIRE
GLOUCESTERSHIRE
OXFORDSHIRE
MONMOUTHSHIRE
CARDIFF
NEWPORT
BRISTOL
Bath
WILTSHIRE
WEST BERKSHIRE
Reading
Bristol Channel
Bridgwater Bay
SOMERSET
EXMOOR NATIONAL PARK
DEVON
Exeter
DORSET
HAMPSHIRE
SOUTHAMPTON
NEW FOREST NATIONAL PARK
BOURNEMOUTH
Poole
ISLE OF WIGHT
Lyme Bay
Salisbury Plain
Cotswold Hills
Mendip Hills
Black Mountains
Brecon Beacons
BRECON BEACONS NATIONAL PARK
Shrewsbury
Hereford
Gloucester
Cheltenham
Worcester
Swindon
Salisbury
Winchester
Weymouth
Swansea
Port Talbot

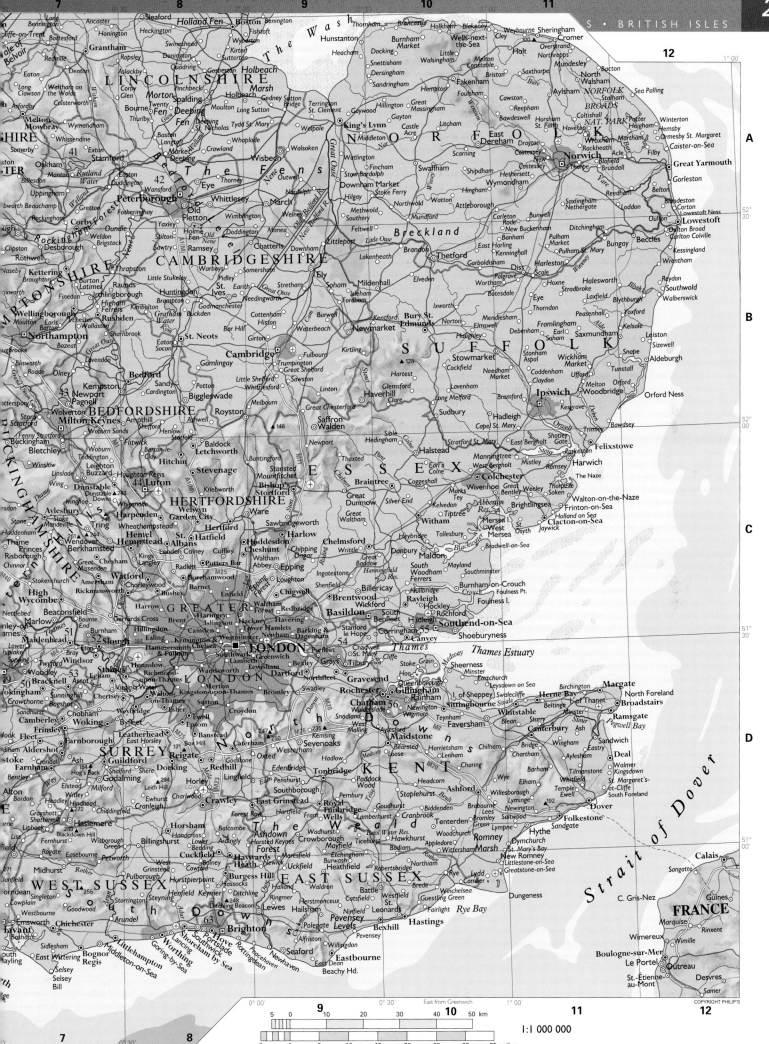

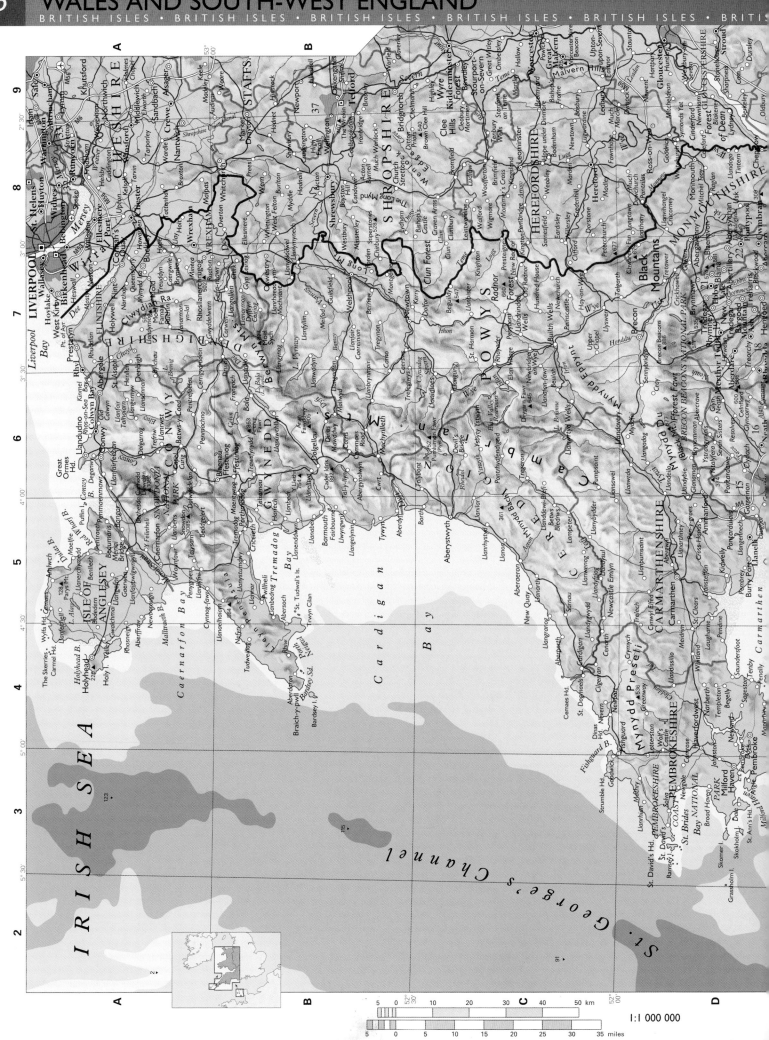

1:1 000 000

FRANCE

CHANNEL ISLANDS
on same scale

Alderney
St. Anne

Passage de la Déroute

Jersey
Trinity
St. Peter
St. Helier
Gorey
Rozel
St. Martin
la Rocque Pt.

Grosnez Pt.
St. Ouens Bay
St. Brelade

Guernsey
St. Sampson
St. Peter Port
Herm
Sark
St. Martin
Torteval

CHANNEL ISLANDS

COPYRIGHT PHILIPS

IS. OF SCILLY
on same scale

Isles of Scilly
Tresco
St. Martin's
Crow Sound
St. Mary's
St. Mary's Sd.
Hugh Town
St. Agnes

Gurnard's Hd.
Pendeen
C. Cornwall
St. Just
Sennen
Land's End
Wolf Rock
Penzance
Newlyn
St. Buryan
St. Levan

Bristol Channel

Gower
Swansea
Port Talbot
Mumbles
Porthcawl
Bridgend

CARDIFF
Newport
BRISTOL
Bath

SOMERSET
Weston-super-Mare
Bridgwater
Minehead
Taunton
Wellington

Exmoor
NATIONAL PARK

DEVON
Barnstaple
Bideford
Exeter

Dartmoor
NATIONAL PARK

PLYMOUTH
Torquay
Torbay
Paignton
Brixham

CORNWALL
Bodmin Moor
Bodmin
Newquay
St. Austell
Truro
Falmouth
Redruth
Camborne
Penzance
St. Ives
Helston
Lizard Pt.

DORSET
Dorchester
Weymouth
Bridport
Lyme Bay
Portland Bill

Projection: Conical with two standard parallels

57 See pages 44–45 for names of Unitary Authorities.

West from Greenwich

m
1000
750
500
400
200
100
0

ft
3000
2250
1500
1200
600
300
0
150
300 m

A T L A N T I C

O C E A N

Projection : Conical with two standard parallels

West from Greenwich

1:1 000 000

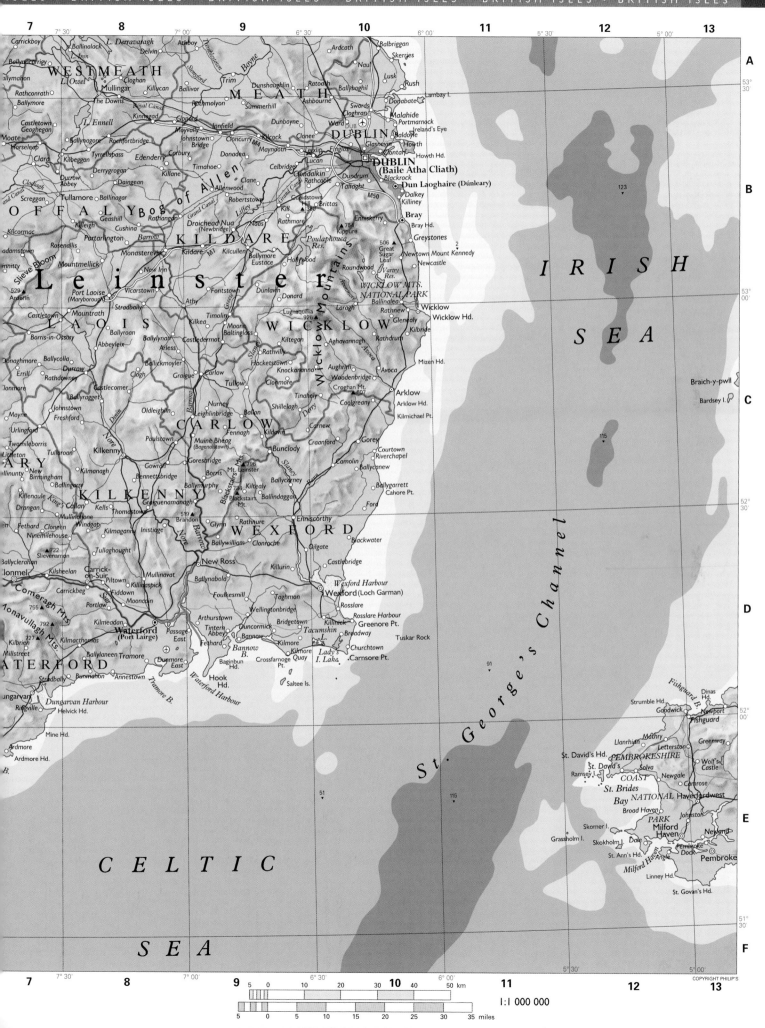

1:1 000 000

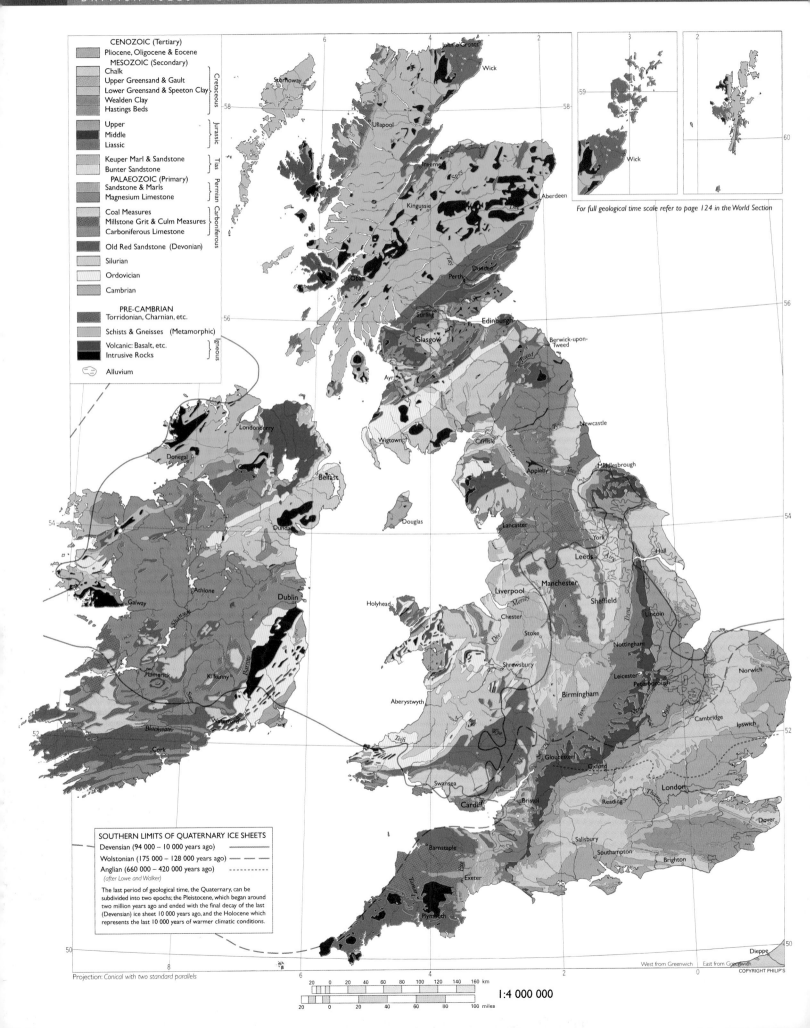

CENOZOIC (Tertiary)
Pliocene, Oligocene & Eocene

MESOZOIC (Secondary)
Chalk
Upper Greensand & Gault
Lower Greensand & Speeton Clay
Wealden Clay
Hastings Beds
⎫ Cretaceous

Upper
Middle
Liassic
⎫ Jurassic

Keuper Marl & Sandstone
Bunter Sandstone
⎫ Trias

PALAEOZOIC (Primary)
Sandstone & Marls
Magnesium Limestone
⎫ Permian

Coal Measures
Millstone Grit & Culm Measures
Carboniferous Limestone
⎫ Carboniferous

Old Red Sandstone (Devonian)
Silurian
Ordovician
Cambrian

PRE-CAMBRIAN
Torridonian, Charnian, etc.
Schists & Gneisses (Metamorphic)
Volcanic: Basalt, etc.
Intrusive Rocks
⎫ Igneous

Alluvium

For full geological time scale refer to page 124 in the World Section

SOUTHERN LIMITS OF QUATERNARY ICE SHEETS
Devensian (94 000 – 10 000 years ago) ————
Wolstonian (175 000 – 128 000 years ago) – – – –
Anglian (660 000 – 420 000 years ago) · · · · · · ·
(after Lowe and Walker)

The last period of geological time, the Quaternary, can be subdivided into two epochs; the Pleistocene, which began around two million years ago and ended with the final decay of the last (Devensian) ice sheet 10 000 years ago, and the Holocene which represents the last 10 000 years of warmer climatic conditions.

Projection: Conical with two standard parallels

West from Greenwich   East from Greenwich
COPYRIGHT PHILIP'S

20 0 20 40 60 80 100 120 140 160 km
20 0 20 40 60 80 100 miles

1:4 000 000

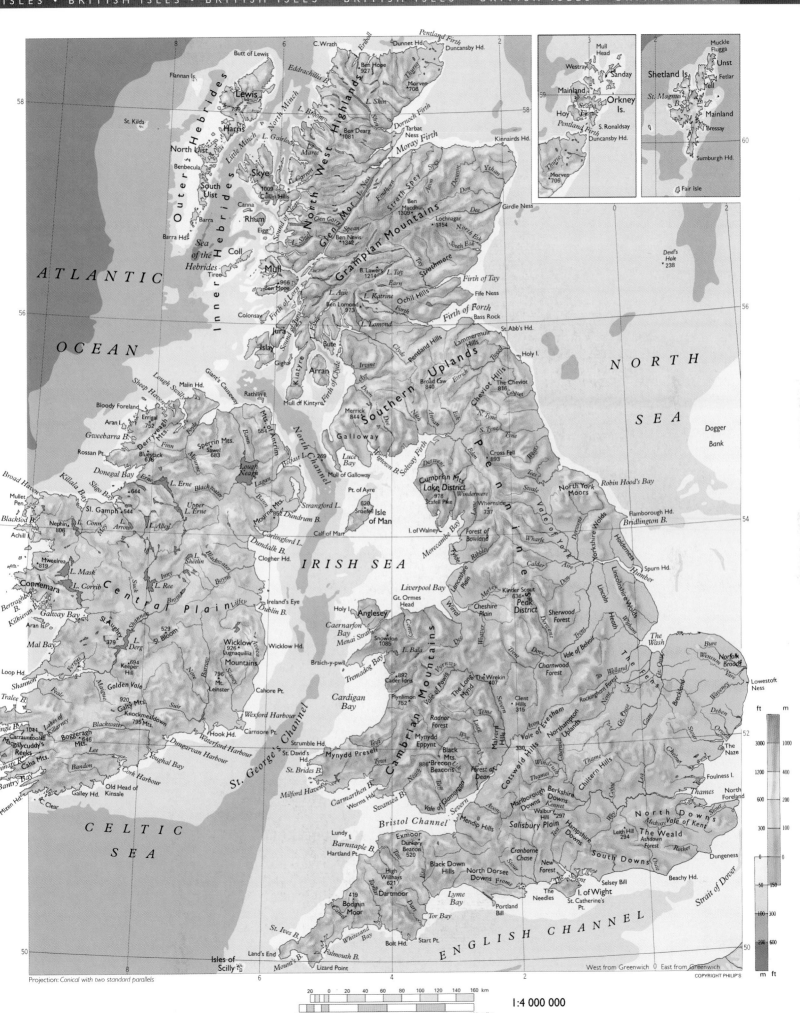

Projection: Conical with two standard parallels

West from Greenwich 0 East from Greenwich

1:4 000 000

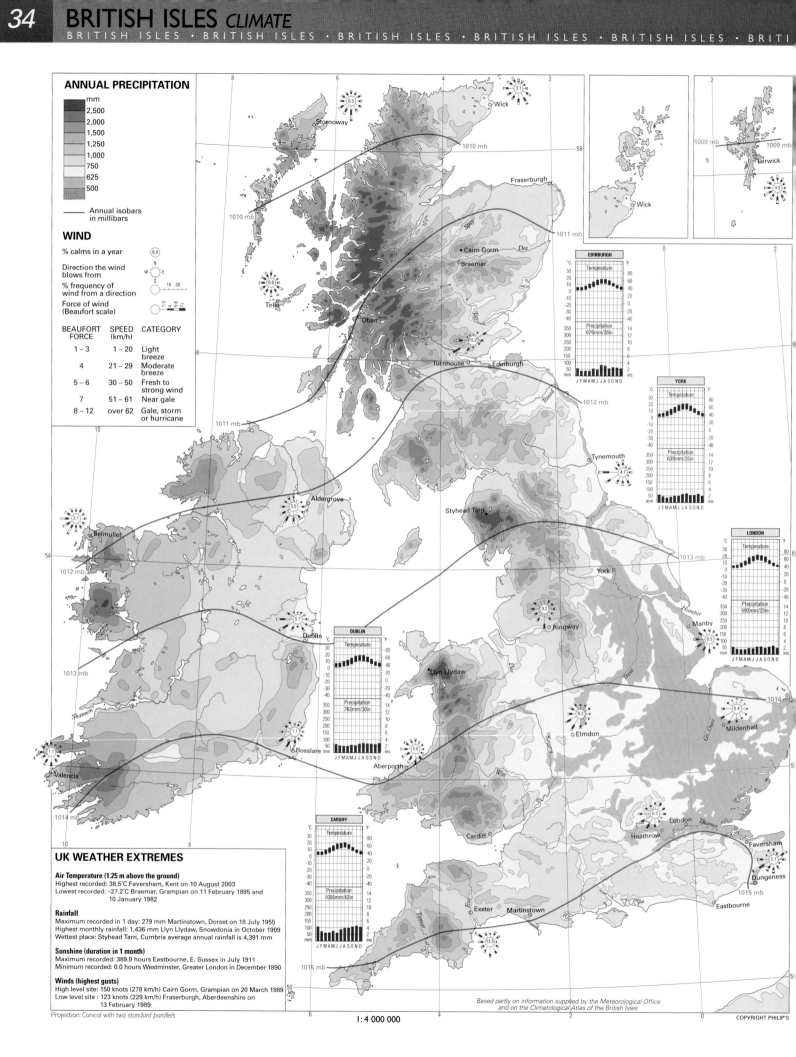

ANNUAL PRECIPITATION

mm
- 2,500
- 2,000
- 1,500
- 1,250
- 1,000
- 750
- 625
- 500

— Annual isobars in millibars

WIND

% calms in a year

Direction the wind blows from

% frequency of wind from a direction

Force of wind (Beaufort scale)

BEAUFORT FORCE	SPEED (km/h)	CATEGORY
1 – 3	1 – 20	Light breeze
4	21 – 29	Moderate breeze
5 – 6	30 – 50	Fresh to strong wind
7	51 – 61	Near gale
8 – 12	over 62	Gale, storm or hurricane

UK WEATHER EXTREMES

Air Temperature (1.25 m above the ground)
Highest recorded: 38.5°C Faversham, Kent on 10 August 2003
Lowest recorded: –27.2°C Braemar, Grampian on 11 February 1895 and 10 January 1982

Rainfall
Maximum recorded in 1 day: 279 mm Martinstown, Dorset on 18 July 1955
Highest monthly rainfall: 1,436 mm Llyn Llydaw, Snowdonia in October 1909
Wettest place: Styhead Tarn, Cumbria average annual rainfall is 4,391 mm

Sunshine (duration in 1 month)
Maximum recorded: 389.9 hours Eastbourne, E. Sussex in July 1911
Minimum recorded: 0.0 hours Westminster, Greater London in December 1890

Winds (highest gusts)
High level site: 150 knots (278 km/h) Cairn Gorm, Grampian on 20 March 1989
Low level site: 123 knots (229 km/h) Fraserburgh, Aberdeenshire on 13 February 1989

Projection: Conical with two standard parallels

1: 4 000 000

Based partly on information supplied by the Meteorological Office and on the Climatological Atlas of the British Isles

COPYRIGHT PHILIP'S

EDINBURGH — Precipitation 676mm/26in
YORK — Precipitation 639mm/25in
LONDON — Precipitation 593mm/23in
DUBLIN — Precipitation 762mm/30in
CARDIFF — Precipitation 1065mm/42in

CLIMATE GRAPHS

Average monthly minimum temperature in degrees Celsius

Average monthly maximum temperature in degrees Celsius

Height of meteorological station above sea level in metres

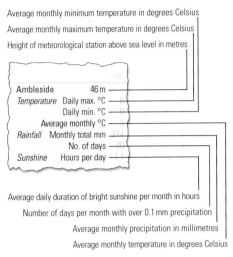

Ambleside   46 m
Temperature   Daily max. °C
          Daily min. °C
      Average monthly °C
Rainfall   Monthly total mm
          No. of days
Sunshine   Hours per day

Average daily duration of bright sunshine per month in hours

Number of days per month with over 0.1 mm precipitation

Average monthly precipitation in millimetres

Average monthly temperature in degrees Celsius

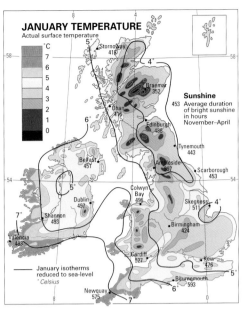

JANUARY TEMPERATURE
Actual surface temperature

°C
7
6
5
4
3
2
1
0

Sunshine
453 Average duration of bright sunshine in hours November–April

January isotherms reduced to sea-level ° Celsius

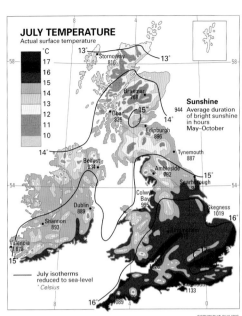

JULY TEMPERATURE
Actual surface temperature

°C
17
16
15
14
13
12
11
10

Sunshine
944 Average duration of bright sunshine in hours May–October

July isotherms reduced to sea-level ° Celsius

COPYRIGHT PHILIP'S

		Jan	Feb	Mar	Apr	May	June	July	Aug	Sept	Oct	Nov	Dec	Year
Ambleside	**46 m**													
Temperature	Daily max. °C	6	7	9	12	16	19	20	19	17	13	9	7	13
	Daily min. °C	0	0	2	4	6	9	11	11	9	6	3	1	5
	Average monthly °C	3	4	6	8	11	14	15	15	13	10	6	4	9
Rainfall	Monthly total mm	214	146	112	101	90	111	134	139	184	196	209	215	1,851
	No. of days	20	17	15	15	14	15	18	17	18	19	19	21	208
Sunshine	Hours per day	1.1	2	3.2	4.5	6	5.7	4.5	4.2	3.3	2.2	1.4	1	3.3
Belfast	**4 m**													
Temperature	Daily max. °C	6	7	9	12	15	18	18	18	16	13	9	7	12
	Daily min. °C	2	2	3	4	6	9	11	11	9	7	4	3	6
	Average monthly °C	4	4	6	8	11	13	15	15	13	10	7	5	9
Rainfall	Monthly total mm	80	52	50	48	52	68	94	77	80	83	72	90	845
	No. of days	20	17	16	16	15	16	19	17	18	19	19	21	213
Sunshine	Hours per day	1.5	2.3	3.4	5	6.3	6	4.4	4.4	3.6	2.6	1.8	1.1	3.5
Birkenhead	**60 m**													
Temperature	Daily max. °C	6	6	9	11	15	17	19	19	16	13	9	7	12
	Daily min. °C	2	2	3	5	8	11	13	13	11	8	5	3	7
	Average monthly °C	4	4	6	8	11	14	16	16	14	10	7	5	10
Rainfall	Monthly total mm	64	46	40	41	55	55	67	80	66	71	76	65	726
	No. of days	18	13	13	13	13	13	15	15	15	17	17	19	181
Sunshine	Hours per day	1.6	2.4	3.5	5.3	6.3	6.7	5.7	5.4	4.2	2.9	1.8	1.3	3.9
Birmingham	**163 m**													
Temperature	Daily max. °C	5	6	9	12	16	19	20	20	17	13	9	6	13
	Daily min. °C	2	2	3	5	7	10	12	12	10	7	5	3	7
	Average monthly °C	3	4	6	8	11	15	16	16	14	10	7	5	10
Rainfall	Monthly total mm	74	54	50	53	64	50	69	69	61	69	84	67	764
	No. of days	17	15	13	14	14	13	15	14	14	15	17	18	178
Sunshine	Hours per day	1.4	2.1	3.2	4.6	5.4	6	5.4	5.1	3.9	2.8	1.6	1.2	3.6
Cambridge	**12 m**													
Temperature	Daily max. °C	6	7	11	14	17	21	22	22	19	15	10	7	14
	Daily min. °C	1	1	2	4	7	10	12	12	10	6	4	2	6
	Average monthly °C	3	4	6	9	12	15	17	17	14	10	7	5	10
Rainfall	Monthly total mm	49	35	36	37	45	45	58	55	51	51	54	41	558
	No. of days	15	13	10	11	11	11	12	12	11	13	14	14	147
Sunshine	Hours per day	1.7	2.5	3.8	5.1	6.2	6.7	6	5.7	4.6	3.4	1.9	1.4	4.1
Craibstone	**91 m**													
Temperature	Daily max. °C	5	6	8	10	13	16	18	17	15	12	8	6	11
	Daily min. °C	0	0	2	3	5	8	10	10	8	6	3	1	5
	Average monthly °C	3	3	5	7	9	12	14	13	12	9	6	4	8
Rainfall	Monthly total mm	78	55	53	51	63	54	95	75	67	92	93	80	856
	No. of days	19	16	15	15	14	14	18	15	16	18	19	18	197
Sunshine	Hours per day	1.8	2.9	3.5	4.9	5.9	6.1	5.1	4.8	4.3	3..1	2	1.5	3.8
Durham	**102 m**													
Temperature	Daily max. °C	6	6	9	12	15	18	20	19	17	13	9	7	13
	Daily min. °C	0	0	1	3	6	9	11	10	9	6	3	2	5
	Average monthly °C	3	3	5	7	10	13	15	15	13	9	6	4	9
Rainfall	Monthly total mm	59	51	38	38	51	49	61	67	60	63	66	55	658
	No. of days	17	15	14	13	13	14	15	14	14	16	17	17	179
Sunshine	Hours per day	1.7	2.5	3.3	4.6	5.4	6	5.1	4.8	4.1	3	1.9	1.4	3.6

		Jan	Feb	Mar	Apr	May	June	July	Aug	Sept	Oct	Nov	Dec	Year
Lerwick	**82 m**													
Temperature	Daily max. °C	5	5	6	8	11	13	14	14	13	10	8	6	9
	Daily min. °C	1	1	2	3	5	7	10	10	8	6	4	3	5
	Average monthly °C	3	3	4	5	8	10	12	12	11	8	6	4	7
Rainfall	Monthly total mm	109	87	69	68	52	55	72	71	87	104	111	118	1,003
	No. of days	25	22	20	21	15	15	17	17	19	23	24	25	243
Sunshine	Hours per day	0.8	1.8	2.9	4.4	5.3	5.3	4	3.8	3.5	2.2	2.2	0.5	3
Plymouth	**27 m**													
Temperature	Daily max. °C	8	8	10	12	15	18	19	19	18	15	11	9	14
	Daily min. °C	4	4	5	6	8	11	13	13	12	9	7	5	8
	Average monthly °C	6	6	7	9	12	15	16	16	15	12	9	7	11
Rainfall	Monthly total mm	99	74	69	53	63	53	70	77	78	91	113	110	950
	No. of days	19	15	14	12	12	12	14	14	15	16	17	18	178
Sunshine	Hours per day	1.9	2.9	4.3	6.1	7.1	7.4	6.4	6.4	5.1	3.7	2.2	1.7	4.6
Renfrew	**6 m**													
Temperature	Daily max. °C	5	7	9	12	15	18	19	19	16	13	9	7	12
	Daily min. °C	1	1	2	4	6	9	11	11	9	6	4	2	6
	Average monthly °C	3	4	6	8	11	14	15	15	13	9	7	4	9
Rainfall	Monthly total mm	111	85	69	67	63	70	97	93	102	119	106	127	1,109
	No. of days	19	16	15	15	14	15	17	17	17	18	18	20	201
Sunshine	Hours per day	1.1	2.1	2.9	4.7	6	6.1	5.1	4.4	3.7	2.3	1.4	0.8	3.4
St Mary's	**50 m**													
Temperature	Daily max. °C	9	9	11	12	14	17	19	19	18	15	12	10	14
	Daily min. °C	6	6	7	7	9	12	13	14	13	11	9	7	9
	Average monthly °C	8	7	9	10	12	14	16	16	15	13	10	9	12
Rainfall	Monthly total mm	91	71	69	46	56	49	61	64	67	80	96	94	844
	No. of days	22	17	16	13	14	14	16	15	16	17	19	21	200
Sunshine	Hours per day	2	2.9	4.2	6.4	7.6	7.6	6.7	6.7	5.2	3.9	2.5	1.8	4.8
Southampton	**20 m**													
Temperature	Daily max. °C	7	8	11	14	17	20	22	22	19	15	11	8	15
	Daily min. °C	2	2	3	5	8	11	13	13	11	7	5	3	7
	Average monthly °C	5	5	7	10	13	16	17	17	15	11	8	6	11
Rainfall	Monthly total mm	83	56	52	45	56	49	60	69	70	86	94	84	804
	No. of days	17	13	13	12	12	12	13	13	14	14	16	17	166
Sunshine	Hours per day	1.8	2.6	4	5.7	6.7	7.2	6.5	6.4	4.9	3.6	2.2	1.6	4.5
Tiree	**9 m**													
Temperature	Daily Max. °C	7	7	9	10	13	15	16	16	15	12	10	8	12
	Daily Min. °C	4	3	4	5	7	10	11	11	10	8	6	5	7
	Average Monthly °C	5	5	6	8	10	12	14	14	13	10	8	6	9
Rainfall	Monthly Total mm	117	77	67	64	55	70	91	90	118	129	122	128	1,128
	No. of Days	23	19	17	17	15	16	20	18	20	23	22	24	234
Sunshine	Hours per Day	1.3	2.6	3.7	5.7	7.5	6.8	5.2	5.3	4.2	2.6	1.6	0.9	4
Valencia	**9 m**													
Temperature	Daily max. °C	9	9	11	13	15	17	18	18	17	14	12	10	14
	Daily min. °C	5	4	5	6	8	11	12	13	11	9	7	6	8
	Average monthly °C	7	7	8	9	11	14	15	15	14	12	9	8	11
Rainfall	Monthly total mm	165	107	103	75	86	81	107	95	122	140	151	168	1,400
	No. of days	20	15	14	13	13	13	15	15	16	17	18	21	190
Sunshine	Hours per day	1.6	2.5	3.5	5.2	6.5	5.9	4.7	4.9	3.8	2.8	2	1.3	3.7

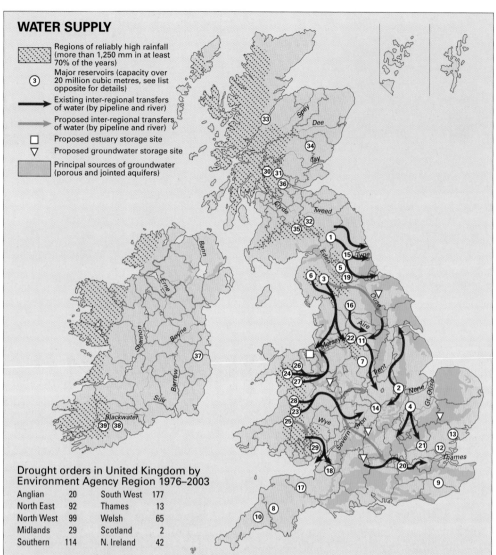

WATER SUPPLY

- Regions of reliably high rainfall (more than 1,250 mm in at least 70% of the years)
- ③ Major reservoirs (capacity over 20 million cubic metres, see list opposite for details)
- ➔ Existing inter-regional transfers of water (by pipeline and river)
- ➔ Proposed inter-regional transfers of water (by pipeline and river)
- ☐ Proposed estuary storage site
- ▽ Proposed groundwater storage site
- Principal sources of groundwater (porous and jointed aquifers)

Drought orders in United Kingdom by Environment Agency Region 1976–2003

Anglian	20	South West	177
North East	92	Thames	13
North West	99	Welsh	65
Midlands	29	Scotland	2
Southern	114	N. Ireland	42

MAJOR RESERVOIRS (with capacity in million m³)

England
1	Kielder Res.	198
2	Rutland Water	123
3	Haweswater	85
4	Grafham Water	59
5	Cow Green Res.	41
6	Thirlmere	41
7	Carsington Res.	36
8	Roadford Res.	35
9	Bewl Water Res.	31
10	Colliford Lake	29
11	Ladybower Res.	28
12	Hanningfield Res.	27
13	Abberton Res.	25
14	Draycote Water	23
15	Derwent Res.	22
16	Grimwith Res.	22
17	Wimbleball Lake	21
18	Chew Valley Lake	20
19	Balderhead Res.	20
20	Thames Valley (linked reservoirs)	
21	Lea Valley (linked reservoirs)	
22	Longendale (linked reservoirs)	

Wales
23	Elan Valley	99
24	Llyn Celyn	74
25	Llyn Brianne	62
26	Llyn Brenig	60
27	Llyn Vyrnwy	60
28	Llyn Clywedog	48
29	Llandegfedd Res.	22

Scotland
30	Loch Lomond	86
31	Loch Katrine	64
32	Megget Res.	64
33	Loch Ness	26
34	Blackwater Res.	25
35	Daer Res.	23
36	Carron Valley Res.	21

Ireland
37	Poulaphouca Res.	168
38	Inishcarra Res.	57
39	Carrigadrohid Res.	33

WATER SUPPLY IN THE UK

The pie graph represents the 16,076 million litres a day that were supplied by the public water authority and services companies in the UK in 2003.

Total water abstraction in England and Wales in 2003 was approximately 58,593 million litres a day.

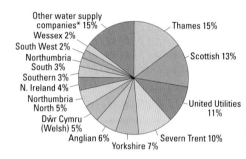

- Other water supply companies* 15%
- Wessex 2%
- South West 2%
- Northumbria South 3%
- Southern 3%
- N. Ireland 4%
- Northumbria North 5%
- Dŵr Cymru (Welsh) 5%
- Anglian 6%
- Yorkshire 7%
- Severn Trent 10%
- United Utilities 11%
- Scottish 13%
- Thames 15%

*This is a group of 12 privately-owned companies who are not connected with the other water authorities

WATER ABSTRACTIONS

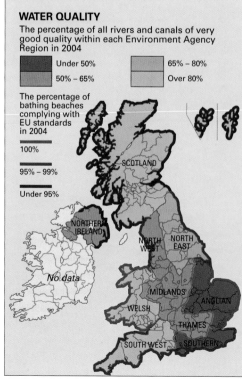

THAMES   Environment Agency Region

1883 (16%)   Water supply* in megalitres per day (with percentage of total abstraction from groundwater in brackets)

*Piped mains water, excluding water abstracted for agricultural and industrial use

- SCOTLAND   2397 (7%)
- N. IRELAND   710 (8%)
- NORTH EAST   2256 (14%)
- NORTH WEST   1602 (11%)
- No data
- MIDLANDS   2637 (36%)
- ANGLIAN   2153 (37%)
- WELSH   1505 (3%)
- THAMES   4214 (35%)
- SOUTH WEST   1249 (30%)
- SOUTHERN   1303 (74%)

WATER QUALITY

The percentage of all rivers and canals of very good quality within each Environment Agency Region in 2004

- Under 50%
- 50% – 65%
- 65% – 80%
- Over 80%

The percentage of bathing beaches complying with EU standards in 2004

- 100%
- 95% – 99%
- Under 95%

No data

FLOOD RISK IN ENGLAND AND WALES

- Areas at greatest risk from flooding (as designated by the Environment Agency in 2002)
- Settlements with over 100 properties flooded in 2001

Ponteland, Skinningrove, Malton and Norton, Stockbridge, York, Barnby, Catcliffe, Gowdall, Ruthin, Mold, Naburn, Shrewsbury, Bewdley, Newport, Waltham Abbey, Woking, Wanstead, Portsmouth, Uckfield, Lewes

EU AIR QUALITY Emissions in thousand tonnes

	Sulphur dioxide			Nitrogen oxides		
	1975	1990	2002	1975	1990	2002
Austria	–	90	204	–	221	36
Belgium/Lux.	–	105	307	–	172	153
Denmark	418	183	200	182	270	25
Finland	–	260	211	–	290	85
France	3,329	1,200	1,434	1,608	1,487	596
Germany	3,325	5,633	1,479	2,532	3,033	608
Greece	–	–	318	–	338	509
Ireland	186	187	121	60	128	96
Italy	3,250	1,682	1,267	1,499	2,041	665
Netherlands	386	204	430	447	575	85
Portugal	178	286	293	104	216	295
Spain	–	2,205	1,929	–	1,247	1,968
Sweden	–	169	243	–	411	59
United Kingdom	5,310	3,754	1,587	2,365	2,731	1,003

ACID RAIN
Average acidity of precipitation in the UK
(pH scale)

- 4.29 and under (most acidic)
- 4.30 – 4.39
- 4.40 – 4.49
- 4.50 – 4.59
- 4.60 – 4.69
- 4.70 – 4.79
- 4.80 and over (least acidic)

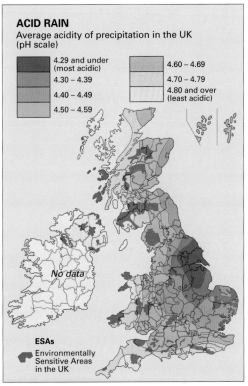

No data

ESAs
Environmentally Sensitive Areas in the UK

GROUND LEVEL OZONE
The number of days each year with 8 hour periods with ozone levels exceeding 50 parts per billion

- More than 50
- 40 – 50
- 30 – 40
- 20 – 30
- Less than 20

Greenhouse Gas Emissions

- Carbon dioxide
- Methane
- Nitrous oxide

131 Total emissions in million tonnes of Carbon Equivalent (2003)

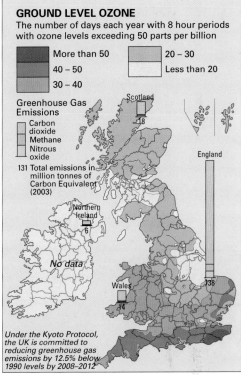

Scotland
18

England
138

Northern Ireland
6

Wales
14

No data

Under the Kyoto Protocol, the UK is committed to reducing greenhouse gas emissions by 12.5% below 1990 levels by 2008–2012

FORESTRY
The percentage of the total area covered by woodland and forest

- Over 20%
- 15% – 20%
- 10% – 15%
- 5% – 10%
- Under 5%

▲ Over 50% coniferous
◆ Over 50% broadleaves

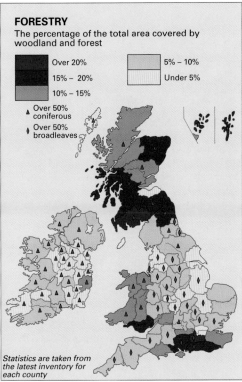

Statistics are taken from the latest inventory for each county

NATURAL VEGETATION
The plant cover associated with a particular environment if it is unaffected by human activity

- Oak
- Beech and oak
- Ash and oak
- Birch and oakwood
- Scots pine
- Heath, moorland, water meadows, fen, bog and marsh

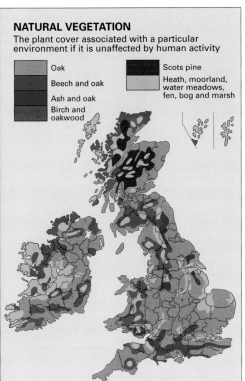

CONSERVATION

- National Parks
- Areas of Outstanding Natural Beauty
- National Scenic Areas
- Forest Parks, Regional Parks in Scotland and Special Protected Areas
- Green Belts (and the urban areas they surround)
- Heritage Coast (England and Wales)/Coastal Conservation Zones (Scotland)

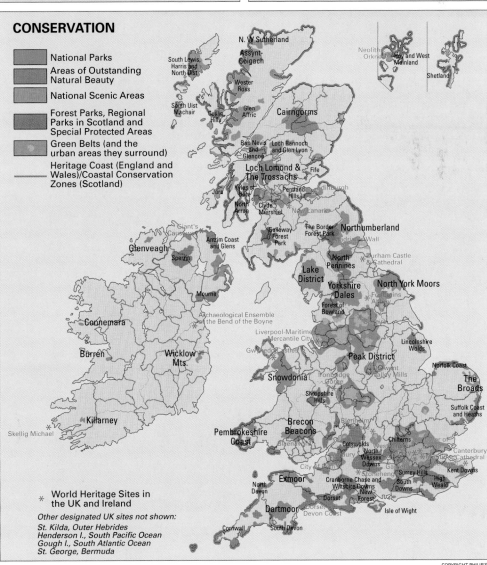

N. W. Sutherland
Assynt-Coigach
South Lewis, Harris and North Uist
Wester Ross
South Uist Machair
Cuillin Hills
Glen Affric
Cairngorms
Ben Nevis and Glencoe
Loch Rannoch and Glen Lyon
Loch Lomond & The Trossachs
Fife
Jura
Kyles of Bute
Pentland Hills
North Arran
Clyde Muirshiel
New Lanark
Galloway Forest Park
The Border Forest Park
Hadrian's Wall
Northumberland
Giant's Causeway
Antrim Coast and Glens
Durham Castle & Cathedral
Glenveagh
Sperrin
North Pennines
Lake District
Yorkshire Dales
North York Moors
Mourne
Forest of Bowland
Fountains
Archaeological Ensemble at the Bend of the Boyne
Liverpool–Maritime Mercantile City
Connemara
Lincolnshire Wolds
Burren
Wicklow Mts.
Peak District
Norfolk Coast
Snowdonia
The Broads
Shropshire Hills
Ironbridge
Suffolk Coast and Heaths
Killarney
Pembrokeshire Coast
Brecon Beacons
Cotswolds
Chilterns
Canterbury Cathedral
Skellig Michael
North Wessex Downs
Surrey Hills
Kent Downs
Stonehenge
North Devon
Exmoor
Cranborne Chase and Wiltshire Downs
New Forest
South Downs
High Weald
Dartmoor
Dorset
Isle of Wight
Cornwall
South Devon
Neolithic Orkney
Hoy and West Mainland
Shetland

* World Heritage Sites in the UK and Ireland

Other designated UK sites not shown:
St. Kilda, Outer Hebrides
Henderson I., South Pacific Ocean
Gough I., South Atlantic Ocean
St. George, Bermuda

38

BRITISH ISLES *AGRICULTURE AND FISHING*
BRITISH ISLES • BRITISH ISLES • BRITISH ISLES • BRITISH ISLES • BRITISH ISLES • BRITI

TYPES OF FARM

- Dairy cattle
- Beef cattle
- Sheep
- ● Pigs and/or poultry
- Mixed farming
- Market gardening (fruit and vegetables)
- Cereals
- Other crops (mainly potatoes, sugar beet)
- ⎯⎯ Northern limit of 9 month growing season
- Forests
- Built-up areas

Areas with over 1,000 mm rainfall per year

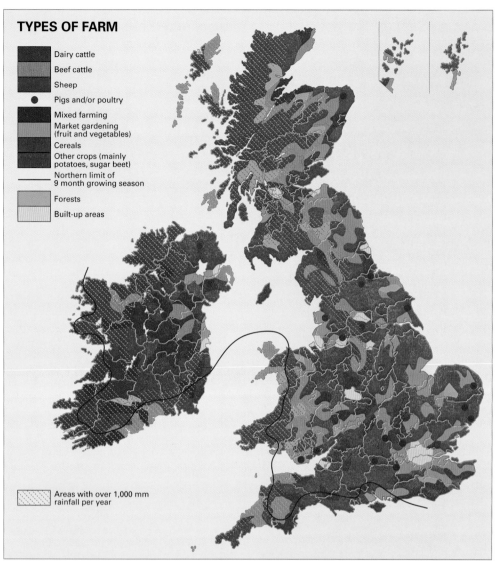

CEREAL FARMING
The percentage of the total farmland used for growing cereals in 2003

- Over 40%
- 30 – 40%
- 20 – 30%
- 10 – 20%
- 0 – 10%
- No data

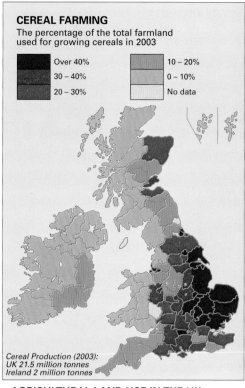

Cereal Production (2003):
UK 21.5 million tonnes
Ireland 2 million tonnes

AGRICULTURAL LAND USE IN THE UK

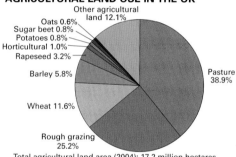

- Other agricultural land 12.1%
- Oats 0.6%
- Sugar beet 0.8%
- Potatoes 0.8%
- Horticultural 1.0%
- Rapeseed 3.2%
- Barley 5.8%
- Wheat 11.6%
- Rough grazing 25.2%
- Pasture 38.9%

Total agricultural land area (2004): 17.2 million hectares

DAIRY FARMING
The number of dairy cows per 100 hectares of farmland in 2003

- Over 40
- 30 – 40
- 20 – 30
- 10 – 20
- 0 – 10
- No data

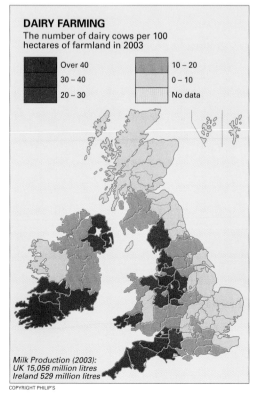

Milk Production (2003):
UK 15,056 million litres
Ireland 529 million litres

LIVESTOCK FARMING
The number of cattle, sheep and pigs per 100 hectares of farmland in 2003

- Over 600
- 450 – 600
- 300 – 450
- 150 – 300
- 0 – 150
- No data

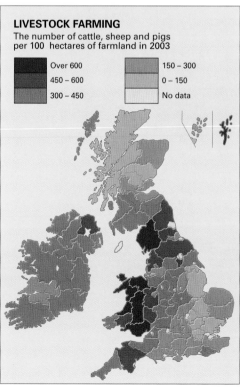

FOOT-AND-MOUTH DISEASE
The number of confirmed cases of foot-and-mouth disease in 2001

- Over 200
- 100 – 200
- 50 – 100
- 25 – 50
- 0 – 25
- Unaffected areas

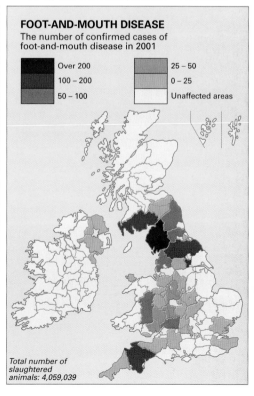

Total number of slaughtered animals: 4,059,039

NUMBER AND SIZE OF AGRICULTURAL HOLDINGS IN THE UK

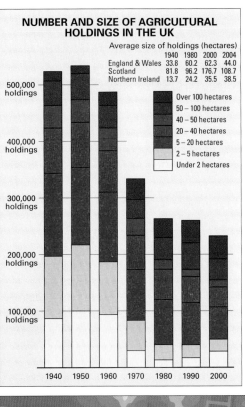

Average size of holdings (hectares)

	1940	1980	2000	2004
England & Wales	33.8	60.2	62.3	44.0
Scotland	81.8	96.2	176.7	108.7
Northern Ireland	13.7	24.2	35.5	38.5

- Over 100 hectares
- 50 – 100 hectares
- 40 – 50 hectares
- 20 – 40 hectares
- 5 – 20 hectares
- 2 – 5 hectares
- Under 2 hectares

LAND UNDER AGRICULTURE

The percentage of the total land area used for agriculture in 2003

- Over 80%
- 60 – 80%
- 40 – 60%
- 20 – 40%
- 0 – 20%
- No data

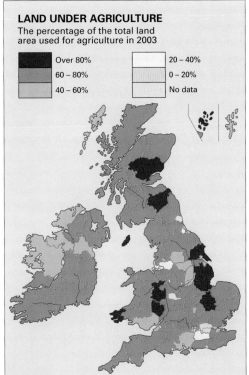

EMPLOYMENT IN AGRICULTURE

The percentage of the total workforce employed in agriculture in 2002

- Over 10%
- 2.5 – 10%
- 1 – 2.5%
- 0 – 1%

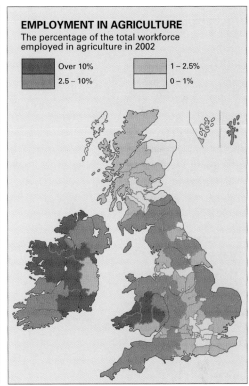

FISHING

Quantities of fish landed at major ports in 2003 (Ireland 2000)

('000 tonnes)
100
50
25
10
5

Type of fish landed
- Demersal (Deep-sea fish)
- Pelagic (Shallow-water fish)
- Shellfish

Fishing Regions
IV	North Sea
VIa	West Scotland
VIIa	Irish Sea
VIIb/h/j	W. Ireland & Sole Bank
VIId/e	English Channel
VIIf/g	Bristol Ch. & S.E. Ireland

Region boundary

Fish landed according to region of capture (2003)
- Demersal
- Pelagic
- Shellfish

Each symbol represents 10,000 tonnes caught

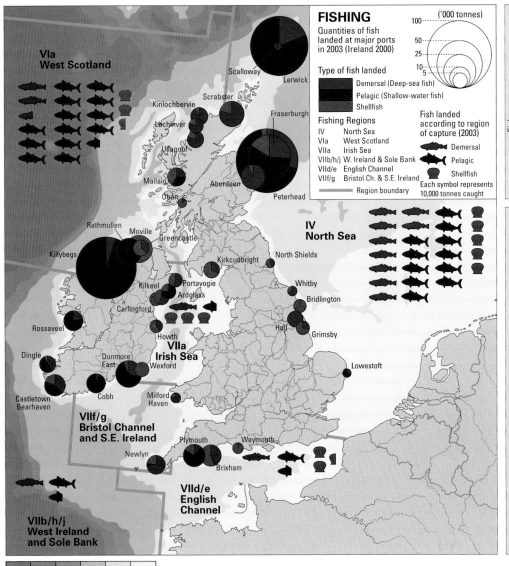

VIa West Scotland

VIIb/h/j West Ireland and Sole Bank

VIIf/g Bristol Channel and S.E. Ireland

VIIa Irish Sea

IV North Sea

VIId/e English Channel

1000 500 200 100 50 m

CHANGES IN THE UK FISHING INDUSTRY

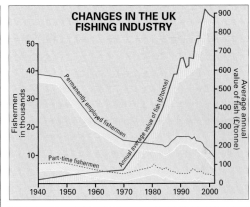

FORESTRY – WOODLAND COVER

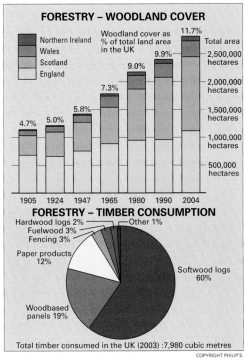

Northern Ireland
Wales
Scotland
England

Woodland cover as % of total land area in the UK

Total area

4.7% 5.0% 5.8% 7.3% 9.0% 9.9% 11.7%

1905 1924 1947 1965 1980 1990 2004

2,500,000 hectares
2,000,000 hectares
1,500,000 hectares
1,000,000 hectares
500,000 hectares

FORESTRY – TIMBER CONSUMPTION

Hardwood logs 2%
Fuelwood 3%
Fencing 3%
Other 1%
Paper products 12%
Softwood logs 60%
Woodbased panels 19%

Total timber consumed in the UK (2003) : 7,980 cubic metres

EMPLOYMENT IN MANUFACTURING

The percentage of the workforce employed in manufacturing in 2003

- Over 25%
- 20 – 25%
- 15 – 20%
- 12.5 – 15%
- 10 – 12.5%
- Under 10%

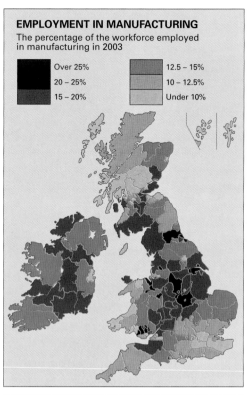

CHANGE IN MANUFACTURING EMPLOYMENT

The percentage change in the number of people employed in manufacturing by region 1991–2004*

- Over 20% gain
- 10 – 20% gain
- 0 – 10% gain
- 0 – 15% loss
- 15 – 25% loss
- Over 25% loss

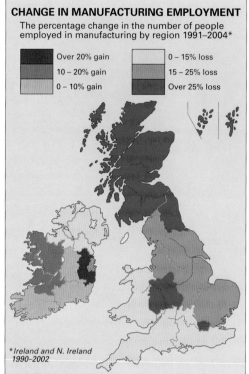

*Ireland and N. Ireland 1990–2002

LOCATION OF MANUFACTURING INDUSTRY

Heavy Industry
- ▲ Chemicals
- ■ Iron and steel
- ● Motor vehicles

Light Industry
- ◆ Electrical engineering
- ○ Science parks

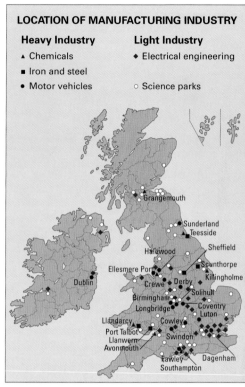

Grangemouth
Sunderland
Teesside
Sheffield
Halewood
Scunthorpe
Ellesmere Port
Killingholme
Dublin
Crewe
Derby
Solihull
Birmingham
Coventry
Longbridge
Luton
Llandarcy
Cowley
Port Talbot
Llanwern
Swindon
Avonmouth
Dagenham
Fawley
Southampton

EMPLOYMENT IN SERVICES

The percentage of the workforce employed in the service industry in 2003

- Over 85%
- 80 – 85%
- 75 – 80%
- 70 – 75%
- Under 70%

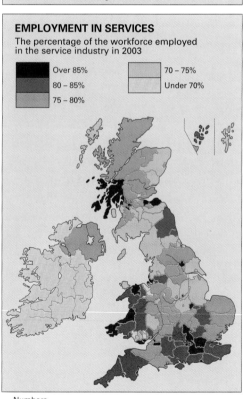

UNEMPLOYMENT

The percentage of the workforce unemployed in 2004

- Over 7%
- 6 – 7%
- 5 – 6%
- 4 – 5%
- 3 – 4%
- Under 3%

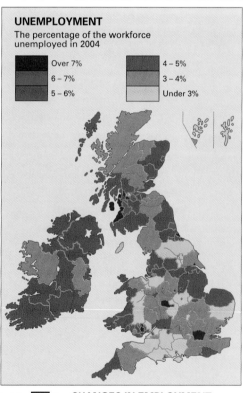

ASSISTED AREAS

The areas in which extra financial support from central government is focused to encourage economic growth

- Tier 1 with 40% aid limit
- Tier 2 with 30% aid limit

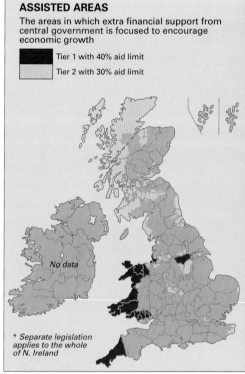

No data

*Separate legislation applies to the whole of N. Ireland

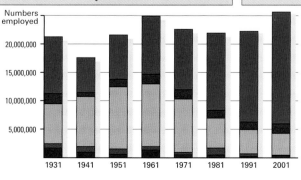

Numbers employed

20,000,000

15,000,000

10,000,000

5,000,000

1931 1941 1951 1961 1971 1981 1991 2001

CHANGES IN EMPLOYMENT IN THE UK

Employment by industry

- Services
- Transport
- Manufacturing
- Mining & energy supply
- Agriculture, forestry & fishing

MANUFACTURING OUTPUT IN THE UK

Total value 2003: £152.8 billion

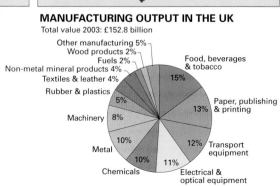

- Other manufacturing 5%
- Wood products 2%
- Fuels 2%
- Non-metal mineral products 4%
- Textiles & leather 4%
- Rubber & plastics 5%
- Machinery 8%
- Metal 10%
- Chemicals 10%
- Electrical & optical equipment 11%
- Transport equipment 12%
- Paper, publishing & printing 13%
- Food, beverages & tobacco 15%

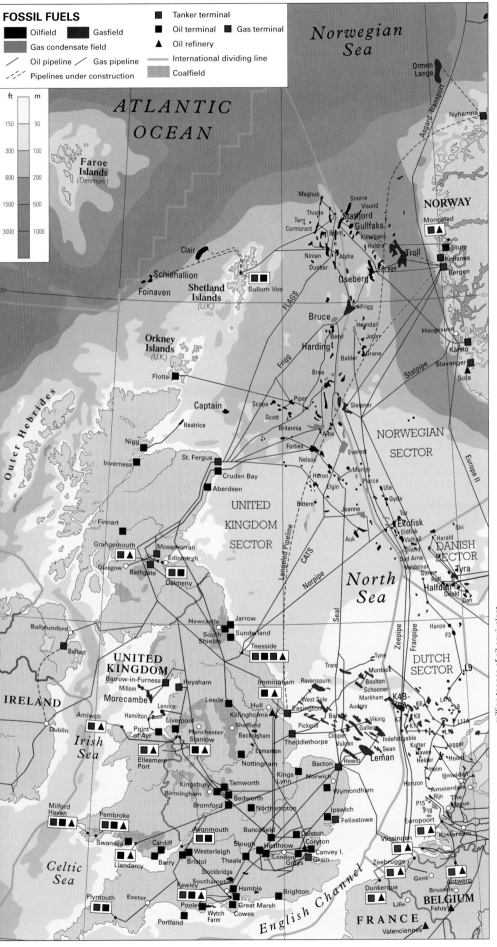

FOSSIL FUELS

- Oilfield
- Gasfield
- Gas condensate field
- Oil pipeline
- Gas pipeline
- Pipelines under construction
- Tanker terminal
- Oil terminal
- Gas terminal
- Oil refinery
- International dividing line
- Coalfield

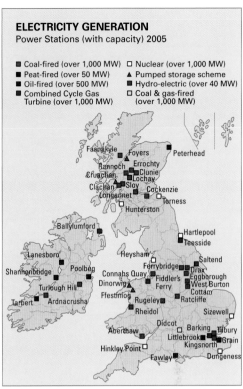

ELECTRICITY GENERATION
Power Stations (with capacity) 2005

- Coal-fired (over 1,000 MW)
- Peat-fired (over 50 MW)
- Oil-fired (over 500 MW)
- Combined Cycle Gas Turbine (over 1,000 MW)
- Nuclear (over 1,000 MW)
- Pumped storage scheme
- Hydro-electric (over 40 MW)
- Coal & gas-fired (over 1,000 MW)

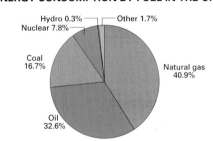

ENERGY CONSUMPTION BY FUEL IN THE UK

Hydro 0.3%
Other 1.7%
Nuclear 7.8%
Coal 16.7%
Natural gas 40.9%
Oil 32.6%

Total consumption in 2004: 234.9 million tonnes of oil equivalent

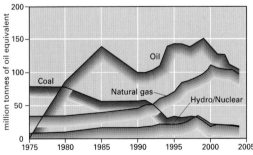

PRODUCTION OF PRIMARY FUELS IN THE UK

Coal
Oil
Natural gas
Hydro/Nuclear

million tonnes of oil equivalent

1975 1980 1985 1990 1995 2000 2005

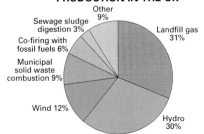

RENEWABLE ENERGY PRODUCTION IN THE UK

Other 9%
Landfill gas 31%
Sewage sludge digestion 3%
Co-firing with fossil fuels 6%
Municipal solid waste combustion 9%
Wind 12%
Hydro 30%

Total generation of renewable energy in 2003 was 2.8 million tonnes of oil equivalent, 3.3% of total energy production in the UK

COPYRIGHT PHILIP'S

ROADS AND FERRIES

- M6 Motorways
- Main primary routes

56 Average 24 hour flow of vehicles for major sections of motorway network. Figures are given in thousands for 2004

- - - - Principal car ferry routes
- - - - Long-haul sea ferry destinations

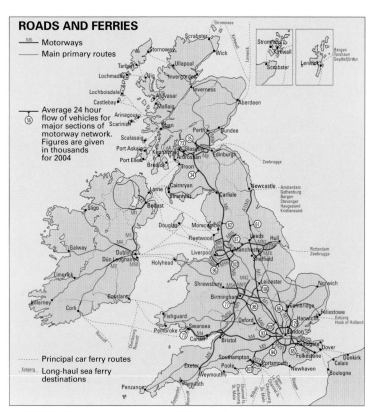

RAILWAYS

- Electrified lines
- Other main lines

Furthest distances from London reached within a journey time of

	3 hours	6 hours
1950	▲	●
2005	▲	●

Channel Tunnel
- - - - Channel Tunnel
- High-speed rail link
- · · · · under construction

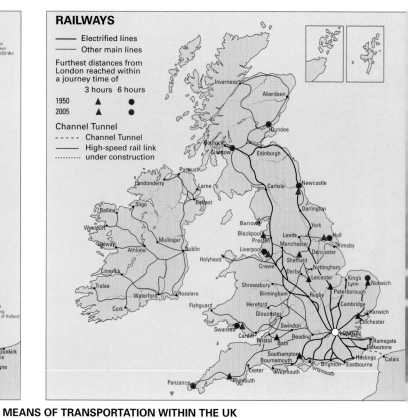

CHANNEL TUNNEL AND HIGH-SPEED LINKS IN EUROPE

Estimated journey times between London and other European cities

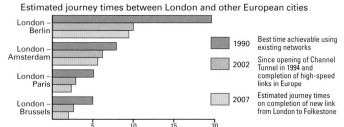

- London – Berlin
- London – Amsterdam
- London – Paris
- London – Brussels

Hours

- 1990 Best time achievable using existing networks
- 2002 Since opening of Channel Tunnel in 1994 and completion of high-speed links in Europe
- 2007 Estimated journey times on completion of new link from London to Folkestone

MEANS OF TRANSPORTATION WITHIN THE UK

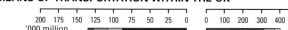

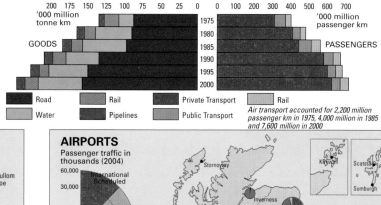

'000 million tonne km — GOODS
'000 million passenger km — PASSENGERS

	200 175 150 125 100 75 50 25 0		0 100 200 300 400 500 600 700
1975			
1980			
1985			
1990			
1995			
2000			

- Road
- Rail
- Water
- Pipelines
- Private Transport
- Public Transport
- Rail

Air transport accounted for 2,200 million passenger km in 1975, 4,000 million in 1985 and 7,600 million in 2000

SEAPORTS

Goods traffic by port in thousand tonnes 2003

50,000
25,000
10,000
5,000

% imports — Foreign Traffic — % exports
% imports — Domestic Traffic — % exports

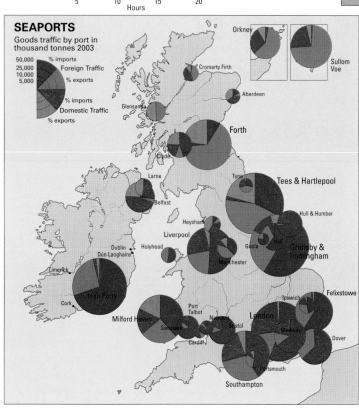

AIRPORTS

Passenger traffic in thousands (2004)

60,000
30,000
5,000
1,000

- International Scheduled
- International Chartered
- Domestic Scheduled
- Domestic Chartered

• Selected airports with over 100,000 passengers (2004)

* Comparable statistics for scheduled and chartered passengers in Ireland are not available

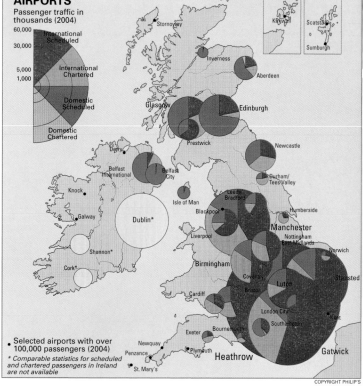

COPYRIGHT PHILIP'S

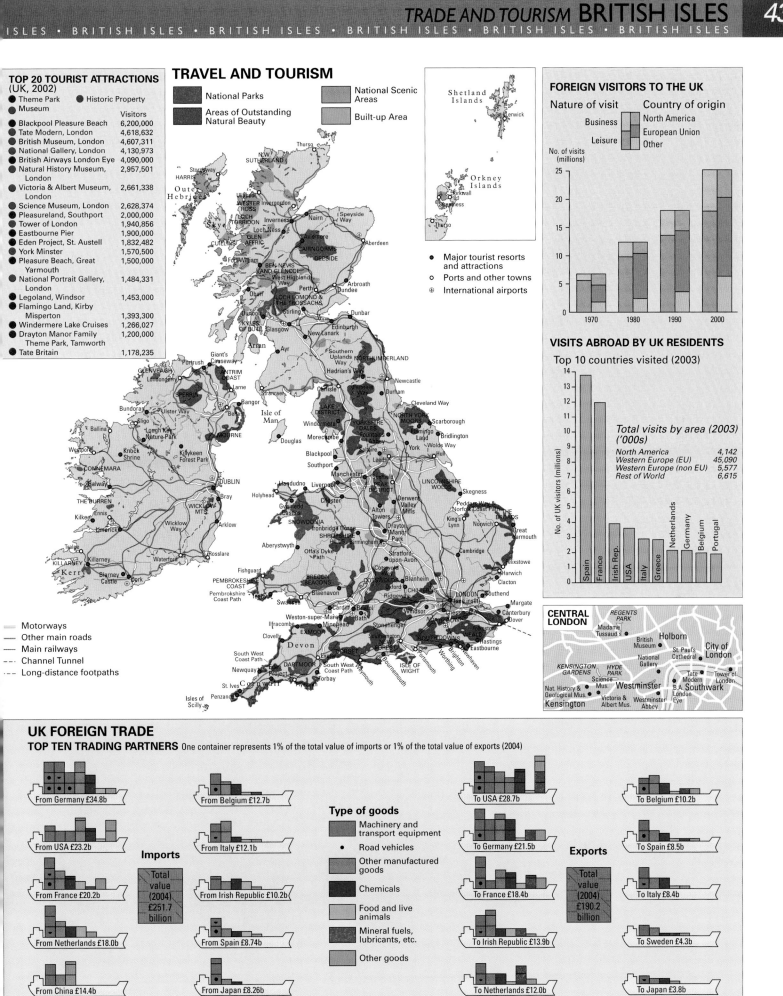

TRAVEL AND TOURISM

TOP 20 TOURIST ATTRACTIONS
(UK, 2002)
● Theme Park   ● Historic Property
● Museum

	Visitors
● Blackpool Pleasure Beach	6,200,000
● Tate Modern, London	4,618,632
● British Museum, London	4,607,311
● National Gallery, London	4,130,973
● British Airways London Eye	4,090,000
● Natural History Museum, London	2,957,501
● Victoria & Albert Museum, London	2,661,338
● Science Museum, London	2,628,374
● Pleasureland, Southport	2,000,000
● Tower of London	1,940,856
● Eastbourne Pier	1,900,000
● Eden Project, St. Austell	1,832,482
● York Minster	1,570,500
● Pleasure Beach, Great Yarmouth	1,500,000
● National Portrait Gallery, London	1,484,331
● Legoland, Windsor	1,453,000
● Flamingo Land, Kirby Misperton	1,393,300
● Windermere Lake Cruises	1,266,027
● Drayton Manor Family Theme Park, Tamworth	1,200,000
● Tate Britain	1,178,235

National Parks
Areas of Outstanding Natural Beauty
National Scenic Areas
Built-up Area

● Major tourist resorts and attractions
○ Ports and other towns
⊕ International airports

== Motorways
— Other main roads
— Main railways
-·- Channel Tunnel
--- Long-distance footpaths

FOREIGN VISITORS TO THE UK

Nature of visit   Country of origin

Business   North America
                   European Union
Leisure   Other

No. of visits (millions)
25
20
15
10
5
0
1970 1980 1990 2000

VISITS ABROAD BY UK RESIDENTS

Top 10 countries visited (2003)

No. of UK visitors (millions)
14
13
12
11
10
9
8
7
6
5
4
3
2
1
0
Spain France Irish Rep. USA Italy Greece Netherlands Germany Belgium Portugal

Total visits by area (2003) ('000s)
North America   4,142
Western Europe (EU)   45,090
Western Europe (non EU) 5,577
Rest of World   6,615

CENTRAL LONDON

UK FOREIGN TRADE

TOP TEN TRADING PARTNERS One container represents 1% of the total value of imports or 1% of the total value of exports (2004)

Imports

From Germany £34.8b
From USA £23.2b
From France £20.2b
From Netherlands £18.0b
From China £14.4b
From Belgium £12.7b
From Italy £12.1b
From Irish Republic £10.2b
From Spain £8.74b
From Japan £8.26b

Total value (2004) £251.7 billion

Type of goods
Machinery and transport equipment
● Road vehicles
Other manufactured goods
Chemicals
Food and live animals
Mineral fuels, lubricants, etc.
Other goods

Exports

To USA £28.7b
To Germany £21.5b
To France £18.4b
To Irish Republic £13.9b
To Netherlands £12.0b
To Belgium £10.2b
To Spain £8.5b
To Italy £8.4b
To Sweden £4.3b
To Japan £3.8b

Total value (2004) £190.2 billion

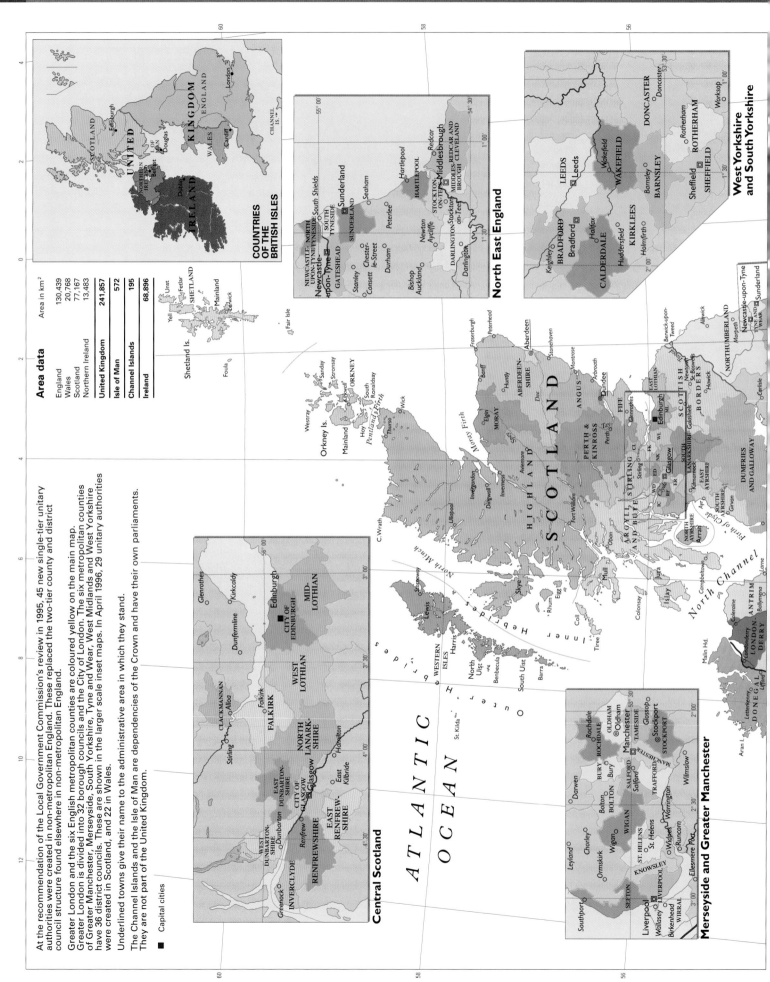

COUNTRIES OF THE BRITISH ISLES

Area data

	Area in km²
England	130,439
Wales	20,768
Scotland	77,167
Northern Ireland	13,483
United Kingdom	**241,857**
Isle of Man	**572**
Channel Islands	**195**
Ireland	**68,896**

At the recommendation of the Local Government Commission's review in 1995, 45 new single-tier unitary authorities were created in non-metropolitan England. These replaced the two-tier county and district council structure found elsewhere in non-metropolitan England.

Greater London and the six English metropolitan counties are coloured yellow on the main map. Greater London is divided into 32 borough councils and the City of London. The six metropolitan counties of Greater Manchester, Merseyside, South Yorkshire, Tyne and Wear, West Midlands and West Yorkshire have 36 district councils. These are shown in the larger scale inset maps. In April 1996, 29 unitary authorities were created in Scotland, and 22 in Wales.

Underlined towns give their name to the administrative area in which they stand.

The Channel Islands and the Isle of Man are dependencies of the Crown and have their own parliaments. They are not part of the United Kingdom.

■ Capital cities

North East England

West Yorkshire and South Yorkshire

Central Scotland

Merseyside and Greater Manchester

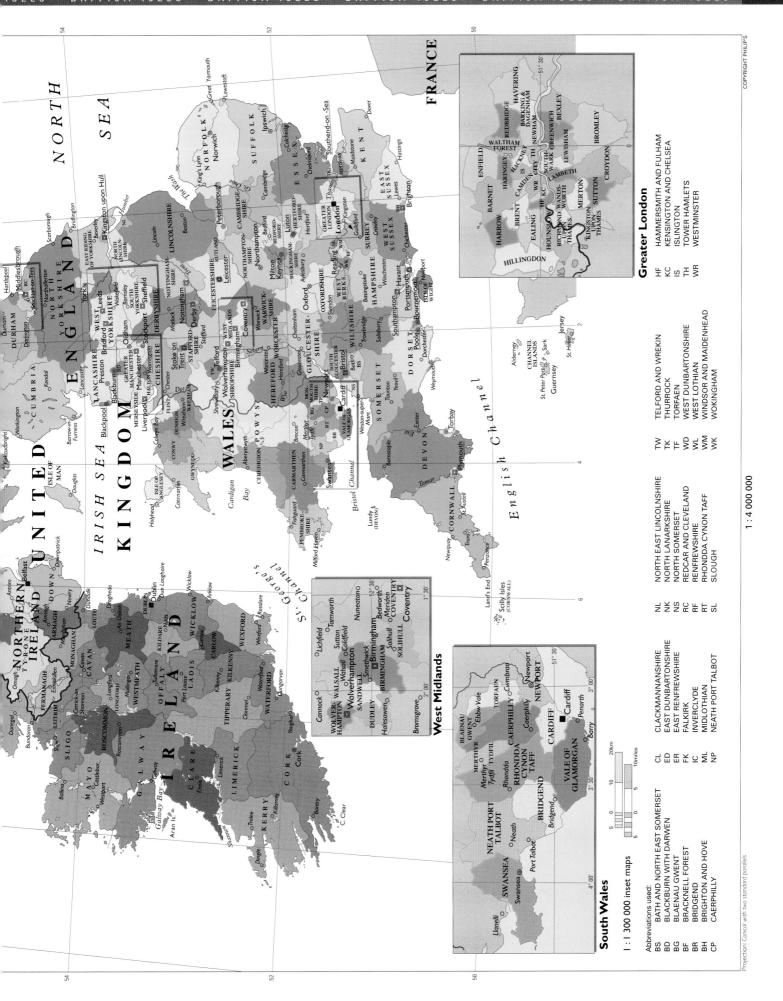

Greater London

HF	HAMMERSMITH AND FULHAM
KC	KENSINGTON AND CHELSEA
IS	ISLINGTON
TH	TOWER HAMLETS
WR	WESTMINSTER

TW	TELFORD AND WREKIN		
TK	THURROCK		
TF	TORFAEN		
WD	WEST DUNBARTONSHIRE		
WL	WEST LOTHIAN		
WM	WINDSOR AND MAIDENHEAD		
WK	WOKINGHAM		

NL	NORTH EAST LINCOLNSHIRE
NK	NORTH LANARKSHIRE
NS	NORTH SOMERSET
RC	REDCAR AND CLEVELAND
RF	RENFREWSHIRE
RT	RHONDDA CYNON TAFF
SL	SLOUGH

1 : 4 000 000

West Midlands

South Wales

1 : 1 300 000 inset maps

Abbreviations used:

BS	BATH AND NORTH EAST SOMERSET
BD	BLACKBURN WITH DARWEN
BG	BLAENAU GWENT
BF	BRACKNELL FOREST
BR	BRIDGEND
BH	BRIGHTON AND HOVE
CP	CAERPHILLY

CL	CLACKMANNANSHIRE
ED	EAST DUNBARTONSHIRE
ER	EAST RENFREWSHIRE
FK	FALKIRK
IC	INVERCLYDE
ML	MIDLOTHIAN
NP	NEATH PORT TALBOT

Projection: Conical with two standard parallels

COPYRIGHT PHILIP'S

POPULATION DENSITY

Persons per sq km (2002)

- Over 5,000
- 2,000 – 5,000
- 1,000 – 2,000
- 500 – 1,000
- 200 – 500
- 100 – 200
- 20 – 100
- Under 20

POPULATION CHANGE 1982–2002

The percentage change in the number of
people between 1981 and 2001

△ Over 20%   ▽ Over 5%
   increase   decrease

POPULATION DATA	% Change 1982–2002	Population 2002 ('000s)	Density (persons per sq km)
England	5.2	49,559	380
Wales	4.1	2,919	141
Scotland	−2.1	5,055	65
Northern Ireland	9.8	1,697	125
United Kingdom	5.2	59,229	244
Ireland	13.0	3,897	57

Projection: Conical with two standard parallels

1 : 4 000 000

COPYRIGHT PHILIP'S

POPULATION DENSITY IN 1891

Persons per sq km

- Over 1,000
- 500 – 1,000
- 200 – 500
- 100 – 200
- 50 – 100
- 25 – 50
- Under 25

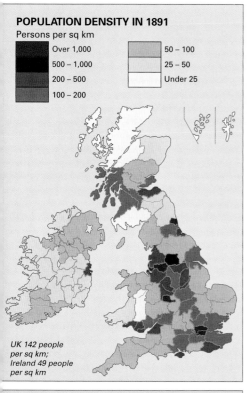

UK 142 people per sq km; Ireland 49 people per sq km

ETHNIC GROUPS

Ethnic minorities as a % of total population in 2000–1

- Over 6%
- 4 – 6%
- 2 – 4%
- 0 – 2%

Ethnic minority groups

- Indian/ Pakistani/ Bangladeshi
- W. Indian/ African
- Other

77 000 Total number of ethnic minority people in each region

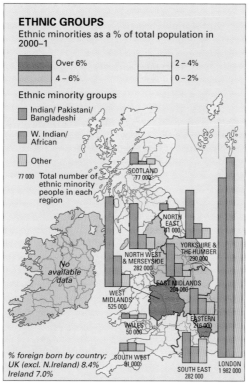

SCOTLAND 77 000
NORTH EAST 41 000
NORTH WEST & MERSEYSIDE 282 000
YORKSHIRE & THE HUMBER 290 000
EAST MIDLANDS 204 000
WEST MIDLANDS 525 000
WALES 50 000
EASTERN 216 000
SOUTH WEST 91 000
SOUTH EAST 282 000
LONDON 1 982 000

% foreign born by country; UK (excl. N.Ireland) 8.4% Ireland 7.0%

No available data

MIGRATION

The difference between the number moving in and the number moving away (per 1,000 inhabitants)*

- Over 10 moved in
- 5 – 10 moved in
- 0 – 5 moved in
- 0 – 5 moved away
- 5 – 10 moved away
- Over 10 moved away

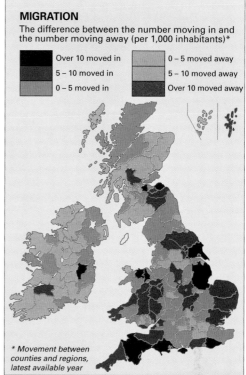

* Movement between counties and regions, latest available year

NATURAL POPULATION CHANGE

The difference between the number of births and the number of deaths per thousand inhabitants in 2001

- Over 7.5 more births
- 5 – 7.5 more births
- 2.5 – 5 more births
- 0 – 2.5 more births
- 0 – 2.5 more deaths
- Over 2.5 more deaths

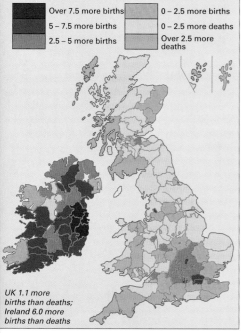

UK 1.1 more births than deaths; Ireland 6.0 more births than deaths

YOUNG PEOPLE

The percentage of the population under 15 years old in 2002

- Over 22.5%
- 20 – 22.5%
- 19 – 20%
- 18 – 19%
- Under 18%

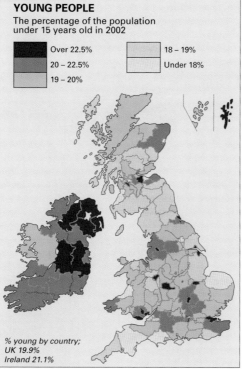

% young by country; UK 19.9% Ireland 21.1%

OLD PEOPLE

The percentage of the population over pensionable age* in 2002

- Over 22.5%
- 20 – 22.5%
- 17.5 – 20%
- 15 – 17.5%
- 12.5 – 15%
- Under 12.5%

*Pensionable age is 65 for males, 60 for females

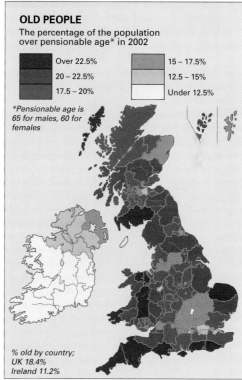

% old by country; UK 18.4% Ireland 11.2%

UK VITAL STATISTICS (1900–2000)

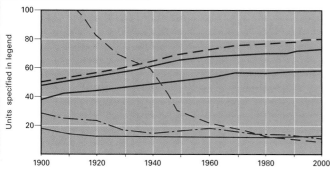

Units specified in legend

- Total population (in millions)
- Infant mortality (deaths per 1,000 live births)
- Birth rate (births per 1,000 of the population)
- Death rate (deaths per 1,000 of the population)
- Male life expectancy (in years)
- Female life expectancy (in years)

COPYRIGHT PHILIP'S

AGE STRUCTURE OF THE UK

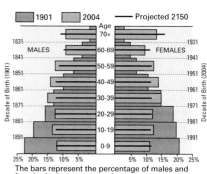

1901   2004   Projected 2150

Age 70+, 60-69, 50-59, 40-49, 30-39, 20-29, 10-19, 0-9

MALES   FEMALES

Decade of Birth (1901): 1831, 1841, 1851, 1861, 1871, 1881, 1891
Decade of Birth (2004): 1931, 1941, 1951, 1961, 1971, 1981, 1991

25% 20% 15% 10% 5%   5% 10% 15% 20% 25%

The bars represent the percentage of males and females in the age group shown

HOME OWNERSHIP
The percentage of dwellings that were owner-occupied in 2003

Over 75%	65 – 70%
70 – 75%	Under 65%

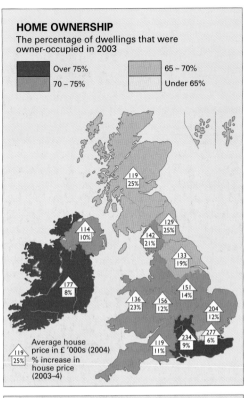

119 / 25%
114 / 10%
129 / 25%
142 / 21%
133 / 19%
177 / 8%
151 / 14%
136 / 23%
156 / 12%
204 / 12%
119 / 11%
234 / 9%
277 / 6%

119 / 25% Average house price in £ '000s (2004)
% increase in house price (2003–4)

CAR OWNERSHIP
The number of new cars per thousand people in 2001*

Over 50	20 – 30
40 – 50	10 – 20
30 – 40	

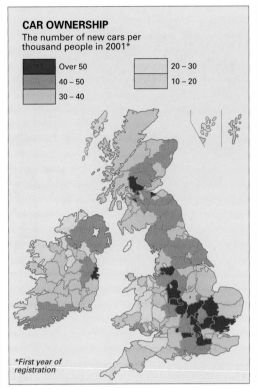

*First year of registration

INCOME
The average gross weekly earnings of males and females in full employment in 2004

Over £450	£375 – £400
£425 – £450	£350 – £375
£400 – £425	Under £350

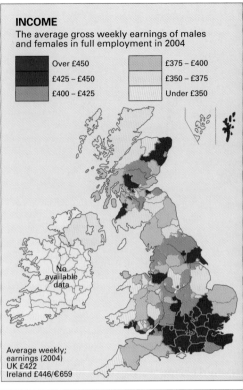

No available data

Average weekly; earnings (2004)
UK £422
Ireland £446/€659

HEALTH
The number of doctors per 100,000 people by region in 2002

Over 70	55 – 60
65 – 70	50 – 55
60 – 65	Under 50

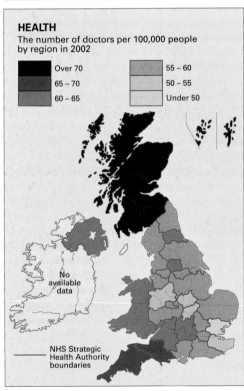

No available data

— NHS Strategic Health Authority boundaries

EDUCATION
The percentage of pupils aged 16 staying on in full-time education in 2003–2004

Over 77.5%	70 – 72.5%
75 – 77.5%	67.5 – 70%
72.5 – 75%	Under 67.5%

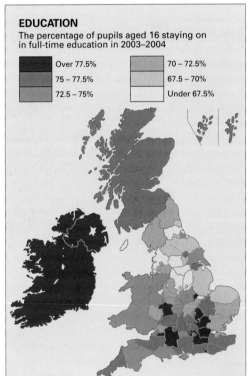

CRIME RATE
The number of recorded crimes per thousand people in 2003–4

Over 125	50 – 75
100 – 125	25 – 50
75 – 100	Under 25

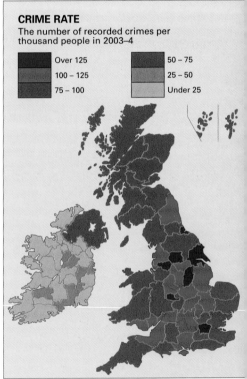

COMPARISON OF HOUSEHOLD EXPENDITURE IN THE UK

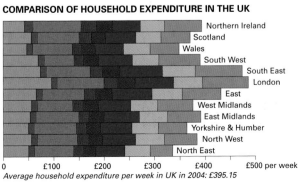

Northern Ireland
Scotland
Wales
South West
South East
London
East
West Midlands
East Midlands
Yorkshire & Humber
North West
North East

0   £100   £200   £300   £400   £500 per week

Average household expenditure per week in UK in 2004: £395.15

■	Housing
■	Fuel, light & power
■	Food, beverages and tobacco
■	Clothing and footwear
■	Household goods & services
■	Transport & communication
■	Leisure goods & services
■	Miscellaneous goods

COPYRIGHT PHILIP'S

CHANGES IN LIFESTYLE IN THE UK
Percentage of households owning goods listed below

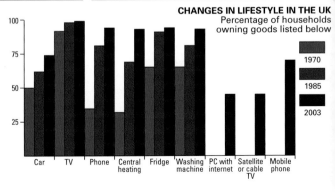

■	1970
■	1985
■	2003

Car   TV   Phone   Central heating   Fridge   Washing machine   PC with internet   Satellite or cable TV   Mobile phone

100
75
50
25

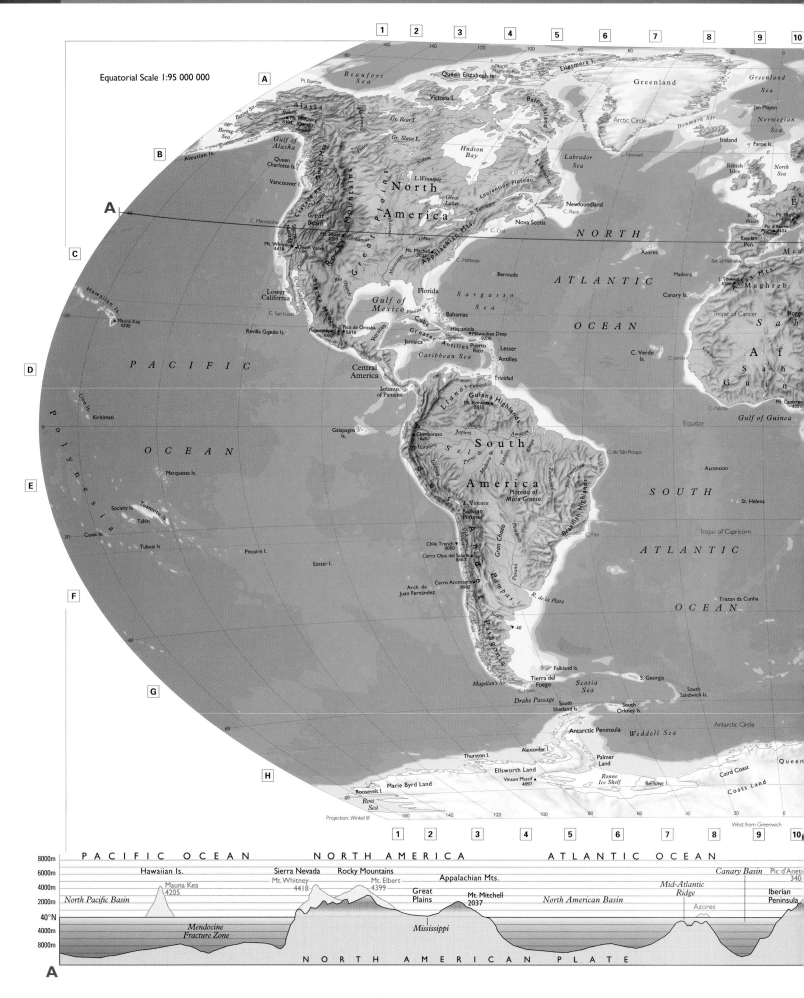

Equatorial Scale 1:95 000 000

Projection: Winkel III

West from Greenwich

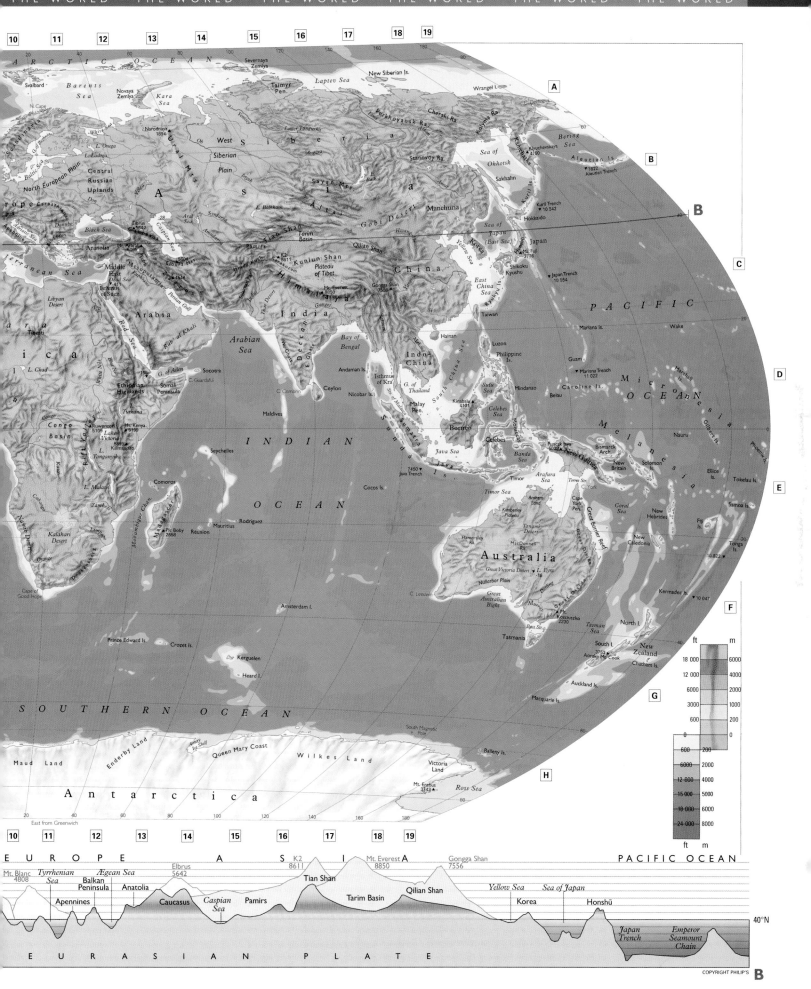

10 **11** **12** **13** **14** **15** **16** **17** **18** **19**

A R C T I C   O C E A N

Svalbard   Barents Sea   Novaya Zemlya   Kara Sea   Severnaya Zemlya   New Siberian Is.   Wrangel I.   **A**

N Cape   Scandinavia   White Sea   L. Onega   L. Ladoga   Ural Mts   Narodnaya 1894   Ob   West Siberian Plain   Lower Tunguska   Taimyr Pen.   Laptev Sea   Verkhoyansk Ra.   Cherski Ra.   Kolyma Ra.   Kamchatka   Klyuchevskaya 4750   Bering Sea   **B**

North European Plain   Central Russian Uplands   Yenisey   Yrtsysh   Angara   S i b e r i a   Stanovoy Ra.   Sea of Okhotsk   Sakhalin   Aleutian Is.   7822 Aleutian Trench   **B**

rope   Carpathians   Danube   Don   Volga   Caspian Sea   L. Balkhash   Baikal   Altai   Sayan Mts.   Gobi Desert   Manchuria   Kuril Trench 10 542   Hokkaido   **B**

Adriatic Sea   Black Sea   Elbrus 5642   Syrdarya   Tarim Basin   Hwang-Ho   Sea of Japan (East Sea)   Japan   **C**

editerranean Sea   Anatolia   Mt Ararat 5165   Elburz Mts   Pamirs   Tian Shan   Kunlun Shan   Qilian Shan   C h i n a   Mt Fuji 3776   **C**

A s i a   Middle East   Mesopotamia   Dead Sea   Isthmus of Suez   Euphrates   Hindu Kush   Karakoram   8611   Plateau of Tibet   Himalaya   Mt. Everest 8850   Gongga Shan 7556   Shikoku   Kyushu   Ryukyu Is.   East China Sea   Japan Trench 10 554   **C**

Libyan Desert   Arabia   Red Sea   Rub' al Khali   Persian Gulf   Indus   Thar Desert   Ganges   Brahmaputra   I n d i a   Si   Taiwan   Mariana Is.   Wake   **D**

f r i c a   Tibesti   L. Chad   White Nile   G. of Aden   Socotra   C. Guardafui   Arabian Sea   W. Ghats   Deccan   E. Ghats   Bay of Bengal   Andaman Is.   Indo-China   Hainan   Luzon   Philippine Is.   Guam   Mariana Trench 11 022   Caroline Is.   M i c r o n e s i a   Marshall   **D**

Ethiopian Highlands   Somali Peninsula   C. Comorin   Ceylon   Nicobar Is.   Isthmus of Kra   G. of Thailand   Malay Pen.   Kinabalu 4101   Sulu Sea   Mindanao   Belau   O C E A N   **D**

Congo Basin   Ruwenzori 5109   Mt Kenya 5199   L. Victoria   Turkana   Maldives   I N D I A N   Sumatra   South China Sea   Borneo   Celebes Sea   Celebes   Moluccas   Nauru   **E**

Kilimanjaro 5895   L. Tanganyika   Seychelles   Sunda Is.   Java Sea   7450 Java Trench   Java   Puncak Jaya 5029   New Guinea   Bismarck Arch.   New Britain   Solomon Is.   Ellice Is.   M e l a n e s i a   Phoenix Is.   **E**

Congo   Kasai   Zambezi   L. Malawi   Comoros   Madagascar   O C E A N   Cocos Is.   Banda Sea   Timor   Arafura Sea   Torres Str.   C. York   New Hebrides   Fiji Is.   Samoa Is.   Tokelau Is.   **E**

Namib Desert   Orange   Drakensberg   Limpopo   Pic Boby 2658   Reunion   Mauritius   Rodriguez   Timor Sea   Kimberley Plateau   Arnhem Land   Cape York Pen.   Great Barrier Reef   Coral Sea   New Caledonia   Tonga Is.   10 822   **E**

Kalahari Desert   Amsterdam I.   Hamersley Ra.   Tanami Desert   MacDonnell Ra.   Great Dividing Range   **F**

Cape of Good Hope   Prince Edward Is.   Crozet Is.   A u s t r a l i a   Great Victoria Desert   L. Eyre -16   Nullarbor Plain   Great Australian Bight   Murray   Mt Kosciuszko 2230   C. Leeuwin   North I.   Tasman Sea   **F**

Kerguelen   Heard I.   Bass Str.   Tasmania   Aoraki Mt Cook 3753   South I.   New Zealand   Chatham Is.   Kermadec Is.   10 047   **G**

S O U T H E R N   O C E A N   Auckland Is.   **G**

South Magnetic Pole   Macquarie Is.   **G**

Maud Land   Enderby Land   Amery Ice Shelf   Queen Mary Coast   W i l k e s   L a n d   Ballery Is.   Victoria Land   **H**

A n t a r c t i c a   Mt Erebus 3743   Ross Sea   **H**

20   40   60   80   100   120   140   160   180

East from Greenwich

10 **11** **12** **13** **14** **15** **16** **17** **18** **19**

PACIFIC

Mariana Trench

P A C I F I C

O C E A N

ft   m   18 000   6000   12 000   4000   6000   2000   3000   1000   600   200   0   0   600   200   6000   2000   12 000   4000   15 000   5000   18 000   6000   24 000   8000   ft   m

F

G

H

E U R O P E   A S I A   PACIFIC OCEAN

K2   Mt Everest   Gongga Shan
8611   8850   7556

Elbrus
5642

Mt Blanc   Tyrrhenian   Tian Shan
4808   Sea

Æegean Sea   Qilian Shan

Balkan   Anatolia   Yellow Sea   Sea of Japan
Peninsula

Apennines   Caucasus   Caspian   Pamirs   Tarim Basin   Korea   Honshū
Sea

40°N

Japan   Emperor
Trench   Seamount
Chain

E U R A S I A N   P L A T E

COPYRIGHT PHILIP'S

B

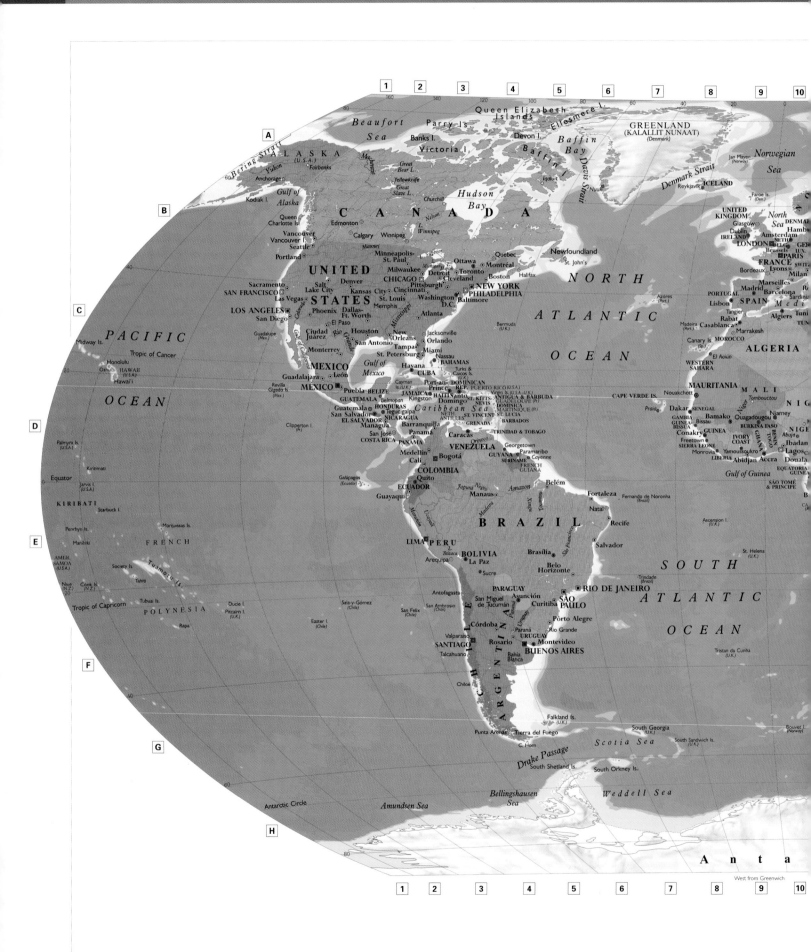

Projection: Winkel III

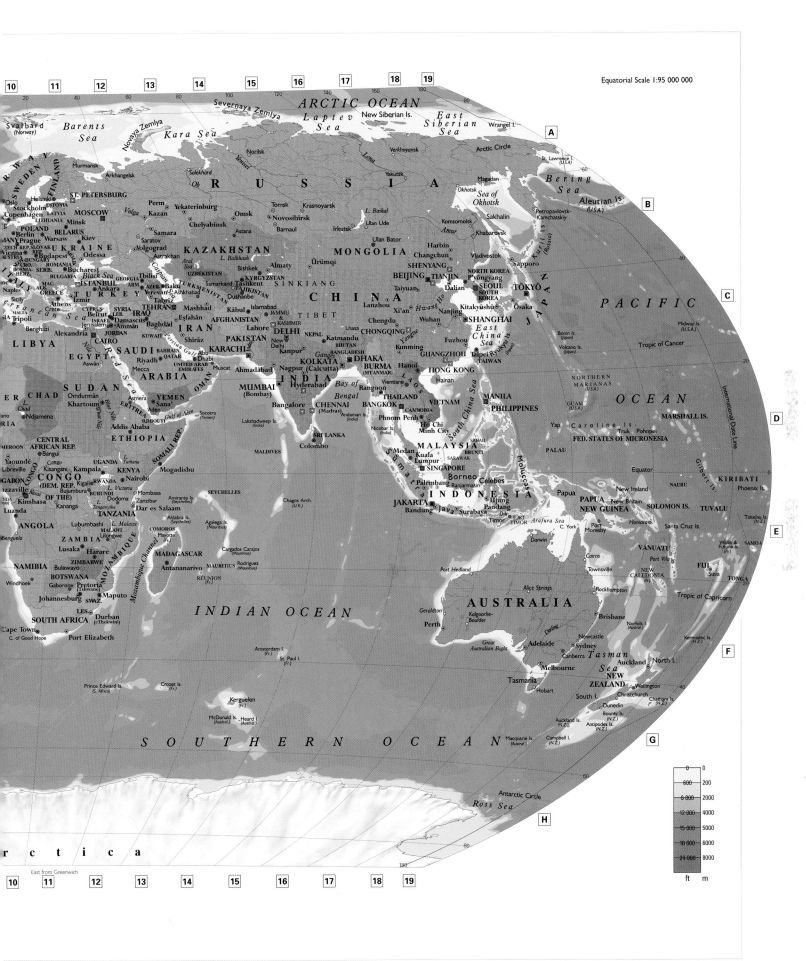

Equatorial Scale 1:95 000 000

East from Greenwich

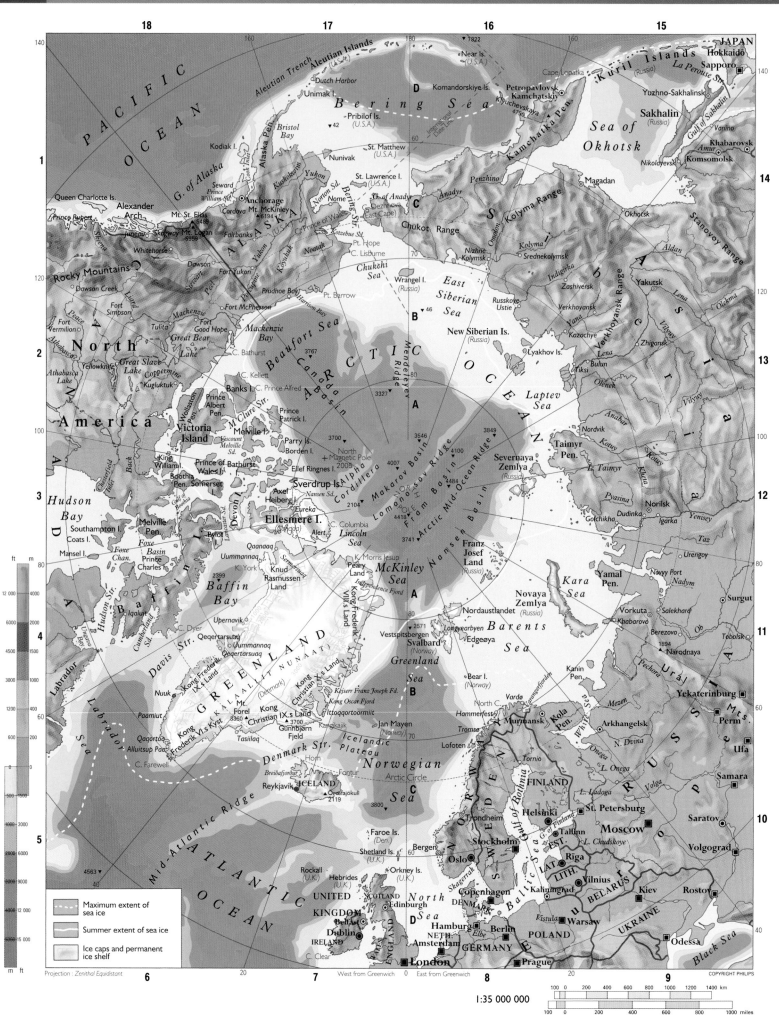

Projection : Zenithal Equidistant

West from Greenwich 0 East from Greenwich

COPYRIGHT PHILIPS

Maximum extent of sea ice

Summer extent of sea ice

Ice caps and permanent ice shelf

1:35 000 000

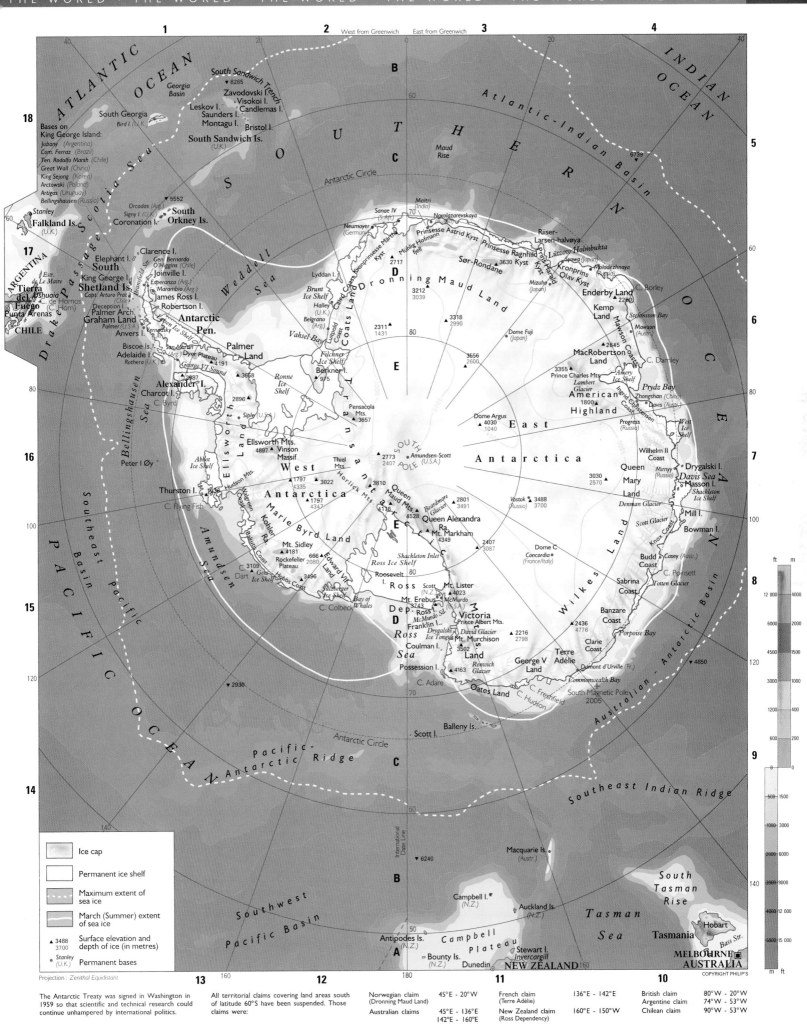

West from Greenwich East from Greenwich

ATLANTIC OCEAN

Georgia Basin

South Sandwich Trench

Zavodovski I.
Visokoi I.
Candlemas I.

Leskov I.
Saunders I.
Montagu I.

Bristol I.

South Sandwich Is.
(U.K.)

▼ 8265

South Georgia

Bird I. (U.K.)

Bases on King George Island:
Jubany (Argentina)
Com. Ferraz (Brazil)
Ten. Rodolfo Marsh (Chile)
Great Wall (China)
King Sejong (Korea)
Arctowski (Poland)
Artigas (Uruguay)
Bellingshausen (Russia)

Maud Rise

SOUTHERN

Atlantic–Indian Basin

INDIAN OCEAN

▼ 6739

Antarctic Circle

Scotia Sea

Orcadas (Arg.) ▲ 5552

Signy I. (U.K.)

Coronation I.

South Orkney Is.

Stanley
Falkland Is.
(U.K.)

ARGENTINA

Tierra del Fuego

Ushuaia
C. de Hornos (C. Horn)

Punta Arenas

CHILE

Drake Passage

Clarence I.
Elephant I.

Gen. Bernardo O'Higgins (Chile)

South Shetland Is.

King George I.

Esperanza (Arg.)
Capt. Arturo Prat (Chile)
Marambio (Arg.)
James Ross I.
Robertson I.

Joinville I.

Deception I.
Palmer Arch.

Antarctic Pen.

Palmer (U.S.A.)
Anvers I.
Vernadsky Ice Shelf

Graham Land

Biscoe Is.
Adelaide I.
Rothera (U.K.)

San Martín (Arg.)

Dyer Plateau

Alexander I.
▲ 2987

Charcot I.
C. Byrd

Bellingshausen Sea

Peter I Øy

▲ 2896

Siple (U.S.A.)

Thurston I.
▲ 1936

C. Flying Fish

Abbot Ice Shelf

Hudson Mts.

Walgreen Coast

Bakutis Coast

Kohler Ra.

Marie Byrd Land

Mt. Sidley ▲ 4181

Rockefeller Plateau
666 ▲ 2080

Edward VII Land

Dart ▲ 3109

Getz Ice Shelf

Hobbs Coast

▲ 3496

C. Colbeck

Sulzberger Ice Shelf

Bay of Whales

Southeast Pacific Basin

PACIFIC OCEAN

Weddell Sea

Lyddan I.

Brunt Ice Shelf

Halley (U.K.)

Belgrano (Arg.)

Filchner Ice Shelf

Berkner I.
975

Vahsel Bay

Ronne Ice Shelf

Pensacola Mts.
▲ 3657

Ellsworth Mts.
Vinson Massif ▲ 4897

Thiel Mts.

West Antarctica

1797 ▲ 3022
4335

1797 ▲
4343

▲ 3810

▲ 4116

▲ 4528

Horlick Mts.

Queen Maud Mts.

Beardmore Glacier ▲ 2801
3491

Mt. Markham ▲ 4349

Queen Alexandra Ra.

▲ 2407
3087

Shackleton Inlet

Ross Ice Shelf

Roosevelt I.

80

Ross Sea

Scott (N.Z.)

Mt. Lister ▲ 4023

Mt. Erebus ▲ 3743

McMurdo (U.S.A.)
Ross I.
McMurdo Sd.

Ross Dep.

Franklin I.

Coulman I.

Drygalski Ice Tongue

Mt. Murchison ▲ 3502

Possession I. ▲ 4163

Renwick Glacier

C. Adare

Oates Land

C. Hudson

Coats Land

Lützow Ice Shelf

Lyddan I.

Dronning Maud Land

Sanae IV

Maitri (India)

Neumayer (Germany)

Sanae IV (S. Afr.)

Novolazarevskaya (Russia)

Prinsesse Astrid Kyst

Prinsesse Ragnhild Kyst

Riiser-Larsen-halvøya

Mühlig Hofmann fjell ▲ 2717

Borg-massivet

▲ 3212
3039

▲ 2311
1431

▲ 3318
2990

Sør-Rondane

Prins Harald Kyst

▲ 3630

Lützow Holmbukta

Syowa (Japan)

Kronprins Olav Kyst

Molodezhnaya (Russia)

Mizuho (Japan)

Enderby Land

C. Borley

▲ 2280

Kemp Land

Stefansson Bay

Mawson (Austr.)

▲ 2645

MacRobertson Land

C. Darnley

Prince Charles Mts. ▲ 3355

Amery Ice Shelf

Lambert Glacier

Prydz Bay

Zhongshan (China)

Davis (Austr.)

Ingrid Christensen Coast

American Highland

▲ 1800

Dome Fuji (Japan)

Dome Argus ▲ 4030
1040

East Antarctica

▲ 3656
2600

▲ 3030
2570

Vostok (Russia) ▲ 3488
3700

Dome C

Concordia (France/Italy)

Progress (Russia)

West Ice Shelf

Wilhelm II Coast

Mirnyy (Russia)

Drygalski I.

Davis Sea

Masson I.

Shackleton Ice Shelf

Mill I.

Denman Glacier

Queen Mary Land

Bowman I.

Scott Glacier

Knox Coast

Budd Coast

Casey (Austr.)

C. Poinsett

Totten Glacier

Sabrina Coast

Wilkes Land

Banzare Coast

▲ 2436
4776

Clarie Coast

Porpoise Bay

Dumont d'Urville (Fr.)

Commonwealth Bay

South Magnetic Pole 2005

Terre Adélie

George V Land

▲ 2216
2798

C. Freshfield

David Glacier

Victoria Land

Prince Albert Mts.

INDIAN OCEAN

Australian–Antarctic Basin

▼ 4650

South

Amundsen-Scott (U.S.A.)

2773
2407

SOUTH POLE

South Pole

Transantarctic Mts.

Sector

Antarctic Circle

Scott I.

Balleny Is.

International Date Line

▼ 6240

Southwest Pacific Basin

Pacific–Antarctic Ridge

Southeast Indian Ridge

Macquarie Is. (Austr.)

Campbell I. (N.Z.)

Auckland Is. (N.Z.)

Antipodes Is. (N.Z.)

Bounty Is. (N.Z.)

Campbell Plateau

Stewart I.

Invercargill

Dunedin

NEW ZEALAND

South Tasman Rise

Tasman Sea

Tasmania

Bass Str.

Hobart

MELBOURNE AUSTRALIA

COPYRIGHT PHILIP'S

Legend:

	Ice cap
	Permanent ice shelf
	Maximum extent of sea ice
	March (Summer) extent of sea ice
▲ 3488 3700	Surface elevation and depth of ice (in metres)
• Stanley (U.K.)	Permanent bases

Projection : Zenithal Equidistant

The Antarctic Treaty was signed in Washington in 1959 so that scientific and technical research could continue unhampered by international politics.

All territorial claims covering land areas south of latitude 60°S have been suspended. Those claims were:

Norwegian claim (Dronning Maud Land)	45°E – 20°W
Australian claims	45°E – 136°E 142°E – 160°E
French claim (Terre Adélie)	136°E – 142°E
New Zealand claim (Ross Dependency)	160°E – 150°W
British claim	80°W – 20°W
Argentine claim	74°W – 53°W
Chilean claim	90°W – 53°W

Elevation scale:
ft / m
12 000 / 4000
9000 / 3000
6000 / 2000
4500 / 1500
3000 / 1000
1200 / 400
600 / 200
0 / 0
500 / 1500
1000 / 3000
2000 / 6000
3000 / 9000
4000 / 12 000
5000 / 15 000
m / ft

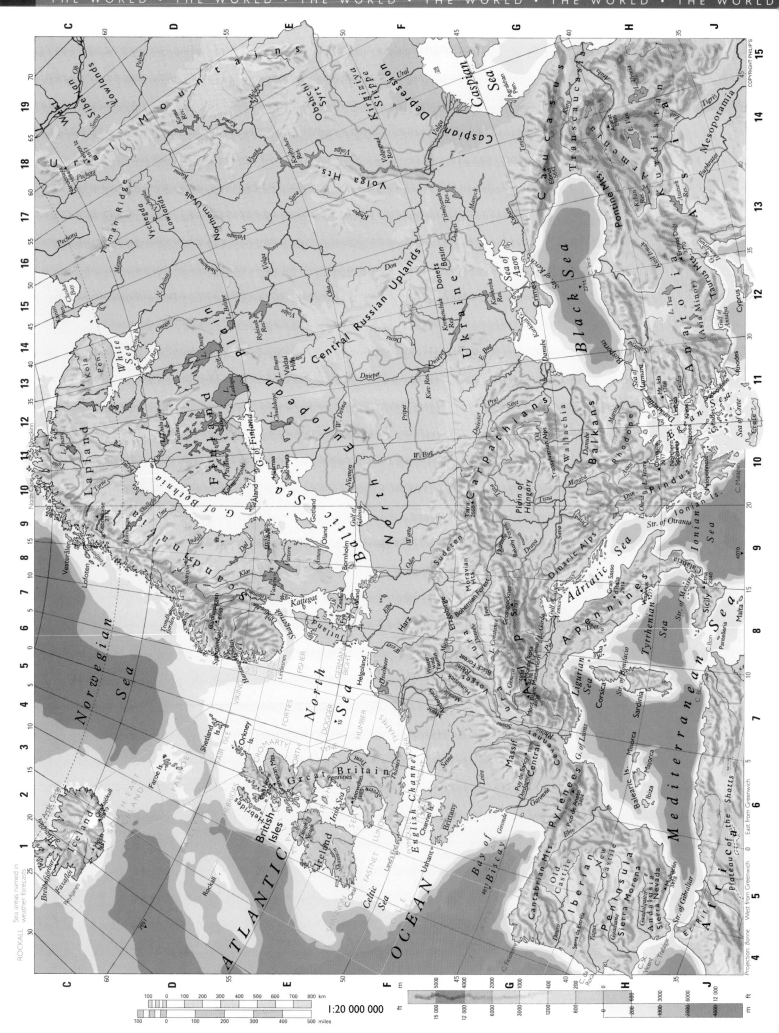

1:20 000 000

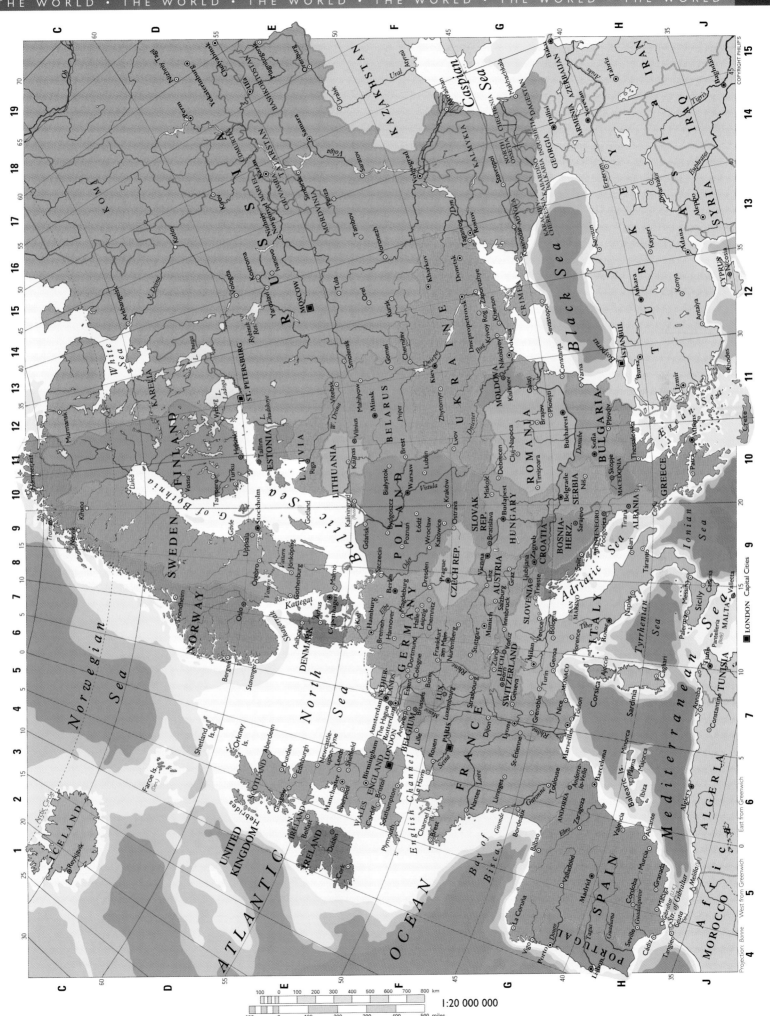

1:20 000 000

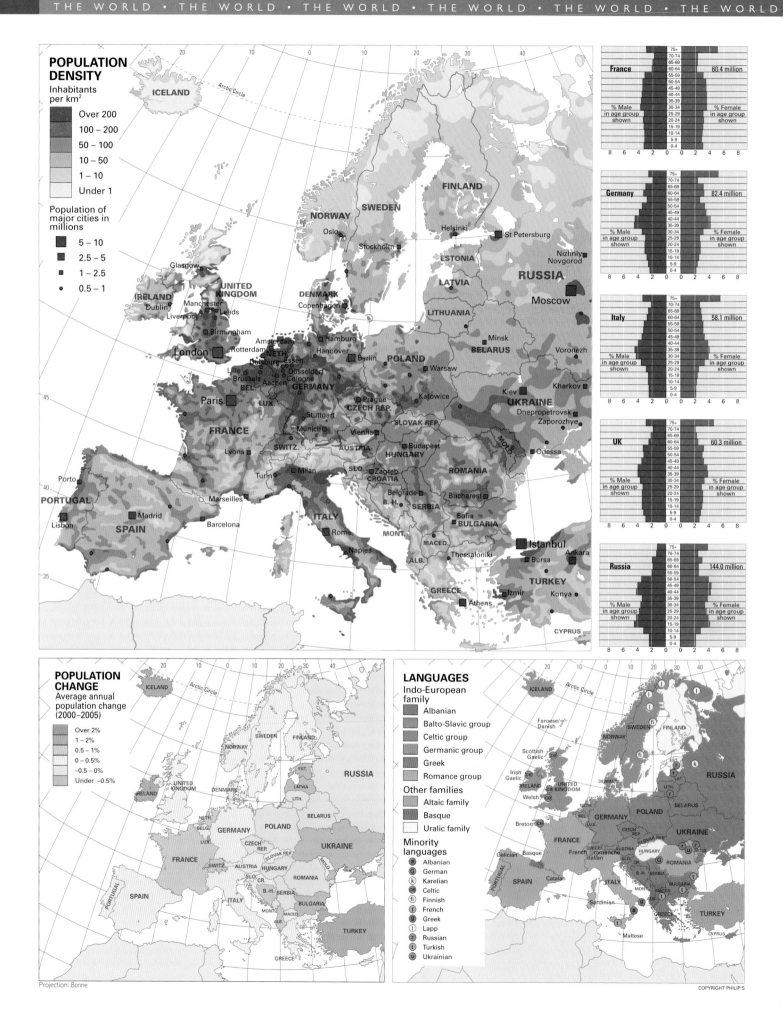

POPULATION DENSITY

Inhabitants per km²

- Over 200
- 100 – 200
- 50 – 100
- 10 – 50
- 1 – 10
- Under 1

Population of major cities in millions

- 5 – 10
- 2.5 – 5
- 1 – 2.5
- 0.5 – 1

France 60.4 million

Germany 82.4 million

Italy 58.1 million

UK 60.3 million

Russia 144.0 million

POPULATION CHANGE

Average annual population change (2000–2005)

- Over 2%
- 1 – 2%
- 0.5 – 1%
- 0 – 0.5%
- –0.5 – 0%
- Under –0.5%

LANGUAGES

Indo-European family

- Albanian
- Balto-Slavic group
- Celtic group
- Germanic group
- Greek
- Romance group

Other families

- Altaic family
- Basque
- Uralic family

Minority languages

- a Albanian
- G German
- k Karelian
- ce Celtic
- fi Finnish
- f French
- g Greek
- l Lapp
- r Russian
- t Turkish
- u Ukrainian

Projection: Bonne

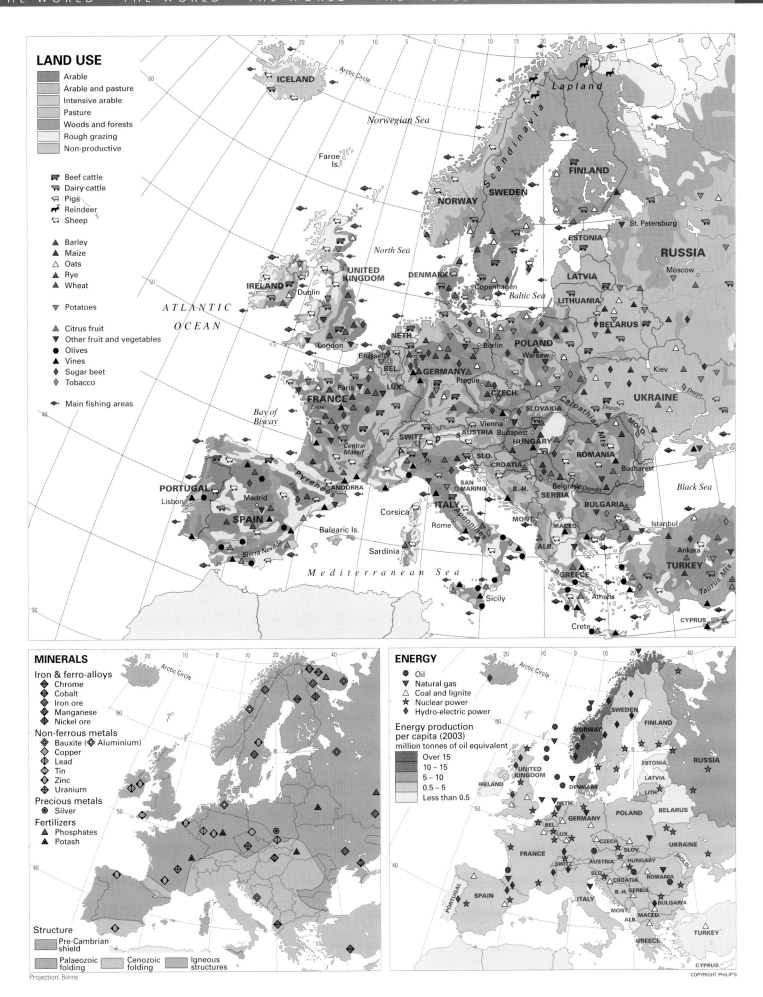

LAND USE

- Arable
- Arable and pasture
- Intensive arable
- Pasture
- Woods and forests
- Rough grazing
- Non-productive

- Beef cattle
- Dairy cattle
- Pigs
- Reindeer
- Sheep

- ▲ Barley
- ▲ Maize
- △ Oats
- ▲ Rye
- ▲ Wheat

- ▽ Potatoes

- △ Citrus fruit
- ▼ Other fruit and vegetables
- ● Olives
- ▲ Vines
- ◆ Sugar beet
- ◆ Tobacco

- Main fishing areas

MINERALS

Iron & ferro-alloys
- ◆ Chrome
- ◆ Cobalt
- ◆ Iron ore
- ◆ Manganese
- ◆ Nickel ore

Non-ferrous metals
- ◈ Bauxite (◇ Aluminium)
- ◇ Copper
- ◇ Lead
- ◇ Tin
- ◇ Zinc
- ⊕ Uranium

Precious metals
- ◉ Silver

Fertilizers
- ▲ Phosphates
- ▲ Potash

Structure
- Pre-Cambrian shield
- Palaeozoic folding
- Cenozoic folding
- Igneous structures

Projection: *Bonne*

ENERGY

- ● Oil
- ▼ Natural gas
- △ Coal and lignite
- ★ Nuclear power
- ◆ Hydro-electric power

Energy production per capita (2003)
million tonnes of oil equivalent
- Over 15
- 10 – 15
- 5 – 10
- 0.5 – 5
- Less than 0.5

COPYRIGHT PHILIP'S

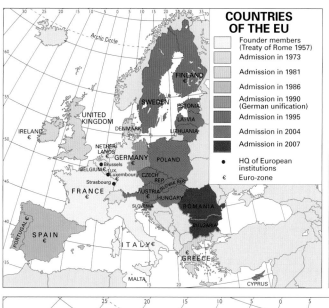

COUNTRIES OF THE EU

- Founder members (Treaty of Rome 1957)
- Admission in 1973
- Admission in 1981
- Admission in 1986
- Admission in 1990 (German unification)
- Admission in 1995
- Admission in 2004
- Admission in 2007
- • HQ of European institutions
- € Euro-zone

EU COUNTRY COMPARISONS	Population (thousands)	Annual Income (US$ per capita)
Austria	8,185	31,300
Belgium	10,364	30,600
Cyprus	780	20,300
Czech Republic	10,241	16,800
Denmark	5,432	32,200
Estonia	1,333	14,300
Finland	5,223	29,000
France	60,656	28,700
Germany	82,431	28,700
Greece	10,688	21,300
Hungary	10,007	14,900
Ireland	4,016	31,900
Italy	58,103	27,700
Latvia	2,290	11,500
Lithuania	3,597	12,500
Luxembourg	469	58,900
Malta	399	18,200
Netherlands	16,407	29,500
Poland	38,635	12,000
Portugal	10,566	17,900
Slovakia	5,431	14,500
Slovenia	2,011	19,600
Spain	40,341	23,300
Sweden	9,002	28,400
United Kingdom	60,041	29,600
Total EU 2005 (25 countries)	**456,648**	**24,144**
Bulgaria	7,450	9,000
Romania	22,330	8,300

REGIONS OF THE EU

Austria (States) — A
1 Niederösterreich
2 Oberösterreich
3 Burgenland
4 Kärnten
5 Salzburg
6 Steiermark
7 Tirol
8 Wien
9 Vorarlberg

Belgium (Regions) — B
1 Bruxelles
2 Vlaanderen
3 Wallonie

Bulgaria (member state from 2007) — BU

Cyprus (member state with no corresponding division) — CY

Czech Republic — CZ
1 Jihovychod
2 Jihozapad
3 Moravskoslezsko
4 Praha
5 Severovychod
6 Severozapad
7 Stredni Cechy
8 Stredni Morava

Denmark (member state with no corresponding division) — DK

Estonia (member state with no corresponding division) — EE

Finland (Provinces) — FIN
1 Åland
2 Itä-Suomi
3 Väli-Suomi
4 Pohjois-Suomi
5 Uusimaa (Suuralue)
6 Etelä-Suomi

France (Regions) — F
1 Alsace
2 Aquitaine
3 Auvergne
4 Bourgogne
5 Bretagne
6 Centre
7 Champagne-Ardenne
8 Corse
9 Franche-Comté
10 Île-de-France
11 Languedoc-Roussillon
12 Limousin
13 Loire (Pays de la)
14 Lorraine
15 Midi-Pyrénées
16 Nord-Pas-de-Calais
17 Normandie (Basse-)
18 Normandie (Haute-)
19 Picardie
20 Poitou-Charentes
21 Provence-Alpes-Côte d'Azur
22 Rhône-Alpes

Germany (Länder) — D
1 Baden-Württemberg
2 Niedersachsen
3 Bayern
4 Berlin
5 Brandenburg
6 Bremen
7 Hamburg
8 Hessen
9 Mecklenburg-Vorpommern
10 Nordrhein-Westfalen
11 Rheinland-Pfalz
12 Saarland
13 Sachsen
14 Sachsen-Anhalt
15 Schleswig-Holstein
16 Thüringen

Greece (Regions) — EL
1 Anatoliki Makedonia kai Thraki
2 Kriti
3 Voreio Aigaio
4 Notio Aigaio
5 Epiros
6 Attiki
7 Sterea Ellas
8 Dytiki Ellas
9 Ionioi Nisoi
10 Dytiki Makedonia
11 Kentriki Makedonia
12 Peloponnese
13 Thessaly

Hungary (Megyék) — HU
1 Del-Alfold
2 Del-Dunantul
3 Eszak-Alfold
4 Eszak-Magyarorszag
5 Kozep-Dunantul
6 Kozep-Magyarorszag
7 Nyugat-Dunantul

Ireland (Provinces) — IRL
1 Border, Midlands & Western
2 Southern & Eastern

Italy (Regions) — I
1 Abruzzo
2 Basilicata
3 Calábria
4 Campánia
5 Emilia-Romagna
6 Friuli-Venézia Giulia
7 Lazio
8 Liguria
9 Lombardia
10 Marche
11 Molise
12 Umbria
13 Piemonte
14 Puglia
15 Sardegna
16 Sicilia
17 Toscana
18 Trentino-Alto Adige
19 Valle d'Aosta
20 Venéto

Latvia (member state with no corresponding division) — LV

Lithuania (member state with no corresponding division) — LT

Luxembourg (member state with no corresponding division) — L

Malta (member state with no corresponding division) — MT

Netherlands (Regions) — NL
1 Noord-Nederland
2 Oost-Nederland
3 West-Nederland
4 Zuid-Nederland

Poland (Voivodships) — PL
1 Dolnośląskie
2 Kujawsko-Pomorskie
3 Łódzkie
4 Lubelskie
5 Lubuskie
6 Małopolskie
7 Mazowieckie
8 Opolskie
9 Podkarpackie
10 Podlaskie
11 Pomorskie
12 Śląskie
13 Swietokrzyskie
14 Warmińsko-Mazurskie
15 Wielkopolskie
16 Zachodniopomorskie

Portugal (Autonomous regions) — P
1 Alentejo
2 Algarve
3 Centro
4 Lisboa-Vale do Tejo
5 Norte

Romania (member state from 2007) — RO

Slovak Republic (Kraj) — SK
1 Bratislavsky Kraj
2 Stredne Slovensko
3 Vychodne Slovensko
4 Zapadne Slovensko

Slovenia (member state with no corresponding division) — SI

Spain (Autonomous communities) — E
1 Andalucía
2 Aragon
3 Asturias
4 Islas Baleares
5 País Vasco
6 Islas Canarias
7 Cantabria
8 Castilla y León
9 Castilla-La Mancha
10 Cataluña
11 Extremadura
12 Galicia
13 Madrid
14 Murcia
15 Navarra
16 Rioja (La)
17 Valencia

Sweden (Regions) — S
1 Stockholm
2 Östra Mellansverige
3 Sydsverige
4 Västsverige
5 Norra Mellansverige
6 Mellersta Norrland
7 Övre Norrland
8 Småland med öarna

United Kingdom (Government Office Regions) — UK
1 North East
2 North West
3 Yorkshire & The Humber
4 East Midlands
5 West Midlands
6 Eastern
7 London
8 South East
9 South West
10 Wales
11 Scotland
12 Northern Ireland

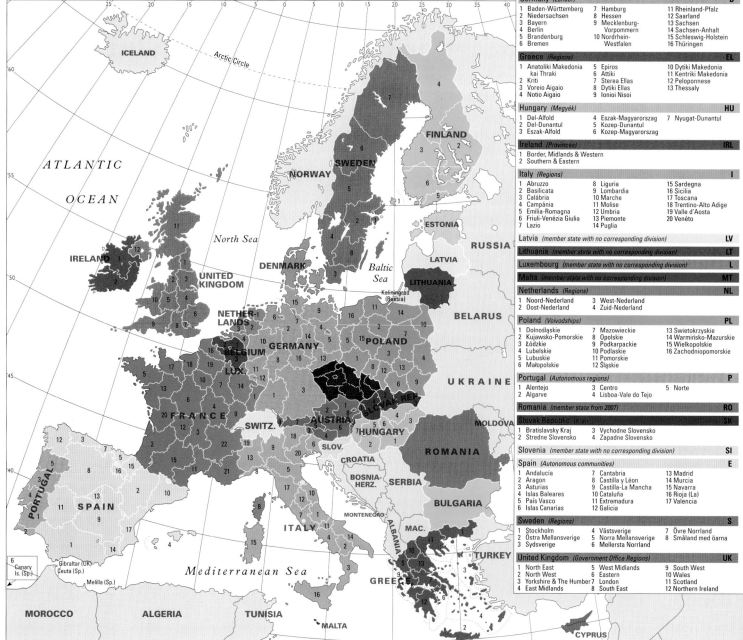

Projection: Bonne

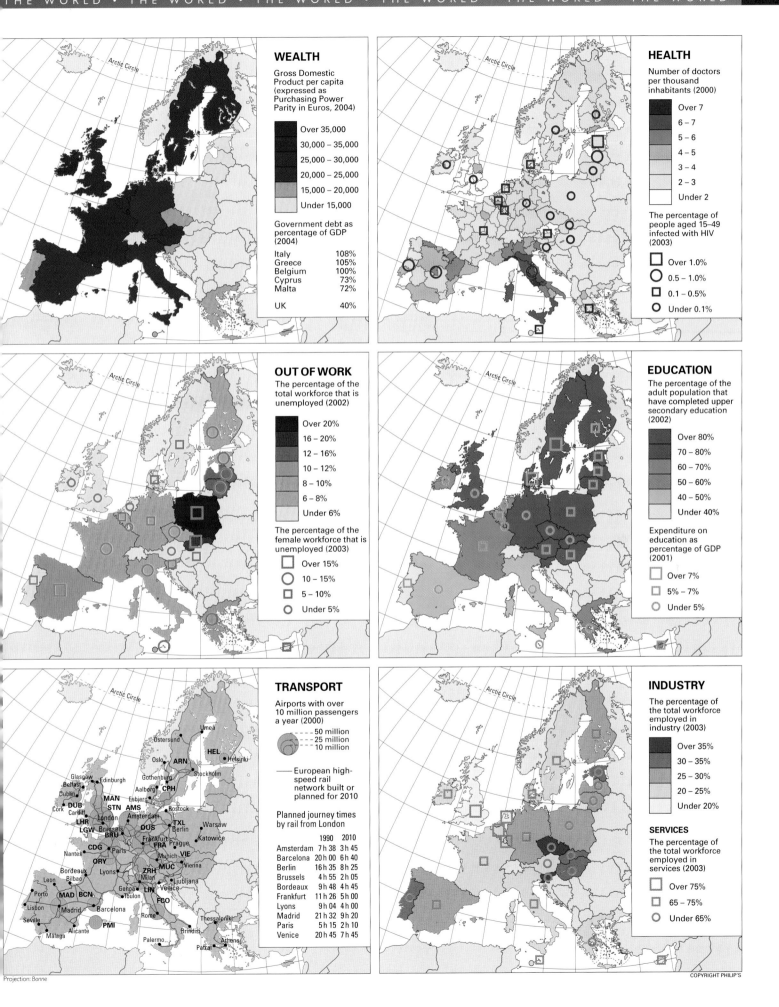

Projection: Bonne

COPYRIGHT PHILIP'S

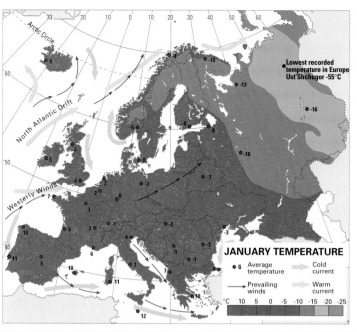

JANUARY TEMPERATURE

Lowest recorded temperature in Europe Ust'Shchugor -55°C

- **6** Average temperature
- → Prevailing winds
- ⇒ Cold current
- ⇒ Warm current

°C 10 5 0 -5 -10 -15 -20 -25

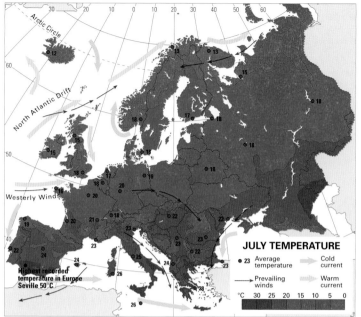

JULY TEMPERATURE

Highest recorded temperature in Europe Seville 50°C

- **23** Average temperature
- → Prevailing winds
- ⇒ Cold current
- ⇒ Warm current

°C 30 25 20 15 10 5 0

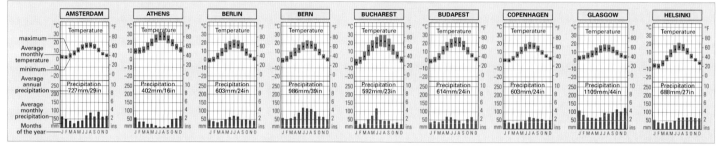

AMSTERDAM	ATHENS	BERLIN	BERN	BUCHAREST	BUDAPEST	COPENHAGEN	GLASGOW	HELSINKI
Temperature	Temperature	Temperature	Temperature	Temperature	Temperature	Temperature	Temperature	Temperature
Precipitation 727mm/29in	Precipitation 402mm/16in	Precipitation 603mm/24in	Precipitation 986mm/39in	Precipitation 592mm/23in	Precipitation 614mm/24in	Precipitation 603mm/24in	Precipitation 1109mm/44in	Precipitation 688mm/27in

- maximum
- Average monthly temperature
- minimum
- Average annual precipitation
- Average monthly precipitation
- Months of the year

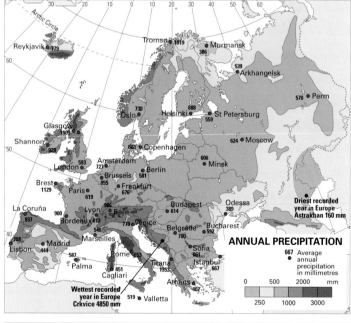

ANNUAL PRECIPITATION

Tromso 1019
Reykjavik 779
Murmansk 386
Arkhangelsk 539
Perm 570
Oslo 730
Helsinki 688
St Petersburg 559
Glasgow 1109
Shannon 929
Moscow 624
London 593
Amsterdam 727
Berlin 581
Minsk 606
Brussels 855
Frankfurt 676
Breste 1129
Paris 619
La Coruña 937
Lyon 886
Bern 900
Bordeaux 813
Venice 770
Budapest 614
Odessa 389
Marseilles 546
Belgrade 700
Bucharest 592
Lisbon 708
Madrid 444
Rome 653
Sofia 661
Titana 1353
Istanbul 667
Palma 451
Cagliari 587
Athens 402
Valletta 519

Driest recorded year in Europe Astrakhan 160 mm

Wettest recorded year in Europe Crkvice 4850 mm

- **667** Average annual precipitation in millimetres

0 500 2000 mm
250 1000 3000

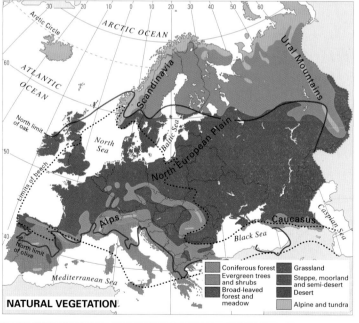

NATURAL VEGETATION

ARCTIC OCEAN
ATLANTIC OCEAN
Scandinavia
Ural Mountains
North Sea
Baltic Sea
North European Plain
North limit of oak
limits of beech
Alps
Caucasus
Caspian Sea
North limit of olive
Black Sea
Mediterranean Sea

- Coniferous forest
- Evergreen trees and shrubs
- Broad-leaved forest and meadow
- Grassland
- Steppe, moorland and semi-desert
- Desert
- Alpine and tundra

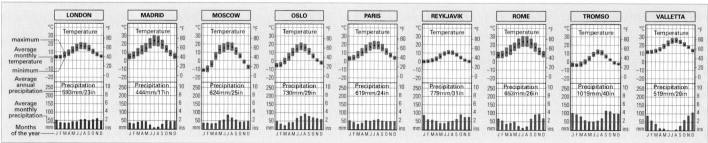

LONDON	MADRID	MOSCOW	OSLO	PARIS	REYKJAVIK	ROME	TROMSO	VALLETTA
Temperature	Temperature	Temperature	Temperature	Temperature	Temperature	Temperature	Temperature	Temperature
Precipitation 593mm/23in	Precipitation 444mm/17in	Precipitation 624mm/25in	Precipitation 730mm/29in	Precipitation 619mm/24in	Precipitation 779mm/31in	Precipitation 653mm/26in	Precipitation 1019mm/40in	Precipitation 519mm/20in

- maximum
- Average monthly temperature
- minimum
- Average annual precipitation
- Average monthly precipitation
- Months of the year

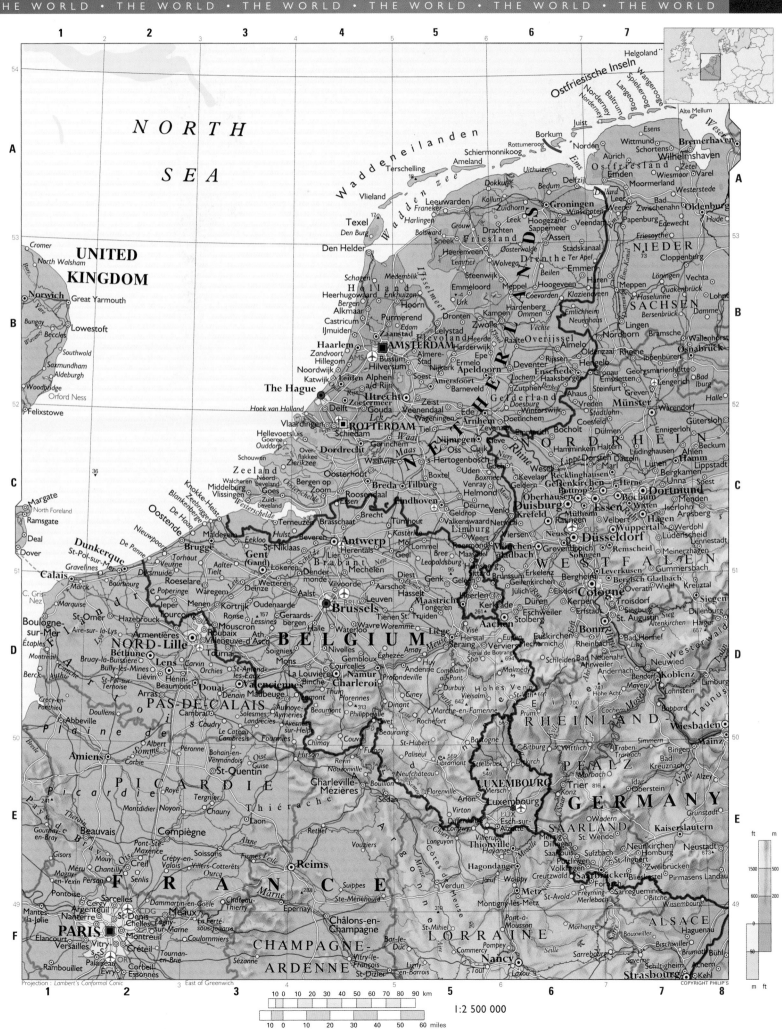

Projection : Lambert's Conformal Conic

1:2 500 000

COPYRIGHT PHILIP'S

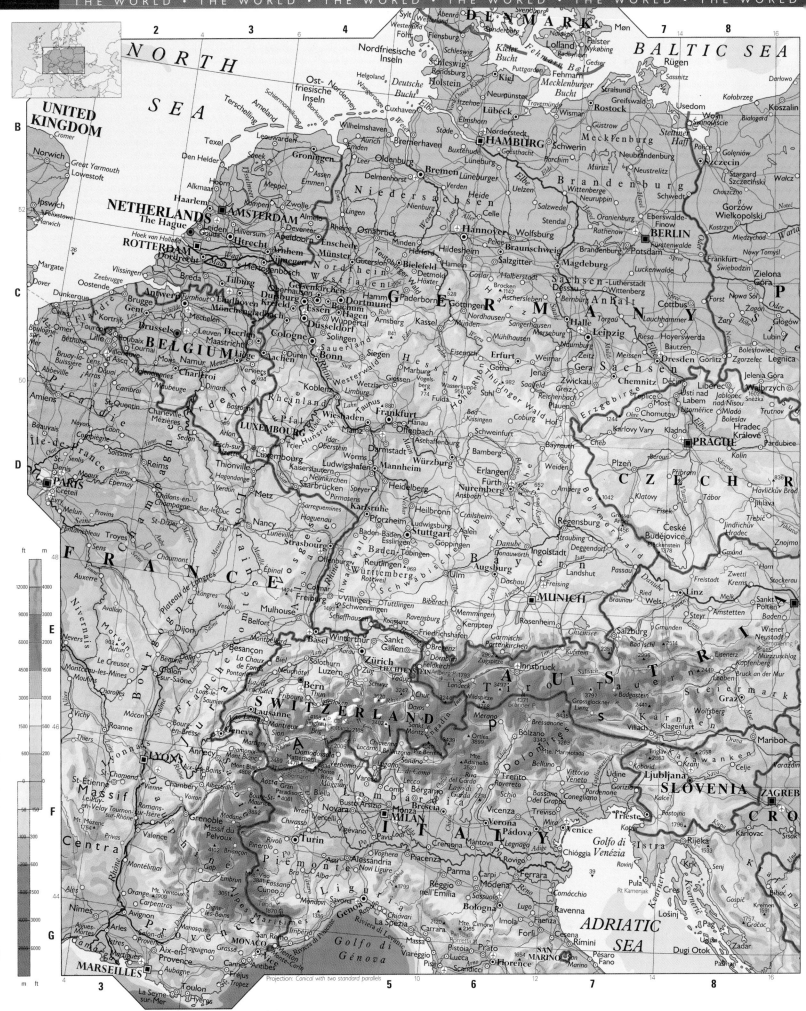

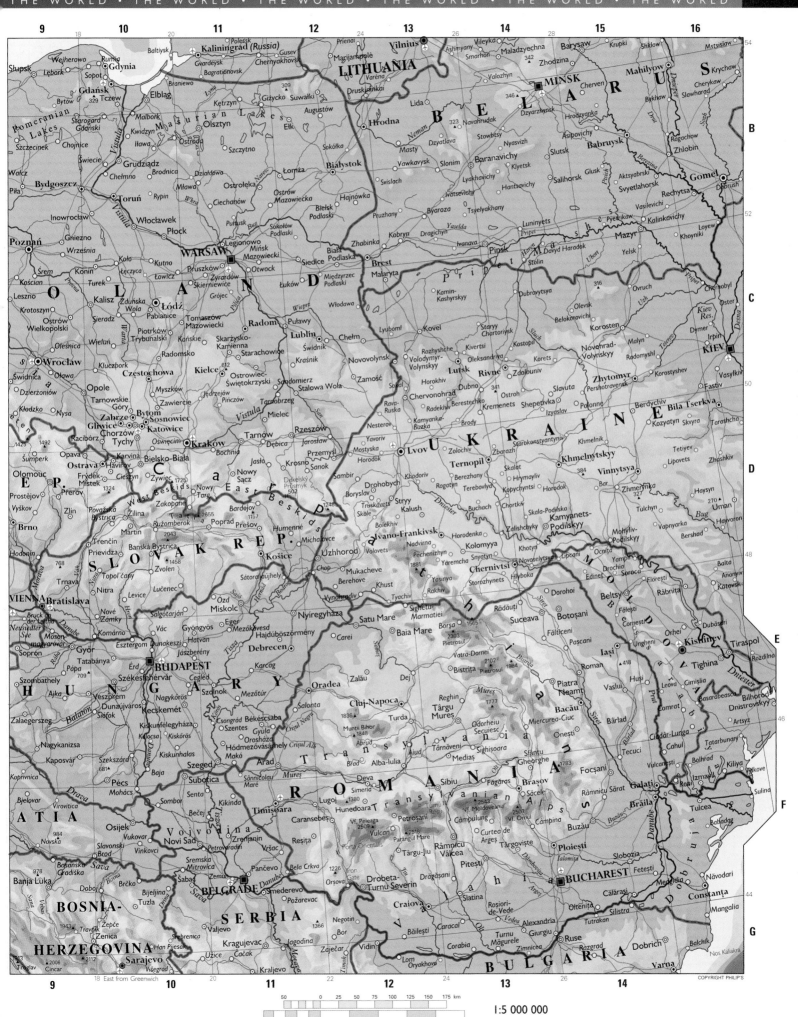

1:5 000 000

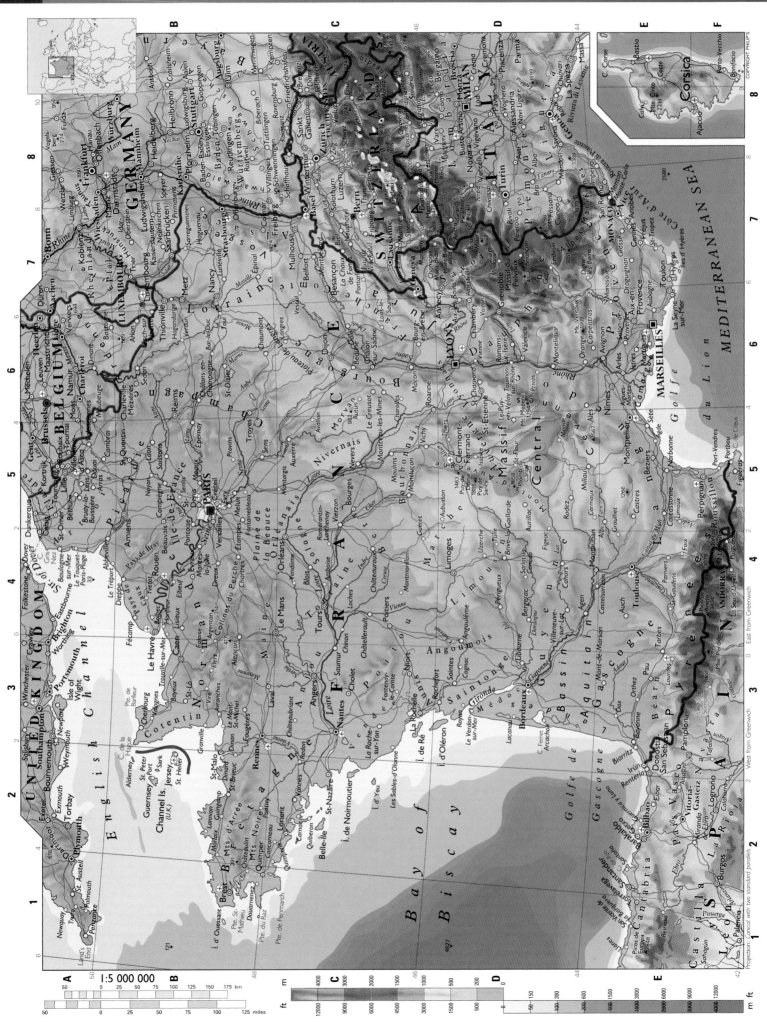

1:5 000 000

Projection: Conical with two standard parallels

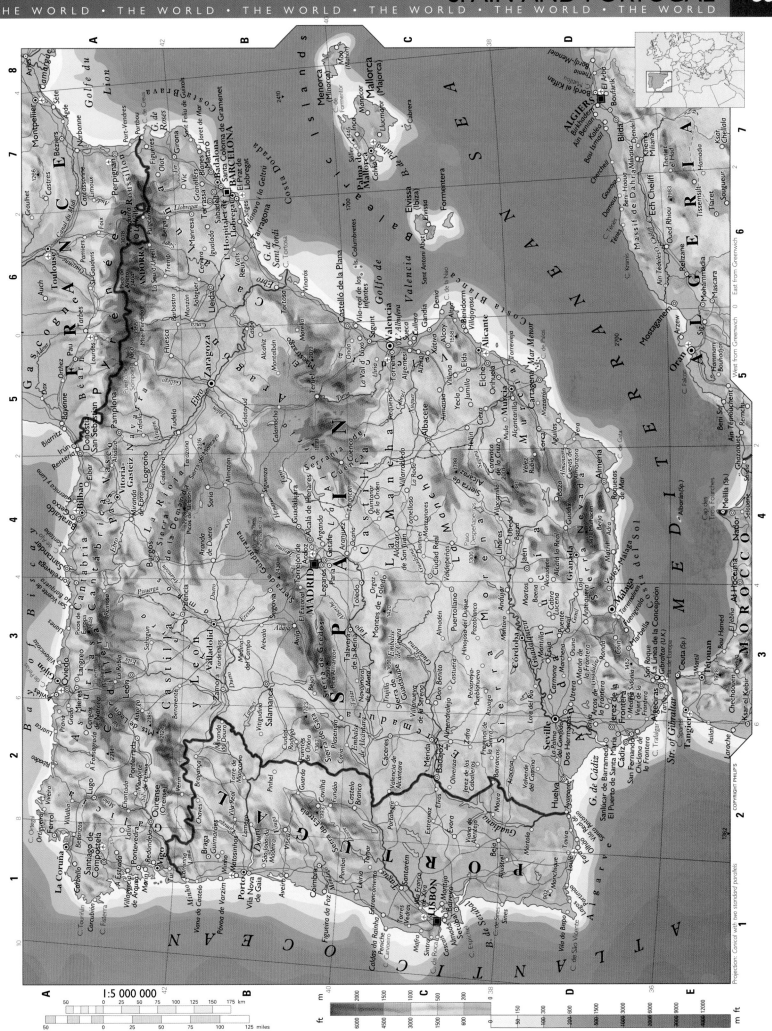

1:5 000 000

Projection: Conical with two standard parallels

COPYRIGHT PHILIP'S

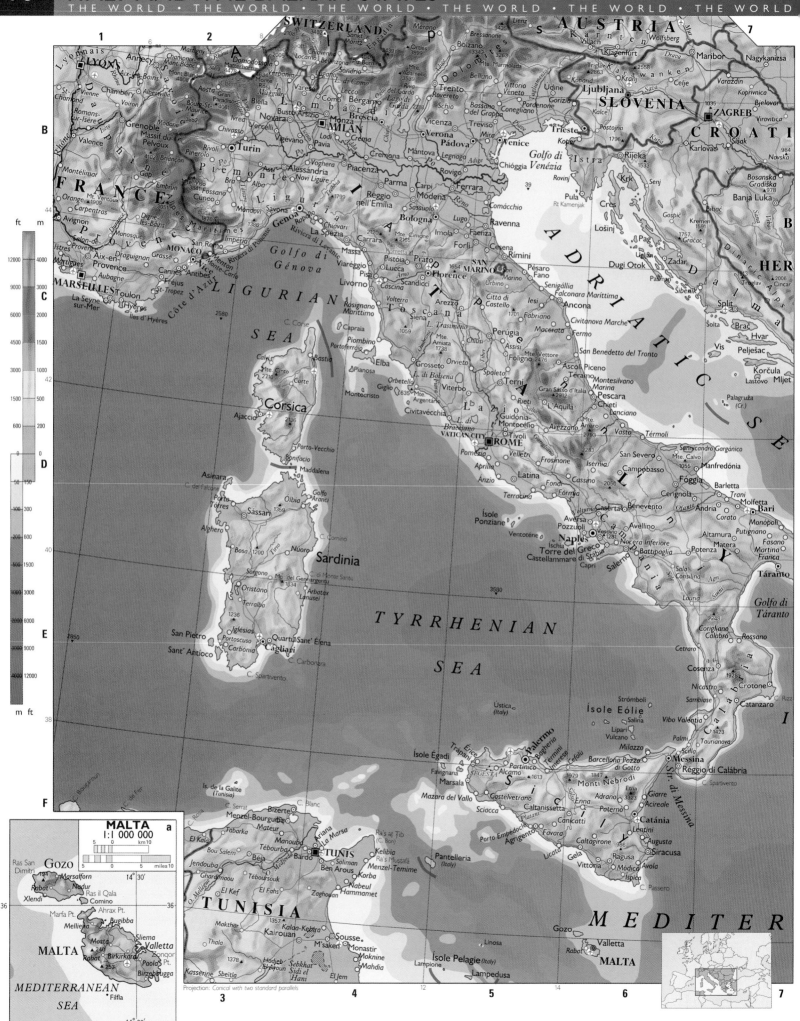

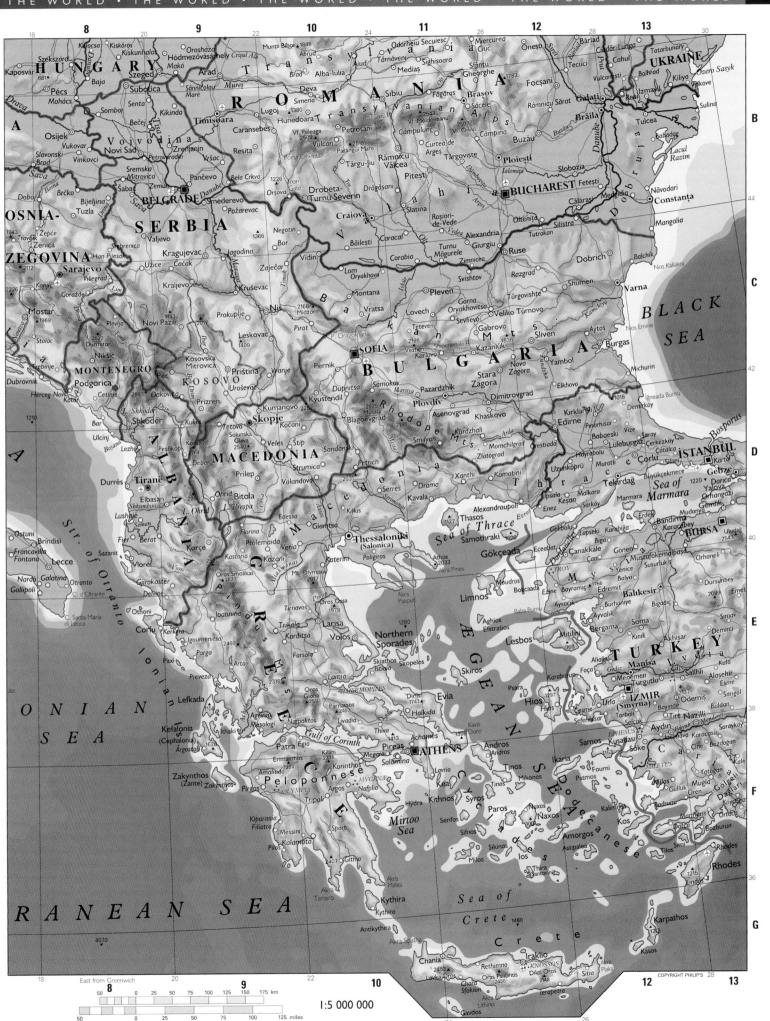

East from Greenwich

1:5 000 000

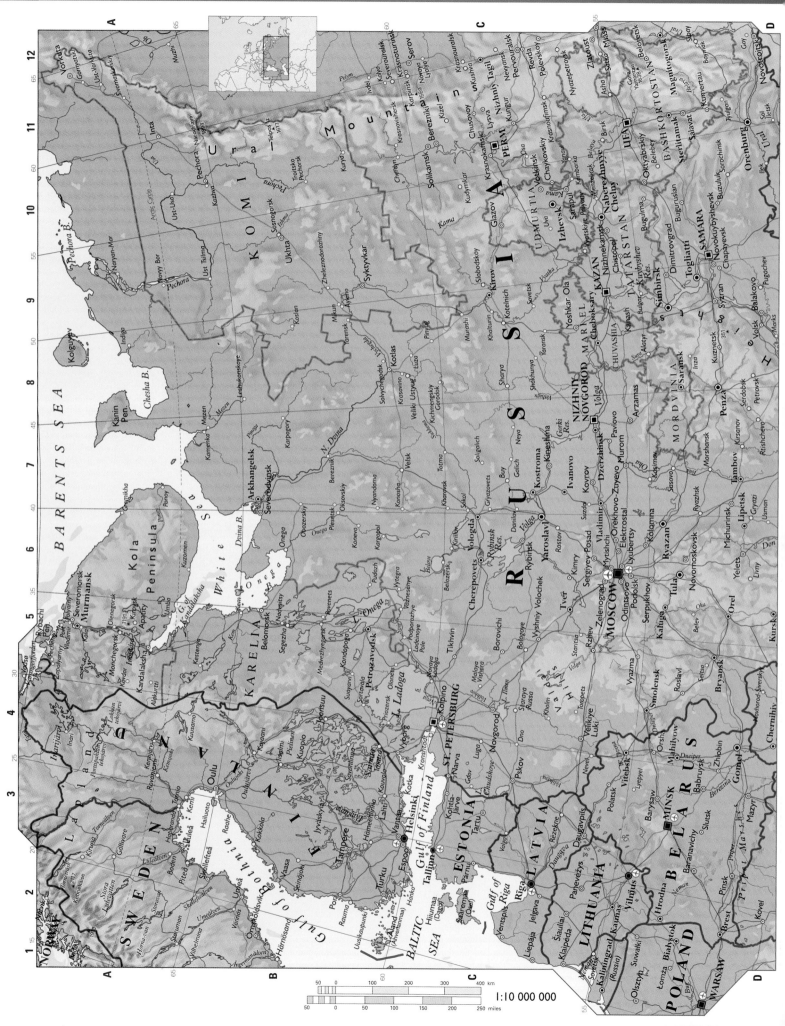

1:10 000 000

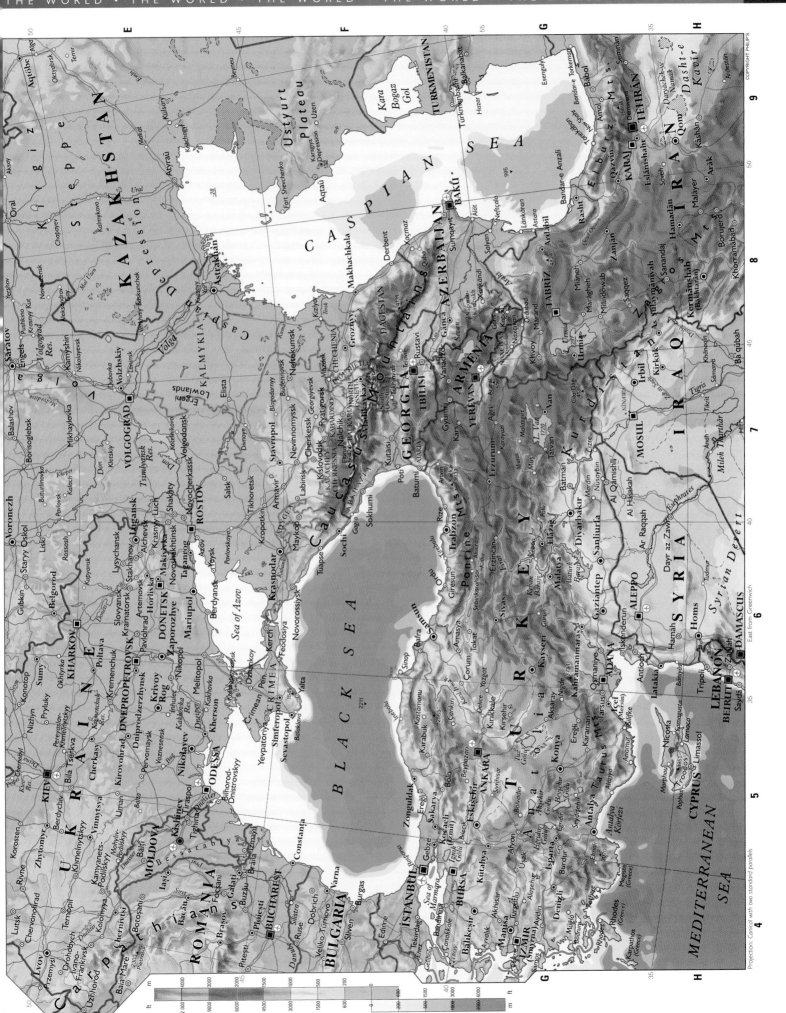

Projection: Conical with two standard parallels

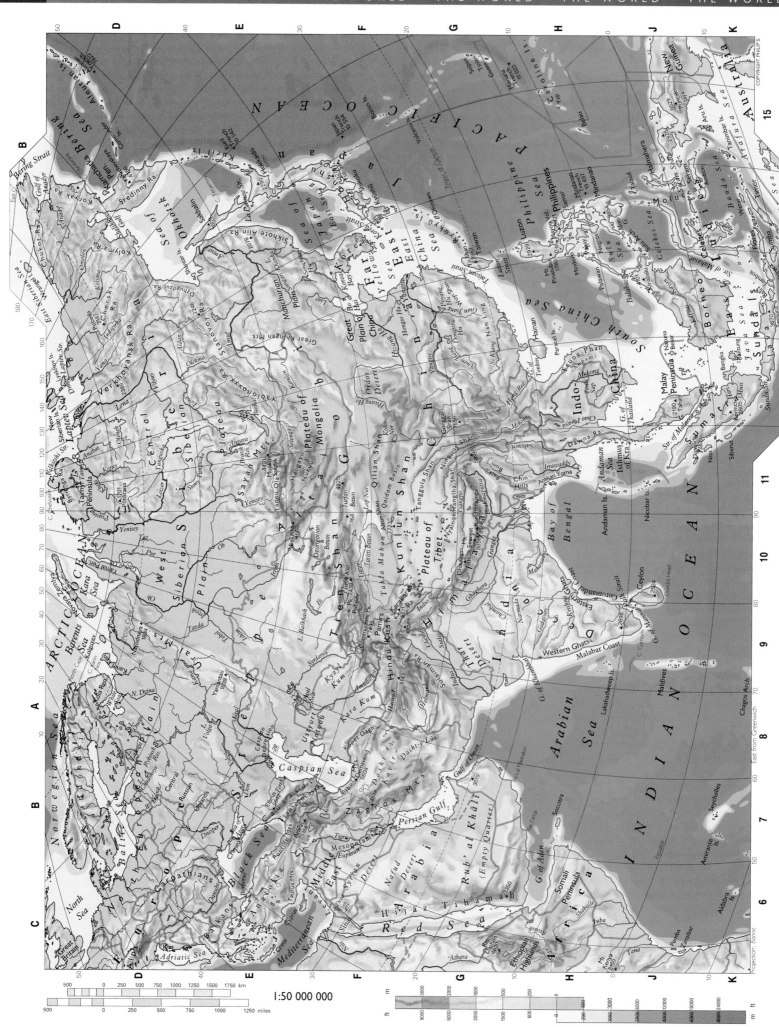

1:50 000 000

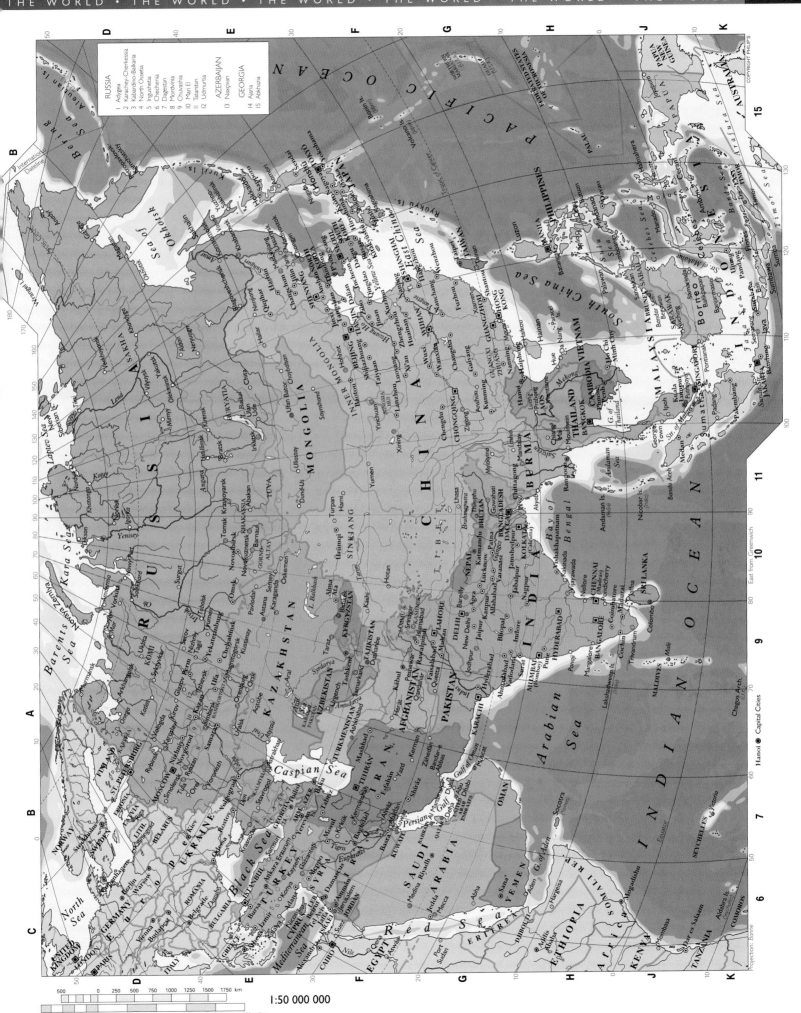

RUSSIA
1 Adygea
2 Karachey-Cherkessia
3 Kabardino-Balkaria
4 North Ossetia
5 Ingushetia
6 Chechenia
7 Dagestan
8 Mordovia
9 Chuvashia
10 Mari El
11 Tatarstan
12 Udmurtia

AZERBAIJAN
13 Naxçıvan

GEORGIA
14 Ajaria
15 Abkhazia

Hanoi ● Capital Cities

1:50 000 000

Projection: Bonne

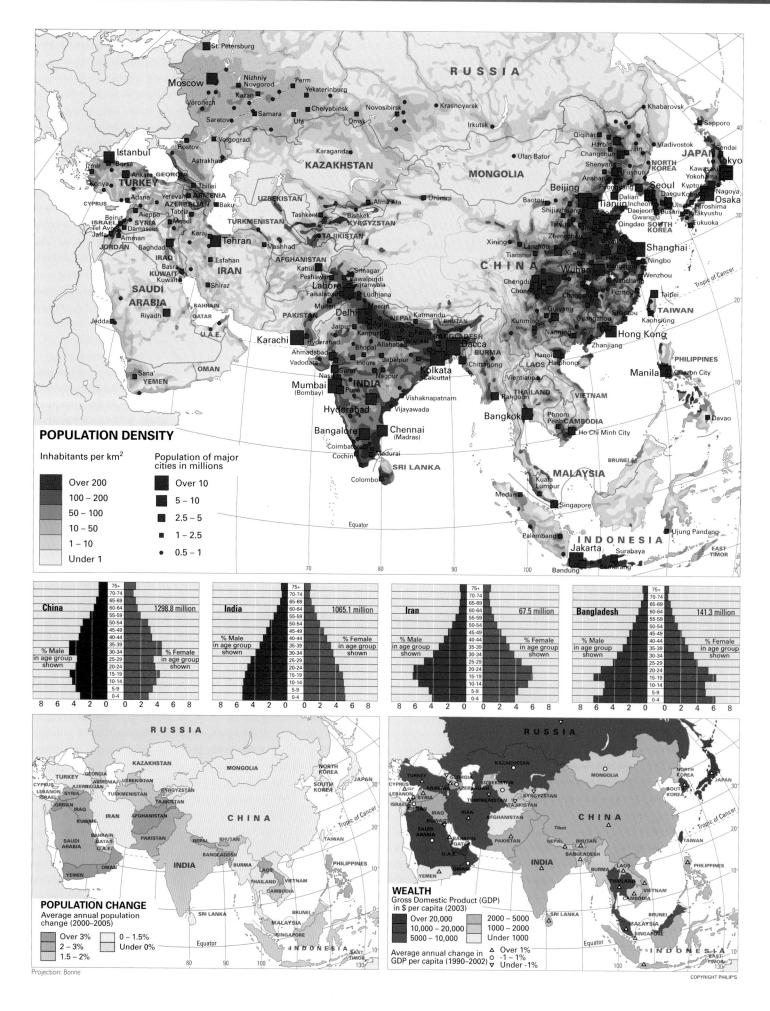

POPULATION DENSITY

Inhabitants per km²

- Over 200
- 100 – 200
- 50 – 100
- 10 – 50
- 1 – 10
- Under 1

Population of major cities in millions

- Over 10
- 5 – 10
- 2.5 – 5
- 1 – 2.5
- 0.5 – 1

China 1298.8 million

| | 75+ |
| 70-74 |
| 65-69 |
| 60-64 |
| 55-59 |
| 50-54 |
| 45-49 |
| 40-44 |
% Male	35-39	% Female
in age group	30-34	in age group
shown	25-29	shown
20-24
15-19
10-14
5-9
0-4
8 6 4 2 0 0 2 4 6 8

India 1065.1 million

% Male in age group shown / % Female in age group shown
8 6 4 2 0 0 2 4 6 8

Iran 67.5 million

% Male in age group shown / % Female in age group shown
8 6 4 2 0 0 2 4 6 8

Bangladesh 141.3 million

% Male in age group shown / % Female in age group shown
8 6 4 2 0 0 2 4 6 8

POPULATION CHANGE

Average annual population change (2000–2005)

- Over 3%
- 2 – 3%
- 1.5 – 2%
- 0 – 1.5%
- Under 0%

WEALTH

Gross Domestic Product (GDP) in $ per capita (2003)

- Over 20,000
- 10,000 – 20,000
- 5000 – 10,000
- 2000 – 5000
- 1000 – 2000
- Under 1000

Average annual change in GDP per capita (1990–2002)

- △ Over 1%
- ○ -1 – 1%
- ▽ Under -1%

Projection: Bonne

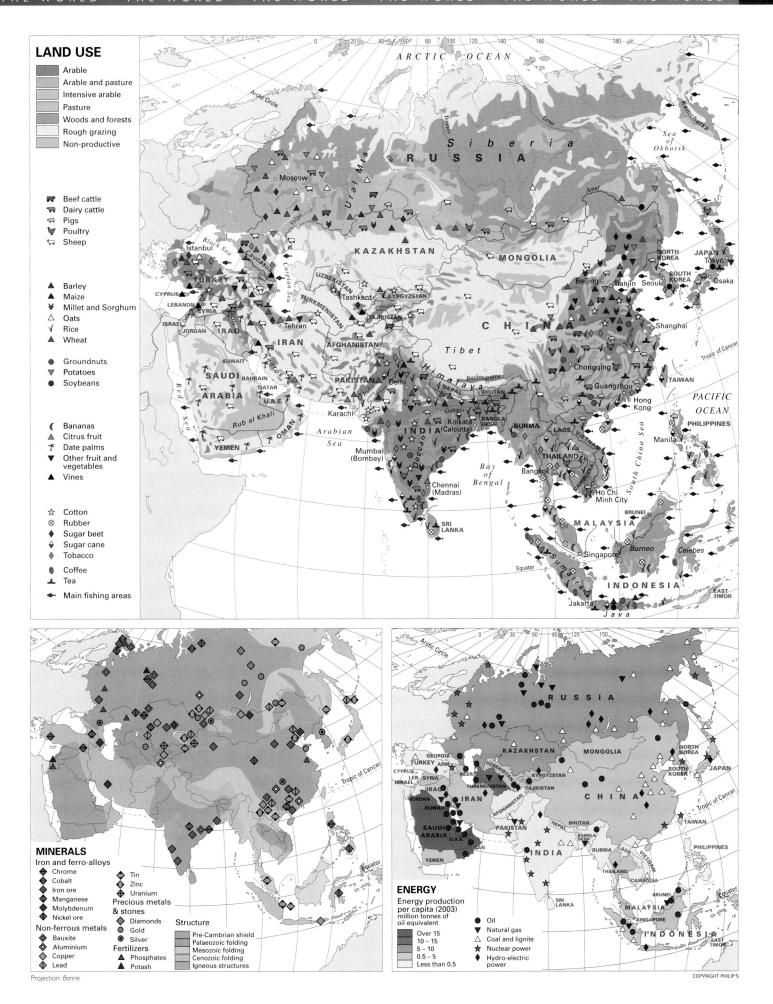

LAND USE

- Arable
- Arable and pasture
- Intensive arable
- Pasture
- Woods and forests
- Rough grazing
- Non-productive

- Beef cattle
- Dairy cattle
- Pigs
- Poultry
- Sheep

- ▲ Barley
- ▲ Maize
- ⌄ Millet and Sorghum
- △ Oats
- √ Rice
- ▲ Wheat

- ● Groundnuts
- ▽ Potatoes
- ● Soybeans

- (Bananas
- ▲ Citrus fruit
- ↟ Date palms
- ▼ Other fruit and vegetables
- ▲ Vines

- ☆ Cotton
- ⊗ Rubber
- ◆ Sugar beet
- ◈ Sugar cane
- ◊ Tobacco
- ◉ Coffee
- ⚘ Tea

- ← Main fishing areas

MINERALS

Iron and ferro-alloys

- ◆ Chrome
- ◆ Cobalt
- ◉ Iron ore
- ◆ Manganese
- ◆ Molybdenum
- ◆ Nickel ore

Non-ferrous metals

- ◆ Bauxite
- ◇ Aluminium
- ◇ Copper
- ◆ Lead
- ◆ Tin
- ◇ Zinc
- ⊕ Uranium

Precious metals & stones

- ◆ Diamonds
- ◉ Gold
- ◉ Silver

Fertilizers

- ▲ Phosphates
- ▲ Potash

Structure

- Pre-Cambrian shield
- Palaeozoic folding
- Mesozoic folding
- Cenozoic folding
- Igneous structures

Projection: Bonne

ENERGY

Energy production per capita (2003)
million tonnes of oil equivalent

- Over 15
- 10 – 15
- 5 – 10
- 0.5 – 5
- Less than 0.5

- ● Oil
- ▼ Natural gas
- △ Coal and lignite
- ★ Nuclear power
- ⬡ Hydro-electric power

COPYRIGHT PHILIP'S

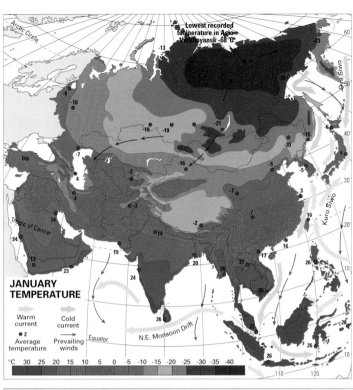

JANUARY TEMPERATURE

Lowest recorded temperature in Asia Verkhoyansk -68°C

→ Warm current
→ Cold current
● 2 Average temperature
→ Prevailing winds
Equator
N.E. Monsoon Drift

°C 30 25 20 15 10 5 0 -5 -10 -15 -20 -25 -30 -35 -40

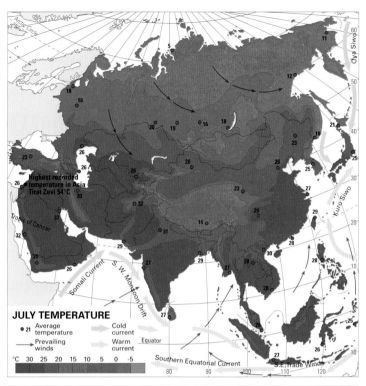

JULY TEMPERATURE

Highest recorded temperature in Asia Tirat Zevi 54°C

● 21 Average temperature
→ Prevailing winds
→ Cold current
→ Warm current
Equator
Somali Current
S.W. Monsoon Drift
Southern Equatorial Current
S.E. Trade Winds
Kuro Siwo
Oya Siwo

°C 30 25 20 15 10 5 0 -5

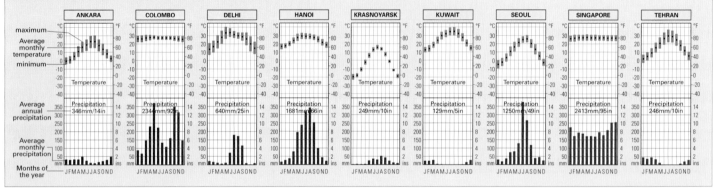

	ANKARA	COLOMBO	DELHI	HANOI	KRASNOYARSK	KUWAIT	SEOUL	SINGAPORE	TEHRAN
maximum / Average monthly temperature / minimum	Temperature	Temperature	Temperature	Temperature	Temperature	Temperature	Temperature	Temperature	Temperature
Average annual precipitation	Precipitation 346mm/14in	Precipitation 2344mm/92in	Precipitation 640mm/25in	Precipitation 1681mm/66in	Precipitation 249mm/10in	Precipitation 129mm/5in	Precipitation 1250mm/49in	Precipitation 2413mm/95in	Precipitation 246mm/10in
Months of the year	JFMAMJJASOND	JFMAMJJASOND	JFMAMJJASOND	JFMAMJJASOND	JFMAMJJASOND	JFMAMJJASOND	JFMAMJJASOND	JFMAMJJASOND	JFMAMJJASOND

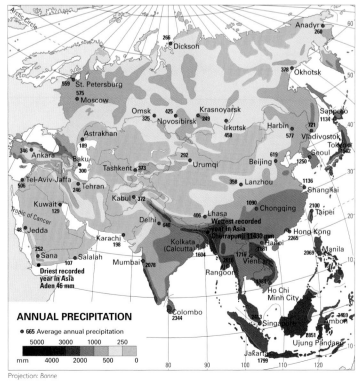

ANNUAL PRECIPITATION

Anadyr 260
Dickson 266
Okhotsk 378
St. Petersburg 559
Moscow 575
Omsk 325
Novosibirsk 425
Krasnoyarsk 249
Irkutsk 458
Harbin 577
Sapporo 1134
Vladivostok 721
Tokyo 1562
Seoul 1250
Astrakhan 189
Ankara 346
Baku
Tashkent 373
Tehran 300 246
Urumqi 292
Beijing 619
Lanzhou 358
Shanghai 1136
Kabul 372
Lhasa 406
Delhi 640
Chongqing 1090
Taipei 2100
Kolkata (Calcutta) 1604
Karachi 198
Hong Kong 2265
Hanoi 1681
Manila 2069
Mumbai 2078
Vientiane 1715
Tel-Aviv-Jaffa 506
Kuwait 129
Jedda 48
Sana 252
Salalah 107
Rangoon
Ho Chi Minh City
Colombo 2344
Singapore
Ujung Pandang 2851
Jakarta 1799
Ambon

Wettest recorded year in Asia Cherrapunji 11430 mm
Driest recorded year in Asia Aden 46 mm

● 665 Average annual precipitation

mm 5000 4000 3000 2000 1000 500 250 0

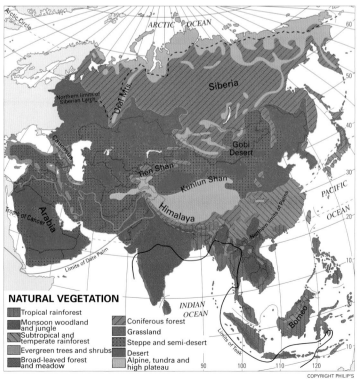

NATURAL VEGETATION

Siberia
Gobi Desert
Ural Mts.
Caucasus
Tien Shan
Kunlun Shan
Himalaya
Arabia
Borneo
ARCTIC OCEAN
PACIFIC OCEAN
INDIAN OCEAN
Northern limits of Siberian Larch
Northern limits of Palm
Limits of Date Palm
Limits of Teak

- Tropical rainforest
- Monsoon woodland and jungle
- Subtropical and temperate rainforest
- Evergreen trees and shrubs
- Broad-leaved forest and meadow
- Coniferous forest
- Grassland
- Steppe and semi-desert
- Desert
- Alpine, tundra and high plateau

Projection: Bonne

COPYRIGHT PHILIP'S

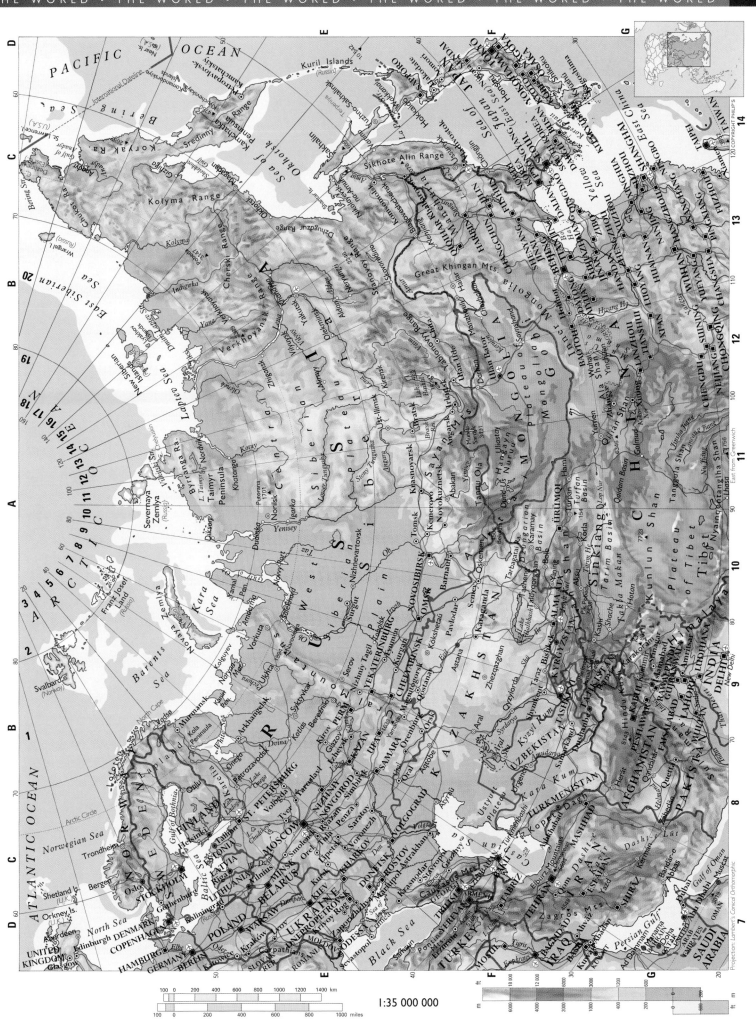

1:35 000 000

Projection: Lambert's Conic Orthomorphic

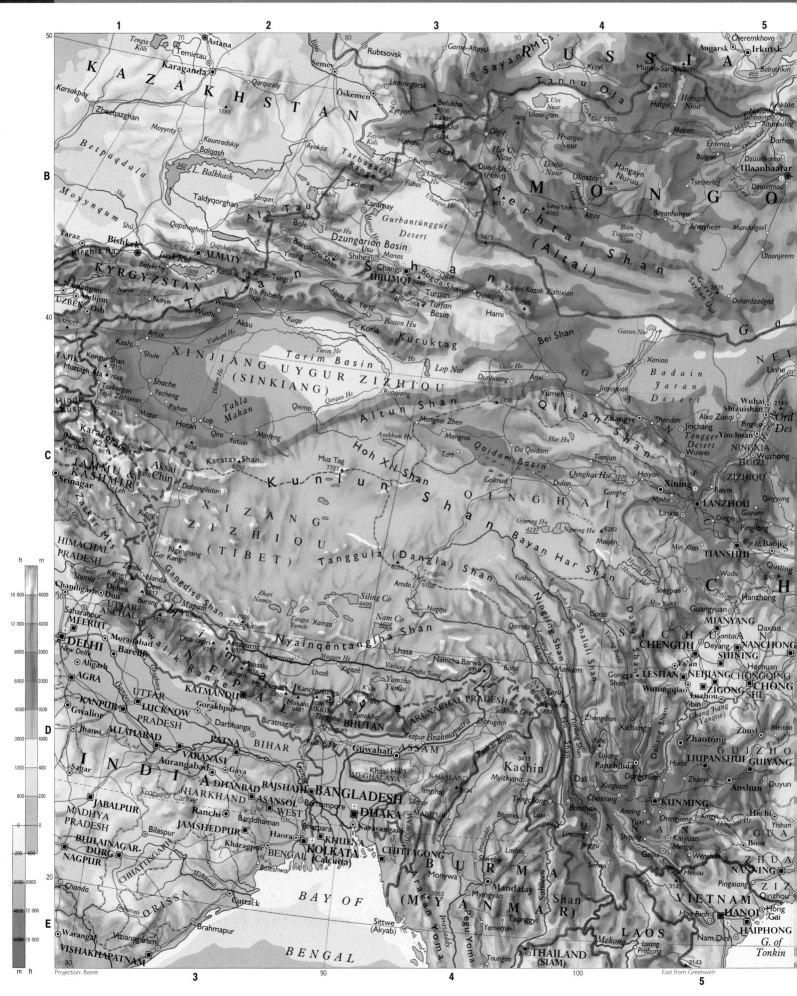

1:15 000 000

CHINA
Jixi
Linkou
Novokachalinsk
Kamen-Rybolov
L. Khanka
Spassk Dalniy
Suifenhe
Lipovcy
Manzovka
Ussuriysk
Artem
Hunchun
1498
Vladivostok
Slavyanka
Nakhodka
Khasan
Najin
Chŏngjin
NORTH
KOREA

RUSSIA
Lesozavodsk
Ariadnoye
Kirovskiy
Rakitnoye
Terney
Plastun
Gornyy
Yakovlevka
Dalnegorsk
Arsenev
Kavalerovo
Sikhote Alin Ra.
1855
Lazo
Margaritovo
Preobrazheniye

Wakkanai
Rebun-Tō
Rishiri-Tō
Teshio
Esashi
Otoineppu
Ōmu
Mombetsu
Yūbetsu
Abashiri-Wan
Rausu-Dake
Embetsu
Nayoro
Engaru
Kitami
Abashiri
1661
Haboro
Shibetsu
Asahigawa
Kunashiri
Rumoi
Bibai
Iwamizawa
2290
Daisetsu-Zan
Shari
Nakeshibetsu
Ishikari-Wan
Atsuta
Ebetsu
Obihiro
Honbetsu
Shibecha
Nemuro
Kamui-Misaki
Otaru
SAPPORO
HOKKAIDŌ
2077
Akkeshi
Iwanai
Sikotu-Ko
Poroshiri-Dake
Kushiro
Suttsu
Toya-Ko
Tomakomai
2052
Setana
Uchiura-Wan
Muroran
Samani
Okushiri-Tō
Yakumo
Hiroo
Erimo-misaki
Esashi
Esan-Misaki
Matsumae
Hakodate
Shiriya-Zaki
Shiragami-Misaki
Tsugaru Strait
Ohata
Mutsu
Mutsu-Wan
Kanagi
Aomori
Goshogawara
Towada-Ko
Towada
Hachinohe
Henashi-Misaki
Hirosaki
Kuji
Noshiro
Odate
Iwaizumi
Oga-Hantō
Oga
Iwate-San
Miyako
2041
Morioka
Akita
Ōmagari
1914
Kamaishi
Honjō
Hanamaki
Kesennuma
Sakata
2230
Ichinoseki
Tsuruoka
Mogami-Gawa
Furukawa
Ishinomaki
1980
Yamagata
Sōma
SENDAI
Sendai-Wan
Sado
Ryōtsu
Niigata
Shibata
Fukushima
Aikawa
Niitsu
Higashijima-San
Haranomachi
Sanjo
2024
Suzu-Misaki
Nagaoka
Aizuwakamatsu
Kōriyama
Wajima
Tōkamachi
Sukagawa
Honshū
Nanao
Suzu-Wan
Tajima
Iwaki
Toyama-Wan
Takada
2578
Tanakura
Himi
Nagano
Kiryū
Utsunomiya
Kitaibaraki
Takaoka
Toyama
Maebashi
Hitachi
8412
Kanazawa
Hodaka-Dake
Takasaki
Oyama
Tsuchiura
Komatsu
3190
Matsumoto
Kumagaya
Kawagoe
Takayama
Ina
Kawaguchi
Fukui
2782
3063
Kōfu
TŌKYŌ
Funabashi
Takefu
Iida
3192
KAWASAKI
Chiba
Tsuruga
Ōgaki
Gifu
Fuji-San
Odawara
YOKOHAMA
Ichihara
Kyō-ga-Saki
Kiso-Gawa
3776
Yokosuka
Izu-Shotō
Wakasa-Wan
Ichinomiya
Toyota
Shizuoka
Itō
Ō-Shima
Maizuru
Ayabe
NAGOYA
Okazaki
Numazu
Tateyama
Tottori
Toyooka
Yokkaichi
Toyohashi
Iwata
Suruga-Wan
Nojima-Zaki
Matsue
Yonago
Fukuchiyama
Ōtsu
Iwata
Irō-Zaki
Izumo
1712
Tsuyama
KYŌTO
Toyohashi
Nii-Jima
Ōda
Chūgoku-Sanchi
Himeji
Amagasaki
Higashiōsaka
Hamamatsu
Miyake-Jima
Hamada
Fuchū
KOBE
OSAKA
Matsusaka
9076
Masuda
Okayama
Izumi-Sano
Ise-Wan
HIROSHIMA
Fukuyama
Takamatsu
Wakayama
Daiō-Misaki
Hagi
Iwakuni
Kure
Marugame
Naruto
Awaji-Shima
1915
Ōwase
Yamaguchi
Tokuyama
Imabari
Ikeda
Tokushima
Kii Channel
Ube
Hofu
Anan
Tanabe
Hachijō-Jima
Shimonoseki
Matsuyama
1955
Mugi
Kushimoto
Shio-no-Misaki
Iki
Nōgata
KITAKYŪSHŪ
Kōchi
Shingū
Aoga-Shima
FUKUOKA
Buzen
Muroto
Karatsu
Beppu
Yawatahama
Tosa-Wan
Muroto-Misaki
Imari
Saga
Kurume
Ōita
Uwajima
Nakamura
Saiki
Shikoku
Sasebo
Ōmuta
1787
Sukumo
Isahaya
Kumamoto
Ashizuri-Zaki
Nagasaki
Yatsushiro
Nobeoka
Fukue-Shima
Amakusa-Shotō
Hyūga
Ushibuka
Kyūshū
Minamata
Miyazaki
Koshikijima-Rettō
Sendai
Miyakonojō
Kagoshima
Nichinan
Makurazaki
Kanoya
Ibusuki
Sata-Misaki

SEA OF
JAPAN
(EAST SEA)
JAPAN
Yeongdeok
SOUTH
KOREA
Pohang
ULSAN
Ulleungdo
(S. Korea)
Tokdo
(Takeshima)
Oki-Shotō
(Japan)
Korea
Strait
Tsushima
(Japan)
PACIFIC OCEAN
Nampo Shoto
Izu-Shotō

ft   m
9000 3000
6000 2000
4500 1500
3000 1000
1200 400
600   200
0   0
600   200
6000 2000
12 000 4000
18 000 6000
24 000 8000
ft   m

Projection: Conical with two standard parallels   East from Greenwich
COPYRIGHT PHILIP'S
1:6 400 000

50 25 0 25 50 75 100 125 150 175 km
50 25 0 25 50 75 100 125 miles

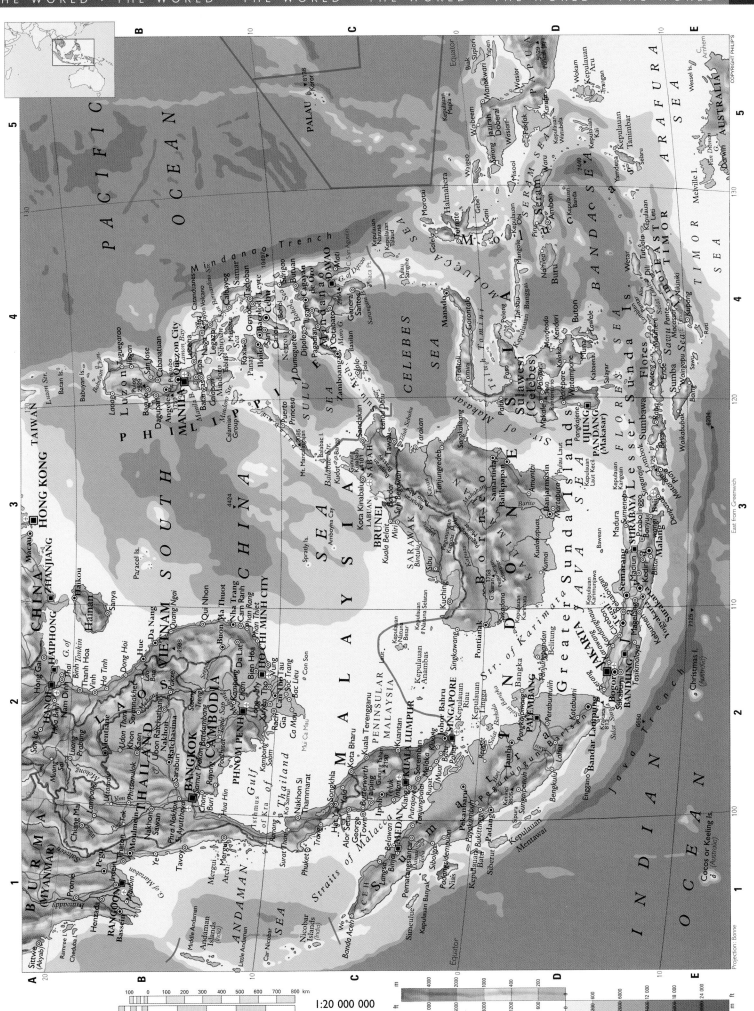

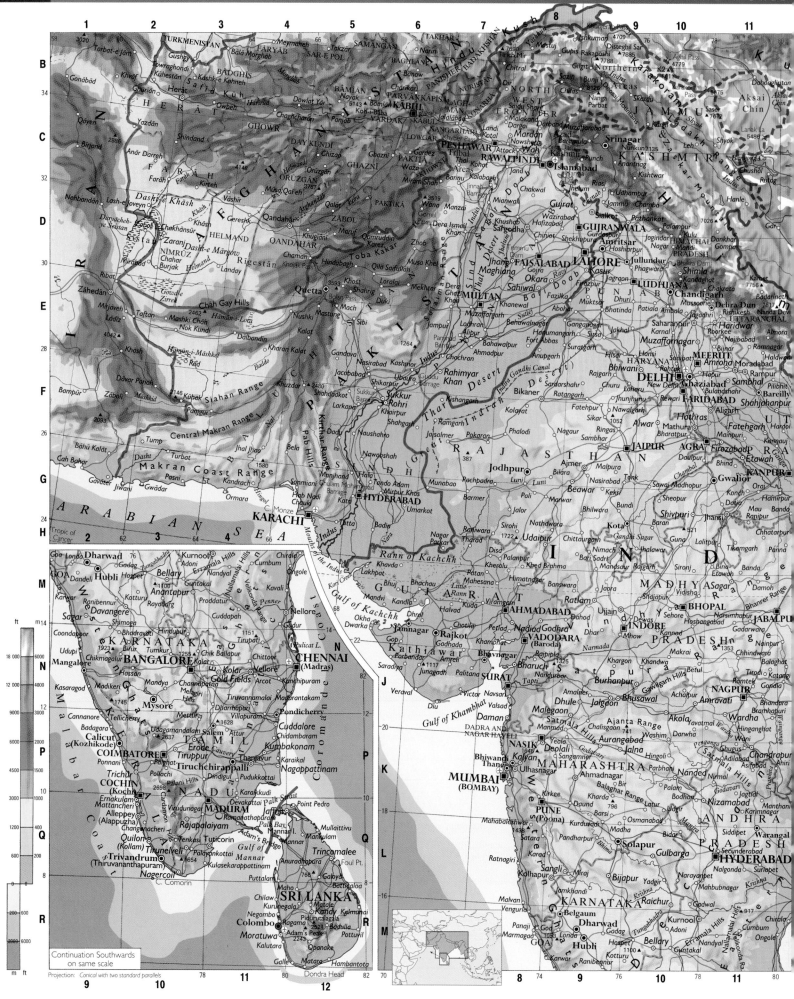

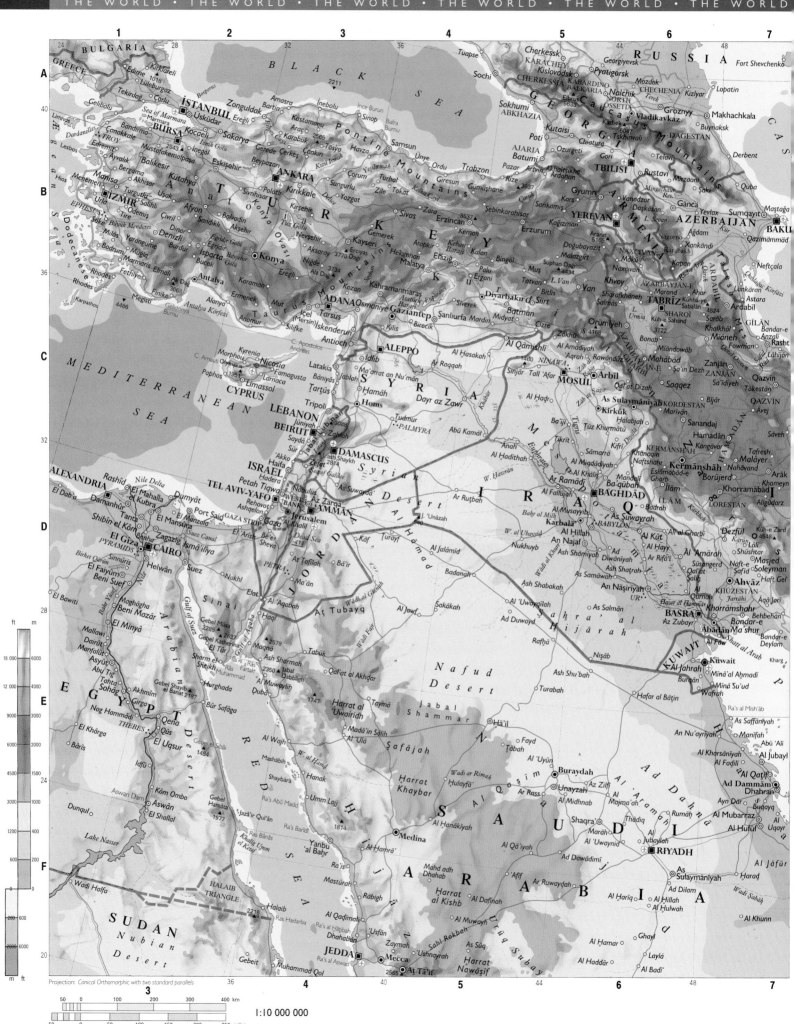

Projection: Conical Orthomorphic with two standard parallels

1:10 000 000

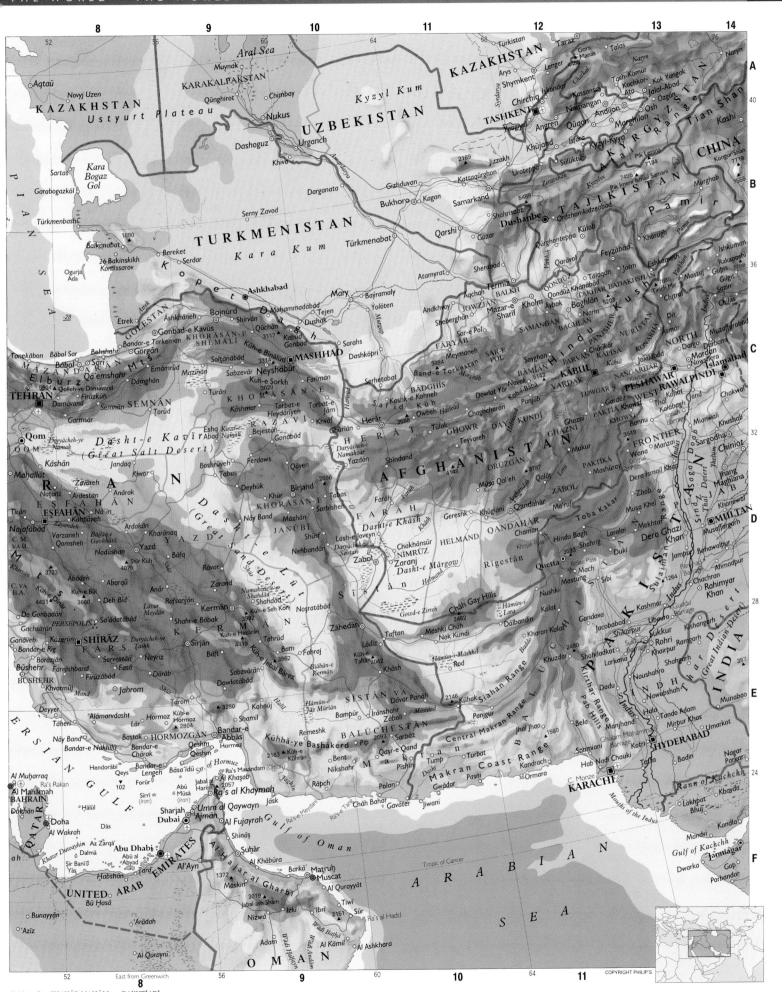

C. M. VA B. = CHAHĀR MAHĀLL VA BAKHTĪARĪ
K. VA B. A. = KOHKĪLŪYEH VA BŪYER AḤMADĪ

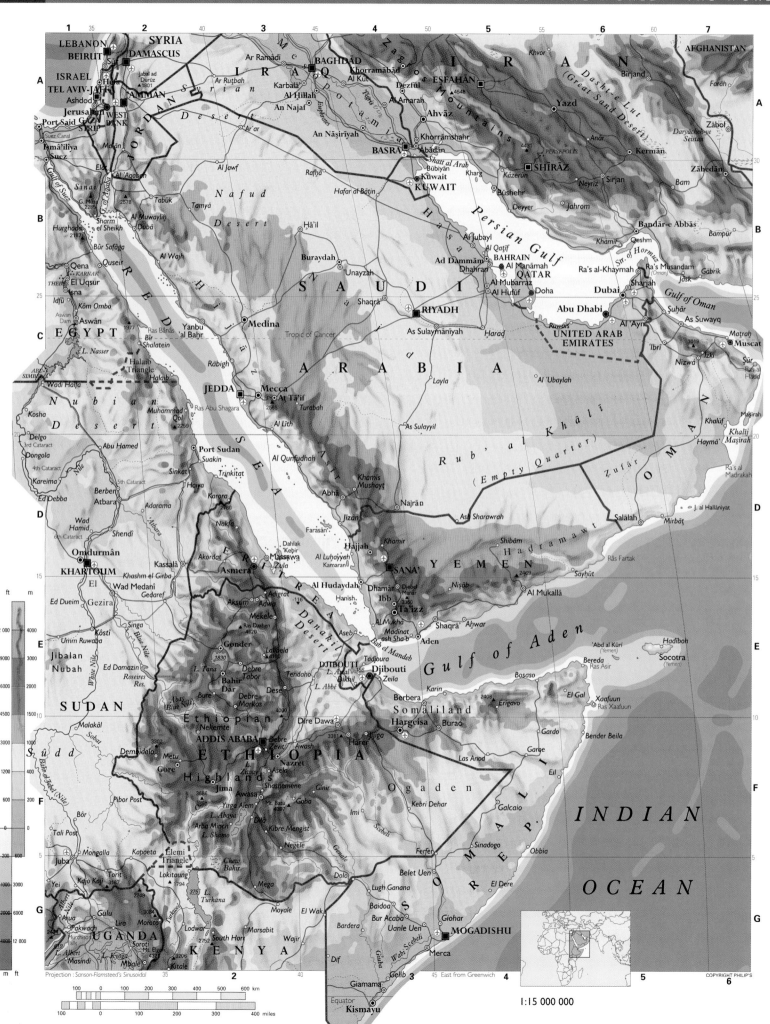

Projection : Sanson-Flamsteed's Sinusoidal

COPYRIGHT PHILIP'S

1:15 000 000

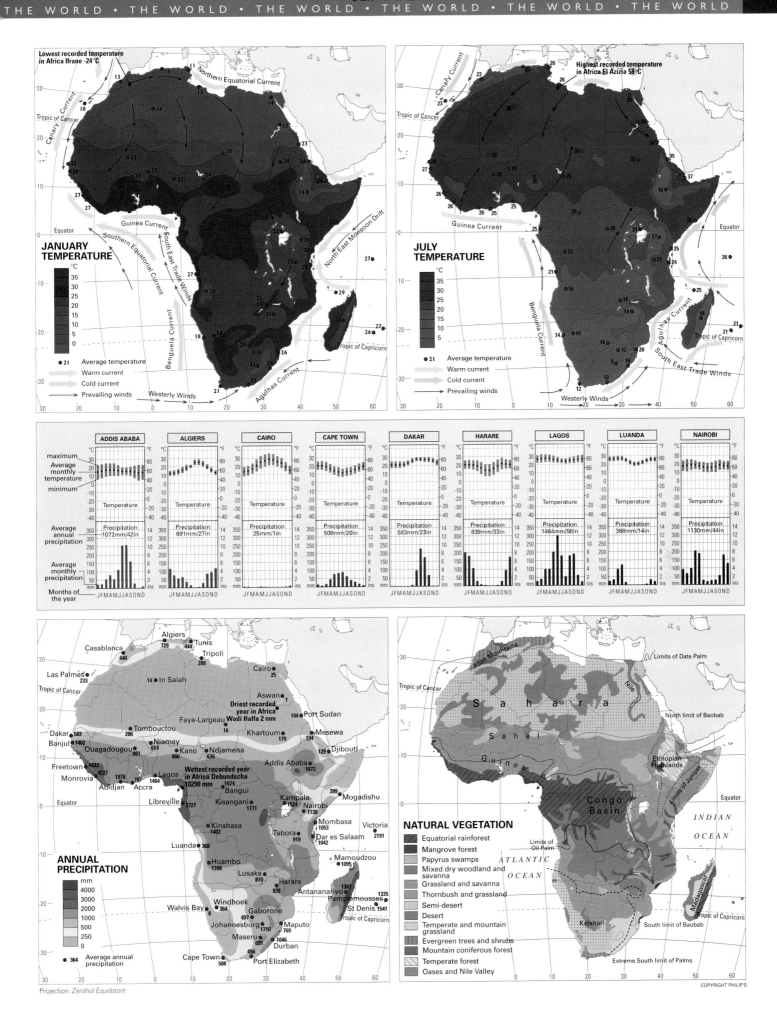

JANUARY TEMPERATURE

Lowest recorded temperature in Africa Ifrane -24°C

°C
35
30
25
20
15
10
5
0

- 21 Average temperature
- Warm current
- Cold current
- Prevailing winds

Northern Equatorial Current, Canary Current, Tropic of Cancer, Guinea Current, Southern Equatorial Current, South East Trade Winds, Benguela Current, Equator, Westerly Winds, Agulhas Current, Tropic of Capricorn, North East Monsoon Drift

JULY TEMPERATURE

Highest recorded temperature in Africa El Azizia 58°C

°C
35
30
25
20
15
10
5

- 21 Average temperature
- Warm current
- Cold current
- Prevailing winds

Canary Current, Tropic of Cancer, Guinea Current, Benguela Current, Equator, Agulhas Current, South East Trade Winds, Westerly Winds, Tropic of Capricorn

Climate graphs

Station	Avg annual precipitation
ADDIS ABABA	1072mm/42in
ALGIERS	691mm/27in
CAIRO	25mm/1in
CAPE TOWN	508mm/20in
DAKAR	583mm/23in
HARARE	839mm/33in
LAGOS	1464mm/58in
LUANDA	368mm/14in
NAIROBI	1130mm/44in

maximum
Average monthly temperature
minimum
Average annual precipitation
Average monthly precipitation
Months of the year — JFMAMJJASOND

ANNUAL PRECIPITATION

mm
4000
3000
2000
1000
500
250
0

- 364 Average annual precipitation

Casablanca 440, Algiers 729, Tunis 444, Tripoli 288, Las Palmas 233, Cairo 25, In Salah 14, Aswan 1, Driest recorded year in Africa Wadi Halfa 2 mm, Faya-Largeau 16, Port Sudan 104, Dakar 583, Tombouctou 206, Khartoum 179, Mesewa 194, Banjul 1402, Niamey 614, Ndjamena 636, Djibouti 129, Ouagadougou 881, Kano 866, Addis Ababa 1072, Freetown 4433, Wettest recorded year in Africa Debundscha 10290 mm, Lagos 1464, Bangui 1574, Monrovia 4227, Abidjan 1978, Accra 787, Kampala 1524, Mogadishu 399, Libreville 2727, Kisangani 1771, Nairobi 1130, Kinshasa 1402, Mombasa 1053, Victoria 2191, Tabora 919, Dar es Salaam 1042, Luanda 368, Mamoudzou 1095, Huambo 1398, Lusaka 810, Harare 839, Antananarivo 1361, Pamplemousses 1335, Walvis Bay 8, Windhoek 364, Gaborone 691, St Denis 1541, Johannesburg 710, Maputo 769, Maseru 497, Durban 1046, Cape Town 508, Port Elizabeth 456

Projection: Zenithal Equidistant

NATURAL VEGETATION

- Equatorial rainforest
- Mangrove forest
- Papyrus swamps
- Mixed dry woodland and savanna
- Grassland and savanna
- Thornbush and grassland
- Semi-desert
- Desert
- Temperate and mountain grassland
- Evergreen trees and shrubs
- Mountain coniferous forest
- Temperate forest
- Oases and Nile Valley

Atlas Mountains, Tropic of Cancer, Sahara, Sahel, Guinea, Nile, North limit of Baobab, Ethiopian Highlands, Limits of Juniper, Limits of Date Palm, Limits of Oil Palm, Congo Basin, Equator, INDIAN OCEAN, ATLANTIC OCEAN, Madagascar, Kalahari, South limit of Baobab, Tropic of Capricorn, Extreme South limit of Palms

COPYRIGHT PHILIP'S

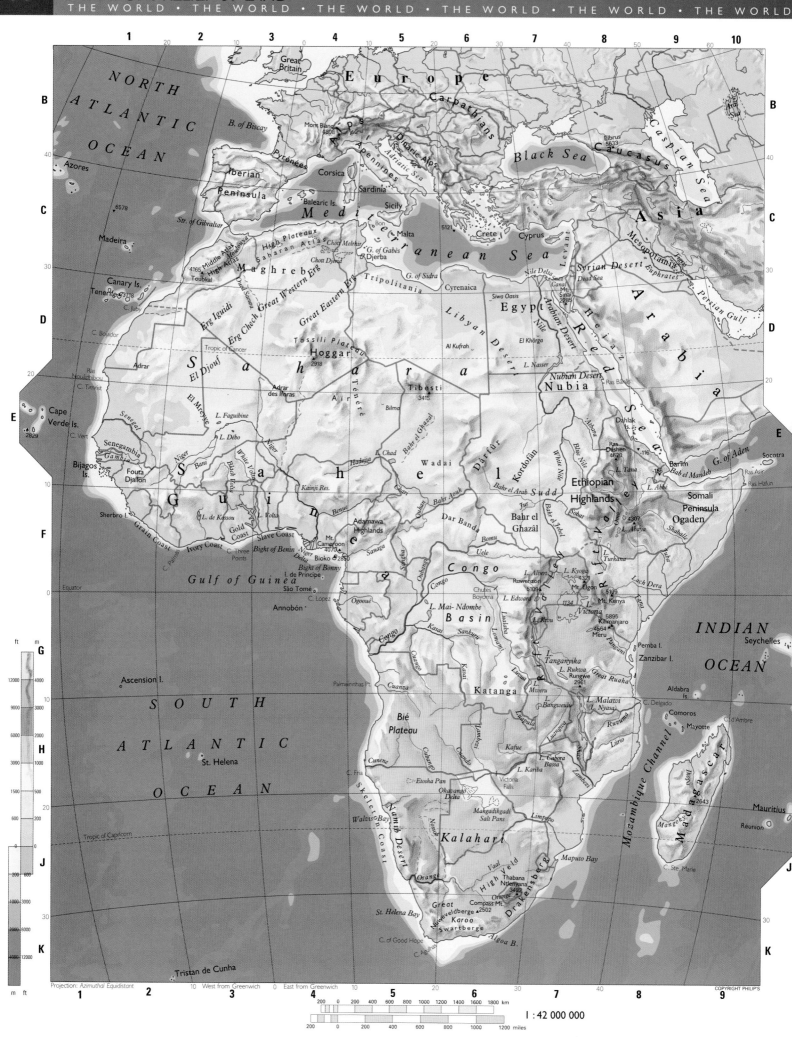

Projection: Azimuthal Equidistant

COPYRIGHT PHILIP'S

1 : 42 000 000

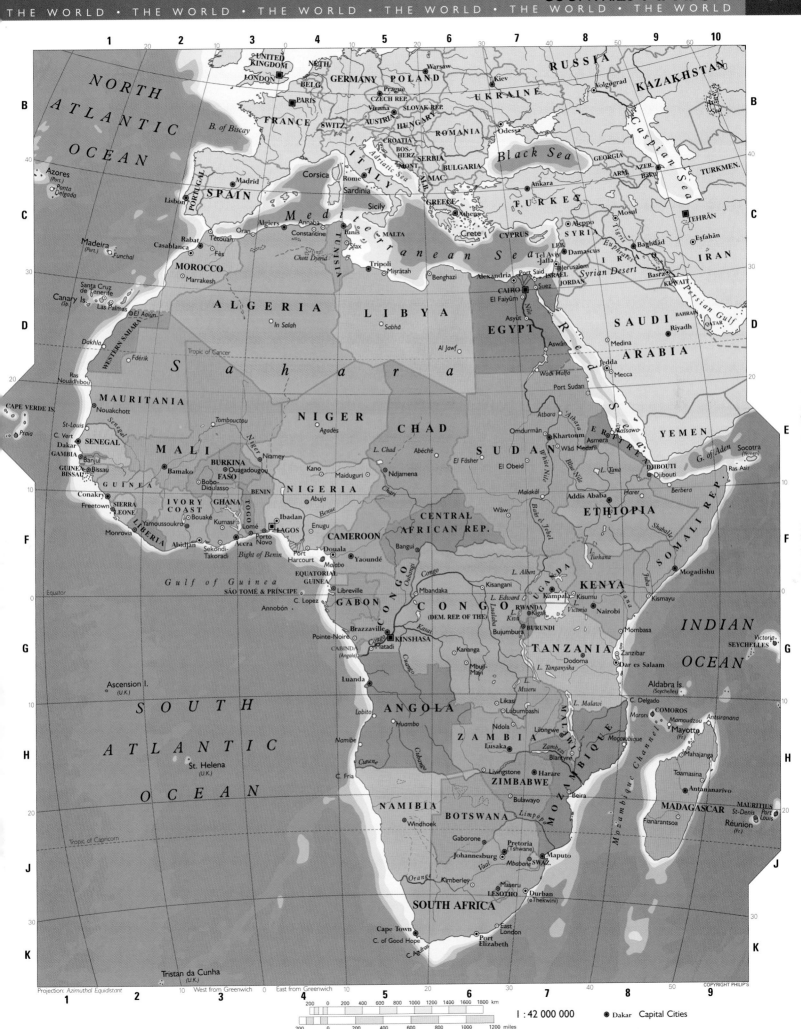

NORTH
ATLANTIC
OCEAN

B. of Biscay

Azores
(Port.)
Ponta
Delgada

UNITED
KINGDOM
LONDON
NETH.
BELG.
GERMANY POLAND
Warsaw
Kiev
RUSSIA
KAZAKHSTAN
Volgograd
PARIS
FRANCE
PRAGUE
CZECH REP.
Vienna
SLOVAK REP.
AUSTRIA
SWITZ.
HUNGARY
CROATIA
BOS.-
HERZ.
MONT.
SERBIA
ROMANIA
BULGARIA
UKRAINE
Odessa
Black Sea
GEORGIA
ARM. AZER.
Baku
TURKMEN.
Caspian Sea

Madrid
SPAIN
PORTUGAL
Lisbon
Corsica
Rome
ITALY
Sardinia
Adriatic Sea
ALB.
MAC.
GREECE
Athens
Crete
CYPRUS
TURKEY
Ankara
Mosul
Aleppo
SYRIA
Tehrān
Esfahān
IRAN
Baghdad

Madeira
(Port.)
Funchal
Rabat
Tetouán
Casablanca
Fès
MOROCCO
Marrakesh
Oran
Algiers
Annaba
Constantine
TUNISIA
Tunis
Sfax
MALTA
Mediterranean Sea
Tripoli
Mişrātah
Benghazi
Alexandria
Port Said
CAIRO
Suez
El Faiyûm
ISRAEL
Tel Aviv-Jaffa
Jerusalem
JORDAN
Damascus
Basra
KUWAIT
Persian Gulf
BAHRAIN
QATAR

Santa Cruz
de Tenerife
Canary Is.
(Sp.)
Las Palmas
El Aaiún
WESTERN SAHARA
Dakhla
Fdérik
Tropic of Cancer
In Salah
Sabhā
ALGERIA
LIBYA
S a h a r a
Al Jawf
EGYPT
Asyût
Aswān
Wādī Halfa
Medina
Jedda
Mecca
SAUDI
ARABIA
Riyadh

Ras
Nouâdhibou
MAURITANIA
Nouakchott
Tombouctou
NIGER
Agades
CHAD
Omdurmân
Khartoum
Wād Medani
Port Sudan
Atbara
Atbara
Massawa
ERITREA
YEMEN
Socotra
(Yemen)

CAPE VERDE IS.
St-Louis
C. Vert
Praia
Dakar
SENEGAL
GAMBIA
Banjul
GUINEA-BISSAU
Bissau
Conakry
GUINEA
Freetown
SIERRA LEONE
MALI
Bamako
Niamey
Senegal
Niger
BURKINA
FASO
Ouagadougou
Bobo-Dioulasso
Kano
Maiduguri
NIGERIA
L. Chad
Abéché
Ndjamena
El Fâsher
El Obeid
SUDAN
Malakâl
White Nile
Blue Nile
L. Tana
Addis Ababa
ETHIOPIA
DJIBOUTI
Djibouti
Berbera
G. of Aden
Ras Asir
Harer

MONROVIA
LIBERIA
Abidjan
IVORY COAST
Bouaké
Yamoussoukro
GHANA
Kumasi
Accra
Sekondi-Takoradi
TOGO
BENIN
Lomé
Porto Novo
LAGOS
Ibadan
Enugu
Abuja
Benue
Douala
Port Harcourt
CAMEROON
Yaoundé
Bangui
CENTRAL
AFRICAN REP.
Chari
Wāw
Bahr el Jebel
L. Turkana
Shabelle
SOMALI REP.
Mogadishu

Bight of Benin
MALABO
EQUATORIAL
GUINEA
SÃO TOMÉ & PRÍNCIPE
Libreville
GABON
C. López
Annobón
Equator
Gulf of Guinea
CONGO
Mbandaka
Congo
Kisangani
CONGO
(DEM. REP. OF THE)
Ubangi
L. Albert
UGANDA
Kampala
L. Edward
RWANDA
Kigali
Kivu
BURUNDI
Bujumbura
L. Victoria
Kisumu
KENYA
Nairobi
Kismayu
Mombasa
INDIAN
OCEAN
SEYCHELLES
Victoria

Ascension I.
(U.K.)
Brazzaville
KINSHASA
Pointe-Noire
CABINDA
(Angola)
Matadi
Kananga
Mbuji-Mayi
Kasai
TANZANIA
Dodoma
Dar es Salaam
Zanzibar
L. Tanganyika
Aldabra Is.
(Seychelles)

SOUTH
ATLANTIC
OCEAN
Luanda
Lobito
ANGOLA
Huambo
Namibe
Likasi
Lubumbashi
Ndola
L. Mweru
L. Malawi
C. Delgado
COMOROS
Moroni
Mamoudzou
Mayotte
(Fr.)
Antsiranana
MALAWI
ZAMBIA
Lilongwe
Lusaka
Zambezi
Blantyre
Moçambique
Mahajanga

St. Helena
(U.K.)
Cunene
Cubango
Livingstone
Harare
ZIMBABWE
Bulawayo
Beira
MOZAMBIQUE
Mozambique Channel
MADAGASCAR
Toamasina
Antananarivo
Fianarantsoa
MAURITIUS
St-Denis
Port Louis
Réunion
(Fr.)

Tropic of Capricorn
NAMIBIA
Windhoek
BOTSWANA
Gaborone
Limpopo
Pretoria
(Tshwane)
Maputo
SWAZ.
Mbabane
Johannesburg
Vaal
C. Fria
Orange
Kimberley
LESOTHO
Maseru
Durban
(eThekwini)
SOUTH AFRICA
East London

Tristan da Cunha
(U.K.)
Cape Town
C. of Good Hope
C. Agulhas
Port Elizabeth

1 : 42 000 000
200 0 200 400 600 800 1000 1200 1400 1600 1800 km
200 0 200 400 600 800 1000 1200 miles
● Dakar Capital Cities

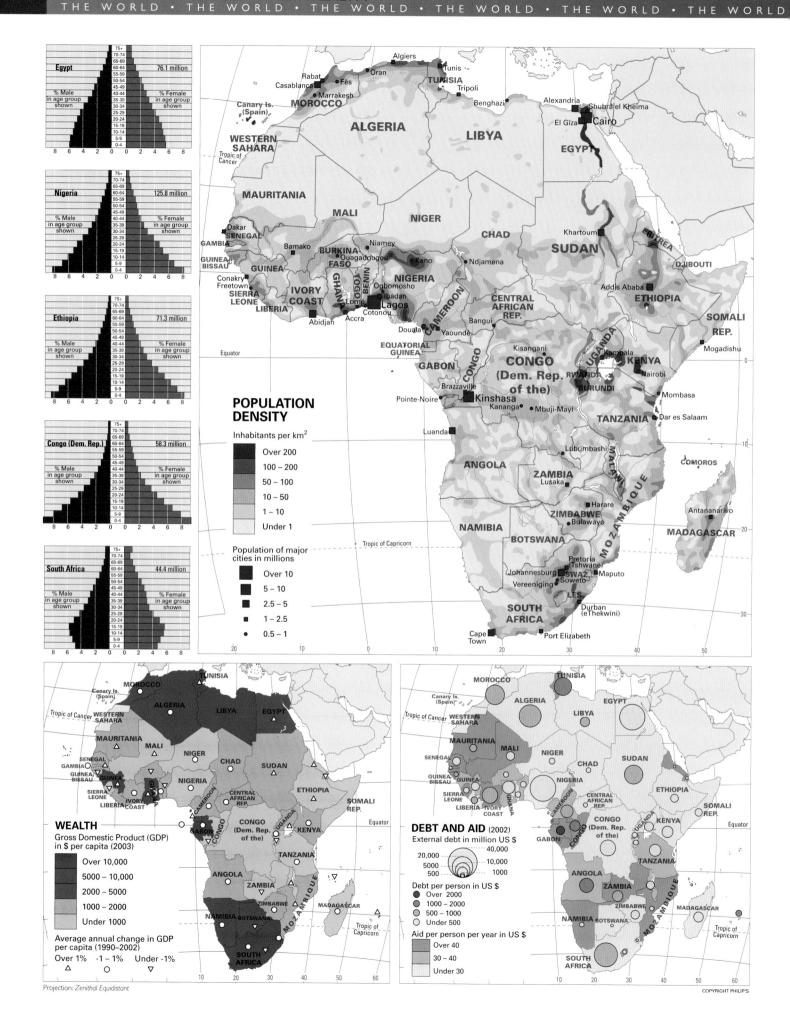

Egypt 76.1 million

% Male in age group shown | % Female in age group shown

Nigeria 125.8 million

% Male in age group shown | % Female in age group shown

Ethiopia 71.3 million

% Male in age group shown | % Female in age group shown

Congo (Dem. Rep.) 58.3 million

% Male in age group shown | % Female in age group shown

South Africa 44.4 million

% Male in age group shown | % Female in age group shown

POPULATION DENSITY

Inhabitants per km²

- Over 200
- 100 – 200
- 50 – 100
- 10 – 50
- 1 – 10
- Under 1

Population of major cities in millions

- Over 10
- 5 – 10
- 2.5 – 5
- 1 – 2.5
- 0.5 – 1

WEALTH

Gross Domestic Product (GDP) in $ per capita (2003)

- Over 10,000
- 5000 – 10,000
- 2000 – 5000
- 1000 – 2000
- Under 1000

Average annual change in GDP per capita (1990–2002)

Over 1% △   -1 – 1% ○   Under -1% ▽

Projection: *Zenithal Equidistant*

DEBT AND AID (2002)

External debt in million US $

- 40,000
- 20,000
- 10,000
- 5000
- 1000
- 500

Debt per person in US $

- Over 2000
- 1000 – 2000
- 500 – 1000
- Under 500

Aid per person per year in US $

- Over 40
- 30 – 40
- Under 30

COPYRIGHT PHILIP'S

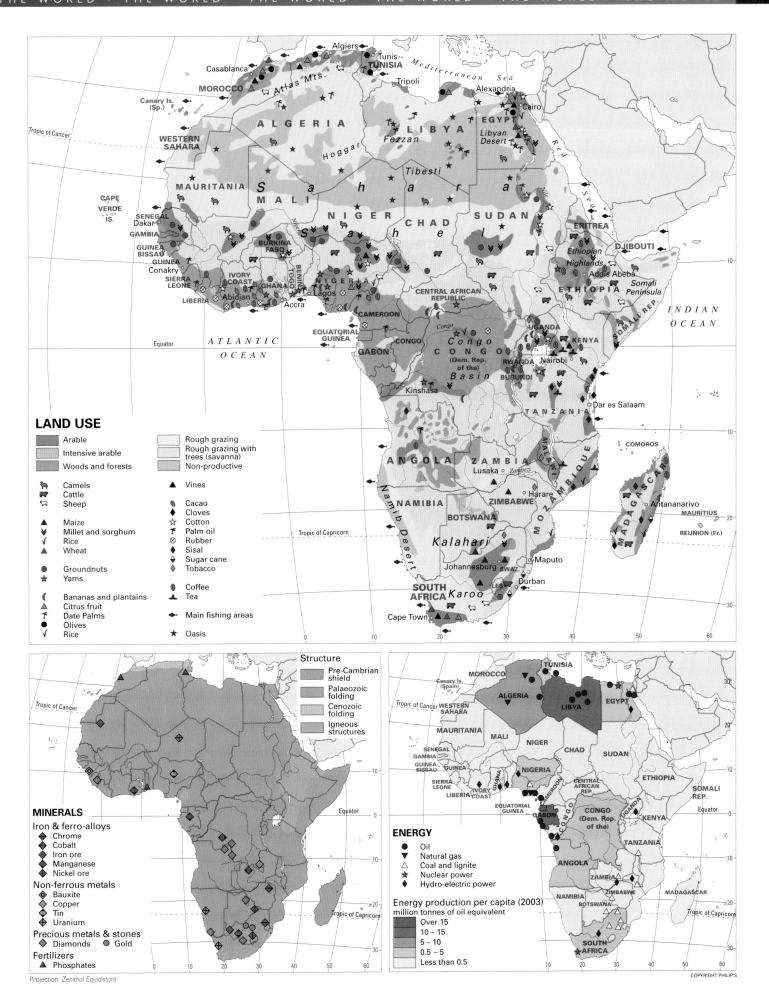

Algiers
Tunis
TUNISIA
Casablanca
Tripoli
Mediterranean Sea
Alexandria
MOROCCO
Cairo
Atlas Mts.
WESTERN
SAHARA
A L G E R I A
L I B Y A
EGYPT
Canary Is.
(Sp.)
Fezzan
Libyan
Desert
Tropic of Cancer
Hoggar
Tibesti
S *a* *h* *a* *r* *a*
Red
MAURITANIA
MALI
NIGER
CHAD
SUDAN
CAPE
VERDE
IS.
S *a* *h* *e* *l*
ERITREA
DJIBOUTI
SENEGAL
Dakar
Ethiopian
Highlands
GAMBIA
BURKINA
FASO
Somali
Peninsula
GUINEA
BISSAU
Addis Abeba
GUINEA
NIGERIA
ETHIOPIA
Conakry
INDIAN
OCEAN
SIERRA
LEONE
IVORY
COAST
GHANA
TOGO
CENTRAL AFRICAN
REPUBLIC
Lagos
LIBERIA
Abidjan
Accra
UGANDA
KENYA
CAMEROON
Congo
Equator
ATLANTIC
OCEAN
EQUATORIAL
GUINEA
CONGO
C o n g o
Nairobi
GABON
CONGO
(Dem. Rep.
of the)
Basin
RWANDA
BURUNDI
Kinshasa
Dar es Salaam
T A N Z A N I A
COMOROS
A N G O L A
Z A M B I A
Lusaka
Zambezi
MADAGASCAR
NAMIBIA
ZIMBABWE
Harare
MAURITIUS
BOTSWANA
Antananarivo
REUNION (Fr.)
Tropic of Capricorn
Kalahari
Namib Desert
Maputo
Johannesburg
SWAZ.
SOUTH
AFRICA
Karoo
LESO.
Durban
Cape Town

LAND USE

◼ Arable	◻ Rough grazing
◼ Intensive arable	◻ Rough grazing with trees (savanna)
◼ Woods and forests	◼ Non-productive

Camels
Cattle
Sheep
▲ Vines
▲ Maize
◗ Cacao
Y Millet and sorghum
◆ Cloves
Y Rice
☆ Cotton
▲ Wheat
↑ Palm oil
● Groundnuts
⊗ Rubber
★ Yams
◇ Sisal
◇ Sugar cane
◗ Bananas and plantains
◆ Tobacco
▲ Citrus fruit
◖ Coffee
↑ Date Palms
⊥ Tea
● Olives
Y Rice
← Main fishing areas
★ Oasis

MINERALS

Iron & ferro-alloys
◆ Chrome
◆ Cobalt
◆ Iron ore
◆ Manganese
◆ Nickel ore

Non-ferrous metals
◇ Bauxite
◇ Copper
◇ Tin
⊕ Uranium

Precious metals & stones
◆ Diamonds   ● Gold

Fertilizers
▲ Phosphates

Structure
◼ Pre-Cambrian shield
◼ Palaeozoic folding
◼ Cenozoic folding
◼ Igneous structures

ENERGY

● Oil
▼ Natural gas
△ Coal and lignite
★ Nuclear power
◆ Hydro-electric power

Energy production per capita (2003)
million tonnes of oil equivalent
◼ Over 15
◼ 10 – 15
◼ 5 – 10
◼ 0.5 – 5
◼ Less than 0.5

Projection: *Zenithal Equidistant*

COPYRIGHT PHILIP'S

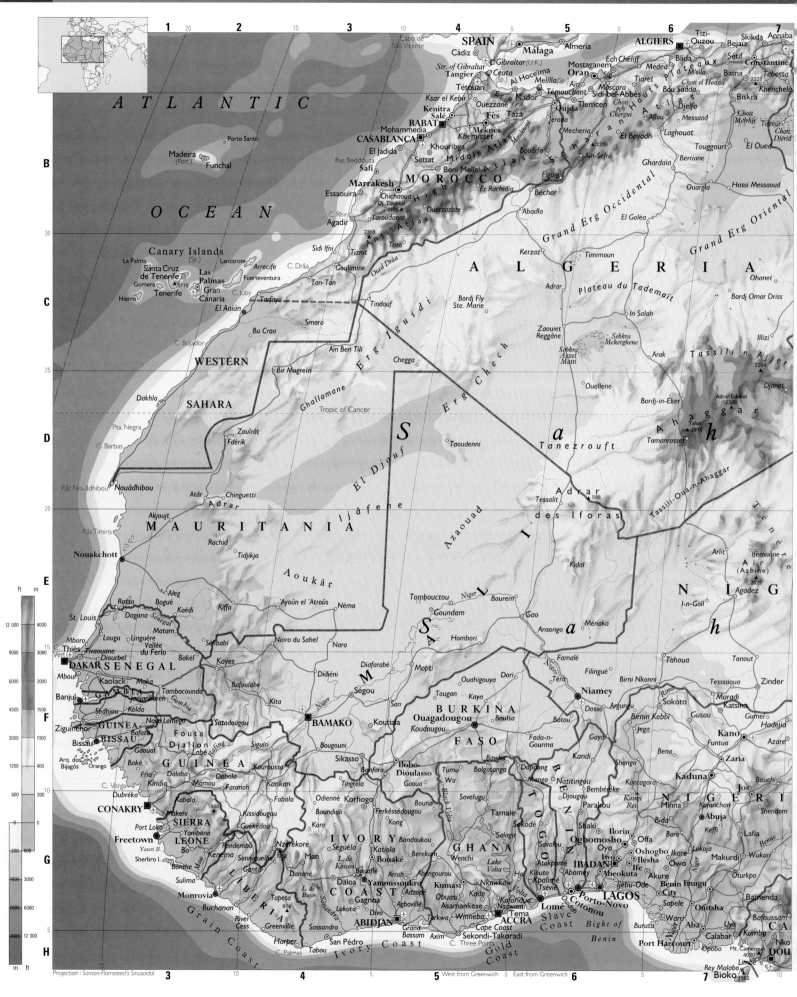

1:15 000 000

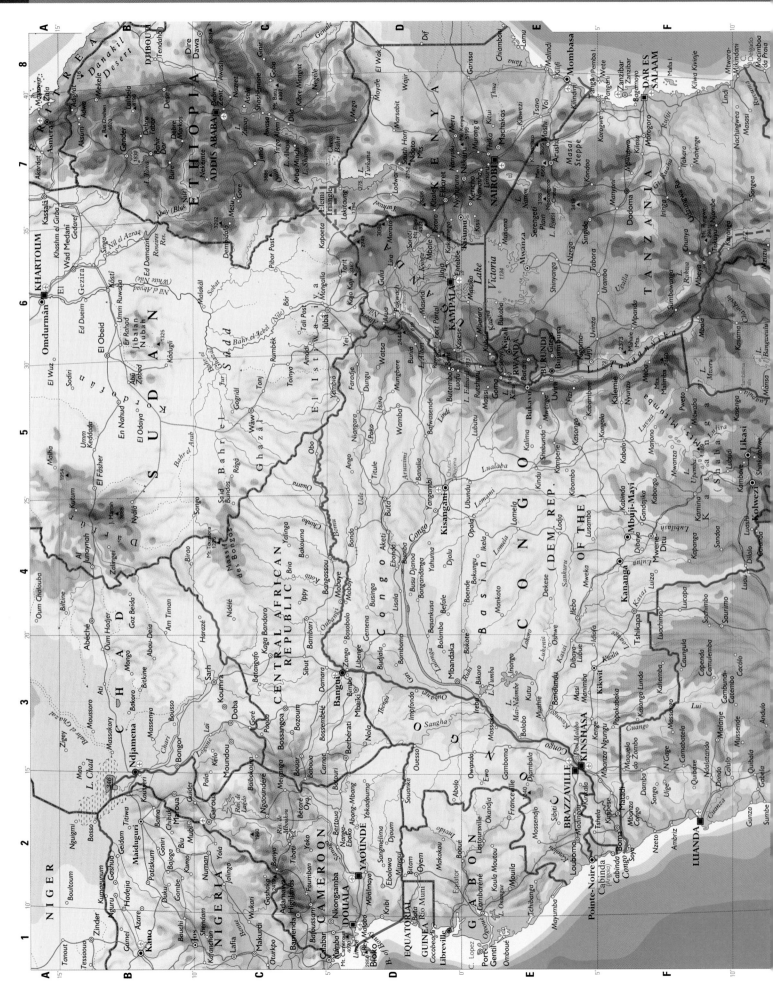

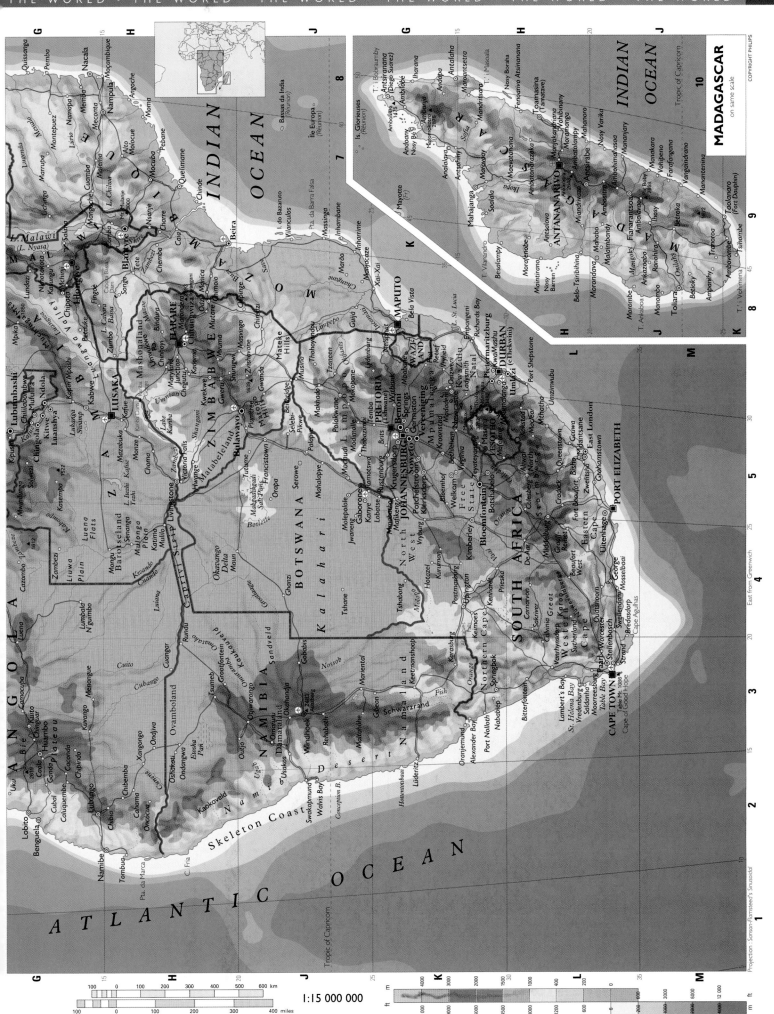

MADAGASCAR
on same scale

COPYRIGHT PHILIPS

INDIAN OCEAN

INDIAN OCEAN

ATLANTIC OCEAN

ANGOLA

ZAMBIA

NAMIBIA

BOTSWANA

ZIMBABWE

MOZAMBIQUE

MALAWI

SOUTH AFRICA

Kalahari Desert

Namib Desert

LUSAKA

HARARE

JOHANNESBURG

PRETORIA

MAPUTO

ANTANANARIVO

CAPE TOWN

DURBAN

PORT ELIZABETH

Windhoek

Gaborone

Bulawayo

Lilongwe

Blantyre

1:15 000 000

Projection: Sanson-Flamsteed's Sinusoidal

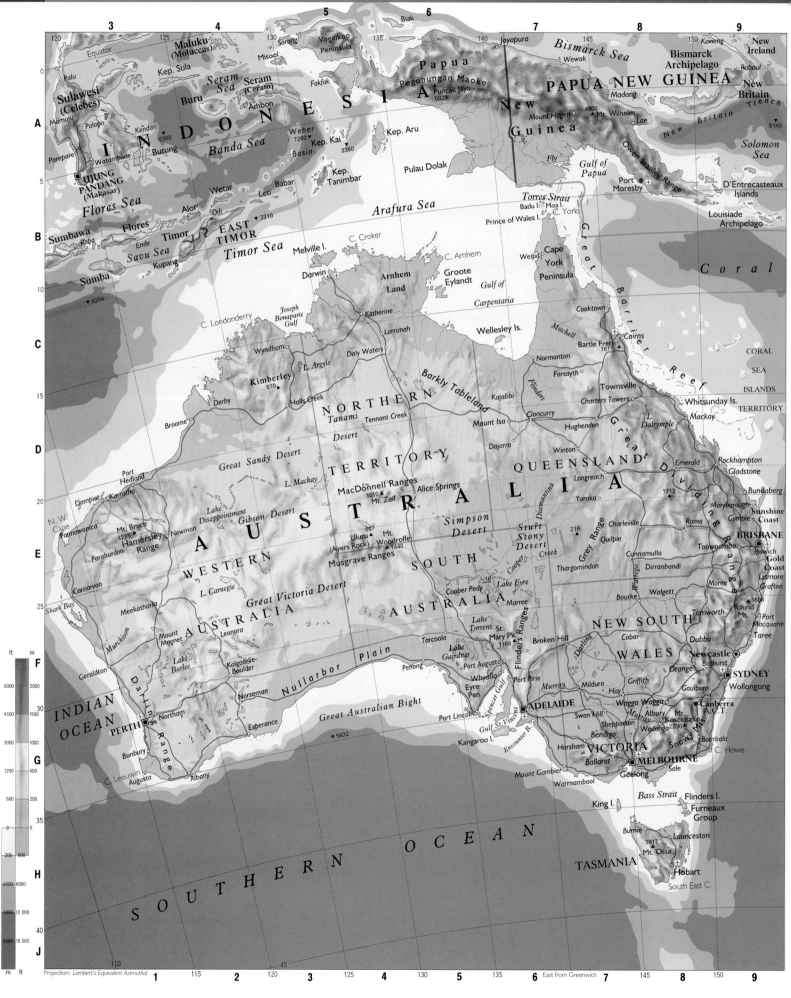

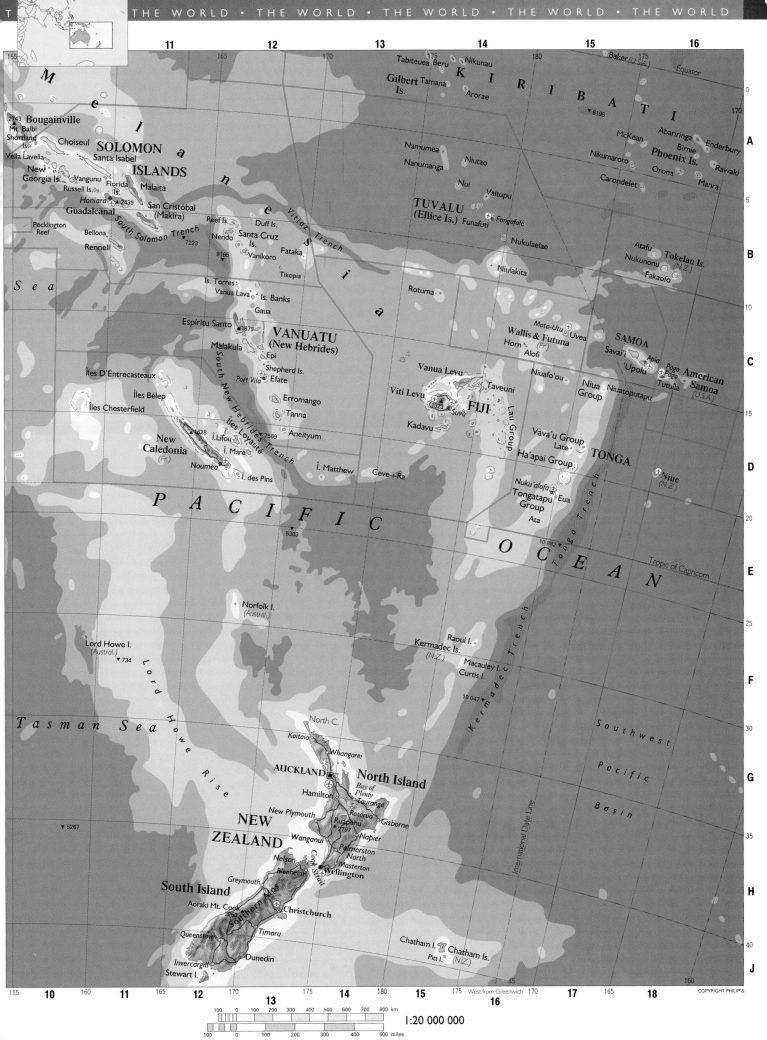

1:20 000 000

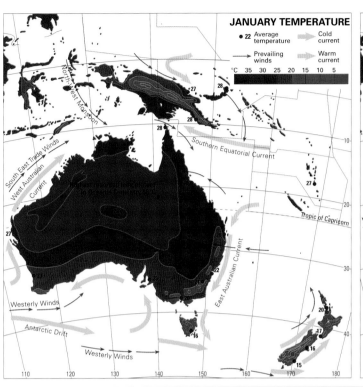

JANUARY TEMPERATURE

- • 22 Average temperature
- → Prevailing winds
- ⇒ Cold current
- ⇒ Warm current

°C 35 30 25 20 15 10 5

Highest recorded temperature in Oceania Cloncurry 53°C

North West Monsoon
South East Trade Winds
West Australian Current
Southern Equatorial Current
Tropic of Capricorn
East Australian Current
Westerly Winds
Antarctic Drift
Westerly Winds

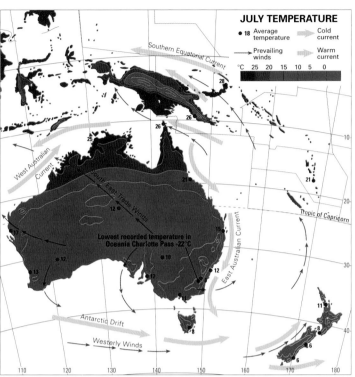

JULY TEMPERATURE

- • 18 Average temperature
- → Prevailing winds
- ⇒ Cold current
- ⇒ Warm current

°C 25 20 15 10 5 0

Southern Equatorial Current
West Australian Current
South East Trade Winds
Lowest recorded temperature in Oceania Charlotte Pass -22°C
Antarctic Drift
Westerly Winds
East Australian Current

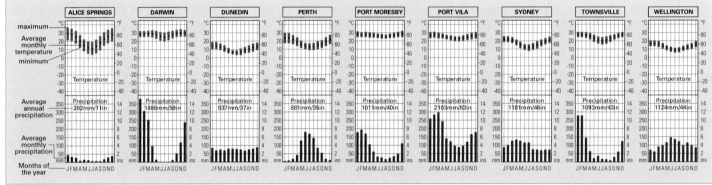

	ALICE SPRINGS	DARWIN	DUNEDIN	PERTH	PORT MORESBY	PORT VILA	SYDNEY	TOWNSVILLE	WELLINGTON
Average annual precipitation	282mm/11in	1488mm/59in	937mm/37in	881mm/35in	1011mm/40in	2103mm/83in	1181mm/46in	1093mm/43in	1124mm/44in

maximum — Average monthly temperature — minimum

Temperature / Precipitation / Average monthly precipitation / Months of the year: J F M A M J J A S O N D

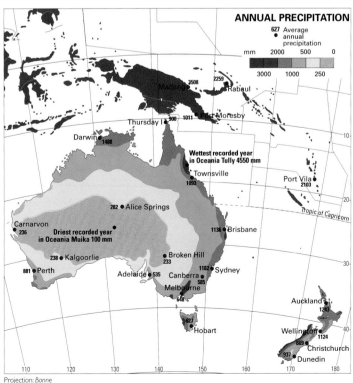

ANNUAL PRECIPITATION

- • 627 Average annual precipitation

mm 2000 500 0
3000 1000 250

Madang 3508
Rabaul 2259
Port Moresby 1011
Thursday I. 900
Darwin 1488
Wettest recorded year in Oceania Tully 4550 mm
Townsville 1093
Port Vila 2103
Alice Springs 282
Carnarvon 236
Driest recorded year in Oceania Muika 100 mm
Brisbane 1136
Kalgoorlie 238
Broken Hill 233
Perth 881
Sydney 1182
Adelaide 535
Canberra 585
Melbourne 648
Auckland 1243
Hobart 621
Wellington 1124
669
Christchurch
Dunedin 937

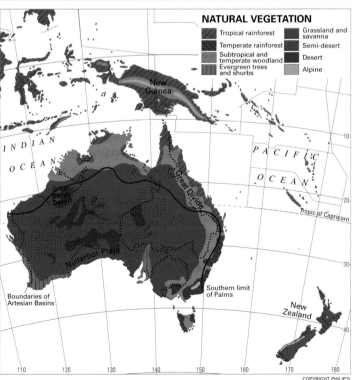

NATURAL VEGETATION

- Tropical rainforest
- Temperate rainforest
- Subtropical and temperate woodland
- Evergreen trees and shrubs
- Grassland and savanna
- Semi-desert
- Desert
- Alpine

INDIAN OCEAN
PACIFIC OCEAN
New Guinea
Great Sandy Desert
Great Divide
Tropic of Capricorn
Nullarbor Plain
Boundaries of Artesian Basins
Southern limit of Palms
New Zealand

Projection: Bonne

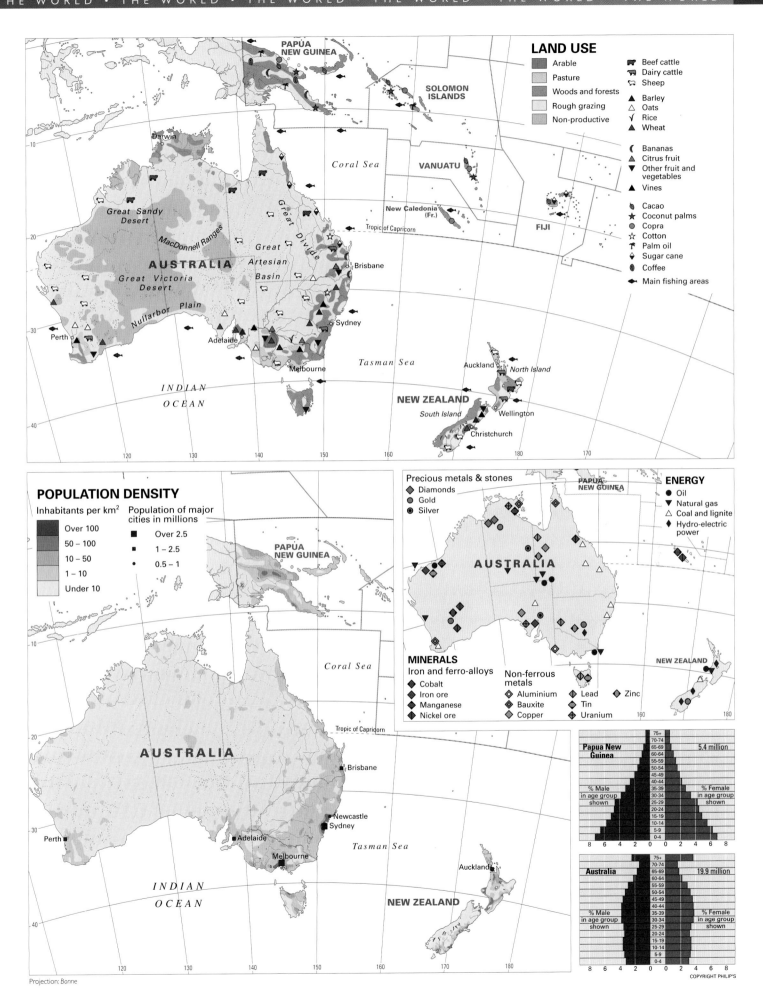

LAND USE

- Arable
- Pasture
- Woods and forests
- Rough grazing
- Non-productive

- Beef cattle
- Dairy cattle
- Sheep
- Barley
- Oats
- Rice
- Wheat
- Bananas
- Citrus fruit
- Other fruit and vegetables
- Vines
- Cacao
- Coconut palms
- Copra
- Cotton
- Palm oil
- Sugar cane
- Coffee
- Main fishing areas

POPULATION DENSITY

Inhabitants per km² | Population of major cities in millions

- Over 100
- 50 – 100
- 10 – 50
- 1 – 10
- Under 10

- Over 2.5
- 1 – 2.5
- 0.5 – 1

Precious metals & stones
- Diamonds
- Gold
- Silver

MINERALS

Iron and ferro-alloys
- Cobalt
- Iron ore
- Manganese
- Nickel ore

Non-ferrous metals
- Aluminium
- Bauxite
- Copper
- Lead
- Tin
- Uranium
- Zinc

ENERGY
- Oil
- Natural gas
- Coal and lignite
- Hydro-electric power

Papua New Guinea — 5.4 million

% Male in age group shown | % Female in age group shown

Australia — 19.9 million

% Male in age group shown | % Female in age group shown

Projection: Bonne

COPYRIGHT PHILIP'S

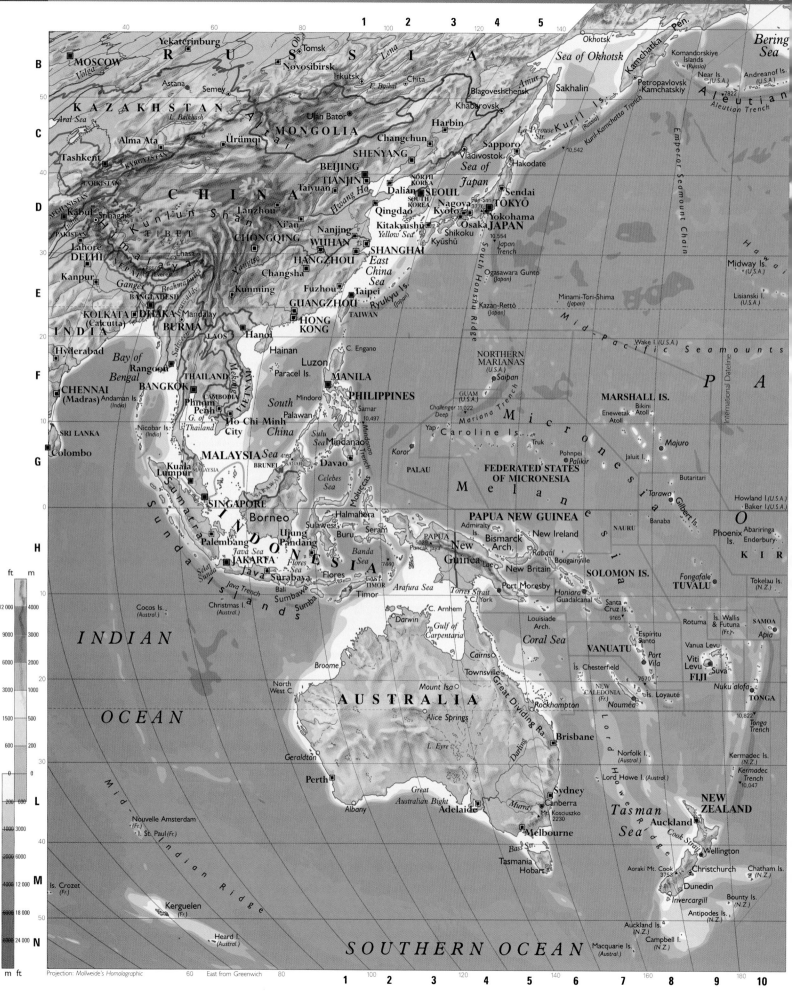

Projection: Mollweide's Homolographic   East from Greenwich

16 17 18 19 20

ALASKA
(U.S.A.)
Anchorage
Juneau
Bristol Bay
Gulf of Alaska
5959
Is. (U.S.A.)
Prince of Wales I.
(U.S.A.) Prince Rupert
Queen Charlotte Is.
(Canada)

C A N A D A

B

Edmonton
L. Winnipeg
Newfoundland

Calgary
Winnipeg
Regina
Vancouver
Vancouver I. Victoria
Seattle
Portland
Boise
L. Superior
Minneapolis
Québec
St. Lawrence
Montréal
St. John's

N O R T H

50

C

Salt Lake City
Detroit
Ottawa
Boston
L. Huron
L. Ontario
Buffalo
L. Erie
Toronto
CHICAGO
Pittsburgh
NEW YORK
PHILADELPHIA
Baltimore
Washington D.C.

C. Mendocino
Denver
Kansas City
St. Louis
Cincinnati
40
Missouri

A T L A N T I C

D

SAN FRANCISCO
Sacramento
U N I T E D   S T A T E S
Oklahoma City
Memphis
Atlanta
C. Hatteras
4418
Appalachian Mts.
Colorado

LOS ANGELES
Phoenix
Dallas
San Diego
Houston
Jacksonville
Bermuda
(U.K.)

Ciudad
Juárez
San Antonio
New Orleans
Mississippi
30

Guadalupe
(Mex.)
Golfo de California
Baja California
M E X I C O
Gulf of Mexico
Miami
BAHAMAS

O C E A N

E

Monterrey

Tropic of Cancer
Havana
Florida
CUBA
West Indies

C. San Lucas
Guadalajara
Mérida
Canal de Yucatán
9200
7680
HAITI
DOMINICAN REP.
Leeward
Is.

Is. de Revillagigedo
(Mex.)
MEXICO
4619
Puebla
BELIZE
JAMAICA
Kingston
PUERTO
RICO
(U.S.A.)

F

Acapulco
GUATEMALA
HONDURAS
Caribbean Sea
BARBADOS
Windward Is.
Guatemala
San Salvador
NICARAGUA
Barranquilla
Maracaibo
EL SALVADOR
Managua
San José
Caracas
Orinoco

I. Clipperton
(Fr.)
COSTA
RICA
Colón Panamá
PANAMA
VENEZUELA

G

I. del Coco
(Costa Rica)
Medellín
Bogotá

I. de Malpelo
(Colombia)
Cali
COLOMBIA

Galápagos
(Ecuador)
Equator
Quito
ECUADOR

0

Guayaquil
Iquitos
Amazonas
H

C. Pariñas
BRAZIL

Trujillo
6369
PERU
10

LIMA
Cuzco
Nevada Ancohuma
6550
Arequipa
L. Titicaca
J
6866
La Paz
Peru-
Arica
BOLIVIA

Iquique
Chile
20

Tropic of Capricorn
Antofagasta
PARAGUAY
Asunción
K
San Félix
(Chile)
8050
Trench
San Ambrosio
(Chile)
San Miguel
de Tucumán

Sala-y-Gómez
(Chile)
Pôrto
Alegre
I. de Pascua
(Chile)
Córdoba
30
Aconcagua
6962
Rosario
Arch. de
Juan Fernández
(Chile)
Valparaíso
URUGUAY

SANTIAGO
BUENOS
AIRES
Montevideo
Río de la Plata
L
Concepción
ARGENTINA

40

SOUTH

M

ATLANTIC

6212
50

OCEAN

N

Punta Arenas
Est. de Magallanes
Falkland Is.
(U.K.)
South Georgia
(U.K.)
Tierra del Fuego
C. de Hornos

West Pacific side (ocean labels):

Honolulu
O'ahu HAWAI'I
4205
(U.S.A.)
Hawai'i

Johnston I.
(U.S.A.)

C I F I C

North West Christmas Ridge

Palmyra Is.
(U.S.A.)
Teraina
Tabuaeran
Kiritimati
Line Is.

Jarvis I.
(U.S.A.)
O C E A N

I B A T I

Malden I.
Starbuck I.

Tongareva
Îs. Marquises
Pukapuka Manihiki
Vostok I.
Caroline I.
(Millennium I.)
Flint I.
AMER.
SAMOA
(U.S.A.)
Suwarrow Is.
Îs. de la
Société
Îs. Tuamotu
Niue
(N.Z.)
Cook Is.
(N.Z.)
Papeete Tahiti
F R E N C H   P O L Y N E S I A

Rarotonga
Îs. Tubuai
Mururoa
Henderson I.

Rapa
Pitcairn I.
(U.K.)

East Pacific Rise

Chile Rise

PATAGONIA
CORDILLERA DE LOS ANDES

Pacific-Antarctic Ridge

East from Greenwich labels: 120 100 80 60 40 20

11 12 13 14 15 16 17 18 19 20

160 140 120 100 80 West from Greenwich 60 40

COPYRIGHT PHILIP'S

Equatorial Scale 1:54 000 000

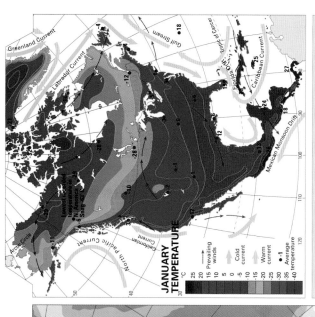

JANUARY TEMPERATURE

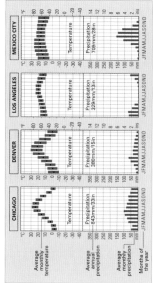

MEXICO CITY

LOS ANGELES

DENVER

CHICAGO

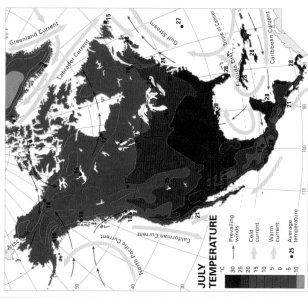

JULY TEMPERATURE

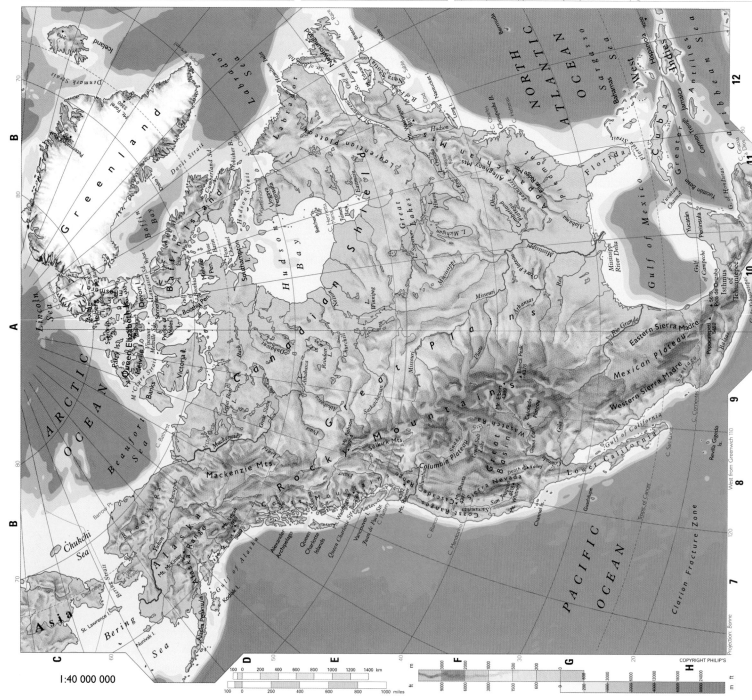

1:40 000 000

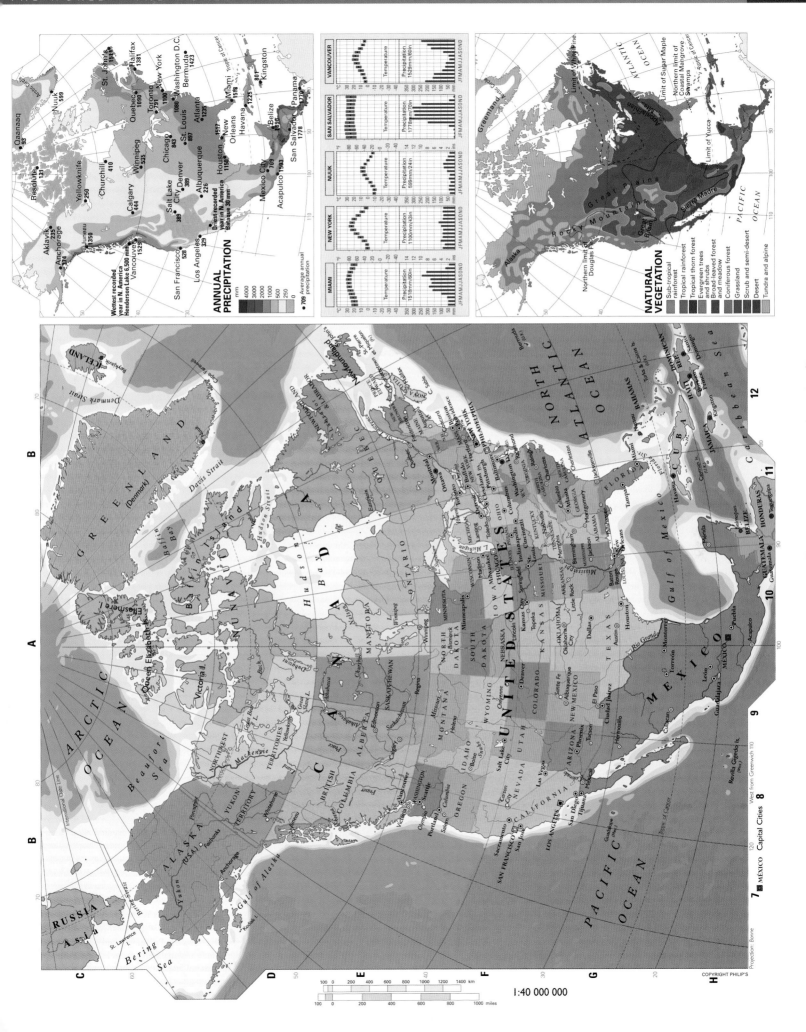

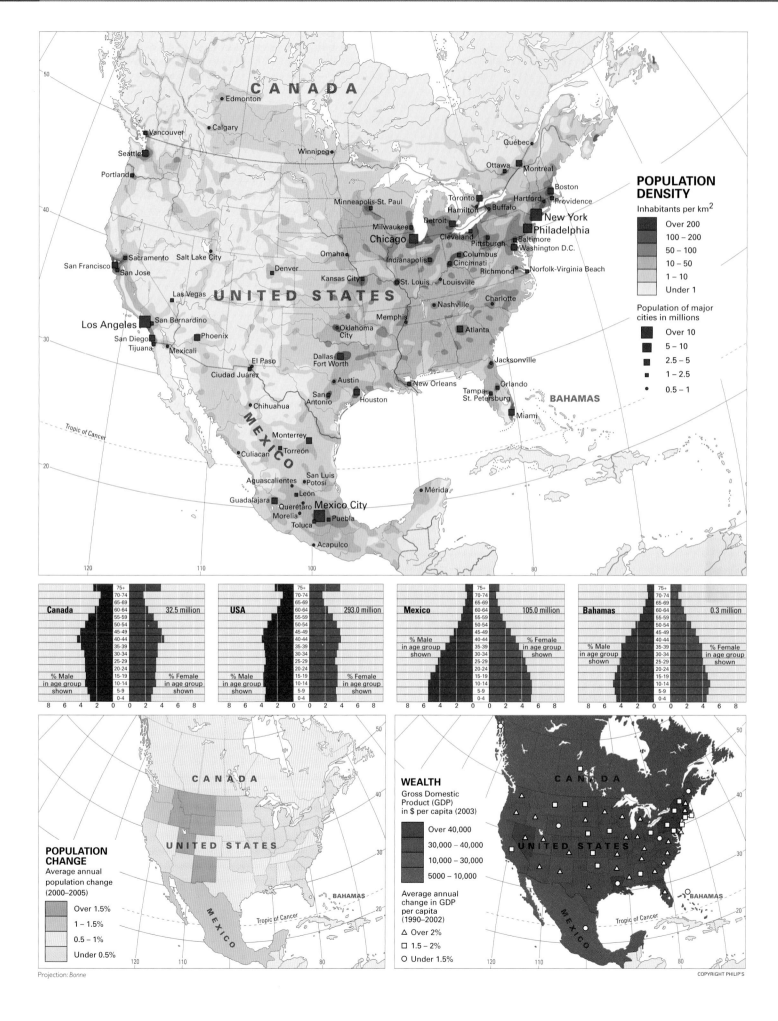

POPULATION DENSITY

Inhabitants per km²

- Over 200
- 100 – 200
- 50 – 100
- 10 – 50
- 1 – 10
- Under 1

Population of major cities in millions

- Over 10
- 5 – 10
- 2.5 – 5
- 1 – 2.5
- 0.5 – 1

Canada 32.5 million
USA 293.0 million
Mexico 105.0 million
Bahamas 0.3 million

% Male in age group shown
% Female in age group shown

POPULATION CHANGE

Average annual population change (2000–2005)

- Over 1.5%
- 1 – 1.5%
- 0.5 – 1%
- Under 0.5%

WEALTH

Gross Domestic Product (GDP) in $ per capita (2003)

- Over 40,000
- 30,000 – 40,000
- 10,000 – 30,000
- 5000 – 10,000

Average annual change in GDP per capita (1990–2002)

- △ Over 2%
- □ 1.5 – 2%
- ○ Under 1.5%

Projection: Bonne

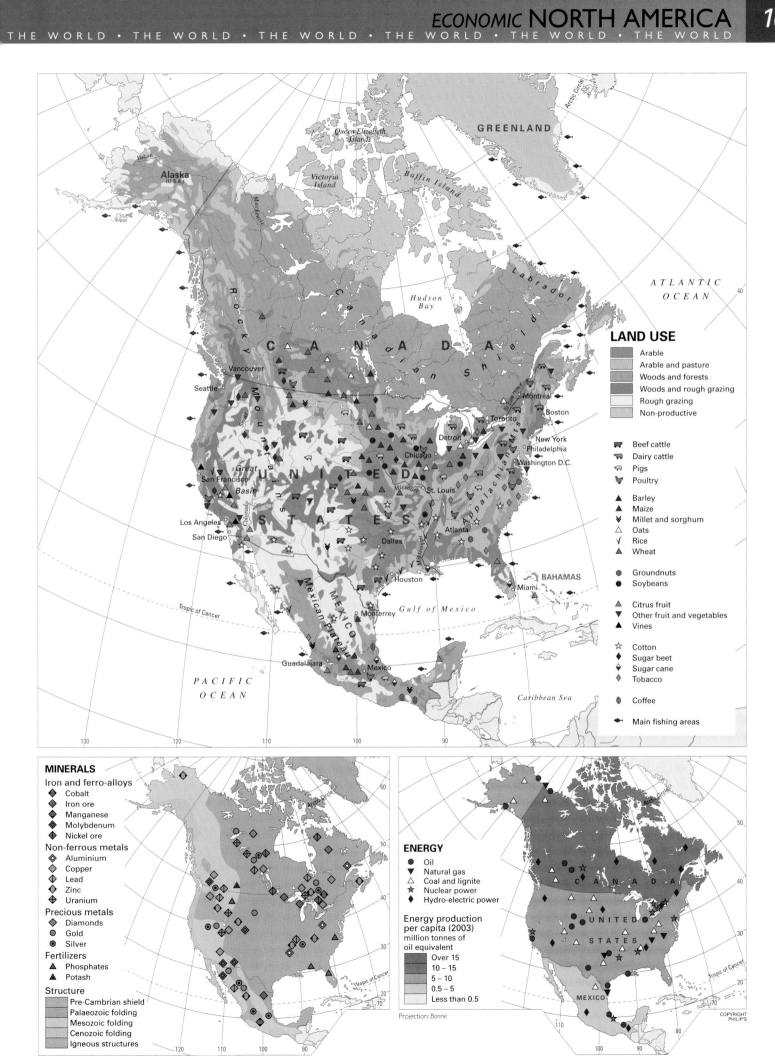

LAND USE

- Arable
- Arable and pasture
- Woods and forests
- Woods and rough grazing
- Rough grazing
- Non-productive

- Beef cattle
- Dairy cattle
- Pigs
- Poultry

- Barley
- Maize
- Millet and sorghum
- Oats
- Rice
- Wheat

- Groundnuts
- Soybeans

- Citrus fruit
- Other fruit and vegetables
- Vines

- Cotton
- Sugar beet
- Sugar cane
- Tobacco

- Coffee

- Main fishing areas

MINERALS

Iron and ferro-alloys
- Cobalt
- Iron ore
- Manganese
- Molybdenum
- Nickel ore

Non-ferrous metals
- Aluminium
- Copper
- Lead
- Zinc
- Uranium

Precious metals
- Diamonds
- Gold
- Silver

Fertilizers
- Phosphates
- Potash

Structure
- Pre-Cambrian shield
- Palaeozoic folding
- Mesozoic folding
- Cenozoic folding
- Igneous structures

ENERGY

- Oil
- Natural gas
- Coal and lignite
- Nuclear power
- Hydro-electric power

Energy production per capita (2003)
million tonnes of oil equivalent

- Over 15
- 10 – 15
- 5 – 10
- 0.5 – 5
- Less than 0.5

Projection: Bonne

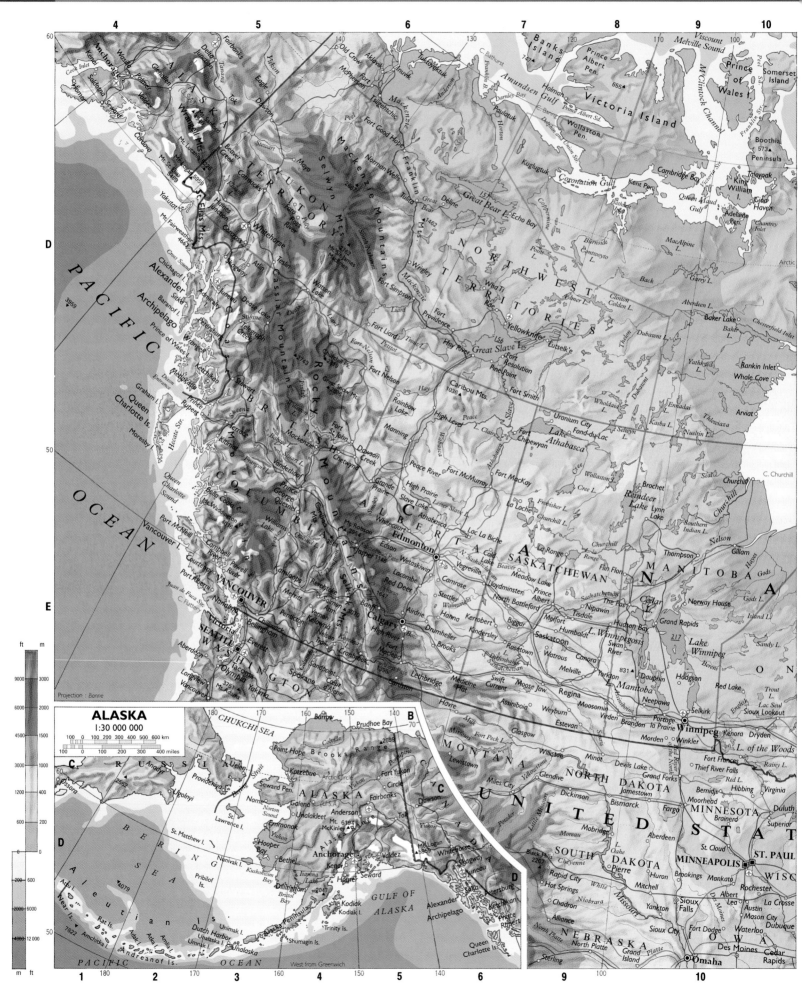

ALASKA
1:30 000 000

NORTHERN CANADA

Continuation northwards on same scale as main map

Main map labels

Devon I.
Lancaster Sound
Baffin Bay
Brodeur Peninsula
Borden Pen.
Arctic Bay
Nanisivik
Bylot I.
Pond Inlet
Clyde River
C. Adair
C. Raper
Home B.
Gulf of Boothia
Fury and Hecla Str.
Igloolik
Baffin Island
Qikiqtarjuaq
Cumberland Peninsula
Pangnirtung
Hoare B.
C. Mercy
Melville Peninsula
Foxe Basin
Prince Charles I.
Air Force I.
Cumberland Sd.
Simpson Pen.
Kugaaruk
Committee B.
Rae Isthmus
Repulse Bay
Arctic Circle
NUNAVUT
C. Dorchester
Foxe Channel
Foxe Pen.
Amadjuak
Cape Dorset
Meta Incognita Peninsula
Iqaluit
Hall Peninsula
Kimmirut
Frobisher Bay
Resolution I.
Southampton I.
Coral Harbour
Bell Pen.
Nottingham I.
Salisbury I.
Wolstenholme
Chesterfield Inlet
Coats I.
Mansel I.
Ivujivik
Salluit
Quaqtaq
Akpatok I.
C. Chidley
Hudson Strait
Kangiqsujuaq
Cratère du Nouveau-Québec
Kangirsuk
Ungava Bay
Kangiqsualujjuaq
Hebron
Puvirnituq
Péninsule d'Ungava
Arnaud
Payne
Kuujjuaq
Nain
Hudson Bay
Ottawa Is.
Feuilles
George
Baleine
Hopedale
C. Harrison
Labrador Sea
Inukjuak
L. Minto
Mélèzes
Rigolet
Cartwright
Sleeper Is.
King George Is.
Baker's Dozen Is.
Sanikiluaq
L. Bienville
Caniapiscau
Kawawachikamach (Schefferville)
Smallwood Res.
North West River
Happy Valley-Goose Bay
Port Hope Simpson
Belle Isle
C. Bauld
St. Anthony
Belcher Is.
Kuujjuarapik
Grande Baleine
Petitsikapau L.
Churchill Falls
Churchill
NEWFOUNDLAND & LABRADOR
C. Tatnam
C. Henrietta Maria
Pte. Louis XIV
Chisasibi
La Grande
Kanaaupscow
Labrador City
Fermont
Ashuanipi
St-Augustin
Romaine
Natashquan
Deer Lake
Corner Brook
Bonavista
James Bay
Akimiski I.
Wemindji
Eastmain
Gagnon
Moisie
I. d'Anticosti
Havre-St-Pierre
Grand Falls-Windsor
Gander
Carbonear
St. John's
Peawanuck
Winisk
Big Trout L.
Attawapiskat
Fort Albany
Waskaganish
Rupert
Mistassini
Manicouagan
Sept-Îles
Port-Cartier
Gulf of St. Lawrence
Stephenville
Channel-Port aux Basques
Marystown
Placentia
C. Race
ONTARIO
Severn
Albany
Moosonee
Charlton
Eastmain
Nottaway
Chibougamau
Baie-Comeau
St. Lawrence
Gaspé
Pén. de la Gaspésie
Îles de la Madeleine
Cabot Str.
St-Pierre et Miquelon (Fr.)
L. St. Joseph
Nakina
Kenogami
Misitaibi
Matagami
L. Matagami
Dolbeau-Mistassini
St-Jean
Roberval
Chicoutimi
Rimouski
Matane
Campbellton
Bathurst
Chatham
PR. EDWARD I.
Summerside
Charlottetown
Sydney
Glace Bay
Cape Breton I.
Port Hawkesbury
New Glasgow
Antigonish
L. Nipigon
Nipigon
Greenstone
Hearst
Kapuskasing
Cochrane
Abitibi L.
Amos
Rés. Gouin
Jonquière
Grand Falls
Edmundston
Woodstock
Fredericton
NEW BRUNSWICK
Moncton
Amherst
NOVA SCOTIA
Kentville
Truro
Dartmouth
Sable I. (Nova Scotia)
Thunder Bay
Marathon
Oba
Chapleau
Timmins
Kirkland Lake
Rouyn-Noranda
Val-d'Or
La Tuque
Québec
Lévis
Thetford Mines
Shawinigan
Trois-Rivières
Joliette
St-Hyacinthe
Sherbrooke
Saint John
B. of Fundy
Digby
Bridgewater
Liverpool
Yarmouth
Lake Superior
Houghton
Sault Ste. Marie
Elliot Lake
Sudbury
North Bay
Pembroke
MONTRÉAL
Hull
OTTAWA
Cornwall
MAINE
Bangor
Augusta
Lewiston
Portland
C. Sable
Gulf of Maine
Ironwood
Marquette
Manistique
Georgian Bay
Parry Sound
Huntsville
Burlington
Montpelier
VERMONT
NEW HAMPSHIRE
Concord
Manchester
C. Cod
Rhinelander
Escanaba
Menominee
Petoskey
Traverse City
Cadillac
Lake Huron
Owen Sound
Barrie
Peterborough
Kingston
Belleville
Champlain
NEW YORK
Albany
Springfield
MASS.
BOSTON
PROVIDENCE
Wausau
Green Bay
Appleton
L. Michigan
Saginaw
Flint
London
TORONTO
Hamilton
Oshawa
L. Ontario
Rochester
Syracuse
Utica
Hartford
CONN.
New Haven
Sheboygan
Grand Rapids
Kitchener
Niagara Falls
Buffalo
Elmira
Binghamton
Bridgeport
NEW YORK
MILWAUKEE
Madison
Racine
Kenosha
Lansing
Flint
Sarnia
L. Erie
Jamestown
Scranton
Newark
N.J.
Rockford
WISCONSIN
CHICAGO
DETROIT
Windsor
Toledo
CLEVELAND
PENNSYLVANIA
Trenton
Allentown
ILLINOIS
Gary
South Bend
INDIANA
OHIO

LABRADOR
Laurentian Plateau
QUÉBEC
ATLANTIC OCEAN

Inset map (Northern Canada continuation)

ARCTIC OCEAN
North Magnetic Pole 2005
GREENLAND
Sverdrup Islands
Borden I.
Brock I.
Mackenzie King I.
Ellef Ringnes
Amund Ringnes
Meighen I.
Axel Heiberg I.
Eureka
Alert
Nares Str.
Prince Patrick I.
Eglinton I.
Emerald I.
Lougheed I.
Cornwall I.
Norwegian Bay
Grise Fiord
Ellesmere Island
C. Prince Alfred
Mackenzie King I.
Parry Islands
Queen Elizabeth Is.
Bathurst I.
Cornwallis I.
Wellington Chan.
Jones Sound
Devon Island
Banks Island
C. Kellet
McClure Strait
Viscount Melville Sound
Resolute
Lancaster Sound
Holman
Prince Albert Pen.
Victoria Island
M'Clintock Channel
Prince of Wales Island
Prince Somerset Island
NUNAVUT
Arctic Bay
Nanisivik
Brodeur Peninsula
Pond Inlet
Baffin Island
NORTHWEST TERRITORIES

Scale

1:15 000 000

100 100 200 300 400 500 600 km

100 100 200 300 400 miles

West from Greenwich

COPYRIGHT PHILIP'S

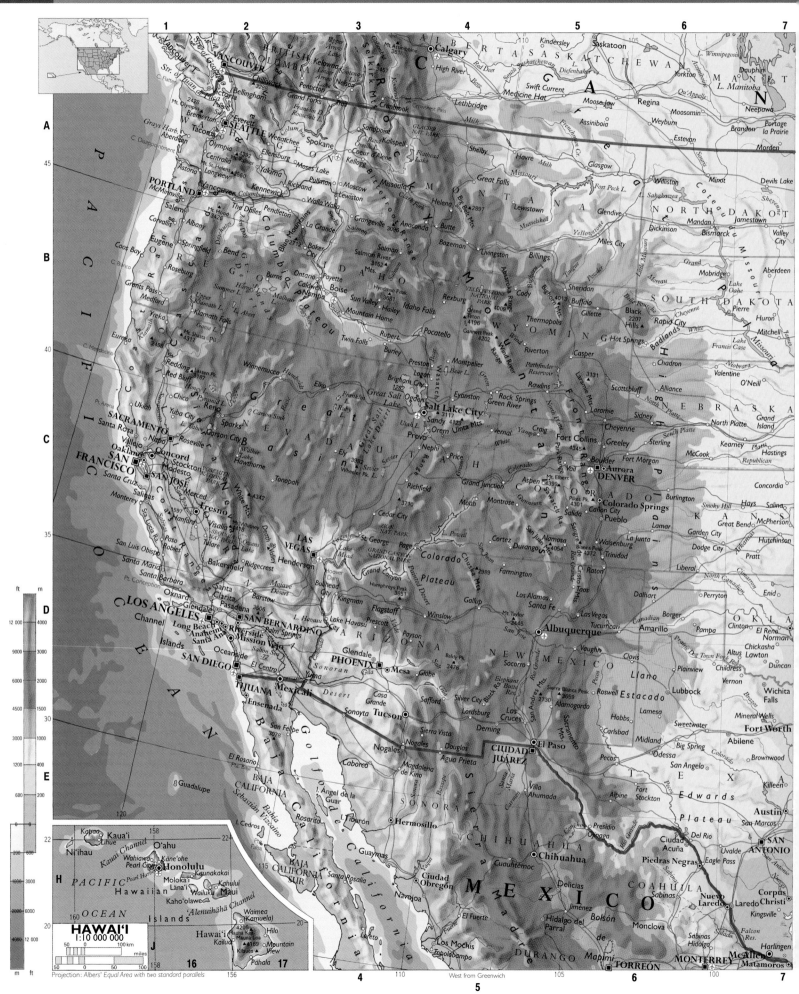

COPYRIGHT PHILIP'S

1:12 000 000

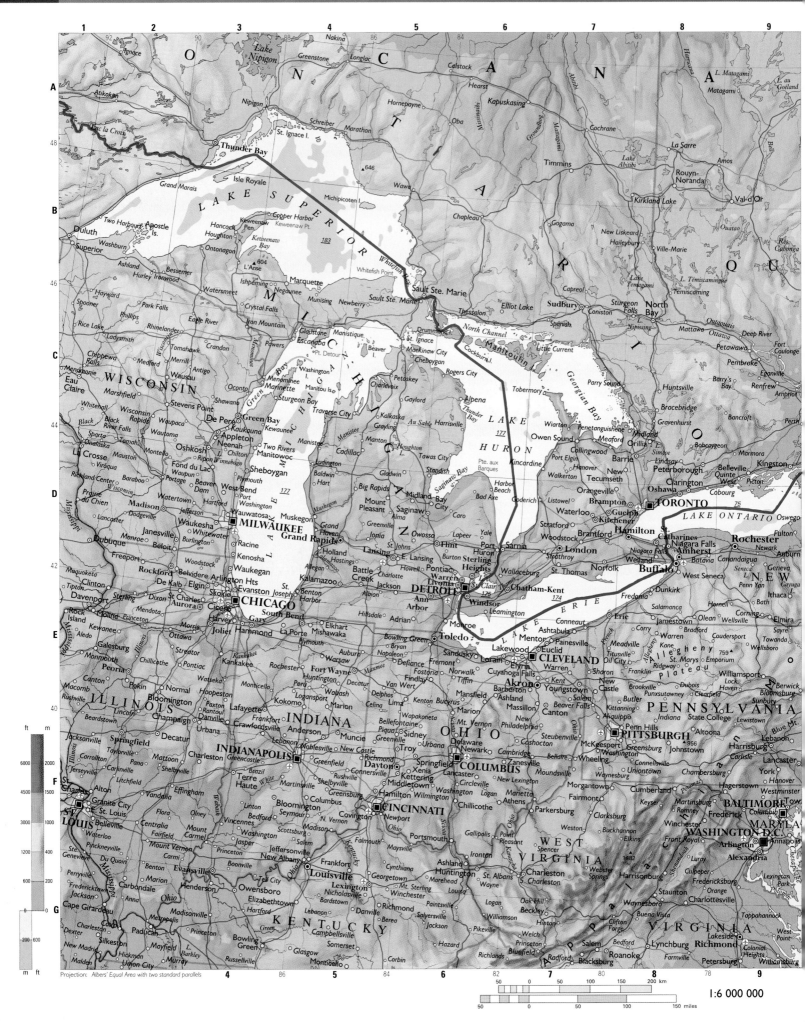

Projection: Albers' Equal Area with two standard parallels

1:6 000 000

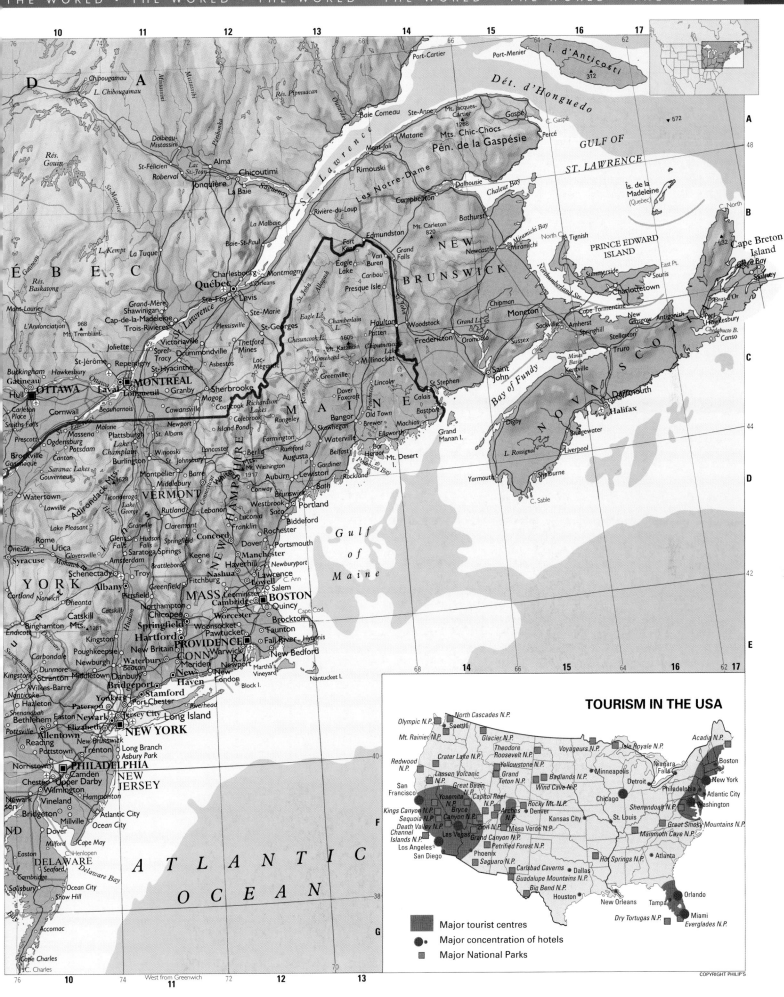

TOURISM IN THE USA

Major tourist centres
Major concentration of hotels
Major National Parks

COPYRIGHT PHILIP'S

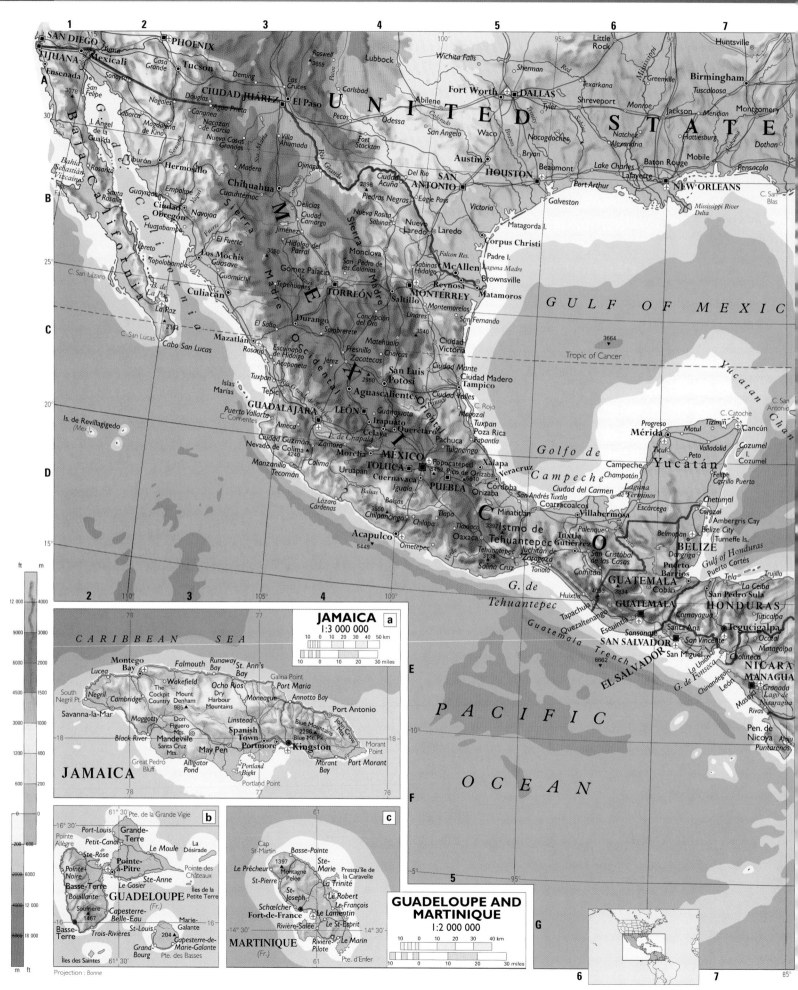

JAMAICA
1:3 000 000

GUADELOUPE AND MARTINIQUE
1:2 000 000

Projection : Bonne

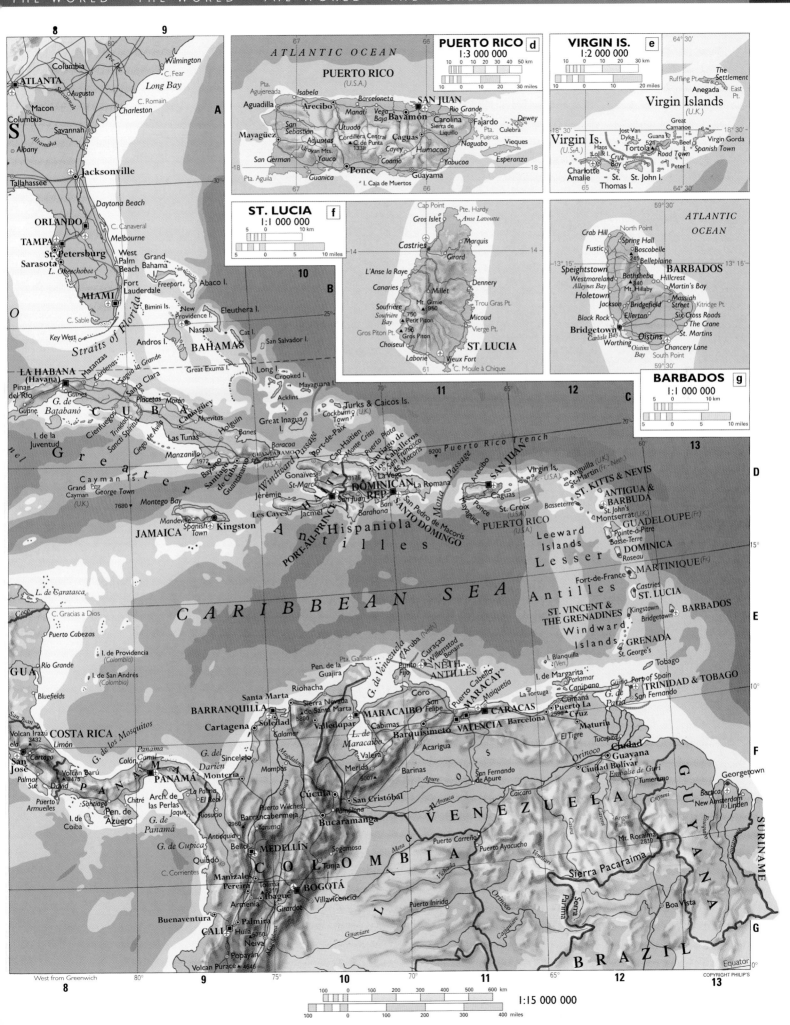

PUERTO RICO d
1:3 000 000

ATLANTIC OCEAN

PUERTO RICO
(U.S.A.)

Pta. Aguijereada
Isabela
Aguadilla
Arecibo
Manati
Vega Baja
Barceloneta
Río Grande
SAN JUAN
Bayamón
Carolina
Fajardo
Dewey
Culebra
Mayagüez
San Sebastián
Utuado
Sierra de Luquillo
Pta. Puerca
Vieques
Adjuntas
Cordillera Central
▲ C. de Punta 1338
Caguas
Humacoa
Naguabo
Esperanza
San German
Yauco
Cayey
Coamo
Yabucoa
Uroyan Mts.
Ponce
Guanica
Guayama
Pta. Aguila
I. Caja de Muertos

VIRGIN IS. e
1:2 000 000

Ruffling Pt.
The Settlement
Anegada
East Pt.

Virgin Islands
(U.K.)

Virgin Is.
(U.S.A.)
Great Camanoe
Jost Van Dyke I.
Guana I.
Beef I.
Virgin Gorda
Haps
Tortola
Road Town
Spanish Town
Lollik I.
Cruz Bay
Peter I.
Charlotte Amalie
St. Thomas I.
St. John I.

ST. LUCIA f
1:1 000 000

Cap Point
Pte. Hardy
Gros Islet
Anse Lavoutte
Castries
Girard
Marquis
L'Anse la Raye
Canaries
Dennery
Soufrière
Soufrière Bay
Mt. Gimie ▲ 950
Millet
Trou Gras Pt.
▲ Petit Piton 750
Micoud
Gros Piton Pt.
▲ Gros Piton 796
Vierge Pt.
Choiseul
Laborie
Vieux Fort
C. Moule à Chique
ST. LUCIA

BARBADOS g
1:1 000 000

ATLANTIC OCEAN

Crab Hill
North Point
Spring Hall
Fustic
Boscobelle
Belleplaine
Speightstown
Bathsheba
Hillcrest
BARBADOS
Westmoreland
Alleynes Bay
▲ Mt. Hillaby 340
Martin's Bay
Massiah Street
Kitridge Pt.
Holetown
Jackson
Bridgefield
Ellerton
Six Cross Roads
The Crane
Black Rock
Worthing
Bridgetown
Oistins
St. Martins
Carlisle Bay
Oistins Bay
Chancery Lane
South Point

Main map (1:15 000 000)

ATLANTA
Columbia
Savannah
Augusta
Macon
C. Fear
Wilmington
Columbus
Charleston
Long Bay
Albany
C. Romain
Jacksonville
Tallahassee
ORLANDO
Daytona Beach
C. Canaveral
TAMPA
Melbourne
St. Petersburg
West Palm Beach
Sarasota
L. Okeechobee
Grand Bahama
MIAMI
Fort Lauderdale
Freeport
Abaco I.
C. Sable
Bimini Is.
New Providence I.
Eleuthera I.
Key West
Nassau
Andros I.
Cat I.
BAHAMAS
San Salvador I.
Straits of Florida
LA HABANA (Havana)
Matanzas
Cardenas
Great Exuma I.
Long I.
Pinar del Rio
Sagua la Grande
Santa Clara
Crooked I.
G. de Batabanó
Guines
Placetas
Moron
Mayaguana I.
Gupne
CUBA
Cienfuegos
Trinidad
Sancti Spiritus
Ciego de Avila
Camaguey
Acklins
Great Inagua
I. de la Juventud
Las Tunas
Holguin
Banes
Turks & Caicos Is.
Greater
Cockburn Town (U.K.)
Manzanillo
1972
Bayamo
Santiago de Cuba
Port-de-Paix
Cap-Haïtien
Puerto Plata
Monte Cristi
Cayman Is.
Grand Cayman (U.K.)
George Town
Los Caballeros
Montego Bay
7680
Baracoa
GUANTANAMO (U.S.A.)
Guantanamo
Windward Passage
Gonaïves
St-Marc
3175
La Vega
San Francisco de Macoris
9200
Puerto Rico Trench
Mandeville
Spanish Town
Jérémie
HAITI
DOMINICAN REP.
Bani
San Juan
La Romana
Mona Passage
Arecibo
SAN JUAN
Virgin Is. (U.K.-U.S.A.)
Anguilla (U.K.)
St-Martin (Fr.-Neth.)
JAMAICA
Kingston
Les Cayes
Jacmel
PORT-AU-PRINCE
Barahona
San Pedro de Macoris
Mayagüez
Ponce
St. Croix (U.S.A.)
St. KITTS & NEVIS
ANTIGUA & BARBUDA
Hispaniola
SANTO DOMINGO
PUERTO RICO
Basseterre
St. John's
Montserrat (U.K.)
Antilles
Leeward Islands
GUADELOUPE (Fr.)
Pointe-à-Pitre
Basse-Terre
DOMINICA
Roseau
Lesser
MARTINIQUE (Fr.)
Fort-de-France
Castries
ST. LUCIA
CARIBBEAN SEA
Antilles
ST. VINCENT & THE GRENADINES
Kingstown
Bridgetown
BARBADOS
L. de Caratasca
Coco
C. Gracias a Dios
Windward
Islands
GRENADA
St. George's
Puerto Cabezas
I. de Providencia (Colombia)
I. Blanquilla (Ven.)
Rio Grande
GUA
I. de San Andres (Colombia)
Bluefields
Tobago
I. de Margarita
Porlamar
Carúpano
Gulf of Paria
Port of Spain
TRINIDAD & TOBAGO
San Fernando
Aruba (Neth.)
Curaçao
Willemstad
Bonaire
NETH. ANTILLES
La Tortuga
Cumaná
Pen. de la Guajira
Pta. Gallinas
G. de Venezuela
Punto Fijo
Coro
MARACAY
Puerto Cabello
CARACAS
Maturin
Volcan Irazú 3432
ela
Riohacha
San Felipe
Puerto La Cruz
Barcelona
El Tigre
San José
Cartago
Volcan Barú 3475
COSTA RICA
Limón
Santa Marta
Sierra Nevada de Santa Marta 5800
MARACAIBO
Cabimas
VALENCIA
BARRANQUILLA
Soledad
Calamar
Barquisimeto
Ciudad Guayana
Palmar Sur
David
Puerto Armuelles
PANAMÁ
Panama Canal
Colón
G. del Darién
Sincelejo
Cartagena
Valledupar
L. de Maracaibo
Valera
Barinas
Apure
San Fernando de Apure
Caicara
Ciudad Bolívar
Embalse de Guri
Tumereng
Georgetown
Chitré
Arch. de las Perlas
La Palma
El Real
Monteria
Mompos
Merida 5007
SURINAME
Pen. de Azuero
I. de Coiba
Santiago
G. de Panamá
Jaque
Riosucio
Antioquia
Barrancabermeja
Yarumal
Puerto Wilches
Cúcuta
Pamplona
San Cristóbal
VENEZUELA
Orinoco
Guayana
Mt. Roraima 2810
New Amsterdam
Linden
G. de Cupica
2960
Bello
MEDELLÍN
Bucaramanga
Puerto Carreño
Puerto Ayacucho
GUYANA
Quibdó
Sogamoso
Tunja
Meta
Sierra Pacaraima
Serra Parima
C. Corrientes
Manizales
Pereira
Tolima 5215
BOGOTÁ
Villavicencio
Puerto Inirida
COLOMBIA
Boa Vista
Armenia
Ibagué
Girardot
Neiva
Guaviare
Buenaventura
CALI
Palmira
Huila 5750
Popayán
Vichada
Venturi
Casiquiare
Volcan Puracé ▲ 4646
BRAZIL
Equator

West from Greenwich
COPYRIGHT PHILIP'S

1:15 000 000

100   0   100   200   300   400   500   600 km
100   0   100   200   300   400 miles

Projection: Lambert's Azimuthal Equal Area

1:35 000 000

COPYRIGHT PHILIP'S

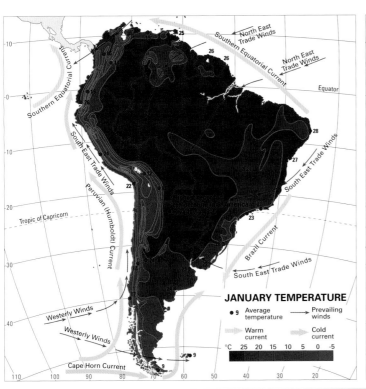

JANUARY TEMPERATURE

- • 9 Average temperature
- → Prevailing winds
- Warm current
- Cold current

°C 25 20 15 10 5 0 -5

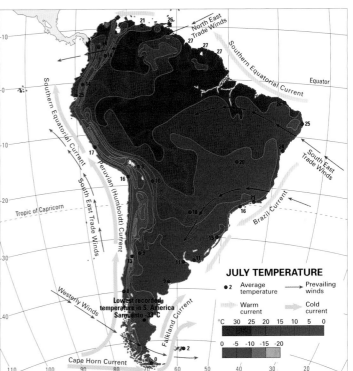

JULY TEMPERATURE

- • 2 Average temperature
- → Prevailing winds
- Warm current
- Cold current

Lowest recorded temperature in S. America Sarmiento -33°C

°C 30 25 20 15 10 5 0

0 -5 -10 -15 -20

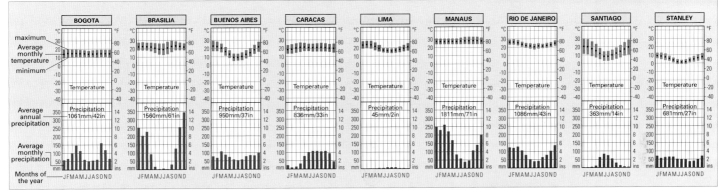

	BOGOTA	BRASILIA	BUENOS AIRES	CARACAS	LIMA	MANAUS	RIO DE JANEIRO	SANTIAGO	STANLEY
maximum / Average monthly temperature / minimum	Temperature	Temperature	Temperature	Temperature	Temperature	Temperature	Temperature	Temperature	Temperature
Average annual precipitation	Precipitation 1061mm/42in	Precipitation 1560mm/61in	Precipitation 950mm/37in	Precipitation 836mm/33in	Precipitation 45mm/2in	Precipitation 1811mm/71in	Precipitation 1086mm/43in	Precipitation 363mm/14in	Precipitation 681mm/27in
Months of the year	JFMAMJJASOND	JFMAMJJASOND	JFMAMJJASOND	JFMAMJJASOND	JFMAMJJASOND	JFMAMJJASOND	JFMAMJJASOND	JFMAMJJASOND	JFMAMJJASOND

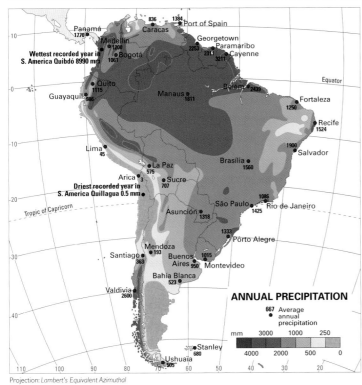

Panamá 1770
Caracas 836 1384 Port of Spain
Medellín 1200
Bogotá 1061
Georgetown
Paramaribo 2253 231
Cayenne 3211
Wettest recorded year in S. America Quibdó 8990 mm
Quito 1115
Guayaquil 896
Manaus 1811
Belém 2439
Fortaleza 1250
Recife 1524
Lima 45
La Paz 575
Arica 3
Sucre 707
Driest recorded year in S. America Quillagua 0.5 mm
Brasília 1560
1900
Salvador
São Paulo 1425 1086 Rio de Janeiro
Asunción 1318
1333
Pôrto Alegre
Mendoza 193
Santiago 363
Buenos Aires 950 1015 Montevideo
Bahía Blanca 523
Valdivia 2600
Stanley 680
Ushuaia 505

ANNUAL PRECIPITATION

- • 667 Average annual precipitation

mm 3000 1000 250

4000 2000 500 0

Guiana Highlands
Amazon Basin
South limit of wild rubber
Atacama Desert
Andes
PACIFIC OCEAN
South limit of Quebracho
Brazilian Highlands
Pampas
Patagonia
ATLANTIC OCEAN

NATURAL VEGETATION

- Tropical rainforest
- Tropical thorn forest
- Temperate rainforest
- Evergreen trees and shrubs
- Grassland and savanna
- Semi-desert
- Desert
- Alpine and high plateau

Projection: Lambert's Equivalent Azimuthal

Venezuela 25.0 million
75+
70-74
65-69
60-64
55-59
50-54
45-49
40-44
35-39
30-34
25-29
20-24
15-19
10-14
5-9
0-4
% Male in age group shown — % Female in age group shown
8 6 4 2 0 0 2 4 6 8

CUBA — Havana
JAMAICA — Kingston
HAITI — Port au Prince
DOM. REP. — Santiago, Santo Domingo
San Juan — Puerto Rico
ANTIGUA & BARBUDA
ST. KITTS & NEVIS — Guadeloupe
DOMINICA
Martinique
ST. LUCIA
ST. VINCENT — BARBADOS
GRENADA
TRINIDAD & TOBAGO

BELIZE
GUATEMALA — Guatemala
HONDURAS — Tegucigalpa
EL SALVADOR — San Salvador
NICARAGUA — Managua
COSTA RICA — San José
PANAMA — Panama

Barranquilla
Cartagena
Maracaibo
Valencia — Maracay
Barquisimeto — Caracas
VENEZUELA — Ciudad Guayana
Cúcuta
Bucaramanga
Medellín
Bogotá
COLOMBIA
Cali

GUYANA
SURINAME
FRENCH GUIANA

POPULATION DENSITY
Inhabitants per km²

Over 200	10 – 50
100 – 200	1 – 10
50 – 100	Under 1

Equator
Galapagos Is.
ECUADOR — Quito, Guayaquil
Belém
São Luís
Manaus
Fortaleza
Teresina
Natal

PERU
Trujillo
Lima
BRAZIL
Recife
Maceió
Salvador

BOLIVIA
Arequipa
La Paz
Santa Cruz
Cochabamba
Goiânia — Brasília

Campo Grande
Belo Horizonte
Nova Iguaçu
Campinas
São Paulo
Santos
Rio de Janeiro
Curitiba
Tropic of Capricorn

PARAGUAY
Asunción

WEALTH
Gross Domestic Product (GDP) in $ per capita (2003)

Over 20,000	2000 – 5000
10,000 – 20,000	1000 – 2000
5000 – 10,000	Under 1000

Average annual change in GDP per capita (1990–2002)
△ Over 2.5%　□ 1.5 – 2.5%　○ Under 1.5%

CHILE
San Miguel de Tucumán
Pôrto Alegre
Córdoba
Santiago — Mendoza — Rosario
URUGUAY
Buenos Aires — Montevideo
La Plata
ARGENTINA
Mar del Plata

Population of major cities in millions

Over 10	1 – 2.5
5 – 10	0.5 – 1
2.5 – 5	

CUBA
NICARAGUA
COSTA RICA
PANAMA
VENEZUELA
GUYANA
SURINAME
FRENCH GUIANA
COLOMBIA
Galapagos Is.
ECUADOR
Equator
BRAZIL
PERU
BOLIVIA
PARAGUAY
Tropic of Capricorn
CHILE
URUGUAY
ARGENTINA
Falkland Is.

Brazil 184.1 million
75+
70-74
65-69
60-64
55-59
50-54
45-49
40-44
35-39
30-34
25-29
20-24
15-19
10-14
5-9
0-4
% Male in age group shown — % Female in age group shown
8 6 4 2 0 0 2 4 6 8

Argentina 39.1 million
75+
70-74
65-69
60-64
55-59
50-54
45-49
40-44
35-39
30-34
25-29
20-24
15-19
10-14
5-9
0-4
% Male in age group shown — % Female in age group shown
8 6 4 2 0 0 2 4 6 8

Falkland Is.

Projection: Lambert's Equivalent Azimuthal

COPYRIGHT PHILIP'S

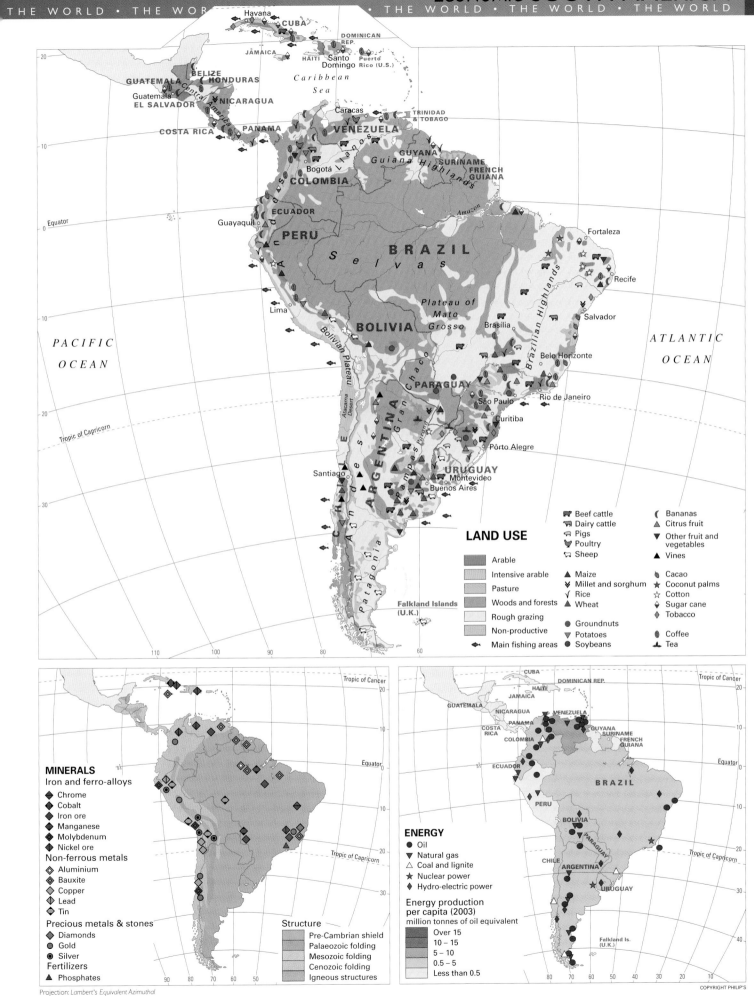

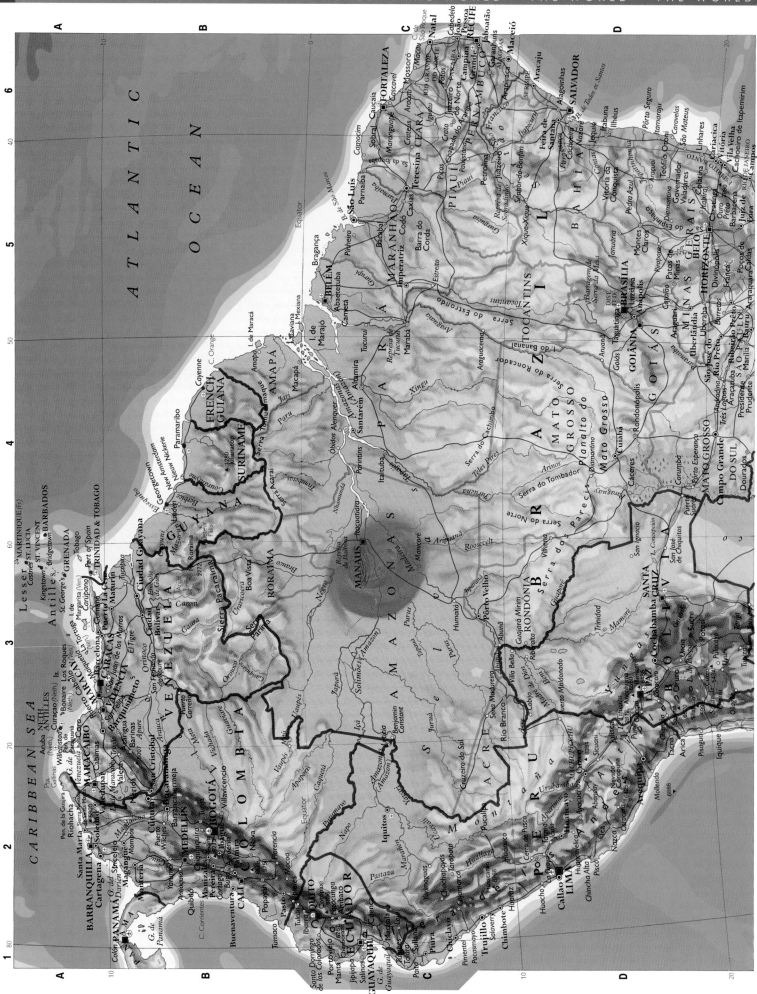

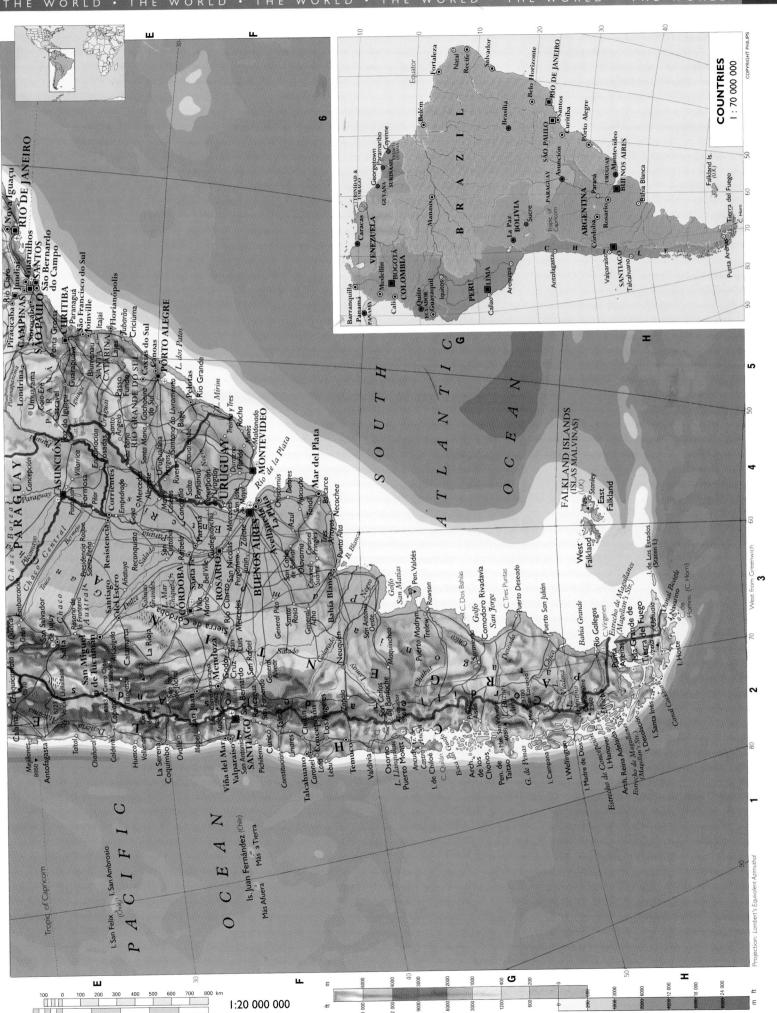

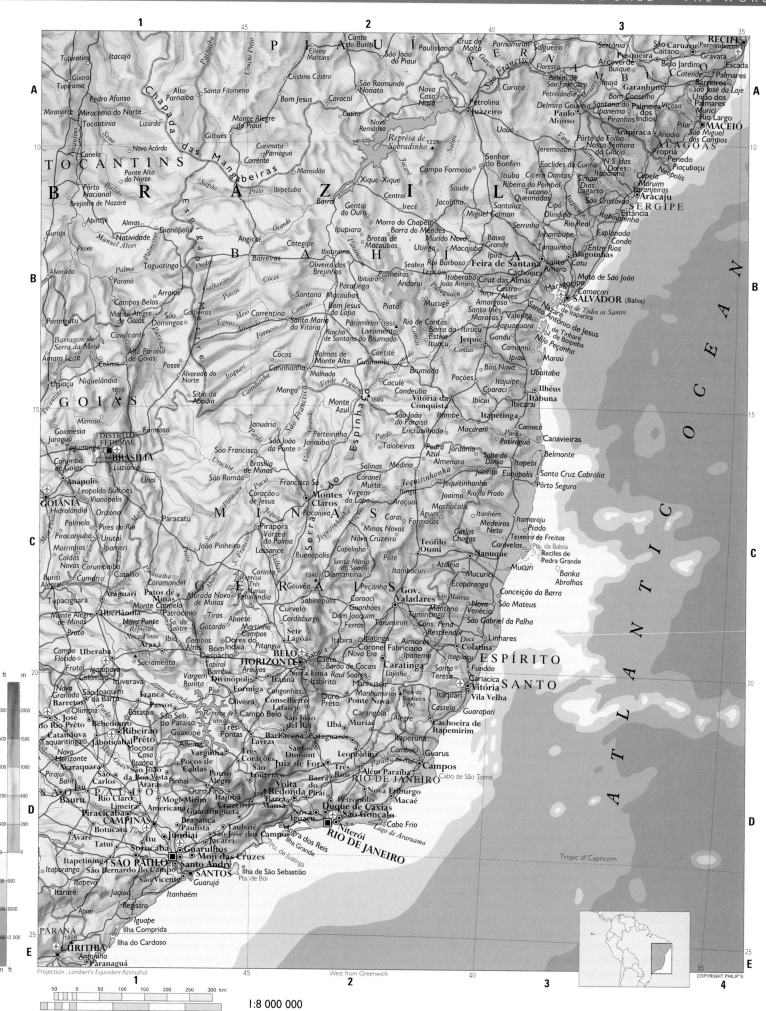

Projection : Lambert's Equivalent Azimuthal

West from Greenwich

1:8 000 000

COPYRIGHT PHILIP'S

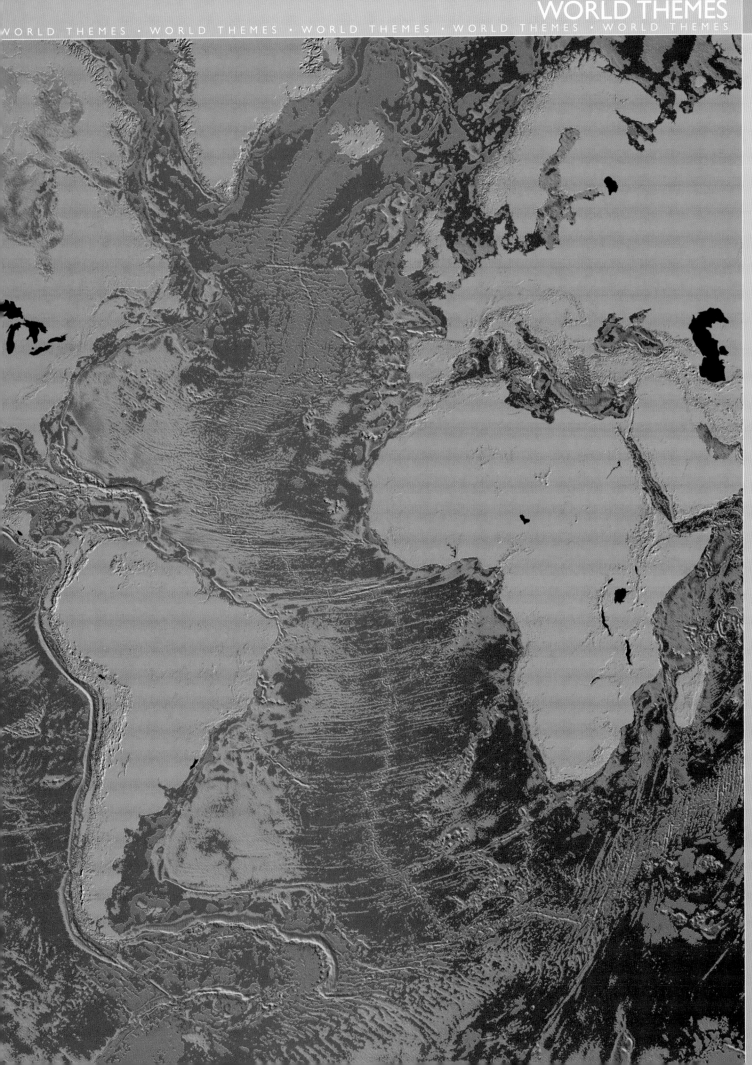

WORLD THEMES

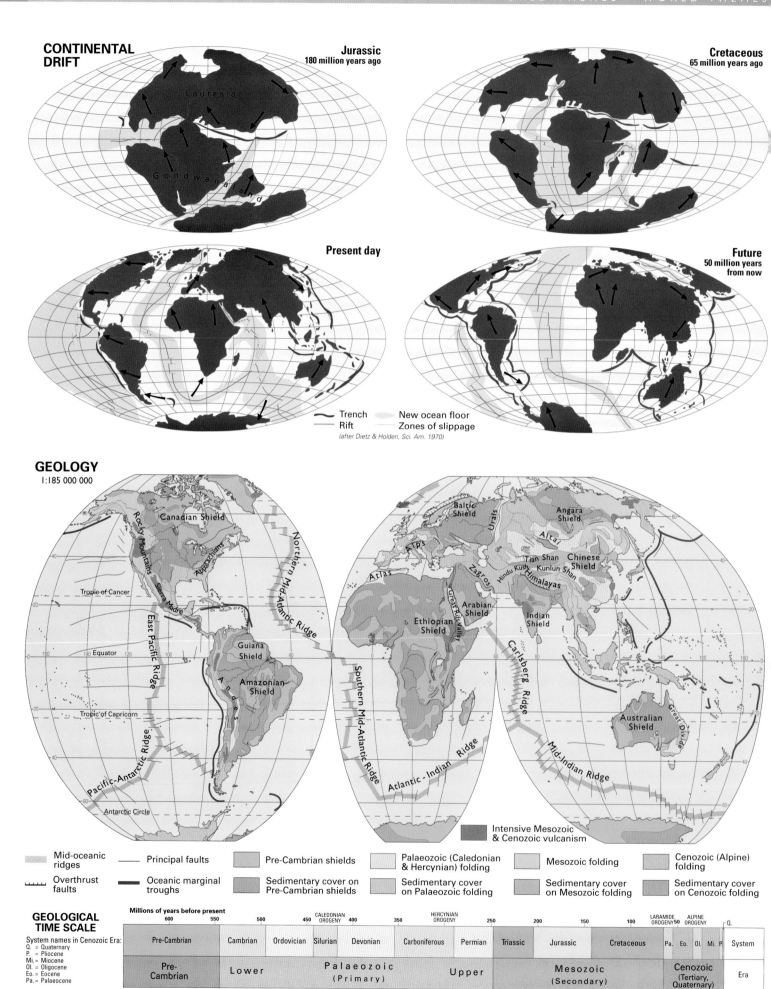

CONTINENTAL DRIFT

Jurassic 180 million years ago

Laurasia

Gondwanaland

Cretaceous 65 million years ago

Present day

Future 50 million years from now

Trench — New ocean floor
Rift — Zones of slippage

(after Dietz & Holden, Sci. Am. 1970)

GEOLOGY

1:185 000 000

Rocky Mountains
Canadian Shield
Appalachians
Northern Mid-Atlantic Ridge
Baltic Shield
Urals
Angara Shield
Altai
Alps
Atlas
Tian Shan
Chinese Shield
Kunlun Shan
Hindu Kush
Himalayas
Zagros
East Pacific Ridge
Sierra Madre
Tropic of Cancer
Great Rift Valley
Arabian Shield
Indian Shield
Equator
Ethiopian Shield
Guiana Shield
Southern Mid-Atlantic Ridge
Carlsberg Ridge
Amazonian Shield
Andes
Tropic of Capricorn
Australian Shield
Great Divide
Pacific-Antarctic Ridge
Atlantic - Indian Ridge
Mid-Indian Ridge
Antarctic Circle

Intensive Mesozoic & Cenozoic vulcanism

Mid-oceanic ridges
Principal faults
Pre-Cambrian shields
Palaeozoic (Caledonian & Hercynian) folding
Mesozoic folding
Cenozoic (Alpine) folding

Overthrust faults
Oceanic marginal troughs
Sedimentary cover on Pre-Cambrian shields
Sedimentary cover on Palaeozoic folding
Sedimentary cover on Mesozoic folding
Sedimentary cover on Cenozoic folding

GEOLOGICAL TIME SCALE

System names in Cenozoic Era:
Q. = Quaternary
P. = Pliocene
Mi. = Miocene
Ol. = Oligocene
Eo. = Eocene
Pa. = Palaeocene

Millions of years before present

| | | | | | CALEDONIAN OROGENY | | | HERCYNIAN OROGENY | | | | | | LARAMIDE OROGENY | ALPINE OROGENY | |
| 600 | 550 | 500 | 450 | 400 | | 350 | | 250 | 200 | 150 | 100 | 50 | | | |

| Pre-Cambrian | Cambrian | Ordovician | Silurian | Devonian | Carboniferous | Permian | Triassic | Jurassic | Cretaceous | Pa. | Eo. | Ol. | Mi. | P. | Q. | System |
| Pre-Cambrian | Lower | Palaeozoic (Primary) | | | | Upper | Mesozoic (Secondary) | | | Cenozoic (Tertiary, Quaternary) | | | | | | Era |

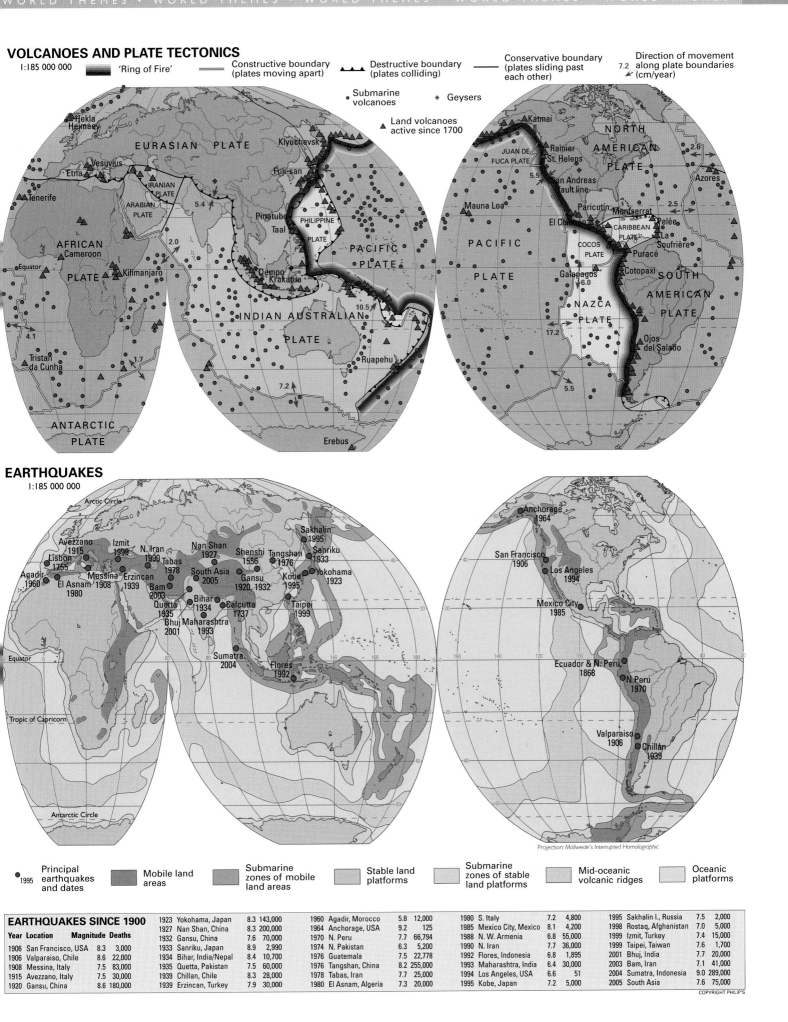

VOLCANOES AND PLATE TECTONICS

1:185 000 000 'Ring of Fire'

| Constructive boundary (plates moving apart) | Destructive boundary (plates colliding) | Conservative boundary (plates sliding past each other) | Direction of movement along plate boundaries (cm/year) |

- Submarine volcanoes
- Geysers
- Land volcanoes active since 1700

EARTHQUAKES

1:185 000 000

Projection: Mollweide's Interrupted Homolographic

- Principal earthquakes and dates
- Mobile land areas
- Submarine zones of mobile land areas
- Stable land platforms
- Submarine zones of stable land platforms
- Mid-oceanic volcanic ridges
- Oceanic platforms

EARTHQUAKES SINCE 1900											
Year	**Location**	**Magnitude**	**Deaths**	1923	Yokohama, Japan	8.3	143,000	1960	Agadir, Morocco	5.8	12,000
				1927	Nan Shan, China	8.3	200,000	1964	Anchorage, USA	9.2	125
1906	San Francisco, USA	8.3	3,000	1932	Gansu, China	7.6	70,000	1970	N. Peru	7.7	66,794
1906	Valparaiso, Chile	8.6	22,000	1933	Sanriku, Japan	8.9	2,990	1974	N. Pakistan	6.3	5,200
1908	Messina, Italy	7.5	83,000	1934	Bihar, India/Nepal	8.4	10,700	1976	Guatemala	7.5	22,778
1915	Avezzano, Italy	7.5	30,000	1935	Quetta, Pakistan	7.5	60,000	1976	Tangshan, China	8.2	255,000
1920	Gansu, China	8.6	180,000	1939	Chillan, Chile	8.3	28,000	1978	Tabas, Iran	7.7	25,000
				1939	Erzincan, Turkey	7.9	30,000	1980	El Asnam, Algeria	7.3	20,000

1980	S. Italy	7.2	4,800	1995	Sakhalin I., Russia	7.5	2,000
1985	Mexico City, Mexico	8.1	4,200	1998	Rostaq, Afghanistan	7.0	5,000
1988	N. W. Armenia	6.8	55,000	1999	Izmit, Turkey	7.4	15,000
1990	N. Iran	7.7	36,000	1999	Taipei, Taiwan	7.6	1,700
1992	Flores, Indonesia	6.8	1,895	2001	Bhuj, India	7.7	20,000
1993	Maharashtra, India	6.4	30,000	2003	Bam, Iran	7.1	41,000
1994	Los Angeles, USA	6.6	51	2004	Sumatra, Indonesia	9.0	289,000
1995	Kobe, Japan	7.2	5,000	2005	South Asia	7.6	75,000

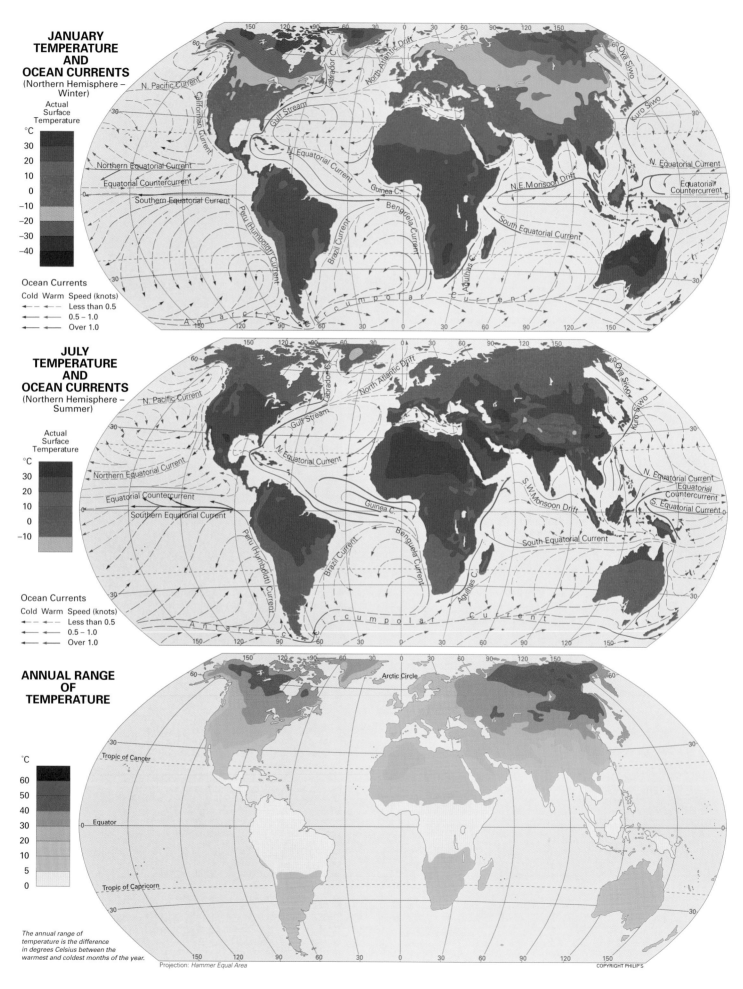

JANUARY TEMPERATURE AND OCEAN CURRENTS
(Northern Hemisphere – Winter)

Actual Surface Temperature

°C
30
20
10
0
−10
−20
−30
−40

Ocean Currents

Cold Warm Speed (knots)
Less than 0.5
0.5 – 1.0
Over 1.0

JULY TEMPERATURE AND OCEAN CURRENTS
(Northern Hemisphere – Summer)

Actual Surface Temperature

°C
30
20
10
0
−10

Ocean Currents

Cold Warm Speed (knots)
Less than 0.5
0.5 – 1.0
Over 1.0

ANNUAL RANGE OF TEMPERATURE

°C
60
50
40
30
20
10
5
0

The annual range of temperature is the difference in degrees Celsius between the warmest and coldest months of the year.

Projection: Hammer Equal Area

COPYRIGHT PHILIP'S

1 : 190 000 000

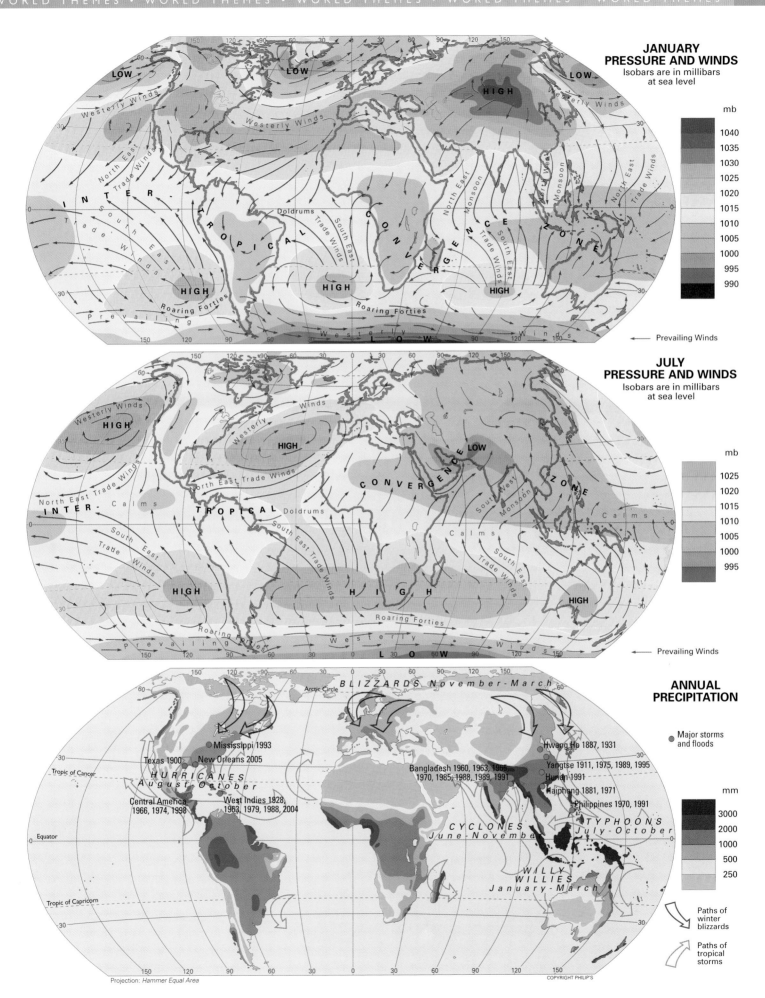

CLIMATE REGIONS *(after Köppen)*

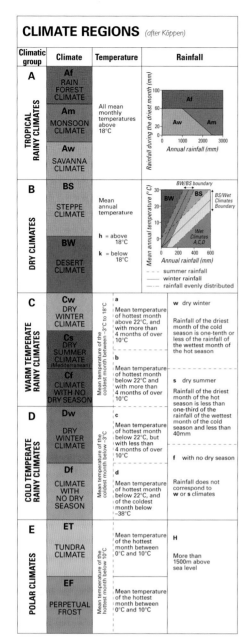

Climatic group	Climate	Temperature	Rainfall
A TROPICAL RAINY CLIMATES	**Af** RAIN FOREST CLIMATE / **Am** MONSOON CLIMATE / **Aw** SAVANNA CLIMATE	All mean monthly temperatures above 18°C	*(graph: Rainfall during the driest month (mm) vs Annual rainfall (mm) showing Af, Aw, Am)*
B DRY CLIMATES	**BS** STEPPE CLIMATE / **BW** DESERT CLIMATE	Mean annual temperature **h** = above 18°C **k** = below 18°C	*(graph: Mean annual temperature (°C) vs Annual rainfall (mm); BW/BS boundary, BS/Wet Climates Boundary, Wet Climates A,C,D; summer rainfall, winter rainfall, rainfall evenly distributed)*
C WARM TEMPERATE RAINY CLIMATES	**Cw** DRY WINTER CLIMATE / **Cs** DRY SUMMER CLIMATE (Mediterranean) / **Cf** CLIMATE WITH NO DRY SEASON	Mean temperature of the coldest month between –3°C to 18°C	**a** Mean temperature of hottest month above 22°C, and with more than 4 months of over 10°C **b** Mean temperature of hottest month below 22°C and with more than 4 months of over 10°C **w** dry winter — Rainfall of the driest month of the cold season is one-tenth or less of the rainfall of the wettest month of the hot season **s** dry summer — Rainfall of the driest month of the hot season is less than one-third of the rainfall of the wettest month of the cold season and less than 40mm
D COLD TEMPERATE RAINY CLIMATES	**Dw** DRY WINTER CLIMATE / **Df** CLIMATE WITH NO DRY SEASON	Mean temperature of the coldest month below –3°C	**c** Mean temperature of hottest month below 22°C, but with less than 4 months of over 10°C **d** Mean temperature of hottest month below 22°C, and of the coldest month below –38°C **f** with no dry season — Rainfall does not correspond to **w** or **s** climates
E POLAR CLIMATES	**ET** TUNDRA CLIMATE / **EF** PERPETUAL FROST	Mean temperature of the hottest month between 0°C and 10°C / Mean temperature of the hottest month below 10°C / Mean temperature of the hottest month between 0°C and 10°C	**H** More than 1500m above sea level

CLIMATE RECORDS

Highest recorded temperature: Al Aziziyah, Libya, 58°C, 13 September 1922.

Lowest recorded temperature (outside poles): Verkhoyansk, Siberia, –68°C, 6 February 1933. Verkhoyansk also registered the greatest annual range of temperature: –70°C to 37°C.

Highest barometric pressure: Agata, Siberia, 1,083.8 mb at altitude 262 m, 31 December 1968.

Lowest barometric pressure: Typhoon Tip, 480 km west of Guam, Pacific Ocean, 870 mb, 12 October 1979.

Driest place: Quillagua, N. Chile, 0.5 mm, 1964–2001.

Wettest place (12 months): Cherrapunji, Meghalaya, N.E. India, August 1860 to August 1861. Cherrapunji also holds the record for rainfall in one month: 2930 mm, July 1861.

Highest recorded wind speed: Mt Washington, New Hampshire, USA, 371 km/h, 12 April 1934. This is three times as strong as hurricane force on the Beaufort Scale.

Windiest place: Commonwealth Bay, George V Coast, Antarctica, where gales frequently reach over 320 km/h.

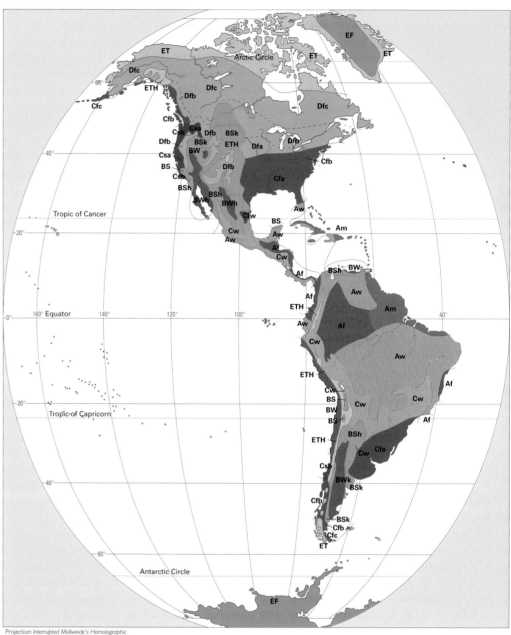

Projection: Interrupted Mollweide's Homolographic

THE MONSOON

In early March, which normally marks the end of the subcontinent's cool season and the start of the hot season, winds blow outwards from the mainland. But as the overhead sun and the ITCZ move northwards, the land is intensely heated, and a low-pressure system develops. The south-east trade winds, which are drawn across the Equator, change direction and are sucked into the interior to become south-westerly winds, bringing heavy rain. By November, the overhead sun and the ITCZ have again moved southwards and the wind directions are again reversed. Cool winds blow from the Asian interior to the sea, losing any moisture on the Himalayas before descending to the coast.

Monthly rainfall
mm
400
200
100
50
25

→ wind direction

━━ ITCZ (intertropical convergence zone)

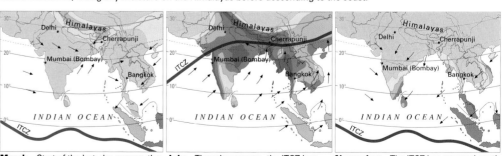

March – Start of the hot, dry season, the ITCZ is over the southern Indian Ocean.

July – The rainy season, the ITCZ has migrated northwards; winds blow onshore.

November – The ITCZ has returned south, the offshore winds are cool and dry.

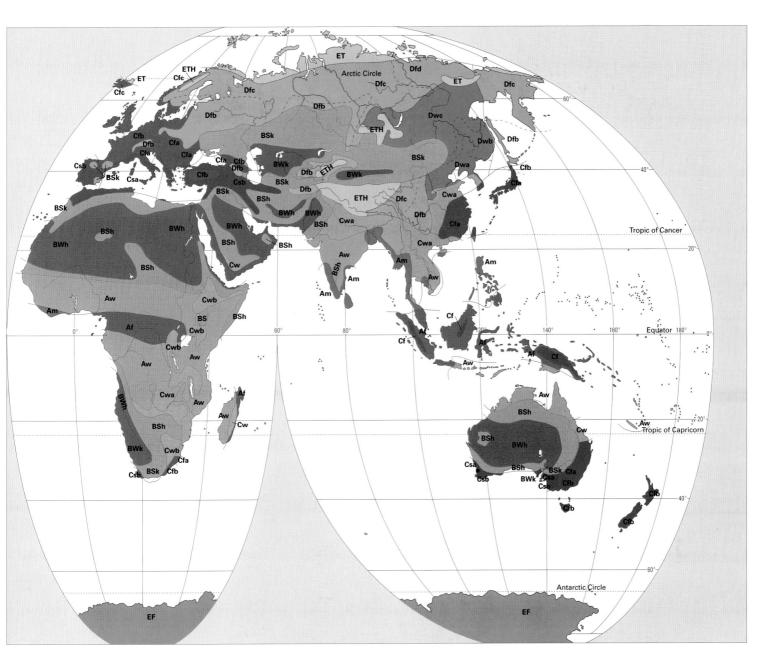

EL NIÑO

In a normal year, south-easterly trade winds drive surface waters westwards off the coast of South America, drawing cold, nutrient-rich water up from below. In an El Niño year (which occurs every 2–7 years), warm water from the west Pacific suppresses up-welling in the east, depriving the region of nutrients. The water is warmed by as much as 7°C, disturbing the tropical atmospheric circulation. During an intense El Niño, the south-east trade winds change direction and become equatorial westerlies, resulting in climatic extremes in many regions of the world, such as drought in parts of Australia and India, and heavy rainfall in south-eastern USA. An intense El Niño occurred in 1997–8, with resultant freak weather conditions across the entire Pacific region.

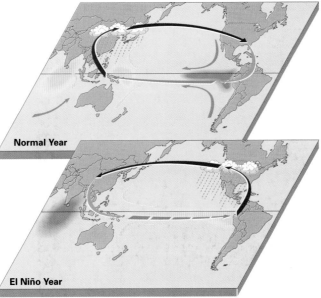

Normal Year

El Niño Year

WINDCHILL FACTOR

In sub-zero weather, even moderate winds significantly reduce effective temperatures. The chart below shows the windchill effect across a range of speeds.

	Wind speed (km/h)				
	16	32	48	64	80
0°C	−8	−14	−17	−19	−20
−5°C	−14	−21	−25	−27	−28
−10°C	−20	−28	−33	−35	−36
−15°C	−26	−36	−40	−43	−44
−20°C	−32	−42	−48	−51	−52
−25°C	−38	−49	−56	−59	−60
−30°C	−44	−57	−63	−66	−68
−35°C	−51	−64	−72	−74	−76
−40°C	−57	−71	−78	−82	−84
−45°C	−63	−78	−86	−90	−92
−50°C	−69	−85	−94	−98	−100

Addis Ababa, Ethiopia 2,410m — Height of meteorological station above sea level in metres
Temperature Daily max. °C — Average monthly maximum temperature in degrees Celsius
Daily min. °C — Average monthly minimum temperature in degrees Celsius
Average monthly °C — Average monthly temperature in degrees Celsius
Rainfall Monthly total mm — Average monthly precipitation in millimetres
Sunshine Hours per day — Average daily duration of bright sunshine per month in hours

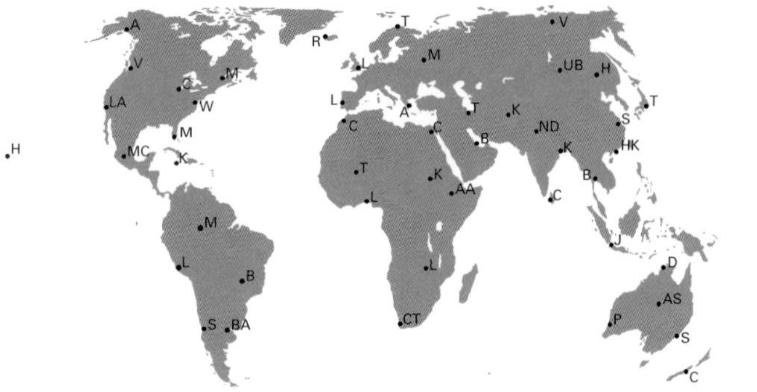

		Jan	Feb	Mar	Apr	May	June	July	Aug	Sept	Oct	Nov	Dec	Year
Addis Ababa, Ethiopia 2,410m														
Temperature	Daily max. °C	23	24	25	24	25	23	20	20	21	22	23	22	23
	Daily min. °C	6	7	9	10	9	10	11	11	10	7	5	5	8
	Average monthly °C	14	15	17	17	17	16	16	15	15	15	14	14	15
Rainfall	Monthly total mm	13	35	67	91	81	117	247	255	167	29	8	5	1,115
Sunshine	Hours per day	8.7	8.2	7.6	8.1	6.5	4.8	2.8	3.2	5.2	7.6	6.7	7	6.4
Alice Springs, Australia 580m														
Temperature	Daily max. °C	35	35	32	27	23	19	19	23	27	31	33	35	28
	Daily min. °C	21	20	17	12	8	5	4	6	10	15	18	20	13
	Average monthly °C	28	27	25	20	15	12	12	14	18	23	25	27	21
Rainfall	Monthly total mm	44	33	27	10	15	13	7	8	7	18	29	38	249
Sunshine	Hours per day	10.3	10.4	9.3	9.2	8	8	8.9	9.8	10	9.7	10.1	10	9.5
Anchorage, USA 183m														
Temperature	Daily max. °C	−7	−3	0	7	13	18	19	17	13	6	−2	−6	−6
	Daily min. °C	−15	−12	−9	−2	4	8	10	9	5	−2	−9	−14	−2
	Average monthly °C	−11	−7	−4	3	9	13	15	13	9	2	−5	−10	−4
Rainfall	Monthly total mm	20	18	13	11	13	25	47	64	64	47	28	24	374
Sunshine	Hours per day	2.4	4.1	6.6	8.3	8.3	9.2	8.5	6	4.4	3.1	2.6	1.6	5.4
Athens, Greece 107m														
Temperature	Daily max. °C	13	14	16	20	25	30	33	33	29	24	19	15	23
	Daily min. °C	6	7	8	11	16	20	23	23	19	15	12	8	14
	Average monthly °C	10	10	12	16	20	25	28	28	24	20	15	11	18
Rainfall	Monthly total mm	62	37	37	23	23	14	6	7	15	51	56	71	402
Sunshine	Hours per day	3.9	5.2	5.8	7.7	8.9	10.7	11.9	11.5	9.4	6.8	4.8	3.8	7.3
Bahrain City, Bahrain 2m														
Temperature	Daily max. °C	20	21	25	29	33	36	37	38	36	32	27	22	30
	Daily min. °C	14	15	18	22	25	29	31	32	29	25	22	16	23
	Average monthly °C	17	18	21	25	29	32	34	35	32	29	25	19	26
Rainfall	Monthly total mm	18	12	10	9	2	0	0	0	0	0.4	3	16	70
Sunshine	Hours per day	5.9	6.9	7.9	8.8	10.6	13.2	12.1	12	12	10.3	7.7	6.4	9.5
Bangkok, Thailand 10m														
Temperature	Daily max. °C	32	33	34	35	34	33	32	32	32	31	31	31	33
	Daily min. °C	20	23	24	26	25	25	25	24	24	24	23	20	24
	Average monthly °C	26	28	29	30	30	29	28	28	28	28	27	26	28
Rainfall	Monthly total mm	9	30	36	82	165	153	168	183	310	239	55	8	1,438
Sunshine	Hours per day	8.2	8	8	10	7.5	6.1	4.7	5.2	5.2	6.1	7.3	7.8	7
Brasilia, Brazil 910m														
Temperature	Daily max. °C	28	28	28	28	27	27	27	29	30	29	28	27	28
	Daily min. °C	18	18	18	17	15	13	13	14	16	18	18	18	16
	Average monthly °C	23	23	23	22	21	20	20	21	23	24	23	22	22
Rainfall	Monthly total mm	252	204	227	93	17	3	6	3	30	127	255	343	1,560
Sunshine	Hours per day	5.8	5.7	6	7.4	8.7	9.3	9.6	9.8	7.9	6.5	4.8	4.4	7.2
Buenos Aires, Argentina 25m														
Temperature	Daily max. °C	30	29	26	22	18	14	14	16	18	21	25	28	22
	Daily min. °C	17	17	16	12	9	5	6	6	8	10	14	16	11
	Average monthly °C	23	23	21	17	13	10	10	11	13	15	19	22	16
Rainfall	Monthly total mm	79	71	109	89	76	61	56	61	79	86	84	99	950
Sunshine	Hours per day	9.2	8.5	7.5	6.8	4.9	3.5	3.8	5.2	6	6.8	8.1	8.5	6.6
Cairo, Egypt 75m														
Temperature	Daily max. °C	19	21	24	28	32	35	35	35	33	30	26	21	28
	Daily min. °C	9	9	12	14	18	20	22	22	20	18	14	10	16
	Average monthly °C	14	15	18	21	25	28	29	28	26	24	20	16	22
Rainfall	Monthly total mm	4	4	3	1	2	1	0	0	1	1	3	7	27
Sunshine	Hours per day	6.9	8.4	8.7	9.7	10.5	11.9	11.7	11.3	10.4	9.4	8.3	6.4	9.5
Cape Town, South Africa 44m														
Temperature	Daily max. °C	26	26	25	23	20	18	17	18	19	21	24	25	22
	Daily min. °C	15	15	14	11	9	7	7	7	8	10	13	15	11
	Average monthly °C	21	20	20	17	14	13	12	12	14	16	18	20	16
Rainfall	Monthly total mm	12	19	17	42	67	98	68	76	36	45	12	13	505
Sunshine	Hours per day	11.4	10.2	9.4	7.7	6.1	5.7	6.4	6.6	7.6	8.6	10.2	10.9	8.4
Casablanca, Morocco 59m														
Temperature	Daily max. °C	17	18	20	21	22	24	26	26	26	24	21	18	22
	Daily min. °C	8	9	11	12	15	18	19	20	18	15	12	10	14
	Average monthly °C	13	13	15	16	18	21	23	23	22	20	17	14	18
Rainfall	Monthly total mm	78	61	54	37	20	3	0	1	6	28	58	94	440
Sunshine	Hours per day	5.2	6.3	7.3	9	9.4	9.7	10.2	9.7	9.1	7.4	5.9	5.3	7.9

		Jan	Feb	Mar	Apr	May	June	July	Aug	Sept	Oct	Nov	Dec	Year
Chicago, USA 186m														
Temperature	Daily max. °C	1	2	6	14	21	26	29	28	24	17	8	2	15
	Daily min. °C	−7	−6	−2	5	11	16	20	19	14	8	0	−5	−6
	Average monthly °C	−3	−2	2	9	16	21	24	23	19	13	4	−2	4
Rainfall	Monthly total mm	47	41	70	77	96	103	86	80	69	71	56	48	844
Sunshine	Hours per day	4	5	6.6	6.9	8.9	10.2	10	9.2	8.2	6.9	4.5	3.7	7
Christchurch, New Zealand 5m														
Temperature	Daily max. °C	21	21	19	17	13	11	10	11	14	17	19	21	16
	Daily min. °C	12	12	10	7	4	2	1	3	5	7	8	11	7
	Average monthly °C	16	16	15	12	9	6	6	7	9	12	13	16	11
Rainfall	Monthly total mm	56	46	43	46	76	69	61	58	51	51	51	61	669
Sunshine	Hours per day	7	6.5	5.6	4.7	4.3	3.9	4.1	4.7	5.6	6.1	6.9	6.3	5.5
Colombo, Sri Lanka 10m														
Temperature	Daily max. °C	30	31	31	31	30	30	29	29	30	29	29	30	30
	Daily min. °C	22	22	23	24	25	25	25	25	25	24	23	22	24
	Average monthly °C	26	26	27	28	28	27	27	27	27	27	26	26	27
Rainfall	Monthly total mm	101	66	118	230	394	220	140	102	174	348	333	142	2,368
Sunshine	Hours per day	7.9	9	8.1	7.2	6.4	5.4	6.1	6.3	6.2	6.5	6.4	7.8	6.9
Darwin, Australia 30m														
Temperature	Daily max. °C	32	32	33	33	33	31	31	32	33	34	34	33	33
	Daily min. °C	25	25	25	24	23	21	19	21	23	25	26	26	24
	Average monthly °C	29	29	29	29	28	26	25	26	28	29	30	29	28
Rainfall	Monthly total mm	405	309	279	77	8	2	0	1	15	48	108	214	1,466
Sunshine	Hours per day	5.8	5.8	6.6	9.8	9.3	10	9.9	10.4	10.1	9.4	9.6	6.8	8.6
Harbin, China 175m														
Temperature	Daily max. °C	−14	−9	0	12	21	26	29	27	20	12	−1	−11	9
	Daily min. °C	−26	−23	−12	−1	7	14	18	16	8	0	−12	−22	−3
	Average monthly °C	−20	−16	−6	6	14	20	23	22	14	6	−7	−17	3
Rainfall	Monthly total mm	4	6	17	23	44	92	167	119	52	36	12	5	577
Sunshine	Hours per day	6.4	7.8	8	7.8	8.3	8.6	8.6	8.2	7.2	6.9	6.1	5.7	7.5
Hong Kong, China 35m														
Temperature	Daily max. °C	18	18	20	24	28	30	31	31	30	27	24	20	25
	Daily min. °C	13	13	16	19	23	26	26	26	25	23	19	15	20
	Average monthly °C	16	15	18	22	25	28	28	28	27	25	21	17	23
Rainfall	Monthly total mm	30	60	70	133	332	479	286	415	364	33	46	17	2,265
Sunshine	Hours per day	4.7	3.5	3.1	3.8	5	5.4	6.8	6.5	6.6	7	6.2	5.5	5.3
Honolulu, Hawaii 5m														
Temperature	Daily max. °C	26	26	26	27	28	29	29	29	30	29	28	26	28
	Daily min. °C	19	19	19	20	21	22	23	23	23	22	21	20	21
	Average monthly °C	23	22	23	23	24	26	26	26	26	26	24	23	24
Rainfall	Monthly total mm	96	84	73	33	25	8	11	23	25	47	55	76	556
Sunshine	Hours per day	7.3	7.7	8.3	8.6	8.8	9.1	9.4	9.3	9.2	8.3	7.5	6.2	8.3
Jakarta, Indonesia 10m														
Temperature	Daily max. °C	29	29	30	31	31	31	31	31	31	31	30	29	30
	Daily min. °C	23	23	23	24	24	23	23	23	23	23	23	23	23
	Average monthly °C	26	26	27	27	27	27	27	27	27	27	27	26	27
Rainfall	Monthly total mm	300	300	211	147	114	97	64	43	66	112	142	203	1,799
Sunshine	Hours per day	6.1	6.5	7.7	8.5	8.4	8.5	9.1	9.5	9.6	9	7.7	7.1	8.1
Kabul, Afghanistan 1,791m														
Temperature	Daily max. °C	2	4	12	19	26	31	33	33	30	22	17	8	20
	Daily min. °C	−8	−6	1	6	11	13	16	15	11	6	1	−3	5
	Average monthly °C	−3	−1	6	13	18	22	25	24	20	14	9	3	12
Rainfall	Monthly total mm	28	61	72	117	33	1	7	1	0	1	37	14	372
Sunshine	Hours per day	5.9	6	5.7	6.8	10.1	11.5	11.4	11.2	9.8	9.4	7.8	6.1	8.5
Khartoum, Sudan 380m														
Temperature	Daily max. °C	32	33	37	40	42	41	38	36	38	39	35	32	37
	Daily min. °C	16	17	20	23	26	27	26	25	25	25	21	17	22
	Average monthly °C	24	25	28	32	34	34	32	30	32	32	28	25	30
Rainfall	Monthly total mm	0	0	0	1	7	5	56	80	28	2	0	0	179
Sunshine	Hours per day	10.6	11.2	10.4	10.8	10.4	10.1	8.6	8.6	9.6	10.3	10.8	10.6	10.2
Kingston, Jamaica 35m														
Temperature	Daily max. °C	30	30	30	31	31	32	32	32	32	31	31	31	31
	Daily min. °C	20	20	20	21	22	24	23	23	23	23	22	21	22
	Average monthly °C	25	25	25	26	26	28	28	28	27	27	26	26	26
Rainfall	Monthly total mm	23	15	23	31	102	89	38	91	99	180	74	36	801
Sunshine	Hours per day	8.3	8.8	8.7	8.7	8.3	7.8	8.5	8.5	7.6	7.3	8.3	7.7	8.2

		Jan	Feb	Mar	Apr	May	June	July	Aug	Sept	Oct	Nov	Dec	Year
Kolkata (Calcutta), India	5 m													
Temperature	Daily max. °C	27	29	34	36	35	34	32	32	32	32	29	26	31
	Daily min. °C	13	15	21	24	25	26	26	26	26	23	18	13	21
	Average monthly °C	20	22	27	30	30	30	29	29	29	28	23	20	26
Rainfall	Monthly total mm	10	30	34	44	140	297	325	332	253	114	20	5	1,604
Sunshine	Hours per day	8.6	8.7	8.9	9	8.7	5.4	4.1	4.1	5.1	6.5	8.3	8.4	7.1
Lagos, Nigeria	40 m													
Temperature	Daily max. °C	32	33	33	32	31	29	28	28	29	30	31	32	31
	Daily min. °C	22	23	23	23	23	22	22	21	22	22	23	22	22
	Average monthly °C	27	28	28	28	27	26	25	24	25	26	27	27	26
Rainfall	Monthly total mm	28	41	99	99	203	300	180	56	180	190	63	25	1,464
Sunshine	Hours per day	5.9	6.8	6.3	6.1	5.6	3.8	2.8	3.3	3	5.1	6.6	6.5	5.2
Lima, Peru	120 m													
Temperature	Daily max. °C	28	29	29	27	24	20	20	19	20	22	24	26	24
	Daily min. °C	19	20	19	17	16	15	14	14	14	15	16	17	16
	Average monthly °C	24	24	24	22	20	17	17	16	17	18	20	21	20
Rainfall	Monthly total mm	1	1	1	1	5	5	8	8	8	3	3	1	45
Sunshine	Hours per day	6.3	6.8	6.9	6.7	4	1.4	1.1	1	1.1	2.5	4.1	5	3.9
Lisbon, Portugal	77 m													
Temperature	Daily max. °C	14	15	17	20	21	25	27	28	26	22	17	15	21
	Daily min. °C	8	8	10	12	13	15	17	17	17	14	11	9	13
	Average monthly °C	11	12	14	16	17	20	22	23	21	18	14	12	17
Rainfall	Monthly total mm	111	76	109	54	44	16	3	4	33	62	93	103	708
Sunshine	Hours per day	4.7	5.9	6	8.3	9.1	10.6	11.4	10.7	8.4	6.7	5.2	4.6	7.7
London (Kew), UK	5 m													
Temperature	Daily max. °C	6	7	10	13	17	20	22	21	19	14	10	7	14
	Daily min. °C	2	2	3	6	8	12	14	13	11	8	5	4	7
	Average monthly °C	4	5	7	9	12	16	18	17	15	11	8	5	11
Rainfall	Monthly total mm	54	40	37	37	46	45	57	59	49	57	64	48	593
Sunshine	Hours per day	1.7	2.3	3.5	5.7	6.7	7	6.6	6	5	3.3	1.9	1.4	4.3
Los Angeles, USA	30 m													
Temperature	Daily max. °C	18	18	18	19	20	22	24	24	24	23	22	19	21
	Daily min. °C	7	8	9	11	13	15	17	17	16	14	11	9	12
	Average monthly °C	12	13	14	15	17	18	21	21	20	18	16	14	17
Rainfall	Monthly total mm	69	74	46	28	3	3	0	0	5	10	28	61	327
Sunshine	Hours per day	6.9	8.2	8.9	8.8	9.5	10.3	11.7	11	10.1	8.6	8.2	7.6	9.2
Lusaka, Zambia	1,154 m													
Temperature	Daily max. °C	26	26	26	27	25	23	23	26	29	31	29	27	27
	Daily min. °C	17	17	16	15	12	10	9	11	15	18	18	17	15
	Average monthly °C	22	22	21	21	18	17	16	19	22	25	23	22	21
Rainfall	Monthly total mm	224	173	90	19	3	1	0	1	1	17	85	196	810
Sunshine	Hours per day	5.1	5.4	6.9	8.9	9	9	9.1	9.6	9.5	9	7	5.5	7.8
Manaus, Brazil	45 m													
Temperature	Daily max. °C	31	31	31	31	31	31	32	33	34	34	33	32	32
	Daily min. °C	24	24	24	24	24	24	24	24	24	25	25	24	24
	Average monthly °C	28	28	28	27	28	28	28	29	29	29	29	28	28
Rainfall	Monthly total mm	278	278	300	287	193	99	61	41	62	112	165	220	2,096
Sunshine	Hours per day	3.9	4	3.6	3.9	5.4	6.9	7.9	8.2	7.5	6.6	5.9	4.9	5.7
Mexico City, Mexico	2,309 m													
Temperature	Daily max. °C	21	23	26	27	26	25	23	24	23	22	21	21	24
	Daily min. °C	5	6	7	9	10	11	11	11	11	9	6	5	8
	Average monthly °C	13	15	16	18	18	18	17	17	17	16	14	13	16
Rainfall	Monthly total mm	8	4	9	23	57	111	160	149	119	46	16	7	709
Sunshine	Hours per day	7.3	8.1	8.5	8.1	7.8	7	6.2	6.4	5.6	6.3	7	7.3	7.1
Miami, USA	2 m													
Temperature	Daily max. °C	24	25	27	28	30	31	32	32	31	29	27	25	28
	Daily min. °C	14	15	16	19	21	23	24	24	24	22	18	15	20
	Average monthly °C	19	20	21	23	25	27	28	28	27	25	22	20	24
Rainfall	Monthly total mm	51	48	58	99	163	188	170	178	241	208	71	43	1,518
Sunshine	Hours per day	7.7	8.3	8.7	9.4	8.9	8.5	8.7	8.4	7.1	6.5	7.5	7.1	8.1
Montreal, Canada	57 m													
Temperature	Daily max. °C	–6	–4	2	11	18	23	26	25	20	14	5	–3	11
	Daily min. °C	–13	–11	–5	2	9	14	17	16	11	6	0	–9	3
	Average monthly °C	–9	–8	–2	6	13	19	22	20	16	10	3	–6	7
Rainfall	Monthly total mm	87	76	86	83	81	91	98	87	96	84	89	89	1,047
Sunshine	Hours per day	2.8	3.4	4.5	5.2	6.7	7.7	8.2	7.7	5.6	4.3	2.4	2.2	5.1
Moscow, Russia	156 m													
Temperature	Daily max. °C	–6	–4	1	9	18	22	24	22	17	10	1	–5	9
	Daily min. °C	–14	–16	–11	–1	5	9	12	9	4	–2	–6	–12	–2
	Average monthly °C	–10	–10	–5	4	12	15	18	16	10	4	–2	–8	4
Rainfall	Monthly total mm	31	28	33	35	52	67	74	74	58	51	36	36	575
Sunshine	Hours per day	1	1.9	3.7	5.2	7.8	8.3	8.4	7.1	4.4	2.4	1	0.6	4.4
New Delhi, India	220 m													
Temperature	Daily max. °C	21	24	29	36	41	39	35	34	34	34	28	23	32
	Daily min. °C	6	10	14	20	26	28	27	26	24	17	11	7	18
	Average monthly °C	14	17	22	28	33	34	31	30	29	26	20	15	25
Rainfall	Monthly total mm	25	21	13	8	13	77	178	184	123	10	2	11	665
Sunshine	Hours per day	7.7	8.2	8.2	8.7	9.2	7.9	6	6.3	6.9	9.4	8.7	8.3	8

		Jan	Feb	Mar	Apr	May	June	July	Aug	Sept	Oct	Nov	Dec	Year
Perth, Australia	60 m													
Temperature	Daily max. °C	29	30	27	25	21	18	17	18	19	21	25	27	23
	Daily min. °C	17	18	16	14	12	10	9	9	10	11	14	16	13
	Average monthly °C	23	24	22	19	16	14	13	13	15	16	19	22	18
Rainfall	Monthly total mm	8	13	22	44	128	189	177	145	84	58	19	13	900
Sunshine	Hours per day	10.4	9.8	8.8	7.5	5.7	4.8	5.4	6	7.2	8.1	9.6	10.4	7.8
Reykjavik, Iceland	18 m													
Temperature	Daily max. °C	2	3	5	6	10	13	15	14	12	8	5	4	8
	Daily min. °C	–3	–3	–1	1	4	7	9	8	6	3	0	–2	3
	Average monthly °C	0	0	2	4	7	10	12	11	9	5	3	1	5
Rainfall	Monthly total mm	89	64	62	56	42	42	50	56	67	94	78	79	779
Sunshine	Hours per day	0.8	2	3.6	4.5	5.9	6.1	5.8	5.4	3.5	2.3	1.1	0.3	3.7
Santiago, Chile	520 m													
Temperature	Daily max. °C	30	29	27	24	19	15	15	17	19	22	26	29	23
	Daily min. °C	12	11	10	7	5	3	3	4	6	7	9	11	7
	Average monthly °C	21	20	18	15	12	9	9	10	12	15	17	20	15
Rainfall	Monthly total mm	3	3	5	13	64	84	76	56	31	15	8	5	363
Sunshine	Hours per day	10.8	8.9	8.5	5.5	3.6	3.3	3.3	3.6	4.8	6.1	8.7	10.1	6.4
Shanghai, China	5 m													
Temperature	Daily max. °C	8	8	13	19	24	28	32	32	27	23	17	10	20
	Daily min. °C	–1	0	4	9	14	19	23	23	19	13	7	2	11
	Average monthly °C	3	4	8	14	19	23	27	27	23	18	12	6	15
Rainfall	Monthly total mm	48	59	84	94	94	180	147	142	130	71	51	36	1,136
Sunshine	Hours per day	4	3.7	4.4	4.8	5.4	4.7	6.9	7.5	5.3	5.6	4.7	4.5	5.1
Sydney, Australia	40 m													
Temperature	Daily max. °C	26	26	25	22	19	17	17	18	20	22	24	25	22
	Daily min. °C	18	19	17	14	11	9	8	9	11	13	16	17	14
	Average monthly °C	22	22	21	18	15	13	12	13	16	18	20	21	18
Rainfall	Monthly total mm	89	101	127	135	127	117	117	76	74	71	74	74	1,182
Sunshine	Hours per day	7.5	7	6.4	6.1	5.7	5.3	6.1	7	7.3	7.5	7.5	7.5	6.8
Tehran, Iran	1,191 m													
Temperature	Daily max. °C	9	11	16	21	29	30	37	36	29	24	16	11	22
	Daily min. °C	–1	1	4	10	16	20	23	23	18	12	6	1	11
	Average monthly °C	4	6	10	15	22	25	30	29	23	18	11	6	17
Rainfall	Monthly total mm	37	23	36	31	14	2	1	1	1	5	29	27	207
Sunshine	Hours per day	5.9	6.7	7.5	7.4	8.6	11.6	11.2	11	10.1	7.6	6.9	6.3	8.4
Timbuktu, Mali	269 m													
Temperature	Daily max. °C	31	35	38	41	43	42	38	35	38	40	37	31	37
	Daily min. °C	13	16	18	22	26	27	25	24	24	23	18	14	21
	Average monthly °C	22	25	28	31	34	34	32	30	31	31	28	23	29
Rainfall	Monthly total mm	0	0	0	1	4	20	54	93	31	3	0	0	206
Sunshine	Hours per day	9.1	9.6	9.6	9.7	9.8	9.4	9.6	9	9.3	9.5	9.5	8.9	9.4
Tokyo, Japan	5 m													
Temperature	Daily max. °C	9	9	12	18	22	25	29	30	27	20	16	11	19
	Daily min. °C	–1	–1	3	4	13	17	22	23	19	13	7	1	10
	Average monthly °C	4	4	8	11	18	21	25	26	23	17	11	6	14
Rainfall	Monthly total mm	48	73	101	135	131	182	146	147	217	220	101	61	1,562
Sunshine	Hours per day	6	5.9	5.7	6	6.2	5	5.8	6.6	4.5	4.4	4.8	5.4	5.5
Tromsø, Norway	100 m													
Temperature	Daily max. °C	–2	–2	0	3	7	12	16	14	10	5	2	0	5
	Daily min. °C	–6	–6	–5	–2	1	6	9	8	5	1	–2	–4	0
	Average monthly °C	–4	–4	–3	0	4	9	13	11	7	3	0	–2	3
Rainfall	Monthly total mm	96	79	91	65	61	59	56	80	109	115	88	95	994
Sunshine	Hours per day	0.1	1.6	2.9	6.1	5.7	6.9	7.9	4.8	3.5	1.7	0.3	0	3.5
Ulan Bator, Mongolia	1,305 m													
Temperature	Daily max. °C	–19	–13	–4	7	13	21	22	21	14	6	–6	–16	4
	Daily min. °C	–32	–29	–22	–8	–2	7	11	8	2	–8	–20	–28	–11
	Average monthly °C	–26	–21	–13	–1	6	14	16	14	8	–1	–13	–22	–4
Rainfall	Monthly total mm	1	1	2	5	10	28	76	51	23	5	5	2	209
Sunshine	Hours per day	6.4	7.8	8	7.8	8.3	8.6	8.6	8.2	7.2	6.9	6.1	5.7	7.5
Vancouver, Canada	5 m													
Temperature	Daily max. °C	6	7	10	14	17	20	23	22	19	14	9	7	14
	Daily min. °C	0	1	3	5	8	11	13	12	10	7	3	2	6
	Average monthly °C	3	4	6	9	13	16	18	17	14	10	6	4	10
Rainfall	Monthly total mm	214	161	151	90	69	65	39	44	83	172	198	243	1,529
Sunshine	Hours per day	1.6	3	3.8	5.9	7.5	7.4	9.5	8.2	6	3.7	2	1.4	5
Verkhoyansk, Russia	137 m													
Temperature	Daily max. °C	–47	–40	–20	–1	11	21	24	21	12	–8	–33	–42	–8
	Daily min. °C	–51	–48	–40	–25	–7	4	6	1	–6	–20	–39	–50	–23
	Average monthly °C	–49	–44	–30	–13	2	12	15	11	3	–14	–36	–46	–16
Rainfall	Monthly total mm	7	5	5	4	5	25	33	30	13	11	10	7	155
Sunshine	Hours per day	0	2.6	6.9	9.6	9.7	10	9.7	7.5	4.1	2.4	0.6	0	5.4
Washington, USA	22 m													
Temperature	Daily max. °C	7	8	12	19	25	29	31	30	26	20	14	8	19
	Daily min. °C	–1	–1	2	8	13	18	21	20	16	10	4	–1	9
	Average monthly °C	3	3	7	13	19	24	26	25	21	15	9	4	14
Rainfall	Monthly total mm	84	68	96	85	103	88	108	120	100	78	75	75	1,080
Sunshine	Hours per day	4.4	5.7	6.7	7.4	8.2	8.8	8.6	8.2	7.5	6.5	5.3	4.5	6.8

Tropical Rain Forest
Tall broadleaved evergreen forest, trees 30–50m high with climbers and epiphytes forming continuous canopies. Associated with wet climate 2–3000mm precipitation per year and high temperatures 24–28°C. High diversity of species, typically 100 per ha including lianas, bamboo, palms, rubber, mahogany. Mangrove swamps form in coastal areas.

Subtropical and Temperate Rain Forest
Precipitation which is less than in the Tropical Rain Forest falls in the long wet season interspersed with a season of reduced rainfall and lower temperatures. As a result there are fewer species, a thinner canopy, fewer lianas and denser ground level foliage. Vegetation consists of evergreen oak, laurel, bamboo, magnolia and tree ferns.

Monsoon Woodland and Open Jungle
Mostly deciduous trees because of the long dry season and lower temperatures. Trees can reach 30m but are sparser than in the rain forests; there is less competition for light and thick jungle vegetation grows at lower levels. High species diversity including lianas, bamboo, teak, sandalwood, sal and banyan.

Diagram shows the highly stratified nature of the tropical rain forest. Crowns of trees form numerous layers at different heights and the dense shade limits undergrowth.

50
25
Metres

Temperate Deciduous and Coniferous Forest
A transition zone between broadleaves and conifers. Broadleaves are better suited to the warmer, damper and flatter locations.

Northern Coniferous Forest (Taiga)
Forming a large continuous belt across Northern America and Eurasia with a uniformity in tree species. Characteristically trees are tall, conical with short branches and wax-covered needle-shaped leaves to retain moisture. Cold climate with prolonged harsh winters and cool summers where average temperatures for more than six months of the year are under 0°C. Undergrowth is sparse with mosses and lichens. Tree species include pine, fir, spruce, larch, tamarisk.

Mountainous Forest, mainly Coniferous
Mild winters, high humidity and high levels of rainfall throughout the year provide habitat for dense needle-leaf evergreen forests and the largest trees in the world, up to 100m, including the Douglas fir, redwood and giant sequoia.

High Plateau Steppe and Tundra
Similar to arctic tundra with frozen ground for the majority of the year. Very sparse ground coverage of low, shallow-rooted herbs, small shrubs, mosses, lichens and heather interspersed with bare soil.

Arctic Tundra
Average temperatures are 0°C, precipitation is mainly snowfall and the ground remains frozen for 10 months of the year. Vegetation flourishes when the shallow surface layer melts in the long summer days. Underlying permafrost remains frozen and surface water cannot drain away, making conditions marshy. Consisting of sedges, snow lichen, arctic meadow grass, cotton grasses and dwarf willow.

Polar and Mountainous Ice Desert
Areas of bare rock and ice with patches of rock-strewn lithosols, low in organic matter and low water content. In sheltered patches only a few mosses, lichens and low shrubs can grow, including woolly moss and purple saxifrage.

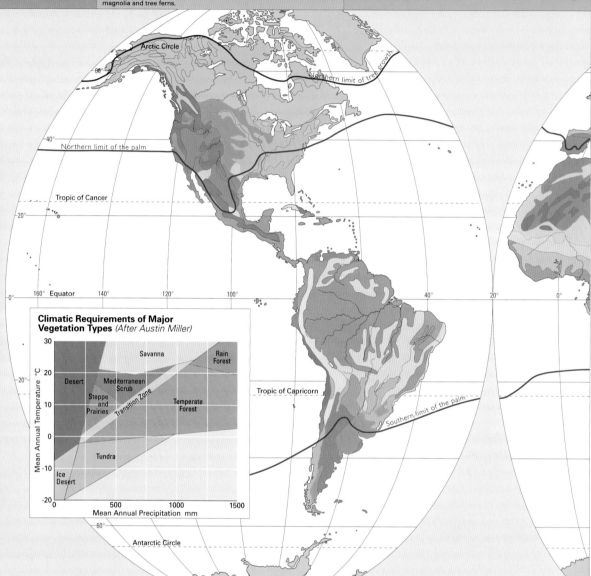

Arctic Circle
Northern limit of tree growth
Northern limit of the palm
Tropic of Cancer
Equator
Tropic of Capricorn
Southern limit of the palm
Antarctic Circle

Climatic Requirements of Major Vegetation Types *(After Austin Miller)*

Desert
Mediterranean Scrub
Savanna
Rain Forest
Steppe and Prairies
Transition Zone
Temperate Forest
Tundra
Ice Desert

Mean Annual Temperature °C
Mean Annual Precipitation mm

SOIL REGIONS
1:220 000 000

- Tundra soil
- Podzols
- Brown forest soil
- Lightly leached dry forest soil
- Red and yellow subtropical forest soil
- Reddish savanna soil and tropical red earths
- Laterites
- Chernozem
- Degraded chernozem
- Black savanna soil
- Chestnut steppe soil
- Desertic (arid) soil
- Alluvium
- Mountain and high plateau soils
- Oases soil
- Tropical and mangrove swamp

(after Glinka, Stremme, Marbut, and others)

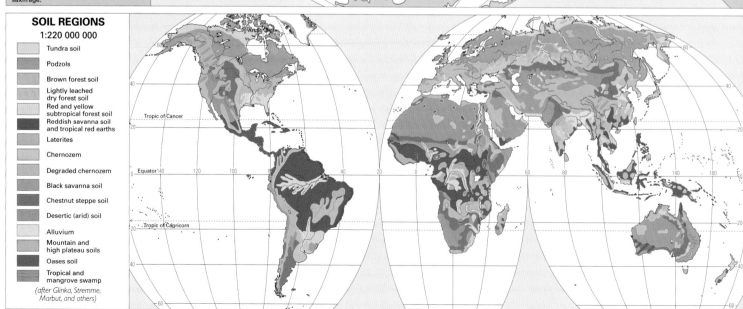

Arctic Circle
Tropic of Cancer
Equator
Tropic of Capricorn

Projection: Interrupted Mollweide's Homolographic

Subtropical and Temperate Woodland, Scrub and Bush
Vast clearings with woody shrubs and tall grasses. Trees are fire-resistant and either deciduous or xerophytic because of long dry periods. Species include eucalyptus, acacia, mimosa and euphorbia.

Tropical Savanna with Low Trees and Bush
Tall, coarse grass with enough precipitation to support a scattering of short deciduous trees and thorn scrub. Vegetation consisting of elephant grass, acacia, palms and baobab is limited by aridity, grazing animals and periodic fires; trees have developed thick, woody bark, small leaves or thorns.

Tropical Savanna and Grassland
Areas with a hot climate and long dry season. Extensive areas of tall grasses often reaching 3.5m with scattered fire and drought resistant bushes, low trees and thickets of elephant grass. Shrubs include acacia, baobab and palms.

NATURAL VEGETATION
(after Austin Miller)

1:116 000 000

Dry Semi-desert with Shrub and Grass
Xerophytic shrubs with thin grass cover and few trees, limited by a long dry season and short, hot, rainy period. Sagebrush, bunch grass and acacia shrubs are common.

Desert Shrub
Scattered xerophytic plants able to withstand daytime extremes in temperature and long periods of drought. There is a large diversity of desert flora such as cacti, yucca, tamarisk, hard grass and artemisia.

Desert
Precipitation less than 250mm per year; vegetation is very sparse, mainly bare rock, sand dunes and salt flats. Vegetation comprises a few xerophytic shrubs and ephemeral flowers.

Dry Steppe and Shrub
Semi-arid with cold, dry winters and hot summers. Bare soil with sparsely distributed short grasses and scattered shrubs and short trees. Species include acacia, artemisia, saksaul and tamarisk.

Temperate Grasslands, Prairie and Steppe
Continuous, tall, dense and deep-rooted swards of ancient grasslands, considered to be natural climax vegetation as determined by soil and climate. Average precipitation 250–750mm with a long dry season, limiting growth of trees and shrubs. Includes Stipa grass, buffalo grass, blue stems and loco weed.

Mediterranean Hardwood Forest and Scrub
Areas with hot and arid summers. Sparse evergreen trees are short and twisted with thick bark, interspersed with areas of scrub land. Trees have waxy leaves or thorns and deep root systems to resist drought. Many of the hardwood forests have been cleared by man, resulting in extensive scrub formation – maquis and chaparral. Species found are evergreen oak, stone pine, cork, olive and myrtle.

Temperate Deciduous Forest and Meadow
Areas of relatively high, well-distributed rainfall and temperatures favourable for forest growth. The tall broadleaved trees form a canopy in the summer, but shed their leaves in the winter. The undergrowth is sparse and poorly developed, but in the spring, herbs and flowers develop quickly. Diverse species with up to 20 per ha, including oak, beech, birch, maple, ash, elm, chestnut and hornbeam. Many of these forests have been cleared for urbanization and farming.

SOIL DEGRADATION
1:220 000 000

Areas of Concern
- Areas of serious concern
- Areas of some concern
- Stable terrain
- Non-vegetated land

Causes of soil degradation (by region)
- Grazing practices
- Other agricultural practices
- Industrialization
- Deforestation
- Fuelwood collection

(after Wageningen 1990)

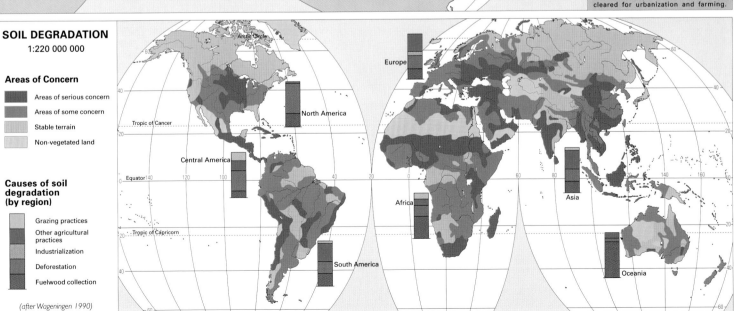

COPYRIGHT PHILIP'S

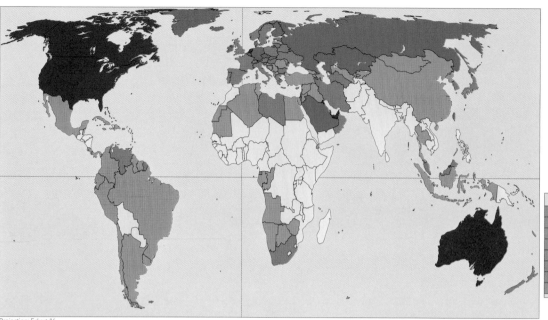

Projection: Eckert IV

CARBON DIOXIDE EMISSIONS

Carbon dioxide emissions in tonnes per capita (2002)

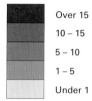

- Over 15
- 10 – 15
- 5 – 10
- 1 – 5
- Under 1

| 5% | 10% | 15% | 20% |

USA
China
Russia
Japan
India
Germany
Canada
UK

Estimated percentage share of total world CO_2 emissions (2002)

THE GREENHOUSE EFFECT

Carbon dioxide is increased by burning fossil fuels and cutting forests

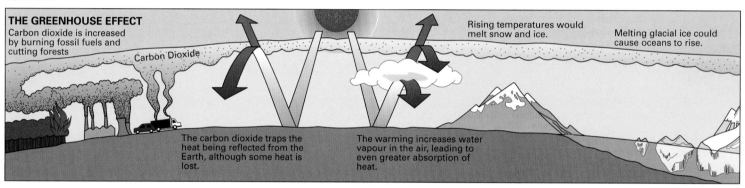

Carbon Dioxide

Rising temperatures would melt snow and ice.

Melting glacial ice could cause oceans to rise.

The carbon dioxide traps the heat being reflected from the Earth, although some heat is lost.

The warming increases water vapour in the air, leading to even greater absorption of heat.

Northern Hemisphere

Southern Hemisphere

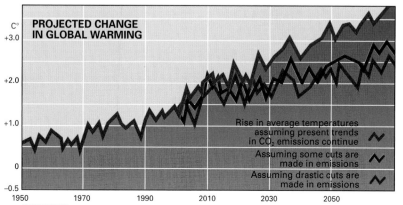

THINNING OZONE LAYER

Total atmospheric ozone concentration in the southern and northern hemispheres (Dobson Units, 2000)

In 1985, scientists working in Antarctica discovered a thinning of the ozone layer, commonly known as an 'ozone hole'. This caused immediate alarm because the ozone layer absorbs most of the Sun's dangerous ultraviolet radiation, which is believed to cause an increase in skin cancer, cataracts and damage to the immune system. Since 1985, ozone depletion has increased and, by 2003, the ozone hole over the South Pole was estimated to be larger than North America. The false-colour images, left, show the total atmospheric ozone concentration in the southern hemisphere (in September 2000) and the northern hemisphere (in March 2000) with the ozone hole clearly identifiable at the centre. The data is from the Tiros Ozone Vertical Sounder, an instrument on the American TIROS weather satellite. The colours represent the ozone concentration in Dobson Units (DU). Scientists agree that ozone depletion is caused by CFCs, a group of manufactured chemicals used in air-conditioning systems and refrigerators. In a 1987 treaty most industrial nations agreed to phase out CFCs and a complete ban on most CFCs was agreed after the end of 1995. However, scientists believe that the chemicals will remain in the atmosphere for 50 to 100 years. As a result, ozone depletion will continue for many years.

PROJECTED CHANGE IN GLOBAL WARMING

C°
+3.0
+2.0
+1.0
0
-0.5

Rise in average temperatures assuming present trends in CO_2 emissions continue

Assuming some cuts are made in emissions

Assuming drastic cuts are made in emissions

1950 1970 1990 2010 2030 2050

COPYRIGHT PHILIP'S

POSSIBLE EFFECT OF SEA LEVEL RISE IN FLORIDA

Sea levels have risen worldwide by about 2 cm since 1900. If CO_2 emissions continue at the same rate, the sea level is expected to rise by 7.4 m by 2200. The map shows the dramatic effects that such a rise could have on the southern part of Florida in the USA.

Submerged land area if sea level rises 7.4 m

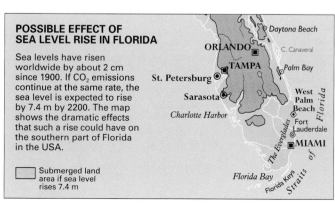

Daytona Beach
ORLANDO
C. Canaveral
TAMPA
Palm Bay
St. Petersburg
Sarasota
West Palm Beach
Charlotte Harbor
Fort Lauderdale
The Everglades
MIAMI
Florida Bay
Florida Keys
Straits of Florida

PREDICTED CHANGE IN TEMPERATURE

The difference between actual annual average surface air temperature, 1969–90, and predicted annual average surface air temperature, 2070–2100. This map shows the predicted increase, assuming a 'medium growth' of the global economy and assuming that no measures to combat the emission of greenhouse gases are taken.

- 5 – 10°C warmer
- 3 – 5°C warmer
- 2 – 3°C warmer
- 1 – 2°C warmer
- 0 – 1°C warmer

Source: The Hadley Centre of Climate Prediction and Research, The Met. Office.

PREDICTED CHANGE IN PRECIPITATION

The difference between actual annual average precipitation, 1960–90, and predicted annual average precipitation, 2070–2100. It should be noted that these predicted annual mean changes mask quite significant seasonal detail.

- Over 2 mm more rain per day
- 1 – 2 mm more rain per day
- 0.5 – 1 mm more rain per day
- 0.2 – 0.5 mm more rain per day
- no change
- 0.2 – 0.5 mm less rain per day
- 0.5 – 1 mm less rain per day
- 1 – 2 mm less rain per day
- Over 2 mm less rain per day

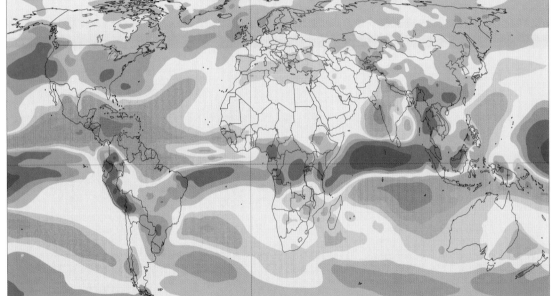

DESERTIFICATION AND DEFORESTATION

- Existing deserts
- Areas with a high risk of desertification
- Areas with a moderate risk of desertification
- Former areas of rainforest
- Existing rainforest

Major famines since 1900 ■
(with dates)

Deforestation 1990–2000

	Annual deforestation (thous. hectares)	Annual deforestation rate (%)
Brazil	2,309	0.4
Indonesia	1,312	1.2
Mexico	631	1.1
Congo (Dem. Rep.)	532	0.4
Burma (Myanmar)	517	1.4
Nigeria	398	2.6
Peru	269	1.4

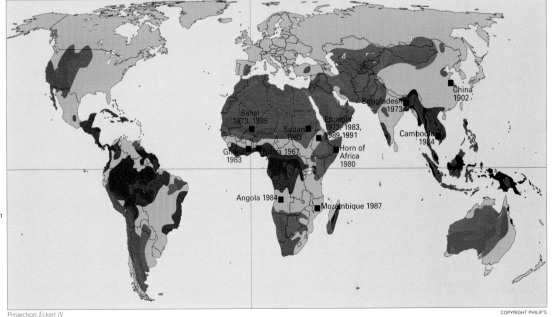

Projection: Eckert IV

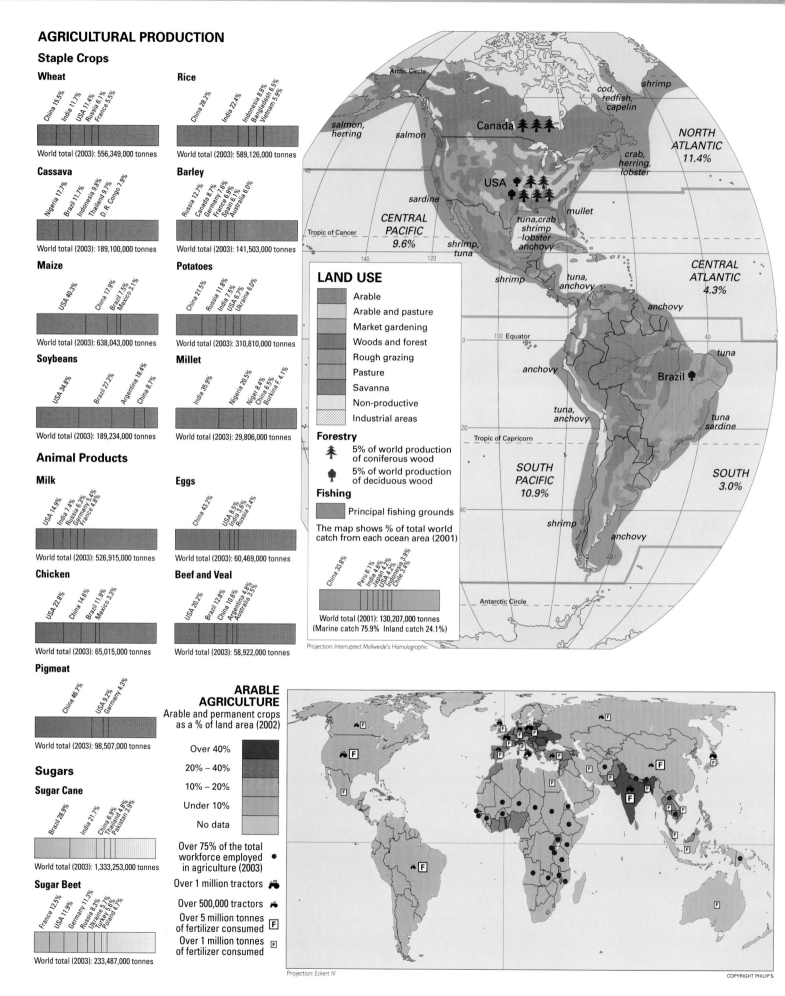

AGRICULTURAL PRODUCTION

Staple Crops

Wheat

China 15.5% | India 11.7% | USA 11.4% | Russia 6.1% | France 5.5%

World total (2003): 556,349,000 tonnes

Rice

China 28.2% | India 22.4% | Indonesia 8.8% | Bangladesh 6.5% | Vietnam 5.9%

World total (2003): 589,126,000 tonnes

Cassava

Nigeria 17.7% | Brazil 11.7% | Indonesia 9.8% | Thailand 9.7% | D. R. Congo 7.9%

World total (2003): 189,100,000 tonnes

Barley

Russia 12.7% | Canada 8.7% | Germany 7.6% | France 6.9% | Spain 6.1% | Australia 6.0%

World total (2003): 141,503,000 tonnes

Maize

USA 40.3% | China 17.9% | Brazil 7.5% | Mexico 3.1%

World total (2003): 638,043,000 tonnes

Potatoes

China 21.5% | Russia 11.8% | India 7.5% | USA 6.7% | Ukraine 6.0%

World total (2003): 310,810,000 tonnes

Soybeans

USA 34.8% | Brazil 27.2% | Argentina 18.4% | China 8.7%

World total (2003): 189,234,000 tonnes

Millet

India 35.9% | Nigeria 20.5% | Niger 8.4% | China 6.5% | Burkina F. 4.1%

World total (2003): 29,806,000 tonnes

Animal Products

Milk

USA 14.9% | India 7.4% | Russia 6.3% | Germany 5.4% | France 4.8%

World total (2003): 526,915,000 tonnes

Eggs

China 43.2% | USA 8.5% | India 3.6% | Russia 3.4%

World total (2003): 60,469,000 tonnes

Chicken

USA 22.8% | China 14.6% | Brazil 11.9% | Mexico 3.3%

World total (2003): 65,015,000 tonnes

Beef and Veal

USA 20.2% | Brazil 12.8% | China 10.6% | Argentina 4.8% | Australia 3.5%

World total (2003): 58,922,000 tonnes

Pigmeat

China 46.7% | USA 9.2% | Germany 4.3%

World total (2003): 98,507,000 tonnes

Sugars

Sugar Cane

Brazil 28.9% | India 21.7% | China 6.9% | Thailand 4.9% | Pakistan 3.9%

World total (2003): 1,333,253,000 tonnes

Sugar Beet

France 12.5% | USA 11.9% | Germany 11.3% | Russia 8.3% | Ukraine 5.7% | Turkey 5.6% | Poland 4.7%

World total (2003): 233,487,000 tonnes

LAND USE

- Arable
- Arable and pasture
- Market gardening
- Woods and forest
- Rough grazing
- Pasture
- Savanna
- Non-productive
- Industrial areas

Forestry

🌲 5% of world production of coniferous wood

🌳 5% of world production of deciduous wood

Fishing

Principal fishing grounds

The map shows % of total world catch from each ocean area (2001)

China 33.8% | Peru 6.1% | India 4.6% | Japan 4.2% | USA 4.2% | Indonesia 3.9% | Chile 3.4%

World total (2001): 130,207,000 tonnes
(Marine catch 75.9% Inland catch 24.1%)

Projection: *Interrupted Mollweide's Homolographic*

NORTH ATLANTIC 11.4%

CENTRAL PACIFIC 9.6%

CENTRAL ATLANTIC 4.3%

SOUTH PACIFIC 10.9%

SOUTH 3.0%

ARABLE AGRICULTURE

Arable and permanent crops as a % of land area (2002)

- Over 40%
- 20% – 40%
- 10% – 20%
- Under 10%
- No data

● Over 75% of the total workforce employed in agriculture (2003)

🚜 Over 1 million tractors

🚜 Over 500,000 tractors

[F] Over 5 million tonnes of fertilizer consumed

[F] Over 1 million tonnes of fertilizer consumed

Projection: *Eckert IV*

COPYRIGHT PHILIP'S

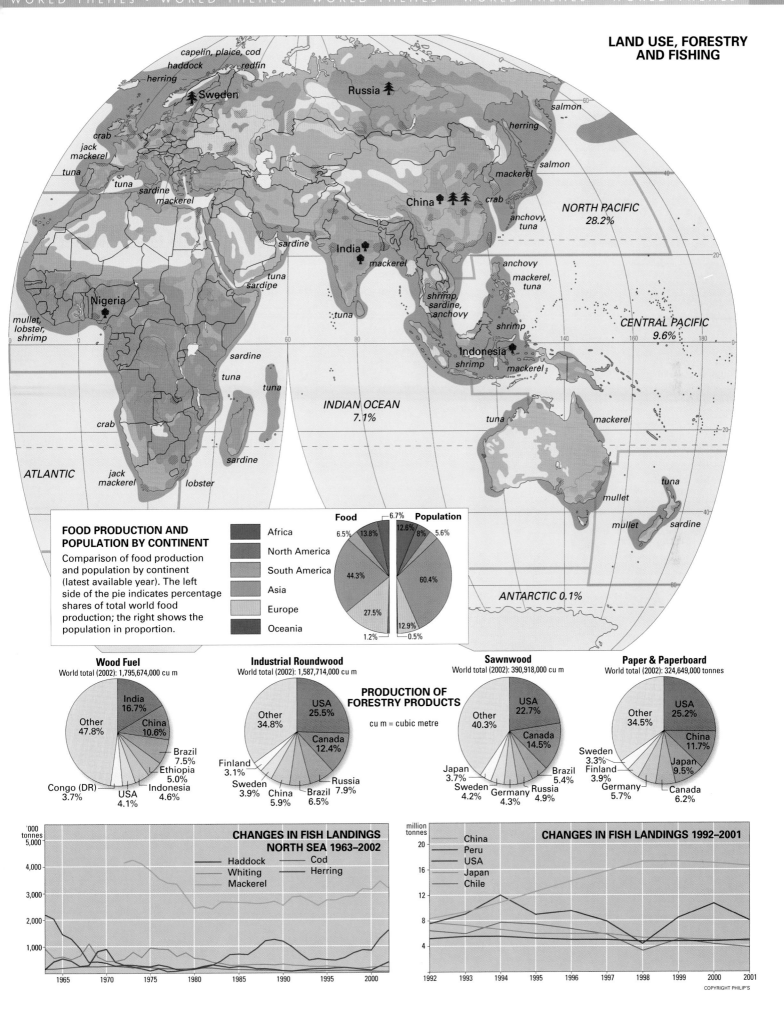

**LAND USE, FORESTRY
AND FISHING**

capelin, plaice, cod
haddock ——— redfin
herring

Sweden

Russia

salmon

crab

herring

jack
mackerel

salmon

tuna

tuna

sardine
mackerel

mackerel

China

crab

NORTH PACIFIC
28.2%

sardine

India

mackerel

anchovy,
tuna

Nigeria

tuna
sardine

tuna

anchovy
mackerel,
tuna

mullet,
lobster,
shrimp

sardine

shrimp,
sardine,
anchovy

shrimp

CENTRAL PACIFIC
9.6%

tuna

Indonesia

shrimp

tuna

mackerel

mackerel

tuna

INDIAN OCEAN
7.1%

crab

sardine

tuna

mullet

tuna

ATLANTIC

jack
mackerel

lobster

mullet

sardine

ANTARCTIC 0.1%

**FOOD PRODUCTION AND
POPULATION BY CONTINENT**

Comparison of food production
and population by continent
(latest available year). The left
side of the pie indicates percentage
shares of total world food
production; the right shows the
population in proportion.

Africa

North America

South America

Asia

Europe

Oceania

Food — 6.7% **Population**
6.5% | 13.8% | 12.6% | 8% | 5.6%
44.3% | 60.4%
27.5%
1.2% | 12.9%
0.5%

Wood Fuel
World total (2002): 1,795,674,000 cu m

India
16.7%

Other
47.8%

China
10.6%

Brazil
7.5%

Ethiopia
5.0%

Congo (DR)
3.7%

USA
4.1%

Indonesia
4.6%

Industrial Roundwood
World total (2002): 1,587,714,000 cu m

USA
25.5%

Other
34.8%

Canada
12.4%

Finland
3.1%

Sweden
3.9%

China
5.9%

Brazil
6.5%

Russia
7.9%

**PRODUCTION OF
FORESTRY PRODUCTS**

cu m = cubic metre

Sawnwood
World total (2002): 390,918,000 cu m

USA
22.7%

Other
40.3%

Canada
14.5%

Japan
3.7%

Sweden
4.2%

Germany
4.3%

Russia
4.9%

Brazil
5.4%

Paper & Paperboard
World total (2002): 324,649,000 tonnes

USA
25.2%

Other
34.5%

China
11.7%

Sweden
3.3%

Finland
3.9%

Japan
9.5%

Germany
5.7%

Canada
6.2%

'000
tonnes
5,000

4,000

3,000

2,000

1,000

**CHANGES IN FISH LANDINGS
NORTH SEA 1963–2002**

Haddock — Cod
Whiting — Herring
Mackerel

1965 1970 1975 1980 1985 1990 1995 2000

million
tonnes
20

16

12

8

4

CHANGES IN FISH LANDINGS 1992–2001

China
Peru
USA
Japan
Chile

1992 1993 1994 1995 1996 1997 1998 1999 2000 2001

COPYRIGHT PHILIP'S

ENERGY PRODUCTION BY REGION
Each square represents 1% of world energy production (2002)

North America
Europe
Eastern Europe & Eurasia
Africa
Middle East
Asia
Japan
South America

ENERGY CONSUMPTION BY REGION
Each square represents 1% of world energy consumption (2002)

North America
Europe
Eastern Europe & Eurasia
Middle East
Africa
Asia
Japan
South America
Australasia

ENERGY BALANCE
Difference between energy production and consumption in millions of tonnes of oil equivalent (MtOe) 2004

↑ **Energy surplus in MtOe**

Over 35 surplus
1 – 35 surplus
1 deficit – 1 surplus (approx. balance)
1 – 35 deficit
Over 35 deficit

↓ **Energy deficit in MtOe**

Fossil fuel production
	Principal	Secondary
Oilfields	●	●
Gasfields	▼	▼
Coalfields	△	△

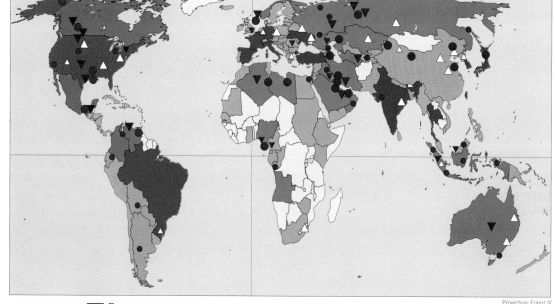

Projection: Eckert IV

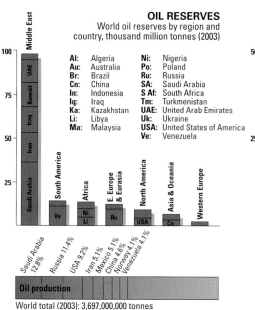

OIL RESERVES
World oil reserves by region and country, thousand million tonnes (2003)

Al: Algeria	**Ni:** Nigeria
Au: Australia	**Po:** Poland
Br: Brazil	**Ru:** Russia
Cn: China	**SA:** Saudi Arabia
In: Indonesia	**S Af:** South Africa
Iq: Iraq	**Tm:** Turkmenistan
Ka: Kazakhstan	**UAE:** United Arab Emirates
Li: Libya	**Uk:** Ukraine
Ma: Malaysia	**USA:** United States of America
	Ve: Venezuela

Middle East
UAE
Kuwait
Iraq
Iran
Saudi Arabia
South America
Ve
Africa
Ni
Li
E. Europe & Eurasia
Ru
North America
USA
Asia & Oceania
Cn
Western Europe

Saudi Arabia 12.8%
Russia 11.4%
USA 9.2%
Iran 5.1%
Mexico 5.1%
China 4.6%
Norway 4.1%
Venezuela 4.1%

Oil production
World total (2003): 3,697,000,000 tonnes

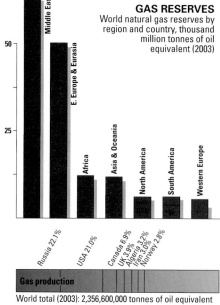

GAS RESERVES
World natural gas reserves by region and country, thousand million tonnes of oil equivalent (2003)

Middle East
E. Europe & Eurasia
Africa
Asia & Oceania
North America
South America
Western Europe

Russia 22.1%
USA 21.0%
Canada 6.9%
UK 3.9%
Algeria 3.2%
Iran 3.0%
Norway 2.8%

Gas production
World total (2003): 2,356,600,000 tonnes of oil equivalent

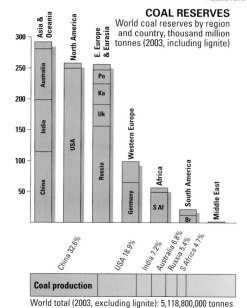

COAL RESERVES
World coal reserves by region and country, thousand million tonnes (2003, including lignite)

Asia & Oceania
Australia
India
China
North America
USA
E. Europe & Eurasia
Po
Ka
Uk
Russia
Western Europe
Germany
Africa
S Af
South America
Br
Middle East

China 32.6%
USA 18.9%
India 7.2%
Australia 6.8%
Russia 5.4%
S Africa 4.7%

Coal production
World total (2003, excluding lignite): 5,118,800,000 tonnes

ELECTRICITY GENERATION
Percentage of electricity generated
by source (2004)

- Over 75% from thermal
- 50 – 75% from thermal
- Over 75% from hydro
- 50 – 75% from hydro
- Over 50% from nuclear
- No dominant source
- No data
- ● Selected geothermal plants
- ◆ Selected hydroelectric plants

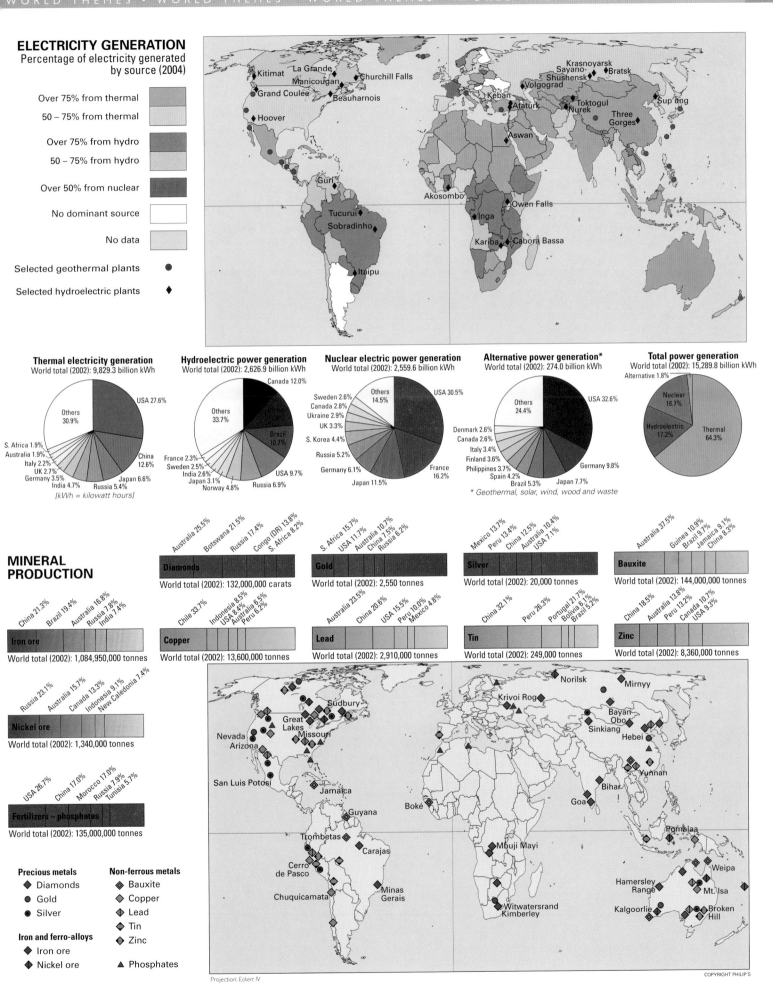

Thermal electricity generation
World total (2002): 9,829.3 billion kWh

USA 27.6%
Others 30.9%
S. Africa 1.9%
Australia 1.9%
Italy 2.2%
UK 2.7%
Germany 3.5%
India 4.7%
Russia 5.4%
Japan 6.6%
China 12.6%

[kWh = kilowatt hours]

Hydroelectric power generation
World total (2002): 2,626.9 billion kWh

Canada 12.0%
Others 33.7%
China
Brazil 10.7%
France 2.3%
Sweden 2.5%
India 2.6%
Japan 3.1%
Norway 4.8%
USA 9.7%
Russia 6.9%

Nuclear electric power generation
World total (2002): 2,559.6 billion kWh

Others 14.5%
USA 30.5%
Sweden 2.6%
Canada 2.8%
Ukraine 2.9%
UK 3.3%
S. Korea 4.4%
Russia 5.2%
Germany 6.1%
France 16.2%
Japan 11.5%

Alternative power generation*
World total (2002): 274.0 billion kWh

Others 24.4%
USA 32.6%
Denmark 2.6%
Canada 2.6%
Italy 3.4%
Finland 3.6%
Philippines 3.7%
Spain 4.2%
Brazil 5.3%
Germany 9.8%
Japan 7.7%

* Geothermal, solar, wind, wood and waste

Total power generation
World total (2002): 15,289.8 billion kWh

Alternative 1.8%
Nuclear 16.7%
Hydroelectric 17.2%
Thermal 64.3%

MINERAL PRODUCTION

Diamonds — World total (2002): 132,000,000 carats
Australia 25.5% | Botswana 21.5% | Russia 17.4% | Congo (DR) 13.8% | S. Africa 8.2%

Gold — World total (2002): 2,550 tonnes
S. Africa 15.7% | USA 11.7% | Australia 10.7% | China 7.5% | Russia 6.2%

Silver — World total (2002): 20,000 tonnes
Mexico 13.7% | Peru 13.4% | China 12.5% | Australia 10.4% | USA 7.1%

Bauxite — World total (2002): 144,000,000 tonnes
Australia 37.5% | Guinea 10.9% | Brazil 9.7% | Jamaica 9.1% | China 8.3%

Iron ore — World total (2002): 1,084,950,000 tonnes
China 21.3% | Brazil 19.4% | Australia 16.8% | Russia 7.8% | India 7.4%

Copper — World total (2002): 13,600,000 tonnes
Chile 33.7% | Indonesia 8.5% | USA 8.4% | Australia 6.5% | Peru 6.2%

Lead — World total (2002): 2,910,000 tonnes
Australia 23.5% | China 20.6% | USA 15.5% | Peru 10.0% | Mexico 4.8%

Tin — World total (2002): 249,000 tonnes
China 32.1% | Peru 26.3% | Portugal 21.7% | Bolivia 6.1% | Brazil 5.2%

Zinc — World total (2002): 8,360,000 tonnes
China 18.5% | Australia 13.8% | Peru 13.2% | Canada 10.7% | USA 9.3%

Nickel ore — World total (2002): 1,340,000 tonnes
Russia 23.1% | Australia 15.7% | Canada 13.3% | Indonesia 9.1% | New Caledonia 7.4%

Fertilizers – phosphates — World total (2002): 135,000,000 tonnes
USA 26.7% | China 17.0% | Morocco 17.0% | Russia 7.9% | Tunisia 5.7%

Precious metals
- ◆ Diamonds
- ● Gold
- ● Silver

Iron and ferro-alloys
- ◆ Iron ore
- ◆ Nickel ore

Non-ferrous metals
- ◆ Bauxite
- ◆ Copper
- ◆ Lead
- ◆ Tin
- ◆ Zinc
- ▲ Phosphates

Projection: Eckert IV

COPYRIGHT PHILIP'S

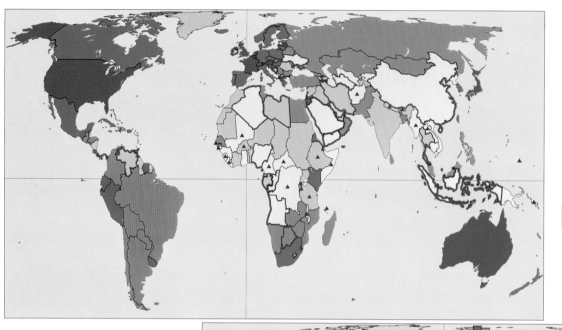

IMPORTANCE OF SERVICE INDUSTRY
Percentage of total GDP from service sector (2003)

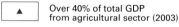

- Over 70%
- 60 – 70%
- 50 – 60%
- 40 – 50%
- Under 40%
- No data

Over 40% of total GDP from industrial sector (2003)

▲ Over 40% of total GDP from agricultural sector (2003)

LOCATION OF MANUFACTURING

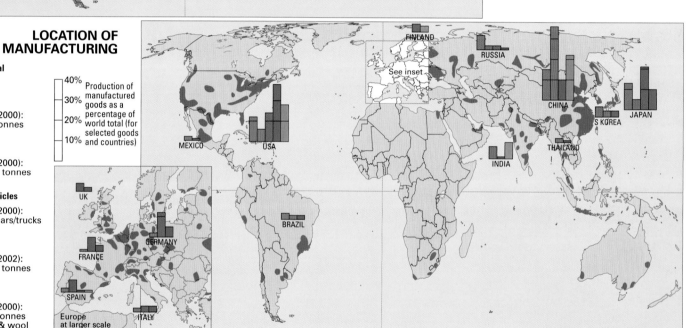

- **Industrial regions**
- **Steel** World total (2000): 845 million tonnes
- **Cement** World total (2000): 1,600 million tonnes
- **Motor vehicles** World total (2000): 40.3 million cars/trucks
- **Paper** World total (2002): 324.6 million tonnes
- **Textiles*** World total (2000): 21.0 million tonnes *cotton, silk & wool

Production of manufactured goods as a percentage of world total (for selected goods and countries)

Europe at larger scale

EMPLOYMENT BY ECONOMIC ACTIVITY Selected countries (2002)

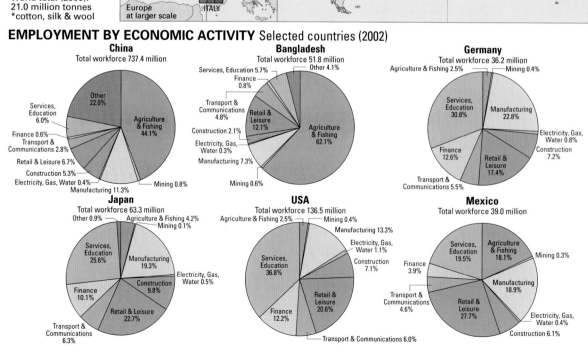

RESEARCH & DEVELOPMENT
Scientists and engineers in R&D (per million people) 1990–2003

Country	Total
Finland	7,431
Iceland	6,592
Sweden	5,171
Japan	5,085
Denmark	4,822
USA	4,526
Norway	4,442
Singapore	4,352
Luxembourg	3,757
Switzerland	3,594
Canada	3,487
Australia	3,446
Russia	3,415
Germany	3,222
Belgium	3,180
France	3,134
South Korea	2,979
Netherlands	2,826
UK	2,691
New Zealand	2,593

WORLD TRADE

Percentage share of total
world exports by value (2003)

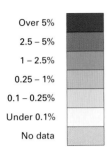

- Over 5%
- 2.5 – 5%
- 1 – 2.5%
- 0.25 – 1%
- 0.1 – 0.25%
- Under 0.1%
- No data

The members of 'G8', the inner circle
of OECD, account for more than half
the total. The majority of nations
contribute less than one quarter of 1%
to the worldwide total of exports;
EU countries account for 35%; the
Pacific Rim nations over 50%.

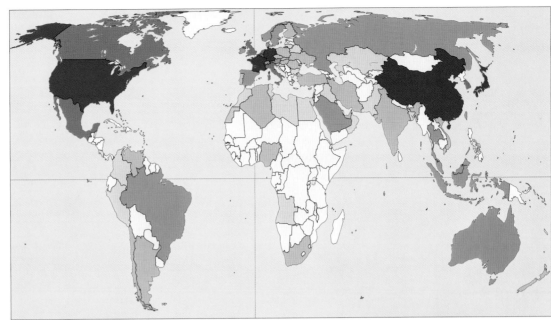

MAJOR EXPORTS Leading manufactured items and their exporters

Motor Vehicles
World total (2004): US$ 265,898 million

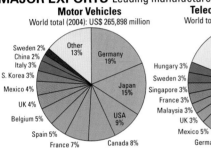

Other 13% — Germany 19% — Japan 15% — USA 9% — Canada 8% — France 7% — Spain 5% — Belgium 5% — UK 4% — Mexico 4% — S. Korea 3% — Italy 3% — China 2% — Sweden 2%

Telecommunications Gear
World total (2004): US$ 405,989 million

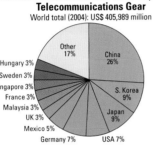

Other 17% — China 26% — S. Korea 9% — Japan 9% — USA 7% — Germany 7% — Mexico 5% — UK 3% — Malaysia 3% — France 3% — Singapore 3% — Sweden 3% — Hungary 3%

Petrol Products
World total (2004): US$ 496,092 million

Other 41% — Russia 15% — Norway 8% — Venezuela 6% — UK 6% — Canada 5% — Mexico 5% — Algeria 4% — Netherlands 4% — Singapore 3% — USA 3%

Computers
World total (2004): US$ 236,396 million

Other 15% — China 26% — USA 10% — Neth. 8% — Germany 7% — Singapore 7% — Malaysia 5% — Mexico 5% — S. Korea 4% — Ireland 4% — UK 4% — Japan 4%

Electrical Components
World total (2004): US$ 838,552 million

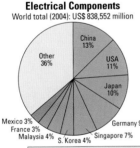

Other 36% — China 13% — USA 11% — Japan 10% — Germany 9% — Singapore 7% — S. Korea 4% — Malaysia 4% — France 3% — Mexico 3%

Pharmaceuticals
World total (2004): US$ 311,399 million

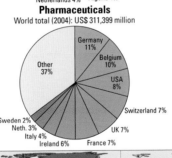

Other 37% — Germany 11% — Belgium 10% — USA 8% — Switzerland 7% — UK 7% — France 7% — Ireland 6% — Italy 4% — Neth. 3% — Sweden 2%

MULTINATIONAL CORPORATIONS (MNCs)

Country of origin of world's top 200 MNCs
(top 200 are ranked by revenue, 2002)

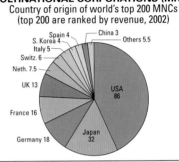

USA 86 — Japan 32 — Germany 18 — France 16 — UK 13 — Neth. 7.5 — Switz. 6 — Italy 5 — S. Korea 4 — Spain 4 — China 3 — Others 5.5

Top ten MNCs by revenue (million US$), 2002

Wal-Mart	Supermarket chain	219,812	USA
Exxon Mobil	Petroleum	191,581	USA
General Motors	Motor vehicles	177,260	USA
BP	Petroleum	174,218	UK
Ford Motor	Motor vehicles	162,412	USA
Enron*	Energy	138,718	USA
DaimlerChrysler	Motor vehicles	136,897	Germany
Royal Dutch/Shell	Petroleum	135,211	Neth/UK
General Electric	Energy and finance	125,913	USA
Toyota Motor	Motor vehicles	120,814	Japan

* Enron ceased trading in 2002

INTERNET AND TELECOMMUNICATIONS

Percentage of total population
using the Internet (2003)

World total 604.1 million Internet users

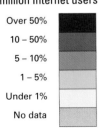

- Over 50%
- 10 – 50%
- 5 – 10%
- 1 – 5%
- Under 1%
- No data

IMPORT   EXPORT

Telecommunications

Trade in office machines and
telecom equipment,
percentage of world total
(2002)

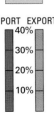

- 40%
- 30%
- 20%
- 10%

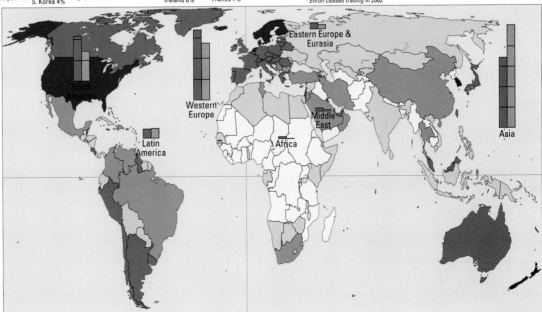

North America — Western Europe — Eastern Europe & Eurasia — Latin America — Africa — Middle East — Asia

Projection: Eckert IV

COPYRIGHT PHILIP'S

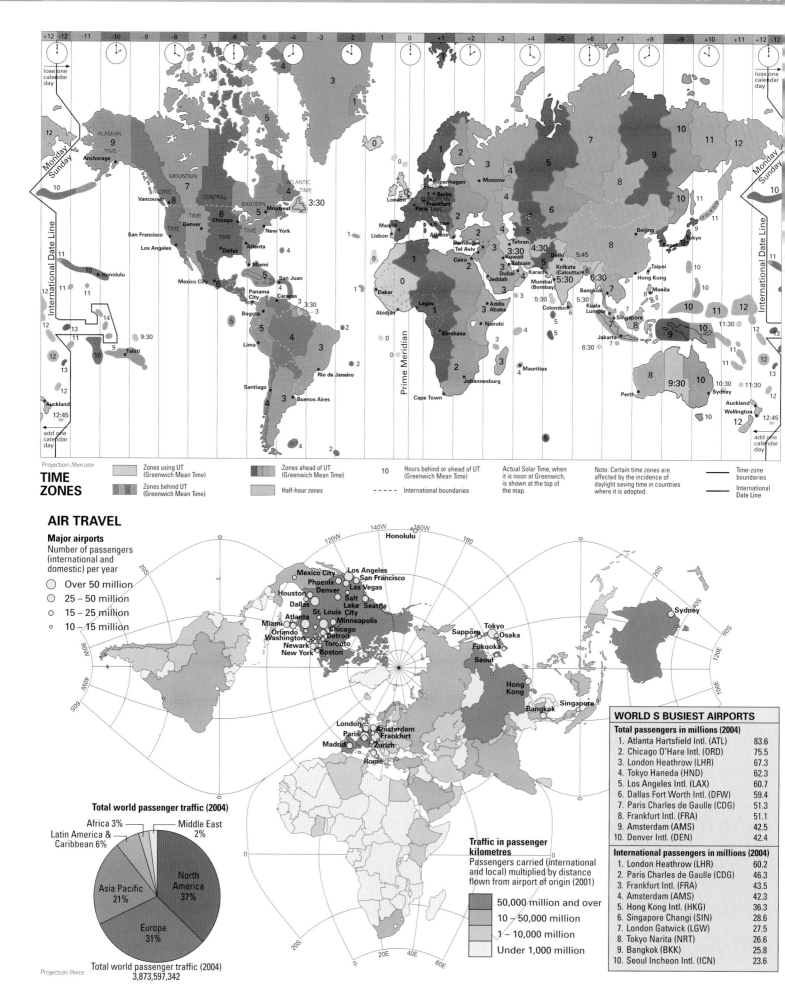

Projection: Mercator

TIME ZONES

(light grey)	Zones using UT (Greenwich Mean Time)	
(dark grey)	Zones behind UT (Greenwich Mean Time)	
	Zones ahead of UT (Greenwich Mean Time)	
	Half-hour zones	

10 Hours behind or ahead of UT (Greenwich Mean Time)

- - - - International boundaries

Actual Solar Time, when it is noon at Greenwich, is shown at the top of the map.

Note: Certain time zones are affected by the incidence of daylight saving time in countries where it is adopted.

——— Time-zone boundaries

——— International Date Line

AIR TRAVEL

Major airports

Number of passengers (international and domestic) per year

- ○ Over 50 million
- ○ 25 – 50 million
- ○ 15 – 25 million
- ○ 10 – 15 million

Total world passenger traffic (2004)

- Africa 3%
- Middle East 2%
- Latin America & Caribbean 6%
- North America 37%
- Asia Pacific 21%
- Europe 31%

Total world passenger traffic (2004)
3,873,597,342

Projection: Peirce

Traffic in passenger kilometres

Passengers carried (international and local) multiplied by distance flown from airport of origin (2001)

- 50,000 million and over
- 10 – 50,000 million
- 1 – 10,000 million
- Under 1,000 million

WORLD S BUSIEST AIRPORTS

Total passengers in millions (2004)

1. Atlanta Hartsfield Intl. (ATL)	83.6
2. Chicago O'Hare Intl. (ORD)	75.5
3. London Heathrow (LHR)	67.3
4. Tokyo Haneda (HND)	62.3
5. Los Angeles Intl. (LAX)	60.7
6. Dallas Fort Worth Intl. (DFW)	59.4
7. Paris Charles de Gaulle (CDG)	51.3
8. Frankfurt Intl. (FRA)	51.1
9. Amsterdam (AMS)	42.5
10. Denver Intl. (DEN)	42.4

International passengers in millions (2004)

1. London Heathrow (LHR)	60.2
2. Paris Charles de Gaulle (CDG)	46.3
3. Frankfurt Intl. (FRA)	43.5
4. Amsterdam (AMS)	42.3
5. Hong Kong Intl. (HKG)	36.3
6. Singapore Changi (SIN)	28.6
7. London Gatwick (LGW)	27.5
8. Tokyo Narita (NRT)	26.6
9. Bangkok (BKK)	25.8
10. Seoul Incheon Intl. (ICN)	23.6

UNESCO WORLD HERITAGE SITES 2005

Total sites = 812 (628 cultural, 160 natural and 24 mixed)

Region	Cultural sites	Natural sites	Mixed sites
Africa	31	32	2
Arab States	56	4	1
Asia & Pacific	112	43	9
Europe & North America	352	48	9
Latin America & Caribbean	77	33	3

Europe at larger scale

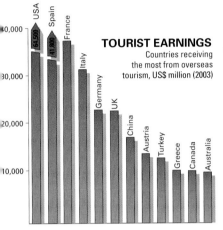

Fjords, Saimaa, St-Petersburg, Edinburgh, Oland, London, Disneyland, Prague, Tatra, Brittany, Paris, Vienna, Budapest, Alps, Lourdes, Venice, Black Sea Coast, Pyrenees, Florence, Costa Brava, Côte d'Azur, Rome, Algarve, Baleanic Is., Aegean Is., Costa del Sol, Costa Blanca, Ionian Islands, Athens, Rhodes, Crete

Destinations

- ■ Cultural & historical centres
- ■ Coastal resorts
- □ Ski resorts
- ■ Centres of entertainment
- ■ Places of pilgrimage
- ■ Places of great natural beauty

□ Other tourist destinations

TOURIST DESTINATIONS

Projection: *Peirce*

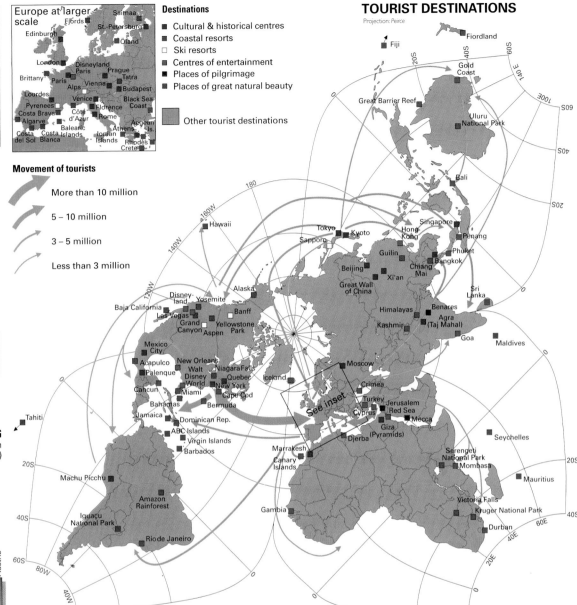

Movement of tourists

- More than 10 million
- 5 – 10 million
- 3 – 5 million
- Less than 3 million

TOURIST EARNINGS

Countries receiving the most from overseas tourism, US$ million (2003)

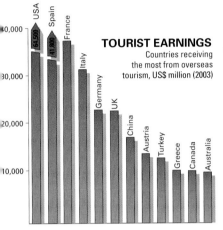

USA 64,500 · Spain 41,800 · France · Italy · Germany · UK · China · Austria · Turkey · Greece · Canada · Australia

(40,000 / 30,000 / 20,000 / 10,000)

TOURIST SPENDING

Countries spending the most on overseas tourism, US$ million (2003)

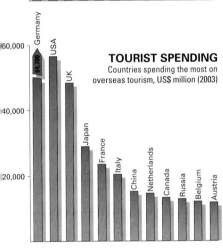

Germany 64,700 · USA · UK · Japan · France · Italy · China · Netherlands · Canada · Russia · Belgium · Austria

(60,000 / 40,000 / 20,000)

IMPORTANCE OF TOURISM

Tourism receipts as a percentage of Gross National Income (2002)

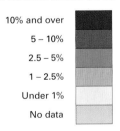

- 10% and over
- 5 – 10%
- 2.5 – 5%
- 1 – 2.5%
- Under 1%
- No data

Arrivals from abroad in millions (2001)

France	75.6
Spain	49.5
USA	45.5
Italy	39.0
China	33.2

(UK = 23.4 million)

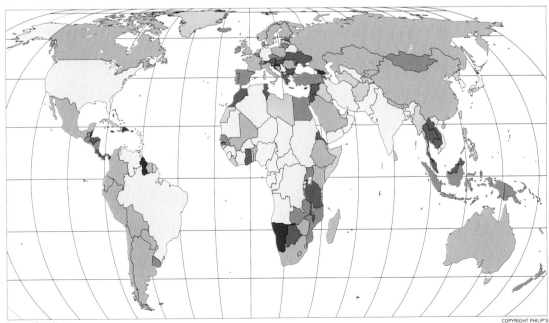

Projection: *Eckert IV*

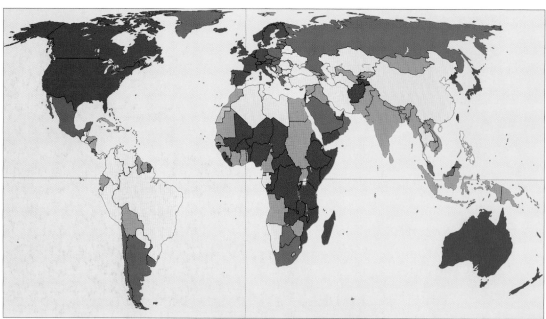

WEALTH

Gross Domestic Product per capita PPP (2003)

Annual value of goods and services divided by the population, using purchasing power parity (PPP) which gives real prices instead of variable exchange rates.

	Over 250% world average
	100 – 250% world average

World average: US$ 8,200

	50 – 100% world average
	15 – 50% world average
	Under 15% world average
	No data

Highest GDP (US$)		Lowest GDP (US$)	
Lux'bourg	55,100	East Timor	500
USA	37,800	Sierra Leone	500
Norway	37,700	Somalia	500
San Marino	34,600	Burundi	600
Switzerland	32,800	Congo (D.Rep.)	600

(UK = US$ 27,700)

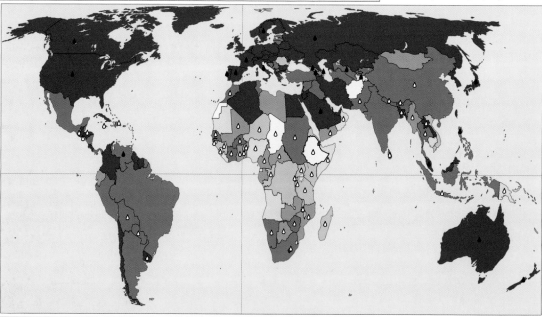

WATER SUPPLY

Percentage of total population with access to safe drinking water (2000)

Over 90%	
75 – 90%	
60 – 75%	
45 – 60%	
30 – 45%	
Under 30%	

Least amount of safe drinking water

Afghanistan	13%	Cambodia	30%
Ethiopia	24%	Mauritania	37%
Chad	27%	Angola	38%
Sierra Leone	28%	Oman	39%

Daily consumption per capita
△ Under 80 litres ▲ Over 320 litres

80 litres a day is considered necessary for a reasonable quality of life

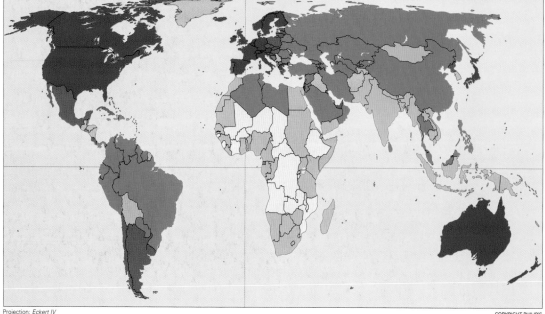

HUMAN DEVELOPMENT INDEX (HDI)

HDI (calculated by the UNDP) gives a value to countries using indicators of life expectancy, education and standards of living in 2002. Higher values show more developed countries.

	Over 0.9
	0.8 – 0.9
	0.7 – 0.8
	0.4 – 0.7
	Under 0.4
	No data

Highest values		Lowest values	
Norway	0.952	Sierra Leone	0.273
Australia	0.946	Niger	0.292
Sweden	0.946	Burkina Faso	0.302
Canada	0.943	Mali	0.326
Netherlands	0.942	Burundi	0.339

(UK = 0.936)

Projection: *Eckert IV*

COPYRIGHT PHILIP'S

HEALTH CARE

Number of qualified doctors
per 100,000 people (2003)

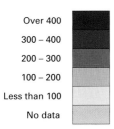

Over 400

300 – 400

200 – 300

100 – 200

Less than 100

No data

Countries with the most and least
doctors per 100,000 people

Most doctors		Least doctors	
Italy	607	Burundi	1
Cuba	596	Mozambique	2
Georgia	463	Rwanda	2
Belarus	450	Chad	3
Greece	438	Ethiopia	3

(UK = 164 doctors)

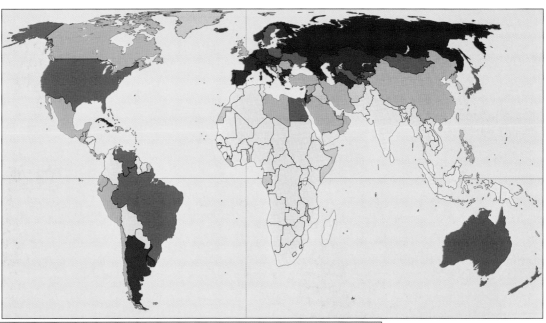

ILLITERACY AND EDUCATION

Percentage of adult population
unable to read or write (2003)

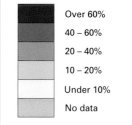

Over 60%

40 – 60%

20 – 40%

10 – 20%

Under 10%

No data

Countries with the highest
and lowest illiteracy rates

Highest (%)		Lowest (%)	
Niger	82	Australia	0
Burkina Faso	73	Denmark	0
Sierra Leone	69	Finland	0
Guinea	64	Liechtenstein	0
Afghanistan	44	Luxembourg	0

(UK = 1%)

GENDER DEVELOPMENT INDEX (GDI)

GDI shows economic and social differences
between men and women by using
various UNDP indicators (2002). Countries
with higher values of GDI have more
equality between men and women.

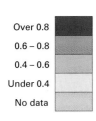

Over 0.8

0.6 – 0.8

0.4 – 0.6

Under 0.4

No data

Highest values		Lowest values	
Norway	0.955	Niger	0.278
Sweden	0.946	Burkina Faso	0.291
Australia	0.945	Mali	0.309
Canada	0.941	Guinea-Bissau	0.329
Netherlands	0.938	Burundi	0.337

(UK = 0.934)

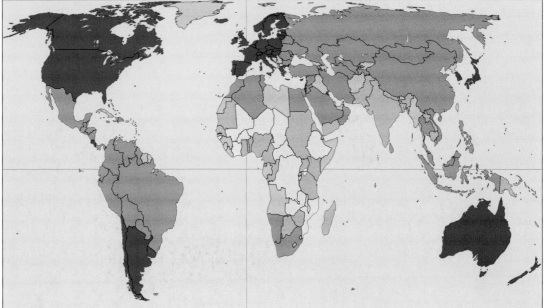

Projection: *Eckert IV*

AGE DISTRIBUTION PYRAMIDS (2005)

The bars represent the percentage of the total population (males plus females) in each age group. Developed countries such as New Zealand have populations spread evenly across age groups and usually a growing percentage of elderly people. Developing countries such as Kenya have the great majority of their people in the younger age groups, about to enter their most fertile years.

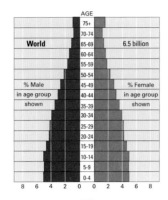

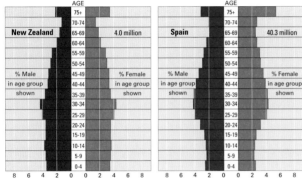

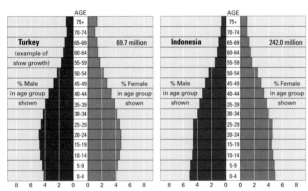

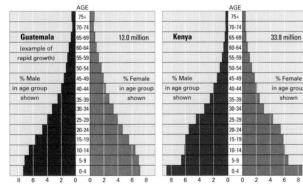

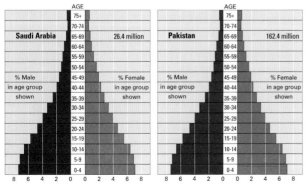

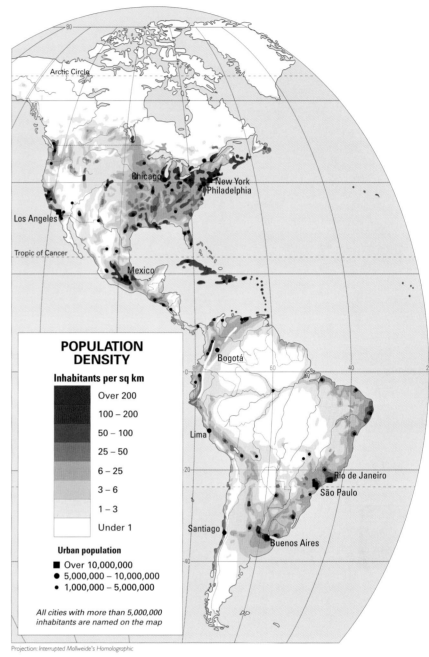

POPULATION DENSITY

Inhabitants per sq km

- Over 200
- 100 – 200
- 50 – 100
- 25 – 50
- 6 – 25
- 3 – 6
- 1 – 3
- Under 1

Urban population

- ■ Over 10,000,000
- ● 5,000,000 – 10,000,000
- • 1,000,000 – 5,000,000

All cities with more than 5,000,000 inhabitants are named on the map

Projection: Interrupted Mollweide's Homolographic

POPULATION CHANGE 1930–2020

Population totals are in millions

Figures in italics represent the percentage average annual increase for the period shown

	1930	1930–1960	1960	1960–1990	1990	1990–2020	2020
World	2,013	*1.4%*	3,019	*1.9%*	5,292	*1.4%*	8,062
Africa	155	*2.0%*	281	*2.9%*	648	*2.7%*	1,441
North America	135	*1.3%*	199	*1.1%*	276	*0.6%*	327
Latin America*	129	*1.8%*	218	*2.4%*	448	*1.6%*	719
Asia	1,073	*1.5%*	1,669	*2.1%*	3,108	*1.4%*	4,680
Europe	355	*0.6%*	425	*0.6%*	498	*0.1%*	514
Oceania	10	*1.4%*	16	*1.8%*	27	*1.1%*	37
CIS	176	*0.7%*	214	*1.0%*	288	*0.6%*	343

* South America plus Central America, Mexico and the West Indies
Commonwealth of Independent States, formerly the USSR

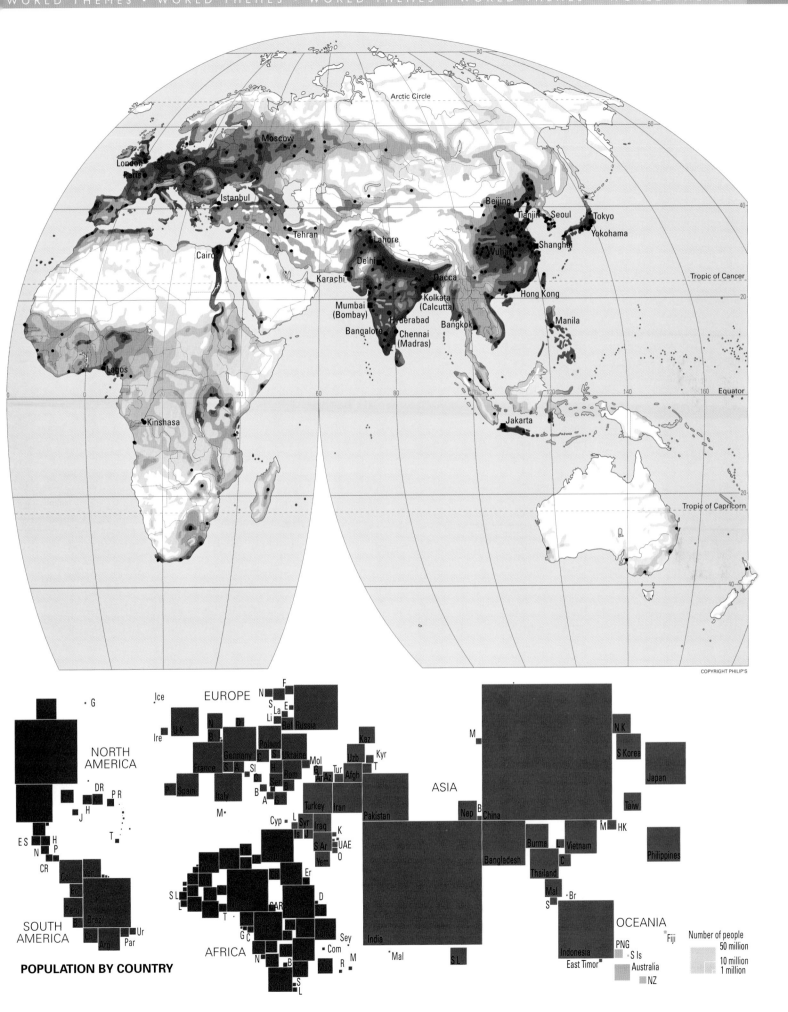

Arctic Circle

Moscow

London
Paris

Istanbul

Tehran

Cairo

Lahore

Delhi

Karachi

Dacca

Beijing

Tianjin · Seoul

Wuhan · Shanghai

Tokyo
Yokohama

Tropic of Cancer

Mumbai
(Bombay)

Kolkata
(Calcutta)

Hyderabad

Bangalore

Chennai
(Madras)

Bangkok

Hong Kong

Manila

Lagos

Kinshasa

Jakarta

Equator

Tropic of Capricorn

COPYRIGHT PHILIP'S

EUROPE

NORTH
AMERICA

ASIA

SOUTH
AMERICA

AFRICA

OCEANIA

POPULATION BY COUNTRY

Number of people
50 million
10 million
1 million

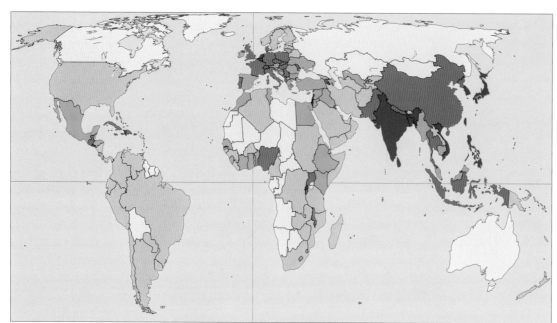

POPULATION DENSITY

Density of people per square kilometre (2004)

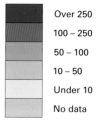

	Over 250
	100 – 250
	50 – 100
	10 – 50
	Under 10
	No data

Most and least densely populated countries

Most		Least	
Singapore	6,283	W. Sahara	1.0
Malta	1,256	Mongolia	1.8
Maldives	1,131	Namibia	2.4
Bahrain	1,019	Australia	2.6
Bangladesh	982	Botswana	2.6

(UK = 246.2 people per square km)

POPULATION CHANGE

Expected change in total population (2000–2010)

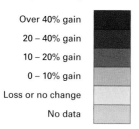

	Over 40% gain
	20 – 40% gain
	10 – 20% gain
	0 – 10% gain
	Loss or no change
	No data

Greatest population gains and losses

Greatest gains (%)		Greatest losses (%)	
Afghanistan	44.4	Bulgaria	– 8.6
Kuwait	41.2	Trinidad & Tob.	– 7.4
Yemen	41.0	Latvia	– 6.7
Uganda	39.8	Estonia	– 6.4
Oman	39.1	Ukraine	– 6.1

(UK = 3% gain)

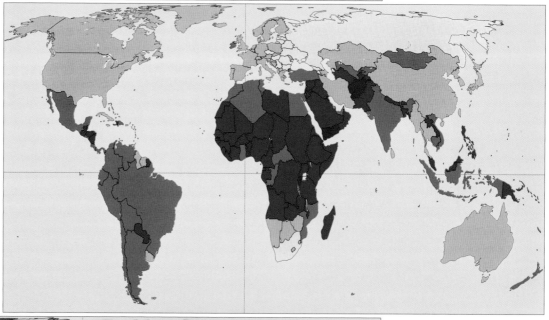

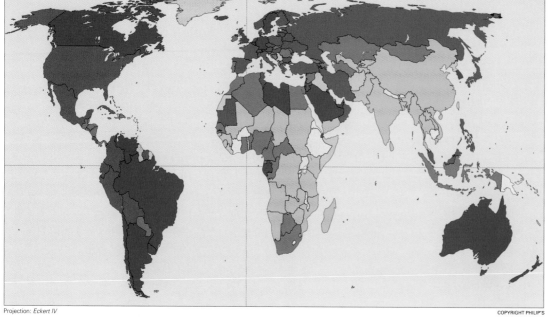

URBAN POPULATION

People living in urban areas as a percentage of total population (2002)

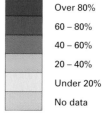

	Over 80%
	60 – 80%
	40 – 60%
	20 – 40%
	Under 20%
	No data

Countries that are the most and least urbanized (%)

Most urbanized		Least urbanized	
Singapore	100	Bhutan	8.2
Belgium	97.2	Burundi	9.6
Kuwait	96.2	Uganda	12.2
Iceland	92.7	Papua N. G.	13.2
Uruguay	92.4	Nepal	14.6

(UK = 89.0%)

Projection: *Eckert IV*

CHILD MORTALITY

Deaths of children under 1 year
old per 1,000 live births (2004)

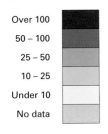

Over 100

50 – 100

25 – 50

10 – 25

Under 10

No data

Countries with the highest and
lowest child mortality

Highest		Lowest	
Angola	193	Singapore	2
Afghanistan	166	Sweden	3
Sierra Leone	145	Japan	3
Mozambique	137	Iceland	3
Liberia	131	Finland	4

(UK = 5 deaths)

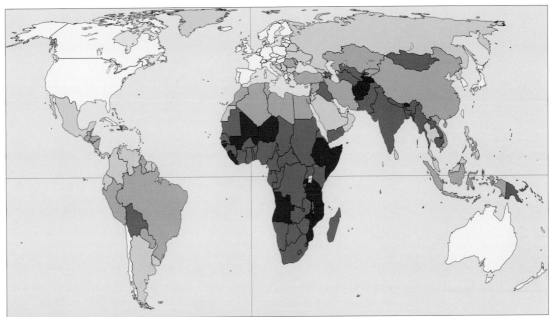

LIFE EXPECTANCY

Life expectancy at birth in years
(2004)

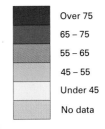

Over 75

65 – 75

55 – 65

45 – 55

Under 45

No data

Countries with the longest and shortest
life expectancy at birth in years

Longest		Shortest	
Andorra	83.5	Botswana	30.8
San Marino	81.5	Zambia	35.2
Singapore	81.5	Angola	36.8
Japan	81.0	Lesotho	36.8
Switzerland	80.3	Mozambique	37.1

(UK = 78.3 years)

FAMILY SIZE

Children born per woman (2004)

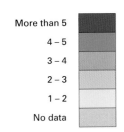

More than 5

4 – 5

3 – 4

2 – 3

1 – 2

No data

Countries with the largest and
smallest family size

Largest		Smallest	
Somalia	6.9	Singapore	1.0
Niger	6.8	Lithuania	1.2
Afghanistan	6.8	Czech Rep.	1.2
Yemen	6.8	Slovenia	1.2
Uganda	6.6	Latvia	1.3

(UK = 1.7 children)

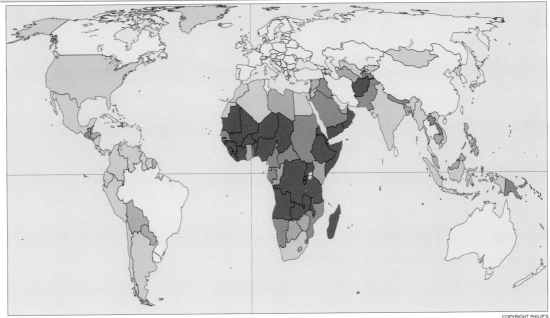

Projection: *Eckert IV*

COPYRIGHT PHILIP'S

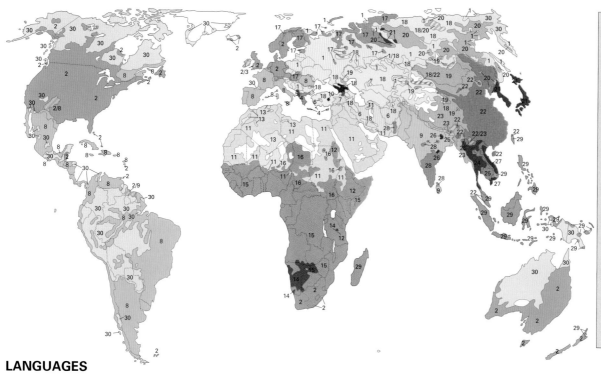

Language can be classified by ancestry and structure. For example, the Romance and Germanic groups are both derived from an Indo-European language believed to have been spoken 5,000 years ago.

First-Language Speakers, in millions (2000)
Mandarin Chinese 874, Hindi 366, English 341, Spanish 336, Bengali 207, Portuguese 176, Russian 167, Japanese 125, German 100, Korean 78, Wu Chinese 77, French 77, Javanese 75, Yue Chinese 71, Telugu 69, Vietnamese 68, Marathi 68, Tamil 66, Italian 62.

Official Languages (% of total world population)
English 27%, Chinese 19%, Hindi 13.5%, Spanish 5.4%, Russian 5.2%, French 4.2%, Arabic 3.3%, Portuguese 3%, Malay 3%, Bengali 2.9%, Japanese 2.3%.

LANGUAGES

INDO-EUROPEAN FAMILY
1 Balto-Slavic group (incl. Russian, Ukrainian)
2 Germanic group (incl. English, German)
3 Celtic group
4 Greek
5 Albanian
6 Iranian group
7 Armenian
8 Romance group (incl. Spanish, Portuguese, French, Italian)
9 Indo-Aryan group (incl. Hindi, Bengali, Urdu, Punjabi, Marathi)

CAUCASIAN FAMILY

AFRO-ASIATIC FAMILY
11 Semitic group (incl. Arabic)
12 Kushitic group
13 Berber group

14 KHOISAN FAMILY

15 NIGER-CONGO FAMILY

16 NILO-SAHARAN FAMILY

17 URALIC FAMILY

ALTAIC FAMILY
18 Turkic group (incl. Turkish)
19 Mongolian group
20 Tungus-Manchu group
21 Japanese and Korean

SINO-TIBETAN FAMILY
22 Sinitic (Chinese) languages (incl. Mandarin, Wu, Yue)
23 Tibetic-Burmic languages

24 TAI FAMILY

AUSTRO-ASIATIC FAMILY
25 Mon-Khmer group
26 Munda group
27 Vietnamese

28 DRAVIDIAN FAMILY (incl. Telugu, Tamil)

29 AUSTRONESIAN FAMILY (incl. Malay-Indonesian, Javanese)

30 OTHER LANGUAGES

RELIGIONS

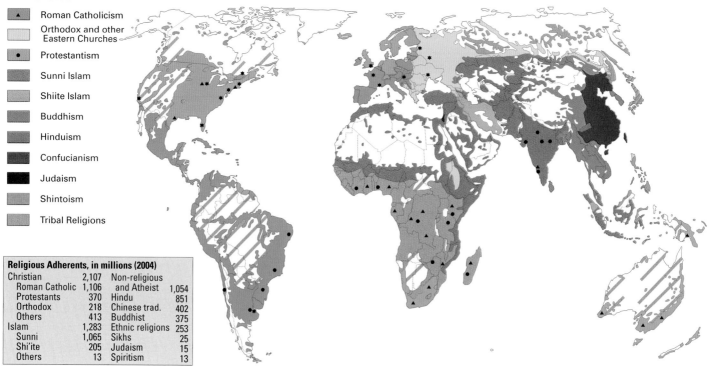

- ▲ Roman Catholicism
- Orthodox and other Eastern Churches
- • Protestantism
- Sunni Islam
- Shiite Islam
- Buddhism
- Hinduism
- Confucianism
- Judaism
- Shintoism
- Tribal Religions

Religious Adherents, in millions (2004)			
Christian	2,107	Non-religious	
Roman Catholic	1,106	and Atheist	1,054
Protestants	370	Hindu	851
Orthodox	218	Chinese trad.	402
Others	413	Buddhist	375
Islam	1,283	Ethnic religions	253
Sunni	1,065	Sikhs	25
Shi'ite	205	Judaism	15
Others	13	Spiritism	13

UNITED NATIONS

Created in 1945 to promote peace and co-operation and based in New York, the United Nations is the world's largest international organization, with an annual budget of US$1.3 billion (2002). Each member of the General Assembly has one vote, while the five permanent members of the 15-nation Security Council – China, France, Russia, UK and USA – hold a veto. The Secretariat is the UN's principal administrative arm. The 54 members of the Economic and Social Council are responsible for economic, social, cultural, educational, health and related matters. The UN has 16 specialized agencies – based in Canada, France, Switzerland and Italy, as well as the USA – which help members in fields such as education (UNESCO), agriculture (FAO), medicine (WHO) and finance (IFC). By the end of 1994, all the original 11 trust territories of the Trusteeship Council had become independent.

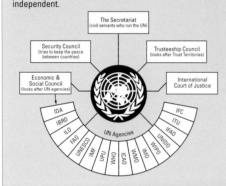

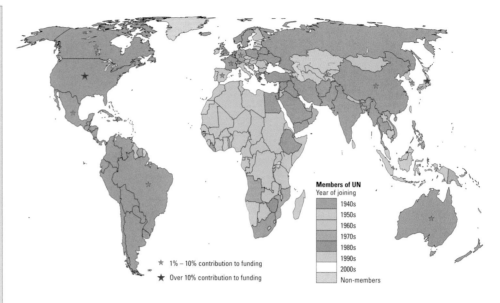

Members of UN
Year of joining

1940s
1950s
1960s
1970s
1980s
1990s
2000s
Non-members

★ 1% – 10% contribution to funding
★ Over 10% contribution to funding

MEMBERSHIP OF THE UN In 1945 there were 51 members; by the end of 2006 membership had increased to 192 following the admission of East Timor, Switzerland and Montenegro. There are 2 independent states which are not members of the UN – Taiwan and the Vatican City. All the successor states of the former USSR had joined by the end of 1992. The official languages of the UN are Chinese, English, French, Russian, Spanish and Arabic.

FUNDING The UN regular budget for 2005 was US$1.8 billion. Contributions are assessed by the members' ability to pay, with the maximum 22% of the total (USA's share), the minimum 0.01%. The European Union pays over 37% of the budget.

PEACEKEEPING The UN has been involved in 54 peace-keeping operations worldwide since 1948.

INTERNATIONAL ORGANIZATIONS

ACP African-Caribbean-Pacific (formed in 1963). Members have economic ties with the EU.
APEC Asia-Pacific Economic Co-operation (formed in 1989). It aims to enhance economic growth and prosperity for the region and to strengthen the Asia-Pacific community. APEC is the only intergovernmental grouping in the world operating on the basis of non-binding commitments, open dialogue, and equal respect for the views of all participants. There are 21 member economies.
ARAB LEAGUE (formed in 1945). The League's aim is to promote economic, social, political and military co-operation. There are 22 member nations.
ASEAN Association of South-east Asian Nations (formed in 1967). Cambodia joined in 1999.
AU The African Union replaced the Organization of African Unity (formed in 1963) in 2002. Its 53 members represent over 94% of Africa's population. Arabic, French, Portuguese and English are recognized as working languages.
COLOMBO PLAN (formed in 1951). Its 25 members aim to promote economic and social development in Asia and the Pacific.
COMMONWEALTH The Commonwealth of Nations evolved from the British Empire. Pakistan was suspended in 1999, and Zimbabwe in 2002. In response to its continued suspension, Zimbabwe left the Commonwealth in December 2003. It now comprises 16 Queen's realms, 31 republics and 6 indigenous monarchies, giving a total of 53 member states.
EU European Union (evolved from the European Community in 1993). Cyprus, the Czech Republic, Estonia, Hungary, Latvia, Lithuania, Malta, Poland, the Slovak Republic and Slovenia joined the EU in May 2004. Bulgaria and Romania joined in January 2007. The other 15 members of the EU are Austria, Belgium, Denmark, Finland, France, Germany, Greece, Ireland, Italy, Luxembourg, Netherlands, Portugal, Spain, Sweden and the UK – together they aim to integrate economies, co-ordinate social developments and bring about political union.
LAIA Latin American Integration Association (1980). Its aim is to promote freer regional trade.
NATO North Atlantic Treaty Organization (formed in 1949). It continues after 1991 despite the winding up of the Warsaw Pact. Bulgaria, Estonia, Latvia, Lithuania, Romania, the Slovak Republic and Slovenia became members in 2004.
OAS Organization of American States (formed in 1948). It aims to promote social and economic co-operation between developed countries of North America and developing nations of Latin America.

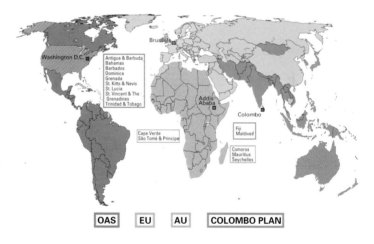

OAS   EU   AU   COLOMBO PLAN

OECD Organization for Economic Co-operation and Development (formed in 1961). It comprises 30 major free-market economies. Poland, Hungary and South Korea joined in 1996, and the Slovak Republic in 2000. 'G8' is its 'inner group' of leading industrial nations, comprising Canada, France, Germany, Italy, Japan, Russia, UK and USA.
OPEC Organization of Petroleum Exporting Countries (formed in 1960). It controls about three-quarters of the world's oil supply. Gabon left the organization in 1996.

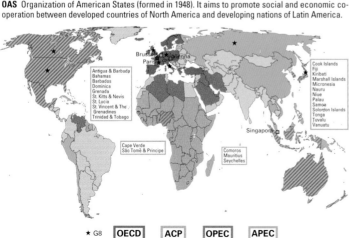

★ G8   OECD   ACP   OPEC   APEC

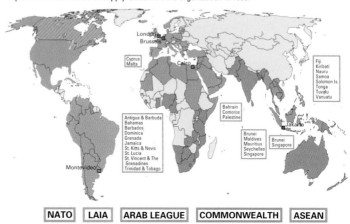

NATO   LAIA   ARAB LEAGUE   COMMONWEALTH   ASEAN

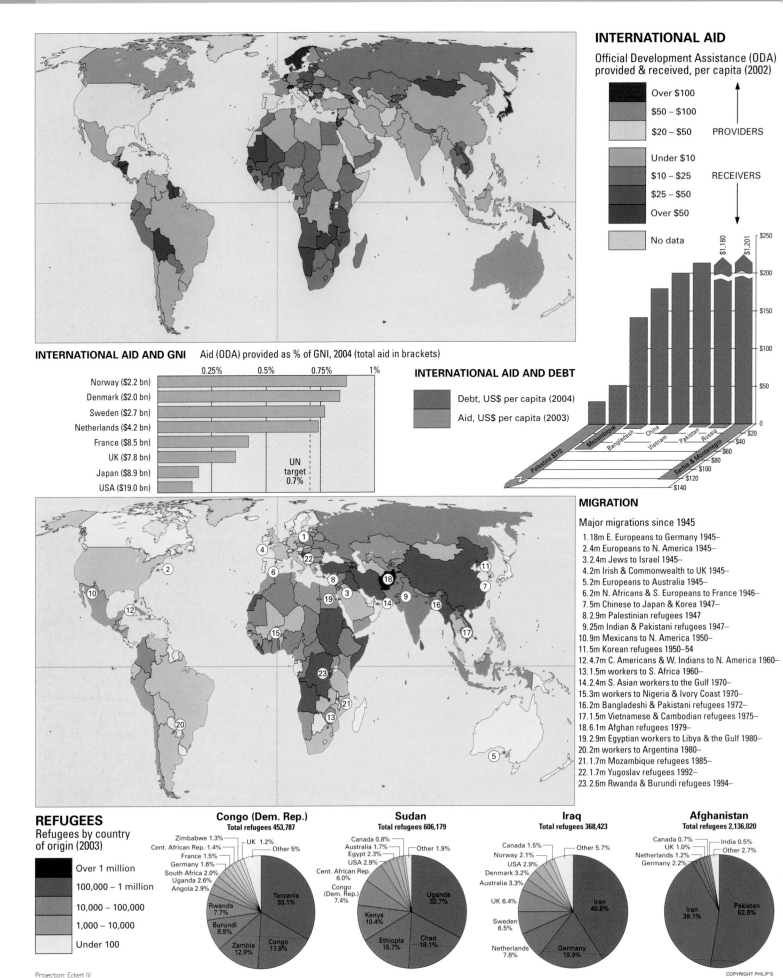

INTERNATIONAL AID

Official Development Assistance (ODA)
provided & received, per capita (2002)

Over $100	
$50 – $100	PROVIDERS
$20 – $50	
Under $10	
$10 – $25	RECEIVERS
$25 – $50	
Over $50	
No data	

INTERNATIONAL AID AND GNI
Aid (ODA) provided as % of GNI, 2004 (total aid in brackets)

Norway ($2.2 bn)
Denmark ($2.0 bn)
Sweden ($2.7 bn)
Netherlands ($4.2 bn)
France ($8.5 bn)
UK ($7.8 bn)
Japan ($8.9 bn)
USA ($19.0 bn)

0.25%   0.5%   0.75%   1%

UN target 0.7%

INTERNATIONAL AID AND DEBT

Debt, US$ per capita (2004)
Aid, US$ per capita (2003)

Palestine $270, Mozambique, Bangladesh, China, Vietnam, Pakistan, Russia, Serbia & Montenegro

$1,180 $1,201

MIGRATION

Major migrations since 1945

1. 18m E. Europeans to Germany 1945–
2. 4m Europeans to N. America 1945–
3. 2.4m Jews to Israel 1945–
4. 2m Irish & Commonwealth to UK 1945–
5. 2m Europeans to Australia 1945–
6. 2m N. Africans & S. Europeans to France 1946–
7. 5m Chinese to Japan & Korea 1947–
8. 2.9m Palestinian refugees 1947
9. 25m Indian & Pakistani refugees 1947–
10. 9m Mexicans to N. America 1950–
11. 5m Korean refugees 1950–54
12. 4.7m C. Americans & W. Indians to N. America 1960–
13. 1.5m workers to S. Africa 1960–
14. 2.4m S. Asian workers to the Gulf 1970–
15. 3m workers to Nigeria & Ivory Coast 1970–
16. 2m Bangladeshi & Pakistani refugees 1972–
17. 1.5m Vietnamese & Cambodian refugees 1975–
18. 6.1m Afghan refugees 1979–
19. 2.9m Egyptian workers to Libya & the Gulf 1980–
20. 2m workers to Argentina 1980–
21. 1.7m Mozambique refugees 1985–
22. 1.7m Yugoslav refugees 1992–
23. 2.6m Rwanda & Burundi refugees 1994–

REFUGEES
Refugees by country
of origin (2003)

Over 1 million	
100,000 – 1 million	
10,000 – 100,000	
1,000 – 10,000	
Under 100	

Congo (Dem. Rep.)
Total refugees 453,787

Zimbabwe 1.3%
Cent. African Rep. 1.4%
France 1.5%
Germany 1.6%
South Africa 2.0%
Uganda 2.6%
Angola 2.9%
Rwanda 7.7%
Burundi 8.9%
Zambia 12.9%
Congo 17.9%
Tanzania 33.1%
UK 1.2%
Other 5%

Sudan
Total refugees 606,179

Canada 0.8%
Australia 1.7%
Egypt 2.3%
USA 2.9%
Cent. African Rep. 6.0%
Congo (Dem. Rep.) 7.4%
Kenya 10.4%
Ethiopia 15.7%
Chad 18.1%
Uganda 32.7%
Other 1.9%

Iraq
Total refugees 368,423

Canada 1.5%
Norway 2.1%
USA 2.9%
Denmark 3.2%
Australia 3.3%
UK 6.4%
Sweden 6.5%
Netherlands 7.8%
Germany 19.9%
Iran 40.8%
Other 5.7%

Afghanistan
Total refugees 2,136,020

Canada 0.7%
UK 1.0%
Netherlands 1.2%
Germany 2.2%
India 0.5%
Other 2.7%
Iran 39.1%
Pakistan 52.6%

Projection: *Eckert IV*

CONFLICTS

Armed conflict since 1994

Countries in the top half of the Human Developement Index (HDI)

Countries in the bottom half of the HDI

No data

Countries with at least one armed conflict between 1994 and mid-2005

MAJOR WARS SINCE 1900	
War	Total deaths
Second World War (1939–45)	55,000,000
First World War (1914–18)	8,500,000
Korean War (1950–53)	4,000,000
Congolese Civil War (1998–)	3,800,000
Vietnam War (1965–73)	3,000,000
Sudanese Civil War (1983–2000)	2,000,000

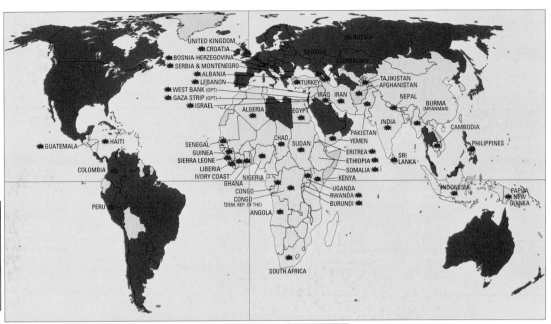

HIV/AIDS

Percentage of adults (15 – 49 years) living with HIV/AIDS (2003)

15 – 40%

5 – 15%

0.5 – 5%

0.1 – 0.5%

Under 0.1%

No data

Total number of adults and children living with HIV/AIDS by region (2004)

Human Immunodeficiency Virus (HIV) is passed from one person to another and attacks the body's defence against illness. It develops into the Acquired Immunodeficiency Syndrome (AIDS) when a particularly severe illness, such as cancer, takes hold. The pandemic started just over 20 years ago and, by 2005, 40.3 millon people were living with HIV or AIDS.

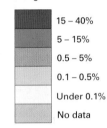

DRUGS

Countries producing illegal drugs

Cannabis

Poppy

Coca leaves

Cocaine

Amphetamines

Major routes of drug trafficking

Opium

Coca leaves

Cocaine

Heroin

Hashish and marijuana

Amphetamines (usually used within producing countries)

Conflicts relating to drug trafficking

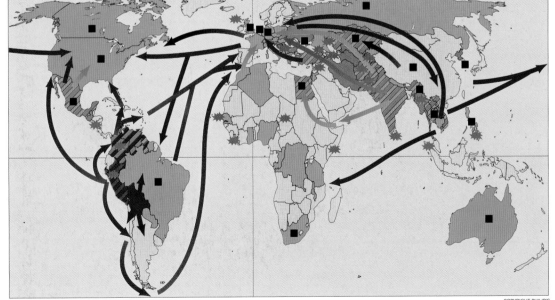

Projection: Eckert IV

COPYRIGHT PHILIP'S

COUNTRY	POPULATION							LAND & AGRICULTURE				TRADE, TOURISM & ENERGY					
	Total population (millions)	Population density (persons per km²)	Life expectancy (years)	Average annual population change (%)	Birth rate (births per thousand people)	Death rate (deaths per thousand people)	Urban population (% of total)	Land area (thousand km²)	Arable & permanent crops (% of land area)	Permanent pasture (% of land area)	Forest (% of land area)	Imports (US$ per capita)	Exports (US$ per capita)	Tourism receipts (US$ per capita)	Energy produced (tonnes of oil equiv. per capita)	Energy consumed (tonnes of oil equiv. per capita)	CO₂ emissions per capita (metric tonnes)
	2005	2005	2005	2005	2005	2005	2005		2002	2002	2000	2004	2004	2003	2002	2002	2003
Afghanistan	29.9	46	43	4.8	47	21	24	652	12	46	2	126	15	–	0.01	0.02	0.03
Albania	3.6	124	77	0.5	15	5	45	29	26	19	36	577	153	145	0.39	0.69	1.16
Algeria	32.5	14	73	1.2	17	5	60	2,382	3	13	1	469	990	5	4.91	1.00	2.65
Angola	11.8	9	37	–0.1	45	26	37	1,247	3	43	56	415	1,081	6	4.41	0.29	1.17
Argentina	39.5	14	76	1.0	17	8	91	2,780	13	52	13	558	855	53	2.23	1.58	3.37
Armenia	3.0	100	72	–0.3	12	8	64	30	20	30	12	433	283	24	0.35	1.34	2.94
Australia	20.1	3	80	0.9	12	7	93	7,741	6	52	21	4,881	4,323	513	13.32	7.03	19.1
Austria	8.2	98	79	0.1	9	10	66	84	18	23	47	12,341	12,524	1,716	1.57	4.25	8.92
Azerbaijan	7.9	91	63	0.6	20	10	50	87	23	31	13	458	401	7.3	2.78	1.92	4.36
Bahamas	0.3	21	66	0.7	18	9	90	14	1	0.2	84	5,433	2,120	2,840	0	3.88	11.26
Bahrain	0.7	700	74	1.5	18	4	90	0.7	9	6	0	8,386	11,721	–	15.29	14.88	30.89
Bangladesh	144.3	1,002	62	2.1	30	8	25	144	65	5	10	70	52	0.4	0.07	0.10	0.24
Barbados	0.3	696	72	0.3	13	9	53	0.4	40	5	5	3,463	687	2,527	0.27	1.88	5.86
Belarus	10.3	50	69	–0.1	11	14	72	208	28	15	45	1,317	1,114	26	0.21	2.80	7.44
Belgium	10.4	335	79	0.2	10	10	97	31	25	21	22	22,596	24,587	782	1.20	6.63	13.66
Belize	0.3	13	67	2.3	29	6	49	23	4	2	59	1,933	1,338	520	0.07	1.14	3.08
Benin	7.6	67	51	2.8	42	14	46	113	25	5	24	123	95	11	0.01	0.09	0.25
Bhutan	2.2	47	54	2.1	34	13	9	47	4	9	64	89	70	3.6	0.24	0.21	0.15
Bolivia	8.9	8	66	1.5	24	8	64	1,099	3	31	49	179	223	13	0.92	0.44	1.23
Bosnia-Herzegovina	4.4	86	73	0.4	12	8	45	51	21	20	45	1,182	386	53	1.37	1.64	3.51
Botswana	1.6	3	34	0.0	23	29	52	582	1	45	22	1,409	1,838	223	0.38	0.81	2.13
Brazil	186.1	22	72	1.1	17	6	84	8,514	8	23	63	328	510	13	0.91	1.17	1.97
Brunei	0.4	67	75	1.9	19	3	78	6	3	1	84	13,000	19,250	–	52.12	5.75	14.97
Bulgaria	7.5	68	72	–0.9	10	14	71	111	32	16	33	1,631	1,218	221	1.42	2.84	6.5
Burkina Faso	13.5	49	44	2.5	44	19	19	274	16	22	26	64	31	1.5	0	0.03	0.09
Burma (Myanmar)	47.0	69	56	0.4	18	12	31	677	16	1	52	37	45	1.2	0.21	0.10	0.2
Burundi	7.8	279	43	2.2	40	17	11	28	52	38	4	18	4,082	0.1	0.01	0.03	0.06
Cambodia	13.6	75	59	1.8	27	9	20	181	22	8	53	230	170	29	0	0.02	0.04
Cameroon	17.0	36	48	1.9	35	15	53	475	15	4	51	116	144	2.1	0.29	0.13	0.39
Canada	32.8	3	80	0.9	11	7	81	9,971	5	3	27	7,808	9,622	323	14.00	10.05	19.05
Cape Verde Is.	0.4	100	71	0.7	25	7	58	4	1	1	21	968	153	213	0	0.15	0.33
Central African Rep.	4.2	7	41	1.5	35	20	44	623	3	5	37	32	41	0.7	0.01	0.04	0.09
Chad	9.7	8	48	3.0	46	16	26	1,284	3	36	10	52	38	2.6	0	0.01	0.02
Chile	16.0	21	77	1.0	16	6	88	757	3	17	21	1,408	1,825	54	0.49	1.67	3.4
China	1,306.3	136	72	0.6	13	7	41	9,597	17	43	18	423	446	13	0.81	0.83	2.72
Colombia	43.0	38	72	1.5	21	6	77	1,139	4	40	48	357	360	19	1.79	0.72	1.18
Comoros	0.7	350	62	2.9	38	8	36	2	66	8	4	126	40	30	0	0.05	0.13
Congo	3.0	9	49	1.3	28	15	54	342	1	29	65	12	37	0.3	4.41	0.14	0.82
Congo (Dem. Rep.)	60.1	25	49	3.0	44	14	33	2,345	3	7	60	259	394	1.9	0.05	0.04	0.03
Costa Rica	4.0	78	77	1.5	19	4	62	51	10	46	39	1,961	1,546	323	0.48	0.96	1.3
Croatia	4.5	79	74	0.0	10	11	60	57	28	28	32	3,711	1,743	1,417	1.01	2.09	5.01
Cuba	11.3	103	77	0.3	12	7	76	111	34	26	21	469	186	163	0.30	1.05	3.05
Cyprus	0.8	89	78	0.5	13	8	70	9	13	0.4	13	7,091	1,429	2,519	0	3.59	10.26
Czech Republic	10.2	129	76	–0.1	9	11	75	79	43	13	34	6,685	6,521	349	2.65	3.87	10.94
Denmark	5.4	126	78	0.3	11	11	86	43	54	9	11	11,750	13,530	975	5.44	3.85	10.94
Djibouti	0.5	22	43	2.1	40	19	85	23	0	57	0	1,330	310	8	0	1.27	2.8
Dominican Republic	9.0	184	67	1.3	23	7	60	49	33	44	28	899	605	346	0.02	0.75	2.21
East Timor	1.0	67	66	2.1	27	6	8	15	–	–	–	167	8	–	–	–	–
Ecuador	13.4	47	76	1.2	23	4	63	284	11	18	38	571	564	30	1.80	0.69	1.82
Egypt	77.5	77	71	1.8	23	5	42	1,001	3	0.0	0	248	142	59	0.89	0.77	1.88
El Salvador	6.7	319	71	1.8	27	6	60	21	43	38	6	891	485	34	0.14	0.45	0.9
Equatorial Guinea	0.5	18	56	2.4	36	12	50	28	8	4	62	2,334	5,542	28	23.55	2.51	8.02
Eritrea	4.7	39	52	2.5	39	14	21	118	4	58	16	132	1,371	16	0	0.05	0.16
Estonia	1.3	29	72	–0.7	10	13	70	45	15	2	49	5,629	4,385	519	0	3.33	13.89
Ethiopia	73.1	65	49	2.4	39	15	16	1,104	10	18	5	29	8	1	0.01	0.26	0.06
Fiji	0.9	50	70	1.4	23	6	53	18	16	10	45	928	677	388	0.17	0.53	1.71
Finland	5.2	15	78	0.2	11	10	61	338	7	0	72	8,687	11,738	364	2.04	5.91	10.41
France	60.7	111	77	0.4	12	9	77	552	36	18	28	6,914	6,903	610	2.12	4.55	6.8
Gabon	1.4	5	56	2.5	36	12	85	268	2	18	85	875	2,650	12	9.86	0.68	3.56
Gambia, The	1.6	145	55	2.9	40	12	26	11	26	46	48	113	72	18	0	0.07	0.2
Gaza Strip (OPT)*	1.4	4,667	72	3.8	40	4	–	0.4	–	–	–	1,357	146	2.9	–	–	–
Georgia	4.7	67	76	–0.4	10	9	52	70	15	28	43	384	193	31	0.32	1.01	0.73
Germany	82.4	231	79	0.0	8	11	89	357	34	14	31	8,698	10,841	279	1.60	4.33	10.21
Ghana	21.9	92	56	1.3	24	11	46	239	28	37	28	169	137	19	0.10	0.17	0.26
Greece	10.7	81	79	0.2	10	10	61	132	30	36	28	5,073	1,449	1,000	0.96	3.25	9.5

WEALTH						SOCIAL INDICATORS										COUNTRY
GNI (million US$) 2004	GNI per capita (PPP US$) 2004	Average annual growth in GDP per capita (%) 1990–2002	Agriculture (% of GDP) 2004	Industry (% of GDP) 2004	Services (% of GDP) 2004	Human Develop. Index (HDI) value 2002	Food intake (calories per capita per day) 2003	Population per doctor 2003	Adults living with HIV/AIDS (% 15–49 year olds) 2003	Gender Develop. Index (GDI) value 2002	Illiteracy rate (% adults) 2003	Motor vehicles per thousand people 2002	Internet usage per thousand people 2003	Aid donated (–)/received (US$ per capita) 2002	Military spending (% of GDP) 2004	
5,543	–	–	60	20	20	–	1,539.0	–	0.1	–	64	0.6	1	63	2.6	Afghanistan
6,641	5,070	6.0	46.2	25.4	28.4	0.781	2,847.8	730	0.1	0.778	13	70.5	10	90	1.5	Albania
73,676	6,260	0.3	10.3	57.4	32.3	0.704	3,021.5	1,176	0.1	0.688	30	88.2	16	6	3.2	Algeria
14,441	2,030	–0.1	8	67	25	0.381	2,082.7	20,000	3.9	–	58	18.4	3	35	10.6	Angola
142,338	12,460	1.7	10.6	35.9	53.5	0.853	2,992.1	329	0.7	0.841	3	197.7	112	256	1.3	Argentina
3,424	4,270	1.7	22.9	36.1	41.1	0.754	2,267.7	348	0.1	0.752	1	–	37	57	6.5	Armenia
541,173	29,200	2.6	3.4	28.2	68.4	0.946	3,053.6	405	0.1	0.945	0	623.8	567	–45	2.7	Australia
262,147	31,790	1.9	2.3	30.8	66.9	0.934	3,673.3	310	0.3	0.924	2	586	462	–63	0.9	Austria
7,828	3,830	0.2	14.1	45.7	40.2	0.746	2,574.8	279	0.1	–	3	57.9	37	18	2.6	Azerbaijan
4,684	16,140	0.1	3	7	90	0.815	2,754.9	613	3.0	0.825	4	342	192	33	–	Bahamas
8,834	18,070	1.5	0.7	41	58.4	0.843	–	592	0.3	0.832	11	325.3	246	214	6.3	Bahrain
61,230	1,980	3.1	21.2	27.1	51.7	0.509	2,205.0	4,348	0.1	0.499	57	1.5	2	11	1.8	Bangladesh
2,507	15,060	1.6	6	16	78	0.888	3,091.1	730	1.5	–	3	268.2	112	30	–	Barbados
20,856	6,900	0.2	11	36.4	52.6	0.790	3,000.3	222	0.3	0.789	1	155.8	141	19	1.4	Belarus
322,837	31,360	1.8	1.3	25.7	73	0.942	3,583.8	239	0.2	0.938	2	523.1	386	–104	1.3	Belgium
1,115	6,510	1.7	17.7	15	67.3	0.737	2,868.6	980	2.4	0.718	6	161	109	230	2.0	Belize
3,667	1,120	2.1	36.3	14.3	49.4	0.421	2,547.9	10,000	1.9	0.406	59	2.3	10	47	2.4	Benin
677	660	3.6	45	10	45	0.536	–	20,000	0.1	–	58	–	15	33	1.8	Bhutan
8,656	2,590	1.1	13	28	59	0.681	2,235.2	1,316	0.1	0.674	13	55.6	32	68	1.6	Bolivia
7,841	7,430	18.0	14.2	30.8	55	0.781	2,893.6	690	0.1	–	–	–	26	163	4.5	Bosnia-Herzegovina
7,490	8,920	2.5	4	44	52	0.589	2,151.4	3,448	37.3	0.581	20	73.7	35	46	3.9	Botswana
552,096	8,020	1.3	10.1	38.6	51.3	0.775	3,049.5	485	0.7	0.768	14	111.9	82	163	1.8	Brazil
–	–	–0.5	5	45	50	0.867	2,855.3	1,010	0.1	0.768	8	629.7	102	11	5.1	Brunei
21,326	7,870	–2.1	11.5	30.1	58.4	0.796	2,847.9	291	0.1	0.795	1	313.5	206	40	2.6	Bulgaria
4,436	1,220	1.6	39.5	19.3	41.3	0.302	2,461.9	25,000	4.2	0.291	73	4	4	36	1.3	Burkina Faso
–	–	5.7	56.6	8.8	34.5	0.551	2,937.1	3,333	1.2	–	17	5.7	1	3	2.1	Burma (Myanmar)
669	660	–3.9	48.1	19	32.9	0.339	1,648.6	100,000	6.0	0.337	48	2.5	2	15	6.0	Burundi
4,430	2,180	4.1	35	30	35	0.568	2,045.8	6,250	2.6	0.557	30	0.9	2	41	3.0	Cambodia
13,138	2,090	–0.1	43.7	20.1	36.2	0.501	2,273.2	14,286	6.9	0.491	21	11	4	78	1.6	Cameroon
905,629	30,660	2.2	2.3	26.4	71.3	0.943	3,589.3	535	0.3	0.941	3	581.6	513	–4	1.1	Canada
852	5,650	3.4	12.1	21.9	66	0.717	3,243.2	5,882	0.1	0.709	23	39.8	36	340	1.5	Cape Verde Is.
1,226	1,110	–0.2	55	20	25	0.361	1,980.4	25,000	13.5	0.345	49	3.1	1	20	1.0	Central African Rep.
2,277	1,420	–0.5	22.6	35.6	41.7	0.379	2,113.5	33,333	4.8	0.368	52	0.9	2	25	2.1	Chad
78,407	10,500	4.4	6.3	38.2	55.5	0.839	2,863.2	870	0.3	0.830	4	135	272	3	3.8	Chile
1,676,846	5,530	8.6	13.8	52.9	33.3	0.745	2,951.0	610	0.1	0.741	14	10.2	63	2	4.3	China
90,626	6,820	0.4	13.4	32.1	54.5	0.773	2,584.6	1,064	0.7	0.770	7	28.4	53	7	3.4	Colombia
328	1,840	–1.4	40	4	56	0.530	1,753.9	14,286	0.1	0.510	43	–	4	14	3.0	Comoros
2,974	750	–1.6	7.4	52	40.6	0.494	2,161.7	4,000	4.9	0.488	16	14.9	4	53	2.8	Congo
6,416	680	–8.1	55	11	34	0.365	1,599.1	14,286	4.2	0.355	34	–	1	3	1.5	Congo (Dem. Rep.)
18,969	9,530	2.7	8.5	29.7	61.8	0.834	2,875.5	625	0.6	0.823	4	136.6	193	3	0.4	Costa Rica
29,700	11,670	2.1	8.2	30.1	61.7	0.830	2,779.0	420	0.1	0.827	1	312.6	232	15	2.4	Croatia
–	–	3.5	6.6	25.5	67.9	0.809	3,151.8	168	0.1	–	3	0.9	11	6	1.8	Cuba
13,633	22,330	3.2	7.35	20.2	72.45	0.883	3,254.6	372	0.1	0.875	2	516.2	294	62	3.8	Cyprus
93,155	18,400	1.4	3.4	39.3	57.3	0.868	3,171.3	292	0.1	0.865	0	394.8	308	11	2.0	Czech Republic
219,422	31,550	2.1	2.2	25.5	72.3	0.932	3,439.3	273	0.2	0.931	0	430.6	513	–302	1.5	Denmark
739	2,270	–3.8	3.5	15.8	80.7	0.454	2,219.7	7,692	2.9	–	32	2.7	7	72	4.4	Djibouti
18,443	6,750	4.2	18	24	58	0.738	2,347.1	526	1.7	0.728	15	99.7	64	27	1.1	Dominican Republic
506	430	–	25.4	17.2	57.4	–	2,805.8	–	–	–	52	–	–	2200	–	East Timor
28,783	3,690	0.0	8.7	30.5	60.9	0.735	2,754.0	690	0.3	0.721	7	47.1	46	9	2.2	Ecuador
90,129	4,120	2.5	17.2	33	49.8	0.653	3,338.0	459	0.1	0.634	42	35.4	39	16	3.4	Egypt
15,613	4,980	2.3	9.2	31.1	59.7	0.720	2,583.8	794	0.7	0.709	20	63.5	84	38	1.1	El Salvador
437	7,400	20.8	3	95.7	1.3	0.703	–	4,000	3.4	0.691	14	–	4	68	2.5	Equatorial Guinea
806	1,050	1.5	12.4	25.9	61.7	0.439	1,512.8	20,000	2.7	0.431	41	–	7	18	13.4	Eritrea
9,435	13,190	2.3	4.1	28.9	67	0.853	3,002.2	319	1.0	0.852	1	359.4	444	83	2.0	Estonia
7,747	810	2.3	47	12.4	40.6	0.359	1,857.3	33,333	4.4	0.346	27	1.7	1	5	4.6	Ethiopia
2,281	5,770	1.8	16.6	22.4	61	0.758	2,893.6	2,941	0.1	0.747	7	126.1	61	45	2.2	Fiji
171,024	29,560	2.5	3.3	30.2	66.5	0.935	3,100.4	322	0.1	0.933	0	485.7	534	–73	2.0	Finland
1,858,731	29,320	1.6	2.7	24.3	73	0.932	3,653.9	303	0.4	0.929	1	590.4	366	–89	2.6	France
5,415	5,600	–0.2	7.4	46.7	45.9	0.648	2,636.8	–	8.1	–	37	16.4	26	236	2.0	Gabon
414	1,900	0.0	26.8	14.5	58.7	0.452	2,272.7	25,000	1.2	0.446	60	4	19	30	0.3	Gambia, The
3,771	1,110	–4.9	9	28	63	–	2,179.8	–	–	–	–	–	40	615	–	Gaza Strip (OPT)*
4,683	2,930	–3.9	20.5	22.6	56.9	0.739	2,354.3	216	0.1	–	1	62.1	31	32	0.6	Georgia
2,488,974	27,950	1.3	1	31	68	0.925	3,495.6	275	0.1	0.921	1	580.5	473	–68	1.5	Germany
8,090	2,280	1.8	34.3	24.2	41.4	0.568	2,667.2	11,111	3.1	0.564	25	10.5	8	332	0.6	Ghana
183,917	22,000	2.2	7	22	71	0.902	3,721.1	228	0.2	0.894	2	414.4	150	509	4.3	Greece

COUNTRY	POPULATION							LAND & AGRICULTURE				TRADE, TOURISM & ENERGY					
	Total population (millions)	Population density (persons per km²)	Life expectancy (years)	Average annual population change (%)	Birth rate (births per thousand people)	Death rate (deaths per thousand people)	Urban population (% of total)	Land area (thousand km²)	Arable & permanent crops (% of land area)	Permanent pasture (% of land area)	Forest (% of land area)	Imports (US$ per capita)	Exports (US$ per capita)	Tourism receipts (US$ per capita)	Energy produced (tonnes of oil equiv. per capita)	Energy consumed (tonnes of oil equiv. per capita)	CO₂ emissions per capita (metric tonnes)
	2005	2005	2005	2005	2005	2005	2005		2002	2002	2000	2004	2004	2003	2002	2002	2003
Guatemala	12.0	110	65	2.6	34	7	47	109	18	24	26	648	243	52	0.12	0.30	0.84
Guinea	9.5	39	50	2.4	42	15	37	246	6	43	28	68	75	0	0.01	0.06	0.16
Guinea-Bissau	1.4	39	47	2.0	38	17	36	36	20	39	78	74	39	1.4	0	0.09	0.25
Guyana	0.8	4	66	0.3	19	8	39	215	3	6	86	813	713	49	0	0.83	2.27
Haiti	8.1	289	53	2.3	37	12	39	28	39	18	3	134	42	12	0.01	0.09	0.21
Honduras	7.2	64	66	2.2	31	7	46	112	13	13	48	463	202	47	0.08	0.37	0.87
Hungary	10.0	108	72	−0.3	10	13	66	93	52	12	20	5,868	5,462	344	1.02	2.63	5.91
Iceland	0.3	3	80	0.9	14	7	93	103	0	23	0	11,023	9,673	1,063	8.20	11.59	10.41
India	1,080.3	329	64	1.4	22	8	29	3,287	57	4	22	83	64	3.3	0.24	0.33	0.96
Indonesia	242.0	126	70	1.5	21	6	48	1,905	19	6	58	186	289	17	0.86	0.47	1.45
Iran	68.0	41	70	0.9	17	6	68	1,648	10	27	5	460	570	26	3.79	2.12	5.4
Iraq	26.1	60	69	2.7	33	5	67	438	14	9	2	379	387	–	4.35	1.14	2.71
Ireland	4.0	57	78	1.2	15	8	60	70	16	48	10	15,163	25,950	969	0.27	3.92	10.26
Israel	6.3	300	79	1.2	18	6	92	21	20	7	6	5,848	5,462	324	0	3.20	10.56
Italy	58.1	193	80	0.1	9	10	68	301	38	15	34	5,668	5,790	537	0.54	3.29	8.11
Ivory Coast	17.3	54	49	2.1	36	15	46	322	22	41	–	194	296	4.9	0.16	0.15	0.32
Jamaica	2.7	245	76	0.7	17	5	52	11	26	21	30	1,342	622	502	0.02	1.39	4.25
Japan	127.4	337	81	0.1	9	9	66	378	13	1	64	3,154	4,229	70	0.84	4.31	9.44
Jordan	5.8	63	78	2.3	22	3	79	89	4	8	1	1,310	552	141	0.05	1.00	2.98
Kazakhstan	15.2	6	67	0.3	16	9	56	2,725	8	69	5	860	1,215	37	6.39	3.46	9.72
Kenya	33.8	58	48	2.6	40	15	42	580	9	37	30	124	77	10	0.03	0.12	0.25
Korea, North	22.9	189	71	0.9	16	7	62	121	23	0.4	68	92	52	–	1.14	1.20	3.13
Korea, South	48.6	496	76	0.4	10	6	80	99	19	1	63	4,407	5,156	108	0.64	4.32	9.84
Kuwait	2.3	128	77	3.4	22	3	96	18	1	8	0	4,835	11,922	51	49.91	10.35	23.17
Kyrgyzstan	5.1	26	68	1.3	22	7	34	200	7	49	5	152	127	9.4	0.59	1.13	0.97
Laos	6.2	26	55	2.4	36	12	22	237	4	4	54	93	59	14	0.14	0.16	0.18
Latvia	2.3	35	71	−0.7	9	13	66	65	30	10	47	2,596	1,552	97	0.34	2.08	3.3
Lebanon	3.8	380	73	1.3	19	6	88	10	31	2	4	2,148	469	267	0.02	1.49	4.33
Lesotho	2.0	67	37	0.1	27	25	18	30	11	67	0	365	242	10	0.04	0.08	0.11
Liberia	2.9	26	48	2.7	44	18	48	111	6	21	36	1,742	372	–	0	0.04	0.15
Libya	5.8	3	77	2.3	27	3	87	1,760	1	8	0	1,246	3,216	14	13.89	2.98	8.96
Lithuania	3.6	55	74	−0.3	9	11	67	65	46	8	31	3,061	2,467	177	1.24	3.12	5.53
Luxembourg	0.5	167	79	1.3	12	8	92	3	–	–	–	32,600	26,800	5,586	0.09	8.48	24.28
Macedonia (FYROM)	2.0	80	74	0.3	12	9	60	26	24	25	36	1,339	815	29	0.82	1.31	4.11
Madagascar	18.0	31	57	3.0	42	11	27	587	6	41	20	64	48	4.2	0.01	0.04	0.13
Malawi	12.7	108	37	2.1	44	23	17	118	26	20	28	41	40	2.6	0.02	0.05	0.07
Malaysia	24.0	73	72	1.8	23	5	65	330	23	1	59	4,138	5,146	246	3.69	2.48	5.81
Mali	11.4	9	45	2.8	47	19	34	1,240	4	25	11	81	80	9.1	0.01	0.03	0.05
Malta	0.4	127	79	0.4	10	8	92	0.3	31	0	0	8,518	6,563	1,740	0	2.31	7.45
Mauritania	3.1	3	53	2.9	42	13	64	1,026	0	38	0	277	175	3.5	0	0.42	1.11
Mauritius	1.2	600	72	0.8	16	7	44	2	53	4	8	1,871	1,677	581	0.02	1.18	3.03
Mexico	106.2	54	75	1.2	21	5	76	1,958	14	42	29	1,797	1,718	89	2.28	1.58	3.91
Micronesia, Fed. States	0.1	100	70	−0.1	25	5	30	0.7	51	16	0	1,490	220	170	–	–	–
Moldova	4.5	132	65	0.2	15	13	46	34	65	12	10	407	229	13	0.02	0.93	2.46
Mongolia	2.8	2	65	1.5	22	7	57	1,567	1	83	7	357	305	51	0.54	0.75	3.19
Morocco	32.7	73	71	1.6	22	6	59	447	21	47	7	478	298	87	0.01	0.36	1.1
Mozambique	19.4	24	40	1.5	36	21	38	802	6	56	39	50	36	5.1	0.12	0.13	0.09
Namibia	2.0	2	44	0.7	25	18	34	824	1	46	10	737	678	167	0.14	0.61	1.15
Nepal	27.7	196	60	2.2	32	9	16	147	23	12	27	51	21	7.2	0.02	0.06	0.11
Netherlands	16.4	390	79	0.5	11	9	67	42	28	29	11	15,409	17,872	564	3.98	6.01	16.07
New Zealand	4.0	15	79	1.0	14	8	86	271	13	52	30	4,943	4,963	994	4.51	5.49	9.91
Nicaragua	5.5	43	70	1.9	25	4	58	130	18	40	27	367	136	28	0.04	0.29	0.73
Niger	12.2	10	42	2.6	48	21	23	1,267	4	9	1	33	23	2.3	0.01	0.04	0.1
Nigeria	128.8	140	47	2.4	41	17	48	924	36	43	15	133	264	2	0.94	0.17	0.75
Norway	4.6	14	79	0.4	12	9	81	324	3	1	29	9,991	16,661	552	57.43	10.83	9.93
Oman	3.0	14	73	3.3	37	4	79	310	0	5	0	2,124	4,380	73	21.41	3.11	8.65
Pakistan	162.4	202	63	2.0	31	8	35	796	29	6	3	86	93	0.7	0.18	0.29	0.68
Panama	3.1	40	72	1.3	20	7	58	76	9	21	39	2,311	1,838	189	0.21	1.72	4.11
Papua New Guinea	5.5	12	65	2.3	30	7	13	463	2	0.2	68	246	443	0.9	0.59	0.21	0.46
Paraguay	6.3	15	75	2.5	30	5	59	407	8	55	59	529	466	10	1.97	1.59	0.61
Peru	27.9	22	70	1.4	21	6	75	1,285	3	21	51	344	441	33	0.37	0.52	1
Philippines	87.9	293	70	1.8	26	5	63	300	36	5	19		0.09	0.37	0.13	0.34	0.9
Poland	38.6	123	74	0.0	11	10	62	323	47	14	31	2,114	1,968	105	1.97	2.17	7.42
Portugal	10.6	115	78	0.4	11	10	56	89	29	16	40	4,915	3,555	654	0.23	2.57	6.18
Qatar	0.9	82	74	2.6	16	5	92	11	2	5	0	6,833	16,667	–	85.75	15.28	45.73

WEALTH						SOCIAL INDICATORS										COUNTRY
GNI (million US$) 2004	GNI per capita (PPP US$) 2004	Average annual growth in GDP per capita (%) 1990–2002	Agriculture (% of GDP) 2004	Industry (% of GDP) 2004	Services (% of GDP) 2004	Human Develop. Index (HDI) value 2002	Food intake (calories per capita per day) 2003	Population per doctor 2003	Adults living with HIV/AIDS (% 15–49 year olds) 2003	Gender Develop. Index (GDI) value 2002	Illiteracy rate (% adults) 2003	Motor vehicles per thousand people 2002	Internet usage per thousand people 2003	Aid donated (−)/received (US$ per capita) 2002	Military spending (% of GDP) 2004	
26,945	4,140	1.3	22.7	19.5	57.9	0.649	2,219.1	917	1.1	0.635	29	61.8	33	17	0.8	Guatemala
3,681	2,130	1.7	25	38.2	36.8	0.425	2,408.9	7,692	3.2	–	64	2.4	5	39	1.7	Guinea
250	690	−2.2	62	12	26	0.350	2,024.2	5,882	10.0	0.329	58	–	15	82	3.1	Guinea-Bissau
765	4,110	4.1	38.3	19.9	41.8	0.719	2,691.7	3,846	2.5	0.715	1	100.8	142	361	0.9	Guyana
3,380	1,680	−3.0	30	20	50	0.463	2,086.2	4,000	5.6	0.458	47	19.3	18	16	0.9	Haiti
7,321	2,710	0.3	12.7	32.1	55.3	0.672	2,355.8	1,149	1.8	0.662	24	11.7	25	82	1.4	Honduras
83,315	15,620	2.4	3.3	31.4	65.3	0.848	3,483.2	282	0.1	0.847	1	305.2	232	25	1.8	Hungary
11,199	32,360	2.1	11.2	9.6	79.2	0.941	3,249.3	284	0.2	0.938	0	639.7	648	–	–	Iceland
674,580	3,100	4.0	23.6	28.4	48	0.595	2,459.0	1,961	0.8	0.572	40	12.9	17	3	2.5	India
248,007	3,460	2.1	14.6	45	40.4	0.692	2,903.9	6,250	0.1	0.685	11	27.6	38	12	3.0	Indonesia
153,984	7,550	2.2	11.2	40.9	48.7	0.732	3,084.9	–	0.1	0.713	21	25.8	72	6	3.3	Iran
–	–	–	13.6	58.6	27.8	–	2,197.0	–	0.1	–	60	47.2	1	32	–	Iraq
137,761	33,170	6.8	5	46	49	0.936	3,656.4	418	0.1	0.929	2	422.8	317	−71	0.9	Ireland
118,124	23,510	1.8	2.8	37.7	59.5	0.908	3,666.1	267	0.1	0.906	5	295.5	301	107	8.7	Israel
1,503,562	27,860	1.5	2.3	28.8	68.9	0.920	3,670.6	165	0.4	0.914	1	641.1	337	−17	1.8	Italy
13,263	1,390	−0.1	27.8	19.4	52.8	0.399	2,630.6	11,111	7.0	0.379	49	6.6	14	58	1.2	Ivory Coast
7,738	3,630	−0.1	6.1	32.7	61.3	0.764	2,684.7	1,176	1.2	0.762	12	74.8	228	6	0.4	Jamaica
4,749,910	30,040	1.0	1.3	24.7	74.1	0.938	2,760.9	495	0.1	0.932	1	566.8	483	−55	1.0	Japan
11,629	4,640	0.9	2.4	26	71.5	0.750	2,673.5	488	0.1	0.734	9	98.1	81	99	14.6	Jordan
33,780	6,980	−0.7	7.4	37.8	54.8	0.766	2,676.5	290	0.1	0.761	2	86.8	16	40	0.9	Kazakhstan
14,987	1,050	−0.6	19.3	18.5	62.4	0.488	2,090.1	7,143	6.7	0.486	15	16.7	13	14	1.3	Kenya
–	–	–	30.2	33.8	36	0.888	2,141.7	556	–	–	1	–	–	–	–	Korea, North
673,036	20,400	4.7	3.2	40.4	56.3	–	3,058.0	–	0.1	0.882	2	293.2	610	−4	2.8	Korea, South
43,052	19,510	−1.7	0.4	60.5	39.1	0.838	3,010.0	625	0.12	0.827	16	399.9	228	−4	5.3	Kuwait
2,050	1,840	−3.2	38.5	22.8	38.7	0.701	2,999.1	368	0.1	...	3	37.2	38	10	1.4	Kyrgyzstan
2,239	1,850	3.8	49.5	27.5	23	0.534	2,311.7	1,639	0.1	0.528	47	–	3	40	0.5	Laos
12,570	11,850	0.2	4.4	24.8	70.8	0.823	2,938.0	344	0.4	0.823	1	314.7	404	42	1.2	Latvia
22,668	5,380	3.1	12	21	67	0.758	3,195.9	365	0.1	0.755	13	416.5	117	230	3.1	Lebanon
1,336	3,210	2.4	15.2	43.9	40.9	0.493	2,638.3	14,286	28.9	0.483	15	–	10	22	2.3	Lesotho
391	130	–	76.9	5.4	17.7	–	1,899.8	781	5.9	–	42	9.7	0	28	0.2	Liberia
25,257	4,490	–	8.7	45.7	45.6	0.794	3,319.8	833	0.2	–	17	140.1	29	3	3.9	Libya
19,727	12,610	−0.3	6.1	33.4	60.5	0.842	3,324.5	248	0.1	0.841	1	375.7	202	63	1.9	Lithuania
25,302	61,220	3.7	0.5	16.3	83.1	0.933	3,701.0	394	0.2	0.926	0	746.9	370	−294	0.9	Luxembourg
4,855	6,480	−0.7	11.2	26	62.8	0.793	2,654.6	457	0.1	–	–	166.5	49	119	6.0	Macedonia (FYROM)
5,181	830	−0.9	29.3	16.7	54	0.469	2,004.6	11,111	1.7	0.462	31	4.9	4	20	1.2	Madagascar
1,922	620	1.1	54.8	19.2	26	0.388	2,154.6	–	14.2	0.374	37	6.9	3	45	0.7	Malawi
117,132	9,630	3.6	7.2	33.6	59.1	0.793	2,881.1	1,471	0.4	0.786	11	18.8	344	7	2.0	Malaysia
4,335	980	1.7	45	17	38	0.326	2,173.9	25,000	1.9	0.309	54	4.1	2	50	0.4	Mali
4,913	18,720	3.6	3	23	74	0.875	3,586.9	344	0.1	0.866	7	713.2	303	63	0.7	Malta
1,210	2,050	1.6	25	29	46	0.465	2,772.0	7,143	0.6	0.456	58	11.2	4	73	1.7	Mauritania
5,730	4,090	4.0	7.6	30	62.4	0.785	2,954.8	1,176	0.1	0.775	14	113.1	123	35	0.2	Mauritius
703,080	9,590	1.4	4	27.2	68.9	0.802	3,144.7	641	0.3	0.792	8	185.2	118	11	0.9	Mexico
252	590	−1.8	50	4	46	–	–	–	–	–	11	–	6	–	–	Micronesia, Fed. States
2,563	1,930	−6.9	22.4	24.8	52.8	0.681	2,806.0	369	0.2	0.678	1	64.3	80	23	0.4	Moldova
1,484	2,020	0.2	20.6	21.5	58	0.668	2,249.1	360	0.1	0.664	1	18	58	119	2.2	Mongolia
46,518	4,100	0.8	21.2	35.8	43	0.620	3,051.8	2,041	0.1	0.604	48	56.9	33	18	5.0	Morocco
4,710	1,160	4.5	21.1	32.1	46.9	0.354	2,078.9	50,000	12.2	0.339	52	8.7	3	34	2.2	Mozambique
4,813	6,960	0.9	11.3	30.8	57.9	0.607	2,277.5	3,448	21.3	0.602	16	38	34	80	3.1	Namibia
6,538	1,470	2.3	40	20	40	0.504	2,453.1	20,000	0.5	0.484	55	5.5	3	16	1.5	Nepal
515,148	31,220	2.2	2.4	24.5	73.1	0.942	3,362.3	305	0.2	0.938	1	438.6	522	−202	1.6	Netherlands
82,465	22,130	2.1	4.6	27.4	68	0.926	3,219.2	457	0.1	0.924	1	632.3	526	−25	1.0	New Zealand
4,452	3,300	1.5	20.7	24.7	54.6	0.667	2,298.0	1,613	0.2	0.66	32	36.5	17	138	0.7	Nicaragua
2,836	830	−0.8	39	17	44	0.292	2,130.4	33,333	1.2	0.278	82	8.9	1	30	1.1	Niger
53,983	930	−0.3	36.3	30.5	33.3	0.466	2,725.5	3,704	5.4	0.458	32	0.6	6	2	0.8	Nigeria
238,398	38,550	3.0	2.2	36.3	61.6	0.956	3,484.2	272	0.1	0.955	0	523.8	346	−304	1.9	Norway
20,508	13,250	0.9	3.1	41.1	55.8	0.770	–	730	0.1	0.747	24	191.6	71	26	11.4	Oman
90,663	2,160	1.1	22.6	24.1	53.3	0.497	2,418.8	1,471	0.1	0.471	54	11.1	10	5	4.9	Pakistan
13,468	6,870	2.5	7.2	13	79.8	0.791	2,271.7	826	0.9	0.785	7	96.3	62	66	1.1	Panama
3,262	2,300	0.5	34.5	34.7	30.8	0.542	2,175.0	16,667	0.6	0.536	34	20.6	14	74	1.4	Papua New Guinea
6,752	4,870	−0.5	25.3	24.9	49.8	0.751	2,565.3	2,041	0.5	0.736	6	66	20	14	0.9	Paraguay
65,043	5,370	2.2	8	27	65	0.752	2,570.9	971	0.5	0.736	9	50.1	104	33	1.4	Peru
96,930	4,890	1.1	14.8	31.9	53.2	0.753	2,379.3	870	0.1	0.751	4	34.3	44	14	1.0	Philippines
232,398	12,640	4.2	2.9	31.3	65.9	0.850	3,374.5	455	0.1	0.848	1	325.1	232	26	1.7	Poland
149,790	19,250	2.5	5.9	30.2	63.9	0.897	3,740.9	314	0.5	0.894	7	734.1	194	−26	2.3	Portugal
–	–	–	0.3	58.2	41.5	0.833	–	455	0.1	–	17	517.3	113	8	10.0	Qatar

COUNTRY	POPULATION							LAND & AGRICULTURE				TRADE, TOURISM & ENERGY					
	Total population (millions)	Population density (persons per km²)	Life expectancy (years)	Average annual population change (%)	Birth rate (births per thousand people)	Death rate (deaths per thousand people)	Urban population (% of total)	Land area (thousand km²)	Arable & permanent crops (% of land area)	Permanent pasture (% of land area)	Forest (% of land area)	Imports (US$ per capita)	Exports (US$ per capita)	Tourism receipts (US$ per capita)	Energy produced (tonnes of oil equiv. per capita)	Energy consumed (tonnes of oil equiv. per capita)	CO_2 emissions per capita (metric tonnes)
	2005	2005	2005	2005	2005	2005	2005		2002	2002	2000	2004	2004	2003	2002	2002	2003
Romania	22.3	94	71	−0.1	11	12	55	238	43	21	28	1,275	1,056	20	1.34	1.91	4.49
Russia	143.4	8	67	−0.4	10	15	73	17,075	7	5	50	648	1,133	31	7.94	4.78	11.21
Rwanda	8.4	323	47	2.4	41	16	22	26	55	19	12	31	8	3.7	0.01	0.04	0.11
St Lucia	0.2	200	74	1.3	20	5	31	0.5	30	3	15	1,335	330	1,410	0	0.63	2.38
Saudi Arabia	26.4	13	75	2.3	30	3	89	2,150	2	79	1	1,372	4,280	130	19.50	4.98	13.52
Senegal	11.7	60	57	2.5	35	11	51	197	13	29	32	182	117	16	0	0.15	0.45
Serbia & Montenegro[†]	10.8	106	75	0.0	12	10	52	102	37	18	2.8	883	300	14	1.06	1.60	4.75
Sierra Leone	5.9	82	73	2.2	43	21	40	72	8	31	67	45	8	10	0	0.06	0.19
Singapore	4.4	4,400	82	1.6	9	4	100	0.7	3	0	3	35,273	32,364	909	0	9.35	27.89
Slovak Republic	5.4	110	75	0.2	11	9	58	49	32	18	42	5,494	5,415	160	1.42	3.89	7.1
Slovenia	2.0	100	76	0.0	9	10	51	20	10	15	55	8,035	7,485	671	1.81	3.78	8.39
Solomon Is.	0.5	18	73	2.7	31	4	17	29	3	1	91	134	148	4	0	0.13	0.39
Somalia	8.6	13	48	3.4	46	17	36	638	2	69	12	40	9	–	0	0.03	0.09
South Africa	44.3	36	43	−0.3	18	21	58	1,221	13	69	7	890	947	96	3.22	2.66	9.13
Spain	40.3	80	80	0.2	10	10	77	498	38	23	29	5,509	4,280	1,037	0.81	3.64	8.27
Sri Lanka	20.1	305	73	0.8	16	6	21	66	29	7	30	361	264	21	0.04	0.24	0.61
Sudan	40.2	16	59	2.6	36	9	41	2,506	7	49	26	87	84	2.9	0.29	0.10	0.26
Suriname	0.4	2	69	0.3	18	7	77	163	0	0	90	1,510	1,238	10	2.39	2.41	3.94
Swaziland	1.1	65	36	0.3	28	25	24	17	11	71	30	1,036	818	24	0.12	0.32	1.25
Sweden	9.0	20	80	0.2	10	10	83	450	7	1	66	10,886	13,522	589	3.83	6.18	6.27
Switzerland	7.5	183	80	0.5	10	8	68	41	11	27	30	16,147	17,427	1,243	2.12	4.24	6
Syria	18.4	99	70	2.3	28	5	50	185	29	45	3	274	331	77	2.03	1.19	2.94
Taiwan	22.9	636	77	0.6	13	6	77	36	23	–	58	7,223	7,445	130	0.52	4.52	12.4
Tajikistan	7.2	50	65	2.2	33	8	24	143	7	23	3	181	157	0.3	0.54	0.82	1.03
Tanzania	36.8	39	45	1.8	38	17	38	945	6	40	44	54	34	12	0.02	0.05	0.1
Thailand	64.2	125	72	0.9	16	7	33	513	38	2	29	1,259	1,369	122	0.53	1.18	3.11
Togo	5.4	95	53	2.1	33	12	36	57	49	19	9	153	123	2.4	0	0.08	0.23
Trinidad & Tobago	1.0	200	69	−0.7	13	9	76	5	24	2	50	4,650	6,671	242	21.21	11.40	24.92
Tunisia	10.0	61	75	1.0	16	5	64	164	32	31	3	1,152	993	158	0.63	0.85	2.17
Turkey	69.7	89	72	1.1	17	6	67	775	37	17	13	1,356	997	189	0.34	1.12	2.86
Turkmenistan	5.0	10	61	1.8	30	9	46	488	4	65	8	570	800	–	12.17	3.01	8.83
Uganda	27.3	116	52	3.3	47	13	12	241	37	26	21	48	23	6.9	0.02	0.03	0.06
Ukraine	47.0	78	67	−0.6	10	16	67	604	55	13	17	669	700	20	1.86	3.43	7.13
United Arab Emirates	2.6	31	75	1.5	19	4	86	84	3	4	4	17,562	26,723	554	64.99	21.18	44.11
United Kingdom	60.4	247	78	0.3	11	10	89	242	24	46	11	7,275	5,748	377	4.50	3.97	9.53
USA	295.7	31	78	0.9	14	8	81	9,629	19	26	25	4,992	2,689	218	6.04	8.33	19.95
Uruguay	3.4	19	76	0.5	14	9	93	175	8	77	7	609	647	102	0.67	1.11	1.62
Uzbekistan	26.9	60	64	1.7	26	8	36	447	12	54	5	105	138	1.8	2.32	2.01	4.42
Venezuela	25.4	28	74	1.4	19	5	88	912	4	21	56	590	1,411	13	8.27	2.90	5.48
Vietnam	83.5	253	71	1.0	17	6	27	332	27	2	30	315	284	1	0.41	0.26	0.75
West Bank (OPT)*	2.4	400	73	3.1	32	4	–	6	–	–	–	625	85	1.7	–	–	–
Western Sahara	0.3	1	–	2.2	–	–	94	266	0	19	0	–	–	–	0	0.32	1.05
Yemen	20.7	39	62	3.5	43	9	26	528	3	30	1	180	216	6.7	1.16	0.19	0.5
Zambia	11.3	15	38	2.1	41	20	37	753	7	40	42	134	137	13	0.21	0.25	0.21
Zimbabwe	12.2	31	37	0.5	30	25	36	394	9	44	49	131	115	3.6	0.32	0.41	0.86

NOTES

SERBIA & MONTENEGRO†
Serbia & Montenegro became separate states in June 2006.

OPT*
Occupied Palestinian Territory.

PER CAPITA
An amount divided by the total population of a country or the amount per person.

PPP
Purchasing Power Parity (PPP) is a method used to enable real comparisons to be made between countries when measuring wealth. The UN International Comparison Programme gives estimates of the PPP for each country, so it can be used as an indicator of real price levels for goods and services rather than using currency exchange rates (see GNI and GNI per capita).

POPULATION TOTAL
These are estimates of the mid-year total in 2005.

POPULATION DENSITY
The total population divided by the land area (both are recorded in the table above).

LIFE EXPECTANCY
The average age that a child born today is expected to live to, if mortality levels of today last throughout its lifetime.

AVERAGE ANNUAL CHANGE
These are estimates of the percentage growth or decline of a country's population as a yearly average.

BIRTH/DEATH RATES
These are 2005 estimates from the CIA World Factbook.

URBAN POPULATION
The urban population shows the percentage of the total population living in towns and cities (each country will differ with regard to the size or type of town that is defined as an urban area).

LAND AREA
This is the total land area of a country, less the area of major lakes and rivers, in square kilometres.

ARABLE AND PERMANENT CROPS
These figures give a percentage of the total land area that is used for crops and fruit (including temporary fallow land or meadows).

PERMANENT PASTURE
This is the percentage of land area that has permanent forage crops for cattle or horses, cultivated or wild. Some land may be classified both as permanent pasture or as forest (see Forest), especially areas of scrub or savanna.

FOREST
Natural/planted trees including cleared land that will be reforested in the near future as a percentage of the land area.

IMPORTS AND EXPORTS
The total value of goods imported into a country and exported to other countries, given in US dollars ($) per capita.

TOURISM RECEIPTS
The amount of income generated from tourism in US dollars per capita.

PRODUCTION AND CONSUMPTION OF ENERGY
The total amount of commercial energy produced or consumed in a country per capita (see note). It is expressed in metric tonnes of oil equivalent (an energy unit giving the heating value derived from one tonne of oil).

CARBON DIOXIDE EMISSIONS
The amount of carbon dioxide that each country produces per capita.

WEALTH						SOCIAL INDICATORS									COUNTRY
GNI (million US$)	GNI per capita (PPP US$)	Average annual growth in GDP per capita (%)	Agriculture (% of GDP)	Industry (% of GDP)	Services (% of GDP)	Human Develop. Index (HDI) value	Food intake (calories per capita per day)	Population per doctor	Adults living with HIV/AIDS (% 15–49 year olds)	Gender Develop. Index (GDI) value	Illiteracy rate (% adults)	Motor vehicles per thousand people	Internet usage per thousand people	Aid donated (–) /received (US$ per capita)	Military spending (% of GDP)	
2004	2004	1990–2002	2004	2004	2004	2002	2003	2003	2003	2002	2003	2002	2003	2002	2004	
63,910	8,190	0.1	13.1	33.7	53.2	0.778	3,454.6	529	0.1	0.775	2	166.2	184	17	2.5	Romania
487,335	9,620	–2.4	4.9	33.9	61.2	0.795	3,071.8	238	0.9	0.794	1	185.1	41	7	–	Russia
1,875	1,300	0.3	41.1	21.2	37.7	0.431	2,084.2	50,000	5.1	0.423	30	3.5	3	47	3.2	Rwanda
706	5,560	0.2	7	20	73	0.777	2,988.2	1,724	–	–	33	172.1	82	259	–	St Lucia
242,180	14,010	–0.6	4.2	67.2	28.6	0.768	2,844.5	654	0.1	0.739	21	372.2	67	–64	10.0	Saudi Arabia
6,967	1,720	1.2	15.9	21.4	62.7	0.437	2,279.5	10,000	0.8	0.429	60	28.3	22	33	1.5	Senegal
21,715	1,910	–	15.5	27.6	56.8	–	2,678.4	–	0.2	–	7	171.8	79	185	–	Serbia & Montenegro†
1,113	790	–5.9	49	30	21	0.273	1,936.0	11,111	7.0	–	69	7.9	2	17	1.7	Sierra Leone
104,994	26,590	3.8	0	32.6	67.4	0.902	–	714	0.2	0.884	7	134.9	509	0.3	4.9	Singapore
34,907	14,370	2.1	3.5	30.1	66.4	0.842	2,888.9	307	0.1	0.84	–	278.1	256	21	1.9	Slovak Republic
29,555	20,730	4.2	3	36	60	0.895	3,001.4	457	0.1	0.892	1	478.9	376	31	1.7	Slovenia
260	1,760	–2.4	42	11	47	0.624	2,264.9	7,692	–	–	–	–	5	56	–	Solomon Is.
–	–	–	65	10	25	–	1,628.0	–	1.0	–	62	1.4	9	7	0.9	Somalia
165,326	10,960	0.0	3.6	31.2	65.2	0.666	2,956.1	4,000	21.5	0.661	14	145.4	68	11	1.5	South Africa
875,817	25,070	2.3	3.5	28.5	68	0.922	3,370.6	304	0.5	0.916	2	545.9	239	–33	1.2	Spain
19,618	4,000	3.4	19.1	26.2	54.7	0.740	2,385.3	2,326	0.1	0.738	8	34	12	29	2.6	Sri Lanka
18,152	1,870	3.1	38.7	20.3	41	0.505	2,227.8	6,250	2.6	0.485	39	3.3	9	4	3.0	Sudan
997	1,990	0.5	13	22	65	0.780	2,652.1	2,000	1.2	–	7	203.5	42	108	0.7	Suriname
1,859	4,970	0.1	16.1	43.4	40.5	0.519	2,322.0	6,667	38.8	0.505	18	87.3	26	87	1.4	Swaziland
321,401	29,770	2.0	2	29	69	0.946	3,185.4	348	0.1	0.946	1	542.7	573	–189	1.7	Sweden
356,052	35,370	0.4	1.5	34	64.5	0.936	3,526.2	286	0.5	0.932	1	562.5	351	–147	1.0	Switzerland
21,125	3,550	1.8	25	31	44	0.710	3,038.0	704	0.1	0.689	23	32	13	11	5.9	Syria
–	–	–	1.7	30.9	67.4	–	–	–	–	–	14	–	–	–	2.6	Taiwan
1,779	1,150	–8.1	23.7	24.3	52	0.671	1,827.6	472	0.1	0.668	1	22	1	9	3.9	Tajikistan
11,560	660	0.7	43.2	17.2	39.6	0.407	1,974.9	25,000	8.8	0.401	22	3.8	7	33	0.2	Tanzania
158,703	8,020	2.9	9	44.3	46.7	0.768	2,467.3	3,333	1.5	0.766	4	126.1	111	2	1.8	Thailand
1,868	1,690	–0.7	39.5	20.4	40.1	0.495	2,345.4	16,667	4.1	0.477	39	16.2	42	14	1.9	Togo
11,360	11,180	2.9	2.7	47	50.3	0.801	2,732.4	1,333	3.2	0.795	2	219.8	106	22	0.6	Trinidad & Tobago
26,301	7,310	3.1	13.8	31.8	54.4	0.745	3,237.8	1,429	0.1	0.734	26	86.7	64	38	1.5	Tunisia
268,741	7,680	1.3	11.7	29.8	58.5	0.751	3,357.0	813	0.1	0.746	13	89.3	85	4	5.3	Turkey
6,615	6,910	–3.2	28.5	42.7	28.8	0.752	2,741.6	333	0.1	0.748	2	–	2	3	3.4	Turkmenistan
6,911	1,520	3.9	35.8	20.8	43.6	0.493	2,409.6	20,000	4.1	0.487	30	5.5	5	53	2.2	Uganda
60,297	6,250	–6.0	18	45.1	36.9	0.777	3,053.6	334	2	0.773	1	107.8	19	13	1.4	Ukraine
48,673	21,000	0.0	4	58.5	37.5	0.824	3,224.7	565	0.2	–	22	441.8	275	2	3.1	United Arab Emirates
2,016,393	31,460	2.4	1	26.3	72.7	0.936	3,412.2	610	0.1	0.934	1	497.9	423	–75	2.4	United Kingdom
12,150,931	39,710	2.0	0.9	19.7	79.4	0.939	3,774.1	358	0.6	0.936	3	800	551	–24	3.3	USA
13,414	9,070	1.4	7.9	27.4	64.8	0.833	2,828.0	258	0.3	0.829	2	217.3	119	7	2.0	Uruguay
11,860	1,860	–0.9	38	26.3	35.7	0.709	2,240.6	341	0.1	0.705	1	–	19	3	2.0	Uzbekistan
104,958	5,760	–1.0	0.1	46.5	53.4	0.778	2,336.3	500	0.5	0.77	7	100.2	60	3	1.5	Venezuela
45,082	2,700	5.9	21.8	40.1	38.1	0.691	2,566.2	1,852	0.4	0.689	6	0.7	43	34	2.5	Vietnam
3,771	1,110	–4.9	9	28	63	–	2,179.8	–	–	–	–	–	40	870	–	West Bank (OPT)*
–	–	–	–	–	40	–	–	–	–	–	–	–	–	–	–	Western Sahara
11,218	820	2.5	15.5	44.7	39.7	0.482	2,038.3	4,545	0.1	0.436	50	50.1	5	23	7.8	Yemen
4,748	890	–1.2	14.9	28.9	56.1	0.389	1,927.4	14,286	16.5	0.375	19	0.8	6	62	1.8	Zambia
6,165	2,180	–0.8	18.1	24.3	57.7	0.491	1,942.6	16,667	33.7	0.482	9	50.7	43	14	4.3	Zimbabwe

GNI
Gross National Income: this used to be referred to as GNP (Gross National Product) and is a good indication of a country's wealth. It is the income in US dollars from goods and services in a country for one year, including income from overseas.

GNI PER CAPITA
The GNI (see above) divided by the total population by using the PPP method (see note).

AVERAGE ANNUAL GROWTH IN GDP
The growth or decline of the Gross Domestic Product per capita (decline shown as a negative [–] number), as an average over the 12 years from 1990 to 2002. The GDP is the value of all goods and services made in a country in one year, but unlike GNI (see above) it does not include income gained from abroad.

AGRICULTURE, INDUSTRY AND SERVICES
The percentage contributions that each of these three sectors makes to a country's GDP (see note).

HUMAN DEVELOPMENT INDEX (HDI)
Produced by the UN Development Programme using indicators of life expectancy, knowledge and standards of living to give a value between 0 and 1 for each country. A high value shows a higher human development.

FOOD INTAKE
The amount of food (measured in calories) supplied, divided by the total population. Belgium and Luxembourg are shown as one country.

POPULATION PER DOCTOR
The total population divided by the number of qualified doctors.

ADULTS LIVING WITH HIV/AIDS
The percentage of all adults (aged 15–49) who have the Human Immunodeficiency Virus or the Acquired Immunodeficiency Syndrome. The total number of adults and children with HIV/AIDS in 2002 was 42 million.

GENDER DEVELOPMENT INDEX (GDI)
Like the HDI (see note), the GDI uses the same UNDP indicators but gives a value between 0 and 1 to measure the social and economic differences between men and women. The higher the value, the more equality exists between men and women.

ILLITERACY
The percentage of all adult men and women (over 15 years) who cannot read or write simple sentences.

MOTOR VEHICLES AND INTERNET USAGE
These are good indicators of a country's development wealth. They are shown in total numbers per 1,000 people.

AID DONATED AND RECEIVED
Aid defined here is Official Development Assistance (ODA) in US dollars per capita. The OECD Development Assistance Committee uses donations from donor countries and redistributes the money in the form of grants or loans to developing countries on their list of aid recipients. Donations are shown in the table with a negative (–) number. The money is given for economic development and welfare and not for military purposes.

MILITARY SPENDING
Government spending on the military or defence as a percentage of GDP.

Each topic list is divided into continents and within a continent the items are listed in order of size. The bottom part of many of the lists is selective in order to give examples from as many different countries as possible. The figures are rounded as appropriate.

World, Continents, Oceans

	km²	miles²	%
The World	509,450,000	196,672,000	–
Land	149,450,000	57,688,000	29.3
Water	360,000,000	138,984,000	70.7
Asia	44,500,000	17,177,000	29.8
Africa	30,302,000	11,697,000	20.3
North America	24,241,000	9,357,000	16.2
South America	17,793,000	6,868,000	11.9
Antarctica	14,100,000	5,443,000	9.4
Europe	9,957,000	3,843,000	6.7
Australia & Oceania	8,557,000	3,303,000	5.7
Pacific Ocean	155,557,000	60,061,000	46.4
Atlantic Ocean	76,762,000	29,638,000	22.9
Indian Ocean	68,556,000	26,470,000	20.4
Southern Ocean	20,327,000	7,848,000	6.1
Arctic Ocean	14,056,000	5,427,000	4.2

Ocean Depths

Atlantic Ocean	m	ft
Puerto Rico (Milwaukee) Deep	9,220	30,249
Cayman Trench	7,680	25,197
Gulf of Mexico	5,203	17,070
Mediterranean Sea	5,121	16,801
Black Sea	2,211	7,254
North Sea	660	2,165

Indian Ocean	m	ft
Java Trench	7,450	24,442
Red Sea	2,635	8,454

Pacific Ocean	m	ft
Mariana Trench	11,022	36,161
Tonga Trench	10,882	35,702
Japan Trench	10,554	34,626
Kuril Trench	10,542	34,587

Arctic Ocean	m	ft
Molloy Deep	5,608	18,399

Mountains

Europe		m	ft
Elbrus	*Russia*	5,642	18,510
Mont Blanc	*France/Italy*	4,807	15,771
Monte Rosa	*Italy/Switzerland*	4,634	15,203
Dom	Switzerland	4,545	14,911
Liskamm	*Switzerland*	4,527	14,852
Weisshorn	*Switzerland*	4,505	14,780
Taschorn	Switzerland	4,490	14,730
Matterhorn/Cervino	*Italy/Switzerland*	4,478	14,691
Mont Maudit	*France/Italy*	4,465	14,649
Dent Blanche	*Switzerland*	4,356	14,291
Nadelhorn	*Switzerland*	4,327	14,196
Grandes Jorasses	*France/Italy*	4,208	13,806
Jungfrau	*Switzerland*	4,158	13,642
Grossglockner	*Austria*	3,797	12,457
Mulhacén	*Spain*	3,478	11,411
Zugspitze	*Germany*	2,962	9,718
Olympus	*Greece*	2,917	9,570
Triglav	*Slovenia*	2,863	9,393
Gerlachovsky	*Slovak Republic*	2,655	8,711
Galdhøpiggen	*Norway*	2,469	8,100
Kebnekaise	*Sweden*	2,117	6,946
Ben Nevis	*UK*	1,342	4,403

Asia		m	ft
Everest	*China/Nepal*	8,850	29,035
K2 (Godwin Austen)	*China/Kashmir*	8,611	28,251
Kanchenjunga	*India/Nepal*	8,598	28,208
Lhotse	*China/Nepal*	8,516	27,939
Makalu	*China/Nepal*	8,481	27,824
Cho Oyu	*China/Nepal*	8,201	26,906
Dhaulagiri	*Nepal*	8,167	26,795
Manaslu	*Nepal*	8,156	26,758
Nanga Parbat	*Kashmir*	8,126	26,660
Annapurna	*Nepal*	8,078	26,502
Gasherbrum	*China/Kashmir*	8,068	26,469
Xixabangma	*China*	8,012	26,286
Kangbachen	*India/Nepal*	7,902	25,925
Trivor	*Pakistan*	7,720	25,328
Pik Kommunizma	*Tajikistan*	7,495	24,590
Demavend	*Iran*	5,604	18,386
Ararat	*Turkey*	5,165	16,945
Gunong Kinabalu	*Malaysia (Borneo)*	4,101	13,455
Fuji-San	*Japan*	3,776	12,388

Africa		m	ft
Kilimanjaro	*Tanzania*	5,895	19,340
Mt Kenya	*Kenya*	5,199	17,057
Ruwenzori	*Uganda/Congo (D.R.)*	5,109	16,762
Ras Dashen	*Ethiopia*	4,620	15,157
Meru	*Tanzania*	4,565	14,977
Karisimbi	*Rwanda/Congo (D.R.)*	4,507	14,787
Mt Elgon	*Kenya/Uganda*	4,321	14,176
Batu	*Ethiopia*	4,307	14,130
Toubkal	*Morocco*	4,165	13,665
Mt Cameroun	*Cameroon*	4,070	13,353

Oceania		m	ft
Puncak Jaya	*Indonesia*	5,029	16,499
Puncak Trikora	*Indonesia*	4,730	15,518
Puncak Mandala	*Indonesia*	4,702	15,427
Mt Wilhelm	*Papua New Guinea*	4,508	14,790
Mauna Kea	*USA (Hawaii)*	4,205	13,796
Mauna Loa	*USA (Hawaii)*	4,169	13,678
Aoraki Mt Cook	*New Zealand*	3,753	12,313
Mt Kosciuszko	*Australia*	2,230	7,316

North America		m	ft
Mt McKinley (Denali)	*USA (Alaska)*	6,194	20,321
Mt Logan	*Canada*	5,959	19,551
Pico de Orizaba	*Mexico*	5,610	18,405
Mt St Elias	*USA/Canada*	5,489	18,008
Popocatépetl	*Mexico*	5,452	17,887
Mt Foraker	*USA (Alaska)*	5,304	17,401
Iztaccihuatl	*Mexico*	5,286	17,342
Lucania	*Canada*	5,226	17,146
Mt Steele	*Canada*	5,073	16,644
Mt Bona	*USA (Alaska)*	5,005	16,420
Mt Whitney	*USA*	4,418	14,495
Tajumulco	*Guatemala*	4,220	13,845
Chirripó Grande	*Costa Rica*	3,837	12,589
Pico Duarte	*Dominican Rep.*	3,175	10,417

South America		m	ft
Aconcagua	*Argentina*	6,962	22,841
Bonete	*Argentina*	6,872	22,546
Ojos del Salado	*Argentina/Chile*	6,863	22,516
Pissis	*Argentina*	6,779	22,241
Mercedario	*Argentina/Chile*	6,770	22,211
Huascarán	*Peru*	6,768	22,204
Llullaillaco	*Argentina/Chile*	6,723	22,057
Nudo de Cachi	*Argentina*	6,720	22,047
Yerupaja	*Peru*	6,632	21,758
Sajama	*Bolivia*	6,520	21,391
Chimborazo	*Ecuador*	6,267	20,561
Pico Cristóbal Colón	*Colombia*	5,800	19,029
Pico Bolivar	*Venezuela*	5,007	16,427

Antarctica	m	ft
Vinson Massif	4,897	16,066
Mt Kirkpatrick	4,528	14,855

Rivers

Europe		km	miles
Volga	*Caspian Sea*	3,700	2,300
Danube	*Black Sea*	2,850	1,770
Ural	*Caspian Sea*	2,535	1,575
Dnepr (Dnipro)	*Black Sea*	2,285	1,420
Kama	*Volga*	2,030	1,260
Don	*Volga*	1,990	1,240
Petchora	*Arctic Ocean*	1,790	1,110
Oka	*Volga*	1,480	920
Dnister (Dniester)	*Black Sea*	1,400	870
Vyatka	*Kama*	1,370	850
Rhine	*North Sea*	1,320	820
N. Dvina	*Arctic Ocean*	1,290	800
Elbe	*North Sea*	1,145	710

Asia		km	miles
Yangtze	*Pacific Ocean*	6,380	3,960
Yenisey–Angara	*Arctic Ocean*	5,550	3,445
Huang He	*Pacific Ocean*	5,464	3,395
Ob–Irtysh	*Arctic Ocean*	5,410	3,360
Mekong	*Pacific Ocean*	4,500	2,795
Amur	*Pacific Ocean*	4,442	2,760
Lena	*Arctic Ocean*	4,402	2,735
Irtysh	*Ob*	4,250	2,640
Yenisey	*Arctic Ocean*	4,090	2,540
Ob	*Arctic Ocean*	3,680	2,285
Indus	*Indian Ocean*	3,100	1,925
Brahmaputra	*Indian Ocean*	2,900	1,800
Syrdarya	*Aral Sea*	2,860	1,775
Salween	*Indian Ocean*	2,800	1,740
Euphrates	*Indian Ocean*	2,700	1,675
Amudarya	*Aral Sea*	2,540	1,575

Africa		km	miles
Nile	*Mediterranean*	6,670	4,140
Congo	*Atlantic Ocean*	4,670	2,900
Niger	*Atlantic Ocean*	4,180	2,595
Zambezi	*Indian Ocean*	3,540	2,200
Oubangi/Uele	*Congo (Dem. Rep.)*	2,250	1,400
Kasai	*Congo (Dem. Rep.)*	1,950	1,210
Shaballe	*Indian Ocean*	1,930	1,200
Orange	*Atlantic Ocean*	1,860	1,155
Cubango	*Okavango Delta*	1,800	1,120
Limpopo	*Indian Ocean*	1,770	1,100
Senegal	*Atlantic Ocean*	1,640	1,020

Australia		km	miles
Murray–Darling	*Southern Ocean*	3,750	2,330
Darling	*Murray*	3,070	1,905
Murray	*Southern Ocean*	2,575	1,600
Murrumbidgee	*Murray*	1,690	1,050

North America		km	miles
Mississippi–Missouri	*Gulf of Mexico*	5,971	3,710
Mackenzie	*Arctic Ocean*	4,240	2,630
Missouri	*Mississippi*	4,088	2,540
Mississippi	*Gulf of Mexico*	3,782	2,350
Yukon	*Pacific Ocean*	3,185	1,980
Rio Grande	*Gulf of Mexico*	3,030	1,880
Arkansas	*Mississippi*	2,340	1,450
Colorado	*Pacific Ocean*	2,330	1,445
Red	*Mississippi*	2,040	1,270
Columbia	*Pacific Ocean*	1,950	1,210
Saskatchewan	*Lake Winnipeg*	1,940	1,205

South America		km	miles
Amazon	*Atlantic Ocean*	6,450	4,010
Paraná–Plate	*Atlantic Ocean*	4,500	2,800
Purus	*Amazon*	3,350	2,080
Madeira	*Amazon*	3,200	1,990
São Francisco	*Atlantic Ocean*	2,900	1,800
Paraná	*Plate*	2,800	1,740
Tocantins	*Atlantic Ocean*	2,750	1,710
Orinoco	*Atlantic Ocean*	2,740	1,700
Paraguay	*Paraná*	2,550	1,580
Pilcomayo	*Paraná*	2,500	1,550
Araguaia	*Tocantins*	2,250	1,400

Lakes

Europe		km²	miles²
Lake Ladoga	*Russia*	17,700	6,800
Lake Onega	*Russia*	9,700	3,700
Saimaa system	*Finland*	8,000	3,100
Vänern	*Sweden*	5,500	2,100

Asia		km²	miles²
Caspian Sea	*Asia*	371,000	143,000
Lake Baikal	*Russia*	30,500	11,780
Aral Sea	*Kazakhstan/Uzbekistan*	28,687	11,086
Tonlé Sap	*Cambodia*	20,000	7,700
Lake Balqash	*Kazakhstan*	18,500	7,100

Africa		km²	miles²
Lake Victoria	*East Africa*	68,000	26,000
Lake Tanganyika	*Central Africa*	33,000	13,000
Lake Malawi/Nyasa	*East Africa*	29,600	11,430
Lake Chad	*Central Africa*	25,000	9,700
Lake Turkana	*Ethiopia/Kenya*	8,500	3,290
Lake Volta	*Ghana*	8,480	3,270

Australia		km²	miles²
Lake Eyre	*Australia*	8,900	3,400
Lake Torrens	*Australia*	5,800	2,200
Lake Gairdner	*Australia*	4,800	1,900

North America		km²	miles²
Lake Superior	*Canada/USA*	82,350	31,800
Lake Huron	*Canada/USA*	59,600	23,010
Lake Michigan	*USA*	58,000	22,400
Great Bear Lake	*Canada*	31,800	12,280
Great Slave Lake	*Canada*	28,500	11,000
Lake Erie	*Canada/USA*	25,700	9,900
Lake Winnipeg	*Canada*	24,400	9,400
Lake Ontario	*Canada/USA*	19,500	7,500
Lake Nicaragua	*Nicaragua*	8,200	3,200

South America		km²	miles²
Lake Titicaca	*Bolivia/Peru*	8,300	3,200
Lake Poopo	*Bolivia*	2,800	1,100

Islands

Europe		km²	miles²
Great Britain	*UK*	229,880	88,700
Iceland	*Atlantic Ocean*	103,000	39,800
Ireland	*Ireland/UK*	84,400	32,600
Novaya Zemlya (N.)	*Russia*	48,200	18,600
Sicily	*Italy*	25,500	9,800
Corsica	*France*	8,700	3,400

Asia		km²	miles²
Borneo	*South-east Asia*	744,360	287,400
Sumatra	*Indonesia*	473,600	182,860
Honshu	*Japan*	230,500	88,980
Celebes	*Indonesia*	189,000	73,000
Java	*Indonesia*	126,700	48,900
Luzon	*Philippines*	104,700	40,400
Hokkaido	*Japan*	78,400	30,300

Africa		km²	miles²
Madagascar	*Indian Ocean*	587,040	226,660
Socotra	*Indian Ocean*	3,600	1,400
Réunion	*Indian Ocean*	2,500	965

Oceania		km²	miles²
New Guinea	*Indonesia/Papua NG*	821,030	317,000
New Zealand (S.)	*Pacific Ocean*	150,500	58,100
New Zealand (N.)	*Pacific Ocean*	114,700	44,300
Tasmania	*Australia*	67,800	26,200
Hawaii	*Pacific Ocean*	10,450	4,000

North America		km²	miles²
Greenland	*Atlantic Ocean*	2,175,600	839,800
Baffin Is.	*Canada*	508,000	196,100
Victoria Is.	*Canada*	212,200	81,900
Ellesmere Is.	*Canada*	212,000	81,800
Cuba	*Caribbean Sea*	110,860	42,800
Hispaniola	*Dominican Rep./Haiti*	76,200	29,400
Jamaica	*Caribbean Sea*	11,400	4,400
Puerto Rico	*Atlantic Ocean*	8,900	3,400

South America		km²	miles²
Tierra del Fuego	*Argentina/Chile*	47,000	18,100
Falkland Is. (E.)	*Atlantic Ocean*	6,800	2,600

How to use the Index

The index contains the names of all the principal places and features shown on the maps. Each name is followed by an additional entry in italics giving the country or region within which it is located. The alphabetical order of names composed of two or more words is governed primarily by the first word and then by the second. This is an example of the rule:

Abbeville *France* 50°6N 1°49E **68** A4
Abbey Town *U.K.* 54°51N 3°17W **22** C2
Abbot Ice Shelf *Antarctica* 73°0S 92°0W **55** D16
Abbots Bromley *U.K.* 52°50N 1°52W **23** G5

Physical features composed of a proper name (Erie) and a description (Lake) are positioned alphabetically by the proper name. The description is positioned after the proper name and is usually abbreviated:

Erie, L. *N. Amer.* 42°15N 81°0W **112** D7

Where a description forms part of a settlement or administrative name, however, it is always written in full and put in its true alphabetical position:

Mount Isa *Australia* 20°42S 139°26E **98** E6

Names beginning with M' and Mc are indexed as if they were spelled Mac. Names beginning St. are alphabetized under Saint, but Santa and San are spelled in full and are alphabetized accordingly. If the same place name occurs two or more times in the index and all are in the same country, each is followed by the name of the administrative subdivision in which it is located.

The geographical co-ordinates that follow each name in the index give the latitude and longitude of each place. The first co-ordinate indicates latitude – the distance north or south of the Equator. The second co-ordinate indicates longitude – the distance east or west of the Greenwich Meridian. Both latitude and longitude are measured in degrees and minutes (there are 60 minutes in a degree).

The latitude is followed by N(orth) or S(outh) and the longitude by E(ast) or W(est).

The number in bold type that follows the geographical co-ordinates refers to the number of the map page where that feature or place will be found. This is usually the largest scale at which the place or feature appears.

The letter and figure that are immediately after the page number give the grid square on the map page, within which the feature is situated. The letter represents the latitude and the figure the longitude. A lower-case letter immediately after the page number refers to an inset map on that page.

In some cases the feature itself may fall within the specified square, while the name is outside. This is usually the case only with features that are larger than a grid square.

Rivers are indexed to their mouths or confluences, and carry the symbol ➜ after their names. The following symbols are also used in the index: ■ country, ▨ overseas territory or dependency, □ first-order administrative area, △ national park, ✈ (LHR) principal airport (and location identifier).

Abbreviations used in the Index

Afghan. – Afghanistan
Ala. – Alabama
Alta. – Alberta
Amer. – America(n)
Arch. – Archipelago
Ariz. – Arizona
Ark. – Arkansas
Atl. Oc. – Atlantic Ocean
B. – Baie, Bahía, Bay, Bucht, Bugt
B.C. – British Columbia
Bangla. – Bangladesh
C. – Cabo, Cap, Cape, Coast
C.A.R. – Central African Republic
Calif. – California
Cent. – Central
Chan. – Channel
Colo. – Colorado
Conn. – Connecticut
Cord. – Cordillera
Cr. – Creek
D.C. – District of Columbia
Del. – Delaware
Dom. Rep. – Dominican Republic
E. – East
El Salv. – El Salvador
Eq. Guin. – Equatorial Guinea
Fla. – Florida
Falk. Is. – Falkland Is.
G. – Golfe, Golfo, Gulf
Ga. – Georgia
Hd. – Head
Hts. – Heights
I.(s). – Île, Ilha, Insel, Isla, Island, Isle(s)
Ill. – Illinois
Ind. – Indiana
Ind. Oc. – Indian Ocean
Ivory C. – Ivory Coast
Kans. – Kansas
Ky. – Kentucky
L. – Lac, Lacul, Lago, Lagoa, Lake, Limni, Loch, Lough
La. – Louisiana
Lux. – Luxembourg
Madag. – Madagascar
Man. – Manitoba
Mass. – Massachusetts
Md. – Maryland
Me. – Maine
Mich. – Michigan
Minn. – Minnesota
Miss. – Mississippi
Mo. – Missouri
Mont. – Montana
Mozam. – Mozambique
Mt.(s) – Mont, Monte, Monti, Montaña, Mountain
N. – Nord, Norte, North, Northern,
N.B. – New Brunswick
N.C. – North Carolina
N. Cal. – New Caledonia
N. Dak. – North Dakota
N.H. – New Hampshire
N.J. – New Jersey
N. Mex. – New Mexico
N.S. – Nova Scotia
N.S.W. – New South Wales
N.W.T. – North West Territory
N.Y. – New York
N.Z. – New Zealand
Nat. Park – National Park
Nebr. – Nebraska
Neths. – Netherlands
Nev. – Nevada
Nfld. – Newfoundland and Labrador
Nic. – Nicaragua
Okla. – Oklahoma
Ont. – Ontario
Oreg. – Oregon
P.E.I. – Prince Edward Island
Pa. – Pennsylvania
Pac. Oc. – Pacific Ocean
Papua N.G. – Papua New Guinea
Pen. – Peninsula, Péninsule
Phil. – Philippines
Pk. – Peak
Plat. – Plateau
Prov. – Province, Provincial
Pt. – Point
Pta. – Ponta, Punta
Pte. – Pointe
Qué. – Québec
Queens. – Queensland
R. – Rio, River
R.I. – Rhode Island
Ra.(s) – Range(s)
Reg. – Region
Rep. – Republic
Res. – Reserve, Reservoir
S. – San, South
Si. Arabia – Saudi Arabia
S.C. – South Carolina
S. Dak. – South Dakota
Sa. – Serra, Sierra
Sask. – Saskatchewan
Scot. – Scotland
Sd. – Sound
Sib. – Siberia
St. – Saint, Sankt, Sint
Str. – Strait, Stretto
Switz. – Switzerland
Tas. – Tasmania
Tenn. – Tennessee
Tex. – Texas
Trin. & Tob.. – Trinidad & Tobago
U.A.E. – United Arab Emirates
U.K. – United Kingdom
U.S.A. – United States of America
Va. – Virginia
Vic. – Victoria
Vol. – Volcano
Vt. – Vermont
W. – West
W. Va. – West Virginia
Wash. – Washington
Wis. – Wisconsin

A

Aachen *Germany* 50°45N 6°6E **66** C4
Aalborg *Denmark* 57°2N 9°54E **63** F5
Aalst *Belgium* 50°56N 4°2E **65** D4
Aarau *Switz.* 47°23N 8°4E **66** E5
Aare ➜ *Switz.* 47°33N 8°14E **66** E5
Aba *Nigeria* 5°10N 7°19E **94** G7
Abaco I. *Bahamas* 26°25N 77°10W **115** B9
Ābādān *Iran* 30°22N 48°20E **86** D7
Abaetetuba *Brazil* 1°40S 48°50W **120** C5
Abakan *Russia* 53°40N 91°10E **79** D11
Abancay *Peru* 13°35S 72°55W **120** D2
Abariringa *Kiribati* 2°50S 171°40W **99** A16
Abaya, L. *Ethiopia* 6°30N 37°50E **88** F2
Abbé, L. *Ethiopia* 11°8N 41°47E **88** E3
Abbeville *France* 50°6N 1°49E **68** A4
Abbey Town *U.K.* 54°51N 3°17W **22** C2
Abbot Ice Shelf *Antarctica* 73°0S 92°0W **55** D16
Abbots Bromley *U.K.* 52°50N 1°52W **23** G5
Abbotsbury *U.K.* 50°40N 2°37W **24** E3
Abéché *Chad* 13°50N 20°35E **95** F10
Abeokuta *Nigeria* 7°3N 3°19E **94** G6
Aberaeron *U.K.* 52°15N 4°15W **26** C5
Aberchirder *U.K.* 57°34N 2°37W **19** G12
Aberdare *U.K.* 51°43N 3°27W **26** D7
Aberdeen *U.K.* 57°9N 2°5W **19** H13
Aberdeen *S. Dak., U.S.A.* 45°28N 98°29W **110** A7
Aberdeen *Wash., U.S.A.* 46°59N 123°50W **110** A2
Aberdeenshire □ *U.K.* 57°17N 2°36W **19** H12
Aberdyfi *U.K.* 52°33N 4°3W **26** B5
Aberfeldy *U.K.* 56°37N 3°51W **21** A8
Aberfoyle *U.K.* 56°11N 4°23W **20** B7
Abergavenny *U.K.* 51°49N 3°1W **26** D7
Abergele *U.K.* 53°17N 3°35W **26** A6
Aberporth *U.K.* 52°8N 4°33W **26** C4
Abersoch *U.K.* 52°49N 4°30W **26** B5
Abersychan *U.K.* 51°44N 3°3W **26** D7
Abert, L. *U.S.A.* 42°38N 120°14W **110** B2
Abertillery *U.K.* 51°44N 3°8W **26** D7
Aberystwyth *U.K.* 52°25N 4°5W **26** C5
Abhā *Si. Arabia* 18°0N 42°34E **88** D3
Abidjan *Ivory C.* 5°26N 3°58W **94** G5
Abilene *U.S.A.* 32°28N 99°43W **110** D7
Abingdon *U.K.* 51°40N 1°17W **24** C6
Abitibi, L. *Canada* 48°40N 79°40W **109** E12
Abkhazia □ *Georgia* 43°12N 41°5E **73** F7
Abomey *Benin* 7°10N 2°5E **94** G6
Aboyne *U.K.* 57°4N 2°47W **19** H12
Absaroka Range *U.S.A.* 44°45N 109°50W **110** B5
Abu Dhabi *U.A.E.* 24°28N 54°22E **87** E8
Abu Hamed *Sudan* 19°32N 33°13E **95** E12
Abuja *Nigeria* 9°5N 7°32E **94** G7
Abunā *Brazil* 9°40S 65°20W **120** C3
Abunā ➜ *Brazil* 9°41S 65°20W **120** C3
Acaponeta *Mexico* 22°30N 105°22W **114** C3
Acapulco *Mexico* 16°51N 99°55W **114** D5
Acarai, Serra *Brazil* 1°50N 57°50W **120** B4
Acarigua *Venezuela* 9°33N 69°12W **120** B3
Accomac *U.S.A.* 37°43N 75°40W **113** G10
Accra *Ghana* 5°35N 0°6W **94** G5
Accrington *U.K.* 53°45N 2°22W **23** E4
Aceh □ *Indonesia* 4°15N 97°30E **83** C1
Acharnes *Greece* 38°5N 23°44E **71** E10
Acheloos ➜ *Greece* 38°19N 21°7E **71** E9
Achill Hd. *Ireland* 53°58N 10°15W **28** D1
Achill I. *Ireland* 53°58N 10°1W **28** D1
Acklins I. *Bahamas* 22°30N 74°0W **115** C10
Acle *U.K.* 52°39N 1°33E **25** A12
Aconcagua, Cerro *Argentina* 32°39S 70°0W **121** F3
Acre □ *Brazil* 9°1S 71°0W **120** C2
Acre ➜ *Brazil* 8°45S 67°22W **120** C3
Acton Burnell *U.K.* 52°37N 2°41W **23** G3
Ad Dammām *Si. Arabia* 26°20N 50°5E **86** E7
Ad Dīwānīyah *Iraq* 32°0N 45°0E **86** D6
Adair, C. *Canada* 71°30N 71°34W **109** B12
Adak I. *U.S.A.* 51°45N 176°45W **108** D2
Adamawa Highlands *Cameroon* 7°20N 12°20E **95** G7
Adam's Bridge *Sri Lanka* 9°15N 79°40E **84** Q11
Adana *Turkey* 37°0N 35°16E **73** G6
Adare, C. *Antarctica* 71°0S 171°0E **55** D11
Addis Ababa *Ethiopia* 9°2N 38°42E **88** F2
Adelaide *Australia* 34°52S 138°30E **98** G6
Adelaide I. *Antarctica* 67°15S 68°30W **55** C17
Adelaide Pen. *Canada* 68°15N 97°30W **108** C10
Adélie, Terre *Antarctica* 68°0S 140°0E **55** C10
Aden *Yemen* 12°45N 45°0E **88** E4
Aden, G. of *Asia* 12°30N 47°30E **88** E4
Adige ➜ *Italy* 45°9N 12°20E **70** B5
Adigrat *Ethiopia* 14°20N 39°26E **88** E2
Adirondack Mts. *U.S.A.* 44°0N 74°0W **113** D10
Adjuntas *Puerto Rico* 18°10N 66°43W **115** d
Admiralty Is. *Papua N. G.* 2°0S 147°0E **102** H6
Adour ➜ *France* 43°32N 1°32W **68** E3
Adrar *Mauritania* 20°30N 7°30E **94** D3
Adrar des Iforas *Africa* 19°40N 1°40E **94** C5
Adrian *U.S.A.* 41°54N 84°2W **112** E5
Adriatic Sea *Medit. S.* 43°0N 16°0E **70** C6
Adwa *Ethiopia* 14°15N 38°52E **88** E2
Adwick le Street *U.K.* 53°34N 1°10W **23** E6
Adygea □ *Russia* 45°0N 40°0E **73** F7
Ægean Sea *Medit. S.* 38°30N 25°0E **71** E11
Aerhtai Shan *Mongolia* 46°40N 92°45E **80** B4
Afghanistan ■ *Asia* 33°0N 65°0E **87** C11
Africa 10°0N 20°0E **90** E6
Afyon *Turkey* 38°45N 30°33E **73** G5
Agadez *Niger* 16°58N 7°59E **94** E7
Agadir *Morocco* 30°28N 9°55W **94** B4
Agartala *India* 23°50N 91°23E **85** H17
Agen *France* 44°12N 0°38E **68** D4
Agra *India* 27°17N 77°58E **84** F10
Ağri *Turkey* 39°44N 43°3E **73** G7
Agrigento *Italy* 37°19N 13°34E **70** F5
Agua Prieta *Mexico* 31°18N 109°34W **114** A3
Aguadilla *Puerto Rico* 18°26N 67°10W **115** d
Aguascalientes *Mexico* 21°53N 102°18W **114** C4
Aguila, Punta *Puerto Rico* 17°57N 67°13W **115** d
Aguja, C. de la *Colombia* 11°18N 74°12W **116** B3
Agujereada, Pta. *Puerto Rico* 18°30N 67°8W **115** d
Agulhas, C. *S. Africa* 34°52S 20°0E **97** L4
Ahaggar *Algeria* 23°0N 6°30E **94** D76
Ahmadabad *India* 23°0N 72°40E **84** H8
Ahmadnagar *India* 19°7N 74°46E **84** K9
Ahmadpur *Pakistan* 29°12N 71°10E **84** E7
Ahvāz *Iran* 31°20N 48°40E **86** D7
Ahvenanmaa *Finland* 60°15N 20°0E **63** E8
Aḩwar *Yemen* 13°30N 46°40E **88** E4
Aihui *China* 50°10N 127°30E **81** A7
Ailsa Craig *U.K.* 55°15N 5°6W **20** D5
Aimorés *Brazil* 19°30S 41°4W **122** C2
Aïn Témouchent *Algeria* 35°16N 1°8W **94** A5
Ainsdale *U.K.* 53°37N 3°2W **23** E2
Aïr *Niger* 18°30N 8°0E **94** E7
Air Force I. *Canada* 67°58N 74°5W **109** C12
Aird, The *U.K.* 57°25N 4°33W **19** H8
Airdrie *Canada* 51°18N 114°2W **108** D8
Airdrie *U.K.* 55°52N 3°57W **21** C8
Aire ➜ *U.K.* 53°43N 0°55W **23** E7
Aisgill *U.K.* 54°23N 2°21W **22** D4
Aisne ➜ *France* 49°26N 2°50E **68** B5
Aix-en-Provence *France* 43°32N 5°27E **68** E6
Aix-les-Bains *France* 45°41N 5°53E **68** D6
Aizawl *India* 23°40N 92°44E **85** H18
Aizuwakamatsu *Japan* 37°30N 139°56E **82** E6
Ajaccio *France* 41°55N 8°40E **68** F8
Ajanta Ra. *India* 20°28N 75°50E **84** J9
Ajaria □ *Georgia* 41°30N 42°0E **73** F7
Ajdābiyā *Libya* 30°54N 20°4E **95** B10
'Ajmān *U.A.E.* 25°25N 55°30E **87** E8
Ajmer *India* 26°28N 74°37E **84** F9
Aketi *Dem. Rep. of the Congo* 2°38N 23°47E **96** D4
Akhisar *Turkey* 38°56N 27°48E **73** G4
Akimiski I. *Canada* 52°50N 81°30W **109** D11
Akita *Japan* 39°45N 140°7E **82** D7
'Akko *Israel* 32°55N 35°4E **86** C3
Aklavik *Canada* 68°12N 135°0W **108** C6
Akola *India* 20°42N 77°2E **84** J10
Akpatok I. *Canada* 60°25N 68°8W **109** C13
Akranes *Iceland* 64°19N 22°5W **63** B1
Akron *U.S.A.* 41°5N 81°31W **112** E7
Aksai Chin *China* 35°15N 79°55E **84** B11
Aksaray *Turkey* 38°25N 34°2E **73** G5
Akşehir Gölü *Turkey* 38°30N 31°25E **73** G5
Aksu *China* 41°5N 80°10E **80** B3
Aksum *Ethiopia* 14°5N 38°40E **88** E2
Akure *Nigeria* 7°15N 5°5E **94** G7
Akureyri *Iceland* 65°40N 18°6W **63** A2
Al 'Amārah *Iraq* 31°55N 47°15E **86** D6
Al 'Aqabah *Jordan* 29°31N 35°0E **86** D3
Al 'Aramah *Si. Arabia* 25°30N 46°0E **86** E6
Al 'Ayn *U.A.E.* 24°15N 55°45E **87** E8
Al Fallūjah *Iraq* 33°20N 43°55E **86** C5
Al Fāw *Iraq* 30°0N 48°30E **86** D7
Al Ḩadīthah *Iraq* 34°0N 41°13E **86** C5
Al Ḩillah *Iraq* 32°30N 44°25E **86** C6
Al Hoceïma *Morocco* 35°8N 3°58W **94** A5
Al Ḩudaydah *Yemen* 14°50N 43°0E **88** E3
Al Hufūf *Si. Arabia* 25°25N 49°45E **86** E7
Al Jahrah *Kuwait* 29°25N 47°40E **86** D6
Al Jawf *Libya* 24°10N 23°24E **95** D10
Al Jawf *Si. Arabia* 29°55N 39°40E **86** D4
Al Jubayl *Si. Arabia* 27°0N 49°50E **86** E7
Al Khalīl *West Bank* 31°32N 35°6E **86** D3
Al Khums *Libya* 32°40N 14°17E **95** B8
Al Kufrah *Libya* 24°17N 23°15E **95** D10
Al Kūt *Iraq* 32°30N 46°0E **86** C6
Al Manāmah *Bahrain* 26°10N 50°30E **87** E7
Al Mubarraz *Si. Arabia* 25°30N 49°40E **86** E7
Al Mukallā *Yemen* 14°33N 49°2E **88** E4
Al Musayyib *Iraq* 32°49N 44°20E **86** C6
Al Qāmishlī *Syria* 37°2N 41°14E **86** B5
Al Qaţīf *Si. Arabia* 26°35N 50°0E **86** E7
Al Qunfudhah *Si. Arabia* 19°3N 41°4E **88** D3
Alabama □ *U.S.A.* 33°0N 87°0W **111** D9
Alabama ➜ *U.S.A.* 31°8N 87°57W **111** D9
Alagoas □ *Brazil* 9°0S 36°0W **122** A3
Alagoinhas *Brazil* 12°7S 38°20W **122** B3
Alai Range *Asia* 39°45N 72°0E **87** B13
Alamogordo *U.S.A.* 32°54N 105°57W **110** D5
Alamosa *U.S.A.* 37°28N 105°52W **110** C5
Åland = Ahvenanmaa *Finland* 60°15N 20°0E **63** E8
Alanya *Turkey* 36°38N 32°0E **73** G5
Alaşehir *Turkey* 38°23N 28°30E **73** G4
Alaska □ *U.S.A.* 64°0N 154°0W **108** C5
Alaska, G. of *Pac. Oc.* 58°0N 145°0W **108** D5
Alaska Peninsula *U.S.A.* 56°0N 159°0W **108** D4
Alaska Range *U.S.A.* 62°50N 151°0W **108** C4
Alba-Iulia *Romania* 46°8N 23°39E **67** E12
Albacete *Spain* 39°0N 1°50W **69** C5
Albanel, L. *Canada* 50°55N 73°12W **109** D12
Albania ■ *Europe* 41°0N 20°0E **71** D9
Albany *Australia* 35°1S 117°58E **98** H2
Albany *Ga., U.S.A.* 31°35N 84°10W **111** D10
Albany *N.Y., U.S.A.* 42°39N 73°45W **113** D11
Albany *Oreg., U.S.A.* 44°38N 123°6W **110** B2
Albany ➜ *Canada* 52°17N 81°31W **109** D11
Albemarle Sd. *U.S.A.* 36°5N 76°0W **111** C11
Albert, L. *Africa* 1°30N 31°0E **96** D6
Albert Lea *U.S.A.* 43°39N 93°22W **111** B8
Albert Nile ➜ *Uganda* 3°36N 32°2E **96** D6
Alberta □ *Canada* 54°40N 115°0W **108** D8
Albertville *France* 45°40N 6°22E **68** D7
Albi *France* 43°56N 2°9E **68** E5
Albion *U.S.A.* 42°15N 84°45W **112** D5
Albrighton *U.K.* 52°38N 2°16W **23** G4
Albuquerque *U.S.A.* 35°5N 106°39W **110** C5
Albury *Australia* 36°3S 146°56E **98** H8
Alcalá de Henares *Spain* 40°28N 3°22W **69** B4
Alcester *U.K.* 52°14N 1°52W **24** B5
Alchevsk *Ukraine* 48°30N 38°45E **73** E6
Alcoy *Spain* 38°43N 0°30W **69** C5
Aldabra Is. *Seychelles* 9°22S 46°28E **91** G8
Aldan *Russia* 58°40N 125°30E **79** D14

Aldan   Azamgarh

Aldan → Russia 63°28N 129°35E 79 C14
Aldborough U.K. 54°5N 1°22W 22 D6
Aldbourne U.K. 51°29N 1°37W 24 D5
Aldbrough U.K. 53°49N 0°6W 23 E8
Aldeburgh U.K. 52°10N 1°37E 25 B12
Alderley Edge U.K. 53°18N 2°13W 23 F4
Alderney France 49°42N 2°11W 27 H9
Aldershot U.K. 51°15N 0°44W 25 D7
Aledo U.S.A. 41°12N 90°45W 112 E2
Alegrete Brazil 29°40S 56°0W 121 E4
Além Paraíba Brazil 21°52S 42°41W 122 D2
Alençon France 48°27N 0°4E 68 B4
Alenquer Brazil 1°56S 54°46W 120 C4
'Alenuihāhā Channel
   U.S.A. 20°30N 156°0W 110 H17
Aleppo Syria 36°10N 37°15E 86 B4
Alert Canada 83°2N 60°0W 109 A13
Alès France 44°9N 4°5E 68 D6
Alessándria Italy 44°54N 8°37E 70 B3
Ålesund Norway 62°28N 6°12E 63 E5
Aleutian Is. Pac. Oc. 52°0N 175°0W 102 B10
Aleutian Trench Pac. Oc. 48°0N 180°0E 102 C10
Alexander Arch. U.S.A. 56°0N 136°0W 108 D6
Alexander I. Antarctica 69°0S 70°0W 55 C17
Alexandria Egypt 31°13N 29°58E 95 B11
Alexandria U.K. 55°59N 4°35W 20 C6
Alexandria La., U.S.A. 31°18N 92°27W 111 D8
Alexandria Va., U.S.A. 38°49N 77°5W 112 F9
Alford Aberds., U.K. 57°14N 2°41W 19 H12
Alford Lincs., U.K. 53°15N 0°10E 23 F9
Alfreton U.K. 53°6N 1°24W 23 F6
Alfriston U.K. 50°48N 0°10E 25 E9
Algarve Portugal 36°58N 8°20W 69 D1
Algeciras Spain 36°9N 5°28W 69 D3
Algeria ■ Africa 28°30N 2°0E 94 C6
Algiers Algeria 36°42N 3°8E 94 A6
Algoa B. S. Africa 33°50S 25°45E 90 K6
Alicante Spain 38°23N 0°30W 69 C5
Alice Springs Australia 23°40S 133°50E 98 E5
Aligarh India 27°55N 78°10E 84 F11
Alipur Duar India 26°30N 89°35E 85 F16
Aliquippa U.S.A. 40°37N 80°15W 112 E7
Aliwal North S. Africa 30°45S 26°45E 97 L5
Alkmaar Neths. 52°37N 4°45E 65 B4
Allahabad India 25°25N 81°58E 85 G12
Allegan U.S.A. 42°32N 85°51W 112 D5
Allegheny → U.S.A. 40°27N 80°1W 112 E8
Allegheny Mts. U.S.A. 38°15N 80°10W 111 C11
Allègre, Pte. Guadeloupe 16°22N 61°46W 114 b
Allen → U.K. 54°58N 2°18W 22 C4
Allen, Bog of Ireland 53°15N 7°0W 31 B9
Allen, L. Ireland 54°8N 8°4W 28 C5
Allendale Town U.K. 54°53N 2°14W 22 C4
Allenheads U.K. 54°49N 2°12W 22 C4
Allentown U.S.A. 40°37N 75°29W 113 E10
Alleppey India 9°30N 76°28E 84 Q10
Alleynes B. Barbados 13°13N 59°39W 115 g
Alliance U.S.A. 42°6N 102°52W 110 B6
Allier → France 46°57N 3°4E 68 C5
Alligator Pond Jamaica 17°52N 77°34W 114 a
Alloa U.K. 56°7N 3°47W 21 B8
Allonby U.K. 54°46N 3°26W 22 C2
Alma U.S.A. 43°23N 84°39W 112 D5
Alma Ata Kazakhstan 43°15N 76°57E 79 E9
Almada Portugal 38°41N 9°8W 69 C1
Almelo Neths. 52°22N 6°42E 65 B6
Almería Spain 36°52N 2°27W 69 D4
Almondsbury U.K. 51°32N 2°34W 24 C3
Aln → U.K. 55°24N 1°37W 22 B5
Alness U.K. 57°41N 4°16W 19 G9
Alnmouth U.K. 55°24N 1°37W 22 B5
Alnwick U.K. 55°24N 1°42W 22 B5
Alor Indonesia 8°15S 124°30E 83 D4
Alor Setar Malaysia 6°7N 100°22E 83 C2
Alpena U.S.A. 45°4N 83°27W 112 C6
Alpes Maritimes Europe 44°10N 7°10E 68 D7
Alphington U.K. 50°43N 3°31W 27 F7
Alpine U.S.A. 30°22N 103°40W 110 D6
Alps Europe 46°30N 9°30E 66 E5
Alrewas U.K. 52°44N 1°44W 23 G5
Alsace □ France 48°15N 7°25E 68 B7
Alsager U.K. 53°6N 2°18W 23 F4
Alston U.K. 54°49N 2°25W 22 C4
Altamira Brazil 3°12S 52°10W 120 C4
Altamura Italy 40°49N 16°33E 70 D7
Altanbulag Mongolia 50°16N 106°30E 80 A5
Altarnun U.K. 50°35N 4°32W 27 F4
Altay China 47°48N 88°10E 80 B3
Altiplano Bolivia 17°0S 68°0W 120 D3
Alton U.K. 51°9N 0°59W 25 D7
Alton U.S.A. 38°53N 90°11W 112 F2
Altoona U.S.A. 40°31N 78°24W 112 E8
Altrincham U.K. 53°24N 2°21W 23 F4
Altun Shan China 38°30N 88°0E 80 C3
Altus U.S.A. 34°38N 99°20W 110 D7
Alucra Turkey 40°22N 38°47E 73 F6
Alvechurch U.K. 52°21N 1°57W 24 B5
Alwar India 27°38N 76°34E 84 F10
Alwinton U.K. 55°21N 2°7W 22 B4
Alxa Zuoqi China 38°50N 105°40E 80 C5
Alyth U.K. 56°38N 3°13W 19 J11
Amadjuak L. Canada 65°0N 71°8W 109 C12
Amagasaki Japan 34°42N 135°23E 82 F4
Amapá Brazil 2°5N 50°50W 120 B4
Amapá □ Brazil 1°40N 52°0W 120 B4
Amarillo U.S.A. 35°13N 101°50W 110 C6
Amasya Turkey 40°40N 35°50E 73 F6
Amazon = Amazonas →
   S. Amer. 0°5S 50°0W 120 C4
Amazonas □ Brazil 5°0S 65°0W 120 C3
Amazonas → S. Amer. 0°5S 50°0W 120 C4
Ambala India 30°23N 76°56E 84 D10
Ambato Ecuador 1°5S 78°42W 120 C2
Ambergris Cay Belize 18°0N 87°55W 114 D7
Ambikapur India 23°15N 83°15E 85 H13
Ambilobé Madag. 13°10S 49°3E 97 G9
Amble U.K. 55°20N 1°36W 22 B5
Ambleside U.K. 54°26N 2°58W 22 D3
Ambon Indonesia 3°43S 128°12E 83 D4
Amchitka I. U.S.A. 51°32N 179°0E 108 D1
Amderma Russia 69°45N 61°30E 79 C8
Ameca Mexico 20°33N 104°2W 114 C4
American Highland Antarctica 73°0S 75°0E 55 D6
American Samoa ☑
   Pac. Oc. 14°20S 170°40W 99 C16
Americana Brazil 22°45S 47°20W 122 D1
Amersfoort Neths. 52°9N 5°23E 65 B5
Amersham U.K. 51°40N 0°36W 25 C7
Ames U.S.A. 42°2N 93°37W 111 B8
Amesbury U.K. 51°10N 1°46W 24 D5
Amherst Canada 45°48N 64°8W 109 E13
Amiens France 49°54N 2°16E 68 B5
Amirante Is. Seychelles 6°0S 53°0E 74 J7
Amlia I. U.S.A. 52°4N 173°30W 108 D2
Amlwch U.K. 53°24N 4°20W 26 A5
'Ammān Jordan 31°57N 35°52E 86 D3
Ammanford U.K. 51°48N 3°59W 26 D6
Amos Canada 48°35N 78°5W 109 E12
Ampleforth U.K. 54°13N 1°6W 22 D6
Ampthill U.K. 52°2N 0°30W 25 B8
Amravati India 20°55N 77°45E 84 J10
Amreli India 21°35N 71°17E 84 J7
Amritsar India 31°35N 74°57E 84 D9
Amroha India 28°53N 78°30E 84 E11
Amsterdam Neths. 52°23N 4°54E 65 B4
Amsterdam U.S.A. 42°56N 74°11W 113 D10
Amsterdam ✈ (AMS) Neths. 52°18N 4°45E 65 B4
Amsterdam I. Ind. Oc. 38°30S 77°30E 53 F13
Amudarya → Uzbekistan 43°58N 59°34E 87 A9
Amund Ringnes I. Canada 78°20N 96°25W 109 B10
Amundsen Gulf Canada 71°0N 124°0W 108 B7
Amundsen Sea Antarctica 72°0S 115°0W 55 D15
Amuntai Indonesia 2°28S 115°25E 83 D3
Amur → Russia 52°56N 141°10E 79 D16
An Najaf Iraq 32°3N 44°15E 86 C6
An Uaimh Ireland 53°39N 6°41W 29 D8
Anaconda U.S.A. 46°8N 112°57W 110 A4
Anadyr Russia 64°35N 177°20E 79 C19
Anadyr, G. of Russia 64°0N 180°0E 79 C20
Anaheim U.S.A. 33°50N 117°55W 110 D3
Anambas, Kepulauan
   Indonesia 3°20N 106°30E 83 C2
Anamur Turkey 36°8N 32°58E 73 G5
Anantapur India 14°39N 77°42E 84 M10
Anápolis Brazil 16°15S 48°50W 122 C1
Anār Iran 30°55N 55°13E 87 D8
Anatolia Turkey 39°0N 30°0E 73 G5
Añatuya Argentina 28°20S 62°50W 121 E3
Ancaster U.K. 52°59N 0°32W 23 G7
Ancholme → U.K. 53°40N 0°32W 23 E7
Anchorage U.S.A. 61°13N 149°54W 108 C5
Anci China 39°20N 116°40E 81 C6
Ancohuma Bolivia 16°0S 68°50W 120 D3
Ancona Italy 43°38N 13°30E 70 C5
Ancrum U.K. 55°31N 2°35W 21 C10
Ancud Chile 42°0S 73°50W 121 G2
Ancud, G. de Chile 42°0S 73°0W 121 G2
Anda China 46°24N 125°19E 81 B7
Andalgalá Argentina 27°40S 66°30W 121 E3
Andalucía □ Spain 37°35N 5°0W 69 D3
Andalusia U.S.A. 31°18N 86°29W 111 D9
Andaman Is. Ind. Oc. 12°30N 92°45E 83 B1
Anderson Alaska, U.S.A. 64°25N 149°15W 108 C5
Anderson Ind., U.S.A. 40°10N 85°41W 112 E5
Anderson S.C., U.S.A. 34°31N 82°39W 111 D10
Anderson → Canada 69°42N 129°0W 108 C7
Andes, Cord. de los S. Amer. 20°0S 68°0W 121 E3
Andhra Pradesh □ India 18°0N 79°0E 84 L11
Andijon Uzbekistan 41°10N 72°15E 87 A13
Andorra ■ Europe 42°30N 1°30E 68 E4
Andorra La Vella Andorra 42°31N 1°32E 68 E4
Andover U.K. 51°12N 1°29W 24 D6
Andradina Brazil 20°54S 51°23W 120 E4
Andreanof Is. U.S.A. 51°30N 176°0W 108 D2
Ándria Italy 41°13N 16°17E 70 D7
Andros Greece 37°50N 24°57E 71 F11
Andros I. Bahamas 24°30N 78°0W 115 C9
Anegada Br. Virgin Is. 18°45N 64°20W 115 e
Aneityum Vanuatu 20°12S 169°45E 99 E12
Angara → Russia 58°6N 94°20E 79 D11
Angarsk Russia 52°30N 104°0E 79 D12
Ånge Sweden 62°31N 15°35E 63 E7
Angel Falls Venezuela 5°57N 62°30W 120 B3
Ángeles Phil. 15°9N 120°33E 83 B4
Ångermanälven → Sweden 64°0N 17°20E 63 E7
Angers France 47°30N 0°35W 68 C3
Anglesey U.K. 53°17N 4°20W 26 A4
Anglesey □ U.K. 53°16N 4°18W 26 A5
Angoche Mozam. 16°8S 39°55E 97 H7
Angola ■ Africa 12°0S 18°0E 97 G3
Angoulême France 45°39N 0°10E 68 D4
Angoumois France 45°50N 0°25E 68 D3
Angra dos Reis Brazil 23°0S 44°10W 122 D2
Angren Uzbekistan 41°1N 70°12E 87 A12
Anguilla ☑ W. Indies 18°14N 63°5W 115 D12
Angus □ U.K. 56°46N 2°56W 19 J11
Angus, Braes of U.K. 56°51N 3°10W 19 J11
Anhui □ China 32°0N 117°0E 81 C6
Anjou France 47°20N 0°15W 68 C3
Ankang China 32°40N 109°1E 81 C5
Ankara Turkey 39°57N 32°54E 73 G5
Ann, C. U.S.A. 42°38N 70°35W 113 D12
Ann Arbor U.S.A. 42°17N 83°45W 112 D6
Annaba Algeria 36°50N 7°46E 94 A7
Annalee → Ireland 54°2N 7°24W 28 C7
Annan U.K. 54°59N 3°16W 21 E9
Annan → U.K. 54°58N 3°16W 21 E9
Annandale U.K. 55°10N 3°25W 21 D9
Annapolis U.S.A. 38°59N 76°30W 112 F9
Annapurna Nepal 28°34N 83°50E 85 E14
Annecy France 45°55N 6°8E 68 D7
Annfield Plain U.K. 54°52N 1°44W 22 C5
Anning China 24°55N 102°26E 80 D5
Anniston U.S.A. 33°39N 85°50W 111 D9
Annobón Atl. Oc. 1°25S 5°36E 90 G4
Annotto B. Jamaica 18°17N 76°45W 114 a
Anqing China 30°30N 117°3E 81 C6
Anshan China 41°5N 122°58E 81 B7
Anshun China 26°18N 105°57E 80 D5
Anstey U.K. 52°41N 1°12W 23 G6
Anstruther U.K. 56°14N 2°41W 21 B10
Antalaha Madag. 14°57S 50°20E 97 G10
Antalya Turkey 36°52N 30°45E 73 G5
Antalya Körfezi Turkey 36°15N 31°30E 73 G5
Antananarivo Madag. 18°55S 47°31E 97 H9
Antarctic Pen. Antarctica 67°0S 60°0W 55 C18
Antarctica 90°0S 0°0 55 E3
Anti Atlas Morocco 30°0N 8°30W 94 C4
Antibes France 43°34N 7°6E 68 E7
Anticosti, Î. d' Canada 49°30N 63°0W 109 E13
Antigo U.S.A. 45°9N 89°9W 112 C3
Antigonish Canada 45°38N 61°58W 109 E13
Antigua & Barbuda ■
   W. Indies 17°20N 61°48W 115 D12
Antioch Turkey 36°14N 36°10E 73 G6
Antioquia Colombia 6°40N 75°55W 120 B2
Antipodes Is. Pac. Oc. 49°45S 178°40E 102 M9
Antofagasta Chile 23°50S 70°30W 121 E2
Antrim U.K. 54°43N 6°14W 29 B9
Antrim □ U.K. 54°56N 6°25W 29 B9
Antrim, Mts. of U.K. 55°3N 6°14W 29 A9
Antsirabe Madag. 19°55S 47°2E 97 H9
Antsiranana Madag. 12°25S 49°20E 97 G9
Antwerp Belgium 51°13N 4°25E 65 C4
Anupshahr India 28°20N 78°16E 84 E11
Anuradhapura Sri Lanka 8°22N 80°28E 84 Q12
Anxi China 40°30N 95°43E 80 B4
Anyang China 36°5N 114°21E 81 C6
Ánzio Italy 41°27N 12°37E 70 D5
Aomori Japan 40°45N 140°45E 82 C7
Aoraki Mount Cook N.Z. 43°36S 170°9E 99 J13
Aosta Italy 45°45N 7°20E 70 B2
Aozou Strip Chad 22°0N 19°0E 95 D9
Apalachee B. U.S.A. 30°0N 84°0W 111 E10
Apaporis → Colombia 1°23S 69°25W 120 C3
Apatity Russia 67°34N 33°22E 72 A5
Apeldoorn Neths. 52°13N 5°57E 65 B5
Apia Samoa 13°50S 171°50W 99 C16
Apostle Is. U.S.A. 47°0N 90°40W 112 B2
Appalachian Mts. U.S.A. 38°0N 80°0W 112 G7
Appennini Italy 44°30N 10°0E 70 B4
Appleby-in-Westmorland
   U.K. 54°35N 2°29W 22 C4
Applecross Forest U.K. 57°27N 5°40W 18 H6
Appledore Devon, U.K. 51°3N 4°13W 27 E5
Appledore Kent, U.K. 51°1N 0°47E 25 D10
Appleton U.S.A. 44°16N 88°25W 112 C3
Apure → Venezuela 7°37N 66°25W 120 B3
Apurímac → Peru 12°17S 73°56W 120 D2
Aqaba, G. of Red Sea 29°0N 34°40E 86 D3
Aqtaü Kazakhstan 43°39N 51°12E 73 F9
Aqtöbe Kazakhstan 50°17N 57°10E 73 D10
Aquitain, Bassin France 44°0N 0°30W 68 D3
Ar Ramādī Iraq 33°25N 43°20E 86 C5
Ara India 25°35N 84°32E 85 G14
'Arab, Bahr el → Sudan 9°0N 29°30E 95 G11
Arab, Shatt al → Asia 29°57N 48°34E 86 D7
Arabia Asia 25°0N 45°0E 74 F6
Arabian Desert Egypt 27°30N 32°30E 95 C12
Arabian Gulf = Persian Gulf
   Asia 27°0N 50°0E 87 E7
Arabian Sea Ind. Oc. 16°0N 65°0E 74 G8
Aracaju Brazil 10°55S 37°4W 122 D3
Aracati Brazil 4°30S 37°44W 120 C6
Araçatuba Brazil 21°10S 50°30W 120 E4
Araçuaí Brazil 16°52S 42°4W 122 C2
Arad Romania 46°10N 21°20E 67 E11
Arafura Sea E. Indies 9°0S 135°0E 83 D5
Aragón □ Spain 41°25N 0°40W 69 B5
Araguacema Brazil 8°50S 49°20W 120 C5
Araguaia → Brazil 5°21S 48°41W 120 C5
Araguari Brazil 18°38S 48°11W 122 C1
Arāk Iran 34°0N 49°40E 86 C7
Arakan Coast Burma 19°0N 94°0E 85 K19
Arakan Yoma Burma 20°0N 94°40E 85 K19
Aral Kazakhstan 46°41N 61°45E 79 E8
Aral Sea Asia 44°30N 60°0E 79 E8
Aran I. Ireland 55°0N 8°30W 28 B4
Aran Is. Ireland 53°6N 9°38W 30 B3
Aransas Pass U.S.A. 27°55N 97°9W 111 E7
Arapiraca Brazil 9°45S 36°39W 122 A3
Araraquara Brazil 21°50S 48°0W 122 D1
Araras Brazil 22°22S 47°23W 122 D1
Ararat Turkey 39°50N 44°15E 73 G7
Araripe, Chapada do Brazil 7°20S 40°0W 120 C5
Aras, Rūd-e → Asia 40°5N 48°29E 86 A7
Arauca → Venezuela 7°24N 66°35W 120 B3
Araxá Brazil 19°35S 46°55W 122 C1
Arbroath U.K. 56°34N 2°35W 21 A10
Arcachon France 44°40N 1°10W 68 D3
Arctic Bay Canada 73°1N 85°7W 109 B11
Arctic Ocean Arctic 78°0N 160°0W 54 B18
Ardabīl Iran 38°15N 48°18E 86 B7
Ardee Ireland 53°52N 6°33W 29 D8
Ardennes Belgium 49°50N 5°5E 65 D5
Arderin Ireland 53°2N 7°39W 31 B7
Ardgour U.K. 56°45N 5°25W 18 J7
Ardingly U.K. 51°3N 0°4W 25 D8
Ardivachar Pt. U.K. 57°23N 7°26W 18 H3
Ardmore U.S.A. 34°10N 97°8W 111 D7
Ardnamurchan, Pt. of U.K. 56°43N 6°14W 18 J5
Ardrossan U.K. 55°39N 4°49W 20 C6
Ards Pen. U.K. 54°33N 5°34W 29 B10
Arecibo Puerto Rico 18°29N 66°43W 115 d
Arena, Pt. U.S.A. 38°57N 123°44W 110 C2
Arendal Norway 58°28N 8°46E 63 F5
Arequipa Peru 16°20S 71°30W 120 D2
Arezzo Italy 43°25N 11°53E 70 C4
Argentan France 48°45N 0°1W 68 B3
Argentina ■ S. Amer. 35°0S 66°0W 121 F3
Argentino, L. Argentina 50°10S 73°0W 121 H2
Argostoli Greece 38°11N 20°29E 71 E9
Argyle, L. Australia 16°20S 128°40E 98 D4
Argyll U.K. 56°10N 5°20W 20 B5
Argyll & Bute □ U.K. 56°13N 5°28W 20 B4
Århus Denmark 56°8N 10°11E 63 F6
Ariana Tunisia 36°52N 10°12E 95 A8
Arica Chile 18°32S 70°20W 120 D2
Arinos → Brazil 10°25S 58°20W 120 D4
Aripuanã → Brazil 5°7S 60°25W 120 C3
Arisaig U.K. 56°55N 5°51W 18 J6
Arizona □ U.S.A. 34°0N 112°0W 110 D4
Arkaig, L. U.K. 56°59N 5°10W 18 J7
Arkansas □ U.S.A. 35°0N 92°30W 111 D8
Arkansas → U.S.A. 33°47N 91°4W 111 D8
Arkansas City U.S.A. 37°4N 97°2W 111 C7
Arkhangelsk Russia 64°38N 40°36E 72 B7
Arklow Ireland 52°48N 6°10W 31 C10
Arkle → U.K. 54°24N 1°56W 22 D5
Arklow Ireland 52°48N 6°10W 31 C10
Arles France 43°41N 4°40E 68 E6
Arlington U.S.A. 38°53N 77°7W 112 F9
Arlon Belgium 49°42N 5°49E 65 E5
Armagh U.K. 54°21N 6°39W 29 C8
Armagh □ U.K. 54°18N 6°37W 29 C8
Armavir Russia 45°2N 41°7E 73 E7
Armenia Colombia 4°35N 75°45W 120 B2
Armenia ■ Asia 40°20N 45°0E 73 F7
Arnaud → Canada 59°59N 69°46W 109 D13
Arnhem Neths. 51°58N 5°55E 65 C5
Arnhem, C. Australia 12°20S 137°30E 98 C6
Arnhem Land Australia 13°10S 134°30E 98 C5
Arno → Italy 43°41N 10°17E 70 C4
Arnold U.K. 53°1N 1°7W 23 F6
Arnprior Canada 45°26N 76°21W 112 C9
Arnside U.K. 54°12N 2°49W 22 D3
Arra Mts. Ireland 52°50N 8°22W 30 C6
Arran U.K. 55°34N 5°12W 20 C5
Arras France 50°17N 2°46E 68 A5
Arrecife Canary Is. 28°57N 13°37W 94 C3
Arrow, L. Ireland 54°3N 8°19W 28 C5
Artemovsk Ukraine 48°35N 38°0E 73 E6
Artigas Uruguay 30°20S 56°30W 121 F4
Artois France 50°20N 2°30E 68 A5
Artux China 39°40N 76°10E 80 C2
Artvin Turkey 41°14N 41°44E 73 F7
Aru, Kepulauan Indonesia 6°0S 134°30E 83 D5
Arua Uganda 3°1N 30°58E 96 D6
Aruanã Brazil 14°54S 51°10W 120 D4
Aruba ☑ W. Indies 12°30N 70°0W 115 E11
Arun → U.K. 50°49N 0°33W 25 E7
Arunachal Pradesh □ India 28°0N 95°0E 85 F19
Arundel U.K. 50°51N 0°33W 25 E7
Arusha Tanzania 3°20S 36°40E 96 E7
Aruwimi →
   Dem. Rep. of the Congo 1°13N 23°36E 96 D4
Arvayheer Mongolia 46°15N 102°48E 80 B5
Arviat Canada 61°6N 93°59W 108 C10
Arxan China 47°11N 119°57E 81 B6
Arzamas Russia 55°27N 43°55E 72 C7
As Sulaymānīyah Iraq 35°35N 45°29E 86 C6
As Sulaymānīyah Si. Arabia 24°9N 47°18E 86 E6
As Suwayq Oman 23°51N 57°26E 88 C6
As Ṣuwayrah Iraq 32°55N 45°0E 86 C6
Asahigawa Japan 43°46N 142°22E 82 B8
Asamankese Ghana 5°50N 0°40W 94 G5
Asansol India 23°40N 87°1E 85 H15
Asbestos Canada 45°47N 71°58W 113 C12
Asbury Park U.S.A. 40°13N 74°1W 113 E10
Ascension I. Atl. Oc. 7°57S 14°23W 90 F9
Áscoli Piceno Italy 42°51N 13°34E 70 C5
Ascot U.K. 51°25N 0°40W 25 D7
Aseb Eritrea 13°0N 42°40E 88 E3
Asenovgrad Bulgaria 42°1N 24°51E 71 C11
Asfordby U.K. 52°46N 0°57W 23 G7
Ash Kent, U.K. 51°16N 1°17E 25 D11
Ash Surrey, U.K. 51°15N 0°43W 25 D7
Ashbourne U.K. 53°2N 1°43W 23 F5
Ashburton U.K. 50°30N 3°46W 27 F6
Ashby de la Zouch U.K. 52°46N 1°29W 23 G6
Ashdown Forest U.K. 51°3N 0°5E 25 D9
Asheville U.S.A. 35°36N 82°33W 111 C10
Ashford Derby, U.K. 53°14N 1°42W 23 F5
Ashford Kent, U.K. 51°8N 0°53E 25 D10
Ashington U.K. 55°11N 1°33W 22 B5
Ashkhabad Turkmenistan 38°0N 57°50E 87 B9
Ashland Ky., U.S.A. 38°28N 82°38W 112 F6
Ashland Ohio, U.S.A. 40°52N 82°19W 112 E6
Ashland Wis., U.S.A. 46°35N 90°53W 111 A8
Ashqelon Israel 31°42N 34°35E 86 D3
Ashtabula U.S.A. 41°52N 80°47W 112 E7
Ashton-in-Makerfield U.K. 53°30N 2°40W 23 F3
Ashton under Lyne U.K. 53°29N 2°6W 23 F4
Ashuanipi, L. Canada 52°45N 66°15W 109 D13
Ashwater U.K. 50°43N 4°19W 27 F5
Ashwick U.K. 51°13N 2°31W 24 D3
Asia 45°0N 75°0E 74 E9
Asinara Italy 41°4N 8°16E 70 D3
'Asīr Si. Arabia 18°40N 42°30E 88 D3
Asir, Ras Somali Rep. 11°55N 51°10E 88 E5
Askrigg U.K. 54°19N 2°6W 22 D4
Aslackby U.K. 52°53N 0°24W 23 G8
Asmera Eritrea 15°19N 38°55E 88 E2
Aspatria U.K. 54°47N 3°19W 22 C2
Aspen U.S.A. 39°11N 106°49W 110 C5
Assal, L. Djibouti 11°40N 42°26E 88 E3
Assam □ India 26°0N 93°0E 85 G18
Assen Neths. 53°0N 6°35E 65 A6
Assiniboia Canada 49°40N 105°59W 108 E9
Assiniboine → Canada 49°53N 97°8W 108 E10
Assisi Italy 43°4N 12°37E 70 C5
Assynt U.K. 58°12N 5°12W 18 F7
Assynt, L. U.K. 58°10N 5°3W 18 F7
Astana Kazakhstan 51°10N 71°30E 79 D9
Asti Italy 44°54N 8°12E 70 B3
Astipalea Greece 36°32N 26°22E 71 F12
Astorga Spain 42°29N 6°8W 69 A2
Astoria U.S.A. 46°11N 123°50W 110 A2
Astrakhan Russia 46°25N 48°5E 73 E8
Asturias □ Spain 43°15N 6°0W 69 A3
Astwood Bank U.K. 52°15N 1°56W 24 B5
Asunción Paraguay 25°10S 57°30W 121 E4
Aswān Egypt 24°4N 32°57E 95 D12
Aswan Dam Egypt 23°54N 32°54E 95 D12
Asyût Egypt 27°11N 31°4E 95 C12
Aṭ Ṭā'if Si. Arabia 21°5N 40°27E 88 C3
Atacama, Desierto de Chile 24°0S 69°20W 121 E3
Atatürk Baraji Turkey 37°28N 38°30E 73 G6
Atbara Sudan 17°42N 33°59E 95 E12
Atbara → Sudan 17°40N 33°56E 95 E12
Atchafalaya B. U.S.A. 29°25N 91°25W 111 E8
Athabasca Canada 54°45N 113°20W 108 D8
Athabasca → Canada 58°40N 110°50W 108 D8
Athabasca, L. Canada 59°15N 109°15W 108 D9
Athboy Ireland 53°37N 6°56W 29 D8
Athenry Ireland 53°18N 8°44W 30 B5
Athens Greece 37°58N 23°43E 71 F10
Athens Ga., U.S.A. 33°57N 83°23W 111 D10
Athens Ohio, U.S.A. 39°20N 82°6W 112 F6
Atherstone U.K. 52°35N 1°33W 23 G5
Atherton U.K. 53°32N 2°30W 23 E4
Athlone Ireland 53°25N 7°56W 30 B7
Atholl, Forest of U.K. 56°51N 3°50W 19 J10
Athos Greece 40°9N 24°22E 71 D11
Athy Ireland 53°0N 7°0W 31 B8
Atikokan Canada 48°45N 91°37W 112 A2
Atka I. U.S.A. 52°7N 174°30W 108 D2
Atlanta U.S.A. 33°45N 84°23W 111 D10
Atlantic City U.S.A. 39°21N 74°27W 113 F10
Atlantic Ocean 0°0 20°0W 52 E9
Atlin Canada 59°31N 133°41W 108 D6
Attawapiskat Canada 52°56N 82°24W 109 D11
Attawapiskat → Canada 52°57N 82°18W 109 D11
Attleborough U.K. 52°32N 1°1E 25 A11
Attu I. U.S.A. 52°55N 172°55E 108 D1
Atyraū Kazakhstan 47°5N 52°0E 73 E9
Au Sable → U.S.A. 44°25N 83°20W 112 C6
Aube → France 48°34N 3°43E 68 B5
Auburn Ind., U.S.A. 41°22N 85°4W 112 E5
Auburn N.Y., U.S.A. 42°56N 76°34W 112 D9
Aubusson France 45°57N 2°11E 68 D5
Auch France 43°39N 0°36E 68 E4
Auchterarder U.K. 56°18N 3°41W 21 B8
Auchtermuchty U.K. 56°18N 3°13W 21 B9
Auckland N.Z. 36°52S 174°46E 99 H13
Auckland Is. Pac. Oc. 50°40S 166°5E 102 N8
Aude → France 43°13N 3°14E 68 E5
Audlem U.K. 52°59N 2°30W 23 G4
Aughnacloy U.K. 54°25N 6°59W 29 C8
Augsburg Germany 48°25N 10°52E 66 D6
Augusta Australia 34°19S 115°9E 98 G2
Augusta U.S.A. 33°28N 81°58W 111 D10
Aunis France 46°5N 0°50W 68 C3
Aurangabad Bihar, India 24°45N 84°18E 85 G14
Aurangabad Maharashtra,
   India 19°50N 75°23E 84 K9
Aurillac France 44°55N 2°26E 68 D5
Aurora Colo., U.S.A. 39°43N 104°49W 110 C6
Aurora Ill., U.S.A. 41°45N 88°19W 112 E3
Austin U.S.A. 30°17N 97°45W 110 D7
Austral Seamount Chain
   Pac. Oc. 24°0S 150°0W 103 K13
Australia ■ Oceania 23°0S 135°0E 98 E3
Australian Capital Territory □
   Australia 35°30S 149°0E 98 H8
Austria ■ Europe 47°0N 14°0E 66 E8
Autun France 46°58N 4°17E 68 C6
Auvergne □ France 45°20N 3°15E 68 D5
Auvergne, Mts. d' France 45°20N 2°55E 68 D5
Auxerre France 47°48N 3°32E 68 C5
Avallon France 47°30N 3°53E 68 C5
Avaré Brazil 23°4S 48°58W 122 D1
Avebury U.K. 51°26N 1°50W 24 D5
Avellaneda Argentina 34°40S 58°22W 121 F4
Avellino Italy 40°54N 14°47E 70 D6
Aversa Italy 40°58N 14°12E 70 D6
Aveton Gifford U.K. 50°18N 3°50W 27 G6
Aviemore U.K. 57°12N 3°50W 19 H10
Avignon France 43°57N 4°50E 68 E6
Ávila Spain 40°39N 4°43W 69 B3
Avilés Spain 43°35N 5°57W 69 A3
Avoca → Ireland 52°48N 6°10W 31 C10
Avon → Bristol, U.K. 51°29N 2°41W 24 D3
Avon → Dorset, U.K. 50°44N 1°46W 24 E5
Avon → Warks., U.K. 52°0N 2°8W 24 B5
Avonmouth U.K. 51°30N 2°42W 24 C3
Avranches France 48°40N 1°20W 68 B3
Awasa Ethiopia 7°2N 38°28E 88 F2
Awash Ethiopia 9°1N 40°10E 88 F3
Awbārī, Idehan Libya 27°10N 11°30E 95 C8
Awe, L. U.K. 56°17N 5°16W 20 B5
Axbridge U.K. 51°17N 2°49W 24 D3
Axe → U.K. 50°42N 3°4W 27 F8
Axe Edge U.K. 53°14N 1°57W 23 F5
Axel Heiberg I. Canada 80°0N 90°0W 109 B11
Axholme, Isle of U.K. 53°32N 0°50W 23 E7
Axios → Greece 40°57N 22°35E 71 D10
Axminster U.K. 50°46N 3°0W 27 F8
Axmouth U.K. 50°42N 3°3W 27 F7
Ayacucho Argentina 37°5S 58°20W 121 F4
Ayacucho Peru 13°0S 74°0W 120 D2
Aydın Turkey 37°51N 27°51E 73 G4
Aydingkol Hu China 42°40N 89°15E 80 B3
Ayers Rock = Uluru Australia 25°23S 131°5E 98 F5
Aylesbury U.K. 51°49N 0°49W 25 C7
Aylesford U.K. 51°18N 0°30E 25 D10
Aylmer, L. Canada 64°5N 108°30E 108 C8
Aylsham U.K. 52°48N 1°15E 25 A11
Aynho U.K. 52°0N 1°15W 24 B6
Ayr U.K. 55°28N 4°38W 20 D6
Ayr → U.K. 55°28N 4°38W 20 D6
Aysgarth U.K. 54°18N 2°1W 22 D4
Ayton Borders, U.K. 55°51N 2°6W 21 C11
Ayton N. Yorks., U.K. 54°15N 0°28W 22 D8
Ayvalık Turkey 39°20N 26°46E 73 G4
Az Zarqā Jordan 32°5N 36°4E 86 C4
Az Zāwīyah Libya 32°52N 12°56E 95 B8
Azad Kashmir □ Pakistan 33°50N 73°50E 84 B8
Azamgarh India 26°5N 83°13E 85 F13

Azare   Biddulph

B

Azare *Nigeria* 11°55N 10°10E **94 F8**
Azerbaijan ■ *Asia* 40°20N 48°0E **73 F8**
Azores *Atl. Oc.* 38°0N 27°0W **91 C1**
Azov *Russia* 47°3N 39°25E **73 E6**
Azov, Sea of *Europe* 46°0N 36°30E **73 E6**
Azuero, Pen. de *Panama* 7°30N 80°30W **115 F8**
Azul *Argentina* 36°42S 59°43W **121 F4**

Bab el Mandeb *Red Sea* 12°35N 43°25E **88 E3**
Bābā, Koh-i- *Afghan.* 34°30N 67°0E **84 B5**
Babine L. *Canada* 54°48N 126°0W **108 D7**
Bābol *Iran* 36°40N 52°50E **87 B8**
Babruysk *Belarus* 53°10N 29°15E **67 B15**
Babuyan Chan. *Phil.* 18°40N 121°30E **83 B4**
Babylon *Iraq* 32°34N 44°22E **86 C5**
Bac Lieu *Vietnam* 9°17N 105°43E **83 C2**
Bacabal *Brazil* 4°15S 44°45W **120 C5**
Bacău *Romania* 46°35N 26°55E **67 E14**
Back → *Canada* 65°10N 104°0W **108 C9**
Bacolod *Phil.* 10°40N 122°57E **83 B4**
Bacton *U.K.* 52°52N 1°27E **25 A11**
Bacup *U.K.* 53°42N 2°11W **23 E4**
Bad Axe *U.S.A.* 43°48N 83°0W **112 D6**
Badagara *India* 11°35N 75°40E **84 P9**
Badajoz *Spain* 38°50N 6°59W **69 C2**
Badakhshān □ *Afghan.* 36°30N 71°0E **87 B12**
Badalona *Spain* 41°26N 2°15E **69 B7**
Baden-Württemberg □
  Germany 48°20N 8°40E **66 D5**
Badenoch *U.K.* 56°59N 4°15W **19 J9**
Bādghīs □ *Afghan.* 35°0N 63°0E **87 C10**
Badlands *U.S.A.* 43°55N 102°30W **110 B6**
Baffin B. *N. Amer.* 72°0N 64°0W **109 B13**
Baffin I. *Canada* 68°0N 75°0W **109 C12**
Bafoulabé *Mali* 13°50N 10°55W **94 F3**
Bafoussam *Cameroon* 5°28N 10°25E **96 C2**
Bafra *Turkey* 41°34N 35°54E **73 F6**
Bagamoyo *Tanzania* 6°28S 38°55E **96 F7**
Bagé *Brazil* 31°20S 54°15W **121 F4**
Baggy Pt. *U.K.* 51°8N 4°16W **27 E5**
Baghdād *Iraq* 33°20N 44°23E **86 C6**
Baghlān *Afghan.* 32°12N 68°46E **87 B12**
Bagshot *U.K.* 51°22N 0°41W **25 D7**
Baguio *Phil.* 16°26N 120°34E **83 B4**
Bahamas ■ *N. Amer.* 24°0N 75°0W **115 C10**
Baharampur *India* 24°2N 88°27E **85 G16**
Bahawalpur *Pakistan* 29°24N 71°40E **84 E7**
Bahia = Salvador *Brazil* 13°0S 38°30W **122 B3**
Bahia □ *Brazil* 12°0S 42°0W **122 B2**
Bahía Blanca *Argentina* 38°35S 62°13W **121 F3**
Bahir Dar *Ethiopia* 11°37N 37°10E **88 E2**
Bahraich *India* 27°38N 81°37E **85 F12**
Bahrain ■ *Asia* 26°0N 50°35E **87 E7**
Baia Mare *Romania* 47°40N 23°35E **67 E12**
Baicheng *China* 45°38N 122°42E **81 B7**
Baidoa *Somali Rep.* 3°8N 43°30E **88 G3**
Baie-Comeau *Canada* 49°12N 68°10W **109 E13**
Baie-St-Paul *Canada* 47°28N 70°32W **113 B12**
Baie Verte *Canada* 49°55N 56°12W **109 E14**
Ba'iji *Iraq* 35°0N 43°30E **86 C5**
Baikal, L. *Russia* 53°0N 108°0E **79 D12**
Baildon *U.K.* 53°51N 1°46W **23 E5**
Bain → *U.K.* 53°6N 0°12W **23 F8**
Bainbridge *U.K.* 54°18N 2°6W **22 D4**
Baiyin *China* 36°45N 104°14E **80 C5**
Baja, Pta. *Mexico* 29°58N 115°49W **114 B1**
Baja California *Mexico* 31°10N 115°12W **114 A1**
Baja California Sur □
  Mexico 25°50N 111°50W **114 B2**
Baker, L. *Canada* 64°0N 96°0W **108 C10**
Baker City *U.S.A.* 44°47N 117°50W **110 B3**
Baker I. *Pac. Oc.* 0°10N 176°35W **99 A15**
Baker Lake *Canada* 64°20N 96°3W **108 C10**
Bakers Dozen Is. *Canada* 56°45N 78°45W **109 D12**
Bakersfield *U.S.A.* 35°23N 119°1W **110 C3**
Bakewell *U.K.* 53°13N 1°40W **23 F5**
Baku *Azerbaijan* 40°29N 49°56E **73 F8**
Bala *U.K.* 52°54N 3°36W **26 B6**
Bala, L. *U.K.* 52°53N 3°37W **26 B6**
Balabac Str. *E. Indies* 7°53N 117°5E **83 C3**
Balaghat Ra. *India* 18°50N 76°30E **84 K10**
Balaklava *Ukraine* 44°30N 33°30E **73 F5**
Balakovo *Russia* 52°4N 47°55E **72 D8**
Balashov *Russia* 51°30N 43°10E **73 D7**
Balaton *Hungary* 46°50N 17°40E **67 E9**
Balbi, Mt. *Papua N. G.* 5°55S 154°58E **99 B10**
Balbina, Reprêsa de *Brazil* 2°0S 59°30W **120 C4**
Balbriggan *Ireland* 53°37N 6°11W **29 D9**
Balcarce *Argentina* 38°0S 58°10W **121 F4**
Balderton *U.K.* 53°3N 0°47W **23 F7**
Baldock *U.K.* 52°0N 0°11W **25 C8**
Baldoyle *Ireland* 53°24N 6°8W **31 B10**
Baldwin *U.S.A.* 43°54N 85°51W **112 D5**
Baldy Peak *U.S.A.* 33°54N 109°34W **110 D5**
Balearic Is. *Spain* 39°30N 3°0E **69 C7**
Baleine → *Canada* 58°15N 67°40W **109 D13**
Baleshare *U.K.* 57°31N 7°22W **18 G3**
Baleshwar *India* 21°35N 87°3E **85 J15**
Bali *Indonesia* 8°20S 115°0E **83 D3**
Balikeşir *Turkey* 39°39N 27°53E **73 G4**
Balikpapan *Indonesia* 1°10S 116°55E **83 D3**
Balkan Mts. *Bulgaria* 43°15N 23°0E **71 C10**
Balkanabat *Turkmenistan* 39°30N 54°22E **87 B8**
Balkhash, L. *Kazakhstan* 46°0N 74°50E **79 E9**
Ballachulish *U.K.* 56°41N 5°8W **18 J7**
Ballaghaderreen *Ireland* 53°55N 8°34W **28 D4**
Ballantrae *U.K.* 55°6N 5°0W **20 D6**
Ballarat *Australia* 37°33S 143°50E **98 H7**
Ballater *U.K.* 57°3N 3°3W **19 H11**
Balleny Is. *Antarctica* 66°30S 163°0E **55 C11**
Ballina *Ireland* 54°7N 9°9W **28 C3**
Ballinasloe *Ireland* 53°20N 8°13W **30 B6**
Ballinrobe *Ireland* 53°38N 9°13W **28 D3**
Ballinskelligs B. *Ireland* 51°48N 10°13W **30 E2**
Ballybunion *Ireland* 52°31N 9°40W **30 C3**
Ballycastle *U.K.* 55°12N 6°15W **29 A9**
Ballyclare *U.K.* 54°46N 6°0W **29 B10**
Ballyhaunis *Ireland* 53°46N 8°46W **28 D4**
Ballyhoura Mts. *Ireland* 52°18N 8°33W **30 D5**

Ballymena *U.K.* 54°52N 6°17W **29 B9**
Ballymoney *U.K.* 55°5N 6°31W **29 A8**
Ballymote *Ireland* 54°5N 8°31W **28 C4**
Ballynahinch *U.K.* 54°24N 5°54W **29 C10**
Ballyquintin Pt. *U.K.* 54°20N 5°30W **29 C11**
Ballyshannon *Ireland* 54°30N 8°11W **28 B5**
Balmoral Forest *U.K.* 57°0N 3°15W **19 J11**
Balrampur *India* 27°30N 82°20E **85 F13**
Balsas → *Mexico* 17°55N 102°10W **114 D4**
Baltic Sea *Europe* 57°0N 19°0E **63 F7**
Baltimore *Ireland* 51°29N 9°22W **30 F4**
Baltimore *U.S.A.* 39°17N 76°36W **112 F9**
Baluchistan □ *Pakistan* 27°30N 65°0E **84 F4**
Bam *Iran* 29°7N 58°14E **87 D9**
Bamako *Mali* 12°34N 7°55W **94 F4**
Bambari *C.A.R.* 5°40N 20°35E **96 C4**
Bamberg *Germany* 49°54N 10°54E **66 D6**
Bamburgh *U.K.* 55°37N 1°43W **22 A5**
Bamenda *Cameroon* 5°57N 10°11E **96 C2**
Bamford *U.K.* 53°22N 1°41W **23 F5**
Bāmiān □ *Afghan.* 35°0N 67°0E **87 C11**
Bampton *Devon, U.K.* 50°59N 3°29W **27 F7**
Bampton *Oxon., U.K.* 51°44N 1°32W **24 C5**
Banaba *Kiribati* 0°45S 169°50E **102 H8**
Bananal, I. do *Brazil* 11°30S 50°30W **120 D4**
Banbridge *U.K.* 54°22N 6°16W **29 C9**
Banbury *U.K.* 52°4N 1°20W **24 B6**
Banchory *U.K.* 57°3N 2°29W **19 H13**
Bancroft *Canada* 45°3N 77°51W **112 C9**
Banda *India* 25°30N 80°26E **84 G12**
Banda, Kepulauan *Indonesia* 4°37S 129°50E **83 D4**
Banda Aceh *Indonesia* 5°35N 95°20E **83 C1**
Banda Sea *Indonesia* 6°0S 130°0E **83 D5**
Bandar-e Abbās *Iran* 27°15N 56°15E **87 E9**
Bandar-e Anzalī *Iran* 37°30N 49°30E **86 B7**
Bandar-e Ma'shur *Iran* 30°35N 49°10E **86 D7**
Bandar-e Torkeman *Iran* 37°0N 54°10E **87 B8**
Bandar Lampung *Indonesia* 5°20S 105°10E **83 D2**
Bandar Seri Begawan *Brunei* 4°52N 115°0E **83 C3**
Bandeira, Pico da *Brazil* 20°26S 41°47W **122 D2**
Bandırma *Turkey* 40°20N 28°0E **73 F4**
Bandon *Ireland* 51°44N 8°44W **30 E5**
Bandon → *Ireland* 51°43N 8°37W **30 E5**
Bandundu
  Dem. Rep. of the Congo 3°15S 17°22E **96 E3**
Bandung *Indonesia* 6°54S 107°36E **83 D2**
Banes *Cuba* 21°0N 75°42W **115 C9**
Banff *Canada* 51°10N 115°34W **108 D8**
Banff *U.K.* 57°40N 2°33W **19 G12**
Bangalore *India* 12°59N 77°40E **84 N10**
Bangassou *C.A.R.* 4°55N 23°7E **96 D4**
Banggai, Kepulauan *Indonesia* 1°40S 123°30E **83 D4**
Banggai *Indonesia* 2°0S 105°50E **83 D2**
Bangka *Thailand* 13°45N 100°35E **83 B2**
Bangladesh ■ *Asia* 24°0N 90°0E **85 H17**
Bangor *Down, U.K.* 54°40N 5°40W **29 B10**
Bangor *Gwynedd, U.K.* 53°14N 4°8W **26 A5**
Bangui *C.A.R.* 4°23N 18°35E **96 D3**
Bangweulu, L. *Zambia* 11°0S 30°0E **96 G6**
Banham *U.K.* 52°27N 1°2E **25 B11**
Bani *Dom. Rep.* 18°16N 70°22W **115 D10**
Banja Luka *Bos.-H.* 44°49N 17°11E **70 B7**
Banjarmasin *Indonesia* 3°20S 114°35E **83 D3**
Banjul *Gambia* 13°28N 16°40W **94 F2**
Bankend *U.K.* 55°1N 3°33W **21 D8**
Banks I. *Canada* 73°15N 121°30W **108 B7**
Banks Is. *Vanuatu* 13°50S 167°30E **99 C12**
Bann → *U.K.* 55°8N 6°41W **29 A8**
Bannockburn *U.K.* 56°5N 3°55W **21 B8**
Bannu *Pakistan* 33°0N 70°18E **84 C7**
Banská Bystrica *Slovak Rep.* 48°46N 19°14E **67 D10**
Bantry *Ireland* 51°41N 9°27W **30 E4**
Bantry B. *Ireland* 51°37N 9°44W **30 E3**
Banwell *U.K.* 51°19N 2°52W **24 D3**
Banyak, Kepulauan *Indonesia* 2°10N 97°10E **83 C1**
Banyuwangi *Indonesia* 8°13S 114°21E **83 D3**
Baoding *China* 38°50N 115°28E **81 C6**
Baoji *China* 34°20N 107°5E **80 C5**
Baoshan *China* 25°10N 99°5E **80 D4**
Baotou *China* 40°32N 110°2E **81 B6**
Ba'qūbah *Iraq* 33°45N 44°50E **86 C6**
Bar Harbor *U.S.A.* 44°23N 68°13W **113 C13**
Bar-le-Duc *France* 48°47N 5°10E **68 B6**
Baraboo *U.S.A.* 43°28N 89°45W **112 D3**
Baracoa *Cuba* 20°20N 74°30W **115 C10**
Barahona *Dom. Rep.* 18°13N 71°7W **115 D10**
Barail Range *India* 25°15N 93°20E **85 G18**
Barakaldo *Spain* 43°18N 2°59W **69 A4**
Baranavichy *Belarus* 53°10N 26°0E **67 B14**
Baranof I. *U.S.A.* 57°0N 135°0W **108 D6**
Barbacena *Brazil* 21°15S 43°56W **122 D2**
Barbados ■ *W. Indies* 13°10N 59°30W **115 g**
Barberton *U.S.A.* 41°1N 81°39W **112 E7**
Barcelona *Spain* 41°22N 2°10E **69 B7**
Barcelona *Venezuela* 10°10N 64°40W **120 A3**
Barceloneta *Puerto Rico* 18°27N 66°32W **115 d**
Barddhaman *India* 23°14N 87°39E **85 H15**
Bardīyah *Libya* 31°45N 25°5E **95 B10**
Bardney *U.K.* 53°13N 0°19W **23 F8**
Bardsey I. *U.K.* 52°45N 4°47W **26 B4**
Bardstown *U.S.A.* 37°49N 85°28W **112 G5**
Bareilly *India* 28°22N 79°27E **84 E11**
Barents Sea *Arctic* 73°0N 39°0E **54 B9**
Barford *U.K.* 52°16N 1°35W **24 B5**
Bargoed *U.K.* 51°42N 3°15W **26 D7**
Barham *U.K.* 51°12N 1°11E **25 D11**
Barhi *India* 24°15N 85°25E **85 G14**
Bari *Italy* 41°8N 16°51E **70 D7**
Bari Doab *Pakistan* 30°20N 73°0E **84 D8**
Barīm *Yemen* 12°39N 43°25E **90 E8**
Barinas *Venezuela* 8°36N 70°15W **120 B2**
Baring, C. *Canada* 70°0N 117°30W **108 C8**
Barisal *Bangla.* 22°45N 90°20E **85 H17**
Barking and Dagenham □
  U.K. 51°32N 0°10E **25 C9**
Barkly Tableland *Australia* 17°50S 136°40E **98 D6**
Barlborough *U.K.* 53°17N 1°17W **23 F6**
Barlby *U.K.* 53°48N 1°2W **23 E6**

Barlee, L. *Australia* 29°15S 119°30E **98 F2**
Barletta *Italy* 41°19N 16°17E **70 D7**
Barmby Moor *U.K.* 53°56N 0°49W **23 E7**
Barmer *India* 25°45N 71°20E **84 G7**
Barmoor Castle *U.K.* 55°39N 1°59W **22 A5**
Barmouth *U.K.* 52°44N 4°4W **26 B5**
Barnard Castle *U.K.* 54°33N 1°55W **22 C5**
Barnaul *Russia* 53°20N 83°40E **79 D10**
Barnet □ *U.K.* 51°38N 0°9W **25 C8**
Barnetby le Wold *U.K.* 53°34N 0°24W **23 E8**
Barnoldswick *U.K.* 53°55N 2°11W **23 E4**
Barnsley *U.K.* 53°34N 1°27W **23 E6**
Barnstaple *U.K.* 51°5N 4°4W **27 E5**
Barotseland *Zambia* 15°0S 24°0E **97 H4**
Barques, Pt. Aux *U.S.A.* 44°4N 82°58W **112 C6**
Barquisimeto *Venezuela* 10°4N 69°19W **120 A3**
Barra *Brazil* 11°5S 43°10W **122 B2**
Barra *U.K.* 57°0N 7°29W **18 J2**
Barra, Sd. of *U.K.* 57°4N 7°25W **18 H3**
Barra do Corda *Brazil* 5°30S 45°10W **120 C5**
Barra do Pirai *Brazil* 22°30S 43°50W **122 D2**
Barra Hd. *U.K.* 56°47N 7°40W **18 J2**
Barra Mansa *Brazil* 22°35S 44°12W **122 D2**
Barrancabermeja *Colombia* 7°0N 73°50W **120 B2**
Barranquilla *Colombia* 11°0N 74°50W **120 A2**
Barre *U.S.A.* 44°12N 72°30W **113 C11**
Barreiras *Brazil* 12°8S 45°0W **122 B2**
Barreiro *Portugal* 38°39N 9°5W **69 C1**
Barreiros *Brazil* 8°49S 35°12W **122 A3**
Barretos *Brazil* 20°30S 48°35W **122 D1**
Barrhead *U.K.* 55°48N 4°23W **20 C7**
Barrie *Canada* 44°24N 79°40W **109 E12**
Barrow *U.S.A.* 71°18N 156°47W **108 B4**
Barrow → *Ireland* 52°25N 6°58W **31 D9**
Barrow-in-Furness *U.K.* 54°7N 3°14W **22 D2**
Barrow upon Humber *U.K.* 53°41N 0°23W **23 E8**
Barrowford *U.K.* 53°51N 2°14W **23 E4**
Barry *U.K.* 51°24N 3°16W **27 F7**
Barry's Bay *Canada* 45°29N 77°41W **112 C9**
Barstow *U.S.A.* 34°54N 117°1W **110 D3**
Bartlesville *U.S.A.* 36°45N 95°59W **111 C7**
Barton *U.K.* 54°29N 1°38W **22 D5**
Barton upon Humber *U.K.* 53°41N 0°25W **23 E8**
Barú, Volcán *Panama* 8°55N 82°35W **115 F8**
Barysaw *Belarus* 54°17N 28°28E **67 A15**
Bashkortostan □ *Russia* 54°0N 57°0E **72 D10**
Basilan *Phil.* 6°35N 122°0E **83 C4**
Basildon *U.K.* 51°34N 0°28E **25 C9**
Basingstoke *U.K.* 51°15N 1°5W **24 D6**
Baskatong, Rés. *Canada* 46°46N 75°50W **113 B10**
Basle *Switz.* 47°35N 7°35E **66 E4**
Basque Provinces = País Vasco □
  Spain 42°50N 2°45W **69 A4**
Basra *Iraq* 30°30N 47°50E **86 D6**
Bass Rock *U.K.* 56°5N 2°38W **21 B10**
Bass Str. *Australia* 39°15S 146°30E **98 H8**
Bassas da India *Ind. Oc.* 22°0S 39°0E **97 J7**
Basse-Pointe *Martinique* 14°52N 61°8W **114 c**
Basse-Terre *Guadeloupe* 16°0N 61°44W **114 b**
Bassein *Burma* 16°45N 94°30E **85 L19**
Bassenthwaite L. *U.K.* 54°40N 3°14W **22 C2**
Basses, Pte. des *Guadeloupe* 15°52N 61°17W **114 b**
Basseterre *St. Kitts & Nevis* 17°17N 62°43W **115 D12**
Basti *India* 26°52N 82°55E **85 F13**
Bastia *France* 42°40N 9°30E **68 E8**
Baston *U.K.* 52°43N 0°21W **23 G8**
Bata *Eq. Guin.* 1°57N 9°50E **96 D1**
Batabanó, G. de *Cuba* 22°30N 82°30W **115 C8**
Batangas *Phil.* 13°35N 121°10E **83 B4**
Batatais *Brazil* 20°54S 47°37W **122 D1**
Batavia *U.S.A.* 43°0N 78°11W **112 D8**
Batdambang *Cambodia* 13°7N 103°12E **83 B2**
Bath *U.K.* 51°23N 2°22W **24 D4**
Bath *Maine, U.S.A.* 43°55N 69°49W **113 D13**
Bath *N.Y., U.S.A.* 42°20N 77°19W **112 D9**
Bathford *U.K.* 51°24N 2°18W **24 D4**
Bathgate *U.K.* 55°54N 3°39W **21 C8**
Bathsheba *Barbados* 13°13N 59°32W **115 g**
Bathurst *Australia* 33°25S 149°31E **98 G8**
Bathurst *Canada* 47°37N 65°43W **109 E13**
Bathurst, C. *Canada* 70°34N 128°0W **108 B7**
Bathurst Inlet *Canada* 66°50N 108°1W **108 C9**
Batley *U.K.* 53°43N 1°38W **23 E5**
Batman *Turkey* 37°55N 41°5E **73 G7**
Batna *Algeria* 35°34N 6°15E **94 A7**
Baton Rouge *U.S.A.* 30°27N 91°11W **111 D8**
Batticaloa *Sri Lanka* 7°43N 81°45E **84 R12**
Battle *U.K.* 50°55N 0°30E **25 E9**
Battle Creek *U.S.A.* 42°19N 85°11W **112 D5**
Batu, Kepulauan *Indonesia* 0°30S 98°25E **83 D1**
Batu Pahat *Malaysia* 1°50N 102°56E **83 C2**
Batumi *Georgia* 41°39N 41°44E **73 F7**
Bauld, C. *Canada* 51°38N 55°26W **109 D14**
Bauru *Brazil* 22°10S 49°0W **122 D1**
Bavaria = Bayern □ *Germany* 48°50N 12°0E **66 D6**
Bawdsey *U.K.* 52°1N 1°27E **25 B11**
Bawtry *U.K.* 53°26N 1°2W **23 F6**
Bay City *U.S.A.* 43°36N 83°54W **112 D6**
Bayamo *Cuba* 20°20N 76°40W **115 C9**
Bayamón *Puerto Rico* 18°24N 66°9W **115 d**
Bayan Har Shan *China* 34°0N 98°0E **80 C4**
Bayanhongor *Mongolia* 46°8N 102°43E **80 B5**
Bayern □ *Germany* 48°50N 12°0E **66 D6**
Bayeux *France* 49°17N 0°42W **68 B3**
Bayonne *France* 43°30N 1°28W **68 E3**
Baza *Spain* 37°30N 2°39W **69 D4**
Bazaruto, I. do *Mozam.* 21°40S 35°28E **97 J7**
Beachley *U.K.* 51°37N 2°39W **24 C3**
Beachy Hd. *U.K.* 50°44N 0°15E **25 E9**
Beacon *U.S.A.* 41°30N 73°58W **113 E11**
Beaconsfield *U.K.* 51°36N 0°38W **25 C7**
Beadnell *U.K.* 55°33N 1°38W **22 A5**
Beagle, Canal *S. Amer.* 55°0S 68°30W **121 H3**
Beaminster *U.K.* 50°48N 2°44W **24 E3**
Bear → *U.S.A.* 41°30N 112°8W **110 B4**
Bear I. *Arctic* 74°30N 19°0E **54 B7**
Bear I. *Ireland* 51°38N 9°50W **30 E3**
Bear L. *U.S.A.* 41°59N 111°21W **110 B4**
Beardmore Glacier *Antarctica* 84°30S 170°0E **55 E11**

Beardstown *U.S.A.* 40°1N 90°26W **112 E2**
Béarn *France* 43°20N 0°30W **68 E3**
Bearsden *U.K.* 55°55N 4°21W **20 C7**
Bearsted *U.K.* 51°16N 0°35E **25 D10**
Beatrice *U.S.A.* 40°16N 96°45W **111 B7**
Beattock *U.K.* 55°20N 3°28W **21 D9**
Beauce, Plaine de la *France* 48°10N 1°45E **68 B4**
Beaufort Sea *Arctic* 72°0N 140°0W **54 B1**
Beaufort West *S. Africa* 32°18S 22°36E **97 L4**
Beauharnois *Canada* 45°20N 73°52W **113 C11**
Beaulieu *U.K.* 50°48N 1°27W **24 E6**
Beauly *U.K.* 57°30N 4°28W **19 H9**
Beauly → *U.K.* 57°29N 4°27W **19 H9**
Beauly Firth *U.K.* 57°30N 4°20W **19 H9**
Beaumaris *U.K.* 53°16N 4°6W **26 A5**
Beaumont *U.S.A.* 30°5N 94°6W **111 D8**
Beaune *France* 47°2N 4°50E **68 C6**
Beauvais *France* 49°25N 2°8E **68 B5**
Beaver → *U.S.A.* 55°26N 107°45W **108 D9**
Beaver Creek *Canada* 63°0N 141°0W **108 C5**
Beaver Dam *U.S.A.* 43°28N 88°50W **112 D3**
Beaver Falls *U.S.A.* 40°46N 80°20W **112 E7**
Beaver I. *U.S.A.* 45°40N 85°33W **112 C5**
Beawar *India* 26°3N 74°18E **84 F9**
Bebedouro *Brazil* 21°0S 48°25W **122 D1**
Bebington *U.K.* 53°22N 3°0W **23 F3**
Beccles *U.K.* 52°27N 1°35E **25 B12**
Béchar *Algeria* 31°38N 2°18W **94 B5**
Beckermet *U.K.* 54°27N 3°30W **22 D1**
Beckfoot *U.K.* 54°50N 3°24W **22 C2**
Beckingham *U.K.* 53°24N 0°50W **23 F7**
Beckley *U.S.A.* 37°47N 81°11W **112 G7**
Bedale *U.K.* 54°18N 1°36W **22 D5**
Beddgelert *U.K.* 53°1N 4°6W **26 A5**
Bedford *U.K.* 52°8N 0°28W **25 B8**
Bedford *Ind., U.S.A.* 38°52N 86°29W **112 F4**
Bedford *Va., U.S.A.* 37°20N 79°31W **112 G8**
Bedford Level *U.K.* 52°32N 0°7W **25 A8**
Bedfordshire □ *U.K.* 52°4N 0°28W **25 B8**
Bedlington *U.K.* 55°8N 1°35W **22 B5**
Bedworth *U.K.* 52°29N 1°28W **24 B6**
Beef I. *Br. Virgin Is.* 18°26N 64°30W **115 e**
Beeford *U.K.* 53°58N 0°17W **23 E8**
Beeston *U.K.* 52°56N 1°11W **23 G6**
Be'er Sheva *Israel* 31°15N 34°48E **86 D3**
Beeston *U.K.* 52°56N 1°11W **23 G6**
Bei Jiang → *China* 23°2N 112°58E **81 D6**
Bei'an *China* 48°10N 126°20E **81 B7**
Beighton *U.K.* 53°21N 1°20W **23 F6**
Beihai *China* 21°28N 109°6E **81 D5**
Beijing *China* 39°53N 116°21E **81 C6**
Beira *Mozam.* 19°50S 34°52E **97 H6**
Beirut *Lebanon* 33°53N 35°31E **86 C3**
Beitbridge *Zimbabwe* 22°12S 30°0E **97 J6**
Beith *U.K.* 55°45N 4°38W **20 C6**
Béja *Tunisia* 36°43N 9°12E **95 A7**
Bejaïa *Algeria* 36°42N 5°2E **94 A7**
Békéscsaba *Hungary* 46°40N 21°5E **67 E11**
Bela *Pakistan* 26°12N 66°20E **84 F5**
Belarus ■ *Europe* 53°30N 27°0E **72 D4**
Belau = Palau ■ *Palau* 7°30N 134°30E **83 C5**
Belbroughton *U.K.* 52°24N 2°7W **24 B4**
Belcher Chan. *Canada* 77°15N 95°0W **109 B10**
Belcher Is. *Canada* 56°15N 78°45W **109 D12**
Belém *Brazil* 1°20S 48°30W **120 C5**
Belep, Îs. *N. Cal.* 19°45S 163°40E **99 D11**
Belet Uen *Somali Rep.* 4°30N 45°5E **88 G4**
Belfast *U.K.* 54°37N 5°56W **29 B10**
Belfast L. *U.K.* 54°40N 5°50W **29 B10**
Belford *U.K.* 55°36N 1°49W **22 A5**
Belfort *France* 47°38N 6°50E **68 C7**
Belgaum *India* 15°55N 74°35E **84 M9**
Belgium ■ *Europe* 50°30N 5°0E **65 D4**
Belgorod *Russia* 50°35N 36°35E **73 D6**
Belgrade *Serbia* 44°50N 20°37E **71 B9**
Belitung *Indonesia* 3°10S 107°50E **83 D2**
Belize ■ *Cent. Amer.* 17°0N 88°30W **114 D7**
Belize City *Belize* 17°25N 88°10W **114 D7**
Bell Peninsula *Canada* 63°50N 82°0W **109 C11**
Bell Ville *Argentina* 32°40S 62°40W **121 F3**
Bella Coola *Canada* 52°25N 126°40W **108 D7**
Bellaire *U.S.A.* 40°1N 80°45W **112 E7**
Bellary *India* 15°10N 76°56E **84 M10**
Belle Fourche → *U.S.A.* 44°26N 102°18W **110 B6**
Belle-Île *France* 47°20N 3°10W **68 C2**
Belle Isle *Canada* 51°57N 55°25W **109 D14**
Belle Isle, Str. of *Canada* 51°30N 56°30W **109 D14**
Bellefontaine *U.S.A.* 40°22N 83°46W **112 E6**
Belleplaine *Barbados* 13°15N 59°34W **115 g**
Belleville *Canada* 44°10N 77°23W **112 C9**
Belleville *U.S.A.* 38°31N 89°59W **112 F3**
Bellingham *U.K.* 55°9N 2°16W **22 B4**
Bellingham *U.S.A.* 48°46N 122°29W **110 A2**
Bellingshausen Sea *Antarctica* 66°0S 80°0W **55 C17**
Bellinzona *Switz.* 46°11N 9°1E **66 E5**
Belmonte *Brazil* 16°0S 39°0W **122 C3**
Belmopan *Belize* 17°18N 88°30W **114 D7**
Belmullet *Ireland* 54°14N 9°58W **28 C2**
Belo Horizonte *Brazil* 19°55S 43°56W **122 C2**
Belo Jardim *Brazil* 8°20S 36°26W **122 A3**
Beloit *U.S.A.* 42°31N 89°2W **112 D3**
Belomorsk *Russia* 64°35N 34°54E **72 B5**
Beloretsk *Russia* 53°58N 58°24E **72 D10**
Beloye, L. *Russia* 60°10N 37°35E **72 B6**
Belper *U.K.* 53°2N 1°29W **23 F6**
Belsay *U.K.* 55°6N 1°51W **22 B5**
Belton *N. Lincs., U.K.* 53°33N 0°48W **23 E7**
Belton *Norfolk, U.K.* 52°35N 1°40E **25 A12**
Beltsy *Moldova* 47°48N 27°58E **67 E14**
Belturbet *Ireland* 54°6N 7°26E **28 B7**
Belvidere *U.S.A.* 42°15N 88°50W **112 D3**
Bembridge *U.K.* 50°41N 1°5W **24 E6**
Bemidji *U.S.A.* 47°28N 94°53W **111 A8**
Ben Cruachan *U.K.* 56°26N 5°8W **20 B5**
Ben Dearg *U.K.* 57°47N 4°56W **19 G8**
Ben Hope *U.K.* 58°25N 4°36W **19 F8**
Ben Lawers *U.K.* 56°32N 4°14W **20 A7**
Ben Lomond *U.K.* 56°11N 4°38W **20 B6**

Ben Macdhui *U.K.* 57°4N 3°40W **19 H10**
Ben Mhor *U.K.* 57°15N 7°18W **18 H3**
Ben More *Argyll & Bute, U.K.* 56°26N 6°1W **20 B3**
Ben More *Stirling, U.K.* 56°23N 4°32W **20 B6**
Ben More Assynt *U.K.* 58°8N 4°52W **19 F8**
Ben Nevis *U.K.* 56°48N 5°1W **18 J7**
Ben Vorlich *U.K.* 56°21N 4°14W **20 B7**
Ben Wyvis *U.K.* 57°40N 4°35W **19 G8**
Benares = Varanasi *India* 25°22N 83°0E **85 G13**
Benbecula *U.K.* 57°26N 7°21W **18 H3**
Bend *U.S.A.* 44°4N 121°19W **110 B2**
Benderloch *U.K.* 56°30N 5°22W **20 A5**
Bendigo *Australia* 36°40S 144°15E **98 H7**
Benevento *Italy* 41°8N 14°45E **70 D6**
Bengal, Bay of *Ind. Oc.* 15°0N 90°0E **85 M17**
Benghazi *Libya* 32°11N 20°3E **95 B10**
Bengkulu *Indonesia* 3°50S 102°12E **83 D2**
Benguela *Angola* 12°37S 13°25E **97 G2**
Beni → *Bolivia* 10°23S 65°24W **120 D3**
Beni Mellal *Morocco* 32°21N 6°21W **94 B4**
Beni Suef *Egypt* 29°5N 31°6E **95 C12**
Benidorm *Spain* 38°33N 0°9W **69 C5**
Benin ■ *Africa* 10°0N 2°0E **94 G6**
Benin, Bight of *W. Afr.* 5°0N 3°0E **94 H6**
Benin City *Nigeria* 6°20N 5°31E **94 G7**
Benington *U.K.* 53°0N 0°5E **23 F9**
Benjamin Constant *Brazil* 4°40S 70°15W **120 C2**
Benoni *S. Africa* 26°11S 28°18E **97 K5**
Benson *U.K.* 51°37N 1°6W **24 C6**
Bentley *Hants., U.K.* 51°12N 0°52W **25 D7**
Bentley *S. Yorks., U.K.* 53°33N 1°8W **23 E6**
Benton *U.S.A.* 38°0N 88°55W **112 G3**
Benton Harbor *U.S.A.* 42°6N 86°27W **112 D4**
Benue → *Nigeria* 7°48N 6°46E **94 G7**
Benxi *China* 41°20N 123°48E **81 B7**
Beppu *Japan* 33°15N 131°30E **82 G2**
Berber *Sudan* 18°0N 34°0E **95 E12**
Berbera *Somali Rep.* 10°30N 45°2E **88 E4**
Berbérati *C.A.R.* 4°15N 15°40E **96 D3**
Berbice → *Guyana* 6°20N 57°32W **120 B4**
Berdyansk *Ukraine* 46°45N 36°50E **73 E6**
Berdychiv *Ukraine* 49°57N 28°30E **73 E4**
Bere Alston *U.K.* 50°29N 4°13W **27 G5**
Bere Regis *U.K.* 50°45N 2°14W **24 E4**
Berea *U.S.A.* 37°34N 84°17W **112 G5**
Berens → *Canada* 52°25N 97°2W **108 D10**
Berezina → *Belarus* 52°33N 30°14E **72 D5**
Berezniki *Russia* 59°24N 56°46E **72 C10**
Bérgamo *Italy* 45°41N 9°43E **70 B3**
Bergen *Norway* 60°20N 5°20E **63 E5**
Bergen op Zoom *Neths.* 51°28N 4°18E **65 C4**
Bergerac *France* 44°51N 0°30E **68 D4**
Bergisch Gladbach *Germany* 50°59N 7°8E **65 D7**
Bering Sea *Pac. Oc.* 58°0N 171°0W **102 B10**
Bering Strait *Pac. Oc.* 65°30N 169°0W **108 C3**
Berkeley *U.S.A.* 51°41N 2°27W **24 C4**
Berkhamsted *U.K.* 51°45N 0°33W **25 C7**
Berkner I. *Antarctica* 79°30S 50°0W **55 D18**
Berkshire Downs *U.K.* 51°33N 1°29W **24 C6**
Berlin *Germany* 52°31N 13°23E **66 B7**
Berlin *U.S.A.* 44°28N 71°11W **113 C12**
Bermejo → *Argentina* 26°51S 58°23W **121 E4**
Bermuda ☑ *Atl. Oc.* 32°45N 65°0W **52 C6**
Bern *Switz.* 46°57N 7°28E **66 E4**
Berneray *U.K.* 57°43N 7°11W **18 G3**
Berry *France* 46°50N 2°0E **68 C5**
Berry Hd. *U.K.* 50°24N 3°29W **27 G7**
Bertraghboy B. *Ireland* 53°22N 9°54W **30 B3**
Berwick *U.S.A.* 41°3N 76°14W **112 E9**
Berwick-upon-Tweed *U.K.* 55°46N 2°0W **22 A5**
Berwyn Mts. *U.K.* 52°54N 3°26W **26 B7**
Besançon *France* 47°15N 6°2E **68 C7**
Bessarabiya *Moldova* 47°0N 28°10E **67 E15**
Bessemer *U.S.A.* 46°29N 90°3W **112 B2**
Bethel *U.S.A.* 60°48N 161°45W **108 C3**
Bethesda *U.K.* 53°9N 4°3W **26 A5**
Bethlehem *S. Africa* 28°14S 28°18E **97 K5**
Bethlehem *U.S.A.* 40°37N 75°23W **113 E10**
Béthune *France* 50°30N 2°38E **68 A5**
Bettiah *India* 26°48N 84°33E **85 F14**
Betul *India* 21°58N 77°59E **84 J10**
Betws-y-Coed *U.K.* 53°5N 3°48W **26 A6**
Beverley *U.K.* 53°51N 0°26W **23 E8**
Bewdley *U.K.* 52°23N 2°19W **24 B4**
Bexhill *U.K.* 50°51N 0°29E **25 E9**
Bexley □ *U.K.* 51°27N 0°9E **25 D9**
Beyneu *Kazakhstan* 45°18N 55°9E **73 E10**
Beypazarı *Turkey* 40°10N 31°56E **73 F5**
Beyşehir Gölü *Turkey* 37°41N 31°33E **73 G5**
Béziers *France* 43°20N 3°12E **68 E5**
Bhagalpur *India* 25°10N 87°0E **85 G15**
Bhakkar *Pakistan* 31°40N 71°5E **84 D7**
Bhaktapur *Nepal* 27°38N 85°24E **84 H11**
Bhanrer Ra. *India* 23°40N 79°45E **84 H11**
Bharatpur *India* 27°15N 77°30E **84 F10**
Bharuch *India* 21°47N 73°0E **84 J8**
Bhatpara *India* 22°50N 88°25E **85 H16**
Bhavnagar *India* 21°45N 72°10E **84 J8**
Bhilainagar-Durg *India* 21°13N 81°26E **85 J12**
Bhilwara *India* 25°25N 74°38E **84 G9**
Bhima → *India* 16°25N 77°17E **84 L10**
Bhiwandi *India* 19°20N 73°0E **84 K8**
Bhiwani *India* 28°50N 76°9E **84 E10**
Bhopal *India* 23°20N 77°30E **84 H10**
Bhubaneshwar *India* 20°15N 85°50E **85 J14**
Bhuj *India* 23°15N 69°49E **84 H6**
Bhusawal *India* 21°3N 75°46E **84 J9**
Bhutan ■ *Asia* 27°25N 90°30E **85 F17**
Biala Podlaska *Poland* 52°4N 23°6E **67 B12**
Białystok *Poland* 53°10N 23°10E **67 B12**
Biarritz *France* 43°29N 1°33W **68 E3**
Bibury *U.K.* 51°45N 1°49W **24 C5**
Bicester *U.K.* 51°54N 1°9W **24 C6**
Bicton *U.K.* 52°44N 2°48W **23 G3**
Bida *Nigeria* 9°3N 5°58E **94 G7**
Biddeford *U.S.A.* 43°30N 70°28W **113 D12**
Biddenden *U.K.* 51°7N 0°40E **25 D10**
Biddulph *U.K.* 53°7N 2°10W **23 F4**

Bideford   Burqin

Bideford U.K. 51°1N 4°13W 27 E5
Bideford Bay U.K. 51°5N 4°20W 27 E5
Bidford-on-Avon U.K. 52°11N 1°50W 24 B5
Bié Plateau Angola 12°0S 16°0E 97 G3
Biel Switz. 47°8N 7°14E 66 E4
Bielefeld Germany 52°1N 8°33E 66 B5
Biella Italy 45°34N 8°3E 70 B3
Bielsko-Biała Poland 49°50N 19°2E 67 D10
Bien Hoa Vietnam 10°57N 106°49E 83 B2
Bienville, L. Canada 55°5N 72°40W 109 D12
Big Belt Mts. U.S.A. 46°30N 111°25W 110 A4
Big Rapids U.S.A. 43°42N 85°29W 112 D5
Big Sioux → U.S.A. 42°29N 96°27W 111 B7
Big Spring U.S.A. 32°15N 101°28W 110 D6
Big Trout L. Canada 53°40N 90°0W 109 D11
Bigbury U.K. 50°18N 3°53W 27 G6
Bigbury B. U.K. 50°16N 3°54W 27 G6
Biggar Canada 52°4N 108°0W 108 D9
Biggar U.K. 55°38N 3°32W 21 C8
Biggleswade U.K. 52°5N 0°14W 25 B8
Bighorn → U.S.A. 46°10N 107°28W 110 A5
Bighorn Mts. U.S.A. 44°25N 107°0W 110 B5
Bihar India 25°5N 85°40E 85 G14
Bihar □ India 25°0N 86°0E 85 G15
Bijagós, Arquipélago dos
    Guinea-Biss. 11°15N 16°10W 94 F2
Bijapur India 16°50N 75°55E 84 L9
Bikaner India 28°2N 73°18E 84 E8
Bikini Atoll Marshall Is. 12°0N 167°30E 102 F8
Bila Tserkva Ukraine 49°45N 30°10E 67 D16
Bilaspur India 22°2N 82°15E 85 H13
Bilbao Spain 43°16N 2°56W 69 A4
Bilecik Turkey 40°5N 30°5E 73 F5
Bilhorod-Dnistrovskyy
    Ukraine 46°11N 30°23E 73 E5
Billericay U.K. 51°38N 0°26E 25 C9
Billesdon U.K. 52°38N 0°54W 23 G7
Billingham U.K. 54°36N 1°17W 22 C6
Billinghay U.K. 53°5N 0°15W 23 F8
Billings U.S.A. 45°47N 108°30W 110 A5
Billingshurst U.K. 51°2N 0°27W 25 D8
Bilma Niger 18°50N 13°30E 95 E8
Biloxi U.S.A. 30°24N 88°53W 111 D9
Bilston U.K. 52°34N 2°4W 23 G4
Bimini Is. Bahamas 25°42N 79°25W 115 B9
Binbrook U.K. 53°26N 0°10W 23 E8
Bingham U.K. 52°57N 0°58W 23 G7
Binghamton U.S.A. 42°6N 75°55W 113 D10
Bingley U.K. 53°51N 1°50W 22 E5
Bioko Eq. Guin. 3°30N 8°40E 96 D1
Biratnagar Nepal 26°27N 87°17E 85 F15
Birchington U.K. 51°22N 1°19E 25 D11
Birdlip U.K. 51°50N 2°5W 24 C4
Birkdale U.K. 53°38N 3°1W 23 E2
Birkenhead U.K. 53°23N 3°2W 23 F2
Birmingham U.K. 52°29N 1°52W 23 H5
Birmingham U.S.A. 33°31N 86°48W 111 D9
Birmingham Int. ✈ (BHX)
    U.K. 52°26N 1°45W 23 H5
Birnin Kebbi Nigeria 12°32N 4°12E 94 F6
Birr Ireland 53°6N 7°54W 30 B7
Birtley Northumberland, U.K. 55°6N 2°12W 22 B4
Birtley Tyne & W., U.K. 54°54N 1°34W 22 C5
Biscay, B. of Atl. Oc. 45°0N 2°0W 68 D1
Bishkek Kyrgyzstan 42°54N 74°46E 79 E9
Bishop Auckland U.K. 54°39N 1°40W 22 C5
Bishop's Castle U.K. 52°30N 2°59W 23 H3
Bishop's Cleeve U.K. 51°57N 2°3W 24 C4
Bishop's Frome U.K. 52°8N 2°29W 24 B4
Bishop's Nympton U.K. 51°0N 3°47W 27 E6
Bishop's Stortford U.K. 51°52N 0°10E 25 C9
Bishop's Waltham U.K. 50°57N 1°11W 24 E6
Bishopsteignton U.K. 50°33N 3°33W 27 F6
Bishopstoke U.K. 50°58N 1°19W 24 E6
Biskra Algeria 34°50N 5°44E 94 B7
Bismarck U.S.A. 46°48N 100°47W 110 A6
Bismarck Arch. Papua N. G. 2°30S 150°0E 98 A9
Bissau Guinea-Biss. 11°45N 15°45W 94 F2
Bitola Macedonia 41°1N 21°20E 71 D9
Bitterfontein S. Africa 31°1S 18°32E 97 L3
Bitterroot Range U.S.A. 46°0N 114°20W 110 A4
Bitton U.K. 51°25N 2°27W 24 D4
Biu Nigeria 10°40N 12°3E 95 F8
Biwa-Ko Japan 35°15N 136°10E 82 F5
Bizerte Tunisia 37°15N 9°50E 95 A7
Blaby U.K. 52°35N 1°10W 23 G6
Black Combe U.K. 54°16N 3°20W 22 D2
Black Esk → U.K. 55°12N 3°11W 21 D9
Black Forest = Schwarzwald
    Germany 48°30N 8°20E 66 D5
Black Hd. Ireland 53°9N 9°16W 30 B4
Black Hd. U.K. 50°0N 5°7W 27 H3
Black Hills U.S.A. 44°0N 103°45W 110 B6
Black Isle U.K. 57°35N 4°16W 19 G9
Black Mts. U.K. 51°55N 3°7W 26 D7
Black Range U.S.A. 33°15N 107°50W 110 D5
Black River Jamaica 18°0N 77°50W 114 a
Black River Falls U.S.A. 44°18N 90°51W 112 C2
Black Rock Barbados 13°7N 59°37W 115 g
Black Sea Eurasia 43°30N 35°0E 73 F6
Blackburn U.K. 53°45N 2°29W 23 E4
Blackdown Hills U.K. 50°57N 3°15W 24 E2
Blackmoor Vale U.K. 50°54N 2°28W 24 E4
Blackpool U.K. 53°49N 3°3W 23 E2
Blackrock Ireland 53°18N 6°11W 31 B10
Blacksburg U.S.A. 37°14N 80°25W 112 G7
Blacksod B. Ireland 54°6N 10°0W 28 C1
Blackwater → Meath, Ireland 53°39N 6°41W 29 D8
Blackwater → Waterford,
    Ireland 52°4N 7°52W 30 D7
Blackwater → Armagh, U.K. 54°31N 6°35W 29 B8
Blackwater → Essex, U.K. 51°44N 0°53E 25 C10
Blaenau Ffestiniog U.K. 53°0N 3°56W 26 B6
Blaenavon U.K. 51°46N 3°5W 26 D7
Blagdon U.K. 51°20N 2°43W 24 D3
Blagoevgrad Bulgaria 42°2N 23°5E 71 C10
Blagoveshchensk Russia 50°20N 127°30E 79 D14
Blair Atholl U.K. 56°46N 3°50W 19 J10
Blairgowrie U.K. 56°35N 3°21W 21 A9

Blakeney Gloucs., U.K. 51°46N 2°28W 24 C4
Blakeney Norfolk, U.K. 52°58N 1°1E 25 A11
Blanc, Mont Europe 45°48N 6°50E 68 D7
Blanca, B. Argentina 39°10S 61°30W 121 F3
Blanca Peak U.S.A. 37°35N 105°29W 110 C5
Blanco, C. U.S.A. 42°51N 124°34W 110 B2
Blandford Forum U.K. 50°51N 2°9W 24 E4
Blanquilla Venezuela 11°51N 64°37W 115 E12
Blantyre Malawi 15°45S 35°0E 97 H6
Blarney Ireland 51°56N 8°33W 30 E5
Blaydon U.K. 54°58N 1°42W 22 C5
Blean U.K. 51°18N 1°3E 25 D11
Bleasdale Moors U.K. 53°55N 2°35W 23 E3
Blenheim N.Z. 41°38S 173°57E 99 J13
Bletchingdon U.K. 51°51N 1°15W 24 C6
Bletchley U.K. 51°59N 0°44W 25 C7
Blida Algeria 36°30N 2°49E 94 A6
Blisworth U.K. 52°10N 0°56W 25 B7
Blitar Indonesia 8°5S 112°11E 83 D3
Blockley U.K. 52°1N 1°44W 24 B5
Bloemfontein S. Africa 29°6S 26°7E 97 K5
Blofield U.K. 52°38N 1°26E 25 A11
Blois France 47°35N 1°20E 68 C4
Bloody Foreland Ireland 55°10N 8°17W 28 A5
Bloomington Ill., U.S.A. 40°28N 89°0W 112 E3
Bloomington Ind., U.S.A. 39°10N 86°32W 112 F4
Bloomsburg U.S.A. 41°0N 76°27W 112 E9
Bloxham U.K. 52°1N 1°21W 24 B6
Blue Mountain Pk. Jamaica 18°3N 76°36W 114 a
Blue Mts. Jamaica 18°3N 76°36W 114 a
Blue Mts. Oreg., U.S.A. 45°0N 118°20W 110 A3
Blue Mts. Pa., U.S.A. 40°30N 76°30W 112 E9
Blue Nile → Sudan 15°38N 32°31E 95 E12
Blue Ridge Mts. U.S.A. 36°30N 80°15W 111 C10
Blue Stack Mts. Ireland 54°42N 8°12W 28 B5
Bluefield U.S.A. 37°15N 81°17W 112 G7
Bluefields Nic. 12°20N 83°50W 114 E8
Blumenau Brazil 27°0S 49°0W 121 E5
Blundeston U.K. 52°31N 1°42E 25 A12
Blyth Northumberland, U.K. 55°8N 1°31W 22 B5
Blyth Notts., U.K. 53°22N 1°3W 23 F6
Blyth → U.K. 55°8N 1°33W 22 B5
Blyth Bridge U.K. 55°42N 3°22W 21 C9
Blyton U.K. 53°27N 0°42W 23 F7
Bo S. Leone 7°55N 11°50W 94 G3
Bo Hai China 39°0N 119°0E 81 C6
Boa Vista Brazil 2°48N 60°30W 120 B3
Bobcaygeon Canada 44°33N 78°33W 112 C8
Bobo-Dioulasso Burkina Faso 11°8N 4°13W 94 F5
Bôbr → Poland 52°4N 15°4E 66 B8
Bochum Germany 51°28N 7°13E 66 C4
Boddam U.K. 59°56N 1°17W 18 C15
Boden Sweden 65°50N 21°42E 63 D8
Bodiam U.K. 51°0N 0°34E 25 D10
Bodinnick U.K. 50°20N 4°38W 27 G4
Bodmin U.K. 50°28N 4°43W 27 G4
Bodmin Moor U.K. 50°33N 4°36W 27 G4
Bodø Norway 67°17N 14°24E 63 D6
Bodrog → Hungary 48°11N 21°22E 67 D11
Bodrum Turkey 37°3N 27°30E 73 G4
Bogalusa U.S.A. 30°47N 89°52W 111 D9
Bogda Shan China 43°35N 89°40E 80 B3
Boggeragh Mts. Ireland 52°2N 8°55W 30 D5
Bognor Regis U.K. 50°47N 0°40W 25 E7
Bogor Indonesia 6°36S 106°48E 83 D2
Bogotá Colombia 4°34N 74°0W 120 B2
Bogra Bangla. 24°51N 89°22E 85 G16
Böhmerwald Germany 49°8N 13°14E 66 D7
Bohol Sea Phil. 9°0N 124°0E 83 C4
Boise U.S.A. 43°37N 116°13W 110 B3
Bole China 45°11N 81°37E 80 B3
Bolivia ■ S. Amer. 17°6S 64°0W 120 D3
Bollington U.K. 53°18N 2°6W 23 F4
Bolney U.K. 50°59N 0°12W 25 E8
Bologna Italy 44°29N 11°20E 70 B4
Bologoye Russia 57°55N 34°5E 72 C5
Bolsena, L. di Italy 42°36N 11°56E 70 C4
Bolsover U.K. 53°14N 1°16W 23 F6
Bolt Head U.K. 50°12N 3°48W 27 G6
Bolt Tail U.K. 50°14N 3°52W 27 G6
Bolton U.K. 53°35N 2°26W 23 E4
Bolton Abbey U.K. 53°59N 1°53W 23 E5
Bolton by Bowland U.K. 53°56N 2°20W 23 E4
Bolton le Sands U.K. 54°6N 2°48W 22 D3
Bolu Turkey 40°45N 31°35E 73 F5
Bolvadin Turkey 38°45N 31°4E 73 G5
Bolzano Italy 46°31N 11°22E 70 A4
Bom Despacho Brazil 19°43S 45°15W 122 C1
Bom Jesus da Lapa Brazil 13°15S 43°25W 122 B2
Boma Dem. Rep. of the Congo 5°50S 13°4E 96 F2
Bombala Australia 36°56S 149°15E 98 H8
Bombay = Mumbai India 18°56N 72°50E 84 K8
Bomu → C.A.R. 4°40N 22°30E 96 D4
Bon, C. Tunisia 37°1N 11°2E 90 C5
Bonaire Neth. Ant. 12°10N 68°15W 115 E11
Bonar Bridge U.K. 57°54N 4°20W 19 G9
Bonavista Canada 48°40N 53°5W 109 E14
Bonchester Bridge U.K. 55°24N 2°39W 21 D10
Bonchurch U.K. 50°37N 1°11W 24 E6
Bo'ness U.K. 56°1N 3°37W 21 B8
Bongor Chad 10°35N 15°20E 95 F9
Bongos, Massif des C.A.R. 8°40N 22°25E 96 C4
Bonifacio France 41°24N 9°10E 68 F8
Bonn Germany 50°46N 7°6E 66 C4
Bonny, Bight of Africa 3°30N 9°20E 96 D1
Bonnyrigg U.K. 55°53N 3°6W 21 C9
Boonville U.S.A. 38°3N 87°16W 112 F4
Boot U.K. 54°24N 3°13W 22 D2
Boothia, Gulf of Canada 71°0N 90°0W 109 B11
Boothia Pen. Canada 71°0N 94°0W 108 B10
Bootle Cumb., U.K. 54°18N 3°22W 22 D2
Bootle Mersey., U.K. 53°28N 3°1W 23 F2
Borås Sweden 57°43N 12°56E 63 F6
Borborema, Planalto da Brazil 7°0S 37°0W 116 D7
Bordeaux France 44°50N 0°36W 68 D3
Borden I. Canada 78°30N 111°30W 109 B8
Borden Pen. Canada 73°0N 83°0W 109 B11
Bordon U.K. 51°8N 0°52W 25 D7
Borehamwood U.K. 51°40N 0°15W 25 C8

Boreland U.K. 55°13N 3°17W 21 D9
Borger U.S.A. 35°39N 101°24W 110 C6
Borhoyn Tal Mongolia 43°50N 111°58E 81 B6
Borisoglebsk Russia 51°27N 42°5E 73 D7
Borkou Chad 18°15N 18°50E 95 E9
Borneo E. Indies 1°0N 115°0E 83 C3
Bornholm Denmark 55°10N 15°0E 63 F7
Borohoro Shan China 44°6N 83°10E 80 B3
Boroughbridge U.K. 54°6N 1°24W 22 D6
Borovichi Russia 58°25N 33°55E 72 C5
Borrowdale U.K. 54°31N 3°10W 22 C2
Borth U.K. 52°29N 4°2W 26 C5
Borūjerd Iran 33°55N 48°50E 86 C7
Bosaso Somali Rep. 11°12N 49°18E 88 E4
Bosbury U.K. 52°5N 2°26W 24 B4
Boscastle U.K. 50°41N 4°42W 27 F4
Boscobelle Barbados 13°17N 59°35W 115 g
Bose China 23°53N 106°35E 80 D5
Bosham U.K. 50°49N 0°51W 25 E7
Bosnia-Herzegovina ■ Europe 44°0N 18°0E 70 B7
Bosporus Turkey 41°5N 29°3E 73 F4
Bossangoa C.A.R. 6°35N 17°30E 96 C3
Bosten Hu China 41°55N 87°40E 80 B3
Boston U.K. 52°59N 0°2W 23 G8
Boston U.S.A. 42°22N 71°3W 113 D12
Bothel U.K. 54°45N 3°15W 22 C2
Bothnia, G. of Europe 62°0N 20°0E 63 E8
Botletle → Botswana 20°10S 23°15E 97 J4
Botoşani Romania 47°42N 26°41E 67 E14
Botswana ■ Africa 22°0S 24°0E 97 J4
Bottesford U.K. 52°57N 0°47W 23 G7
Bottrop Germany 51°31N 6°58E 65 C6
Botucatu Brazil 22°55S 48°30W 122 D1
Bou Saâda Algeria 35°11N 4°9E 94 A6
Bouaké Ivory C. 7°40N 5°2W 94 G4
Bouar C.A.R. 6°0N 15°40E 96 C3
Bouârfa Morocco 32°32N 1°58W 94 B5
Bougainville I. Papua N. G. 6°0S 155°0E 99 B10
Bouillante Guadeloupe 16°8N 61°46W 114 b
Boulder U.S.A. 40°1N 105°17W 110 B5
Boulogne-sur-Mer France 50°42N 1°36E 68 A4
Bounty Is. Pac. Oc. 48°0S 178°30E 102 M9
Bourbonnais France 46°28N 3°0E 68 C5
Bourg-en-Bresse France 46°13N 5°12E 68 C6
Bourges France 47°9N 2°25E 68 C5
Bourgogne □ France 47°0N 4°50E 68 C6
Bourke Australia 30°8S 145°55E 98 G8
Bourne U.K. 52°47N 0°22W 23 G8
Bournemouth U.K. 50°43N 1°52W 24 E5
Bourton-on-the-Water U.K. 51°52N 1°45W 24 C5
Bouvet I. Antarctica 54°26S 3°24E 52 G10
Bovey Tracey U.K. 50°36N 3°41W 27 F6
Bow → Canada 49°57N 111°41W 108 D8
Bowes U.K. 54°32N 1°59W 22 C5
Bowland, Forest of U.K. 54°0N 2°30W 23 E3
Bowling Green Ky., U.S.A. 36°59N 86°27W 112 G4
Bowling Green Ohio, U.S.A. 41°23N 83°39W 112 E6
Bowmore U.K. 55°45N 6°17W 20 C3
Bowness-on-Solway U.K. 54°57N 3°12W 22 C2
Bowness-on-Windermere
    U.K. 54°22N 2°55W 22 D3
Box U.K. 51°25N 2°15W 24 D4
Box Hill U.K. 51°15N 0°16W 25 D8
Boyle Ireland 53°59N 8°18W 28 D5
Boyne → Ireland 53°43N 6°15W 29 D9
Boyoma, Chutes
    Dem. Rep. of the Congo 0°35N 25°23E 90 F6
Bozeat U.K. 52°14N 0°40W 25 B7
Bozeman U.S.A. 45°41N 111°2W 110 A4
Bozoum C.A.R. 6°25N 16°35E 96 C3
Brabant □ Belgium 50°46N 4°30E 65 D4
Brač Croatia 43°20N 16°40E 70 C7
Bracadale, L. U.K. 57°20N 6°30W 18 H4
Bracebridge Canada 45°2N 79°19W 112 C8
Bracebridge Heath U.K. 53°12N 0°32W 23 F7
Bräcke Sweden 62°45N 15°26E 63 E7
Brackley U.K. 52°2N 1°8W 24 B6
Bracknell U.K. 51°25N 0°43W 25 D7
Bradford U.K. 53°47N 1°45W 23 E5
Bradford U.S.A. 41°58N 78°38W 112 E8
Bradford on Avon U.K. 51°21N 2°14W 24 D4
Brading U.K. 50°41N 1°8W 24 E6
Bradwell-on-Sea U.K. 51°43N 0°56E 25 C10
Bradworthy U.K. 50°53N 4°24W 27 F5
Braemar U.K. 57°2N 3°26W 19 H11
Braga Portugal 41°35N 8°25W 69 B1
Bragança Brazil 1°0S 47°2W 120 C5
Bragança Paulista Brazil 22°55S 46°32W 122 D1
Brahmanbaria Bangla. 23°58N 91°15E 85 H17
Brahmani → India 20°39N 86°46E 85 J15
Brahmapur India 19°15N 84°54E 85 K14
Brahmaputra → Asia 23°40N 90°35E 85 H16
Braich-y-pwll U.K. 52°47N 4°46W 26 B4
Brăila Romania 45°19N 27°59E 67 F14
Brailsford U.K. 52°58N 1°35W 23 G5
Brainerd U.S.A. 46°22N 94°12W 111 A8
Braintree U.K. 51°53N 0°34E 25 C10
Bramford U.K. 52°4N 1°7E 25 B11
Brampton Canada 43°45N 79°45W 112 D8
Brampton Cambs., U.K. 52°19N 0°14W 25 B8
Brampton Cumb., U.K. 54°57N 2°44W 22 C3
Brancaster U.K. 52°58N 0°39E 25 A10
Branco → Brazil 1°20S 61°50W 120 C3
Brandenburg Germany 52°25N 12°33E 66 B7
Brandenburg □ Germany 52°50N 13°0E 66 B6
Branderburgh U.K. 57°43N 3°17W 19 G11
Brandon Canada 49°50N 99°57W 108 E10
Brandon Durham, U.K. 54°46N 1°37W 22 C5
Brandon Suffolk, U.K. 52°27N 0°38E 25 B10
Brandon B. Ireland 52°17N 10°8W 30 D2
Brandon Mt. Ireland 52°15N 10°15W 30 D2
Branston U.K. 53°12N 0°27W 23 F8
Brantford Canada 43°10N 80°15W 112 D7
Bras d'Or L. Canada 45°50N 60°50W 113 C17
Brasília Brazil 15°47S 47°55W 122 C1
Braşov Romania 45°38N 25°35E 67 F13
Bratislava Slovak Rep. 48°10N 17°7E 67 D9
Bratsk Russia 56°10N 101°30E 79 D12
Brattleboro U.S.A. 42°51N 72°34W 113 D11

Braunschweig Germany 52°15N 10°31E 66 B6
Braunton U.K. 51°7N 4°10W 27 E5
Bray Ireland 53°13N 6°7W 31 B10
Bray U.K. 51°30N 0°41W 25 D7
Brazil ■ S. Amer. 12°0S 50°0W 120 D4
Brazil U.S.A. 39°32N 87°8W 112 F4
Brazilian Highlands Brazil 18°0S 46°30W 116 E6
Brazos → U.S.A. 28°53N 95°23W 111 E7
Brazzaville Congo 4°9S 15°12E 96 E3
Breadalbane U.K. 56°30N 4°15W 20 A7
Breage U.K. 50°6N 5°20W 27 G3
Breamish → U.K. 55°35N 2°2W 22 A4
Brechin U.K. 56°44N 2°39W 19 J12
Breckland U.K. 52°30N 0°40E 25 B10
Brecon U.K. 51°57N 3°23W 26 D7
Brecon Beacons U.K. 51°53N 3°26W 26 D7
Brecon Beacons △ U.K. 51°50N 3°30W 26 D6
Breda Neths. 51°35N 4°45E 65 C4
Brede U.K. 50°56N 0°36E 25 E10
Bredon Hill U.K. 52°3N 2°2W 24 B4
Bregenz Austria 47°30N 9°45E 66 E5
Breiðafjörður Iceland 65°15N 23°15W 63 A1
Bremen Germany 53°4N 8°47E 66 B5
Bremerhaven Germany 53°33N 8°36E 66 B5
Bremerton U.S.A. 47°34N 122°37W 110 A2
Brendon Hills U.K. 51°6N 3°25W 24 D2
Brennerpass Austria 47°2N 11°30E 66 E6
Brent □ U.K. 51°33N 0°16W 25 C8
Brentwood U.K. 51°37N 0°19E 25 C9
Bréscia Italy 45°33N 10°15E 70 B4
Bressay U.K. 60°9N 1°6W 18 B15
Brest Belarus 52°10N 23°40E 67 B12
Brest France 48°24N 4°31W 68 B1
Bretagne □ France 48°10N 3°0W 68 B2
Breton Sd. U.S.A. 29°35N 89°15W 111 E9
Brewer U.S.A. 44°48N 68°46W 113 C13
Brewood U.K. 52°41N 2°9W 23 G4
Briançon France 44°54N 6°39E 68 D7
Bridestowe U.K. 50°41N 4°7W 27 F5
Bridge U.K. 51°15N 1°8E 25 D11
Bridgefield Barbados 13°9N 59°36W 115 g
Bridgend U.K. 51°30N 3°34W 27 D6
Bridgeport U.S.A. 41°11N 73°12W 113 E11
Bridgeton U.S.A. 39°26N 75°14W 113 F10
Bridgetown Barbados 13°6N 59°37W 115 g
Bridgewater Canada 44°25N 64°31W 109 E13
Bridgnorth U.K. 52°32N 2°25W 23 G4
Bridgwater U.K. 51°8N 2°59W 24 D3
Bridgwater B. U.K. 51°15N 3°15W 24 D2
Bridlington U.K. 54°5N 0°12W 22 D8
Bridlington B. U.K. 54°4N 0°10W 22 D8
Bridport U.K. 50°44N 2°45W 24 E3
Brierfield U.K. 53°49N 2°14W 23 E4
Brierley Hill U.K. 52°29N 2°6W 23 H4
Brigg U.K. 53°34N 0°28W 23 E8
Brigham City U.S.A. 41°31N 112°1W 110 B4
Brighouse U.K. 53°42N 1°46W 23 E5
Brighstone U.K. 50°38N 1°23W 24 E6
Brightlingsea U.K. 51°49N 1°2E 25 C11
Brighton U.K. 50°49N 0°7W 25 E8
Brigstock U.K. 52°27N 0°36W 25 B7
Brill U.K. 51°49N 1°1W 24 C6
Brimfield U.K. 52°18N 2°41W 24 B3
Brindisi Italy 40°39N 17°55E 71 D7
Brinklow U.K. 52°25N 1°22W 24 B6
Brinkworth U.K. 51°33N 1°59W 24 C5
Brisbane Australia 27°25S 153°2E 98 F9
Bristol U.K. 51°26N 2°35W 24 D3
Bristol B. U.S.A. 58°0N 160°0W 108 D4
Bristol Channel U.K. 51°18N 4°30W 27 E5
Briston U.K. 52°51N 1°4E 25 A11
British Columbia □ Canada 55°0N 125°15W 108 D7
British Virgin Is. □ W. Indies 18°30N 64°30W 115 e
Brittany = Bretagne □ France 48°10N 3°0W 68 B2
Brive-la-Gaillarde France 45°10N 1°32E 68 D4
Brixham U.K. 50°23N 3°31W 27 G6
Brixworth U.K. 52°20N 0°54W 25 B7
Brize Norton U.K. 51°46N 1°34W 24 C5
Brno Czech Rep. 49°10N 16°35E 67 D9
Broad B. U.K. 58°14N 6°18W 18 F5
Broad Chalke U.K. 51°2N 1°56W 24 D5
Broad Haven Ireland 54°20N 9°55W 28 C2
Broad Law U.K. 55°30N 3°21W 21 C9
Broad Sd. U.K. 49°55N 6°21W 27 H1
Broadclyst U.K. 50°46N 3°27W 27 F7
Broadhembury U.K. 50°49N 3°18W 27 F7
Broadstairs U.K. 51°21N 1°27E 25 D11
Broadway U.K. 52°2N 1°50W 24 B5
Broadwindsor U.K. 50°48N 2°47W 24 E3
Brochet Canada 57°53N 101°40W 108 D9
Brock I. Canada 77°52N 114°19W 109 B8
Brocken Germany 51°47N 10°37E 66 C6
Brockenhurst U.K. 50°49N 1°34W 24 E5
Brockville Canada 44°35N 75°41W 113 C10
Brockworth U.K. 51°51N 2°9W 24 C4
Brodeur Pen. Canada 72°30N 88°10W 109 B11
Brodick U.K. 55°35N 5°9W 20 C5
Broken Hill Australia 31°58S 141°29E 98 G7
Bromfield U.K. 52°24N 2°45W 23 H3
Bromham U.K. 51°23N 2°1W 24 D4
Bromley □ U.K. 51°24N 0°2E 25 D9
Brompton U.K. 54°21N 1°25W 22 D6
Bromsgrove U.K. 52°21N 2°2W 24 B4
Bromyard U.K. 52°11N 2°30W 24 B4
Brookings U.S.A. 44°19N 96°48W 111 B7
Brooks Canada 50°35N 111°55W 108 D8
Brooks Range U.S.A. 68°0N 152°0W 108 C5
Broom, L. U.K. 57°55N 5°15W 18 G7
Broome Australia 18°0S 122°15E 98 D3
Broomhill U.K. 55°18N 1°36W 22 B5
Brora U.K. 58°0N 3°52W 19 F10
Brora → U.K. 58°0N 3°51W 19 F10
Brosna → Ireland 53°14N 7°58W 30 B7
Brothertoft U.K. 53°0N 0°7W 23 F8
Brotton U.K. 54°35N 0°56W 22 C7
Brough Cumb., U.K. 54°32N 2°18W 22 C4
Brough E. Riding, U.K. 53°44N 0°36W 23 E7

Brough Hd. U.K. 59°8N 3°20W 19 D11
Broughton Borders, U.K. 55°37N 3°24W 21 C9
Broughton N. Lincs., U.K. 53°34N 0°34W 23 E7
Broughton Northants., U.K. 52°22N 0°46W 25 B7
Broughton-in-Furness U.K. 54°17N 3°13W 22 D2
Broughty Ferry U.K. 56°29N 2°51W 21 B10
Brown Willy U.K. 50°35N 4°37W 27 F4
Brownhills U.K. 52°39N 1°54W 23 G5
Brownsville U.S.A. 25°54N 97°30W 111 E7
Brownwood U.S.A. 31°43N 98°59W 110 D7
Broxburn U.K. 55°56N 3°28W 21 C9
Bruay-la-Buissière France 50°29N 2°33E 68 A5
Bruce, Mt. Australia 22°37S 118°8E 98 E2
Brue → U.K. 51°13N 2°59W 24 D3
Brugge Belgium 51°13N 3°13E 65 C3
Brumado Brazil 14°14S 41°40W 122 B2
Brunei ■ Asia 4°50N 115°0E 83 C3
Brunswick Ga., U.S.A. 31°10N 81°30W 111 D10
Brunswick Maine, U.S.A. 43°55N 69°58W 113 D13
Brunton U.K. 55°2N 2°6W 22 B4
Brussels Belgium 50°51N 4°21E 65 D4
Bruton U.K. 51°7N 2°27W 24 D4
Bryan Ohio, U.S.A. 41°28N 84°33W 112 E5
Bryan Tex., U.S.A. 30°40N 96°22W 111 D7
Bryansk Russia 53°13N 34°25E 72 D4
Bryher U.K. 49°57N 6°22W 27 H1
Brynamman U.K. 51°49N 3°51W 26 D6
Brynmawr U.K. 51°48N 3°10W 26 D7
Bucaramanga Colombia 7°0N 73°0W 120 B2
Buchan U.K. 57°32N 2°21W 19 G13
Buchan Ness U.K. 57°29N 1°46W 19 H14
Buchanan Liberia 5°57N 10°2W 94 G3
Bucharest Romania 44°27N 26°10E 67 F14
Buckden U.K. 52°18N 0°14W 25 B8
Buckfastleigh U.K. 50°28N 3°48W 27 G6
Buckhannon U.S.A. 39°0N 80°8W 112 F7
Buckhaven U.K. 56°11N 3°3W 21 B9
Buckie U.K. 57°41N 2°58W 19 G12
Buckingham Canada 45°37N 75°24W 113 C10
Buckingham U.K. 51°59N 0°57W 25 C7
Buckinghamshire □ U.K. 51°53N 0°55W 25 C7
Buckland Brewer U.K. 50°58N 4°15W 27 F5
Buckland Newton U.K. 50°50N 2°26W 24 E4
Buckley U.K. 53°10N 3°5W 26 A7
Budapest Hungary 47°29N 19°3E 67 E10
Bude U.K. 50°49N 4°34W 27 F4
Bude B. U.K. 50°49N 4°35W 27 F4
Budle B. U.K. 55°37N 1°45W 22 A5
Budleigh Salterton U.K. 50°37N 3°19W 27 F7
Buena Vista U.S.A. 37°44N 79°21W 112 G8
Buenaventura Colombia 3°53N 77°4W 120 B2
Buenos Aires Argentina 34°36S 58°22W 121 F4
Buenos Aires, L. Argentina 46°35S 72°30W 121 G2
Buffalo N.Y., U.S.A. 42°53N 78°53W 112 D8
Buffalo Wyo., U.S.A. 44°21N 106°42W 110 B5
Bug → Poland 52°31N 21°5E 67 B11
Bug → Ukraine 46°59N 31°58E 73 E5
Bugle U.K. 50°24N 4°47W 27 G4
Bugulma Russia 54°33N 52°48E 72 D9
Buguruslan Russia 53°39N 52°26E 72 D9
Builth Wells U.K. 52°9N 3°25W 26 C7
Buir Nur Mongolia 47°50N 117°42E 81 B6
Bujumbura Burundi 3°16S 29°18E 96 E5
Bukavu Dem. Rep. of the Congo 2°20S 28°52E 96 E5
Bukhoro Uzbekistan 39°48N 64°25E 87 B11
Bukittinggi Indonesia 0°20S 100°20E 83 D2
Bulawayo Zimbabwe 20°7S 28°32E 97 J5
Bulford U.K. 51°11N 1°45W 24 D5
Bulgan Mongolia 48°45N 103°34E 80 B5
Bulgaria ■ Europe 42°35N 25°30E 71 C11
Bullhead City U.S.A. 35°8N 114°32W 110 C4
Bunbury Australia 33°20S 115°35E 98 G2
Bunclody Ireland 52°39N 6°40W 31 C9
Buncrana Ireland 55°8N 7°27W 28 A7
Bundaberg Australia 24°54S 152°22E 98 E9
Bundi India 25°30N 75°35E 84 G9
Bundoran Ireland 54°28N 8°16W 28 C5
Bungay U.K. 52°27N 1°28E 25 B11
Buntingford U.K. 51°56N 0°0 25 C8
Bunwell U.K. 52°30N 1°9E 25 A11
Buon Ma Thuot Vietnam 12°40N 108°3E 83 B2
Bur Acaba Somali Rep. 3°12N 44°20E 88 G3
Bûr Safâga Egypt 26°43N 33°57E 95 C12
Burao Somali Rep. 9°32N 45°32E 88 F4
Buraydah Si. Arabia 26°20N 43°59E 86 E5
Burbage Derby, U.K. 53°15N 1°55W 23 F5
Burbage Leics., U.K. 52°32N 1°21W 23 G6
Burbage Wilts., U.K. 51°21N 1°39W 24 D5
Burdur Turkey 37°45N 30°17E 73 G5
Bure → U.K. 52°38N 1°43E 25 A12
Burford U.K. 51°49N 1°38W 24 C5
Burgas Bulgaria 42°33N 27°29E 71 C12
Burgess Hill U.K. 50°58N 0°6W 25 E8
Burgh le Marsh U.K. 53°9N 0°15E 23 F9
Burghead U.K. 57°43N 3°30W 19 G11
Burgos Spain 42°21N 3°41W 69 A4
Burgundy = Bourgogne □
    France 47°0N 4°50E 68 C6
Burhanpur India 21°18N 76°14E 84 J10
Burkina Faso ■ Africa 12°0N 1°0W 94 F5
Burley Hants., U.K. 50°49N 1°43W 24 E5
Burley W. Yorks., U.K. 53°54N 1°45W 23 E5
Burlington Colo., U.S.A. 39°18N 102°16W 110 C6
Burlington Iowa, U.S.A. 40°49N 91°14W 111 B8
Burlington Vt., U.S.A. 44°29N 73°12W 113 C11
Burlington Wis., U.S.A. 42°41N 88°17W 112 D3
Burma ■ Asia 21°0N 96°30E 85 J20
Burnham Market U.K. 52°57N 0°44E 25 A10
Burnham-on-Crouch U.K. 51°38N 0°49E 25 C10
Burnham-on-Sea U.K. 51°14N 3°0W 24 D2
Burnie Australia 41°4S 145°56E 98 J8
Burnley U.K. 53°47N 2°14W 23 E4
Burnmouth U.K. 55°50N 2°4W 21 C11
Burns U.S.A. 43°35N 119°3W 110 B3
Burnside → Canada 66°51N 108°4W 108 C9
Burntisland U.K. 56°4N 3°13W 21 B9
Burqin China 47°43N 87°0E 80 B3

Burray · **Chesha B.**

Burray U.K. 58°51N 2°54W 19 E12
Burren △ Ireland 53°1N 8°58W 30 B4
Burrow Hd. U.K. 54°41N 4°24W 20 E7
Burry Port U.K. 51°41N 4°15W 26 D5
Bursa Turkey 40°15N 29°5E 73 F4
Burstwick U.K. 53°44N 0°8W 23 E8
Burton U.K. 54°11N 2°43W 22 D3
Burton Agnes U.K. 54°4N 0°18W 22 D8
Burton Bradstock U.K. 50°42N 2°43W 24 E3
Burton Fleming U.K. 54°8N 0°20W 22 D8
Burton Latimer U.K. 52°22N 0°41W 25 B7
Burton upon Stather U.K. 53°39N 0°41W 23 E7
Burton upon Trent U.K. 52°48N 1°38W 23 G5
Buru Indonesia 3°30S 126°30E 83 D4
Burundi ■ Africa 3°15S 30°0E 96 E5
Burwash U.K. 50°59N 0°23E 25 E9
Burwell U.K. 52°17N 0°20E 25 B9
Burwick U.K. 58°45N 2°58W 19 E12
Bury U.K. 53°35N 2°17W 23 E4
Bury St. Edmunds U.K. 52°15N 0°43E 25 B10
Busan S. Korea 35°5N 129°0E 81 C7
Büshehr Iran 28°55N 50°55E 87 D7
Bushey U.K. 51°38N 0°22W 25 C8
Busto Arsízio Italy 45°37N 8°51E 70 B3
Buta Dem. Rep. of the Congo 2°50N 24°53E 96 D4
Butare Rwanda 2°31S 29°52E 96 E5
Butaritari Kiribati 3°30N 174°0E 102 G9
Bute U.K. 55°48N 5°2W 20 C5
Bute, Kyles of U.K. 55°55N 5°10W 20 C5
Butembo Dem. Rep. of the Congo 0°9N 29°18E 96 D5
Butha Qi China 48°0N 122°32E 81 B7
Butler U.S.A. 40°52N 79°54W 112 E8
Buton Indonesia 5°0S 122°45E 83 D4
Butte U.S.A. 46°0N 112°32W 110 A4
Buttermere U.K. 54°32N 3°16W 22 C2
Butterworth Malaysia 5°24N 100°23E 83 C2
Buttevant Ireland 52°14N 8°40W 30 D5
Butuan Phil. 8°57N 125°33E 83 C4
Buxton U.K. 53°16N 1°54W 23 F5
Buyant-Uhaa Mongolia 44°55N 110°11E 81 B6
Buzău Romania 45°10N 26°50E 67 F14
Buzuluk Russia 52°48N 52°12E 72 D9
Bydgoszcz Poland 53°10N 18°0E 67 B9
Byfield U.K. 52°10N 1°14W 24 B6
Bylot I. Canada 73°13N 78°34W 109 B12
Byrranga Ra. Russia 75°0N 100°0E 79 B12
Bytom Poland 50°25N 18°54E 67 C10

C

Ca Mau Vietnam 9°7N 105°8E 83 C2
Cabanatuan Phil. 15°30N 120°58E 83 B4
Cabedelo Brazil 7°0S 34°50W 120 C6
Cabimas Venezuela 10°23N 71°25W 120 A2
Cabinda Angola 5°33S 12°11E 96 F2
Cabinda □ Angola 5°0S 12°30E 96 F2
Cabo Frio Brazil 22°51S 42°3W 122 D2
Cabo San Lucas Mexico 22°53N 109°54W 114 C3
Cabonga, Réservoir Canada 47°20N 76°40W 109 E12
Cabora Bassa Dam Mozam. 15°20S 32°50E 97 H6
Cabot Str. Canada 47°15N 59°40W 109 E14
Čačak Serbia 43°54N 20°20E 71 C9
Cáceres Brazil 16°5S 57°40W 120 D4
Cáceres Spain 39°26N 6°23W 69 C2
Cachimbo, Serra do Brazil 9°30S 55°30W 120 C4
Cachoeira Brazil 12°30S 39°0W 122 B3
Cachoeira do Sul Brazil 30°3S 52°53W 121 F4
Cachoeiro de Itapemirim Brazil 20°51S 41°7W 122 D2
Cader Idris U.K. 52°42N 3°53W 26 B6
Cadillac U.S.A. 44°15N 85°24W 112 C5
Cádiz Spain 36°30N 6°20W 69 D2
Cádiz, G. de Spain 36°40N 7°0W 69 D2
Caen France 49°10N 0°22W 68 B3
Caenby Corner U.K. 53°24N 0°33W 23 F7
Caernarfon U.K. 53°8N 4°16W 26 A5
Caernarfon B. U.K. 53°4N 4°40W 26 A4
Caerphilly U.K. 51°35N 3°13W 27 D7
Caersws U.K. 52°31N 3°26W 26 B7
Caeté Brazil 19°55S 43°40W 122 C2
Caetité Brazil 13°50S 42°32W 122 B2
Cagayan de Oro Phil. 8°30N 124°40E 83 C4
Cágliari Italy 39°13N 9°7E 70 E3
Caguas Puerto Rico 18°14N 66°2W 115 d
Caha Mts. Ireland 51°45N 9°40W 30 E2
Caher Ireland 52°22N 7°56W 30 D7
Cahersiveen Ireland 51°56N 10°14W 30 E2
Cahore Pt. Ireland 52°33N 6°12W 31 C10
Cahors France 44°27N 1°27E 68 D4
Cairn Gorm U.K. 57°7N 3°39W 19 H10
Cairngorm Mts. U.K. 57°6N 3°42W 19 H10
Cairngorms △ U.K. 57°10N 3°50W 19 H10
Cairnryan U.K. 54°59N 5°1W 20 E5
Cairns Australia 16°57S 145°45E 98 D8
Cairnsmore of Fleet U.K. 54°59N 4°20W 20 D5
Cairo Egypt 30°2N 31°13E 95 B12
Cairo U.S.A. 37°0N 89°11W 112 G3
Caister-on-Sea U.K. 52°40N 1°43E 25 A12
Caistor U.K. 53°30N 0°18W 23 F8
Caithness U.K. 58°25N 3°35W 19 F10
Caithness, Ord of U.K. 58°8N 3°36W 19 F10
Caja de Muertos, I. Puerto Rico 17°54N 66°32W 115 d
Cajamarca Peru 7°5S 78°28W 120 C2
Calabar Nigeria 4°57N 8°20E 94 H7
Calábria □ Italy 39°0N 16°30E 70 E7
Calais France 50°57N 1°56E 68 A4
Calais U.S.A. 45°11N 67°17W 113 C14
Calama Chile 22°30S 68°55W 121 E3
Calamian Group Phil. 11°50N 119°55E 83 B3
Calanscio, Sarir Libya 27°30N 21°30E 95 C10
Calapan Phil. 13°25N 121°7E 83 B4
Calbayog Phil. 12°4N 124°38E 83 B4
Calcutta = Kolkata India 22°34N 88°21E 85 H16
Caldbeck U.K. 54°45N 3°3W 22 C2
Calder → U.K. 53°44N 1°22W 23 E6
Calder Bridge U.K. 54°27N 3°29W 22 D2
Caldera Chile 27°5S 70°55W 121 E2

Caldew → U.K. 54°54N 2°56W 22 C3
Caldwell U.S.A. 43°40N 116°41W 110 B3
Caledonian Canal U.K. 57°29N 4°15W 19 H9
Calgary Canada 51°0N 114°10W 108 D8
Cali Colombia 3°25N 76°35W 120 B2
Calicut India 11°15N 75°43E 84 P9
California □ U.S.A. 37°30N 119°30W 110 C2
California, G. de Mexico 27°0N 111°0W 114 B2
Callan Ireland 52°32N 7°24W 31 C8
Callander U.K. 56°15N 4°13W 20 B7
Callao Peru 12°3S 77°8W 120 D2
Calne U.K. 51°26N 2°0W 24 D5
Calshot U.K. 50°48N 1°19W 24 E6
Calstock U.K. 50°30N 4°13W 27 F5
Caltanissetta Italy 37°29N 14°4E 70 F6
Calvi France 42°34N 8°45E 68 E8
Calvinia S. Africa 31°28S 19°45E 97 L3
Cam → U.K. 52°21N 0°16E 25 B9
Cam Ranh Vietnam 11°54N 109°12E 83 B2
Camagüey Cuba 21°20N 77°55W 115 C9
Camargue France 43°34N 4°34E 68 E6
Camberley U.K. 51°20N 0°44W 25 D7
Cambo U.K. 55°10N 1°57W 22 B5
Cambodia ■ Asia 12°15N 105°0E 83 B2
Camborne U.K. 50°12N 5°19W 27 G3
Cambrai France 50°11N 3°14E 68 A5
Cambrian Mts. U.K. 52°3N 3°57W 26 C6
Cambridge Jamaica 18°18N 77°54W 114 a
Cambridge U.K. 52°12N 0°8E 25 B9
Cambridge Mass., U.S.A. 42°23N 71°7W 113 D12
Cambridge Md., U.S.A. 38°34N 76°5W 113 F9
Cambridge Ohio, U.S.A. 40°2N 81°35W 112 E7
Cambridge Bay Canada 69°10N 105°0W 108 C9
Cambridgeshire □ U.K. 52°25N 0°7W 25 B8
Camden Ark., U.S.A. 33°35N 92°50W 111 D8
Camden N.J., U.S.A. 39°55N 75°7W 113 F10
Camden □ U.K. 51°32N 0°8W 25 C8
Camel → U.K. 50°31N 4°51W 27 F4
Camelford U.K. 50°37N 4°42W 27 F4
Cameroon ■ Africa 6°0N 12°30E 96 C2
Cameroun, Mt. Cameroon 4°13N 9°10E 96 D1
Cametá Brazil 2°12S 49°30W 120 C5
Camocim Brazil 2°55S 40°50W 120 C5
Campana, I. Chile 48°20S 75°20W 121 G2
Campánia □ Italy 41°0N 14°30E 70 D6
Campbell I. Pac. Oc. 52°30S 169°0E 102 N8
Campbell River Canada 50°5N 125°20W 108 D7
Campbellsville U.S.A. 37°21N 85°20W 112 G5
Campbellton Canada 47°57N 66°43W 109 E13
Campbeltown U.K. 55°26N 5°36W 20 D4
Campeche Mexico 19°51N 90°32W 114 D6
Campeche, Golfo de Mexico 19°30N 93°0W 114 D6
Campina Grande Brazil 7°20S 35°47W 120 C6
Campinas Brazil 22°50S 47°0W 122 D1
Campo Belo Brazil 20°52S 45°16W 122 D1
Campo Grande Brazil 20°25S 54°40W 122 D1
Campos Brazil 21°50S 41°20W 122 D2
Campos Belos Brazil 13°10S 47°3W 122 B1
Camrose Canada 53°0N 112°50W 108 D8
Can Tho Vietnam 10°2N 105°46E 83 B2
Canada ■ N. Amer. 60°0N 100°0W 108 D10
Canadian → U.S.A. 35°28N 95°3W 111 C7
Canadian Shield Canada 53°0N 75°0W 104 C9
Çanakkale Turkey 40°8N 26°24E 73 F4
Canandaigua U.S.A. 42°54N 77°17W 112 D9
Cananea Mexico 31°0N 110°18W 114 A2
Canaries St. Lucia 13°55N 61°4W 115 f
Canary Is. Atl. Oc. 28°30N 16°0W 94 C2
Canaveral, C. U.S.A. 28°27N 80°32W 111 E10
Canavieiras Brazil 15°39S 39°0W 122 C3
Canberra Australia 35°15S 149°8E 98 H8
Cancún Mexico 21°8N 86°44W 114 C7
Cangzhou China 38°19N 116°52E 81 C6
Caniapiscau → Canada 56°40N 69°30W 109 D13
Caniapiscau, L. de Canada 54°10N 69°55W 109 D13
Çankırı Turkey 40°40N 33°37E 73 F5
Canna U.K. 57°3N 6°33W 18 H4
Canna, Sd. of U.K. 57°1N 6°30W 18 H5
Cannanore India 11°53N 75°27E 84 P9
Cannes France 43°32N 7°1E 68 E7
Cannington U.K. 51°9N 3°4W 24 D2
Cannock U.K. 52°41N 2°1W 23 G4
Cannock Chase U.K. 52°44N 2°4W 23 G4
Canoas Brazil 29°56S 51°11W 121 E4
Cañon City U.S.A. 38°27N 105°14W 110 C5
Canonbie U.K. 55°5N 2°58W 21 D10
Canora Canada 51°40N 102°30W 108 D9
Canso Canada 45°20N 61°0W 113 C17
Cantabria □ Spain 43°10N 4°0W 69 A4
Cantábrica, Cordillera Spain 43°0N 5°10W 69 A3
Canterbury U.K. 51°16N 1°6E 25 D11
Canton = Guangzhou China 23°6N 113°13E 81 D6
Canton Ill., U.S.A. 40°33N 90°2W 112 E2
Canton N.Y., U.S.A. 44°36N 75°10W 113 C10
Canton Ohio, U.S.A. 40°48N 81°23W 112 E7
Canvey U.K. 51°31N 0°37E 25 C10
Cap-de-la-Madeleine Canada 46°22N 72°31W 113 B11
Cap-Haïtien Haiti 19°40N 72°20W 115 D10
Cap Pt. St. Lucia 14°7N 60°57W 115 f
Cape Breton I. Canada 46°0N 60°30W 113 C17
Cape Charles U.S.A. 37°16N 76°1W 113 G10
Cape Coast Ghana 5°5N 1°15W 94 G5
Cape Coral U.S.A. 26°33N 81°57W 111 E10
Cape Dorset Canada 64°14N 76°32W 109 C12
Cape Fear → U.S.A. 33°53N 78°1W 111 D11
Cape Girardeau U.S.A. 37°19N 89°32W 112 G3
Cape May U.S.A. 38°56N 74°56W 113 F10
Cape Town S. Africa 33°55S 18°22E 97 L3
Cape Verde Is. ■ Atl. Oc. 16°0N 24°0W 91 E1
Cape York Peninsula Australia 12°0S 142°30E 98 C7
Capela Brazil 10°30S 37°0W 122 B3
Capesterre-Belle-Eau Guadeloupe 16°4N 61°36W 114 b
Capesterre-de-Marie-Galante Guadeloupe 15°53N 61°14W 114 b

Capreol Canada 46°43N 80°56W 112 B7
Capri Italy 40°33N 14°14E 70 D6
Caprivi Strip Namibia 18°0S 23°0E 97 H4
Caquetá → Colombia 1°15S 69°15W 120 C3
Caracas Venezuela 10°30N 66°55W 120 A3
Caracol Brazil 9°15S 43°22W 122 A2
Carangola Brazil 20°44S 42°5W 122 D2
Caratasca, L. Honduras 15°20N 83°40W 115 D8
Caratinga Brazil 19°50S 42°10W 122 C2
Caravelas Brazil 17°45S 39°15W 122 C3
Caravelle, Presqu'île de la Martinique 14°46N 60°48W 114 c
Carbondale Ill., U.S.A. 37°44N 89°13W 112 G3
Carbondale Pa., U.S.A. 41°35N 75°30W 113 E10
Carbonear Canada 47°42N 53°13W 109 E14
Carcassonne France 43°13N 2°20E 68 E5
Carcross Canada 60°13N 134°45W 108 C6
Cardamon Hills India 9°30N 77°15E 84 Q10
Cárdenas Cuba 23°0N 81°30W 115 C8
Cardiff U.K. 51°29N 3°10W 27 F7
Cardigan U.K. 52°5N 4°40W 26 C4
Cardigan B. U.K. 52°30N 4°30W 26 B4
Cardington U.K. 52°6N 0°25W 25 B8
Cardston Canada 49°15N 113°20W 108 E8
Cariacica Brazil 20°16S 40°25W 122 D2
Caribbean Sea W. Indies 15°0N 75°0W 115 E10
Cariboo Mts. Canada 53°0N 121°0W 108 D7
Caribou U.S.A. 46°52N 68°1W 113 B13
Caribou Mts. Canada 59°12N 115°40W 108 D8
Carinhanha Brazil 14°15S 44°46W 122 B2
Carinhanha → Brazil 14°20S 43°47W 122 B2
Carinthia = Kärnten □ Austria 46°52N 13°30E 66 E8
Carisbrooke U.K. 50°41N 1°19W 24 E6
Cark U.K. 54°11N 2°58W 22 D3
Carleton Place Canada 45°8N 76°9W 113 C9
Carleton Rode U.K. 52°30N 1°7E 25 A11
Carlingford L. U.K. 54°3N 6°9W 29 C9
Carlinville U.S.A. 39°17N 89°53W 112 F3
Carlisle U.K. 54°54N 2°56W 22 C3
Carlisle U.S.A. 40°12N 77°12W 112 E9
Carlisle B. Barbados 13°5N 59°37W 115 g
Carlops U.K. 55°47N 3°20W 21 C9
Carlow Ireland 52°50N 6°56W 31 C9
Carlow □ Ireland 52°43N 6°50W 31 C9
Carlsbad U.S.A. 32°25N 104°14W 110 D6
Carlton U.K. 52°59N 1°5W 23 G6
Carlton Colville U.K. 52°27N 1°43E 25 B12
Carlton Miniott U.K. 54°12N 1°22W 22 D6
Carluke U.K. 55°45N 3°50W 21 C8
Carmacks Canada 62°5N 136°16W 108 C6
Carmarthen U.K. 51°52N 4°19W 26 D5
Carmarthen B. U.K. 51°40N 4°30W 26 D4
Carmarthenshire □ U.K. 51°55N 4°13W 26 D5
Carmaux France 44°3N 2°10E 68 D5
Carmi U.S.A. 38°5N 88°10W 112 F3
Carn Ban U.K. 57°7N 4°15W 19 H9
Carn Eige U.K. 57°17N 5°8W 18 H7
Carnarvon Australia 24°51S 113°42E 98 E1
Carnarvon S. Africa 30°56S 22°8E 97 L4
Carndonagh Ireland 55°16N 7°15W 29 A7
Carnegie, L. Australia 26°5S 122°30E 98 F3
Carnforth U.K. 54°7N 2°45W 22 D3
Carno U.K. 52°34N 3°30W 26 B6
Carnoustie U.K. 56°30N 2°42W 21 A10
Carnsore Pt. Ireland 52°10N 6°22W 31 D10
Caro U.S.A. 43°29N 83°24W 112 D6
Carolina Puerto Rico 18°23N 65°58W 115 d
Caroline I. Kiribati 9°58S 150°13W 103 H12
Carondelet Kiribati 5°33S 173°50E 99 B16
Caroni → Venezuela 8°21N 62°43W 120 B3
Carpathians Europe 49°30N 21°0E 67 D11
Carpentaria, G. of Australia 14°0S 139°0E 98 C6
Carpentras France 44°3N 5°2E 68 D6
Carpi Italy 44°47N 10°53E 70 B4
Carrara Italy 44°5N 10°6E 70 B4
Carrauntoohill Ireland 52°0N 9°49W 30 E3
Carrick-on-Shannon Ireland 53°57N 8°5W 28 D5
Carrick-on-Suir Ireland 52°21N 7°24W 31 D8
Carrickfergus U.K. 54°43N 5°49W 29 B10
Carrickmacross Ireland 53°59N 6°43W 29 D8
Carrollton U.S.A. 39°18N 90°24W 112 F2
Carron → U.K. 57°53N 4°22W 19 G9
Carron, L. U.K. 57°22N 5°35W 18 H6
Carson City U.S.A. 39°10N 119°46W 110 C3
Carson Sink U.S.A. 39°50N 118°25W 110 C3
Cartagena Colombia 10°25N 75°33W 120 A2
Cartagena Spain 37°38N 0°59W 69 D5
Cartago Colombia 4°45N 75°55W 120 B2
Cartago Costa Rica 9°50N 83°55W 115 F8
Carthage Tunisia 36°52N 10°20E 95 A8
Cartmel U.K. 54°12N 2°57W 22 D3
Cartwright Canada 53°41N 56°58W 109 D14
Caruaru Brazil 8°15S 35°55W 122 A3
Carúpano Venezuela 10°39N 63°15W 120 A3
Casa Grande U.S.A. 32°53N 111°45W 110 D4
Casablanca Morocco 33°36N 7°36W 94 B4
Cascade Ra. U.S.A. 47°0N 121°30W 110 A2
Cascavel Ceará, Brazil 4°7S 38°14W 120 C6
Cascavel Paraná, Brazil 24°57S 53°28W 121 E4
Caserta Italy 41°4N 14°20E 70 D6
Cashel Ireland 52°30N 7°53W 30 D7
Casiquiare → Venezuela 2°1N 67°7W 120 B3
Casper U.S.A. 42°51N 106°19W 110 B5
Caspian Depression Eurasia 47°0N 48°0E 73 E8
Caspian Sea Eurasia 43°0N 50°0E 73 F9
Cassiar Mts. Canada 59°30N 130°30W 108 D6
Castellammare di Stábia Italy 40°42N 14°29E 70 D6
Castelló de la Plana Spain 39°58N 0°3W 69 C5
Castelsarrasin France 44°2N 1°7E 68 E4
Castilla-La Mancha □ Spain 39°30N 3°30W 69 C4
Castilla y Leon □ Spain 42°0N 5°0W 69 B3
Castle Acre U.K. 52°42N 0°42E 25 A10
Castle Cary U.K. 51°6N 2°31W 24 D3
Castle Donington U.K. 52°51N 1°19W 23 G6
Castle Douglas U.K. 54°56N 3°56W 21 E8
Castlebar Ireland 53°52N 9°18W 28 D2
Castlebay U.K. 56°57N 7°31W 18 J2

Castleblaney Ireland 54°7N 6°44W 29 C8
Castlederg U.K. 54°42N 7°35W 28 B6
Castleford U.K. 53°43N 1°21W 23 E6
Castlemaine Harbour Ireland 52°8N 9°50W 30 D3
Castlepollard Ireland 53°41N 7°19W 28 D7
Castlerea Ireland 53°46N 8°29W 28 D5
Castleside U.K. 54°50N 1°52W 22 C5
Castleton Derby, U.K. 53°22N 1°46W 23 F5
Castleton N. Yorks., U.K. 54°28N 0°57W 22 D7
Castletown I. of Man 54°5N 4°38W 29 C12
Castletown Bearhaven Ireland 51°39N 9°55W 30 E3
Castres France 43°37N 2°13E 68 E5
Castries St. Lucia 14°2N 60°58W 115 f
Castro Chile 42°30S 73°50W 121 G2
Castro Alves Brazil 12°46S 39°33W 122 B3
Cat I. Bahamas 24°30N 75°30W 115 C9
Cataguases Brazil 21°23S 42°39W 122 D2
Catalão Brazil 18°10S 47°57W 122 C1
Cataluña □ Spain 41°40N 1°15E 69 B6
Catamarca Argentina 28°30S 65°50W 121 E3
Catanduanes □ Phil. 13°50N 124°20E 83 B4
Catanduva Brazil 21°5S 48°58W 122 D1
Catánia Italy 37°30N 15°6E 70 F6
Catanzaro Italy 38°54N 16°35E 70 E7
Catcleugh U.K. 55°20N 2°24W 22 B4
Caterham U.K. 51°15N 0°4W 25 D8
Catoche, C. Mexico 21°35N 87°5W 114 C7
Caton U.K. 54°5N 2°42W 22 D3
Catsfield U.K. 50°54N 0°28E 25 E9
Catskill U.S.A. 42°14N 73°52W 113 D11
Catskill Mts. U.S.A. 42°10N 74°25W 113 D10
Catterick U.K. 54°23N 1°37W 22 D5
Catterick Camp U.K. 54°22N 1°42W 22 D5
Catton U.K. 54°55N 2°15W 22 C4
Cauca → Colombia 8°54N 74°28W 120 B2
Caucaia Brazil 3°40S 38°35W 120 C6
Caucasus Mountains Eurasia 42°50N 44°0E 73 F7
Caulkerbush U.K. 54°54N 3°41W 21 E9
Caura → Venezuela 7°38N 64°53W 120 B3
Cauvery → India 11°9N 78°52E 84 P11
Cavan Ireland 54°0N 7°22W 28 D7
Cavan □ Ireland 54°1N 7°16W 29 C7
Caviana, I. Brazil 0°10N 50°10W 120 B4
Cawood U.K. 53°50N 1°8W 23 E6
Cawston U.K. 52°47N 1°9E 25 A11
Caxias Brazil 4°55S 43°20W 120 C5
Caxias do Sul Brazil 29°10S 51°10W 121 E4
Cayenne Fr. Guiana 5°5N 52°18W 120 B4
Cayey Puerto Rico 18°7N 66°10W 115 d
Cayman Is. ☑ W. Indies 19°40N 80°30W 115 D8
Cayuga L. U.S.A. 42°41N 76°41W 112 D9
Ceanannus Mor Ireland 53°44N 6°53W 29 D8
Ceará □ Brazil 5°0S 40°0W 120 C6
Cebu Phil. 10°18N 123°54E 83 B4
Cedar → U.S.A. 41°17N 91°21W 112 E2
Cedar L. Canada 53°10N 100°0W 108 D9
Cedar Rapids U.S.A. 41°59N 91°40W 111 B8
Cefalù Italy 38°2N 14°1E 70 E6
Cegléd Hungary 47°11N 19°47E 67 E10
Celaya Mexico 20°31N 100°37W 114 C4
Celebes Sea Indonesia 3°0N 123°0E 83 C4
Celina U.S.A. 40°33N 84°35W 112 E5
Cellar Hd. U.K. 58°25N 6°11W 18 F5
Celtic Sea Atl. Oc. 50°9N 9°34W 14 E7
Cemaes U.K. 53°24N 4°27W 26 A5
Central, Cordillera Colombia 5°0N 75°0W 116 C3
Central, Cordillera Puerto Rico 18°8N 66°35W 115 d
Central African Rep. ■ Africa 7°0N 20°0E 96 C4
Central Makran Range Pakistan 26°30N 64°15E 84 F4
Central Russian Uplands Europe 54°0N 36°0E 56 E13
Central Siberian Plateau Russia 65°0N 105°0E 74 B12
Centralia Ill., U.S.A. 38°32N 89°8W 112 F3
Centralia Wash., U.S.A. 46°43N 122°58W 110 A2
Cephalonia = Kefalonia Greece 38°15N 20°30E 71 E9
Ceredigion □ U.K. 52°16N 4°15W 26 C5
Cerignola Italy 41°17N 15°53E 70 D6
Cerne Abbas U.K. 50°49N 2°29W 24 E4
Cerrigydrudion U.K. 53°1N 3°35W 26 A6
Cesena Italy 44°8N 12°15E 70 B5
České Budějovice Czech Rep. 48°55N 14°25E 66 D8
Çeşme Turkey 38°20N 26°23E 73 G4
Ceuta N. Afr. 35°52N 5°18W 69 E3
Ceve-i-Ra Fiji 21°46S 174°31E 99 E13
Cévennes France 44°10N 3°50E 68 D5
Chacewater U.K. 50°15N 5°11W 27 G3
Chachapoyas Peru 6°15S 77°50W 120 C2
Chaco Austral S. Amer. 27°0S 61°30W 121 E3
Chaco Boreal S. Amer. 22°0S 60°0W 121 E4
Chaco Central S. Amer. 24°0S 61°0W 121 E3
Chad ■ Africa 15°0N 17°15E 95 F8
Chad, L. Chad 13°30N 14°30E 95 F8
Chadron U.S.A. 42°50N 103°0W 110 B6
Chagford U.K. 50°40N 3°50W 27 F6
Chaghcharān Afghan. 34°31N 65°15E 87 C11
Chagos Arch. ☑ Ind. Oc. 6°0S 72°0E 75 J9
Chāh Gay Hills Afghan. 29°30N 64°0E 87 D10
Chakradharpur India 22°45N 85°40E 85 H14
Chaleur B. Canada 47°55N 65°30W 113 B15
Chalisgaon India 20°30N 75°10E 84 J9
Challenger Deep Pac. Oc. 11°30N 142°0E 102 F6
Chalon-sur-Saône France 46°48N 4°50E 68 C6
Châlons-en-Champagne France 48°58N 4°20E 68 B6
Chambal → India 26°29N 79°15E 84 F11
Chambersburg U.S.A. 39°56N 77°40W 112 F9
Chambéry France 45°34N 5°55E 68 D6
Chamonix-Mont Blanc France 45°55N 6°51E 68 D7
Champagne France 48°40N 4°20E 68 B6
Champaign U.S.A. 40°7N 88°15W 112 E3
Champlain, L. U.S.A. 44°40N 73°20W 113 C11
Chañaral Chile 26°23S 70°40W 121 E2
Chancery Lane Barbados 13°3N 59°30W 115 g
Chandigarh India 30°43N 76°47E 84 D10
Chandler's Ford U.K. 50°59N 1°22W 24 E6

Chandpur Bangla. 23°8N 90°45E 85 H17
Chandrapur India 19°57N 79°25E 84 K11
Changbai Shan China 42°20N 129°0E 81 B7
Changchun China 43°57N 125°17E 81 B7
Changde China 29°4N 111°35E 81 D6
Changhua Taiwan 24°2N 120°30E 81 D7
Changji China 44°1N 87°19E 80 B3
Changsha China 28°12N 113°0E 81 D6
Changzhi China 36°10N 113°6E 81 C6
Changzhou China 31°47N 119°58E 81 C6
Chania Greece 35°30N 24°4E 71 G11
Channel Is. U.K. 49°19N 2°24W 27 J9
Channel Is. U.S.A. 33°40N 119°15W 110 D2
Channel-Port aux Basques Canada 47°30N 59°9W 109 E14
Chantrey Inlet Canada 67°48N 96°20W 108 C10
Chaoyang China 41°35N 120°22E 81 B7
Chaozhou China 23°42N 116°32E 81 D6
Chapala, L. de Mexico 20°15N 103°0W 114 C4
Chapayevsk Russia 53°0N 49°40E 72 D8
Chapel-en-le-Frith U.K. 53°20N 1°54W 23 F5
Chapel St. Leonards U.K. 53°13N 0°20E 23 F9
Chapleau Canada 47°50N 83°24W 109 E11
Charaña Bolivia 17°30S 69°25W 120 D3
Chard U.K. 50°52N 2°58W 24 E3
Chari → Chad 12°58N 14°31E 95 F8
Chārīkār Afghan. 35°0N 69°10E 87 C12
Charing U.K. 51°12N 0°49E 25 D10
Charlbury U.K. 51°53N 1°28W 24 C6
Charleroi Belgium 50°24N 4°27E 65 C4
Charles, C. U.S.A. 37°7N 75°58W 113 G10
Charles City U.S.A. 43°4N 92°41W 111 B8
Charleston Ill., U.S.A. 39°30N 88°10W 112 F3
Charleston Mo., U.S.A. 36°55N 89°21W 112 G3
Charleston S.C., U.S.A. 32°46N 79°56W 111 D11
Charleston W. Va., U.S.A. 38°21N 81°38W 112 F7
Charlestown Ireland 53°58N 8°48W 28 D4
Charlestown of Aberlour U.K. 57°28N 3°14W 19 H11
Charleville Australia 26°24S 146°15E 98 F8
Charleville-Mézières France 49°44N 4°40E 68 B6
Charlevoix U.S.A. 45°19N 85°16W 112 C5
Charlotte Mich., U.S.A. 42°34N 84°50W 112 D5
Charlotte N.C., U.S.A. 35°13N 80°50W 111 C10
Charlotte Amalie U.S. Virgin Is. 18°21N 64°56W 115 e
Charlotte Harbor U.S.A. 26°57N 82°4W 111 E10
Charlottesville U.S.A. 38°2N 78°30W 112 F8
Charlottetown Canada 46°14N 63°8W 113 B16
Charlton I. Canada 52°0N 79°20W 109 D12
Charlton Kings U.K. 51°53N 2°3W 24 C4
Charlwood U.K. 51°9N 0°13W 25 D8
Charminster U.K. 50°44N 2°28W 24 E4
Charmouth U.K. 50°44N 2°54W 24 E3
Charnwood Forest U.K. 52°44N 1°17W 23 G6
Charolles France 46°27N 4°16E 68 C6
Charters Towers Australia 20°5S 146°13E 98 E8
Chartham U.K. 51°14N 1°1E 25 D11
Chartres France 48°29N 1°30E 68 B4
Chascomús Argentina 35°30S 58°0W 121 F4
Châteaubriant France 47°43N 1°23W 68 C3
Châteaulin France 48°11N 4°8W 68 B1
Châteauroux France 46°50N 1°40E 68 C4
Châteaux, Pte. des Guadeloupe 16°15N 61°10W 114 b
Châtellerault France 46°50N 0°30E 68 C4
Chatham Canada 47°2N 65°28W 109 E13
Chatham U.K. 51°22N 0°32E 25 D10
Chatham Is. Pac. Oc. 44°0S 176°40W 99 J15
Chatham-Kent Canada 42°24N 82°11W 112 D6
Chattanooga U.S.A. 35°3N 85°19W 111 C9
Chatteris U.K. 52°28N 0°2E 25 B9
Chatton U.K. 55°35N 2°0W 22 A5
Chaumont France 48°7N 5°8E 68 B6
Chaykovskiy Russia 56°47N 54°9E 72 C9
Cheadle Gt. Man., U.K. 53°23N 2°12W 23 F4
Cheadle Staffs., U.K. 52°59N 1°58W 23 G5
Cheb Czech Rep. 50°9N 12°28E 66 C7
Cheboksary Russia 56°8N 47°12E 72 C8
Cheboygan U.S.A. 45°39N 84°29W 112 C5
Chech, Erg Africa 25°0N 2°15W 94 D5
Chechenia □ Russia 43°30N 45°29E 73 F8
Chedabucto B. Canada 45°25N 61°8W 113 C17
Cheddar U.K. 51°17N 2°46W 24 D3
Cheddleton U.K. 53°4N 2°2W 23 F4
Cheduba I. Burma 18°45N 93°40E 85 K18
Chegutu Zimbabwe 18°10S 30°14E 97 H6
Chelm Poland 51°8N 23°30E 67 C12
Chelmer → U.K. 51°44N 0°30E 25 C10
Chelmsford U.K. 51°44N 0°29E 25 C9
Cheltenham U.K. 51°54N 2°4W 24 C4
Chelyabinsk Russia 55°10N 61°24E 79 D8
Chelyuskin, C. Russia 77°30N 103°0E 74 B12
Chemnitz Germany 50°51N 12°54E 66 C7
Chenab → Pakistan 30°23N 71°2E 84 D7
Chengde China 40°59N 117°58E 81 B6
Chengdu China 30°38N 104°2E 80 C5
Chengjiang China 24°39N 103°0E 80 D5
Chennai India 13°8N 80°19E 84 N12
Chepstow U.K. 51°38N 2°41W 26 D8
Cher → France 47°21N 0°29E 68 C4
Cherbourg France 49°39N 1°40W 68 B3
Cherepovets Russia 59°5N 37°55E 72 C6
Chergui, Chott ech Algeria 34°21N 0°25E 94 B6
Cheriton U.K. 51°3N 1°8W 24 D6
Cheriton Fitzpaine U.K. 50°51N 3°35W 27 F6
Cherkasy Ukraine 49°27N 32°4E 73 E5
Cherkessk Russia 44°15N 42°5E 73 F7
Chernihiv Ukraine 51°28N 31°20E 72 D5
Chernivtsi Ukraine 48°15N 25°52E 67 D13
Chernobyl Ukraine 51°20N 30°15E 72 D5
Cherokee U.S.A. 42°45N 95°33W 111 B7
Cherrapunji India 25°17N 91°47E 85 G17
Cherski Ra. Russia 65°0N 143°0E 79 C16
Chertsey U.K. 51°23N 0°30W 25 D7
Chervonohrad Ukraine 50°25N 24°10E 67 C13
Cherwell → U.K. 51°44N 1°14W 24 C6
Chesapeake B. U.S.A. 38°0N 76°10W 112 F9
Chesha B. Russia 67°20N 47°0E 72 A8

Chesham | | Cuanza

Place	Coordinates	Ref.
Chesham U.K.	51°43N 0°36W	25 C7
Cheshire □ U.K.	53°14N 2°30W	23 F4
Cheshunt U.K.	51°43N 0°1W	25 C8
Chesil Beach U.K.	50°37N 2°33W	24 E3
Chester U.K.	53°12N 2°53W	23 F3
Chester U.S.A.	39°51N 75°22W	113 F10
Chester-le-Street U.K.	54°51N 1°34W	22 C5
Chesterfield U.K.	53°15N 1°25W	23 F6
Chesterfield, Îs. N. Cal.	19°52S 158°15E	99 D10
Chesterfield Inlet Canada	63°30N 90°45W	108 C10
Chesuncook L. U.S.A.	46°0N 69°21W	113 B13
Chetumal Mexico	18°30N 88°20W	114 D7
Chetwynd Canada	55°45N 121°36W	108 D7
Cheviot, The U.K.	55°29N 2°9W	22 B4
Cheviot Hills U.K.	55°20N 2°30W	22 B3
Chew Bahir Ethiopia	4°40N 36°50E	88 G2
Chew Magna U.K.	51°22N 2°37W	24 D3
Cheyenne U.S.A.	41°8N 104°49W	110 B6
Cheyenne → U.S.A.	44°41N 101°18W	110 B6
Chhapra India	25°48N 84°44E	85 G14
Chhattisgarh □ India	22°0N 82°0E	85 J12
Chi → Thailand	15°11N 104°43E	83 B2
Chiai Taiwan	23°29N 120°25E	81 D7
Chiang Mai Thailand	18°47N 98°59E	83 B1
Chiávari Italy	44°19N 9°19E	70 B3
Chiba Japan	35°30N 140°7E	82 F7
Chibougamau Canada	49°56N 74°24W	109 E12
Chibougamau, L. Canada	49°50N 74°20W	113 A10
Chic-Chocs, Mts. Canada	48°55N 66°0W	113 A14
Chicago U.S.A.	41°52N 87°38W	112 E4
Chichagof I. U.S.A.	57°30N 135°30W	108 D6
Chichester U.K.	50°50N 0°47W	25 E7
Chickasha U.S.A.	35°3N 97°58W	110 C7
Chiclayo Peru	6°42S 79°50W	120 C2
Chico U.S.A.	39°44N 121°50W	110 C2
Chico → Chubut, Argentina	44°0S 67°0W	121 G3
Chico → Santa Cruz, Argentina	50°0S 68°30W	121 G3
Chicopee U.S.A.	42°9N 72°37W	113 D11
Chicoutimi Canada	48°28N 71°5W	113 A12
Chiddingfold U.K.	51°7N 0°37W	25 D7
Chidley, C. Canada	60°23N 64°26W	109 C13
Chieti Italy	42°21N 14°10E	70 C6
Chifeng China	42°18N 118°58E	81 B6
Chihuahua Mexico	28°38N 106°5W	114 B3
Chilapa Mexico	17°36N 99°10W	114 D5
Chilaw Sri Lanka	7°30N 79°50E	84 R11
Childress U.S.A.	34°25N 100°13W	110 D6
Chile ■ S. Amer.	35°0S 72°0W	121 F2
Chile Rise Pac. Oc.	38°0S 92°0W	103 L18
Chilham U.K.	51°15N 0°59E	25 D10
Chililabombwe Zambia	12°18S 27°43E	97 G5
Chilka L. India	19°40N 85°25E	85 K14
Chillán Chile	36°40S 72°10W	121 F2
Chillicothe Ill., U.S.A.	40°55N 89°29W	112 E3
Chillicothe Ohio, U.S.A.	39°20N 82°59W	112 F6
Chilliwack Canada	49°10N 121°54W	108 E7
Chiloé, I. de Chile	42°30S 73°50W	121 G2
Chilpancingo Mexico	17°33N 99°30W	114 D5
Chiltern Hills U.K.	51°40N 0°53W	25 C7
Chilton U.S.A.	44°2N 88°10W	112 C3
Chilung Taiwan	25°3N 121°45E	81 D7
Chilwa, L. Malawi	15°15S 35°40E	97 H7
Chimborazo Ecuador	1°29S 78°55W	120 C2
Chimbote Peru	9°0S 78°35W	120 C2
Chimkent Kazakhstan	42°18N 69°36E	87 A12
Chin □ Burma	22°0N 93°0E	85 J18
Chin Hills Burma	22°30N 93°30E	85 H18
China ■ Asia	30°0N 110°0E	81 C6
China, Great Plain of Asia	35°0N 115°0E	74 E13
Chinandega Nic.	12°35N 87°12W	114 E7
Chincha Alta Peru	13°25S 76°7W	120 D2
Chindwin → Burma	21°26N 95°15E	85 J19
Chingola Zambia	12°31S 27°53E	97 G5
Chinhoyi Zimbabwe	17°20S 30°8E	97 H6
Chiniot Pakistan	31°45N 73°0E	84 D8
Chinon France	47°10N 0°15E	68 C4
Chióggia Italy	45°13N 12°17E	70 B5
Chíos Greece	38°27N 26°9E	71 E12
Chipata Zambia	13°38S 32°28E	97 G6
Chipman Canada	46°6N 65°53W	113 B15
Chippenham U.K.	51°27N 2°6W	24 D4
Chippewa Falls U.S.A.	44°56N 91°24W	112 C2
Chipping Campden U.K.	52°3N 1°45W	24 B5
Chipping Norton U.K.	51°56N 1°32W	24 C5
Chipping Ongar U.K.	51°42N 0°15E	25 C9
Chipping Sodbury U.K.	51°33N 2°23W	24 C4
Chiquinquira Colombia	5°37N 73°50W	120 B2
Chirbury U.K.	52°35N 3°4W	23 G2
Chirchiq Uzbekistan	41°29N 69°35E	87 A12
Chiredzi Zimbabwe	21°0S 31°38E	97 J6
Chirnside U.K.	55°48N 2°12W	21 C11
Chisasibi Canada	53°50N 79°0W	109 D12
Chiseldon U.K.	51°31N 1°44W	24 C5
Chistopol Russia	55°25N 50°38E	72 C9
Chita Russia	52°0N 113°35E	79 D13
Chitral Pakistan	35°50N 71°56E	84 B7
Chittagong Bangla.	22°19N 91°48E	85 H17
Chittagong □ Bangla.	24°5N 91°0E	85 G17
Chitungwiza Zimbabwe	18°0S 31°6E	97 H6
Choiseul St. Lucia	13°47N 61°3W	115 f
Choiseul Solomon Is.	7°0S 156°40E	99 B10
Cholet France	47°4N 0°52W	68 C3
Chollerton U.K.	55°4N 2°7W	22 B4
Cholsey U.K.	51°35N 1°8W	24 C6
Choluteca Honduras	13°20N 87°14W	114 E7
Chon Buri Thailand	13°21N 101°1E	83 B2
Ch'ŏngjin N. Korea	41°47N 129°50E	81 B7
Chongqing China	29°35N 106°25E	80 D5
Chongqing Shi □ China	30°0N 108°0E	80 C5
Chonos, Arch. de los Chile	45°0S 75°0W	121 G2
Chorley U.K.	53°39N 2°38W	23 E3
Chorzów Poland	50°18N 18°57E	67 C10
Choybalsan Mongolia	48°4N 114°30E	81 B6
Christchurch N.Z.	43°33S 172°47E	99 J13
Christchurch U.K.	50°44N 1°47W	24 E5
Christmas I. Ind. Oc.	10°30S 105°40E	83 E2
Chubut → Argentina	43°20S 65°5W	121 G3
Chudleigh U.K.	50°36N 3°36W	27 F6
Chudskoye, L. Russia	58°13N 27°30E	72 C4
Chukchi Sea Russia	68°0N 175°0W	54 B17
Chukot Ra. Russia	68°0N 175°0E	79 C19
Chulmleigh U.K.	50°54N 3°51W	27 F6
Chuncheon S. Korea	37°58N 127°44E	81 C7
Chuquicamata Chile	22°15S 69°0W	121 E3
Chur Switz.	46°52N 9°32E	66 E5
Church Stretton U.K.	52°32N 2°48W	23 G3
Churchdown U.K.	51°52N 2°10W	24 C4
Churchill Canada	58°47N 94°11W	108 D10
Churchill → Man., Canada	58°47N 94°12W	108 D10
Churchill → Nfld. & L., Canada	53°19N 60°10W	109 D13
Churchill, C. Canada	58°46N 93°12W	108 D10
Churchill Falls Canada	53°36N 64°19W	109 D13
Churchill Pk. Canada	58°10N 125°10W	108 D7
Churu India	28°20N 74°50E	84 E9
Chuska Mts. U.S.A.	36°15N 108°50W	110 C5
Chusovoy Russia	58°22N 57°50E	72 C10
Chuuk Micronesia	7°25N 151°46E	102 G7
Chuvashia □ Russia	55°30N 47°0E	72 C8
Cicero U.S.A.	41°51N 87°44W	112 E4
Ciechanów Poland	52°52N 20°38E	67 B11
Ciego de Ávila Cuba	21°50N 78°50W	115 C9
Cienfuegos Cuba	22°10N 80°30W	115 C8
Çilo Dağı Turkey	37°28N 43°55E	73 G7
Cimarron → U.S.A.	36°10N 96°16W	111 C7
Cincinnati U.S.A.	39°9N 84°27W	112 F5
Cinderford U.K.	51°49N 2°30W	24 C3
Cinto, Mte. France	42°24N 8°54E	68 E8
Circle U.S.A.	65°50N 144°4W	108 C5
Circleville U.S.A.	39°36N 82°57W	112 F6
Cirebon Indonesia	6°45S 108°32E	83 D2
Cirencester U.K.	51°43N 1°57W	24 C6
Ciudad Acuña Mexico	29°18N 100°55W	114 B4
Ciudad Bolívar Venezuela	8°5N 63°36W	120 B3
Ciudad del Carmen Mexico	18°38N 91°50W	114 D6
Ciudad Guayana Venezuela	8°0N 62°30W	120 B3
Ciudad Guzmán Mexico	19°41N 103°29W	114 D4
Ciudad Juárez Mexico	31°44N 106°29W	114 A3
Ciudad Madero Mexico	22°19N 97°50W	114 C5
Ciudad Mante Mexico	22°44N 98°59W	114 C5
Ciudad Obregón Mexico	27°29N 109°56W	114 B3
Ciudad Real Spain	38°59N 3°55W	69 C4
Ciudad Valles Mexico	21°59N 99°1W	114 C5
Ciudad Victoria Mexico	23°44N 99°8W	114 C5
Civitavécchia Italy	42°6N 11°48E	70 C4
Cizre Turkey	37°19N 42°10E	73 G7
Clackmannan U.K.	56°7N 3°45W	21 B8
Clacton-on-Sea U.K.	51°47N 1°11E	25 C11
Claire, L. Canada	58°35N 112°5W	108 D8
Clara Ireland	53°21N 7°37W	28 E6
Clare U.K.	52°4N 0°34E	25 B10
Clare □ Ireland	52°45N 9°0W	30 C4
Clare → Ireland	53°20N 9°2W	28 E3
Clare I. Ireland	53°49N 10°0W	28 D1
Claremont U.S.A.	43°23N 72°20W	113 D11
Clark Fork → U.S.A.	48°9N 116°15W	110 A3
Clarksburg U.S.A.	39°17N 80°30W	112 F7
Clarksdale U.S.A.	34°12N 90°35W	111 D8
Clarksville U.S.A.	36°32N 87°21W	111 C9
Claverley U.K.	52°32N 2°18W	23 G4
Clay Cross U.K.	53°10N 1°25W	23 F6
Claydon U.K.	52°7N 1°8E	25 B11
Clear, C. Ireland	51°25N 9°32W	30 F3
Clear I. Ireland	51°26N 9°30W	30 F4
Clearfield U.S.A.	41°2N 78°27W	112 E8
Clearwater U.S.A.	27°59N 82°48W	111 E10
Cleator Moor U.K.	54°32N 3°30W	22 C2
Clee Hills U.K.	52°26N 2°35W	23 H3
Cleethorpes U.K.	53°33N 0°3W	23 E8
Cleeve Cloud U.K.	51°56N 2°0W	24 C5
Clent Hills U.K.	52°25N 2°4W	24 B4
Cleobury Mortimer U.K.	52°22N 2°28W	23 H4
Clermont-Ferrand France	45°46N 3°4E	68 D5
Clevedon U.K.	51°26N 2°52W	24 D3
Cleveland Miss., U.S.A.	33°45N 90°43W	111 D8
Cleveland Ohio, U.S.A.	41°29N 81°41W	112 E7
Cleveland Hills U.K.	54°25N 1°11W	22 D6
Clew B. Ireland	53°50N 9°49W	28 D2
Cley U.K.	52°57N 1°2E	25 A11
Clifden Ireland	53°29N 10°1W	28 D1
Cliffe U.K.	51°28N 0°31E	25 D10
Clifford U.K.	52°7N 3°6W	23 G2
Clinton Iowa, U.S.A.	41°51N 90°12W	112 E2
Clinton Okla., U.S.A.	35°31N 98°58W	110 C7
Clinton Colden L. Canada	63°58N 107°27W	108 C9
Clipperton, I. Pac. Oc.	10°18N 109°13W	103 F17
Clipston U.K.	52°27N 0°58W	23 G7
Clitheroe U.K.	53°53N 2°22W	23 E4
Clogher Hd. Ireland	53°48N 6°14W	29 D9
Cloghran Ireland	53°27N 6°14W	31 B10
Clonakilty Ireland	51°37N 8°53W	30 E5
Clonakilty B. Ireland	51°35N 8°51W	30 E5
Cloncurry → Australia	18°37S 140°40E	98 E7
Clondalkin Ireland	53°19N 6°25W	31 B10
Clones Ireland	54°11N 7°15W	29 C7
Clonmel Ireland	52°21N 7°42W	31 D7
Clontarf Ireland	53°22N 6°11W	31 B10
Cloughton U.K.	54°20N 0°26W	22 D8
Clovelly U.K.	51°0N 4°25W	27 F5
Clovis U.S.A.	34°24N 103°12W	110 D6
Clowne U.K.	53°16N 1°17W	23 F6
Cluj-Napoca Romania	46°47N 23°38E	67 E12
Clun Forest U.K.	52°27N 3°7W	23 H2
Clunbury U.K.	52°25N 2°55W	23 H3
Clwyd □ U.K.	53°19N 3°31W	26 A6
Clwyd → U.K.	53°19N 3°30W	26 A6
Clyde → U.K.	55°55N 4°30W	20 C6
Clyde, Firth of U.K.	55°22N 5°1W	20 D5
Clyde River Canada	70°30N 68°30W	109 B13
Clydebank U.K.	55°54N 4°23W	20 C7
Clydesdale U.K.	55°43N 3°51W	21 C8
Coalbrookdale U.K.	52°39N 2°30W	23 G4
Coalisland U.K.	54°33N 6°42W	29 B8
Coalville U.K.	52°44N 1°23W	23 G6
Coamo Puerto Rico	18°5N 66°22W	115 d
Coast Mts. Canada	55°0N 129°20W	108 D7
Coast Ranges U.S.A.	39°0N 123°0W	110 B2
Coatbridge U.K.	55°52N 4°6W	20 C7
Coaticook Canada	45°10N 71°46W	113 C12
Coats I. Canada	62°30N 83°0W	109 C11
Coats Land Antarctica	77°0S 25°0W	55 D1
Coatzacoalcos Mexico	18°7N 94°25W	114 D6
Cobán Guatemala	15°30N 90°21W	114 D6
Cobar Australia	31°27S 145°48E	98 G8
Cóbh Ireland	51°51N 8°17W	30 E6
Cobija Bolivia	11°0S 68°50W	120 D3
Cobourg Canada	43°58N 78°10W	112 D8
Cochabamba Bolivia	17°26S 66°10W	120 D3
Cochin India	9°58N 76°20E	84 Q10
Cochrane Canada	49°0N 81°0W	109 E11
Cockburn, Canal Chile	54°30S 72°0W	121 H2
Cockburn I. Canada	45°55N 83°22W	112 C6
Cockburn Town Bahamas	24°2N 74°31W	115 C10
Cockerham U.K.	53°58N 2°49W	23 E3
Cockermouth U.K.	54°40N 3°22W	22 C2
Cockfield U.K.	52°10N 0°48E	25 B10
Cockpit Country, The Jamaica	18°15N 77°45W	114 a
Coco → Cent. Amer.	15°0N 83°8W	115 E8
Coco, I. del Pac. Oc.	5°25N 87°55W	103 G19
Cocos Is. Ind. Oc.	12°10S 96°55E	83 E1
Cod, C. U.S.A.	42°5N 70°10W	113 D12
Coddenham U.K.	52°9N 1°8E	25 B11
Codó Brazil	4°30S 43°55W	120 C5
Cody U.S.A.	44°32N 109°3W	110 B5
Coeur d'Alene U.S.A.	47°41N 116°46W	110 A3
Coggeshall U.K.	51°52N 0°42E	25 C10
Cognac France	45°41N 0°20W	68 D3
Coigach U.K.	57°59N 5°14W	18 G7
Coigeach, Rubha U.K.	58°6N 5°26W	18 F7
Coimbatore India	11°2N 76°59E	84 P10
Coimbra Portugal	40°15N 8°27W	69 B1
Colatina Brazil	19°32S 40°37W	122 C2
Colchester U.K.	51°54N 0°55E	25 C10
Cold Fell U.K.	54°53N 2°36W	22 C3
Coldstream U.K.	55°39N 2°15W	21 C11
Colebrook U.S.A.	44°54N 71°30W	113 C12
Colebrooke U.K.	50°47N 3°44W	27 F6
Coleford U.K.	51°47N 2°36W	24 C3
Coleraine U.K.	55°8N 6°41W	29 A8
Coleshill U.K.	52°30N 1°41W	23 G5
Colgrave Sd. U.K.	60°36N 0°58W	18 A16
Colima Mexico	19°14N 103°43W	114 D4
Colima, Nevado de Mexico	19°33N 103°38W	114 D4
Coll U.K.	56°39N 6°34W	20 J4
Collier Law U.K.	54°47N 1°59W	22 C5
Collin U.K.	55°4N 3°31W	21 D8
Collingbourne Kingston U.K.	51°18N 1°40W	24 D5
Collingham U.K.	53°8N 0°46W	23 F7
Collingwood Canada	44°29N 80°13W	112 D7
Collooney Ireland	54°11N 8°29W	28 C5
Colmar France	48°5N 7°20E	66 B7
Colne U.K.	53°51N 2°9W	23 E4
Colne → Bucks., U.K.	51°27N 0°32W	25 D7
Colne → Essex, U.K.	51°51N 0°58E	25 C10
Cologne Germany	50°56N 6°57E	66 C4
Colombia ■ S. Amer.	3°45N 73°0W	120 B2
Colombo Sri Lanka	6°56N 79°58E	84 R11
Colonsay U.K.	56°5N 6°12W	20 B3
Colorado □ U.S.A.	39°30N 105°30W	110 C5
Colorado → Argentina	39°50S 62°8W	121 F3
Colorado → N. Amer.	31°45N 114°40W	110 D4
Colorado → U.S.A.	28°36N 95°59W	111 E7
Colorado Plateau U.S.A.	37°0N 111°0W	110 C4
Colorado Springs U.S.A.	38°50N 104°49W	110 C6
Colsterworth U.K.	52°49N 0°37W	23 G7
Coltishall U.K.	52°44N 1°21E	25 A11
Columbia Mo., U.S.A.	38°57N 92°20W	111 C8
Columbia S.C., U.S.A.	34°0N 81°2W	111 D10
Columbia Tenn., U.S.A.	35°37N 87°2W	111 C9
Columbia → N. Amer.	46°15N 124°5W	110 A2
Columbia, District of □ U.S.A.	38°55N 77°0W	112 F9
Columbia Plateau U.S.A.	44°0N 117°30W	110 B3
Columbus Ga., U.S.A.	32°28N 84°59W	111 D10
Columbus Ind., U.S.A.	39°13N 85°55W	112 F5
Columbus Miss., U.S.A.	33°30N 88°25W	111 D9
Columbus Nebr., U.S.A.	41°26N 97°22W	111 E7
Columbus Ohio, U.S.A.	39°58N 83°0W	112 F6
Colville → U.S.A.	70°25N 150°30W	108 A4
Colville, C. N.Z.	36°29S 175°21E	99 H14
Colwell U.K.	55°5N 2°4W	22 B4
Colwich U.K.	52°48N 1°58W	23 G5
Colwyn Bay U.K.	53°18N 3°44W	26 A6
Colyton U.K.	50°44N 3°5W	27 F7
Comayagua Honduras	14°25N 87°37W	114 E7
Combe Martin U.K.	51°12N 4°3W	27 E5
Comber U.K.	54°33N 5°45W	29 B10
Comeragh Mts. Ireland	52°18N 7°34W	31 D7
Comilla Bangla.	23°28N 91°8E	85 H17
Comitán Mexico	16°15N 92°8W	114 D6
Committee B. Canada	68°30N 86°30W	109 C11
Communism Pk. Tajikistan	39°0N 72°2E	87 B13
Como Italy	45°47N 9°5E	70 B3
Como, Lago di Italy	46°0N 9°11E	70 B3
Comodoro Rivadavia Argentina	45°50S 67°40W	121 G3
Comorin, C. India	8°3N 77°40E	84 Q10
Comoros ■ Ind. Oc.	12°10S 44°15E	91 H8
Compass Mt. S. Africa	31°45S 24°32E	90 K6
Compiègne France	49°24N 2°50E	68 B5
Conakry Guinea	9°29N 13°49W	94 G3
Conceição da Barra Brazil	18°35S 39°45W	122 C3
Conceição Chile	36°50S 73°0W	121 F2
Concepción Paraguay	23°22S 57°26W	121 E4
Concepción, Est. de Chile	50°30S 74°55W	121 H2
Concepción del Oro Mexico	24°38N 101°25W	114 C4
Concepción del Uruguay Argentina	32°35S 58°20W	121 F4
Conception, Pt. U.S.A.	34°27N 120°28W	110 D2
Conchos → Mexico	29°35N 104°25W	114 B4
Concord U.S.A.	43°12N 71°32W	113 D12
Concordia Argentina	31°20S 58°2W	121 F4
Concordia U.S.A.	39°34N 97°40W	110 C7
Condeúba Brazil	14°52S 42°0W	122 B2
Condover U.K.	52°39N 2°44W	23 G3
Congleton U.K.	53°10N 2°13W	23 F4
Congo ■ Africa	1°0S 16°0E	96 E3
Congo → Africa	6°4S 12°24E	96 F2
Congo, Dem. Rep. of the ■ Africa	3°0S 23°0E	96 E4
Congo Basin Africa	0°10S 24°30E	96 E4
Congresbury U.K.	51°22N 2°48W	24 D3
Coningsby U.K.	53°7N 0°10W	23 F8
Conisbrough U.K.	53°29N 1°14W	23 F6
Coniston Canada	46°29N 80°51W	112 B7
Coniston U.K.	54°22N 3°5W	22 D2
Coniston Water U.K.	54°20N 3°5W	22 D2
Conn, L. Ireland	54°3N 9°15W	28 C3
Connacht □ Ireland	53°43N 9°12W	28 D3
Connah's Quay U.K.	53°13N 3°4W	26 A7
Conneaut U.S.A.	41°57N 80°34W	112 E7
Connecticut □ U.S.A.	41°30N 72°45W	113 E11
Connecticut → U.S.A.	41°16N 72°20W	113 E11
Connellsville U.S.A.	40°1N 79°35W	112 E8
Connemara Ireland	53°29N 9°45W	28 D2
Connemara △ Ireland	53°32N 9°52W	28 D2
Connersville U.S.A.	39°39N 85°8W	112 F5
Conselheiro Lafaiete Brazil	20°40S 43°48W	122 D2
Consett U.K.	54°51N 1°50W	22 C5
Constance, L. Europe	47°35N 9°25E	66 E5
Constanţa Romania	44°14N 28°38E	67 F15
Constantine Algeria	36°25N 6°42E	94 A7
Constitución Chile	35°20S 72°30W	121 F2
Contas → Brazil	14°17S 39°1W	122 B3
Contwoyto L. Canada	65°42N 110°50W	108 C8
Conway Ark., U.S.A.	35°5N 92°26W	111 D8
Conway N.H., U.S.A.	43°59N 71°7W	113 D12
Conwy U.K.	53°17N 3°50W	26 A6
Conwy □ U.K.	53°10N 3°44W	26 A6
Conwy → U.K.	53°17N 3°50W	26 A6
Coober Pedy Australia	29°1S 134°43E	98 F6
Cook Inlet U.S.A.	60°0N 152°0W	108 D4
Cook Is. Pac. Oc.	17°0S 160°0W	103 J12
Cook Strait N.Z.	41°15S 174°29E	99 J13
Cookstown U.K.	54°39N 6°45W	29 B8
Cooktown Australia	15°30S 145°16E	98 D8
Coondapoor India	13°42N 74°40E	84 N9
Coos Bay U.S.A.	43°22N 124°13W	110 B2
Cootehill Ireland	54°4N 7°5W	29 C7
Copenhagen Denmark	55°40N 12°26E	63 F6
Copiapó Chile	27°30S 70°20W	121 E2
Copper Harbor U.S.A.	47°28N 87°53W	112 B4
Coppermine → Canada	67°49N 116°4W	108 C8
Coquet → U.K.	55°20N 1°32W	22 B5
Coquet U.K.	55°20N 1°36W	22 B5
Coquimbo Chile	30°0S 71°20W	121 E2
Coracora Peru	15°5S 73°45W	120 D2
Coral Harbour Canada	64°8N 83°10W	109 C11
Coral Sea Pac. Oc.	15°0S 150°0E	98 C9
Corbin U.S.A.	36°57N 84°6W	112 G5
Corbridge U.K.	54°58N 2°0W	22 C5
Corby U.K.	52°30N 0°41W	25 A7
Corby Glen U.K.	52°49N 0°30W	23 G7
Cordele U.S.A.	31°58N 83°47W	111 D10
Córdoba Argentina	31°20S 64°10W	121 F3
Córdoba Mexico	18°53N 96°56W	114 D5
Córdoba Spain	37°50N 4°50W	69 D3
Córdoba, Sierra de Argentina	31°10S 64°25W	121 F3
Cordova U.S.A.	60°33N 145°45W	108 C5
Corfe Castle U.K.	50°38N 2°3W	24 E4
Corfe Mullen U.K.	50°46N 2°1W	24 E4
Corfu Greece	39°38N 19°50E	71 E8
Corinth Greece	37°56N 22°55E	71 F10
Corinth U.S.A.	34°56N 88°31W	111 D9
Corinth, G. of Greece	38°16N 22°30E	71 E10
Corinto Brazil	18°20S 44°30W	122 C2
Cork Ireland	51°54N 8°29W	30 E6
Cork □ Ireland	51°57N 8°40W	30 E6
Cork Harbour Ireland	51°47N 8°16W	30 E6
Corner Brook Canada	48°57N 57°58W	109 E14
Corning U.S.A.	42°9N 77°3W	112 D9
Cornwall Canada	45°2N 74°44W	113 C10
Cornwall □ U.K.	50°26N 4°40W	27 G4
Cornwall, C. U.K.	50°8N 5°43W	27 G2
Cornwall I. Canada	77°37N 94°38W	109 B10
Cornwallis I. Canada	75°8N 95°0W	109 B10
Coro Venezuela	11°25N 69°41W	120 A3
Corocoro Bolivia	17°15S 68°28W	120 D3
Coromandel Coast India	12°30N 81°0E	84 N12
Coronation Gulf Canada	68°25N 110°0W	108 B8
Coronel Chile	37°0S 73°10W	121 F2
Coronel Fabriciano Brazil	19°31S 42°38W	122 C2
Coronel Pringles Argentina	38°0S 61°30W	121 F3
Coronel Suárez Argentina	37°30S 61°52W	121 F3
Coropuna, Nevado Peru	15°30S 72°41W	120 D2
Corpus Christi U.S.A.	27°47N 97°24W	110 E7
Corraun Pen. Ireland	53°54N 9°54W	28 D2
Corrib, L. Ireland	53°27N 9°16W	30 B4
Corrientes Argentina	27°30S 58°45W	121 E4
Corrientes, C. Colombia	5°30N 77°34W	120 B2
Corrientes, C. Mexico	20°25N 105°42W	114 C3
Corringham U.K.	53°25N 0°41W	23 F7
Corry U.S.A.	41°55N 79°39W	112 E8
Corse, C. France	43°1N 9°25E	68 E8
Corsham U.K.	51°27N 2°10W	24 D4
Corsica □ France	42°0N 9°0E	68 F8
Corsicana U.S.A.	32°6N 96°28W	111 D7
Corsley U.K.	51°13N 2°14W	24 D4
Corte France	42°19N 9°11E	68 E8
Cortez U.S.A.	37°21N 108°35W	110 C5
Cortland U.S.A.	42°36N 76°11W	113 D9
Çorum Turkey	40°30N 34°57E	73 F5
Corumbá Brazil	19°0S 57°30W	120 D4
Corunna = La Coruña Spain	43°20N 8°25W	69 A1
Corvallis U.S.A.	44°34N 123°16W	110 B2
Corve → U.K.	52°22N 2°43W	23 H3
Coseley U.K.	52°33N 2°5W	23 G4
Cosenza Italy	39°18N 16°15E	70 E7
Cosham U.K.	50°51N 1°2W	24 E6
Coshocton U.S.A.	40°16N 81°51W	112 E7
Costa Blanca Spain	38°25N 0°10W	69 C5
Costa Brava Spain	41°30N 3°0E	69 B7
Costa del Sol Spain	36°30N 4°30W	69 D3
Costa Dorada Spain	41°12N 1°15E	69 B6
Costa Rica ■ Cent. Amer.	10°0N 84°0W	115 F8
Costessey U.K.	52°40N 1°13E	25 A11
Cotabato Phil.	7°14N 124°15E	83 C4
Côte d'Azur France	43°25N 7°10E	68 E7
Côte-d'Ivoire = Ivory Coast ■ Africa	7°30N 5°0W	94 G4
Coteau du Missouri U.S.A.	47°0N 100°0W	110 A6
Cotentin France	49°15N 1°30W	68 B3
Cotherstone U.K.	54°35N 1°59W	22 C5
Cotonou Benin	6°20N 2°25E	94 G6
Cotopaxi Ecuador	0°40S 78°30W	120 C2
Cotswold Hills U.K.	51°42N 2°10W	24 C4
Cottbus Germany	51°45N 14°20E	66 C8
Cottenham U.K.	52°18N 0°9E	25 B9
Coudersport U.S.A.	41°46N 78°1W	112 E8
Council Bluffs U.S.A.	41°16N 95°52W	111 E7
Courantyne → S. Amer.	5°55N 57°5W	120 B4
Courtenay Canada	49°45N 125°0W	108 E7
Cove U.K.	56°0N 4°51W	20 B6
Coventry U.K.	52°25N 1°28W	24 B6
Cover → U.K.	54°17N 1°47W	22 D5
Coverack U.K.	50°1N 5°7W	27 G3
Covington U.S.A.	39°5N 84°30W	112 F5
Cowal U.K.	56°5N 5°8W	20 B5
Cowbridge U.K.	51°27N 3°27W	27 F9
Cowdenbeath U.K.	56°7N 3°21W	21 B9
Cowes U.K.	50°45N 1°18W	24 E6
Cowfold U.K.	50°59N 0°16W	25 E8
Cowpen U.K.	55°8N 1°32W	22 B5
Cox's Bazar Bangla.	21°26N 91°59E	85 J17
Cozumel, Isla Mexico	20°30N 86°40W	114 C7
Crab Hill Barbados	13°19N 59°38W	115 g
Cradock S. Africa	32°8S 25°36E	97 L5
Craig U.S.A.	40°31N 107°33W	110 B5
Craigavon U.K.	54°27N 6°23W	29 C9
Crail U.K.	56°16N 2°37W	21 B10
Craiova Romania	44°21N 23°48E	67 F12
Cramlington U.K.	55°6N 1°34W	22 B5
Cranborne U.K.	50°55N 1°54W	24 E5
Cranborne Chase U.K.	50°56N 2°6W	24 E4
Cranbrook Canada	49°30N 115°46W	108 E8
Cranbrook U.K.	51°6N 0°34E	25 D10
Crandon U.S.A.	45°34N 88°54W	112 C3
Crane, The Barbados	13°6N 59°27W	115 g
Cranleigh U.K.	51°8N 0°28W	25 D8
Cranwell U.K.	53°3N 0°27W	23 F8
Crateús Brazil	5°10S 40°39W	120 C5
Crato Brazil	7°10S 39°25W	120 C6
Craven Arms U.K.	52°26N 2°50W	23 H3
Crawfordsville U.S.A.	40°2N 86°54W	112 E4
Crawley U.K.	51°7N 0°11W	25 D8
Credenhill U.K.	52°5N 2°48W	24 B3
Crediton U.K.	50°47N 3°40W	27 F6
Cree → Canada	58°57N 105°47W	108 D9
Cree → U.K.	54°55N 4°25W	20 E7
Cree L. Canada	57°30N 106°30W	108 D9
Cremona Italy	45°7N 10°2E	70 B4
Cres Croatia	44°58N 14°25E	70 B6
Crete Greece	35°15N 25°0E	71 G11
Créteil France	48°47N 2°27E	68 C5
Creuse → France	47°0N 0°34E	68 C4
Crewe U.K.	53°6N 2°26W	23 F4
Crewkerne U.K.	50°53N 2°48W	24 E3
Crianlarich U.K.	56°24N 4°37W	20 B6
Criccieth U.K.	52°55N 4°13W	26 B5
Crick U.K.	52°22N 1°8W	24 B6
Crickhowell U.K.	51°52N 3°8W	26 D7
Cricklade U.K.	51°38N 1°50W	24 C5
Crieff U.K.	56°22N 3°50W	21 B8
Criffell U.K.	54°56N 3°39W	21 E9
Crimea □ Ukraine	45°0N 34°0E	73 F5
Crimean Pen. Ukraine	45°0N 34°0E	73 F5
Crişul Alb → Romania	46°42N 21°17E	67 E11
Crişul Negru → Romania	46°42N 21°16E	67 E11
Croagh Patrick Ireland	53°46N 9°40W	28 D2
Croatia ■ Europe	45°20N 16°0E	70 B7
Croglin U.K.	54°50N 2°39W	22 C5
Crohy Hd. Ireland	54°55N 8°26W	28 B5
Croker, C. Australia	10°58S 132°35E	98 C5
Cromarty U.K.	57°40N 4°2W	19 G8
Cromarty Firth U.K.	57°40N 4°15W	19 G8
Cromdale, Hills of U.K.	57°20N 3°28W	19 H11
Cromer U.K.	52°56N 1°17E	25 A11
Crondall U.K.	51°14N 0°51W	25 D7
Crook U.K.	54°43N 1°45W	22 C5
Crooked I. Bahamas	22°50N 74°10W	115 C10
Crooklands U.K.	54°16N 2°42W	22 D3
Crosby Cumb., U.K.	54°45N 3°25W	22 C2
Crosby Mersey., U.K.	53°30N 3°3W	23 F2
Crosby Ravensworth U.K.	54°33N 2°35W	22 C3
Cross Fell U.K.	54°43N 2°28W	22 C3
Cross Sound U.S.A.	58°0N 135°0W	108 D6
Crosshaven Ireland	51°47N 8°17W	30 E6
Crossmaglen U.K.	54°5N 6°36W	29 C8
Crotone Italy	39°5N 17°8E	70 E7
Crouch → U.K.	51°37N 0°53E	25 C10
Crow Hd. Ireland	51°35N 10°9W	30 E2
Crow Sound U.K.	49°56N 6°16W	27 H1
Crowborough U.K.	51°3N 0°11E	25 D9
Crowland U.K.	52°41N 0°10W	23 G8
Crowle U.K.	53°36N 0°49W	23 E7
Crowsnest Pass Canada	49°40N 114°40W	108 E8
Croyde U.K.	51°7N 4°14W	27 E5
Croydon □ U.K.	51°22N 0°5W	25 D8
Crozet, Is. Ind. Oc.	46°27S 52°0E	53 G12
Cruden Bay U.K.	57°25N 1°52W	19 H14
Crudgington U.K.	52°46N 2°33W	23 G3
Crummock Water U.K.	54°33N 3°18W	22 C2
Cruz Bay U.S. Virgin Is.	18°20N 64°48W	115 e
Cruz das Almas Brazil	12°0S 39°6W	122 B3
Cruzeiro Brazil	22°33S 45°0W	122 D1
Cruzeiro do Sul Brazil	7°35S 72°35W	120 C2
Crystal Falls U.S.A.	46°5N 88°20W	112 B3
Cuando → Angola	17°30S 23°15E	97 H4
Cuango → Dem. Rep. of the Congo	3°14S 17°22E	96 E3
Cuanza → Angola	9°21S 13°9E	96 F2

Cuauhtémoc   East Fen

Cuauhtémoc *Mexico* 28°25N 106°52W **114 B3**
Cuba ■ *W. Indies* 22°0N 79°0W **115 C9**
Cubango → *Africa* 18°50S 22°25E **97 H4**
Cuckfield *U.K.* 51°1N 0°8W **25 D8**
Cúcuta *Colombia* 7°54N 72°31W **120 B2**
Cuddalore *India* 11°46N 79°45E **84 P11**
Cuenca *Ecuador* 2°50S 79°9W **120 C2**
Cuenca *Spain* 40°5N 2°10W **69 B4**
Cuernavaca *Mexico* 18°55N 99°15W **114 D5**
Cuiabá *Brazil* 15°30S 56°0W **120 D4**
Cuillin Hills *U.K.* 57°13N 6°15W **18 H5**
Cuillin Sd. *U.K.* 57°4N 6°20W **18 H5**
Cuito → *Angola* 18°1S 20°48E **97 H4**
Culebra *Puerto Rico* 18°19N 65°18W **115 d**
Culiacán *Mexico* 24°50N 107°23W **114 C3**
Cullen *U.K.* 57°42N 2°49W **19 G12**
Cullompton *U.K.* 50°51N 3°24W **27 F7**
Culm → *U.K.* 50°46N 3°31W **27 F6**
Culpeper *U.S.A.* 38°30N 78°0W **112 F9**
Cumaná *Venezuela* 10°30N 64°5W **120 A3**
Cumberland *U.S.A.* 39°39N 78°46W **112 F8**
Cumberland → *U.S.A.* 37°9N 88°25W **111 C9**
Cumberland Pen. *Canada* 67°0N 64°0W **109 C13**
Cumberland Plateau *U.S.A.* 36°0N 85°0W **111 C10**
Cumberland Sd. *Canada* 65°30N 66°0W **109 C13**
Cumbernauld *U.K.* 55°57N 3°58W **21 C8**
Cumbrae Is. *U.K.* 55°46N 4°54W **20 C6**
Cumbria □ *U.K.* 54°42N 2°52W **22 C3**
Cumbrian Mts. *U.K.* 54°30N 3°0W **22 C2**
Cummertrees *U.K.* 54°59N 3°20W **21 E9**
Cumnock *U.K.* 55°28N 4°17W **20 D7**
Cumnor *U.K.* 51°44N 1°19W **24 C6**
Cumwhinton *U.K.* 54°52N 2°50W **22 C3**
Cunene → *Angola* 17°20S 11°50E **97 H2**
Cúneo *Italy* 44°23N 7°32E **70 B2**
Cunnamulla *Australia* 28°2S 145°38E **98 F8**
Cunninghame *U.K.* 55°38N 4°35W **20 C6**
Cupar *U.K.* 56°19N 3°1W **21 B9**
Curaçao *Neth. Ant.* 12°10N 69°0W **115 E11**
Curicó *Chile* 34°55S 71°20W **121 F2**
Curitiba *Brazil* 25°20S 49°10W **122 E1**
Curlew Mts. *Ireland* 54°0N 8°20W **28 D5**
Curry Rivel *U.K.* 51°1N 2°52W **24 D3**
Curvelo *Brazil* 18°45S 44°27W **122 C2**
Cuttack *India* 20°25N 85°57E **85 J14**
Cuxhaven *Germany* 53°51N 8°41E **66 B5**
Cuyahoga Falls *U.S.A.* 41°8N 81°29W **112 E7**
Cuyuni → *Guyana* 6°23N 58°41W **120 B4**
Cuzco *Peru* 13°32S 72°0W **120 D2**
Cwmbran *U.K.* 51°39N 3°2W **26 D7**
Cyclades *Greece* 37°0N 24°30E **71 F11**
Cynthiana *U.S.A.* 38°23N 84°18W **112 F5**
Cyprus ■ *Asia* 35°0N 33°0E **86 C3**
Cyrenaica *Libya* 27°0N 23°0E **95 C10**
Czech Rep. ■ *Europe* 50°0N 15°0E **66 D8**
Częstochowa *Poland* 50°49N 19°7E **67 C10**

D

Da Lat *Vietnam* 11°56N 108°25E **83 B2**
Da Nang *Vietnam* 16°4N 108°13E **83 B2**
Da Qaidam *China* 37°50N 95°15E **80 C4**
Daba Shan *China* 32°0N 109°0E **81 C6**
Dabie Shan *China* 31°20N 115°20E **81 C6**
Dadra & Nagar Haveli □ *India* 20°5N 73°0E **84 J8**
Dadu *Pakistan* 26°45N 67°45E **84 F5**
Daegu *S. Korea* 35°50N 128°37E **81 C7**
Daejeon *S. Korea* 36°20N 127°28E **81 C7**
Dagestan □ *Russia* 42°30N 47°0E **73 F8**
Dagupan *Phil.* 16°3N 120°20E **83 A6**
Dahod *India* 22°50N 74°15E **84 H9**
Dahongliutan *China* 35°45N 79°20E **80 C2**
Daingean *Ireland* 53°18N 7°17W **31 B8**
Dajarra *Australia* 21°42S 139°30E **98 E6**
Dakar *Senegal* 14°34N 17°29W **94 F2**
Dakhla *W. Sahara* 23°50N 15°53W **94 D2**
Dakhla, El Wâhât el- *Egypt* 25°30N 28°50E **95 C11**
Dalandzadgad *Mongolia* 43°27N 104°30E **80 B5**
Dalbeattie *U.K.* 54°56N 3°50W **21 E8**
Dalhart *U.S.A.* 36°4N 102°31W **110 C6**
Dalhousie *Canada* 48°5N 66°26W **113 A14**
Dali *China* 25°40N 100°10E **80 D5**
Dalian *China* 38°50N 121°40E **81 C7**
Daliang Shan *China* 28°0N 102°45E **80 D5**
Dalkeith *U.K.* 55°54N 3°4W **21 C9**
Dalkey *Ireland* 53°16N 6°6W **31 B10**
Dallas *U.S.A.* 32°47N 96°48W **111 D7**
Dalles, The *U.S.A.* 45°36N 121°10W **110 A2**
Dalmatia *Croatia* 43°20N 17°0E **70 C7**
Dalmellington *U.K.* 55°19N 4°23W **20 D7**
Daloa *Ivory C.* 7°0N 6°30W **94 G4**
Dalry *U.K.* 55°42N 4°43W **20 C6**
Dalrymple, L. *Australia* 20°40S 147°0E **98 E8**
Dalton *Dumf. & Gall., U.K.* 55°4N 3°24W **21 D9**
Dalton *N. Yorks., U.K.* 54°28N 1°32W **22 D5**
Dalton-in-Furness *U.K.* 54°10N 3°11W **22 D2**
Daly Waters *Australia* 16°15S 133°24E **98 D5**
Daman *India* 20°25N 72°57E **84 J8**
Damanhûr *Egypt* 31°0N 30°30E **95 B12**
Damaraland *Namibia* 20°0S 15°0E **97 H2**
Damascus *Syria* 33°30N 36°18E **86 C4**
Damāvand, Qolleh-ye *Iran* 35°56N 52°10E **87 C8**
Damerham *U.K.* 50°56N 1°51W **24 E5**
Dampier *Australia* 20°41S 116°42E **98 E2**
Danakil Desert *Ethiopia* 12°45N 41°0E **88 E3**
Danbury *U.S.A.* 41°24N 73°28W **113 E11**
Dandong *China* 40°10N 124°20E **81 B7**
Danube → *Europe* 45°20N 29°40E **67 F15**
Danville *Ill., U.S.A.* 40°8N 87°37W **112 E4**
Danville *Ky., U.S.A.* 37°39N 84°46W **112 G5**
Danville *Va., U.S.A.* 36°36N 79°23W **111 C11**
Dar Banda *Africa* 8°0N 23°0E **90 F6**
Dar es Salaam *Tanzania* 6°50S 39°12E **96 F7**
Darbhanga *India* 26°15N 85°55E **85 F14**
Dardanelles *Turkey* 40°17N 26°32E **71 D12**
Darent → *U.K.* 51°28N 0°14E **25 D9**
Dârfûr *Sudan* 13°40N 24°0E **95 F10**
Darhan *Mongolia* 49°37N 106°21E **80 B5**

Darién, G. del *Colombia* 9°0N 77°0W **120 B2**
Darjiling *India* 27°3N 88°18E **85 F16**
Darling → *Australia* 34°4S 141°54E **98 G7**
Darling Ra. *Australia* 32°30S 116°20E **98 G2**
Darlington *U.K.* 54°32N 1°33W **22 C5**
Darmstadt *Germany* 49°51N 8°39E **66 D5**
Darnah *Libya* 32°45N 22°45E **95 B10**
Darnley, C. *Antarctica* 68°0S 69°0E **55 C6**
Darnley B. *Canada* 69°30N 123°30W **108 C7**
Dart → *U.K.* 50°24N 3°39W **27 G6**
Dartford *U.K.* 51°26N 0°13E **25 D9**
Dartington *U.K.* 50°27N 3°43W **27 G6**
Dartmoor *U.K.* 50°38N 3°57W **27 F6**
Dartmoor △ *U.K.* 50°37N 3°59W **27 F6**
Dartmouth *Canada* 44°40N 63°30W **113 C16**
Dartmouth *U.K.* 50°21N 3°36W **27 G6**
Darton *U.K.* 53°35N 1°31W **23 E5**
Darwen *U.K.* 53°42N 2°29W **23 E4**
Darwin *Australia* 12°25S 130°51E **98 C5**
Dashen, Ras *Ethiopia* 13°8N 38°26E **88 E2**
Dashoguz *Turkmenistan* 41°49N 59°58E **87 A9**
Dasht → *Pakistan* 25°10N 61°40E **84 G2**
Datong *China* 40°6N 113°18E **81 B6**
Daugava → *Latvia* 57°4N 24°3E **63 F9**
Daugavpils *Latvia* 55°53N 26°32E **63 F9**
Dauphin *Canada* 51°9N 100°5W **108 D9**
Dauphiné *France* 45°15N 5°25E **68 D6**
Davangere *India* 14°25N 75°55E **84 M9**
Davao *Phil.* 7°0N 125°40E **83 C4**
Davenport *U.S.A.* 41°32N 90°35W **112 E2**
Daventry *U.K.* 52°16N 1°10W **24 B6**
David *Panama* 8°30N 82°30W **115 F8**
Davis Str. *N. Amer.* 65°0N 58°0W **104 C14**
Dawlish *U.K.* 50°35N 3°28W **27 F7**
Dawna Ra. *Burma* 16°30N 98°30E **85 L21**
Dawros Hd. *Ireland* 54°50N 8°33W **28 B4**
Dawson *Canada* 64°10N 139°30W **108 C6**
Dawson Creek *Canada* 55°45N 120°15W **108 D7**
Dax *France* 43°44N 1°3W **68 E3**
Daxian *China* 31°15N 107°23E **80 C5**
Daxue Shan *China* 30°30N 101°30E **80 C5**
Dayr az Zawr *Syria* 35°20N 40°5E **86 C5**
Dayton *U.S.A.* 39°45N 84°12W **112 F5**
Daytona Beach *U.S.A.* 29°13N 81°1W **111 E10**
De Aar *S. Africa* 30°39S 24°0E **97 L4**
De Pere *U.S.A.* 44°27N 88°4W **112 C3**
Dead Sea *Asia* 31°30N 35°30E **86 D3**
Deal *U.K.* 51°13N 1°25E **25 D11**
Dean, Forest of *U.K.* 51°45N 2°33W **24 C3**
Dearham *U.K.* 54°44N 3°25W **22 C2**
Dease → *Canada* 59°56N 128°32W **108 D6**
Dease Lake *Canada* 58°25N 130°6W **108 D6**
Death Valley *U.S.A.* 36°15N 116°50W **110 C3**
Deben → *U.K.* 52°0N 1°25E **25 B11**
Debenham *U.K.* 52°14N 1°12E **25 B11**
Debre Markos *Ethiopia* 10°20N 37°40E **88 E2**
Debre Tabor *Ethiopia* 11°50N 38°26E **88 E2**
Debrecen *Hungary* 47°33N 21°42E **67 E11**
Decatur *Ala., U.S.A.* 34°36N 86°59W **111 D9**
Decatur *Ill., U.S.A.* 39°51N 88°57W **112 F3**
Decatur *Ind., U.S.A.* 40°50N 84°56W **112 E5**
Deccan *India* 18°0N 79°0E **84 L11**
Deddington *U.K.* 51°59N 1°18W **24 C6**
Dee → *Aberds., U.K.* 57°9N 2°5W **19 H13**
Dee → *Dumf. & Gall., U.K.* 54°51N 4°3W **20 E7**
Dee → *Wales, U.K.* 53°22N 3°17W **26 A7**
Deeping St. Nicholas *U.K.* 52°44N 0°12W **23 G8**
Deer Lake *Canada* 49°11N 57°27W **109 E14**
Defiance *U.S.A.* 41°17N 84°22W **112 E5**
Dehra Dun *India* 30°20N 78°4E **84 D11**
DeKalb *U.S.A.* 41°56N 88°46W **112 E3**
Delabole *U.K.* 50°37N 4°46W **27 F4**
Del Rio *U.S.A.* 29°22N 100°54W **110 E6**
Delaware *U.S.A.* 40°18N 83°4W **112 E6**
Delaware □ *U.S.A.* 39°0N 75°20W **113 F10**
Delaware → *U.S.A.* 39°15N 75°20W **113 F10**
Delaware B. *U.S.A.* 39°0N 75°10W **111 C12**
Delft *Neths.* 52°1N 4°22E **65 B4**
Delfzijl *Neths.* 53°20N 6°55E **65 A6**
Delgado, C. *Mozam.* 10°45S 40°40E **96 G8**
Delhi *India* 28°39N 77°13E **84 E10**
Delice *Turkey* 39°54N 34°2E **73 G5**
Delicias *Mexico* 28°13N 105°28W **114 B3**
Déline *Canada* 65°11N 123°25W **108 C7**
Delphos *U.S.A.* 40°51N 84°21W **112 E5**
Delta Junction *U.S.A.* 64°2N 145°44W **108 C5**
Demanda, Sierra de la *Spain* 42°15N 3°0W **69 A4**
Deming *U.S.A.* 32°16N 107°46W **110 D5**
Demopolis *U.S.A.* 32°31N 87°50W **111 D9**
Den Helder *Neths.* 52°57N 4°45E **65 B4**
Denbigh *U.K.* 53°12N 3°25W **26 A7**
Denbighshire □ *U.K.* 53°8N 3°22W **26 A7**
Denby Dale *U.K.* 53°34N 1°40W **23 E5**
Denham, Mt. *Jamaica* 18°13N 77°32W **114 a**
Denia *Spain* 38°49N 0°8E **69 C6**
Denizli *Turkey* 37°42N 29°2E **73 G4**
Denmark ■ *Europe* 55°45N 10°0E **63 F6**
Denmark Str. *Atl. Oc.* 66°0N 30°0W **54 C6**
Dennery *St. Lucia* 13°55N 60°54W **115 f**
Denny *U.K.* 56°1N 3°55W **21 B8**
Denpasar *Indonesia* 8°39S 115°13E **83 D3**
Dent *U.K.* 54°17N 2°27W **22 D4**
Denton *Gt. Man., U.K.* 53°27N 2°9W **23 F4**
Denton *Lincs., U.K.* 52°53N 0°43W **23 G7**
D'Entrecasteaux Is. *Papua N. G.* 9°0S 151°0E **98 B9**
Denver *U.S.A.* 39°42N 104°59W **110 C5**
Deoghar *India* 24°30N 86°42E **85 G15**
Deolali *India* 19°58N 73°50E **84 K8**
Deosai Mts. *Pakistan* 35°40N 75°0E **84 B9**
Dera Ghazi Khan *Pakistan* 30°5N 70°43E **84 D7**
Dera Ismail Khan *Pakistan* 31°50N 70°50E **84 D7**
Derbent *Russia* 42°5N 48°15E **73 F8**
Derby *Australia* 17°18S 123°38E **98 D3**
Derby *U.K.* 52°56N 1°28W **23 G6**
Derbyshire □ *U.K.* 53°11N 1°38W **23 F5**
Dereham *U.K.* 52°41N 0°57E **25 A10**

Derg → *U.K.* 54°44N 7°26W **28 B7**
Derg, L. *Ireland* 53°0N 8°20W **30 C6**
Deridder *U.S.A.* 30°51N 93°17W **111 D8**
Derry = Londonderry *U.K.* 55°0N 7°20W **28 A7**
Derrynasaggart Mts. *Ireland* 51°58N 9°15W **30 E4**
Derryveagh Mts. *Ireland* 54°56N 8°11W **28 B5**
Derwent → *Derby, U.K.* 52°57N 1°28W **23 G6**
Derwent → *N. Yorks., U.K.* 53°45N 0°58W **23 E7**
Derwent → *Tyne & W., U.K.* 54°58N 1°41W **22 C5**
Derwent Water *U.K.* 54°35N 3°9W **22 C2**
Des Moines *U.S.A.* 41°35N 93°37W **111 B8**
Des Moines → *U.S.A.* 40°23N 91°25W **111 B81**
Desborough *U.K.* 52°27N 0°49W **25 B7**
Deseado → *Argentina* 47°45S 65°54W **121 G3**
Desford *U.K.* 52°37N 1°17W **23 G6**
Desolación, I. *Chile* 53°0S 74°0W **121 H2**
Dessau *Germany* 51°51N 12°14E **66 C7**
Detour, Pt. *U.S.A.* 45°40N 86°40W **112 C4**
Detroit *U.S.A.* 42°19N 83°12W **112 D6**
Deutsche Bucht *Germany* 54°15N 8°0E **66 A5**
Deventer *Neths.* 52°15N 6°10E **65 B6**
Deveron → *U.K.* 57°41N 2°32W **19 G12**
Devils Lake *U.S.A.* 48°7N 98°52W **110 A7**
Devizes *U.K.* 51°22N 1°58W **24 D5**
Devon □ *U.K.* 50°50N 3°40W **27 F6**
Devon I. *Canada* 75°10N 85°0W **109 B11**
Devonport *U.K.* 50°22N 4°11W **27 G5**
Dewey *Puerto Rico* 18°18N 65°18W **115 d**
Dewsbury *U.K.* 53°42N 1°37W **23 E5**
Dexter *U.S.A.* 36°48N 89°57W **112 G3**
Deyang *China* 31°3N 104°27E **80 C5**
Dezful *Iran* 32°20N 48°30E **86 C7**
Dezhneva, Mys. *Russia* 66°5N 169°40W **79 C20**
Dezhou *China* 37°26N 116°18E **81 C6**
Dhahran *Si. Arabia* 26°10N 50°7E **86 E7**
Dhaka *Bangla.* 23°43N 90°26E **85 H17**
Dhaka □ *Bangla.* 24°25N 90°25E **85 G17**
Dhamār *Yemen* 14°30N 44°20E **88 E3**
Dhamtari *India* 20°42N 81°35E **85 J12**
Dhanbad *India* 23°50N 86°30E **85 H15**
Dharwad *India* 15°30N 75°4E **84 M9**
Dhaulagiri *Nepal* 28°39N 83°28E **85 E13**
Dhenkanal *India* 20°45N 85°35E **85 J14**
Dhuburi *India* 26°2N 89°59E **85 F16**
Dhule *India* 20°58N 74°50E **84 J9**
Diamantina *Brazil* 18°17S 43°40W **122 C2**
Diamantina → *Australia* 26°45S 139°10E **98 F6**
Diamantino *Brazil* 14°30S 56°30W **120 D4**
Dibrugarh *India* 27°29N 94°55E **85 F19**
Dickinson *U.S.A.* 46°53N 102°47W **110 A6**
Didcot *U.K.* 51°36N 1°14W **24 C6**
Diefenbaker, L. *Canada* 51°0N 106°55W **108 D9**
Dieppe *France* 49°54N 1°4E **68 B4**
Digby *Canada* 44°38N 65°50W **109 E13**
Digne-les-Bains *France* 44°5N 6°12E **68 D7**
Dijon *France* 47°20N 5°3E **68 C6**
Dikson *Russia* 73°40N 80°5E **79 B10**
Dili *E. Timor* 8°39S 125°34E **83 D4**
Dillingham *U.S.A.* 59°3N 158°28W **108 D4**
Dimitrovgrad *Bulgaria* 42°5N 25°35E **71 C11**
Dimitrovgrad *Russia* 54°14N 49°39E **72 D8**
Dinajpur *Bangla.* 25°33N 88°43E **85 G16**
Dinan *France* 48°28N 2°2W **68 B2**
Dinant *Belgium* 50°16N 4°55E **65 D4**
Dinaric Alps *Croatia* 44°0N 16°30E **70 C7**
Dingle *Ireland* 52°9N 10°17W **30 D2**
Dingle B. *Ireland* 52°3N 10°20W **30 D2**
Dingwall *U.K.* 57°36N 4°26W **19 G9**
Dipolog *Phil.* 8°36N 123°20E **83 C4**
Dire Dawa *Ethiopia* 9°35N 41°45E **88 F3**
Dirranbandi *Australia* 28°33S 148°17E **98 F8**
Disappointment, C. *U.S.A.* 46°18N 124°5W **110 A2**
Disappointment, L. *Australia* 23°20S 122°40E **98 E3**
Diss *U.K.* 52°23N 1°7E **25 B11**
Distington *U.K.* 54°36N 3°32W **22 C1**
District of Columbia □ *U.S.A.* 38°55N 77°0W **112 F9**
Distrito Federal □ *Brazil* 15°45S 47°45W **122 C1**
Ditchingham *U.K.* 52°28N 1°28E **25 B11**
Ditchling Beacon *U.K.* 50°54N 0°6W **25 E8**
Ditton Priors *U.K.* 52°30N 2°34W **23 G3**
Diu *India* 20°45N 70°58E **84 J7**
Divinópolis *Brazil* 20°10S 44°54W **122 D2**
Dixon *U.S.A.* 41°50N 89°29W **112 E3**
Dixon Entrance *U.S.A.* 54°30N 132°0W **108 D6**
Diyarbakır *Turkey* 37°55N 40°18E **73 G7**
Dizzard Pt. *U.K.* 50°44N 4°40W **27 F4**
Djelfa, Î. de *Tunisia* 33°50N 10°48E **95 B86**
Djerid, Chott *Tunisia* 33°42N 8°30E **95 B7**
Djibouti *Djibouti* 11°30N 43°5E **88 E3**
Djibouti ■ *Africa* 12°0N 43°0E **88 E3**
Djourab, Erg du *Chad* 16°40N 18°50E **95 E9**
Dmitriy Laptev Str. *Russia* 73°0N 140°0E **79 B16**
Dnepropetrovsk *Ukraine* 48°30N 35°0E **73 E6**
Dnieper → *Ukraine* 46°30N 32°18E **73 E5**
Dniester → *Europe* 46°18N 30°17E **67 E16**
Dniprodzerzhynsk *Ukraine* 48°32N 34°37E **73 E5**
Doba *Chad* 8°40N 16°50E **95 G9**
Doberai, Jazirah *Indonesia* 1°25S 133°0E **83 D5**
Dobrich *Bulgaria* 43°37N 27°49E **71 C12**
Dobruja *Europe* 44°30N 28°15E **67 F15**
Docking *U.K.* 52°54N 0°38E **25 A10**
Doddington *Cambs., U.K.* 52°30N 0°3E **25 B9**
Doddington *Northumberland, U.K.* 55°33N 1°54W **22 A5**
Dodecanese *Greece* 36°35N 27°0E **71 F12**
Dodge City *U.S.A.* 37°45N 100°1W **110 C6**
Dodman Pt. *U.K.* 50°13N 4°48W **27 G4**
Dodoma *Tanzania* 6°8S 35°45E **96 F7**
Doha *Qatar* 25°15N 51°35E **87 E7**
Dolbeau-Mistassini *Canada* 48°53N 72°14W **109 E12**
Dole *France* 47°7N 5°31E **68 C6**
Dolgarrog *U.K.* 53°11N 3°50W **26 A6**
Dolgellau *U.K.* 52°45N 3°53W **26 B6**
Dolo *Ethiopia* 4°11N 42°3E **88 G3**
Dolomites *Italy* 46°23N 11°51E **70 A4**

Dolores *Argentina* 36°20S 57°40W **121 F4**
Dolphin and Union Str. *Canada* 69°5N 114°45W **108 C8**
Dolphinton *U.K.* 55°42N 3°25W **21 C9**
Dolton *U.K.* 50°53N 4°2W **27 F5**
Dominica ■ *W. Indies* 15°20N 61°20W **115 D12**
Dominican Rep. ■ *W. Indies* 19°0N 70°30W **115 D10**
Don → *Russia* 47°4N 39°18E **73 E6**
Don → *Aberds., U.K.* 57°11N 2°5W **19 H13**
Don → *S. Yorks., U.K.* 53°41N 0°52W **23 E7**
Don Figuerero Mts. *Jamaica* 18°5N 77°36W **114 a**
Donaghadee *U.K.* 54°39N 5°33W **29 B10**
Doncaster *U.K.* 53°32N 1°6W **23 E6**
Dondra Head *Sri Lanka* 5°55N 80°40E **84 S12**
Donegal *Ireland* 54°39N 8°5W **28 B5**
Donegal □ *Ireland* 54°53N 8°0W **28 B5**
Donegal B. *Ireland* 54°31N 8°49W **28 B4**
Donets → *Russia* 47°33N 40°55E **73 E7**
Donetsk *Ukraine* 48°0N 37°45E **73 E6**
Dong Hoi *Vietnam* 17°29N 106°36E **83 B2**
Dongola *Sudan* 19°9N 30°22E **95 E12**
Dongting Hu *China* 29°18N 112°45E **81 D6**
Donhead *U.K.* 51°1N 2°7W **24 D4**
Donington *U.K.* 52°54N 0°12W **23 G8**
Donna Nook *U.K.* 53°29N 0°8E **23 F9**
Donostia-San Sebastián *Spain* 43°17N 1°58W **69 A5**
Doon → *U.K.* 55°27N 4°39W **20 D6**
Dorchester *Dorset, U.K.* 50°42N 2°27W **24 E4**
Dorchester *Oxon., U.K.* 51°39N 1°10W **24 C6**
Dorchester, C. *Canada* 65°27N 77°27W **109 C12**
Dordogne → *France* 45°2N 0°36W **68 D3**
Dordrecht *Neths.* 51°48N 4°39E **65 C4**
Dores do Indaiá *Brazil* 19°27S 45°36W **122 C1**
Dorking *U.K.* 51°14N 0°19W **25 D8**
Dornie *U.K.* 57°17N 5°31W **18 H6**
Dornoch *U.K.* 57°53N 4°2W **19 G9**
Dornoch Firth *U.K.* 57°51N 4°4W **19 G9**
Döröö Nuur *Mongolia* 48°0N 93°0E **80 B4**
Dorset □ *U.K.* 50°45N 2°26W **24 E4**
Dorstone *U.K.* 52°3N 2°59W **24 B3**
Dortmund *Germany* 51°30N 7°28E **66 C4**
Dos Bahías, C. *Argentina* 44°58S 65°32W **121 G3**
Dos Hermanas *Spain* 37°16N 5°55W **69 D3**
Dothan *U.S.A.* 31°13N 85°24W **111 D9**
Douai *France* 50°21N 3°4E **68 A5**
Douala *Cameroon* 4°0N 9°45E **96 D1**
Doubs → *France* 46°53N 5°1E **68 C6**
Douglas *I. of Man* 54°10N 4°28W **29 C13**
Douglas *U.S.A.* 31°21N 109°33W **110 D5**
Dounreay *U.K.* 58°35N 3°44W **19 E10**
Dourados *Brazil* 22°9S 54°50W **120 E4**
Douro → *Europe* 41°8N 8°40W **69 B1**
Dove → *Derby, U.K.* 52°51N 1°36W **23 G5**
Dove → *N. Yorks., U.K.* 54°15N 0°55W **22 D7**
Dove Dale *U.K.* 53°7N 1°46W **23 F5**
Dover *U.K.* 51°7N 1°19E **25 D11**
Dover *Del., U.S.A.* 39°10N 75°32W **113 F10**
Dover *N.H., U.S.A.* 43°12N 70°56W **113 D12**
Dover, Str. of *Europe* 51°0N 1°30E **64 F7**
Dover-Foxcroft *U.S.A.* 45°11N 69°13W **113 C13**
Doveridge *U.K.* 52°54N 1°49W **23 G5**
Dovrefjell *Norway* 62°15N 9°33E **63 E5**
Down □ *U.K.* 54°23N 6°2W **29 C9**
Downham *U.K.* 52°26N 0°14E **25 B9**
Downham Market *U.K.* 52°37N 0°23E **25 A9**
Downpatrick *U.K.* 54°20N 5°43W **29 C10**
Downpatrick Hd. *Ireland* 54°20N 9°21W **28 B3**
Downton *U.K.* 50°59N 1°44W **24 E5**
Dra, Oued → *Morocco* 28°40N 11°10W **94 C3**
Draguignan *France* 43°32N 6°27E **68 E7**
Drake Passage *S. Ocean* 58°0S 68°0W **55 B17**
Drakensberg *S. Africa* 31°0S 28°0E **97 L5**
Drammen *Norway* 59°42N 10°12E **63 F6**
Drava → *Croatia* 45°33N 18°55E **71 B8**
Drenthe □ *Neths.* 52°52N 6°40E **65 B6**
Dresden *Germany* 51°3N 13°44E **66 C7**
Dreux *France* 48°44N 1°23E **68 B4**
Driffield *U.K.* 54°0N 0°26W **23 D8**
Drina → *Bos.-H.* 44°53N 19°21E **71 B8**
Drobeta-Turnu Severin *Romania* 44°39N 22°41E **67 F12**
Drogheda *Ireland* 53°43N 6°22W **29 D9**
Drohobych *Ukraine* 49°20N 23°30E **73 E3**
Droichead Nua *Ireland* 53°11N 6°48W **31 B9**
Droitwich *U.K.* 52°16N 2°8W **24 B4**
Dromore *U.K.* 54°31N 7°28W **28 B7**
Dromore West *Ireland* 54°15N 8°52W **28 B4**
Dronfield *U.K.* 53°19N 1°27W **23 F6**
Dronning Maud Land *Antarctica* 72°30S 12°0E **55 D3**
Drumheller *Canada* 51°25N 112°40W **108 D8**
Drummond I. *U.S.A.* 46°1N 83°39W **112 C6**
Drummondville *Canada* 45°55N 72°25W **113 C11**
Druridge B. *U.K.* 55°17N 1°32W **22 A5**
Dry Harbour Mts. *Jamaica* 18°19N 77°24W **114 a**
Dryden *Canada* 49°47N 92°50W **108 E10**
Drygalski I. *Antarctica* 66°0S 92°0E **55 C7**
Ďumbá *Si. Arabia* 27°10N 35°40E **86 E3**
Dubai *U.A.E.* 25°18N 55°20E **87 E8**
Dubawnt → *Canada* 64°33N 100°6W **108 C9**
Dubawnt L. *Canada* 63°8N 101°28W **108 C9**
Dubbo *Australia* 32°11S 148°35E **98 G8**
Dublin *Ireland* 53°21N 6°15W **31 B10**
Dublin *U.S.A.* 32°32N 82°54W **111 D10**
Dublin □ *Ireland* 53°24N 6°20W **31 B10**
Dublin ✈ (DUB) *Ireland* 53°26N 6°15W **31 B10**
Dubois *U.S.A.* 41°7N 78°46W **112 E8**
Dubrovnik *Croatia* 42°39N 18°6E **71 C8**
Dubuque *U.S.A.* 42°30N 90°41W **112 D2**
Duddington *U.K.* 52°36N 0°32E **23 G7**
Duddon → *U.K.* 54°12N 3°15W **22 D2**
Dudinka *Russia* 69°30N 86°13E **79 C10**
Dudley *U.K.* 52°31N 2°5W **23 G4**
Duffield *U.K.* 52°59N 1°29W **23 G6**
Dufftown *U.K.* 57°27N 3°8W **19 H11**
Dugi Otok *Croatia* 44°0N 15°3E **70 C6**
Duisburg *Germany* 51°26N 6°45E **66 C4**

Dukinfield *U.K.* 53°28N 2°6W **23 F4**
Dulce → *Argentina* 30°32S 62°33W **121 F3**
Duluth *U.S.A.* 46°47N 92°6W **112 B1**
Dulverton *U.K.* 51°2N 3°33W **27 E6**
Dumaguete *Phil.* 9°17N 123°15E **83 C4**
Dumbarton *U.K.* 55°57N 4°33W **20 C6**
Dumfries *U.K.* 55°4N 3°37W **21 D8**
Dumfries & Galloway □ *U.K.* 55°9N 3°58W **21 D8**
Dumyât *Egypt* 31°24N 31°48E **95 B12**
Dún Laoghaire *Ireland* 53°17N 6°8W **31 B10**
Dunbar *U.K.* 56°0N 2°31W **21 B10**
Dunblane *U.K.* 56°11N 3°58W **21 B8**
Duncan *U.S.A.* 34°30N 97°57W **110 D7**
Duncansby Head *U.K.* 58°38N 3°1W **19 E11**
Dunchurch *U.K.* 52°21N 1°17W **24 B6**
Dundalk *Ireland* 54°1N 6°24W **29 C9**
Dundalk Bay *Ireland* 53°55N 6°15W **29 D9**
Dundee *U.K.* 56°28N 2°59W **21 B10**
Dundrum *Ireland* 53°18N 6°14W **31 B10**
Dundrum *U.K.* 54°16N 5°52W **29 C10**
Dundrum B. *U.K.* 54°13N 5°47W **29 C10**
Dunedin *N.Z.* 45°50S 170°33E **99 K13**
Dunfermline *U.K.* 56°5N 3°27W **21 B9**
Dungannon *U.K.* 54°31N 6°46W **29 B8**
Dungarvan *Ireland* 52°5N 7°37W **31 D7**
Dungarvan Harbour *Ireland* 52°4N 7°35W **31 D7**
Dungeness *U.K.* 50°54N 0°59E **25 E10**
Dunhua *China* 43°20N 128°14E **81 B7**
Dunhuang *China* 40°8N 94°36E **80 B4**
Dunkeld *U.K.* 56°34N 3°35W **21 A8**
Dunkerque *France* 51°2N 2°20E **68 A5**
Dunkery Beacon *U.K.* 51°9N 3°36W **27 E6**
Dunkirk *U.S.A.* 42°29N 79°20W **112 D8**
Dunleer *Ireland* 53°50N 6°24W **29 D9**
Dunmanway *Ireland* 51°43N 9°6W **30 E4**
Dunmore *U.S.A.* 41°25N 75°38W **113 E10**
Dunnet Hd. *U.K.* 58°40N 3°21W **19 E11**
Dunoon *U.K.* 55°57N 4°56W **20 C6**
Duns *U.K.* 55°47N 2°20W **21 C11**
Dunsford *U.K.* 50°41N 3°42W **27 F6**
Dunstable *U.K.* 51°53N 0°32W **25 C7**
Dunster *U.K.* 51°11N 3°27W **24 D2**
Dunston *U.K.* 52°46N 2°7W **23 G4**
Dunvegan *U.K.* 57°27N 6°35W **18 H4**
Duque de Caxias *Brazil* 22°46S 43°18W **122 D2**
Durance → *France* 43°55N 4°45E **68 E6**
Durango *Mexico* 24°3N 104°39W **114 C4**
Durango *U.S.A.* 37°16N 107°53W **110 C5**
Durant *U.S.A.* 33°59N 96°25W **111 D7**
Durazno *Uruguay* 33°25S 56°31W **121 F4**
Durban *S. Africa* 29°49S 31°1E **97 K6**
Düren *Germany* 50°48N 6°29E **66 C4**
Durgapur *India* 23°30N 87°20E **85 H15**
Durham *U.K.* 54°47N 1°34W **22 C5**
Durham *U.S.A.* 35°59N 78°54W **111 C11**
Durham □ *U.K.* 54°42N 1°45W **22 C5**
Durlston Hd. *U.K.* 50°36N 1°57W **24 E5**
Durness *U.K.* 58°34N 4°45W **19 E8**
Durrës *Albania* 41°19N 19°28E **71 D8**
Durrington *U.K.* 51°12N 1°47W **24 D5**
Durrow *Ireland* 52°51N 7°24W **31 C8**
Dursey I. *Ireland* 51°36N 10°12W **30 E2**
Dursley *U.K.* 51°40N 2°21W **24 C4**
Dushanbe *Tajikistan* 38°33N 68°48E **87 B12**
Düsseldorf *Germany* 51°14N 6°47E **66 C4**
Dutch Harbor *U.S.A.* 53°53N 166°32W **108 D3**
Duyun *China* 26°18N 107°29E **80 D5**
Dvina, N. → *Russia* 64°32N 40°30E **72 B7**
Dvina B. *Russia* 65°0N 39°0E **72 B6**
Dwarka *India* 22°18N 69°8E **84 H6**
Dyce *U.K.* 57°13N 2°12W **19 H13**
Dyer, C. *Canada* 66°37N 61°16W **109 C13**
Dyersburg *U.S.A.* 36°3N 89°23W **111 C91**
Dyfi → *U.K.* 52°32N 4°3W **26 B5**
Dymchurch *U.K.* 51°1N 1°0E **25 D11**
Dymock *U.K.* 51°59N 2°26W **24 C4**
Dzerzhinsk *Russia* 56°14N 43°30E **72 C7**
Dzhankoy *Ukraine* 45°40N 34°20E **73 E5**
Dzhugdzur Ra. *Russia* 57°30N 138°0E **79 D15**
Dzungarian Basin *China* 44°30N 86°0E **80 B3**
Dzuumod *Mongolia* 47°45N 106°58E **80 B5**

E

Eagle *U.S.A.* 64°47N 141°12W **108 C5**
Eagle L. *U.S.A.* 46°20N 69°22W **113 B13**
Eagle Pass *U.S.A.* 28°43N 100°30W **110 E6**
Eagle River *U.S.A.* 47°25N 88°18W **112 B3**
Eaglesfield *U.K.* 55°4N 3°12W **21 D9**
Eakring *U.K.* 53°9N 0°58W **23 F7**
Ealing □ *U.K.* 51°31N 0°20W **25 C8**
Earby *U.K.* 53°55N 2°7W **23 E4**
Eardisley *U.K.* 52°8N 3°1W **24 B2**
Earith *U.K.* 52°22N 0°2E **25 B9**
Earl Shilton *U.K.* 52°35N 1°18W **23 G6**
Earl Soham *U.K.* 52°14N 1°18E **25 B11**
Earls Barton *U.K.* 52°16N 0°45W **25 B7**
Earl's Colne *U.K.* 51°56N 0°43E **25 C10**
Earlston *U.K.* 55°39N 2°40W **21 C10**
Earn → *U.K.* 56°21N 3°18W **21 B9**
Earn, L. *U.K.* 56°23N 4°13W **20 B7**
Earsdon *U.K.* 55°3N 1°29W **22 B6**
Easebourne *U.K.* 51°0N 0°43W **25 E7**
Easington *Durham, U.K.* 54°47N 1°21W **22 C6**
Easington *E. Riding, U.K.* 53°39N 0°6E **23 E9**
Easington Colliery *U.K.* 54°49N 1°19W **22 C6**
Easingwold *U.K.* 54°8N 1°11W **22 D6**
East Ayrshire □ *U.K.* 55°26N 4°11W **20 D7**
East Bengal *Bangla.* 24°0N 90°0E **85 H17**
East Bergholt *U.K.* 51°59N 1°3E **25 C11**
East Beskids *Europe* 49°20N 22°0E **67 D11**
East Brent *U.K.* 51°15N 2°56W **24 D3**
East C. = Dezhneva, Mys. *Russia* 66°5N 169°40W **79 C20**
East China Sea *Asia* 30°0N 126°0E **81 D7**
East Cowes *U.K.* 50°45N 1°16W **24 E6**
East Falkland *Falk. Is.* 51°30S 58°30W **121 H4**
East Fen *U.K.* 53°4N 0°5E **23 F9**

East Grinstead U.K. 51°7N 0°0 25 D9
East Harling U.K. 52°26N 0°56E 25 B10
East Ilsley U.K. 51°31N 1°16W 24 C6
East Indies Asia 0°0 120°0E 74 J14
East Kilbride U.K. 55°47N 4°11W 20 C7
East Lansing U.S.A. 42°44N 84°29W 112 D5
East London S. Africa 33°0S 27°55E 97 L5
East Lothian ☐ U.K. 55°58N 2°44W 21 C10
East Markham U.K. 53°15N 0°53W 23 F7
East Moor U.K. 53°16N 1°34W 23 F5
East Pacific Rise Pac. Oc. 15°0S 110°0W 103 J17
East Pt. Br. Virgin Is. 18°40N 64°18W 115 e
East Pt. Canada 46°27N 61°58W 113 B17
East St. Louis U.S.A. 38°37N 90°9W 112 F2
East Sea = Japan, Sea of Asia 40°0N 135°0E 82 D4
East Siberian Sea Russia 73°0N 160°0E 79 B18
East Sussex ☐ U.K. 50°56N 0°19E 25 E9
East Timor ■ Asia 8°50S 126°0E 83 D4
East Wittering U.K. 50°46N 0°52W 25 E7
East Woodhay U.K. 51°21N 1°25W 24 D6
Eastbourne U.K. 50°46N 0°18E 25 E9
Eastchurch U.K. 51°24N 0°53E 25 D10
Eastern Ghats India 14°0N 78°50E 84 N11
Eastern Group Fiji 17°0S 178°30W 99 D15
Eastleigh U.K. 50°58N 1°21W 24 E6
Eastmain Canada 52°10N 78°30W 109 D12
Eastmain → Canada 52°27N 78°26W 109 D12
Eastnor U.K. 52°2N 2°23W 24 B4
Easton Dorset, U.K. 50°33N 2°26W 24 E4
Easton Northants., U.K. 52°37N 0°31W 25 A7
Easton Md., U.S.A. 38°47N 76°5W 113 F9
Easton Pa., U.S.A. 40°41N 75°13W 113 E10
Easton-in-Gordano U.K. 51°28N 2°42W 24 D3
Eastport U.S.A. 44°56N 67°0W 113 C14
Eastry U.K. 51°14N 1°19E 25 D11
Eastwood U.K. 53°1N 1°18W 23 F6
Eaton U.K. 52°51N 0°49W 23 G7
Eaton Socon U.K. 52°14N 0°17W 25 B8
Eau Claire U.S.A. 44°49N 91°30W 112 C2
Eau Claire, L. à l' Canada 56°10N 74°25W 109 D12
Ebberston U.K. 54°14N 0°37W 22 D7
Ebbw Vale U.K. 51°46N 3°12W 26 D7
Eberswalde-Finow Germany 52°50N 13°49E 66 B7
Ebetsu Japan 43°7N 141°34E 82 B7
Ebinur Hu China 44°55N 82°55E 80 B3
Ebolowa Cameroon 2°55N 11°10E 96 D2
Ebro → Spain 40°43N 0°54E 69 B6
Ecclefechan U.K. 55°4N 3°16W 21 D9
Eccleshall U.K. 52°52N 2°15W 23 G4
Ech Chéliff Algeria 36°10N 1°20E 94 A6
Echo Bay Canada 66°5N 117°55W 108 C8
Eckington U.K. 53°18N 1°22W 23 F6
Eclipse Sd. Canada 72°38N 79°0W 109 B12
Ecuador ■ S. Amer. 2°0S 78°0W 120 C2
Ed Damazin Sudan 11°46N 34°21E 95 F12
Edam Neths. 52°31N 5°3E 65 B5
Eday U.K. 59°11N 2°47W 19 D12
Eddrachillis B. U.K. 58°17N 5°14W 18 F7
Eddystone U.K. 50°11N 4°16W 27 G5
Eden → U.K. 54°57N 3°1W 22 C2
Edenbridge U.K. 51°12N 0°5E 25 D9
Edenderry Ireland 53°21N 7°4W 31 B8
Edge Hill U.K. 52°8N 1°26W 24 B6
Edinburgh U.K. 55°57N 3°13W 21 C9
Edinburgh ✕ (EDI) U.K. 55°54N 3°22W 21 C9
Edington U.K. 51°17N 2°5W 24 D4
Edirne Turkey 41°40N 26°34E 73 F4
Edmonton Canada 53°30N 113°30W 108 D8
Edmundbyers U.K. 54°50N 1°58W 22 C5
Edmundston Canada 47°23N 68°20W 109 E13
Edremit Turkey 39°34N 27°0E 86 B1
Edson Canada 53°35N 116°28W 108 D8
Edward, L. Africa 0°25S 29°40E 96 E5
Edward VII Land Antarctica 80°0S 150°0W 55 E13
Edwards Plateau U.S.A. 30°45N 101°20W 110 D6
Effingham U.S.A. 39°7N 88°33W 112 F3
Égadi, Ísole Italy 37°55N 12°16E 70 F5
Eganville Canada 45°32N 77°5W 112 C9
Eger Hungary 47°53N 20°27E 67 E11
Egham U.K. 51°25N 0°32W 25 D7
Eglinton I. Canada 75°48N 118°30W 109 B8
Egremont U.K. 54°29N 3°32W 22 D1
Eğridir Turkey 37°52N 30°51E 73 G5
Eğridir Gölü Turkey 37°53N 30°50E 73 G5
Egton U.K. 54°28N 0°44W 22 D7
Egypt ■ Africa 28°0N 31°0E 95 C12
Eifel Germany 50°15N 6°50E 66 C4
Eigg U.K. 56°54N 6°10W 18 J5
Eil, L. U.K. 56°51N 5°16W 18 J7
Eindhoven Neths. 51°26N 5°28E 65 C5
Eire = Ireland ■ Europe 53°50N 7°52W 64 E2
Eivissa Spain 38°54N 1°26E 69 C6
El Aaiún W. Sahara 27°9N 13°12W 94 C3
El 'Alamein Egypt 30°48N 28°58E 95 B11
El Centro U.S.A. 32°48N 115°34W 110 D3
El Djouf Mauritania 20°0N 9°0W 94 D4
El Dorado U.S.A. 33°12N 92°40W 111 D8
El Faiyûm Egypt 29°19N 30°50E 95 C12
El Fâsher Sudan 13°33N 25°26E 95 F11
El Fuerte Mexico 26°25N 108°39W 114 B3
El Geneina Sudan 13°27N 22°45E 95 F10
El Gezira ☐ Sudan 15°0N 33°0E 95 F12
El Gîza Egypt 30°0N 31°12E 95 C12
El Istiwa'iya Sudan 5°0N 28°0E 95 G11
El Jadida Morocco 33°11N 8°17W 94 B4
El Khârga Egypt 25°30N 30°33E 95 C12
El Mahalla el Kubra Egypt 31°0N 31°0E 95 B12
El Mansûra Egypt 31°0N 31°19E 95 B12
El Minyâ Egypt 28°7N 30°33E 95 C12
El Obeid Sudan 13°8N 30°10E 95 F12
El Oued Algeria 33°20N 6°58E 94 B7
El Paso U.S.A. 31°45N 106°29W 110 D5
El Puerto de Santa María Spain 36°36N 6°13W 69 D2
El Reno U.S.A. 35°32N 97°57W 110 C7
El Salvador ■ Cent. Amer. 13°50N 89°0W 114 E7
El Tigre Venezuela 8°44N 64°15W 120 B3
El Uqsur Egypt 25°41N 32°38E 95 C12
Elat Israel 29°30N 34°56E 86 D3
Elâzığ Turkey 38°37N 39°14E 73 G6
Elba Italy 42°46N 10°17E 70 C4
Elbasan Albania 41°9N 20°9E 71 D9
Elbe → Europe 53°50N 9°0E 66 B5
Elbert, Mt. U.S.A. 39°7N 106°27W 110 C5
Elbeuf France 49°17N 1°2E 68 B4
Elbląg Poland 54°10N 19°25E 67 A10
Elbrus Asia 43°21N 42°30E 73 F7
Elburz Mts. Iran 36°0N 52°0E 87 B8
Elche Spain 38°15N 0°42W 69 C5
Elda Spain 38°29N 0°47W 69 C5
Eldoret Kenya 0°30N 35°17E 96 D7
Elektrostal Russia 55°41N 38°32E 72 C6
Elemi Triangle Africa 5°0N 35°20E 96 D7
Elephant Butte Res. U.S.A. 33°9N 107°11W 110 D5
Elephant I. Antarctica 61°0S 55°0W 55 C18
Eleuthera Bahamas 25°0N 76°20W 115 C9
Elgin U.K. 57°39N 3°19W 19 G11
Elgin U.S.A. 42°2N 88°17W 112 D3
Elgon, Mt. Africa 1°10N 34°30E 96 D6
Elham U.K. 51°9N 1°8E 25 D11
Elishaw U.K. 55°15N 2°14W 22 B4
Elista Russia 46°16N 44°14E 73 E7
Elizabeth U.S.A. 40°39N 74°12W 113 E10
Elizabeth City U.S.A. 36°18N 76°14W 111 C11
Elizabethtown U.S.A. 37°42N 85°52W 112 G5
Elkhart U.S.A. 41°41N 85°58W 112 E5
Elkins U.S.A. 38°55N 79°51W 112 F8
Elko U.S.A. 40°50N 115°46W 110 B3
Elland U.K. 53°41N 1°50W 23 E5
Ellef Ringnes I. Canada 78°30N 102°2W 109 B9
Ellen → U.K. 54°44N 3°30W 22 C2
Ellensburg U.S.A. 46°59N 120°34W 110 A2
Ellerton Barbados 13°7N 59°33W 115 g
Ellesmere U.K. 52°55N 2°53W 23 G3
Ellesmere I. Canada 79°30N 80°0W 109 B12
Ellesmere Port U.K. 53°17N 2°54W 23 F3
Ellington U.K. 55°14N 1°33W 22 B5
Elliot Lake Canada 46°25N 82°35W 109 E11
Ellon U.K. 57°22N 2°4W 19 H13
Ellsworth Land Antarctica 76°0S 89°0W 55 D16
Elmalı Turkey 36°44N 29°56E 73 G4
Elmira U.S.A. 42°6N 76°48W 112 D9
Elmswell U.K. 52°15N 0°55E 25 B10
Eluru India 16°48N 81°8E 85 L12
Ely U.K. 52°24N 0°16E 25 B9
Ely U.S.A. 39°15N 114°54W 110 C4
Elyria U.S.A. 41°22N 82°7W 112 E6
Emāmrūd Iran 36°30N 55°0E 87 B8
Embarcación Argentina 23°10S 64°0W 121 E3
Embleton U.K. 55°29N 1°38W 22 B5
Emden Germany 53°21N 7°12E 66 B4
Emerald Australia 37°56S 145°29E 98 E8
Emmeloord Neths. 52°44N 5°46E 65 B5
Emmen Neths. 52°48N 6°57E 65 B6
Emmonak U.S.A. 62°47N 164°31W 108 C3
Empalme Mexico 27°58N 110°51W 114 B2
Empangeni S. Africa 28°50S 31°52E 97 K6
Empedrado Argentina 28°0S 58°46W 121 E4
Emperor Seamount Chain Pac. Oc. 40°0N 170°0E 102 D9
Emporia U.S.A. 38°25N 96°11W 111 C7
Emporium U.S.A. 41°31N 78°14W 112 E8
Empty Quarter = Rub' al Khālī Si. Arabia 19°0N 48°0E 88 D4
Ems → Germany 53°20N 7°12E 66 B4
En Nahud Sudan 12°45N 28°25E 95 F11
Enard B. U.K. 58°5N 5°20W 18 F7
Encarnación Paraguay 27°15S 55°50W 121 E4
Encounter B. Australia 35°45S 138°45E 98 H6
Ende Indonesia 8°45S 121°40E 83 D4
Enderbury I. Kiribati 3°8S 171°5W 102 H10
Enderby U.K. 52°36N 1°13W 23 G6
Enderby Land Antarctica 66°0S 53°0E 55 C5
Endicott U.S.A. 42°6N 76°4W 113 D9
Enewetak Atoll Marshall Is. 11°30N 162°15E 102 F8
Enez Turkey 40°45N 26°5E 73 F4
Enfer, Pte. d' Martinique 14°22N 60°54W 114 c
Enfield ☐ U.K. 51°38N 0°5W 25 C8
Engadin Switz. 46°45N 10°10E 66 E6
Engels Russia 51°28N 46°6E 73 D8
Enggano Indonesia 5°20S 102°40E 83 D2
England ☐ U.K. 53°0N 2°0W 64 E6
English → Canada 49°12N 91°5W 108 D10
English Channel Europe 50°0N 2°0W 64 F6
Enid U.S.A. 36°24N 97°53W 110 C7
Ennadai L. Canada 60°58N 101°20W 108 C9
Ennedi Chad 17°15N 22°0E 95 E10
Ennerdale Water U.K. 54°32N 3°24W 22 C2
Ennis Ireland 52°51N 8°59W 30 C5
Enniscorthy Ireland 52°30N 6°34W 31 D9
Enniskillen U.K. 54°21N 7°39W 28 C6
Ennistimon Ireland 52°57N 9°17W 30 C4
Enns → Austria 48°14N 14°32E 66 D8
Enschede Neths. 52°13N 6°53E 65 B6
Ensenada Mexico 31°52N 116°37W 114 A1
Enshi China 30°18N 109°29E 81 C5
Enstone U.K. 51°55N 1°27W 24 C6
Entebbe Uganda 0°4N 32°28E 96 D6
Entre Rios ☐ Argentina 30°30S 58°30W 121 F4
Enugu Nigeria 6°30N 7°30E 94 G7
Eólie, Ís. Italy 38°30N 14°57E 70 E6
Épernay France 49°3N 3°56E 68 B5
Épinal France 48°10N 6°27E 68 B7
Epping U.K. 51°41N 0°7E 25 C9
Epping Forest U.K. 51°40N 0°5E 25 C9
Epsom U.K. 51°19N 0°16W 25 D8
Epworth U.K. 53°32N 0°48W 23 E7
Equatorial Guinea ■ Africa 2°0N 8°0E 96 D1
Er Rachidia Morocco 31°58N 4°20W 94 B5
Erciyaş Dağı Turkey 38°30N 35°30E 86 B3
Erdenet Mongolia 49°2N 104°5E 80 B5
Erebus, Mt. Antarctica 77°35S 167°0E 55 D11
Ereğli Konya, Turkey 37°31N 34°4E 73 G5
Ereğli Zonguldak, Turkey 41°15N 31°24E 73 F5
Erfurt Germany 50°58N 11°2E 66 C6
Ergeni Lowlands Russia 47°0N 44°0E 73 E7
Eriboll, L. U.K. 58°30N 4°42W 19 E8
Erie U.S.A. 42°8N 80°5W 112 D7
Erie, L. N. Amer. 42°15N 81°0W 112 D7
Eriskay U.K. 57°4N 7°18W 18 H3
Eritrea ■ Africa 14°0N 38°30E 88 D2
Erlangen Germany 49°36N 11°0E 66 D6
Ernakulam India 9°59N 76°22E 84 Q10
Erne → Ireland 54°30N 8°16W 28 C5
Erne, Lower L. U.K. 54°28N 7°47W 28 C6
Erne, Upper L. U.K. 54°14N 7°32W 28 C6
Erode India 11°24N 77°45E 84 P10
Erramala Hills India 15°30N 78°15E 84 M11
Errigal Ireland 55°2N 8°6W 28 A5
Erris Hd. Ireland 54°19N 10°0W 28 C1
Erromango Vanuatu 18°45S 169°5E 99 D12
Erzgebirge Germany 50°27N 12°55E 66 C7
Erzincan Turkey 39°46N 39°30E 73 G6
Erzurum Turkey 39°57N 41°15E 73 G7
Esbjerg Denmark 55°29N 8°29E 63 F5
Escada Brazil 8°22S 35°8W 122 A3
Escanaba U.S.A. 45°45N 87°4W 112 C4
Esch-sur-Alzette Lux. 49°32N 6°0E 65 E6
Escrick U.K. 53°53N 1°2W 23 E6
Escuinapa de Hidalgo Mexico 22°50N 105°50W 114 C3
Escuintla Guatemala 14°20N 90°48W 114 E6
Eşfahān Iran 32°39N 51°43E 87 C7
Esha Ness U.K. 60°29N 1°38W 18 B14
Esil → Russia 57°45N 71°10E 79 D9
Esk → Cumb., U.K. 54°20N 3°24W 22 D2
Esk → Dumf. & Gall., U.K. 54°58N 3°2W 21 E9
Esk → N. Yorks., U.K. 54°30N 0°37W 22 D7
Eskdale U.K. 55°12N 3°4W 21 D9
Esker Canada 53°53N 66°25W 109 D13
Eskilstuna Sweden 59°22N 16°32E 63 F7
Eskişehir Turkey 39°50N 30°30E 73 G5
Eslāmābād-e Gharb Iran 34°10N 46°30E 86 C6
Esperance Australia 33°45S 121°55E 98 G3
Esperanza Puerto Rico 18°6N 65°28W 115 d
Espinhaço, Serra do Brazil 17°30S 43°30W 122 C2
Espírito Santo ☐ Brazil 20°0S 40°45W 122 C2
Espíritu Santo Vanuatu 15°15S 166°50E 99 D12
Espoo Finland 60°12N 24°40E 63 E8
Essaouira Morocco 31°32N 9°42W 94 B4
Essen Germany 51°28N 7°2E 66 C4
Essequibo → Guyana 6°50N 58°30W 120 B4
Essex ☐ U.K. 51°54N 0°27E 25 C9
Esslingen Germany 48°44N 9°18E 66 D5
Estados, I. de Los Argentina 54°40S 64°30W 121 H3
Estância Brazil 11°16S 37°26W 122 B3
Estevan Canada 49°10N 102°59W 108 E9
Eston U.K. 54°34N 1°8W 22 C6
Estonia ■ Europe 58°30N 25°30E 63 F8
Estrela, Serra da Portugal 40°10N 7°45W 69 B2
Estrondo, Serra do Brazil 7°20S 48°0W 120 C5
Etawah India 26°48N 79°6E 84 F11
Etchingham U.K. 51°0N 0°26E 25 D9
eThekwini = Durban S. Africa 29°49S 31°1E 97 K6
Ethiopia ■ Africa 8°0N 40°0E 88 F3
Ethiopian Highlands Ethiopia 10°0N 37°0E 88 F2
Etive, L. U.K. 56°29N 5°10W 20 B5
Etna Italy 37°50N 14°55E 70 F6
Eton U.K. 51°30N 0°36W 25 C7
Etosha Pan Namibia 18°40S 16°30E 97 H3
Ettington U.K. 52°8N 1°35W 24 B5
Ettrick Forest U.K. 55°30N 3°0W 21 C9
Ettrick Water → U.K. 55°31N 2°55W 21 C10
Euclid U.S.A. 41°34N 81°32W 112 E7
Eugene U.S.A. 44°5N 123°4W 110 B2
Euphrates → Asia 31°0N 47°25E 86 D6
Eureka Canada 80°0N 85°56W 109 B11
Eureka U.S.A. 40°47N 124°9W 110 B2
Europa, Île Ind. Oc. 22°20S 40°22E 97 J8
Europa, Picos de Spain 43°10N 4°49W 69 A3
Europe 50°0N 20°0E 56 E10
Euxton U.K. 53°41N 2°41W 23 E3
Evanston Ill., U.S.A. 42°3N 87°40W 112 D4
Evanston Wyo., U.S.A. 41°16N 110°58W 110 B4
Evansville U.S.A. 37°58N 87°35W 112 G4
Evercreech U.K. 51°9N 2°30W 24 D4
Everest, Mt. Nepal 28°5N 86°58E 85 E15
Everett U.S.A. 47°59N 122°12W 110 A2
Everglades, The U.S.A. 25°50N 81°0W 111 E10
Evesham U.K. 52°6N 1°56W 24 B5
Evia Greece 38°30N 24°0E 71 E11
Évora Portugal 38°33N 7°57W 69 C2
Évreux France 49°3N 1°8E 68 B4
Evros → Greece 41°40N 26°34E 71 D12
Ewe, L. U.K. 57°49N 5°38W 18 G6
Ewell U.K. 51°20N 0°14W 25 D8
Ewhurst U.K. 51°9N 0°25W 25 D8
Exe → U.K. 50°41N 3°29W 27 F7
Exeter U.K. 50°43N 3°31W 27 F6
Exminster U.K. 50°40N 3°29W 27 F7
Exmoor U.K. 51°12N 3°45W 27 E6
Exmoor △ U.K. 51°8N 3°42W 27 E6
Exmouth U.K. 50°37N 3°25W 27 F7
Exton U.K. 52°42N 0°38W 23 G7
Extremadura ☐ Spain 39°30N 6°5W 69 C2
Eyam U.K. 53°17N 1°40W 23 F5
Eyasi, L. Tanzania 3°30S 35°0E 96 E6
Eye Cambs., U.K. 52°37N 0°11W 25 A8
Eye Suffolk, U.K. 52°19N 1°9E 25 B11
Eye Pen. U.K. 58°13N 6°10W 18 F5
Eyemouth U.K. 55°52N 2°5W 21 C11
Eynsham U.K. 51°47N 1°22W 24 C6
Eyre, L. Australia 29°30S 137°26E 98 F6
Eyre Pen. Australia 33°30S 136°17E 98 G6

F

F.Y.R.O.M. = Macedonia ■ Europe 41°53N 21°40E 71 D9
Faenza Italy 44°17N 11°53E 70 B4
Fair Hd. U.K. 55°14N 6°9W 29 A9
Fair Isle U.K. 59°32N 1°38W 18 C14
Fairbanks U.S.A. 64°51N 147°43W 108 C5
Fairfield U.S.A. 38°23N 88°22W 112 F3
Fairford U.K. 51°43N 1°46W 24 C5
Fairlight U.K. 50°52N 0°40E 25 E10
Fairmont U.S.A. 39°29N 80°9W 112 F7
Fairweather, Mt. U.S.A. 58°55N 137°32W 108 D6
Faisalabad Pakistan 31°30N 73°5E 84 D8
Faizabad India 26°45N 82°10E 85 F13
Fajardo Puerto Rico 18°20N 65°39W 115 d
Fakenham U.K. 52°51N 0°51E 25 A10
Falcon Res. U.S.A. 26°34N 99°10W 110 E7
Faldingworth U.K. 53°21N 0°24W 23 F8
Falkirk U.K. 56°0N 3°47W 21 C8
Falkland U.K. 56°16N 3°12W 21 B9
Falkland Is. ☒ Atl. Oc. 51°30S 59°0W 121 H4
Fall River U.S.A. 41°43N 71°10W 113 E12
Falmouth Jamaica 18°30N 77°40W 114 a
Falmouth U.K. 50°9N 5°5W 27 G3
Falmouth B. U.K. 50°6N 5°5W 27 G3
Falstone U.K. 55°11N 2°26W 22 B4
Falun Sweden 60°37N 15°37E 63 E7
Famagusta Cyprus 35°8N 33°55E 86 C3
Fanad Hd. Ireland 55°17N 7°38W 28 A6
Fannich, L. U.K. 57°38N 4°59W 19 G8
Fano Italy 43°50N 13°1E 70 C5
Far East Asia 40°0N 130°0E 74 E14
Farāh Afghan. 32°20N 62°7E 87 C10
Farasān Si. Arabia 16°45N 41°55E 88 D3
Fareham U.K. 50°51N 1°11W 24 E6
Farewell C. Greenland 59°48N 43°55W 54 D5
Fargo U.S.A. 46°53N 96°48W 111 A7
Faridabad India 28°26N 77°19E 84 E10
Faringdon U.K. 51°39N 1°34W 24 C5
Farmington U.S.A. 36°44N 108°12W 110 C5
Farmville U.S.A. 37°18N 78°24W 112 G8
Farnborough U.K. 51°16N 0°45W 25 D7
Farne Is. U.K. 55°38N 1°37W 22 A5
Farnham U.K. 51°13N 0°47W 25 D7
Farnworth U.K. 53°34N 2°25W 23 E4
Faro Canada 62°11N 133°22W 108 C6
Faro Portugal 37°2N 7°55W 69 D2
Faroe Is. ☒ Atl. Oc. 62°0N 7°0W 57 C4
Fārs ☐ Iran 29°30N 55°0E 87 D8
Fāryāb ☐ Afghan. 36°0N 65°0E 87 B11
Faslane U.K. 56°5N 4°49W 20 B6
Fataka Solomon Is. 11°55S 170°12E 99 C12
Fatehgarh India 27°25N 79°35E 84 F11
Fatehpur Raj., India 28°0N 74°40E 84 F9
Fatehpur Ut. P., India 25°56N 81°13E 85 G12
Fauldhouse U.K. 55°50N 3°43W 21 C8
Faversham U.K. 51°19N 0°56E 25 D10
Fawley U.K. 50°50N 1°20W 24 E6
Fayetteville Ark., U.S.A. 36°4N 94°10W 111 C8
Fayetteville N.C., U.S.A. 35°3N 78°53W 111 D11
Fazeley U.K. 52°37N 1°40W 23 G5
Fazilka India 30°27N 74°2E 84 D9
Fdérik Mauritania 22°40N 12°45W 94 D3
Feale → Ireland 52°27N 9°37W 30 D3
Fear, C. U.S.A. 33°50N 77°58W 111 D11
Fécamp France 49°45N 0°22E 68 B4
Fehmarn Germany 54°27N 11°7E 66 A6
Feira de Santana Brazil 12°15S 38°57W 122 B3
Felipe Carrillo Puerto Mexico 19°38N 88°3W 114 D7
Felixstowe U.K. 51°58N 1°23E 25 C11
Felton U.K. 55°18N 1°42W 22 B5
Feltwell U.K. 52°30N 0°32E 25 B10
Fenny Bentley U.K. 53°3N 1°45W 23 F5
Fenny Compton U.K. 52°10N 1°23W 24 B6
Fenny Stratford U.K. 52°0N 0°44W 25 C7
Fens, The U.K. 52°38N 0°2W 25 A8
Fenyang China 37°18N 111°48E 81 C6
Feodosiya Ukraine 45°2N 35°16E 73 E6
Fergus Falls U.S.A. 46°17N 96°4W 111 A7
Ferkéssédougou Ivory C. 9°35N 5°6W 94 G4
Fermanagh ☐ U.K. 54°21N 7°40W 28 C6
Fermont Canada 52°47N 67°5W 109 D13
Fermoy Ireland 52°9N 8°16W 30 D6
Fernhurst U.K. 51°3N 0°43W 25 D7
Ferrara Italy 44°50N 11°35E 70 B4
Ferret, C. France 44°38N 1°15W 68 D3
Ferrol Spain 43°29N 8°15W 69 A1
Ferryhill U.K. 54°41N 1°33W 22 C5
Fès Morocco 34°0N 5°0W 94 B5
Fethiye Turkey 36°36N 29°6E 73 G4
Fetlar U.K. 60°36N 0°52W 18 A16
Feuilles → Canada 58°47N 70°4W 109 D12
Feyzābād Afghan. 37°7N 70°33E 87 B12
Fezzan Libya 27°0N 13°0E 95 C8
Ffestiniog U.K. 52°57N 3°55W 26 B6
Fianarantsoa Madag. 21°26S 47°5E 97 J9
Fife ☐ U.K. 56°16N 3°1W 21 B9
Fife Ness U.K. 56°17N 2°35W 21 B10
Figeac France 44°37N 2°2E 68 D5
Figueres Spain 42°18N 2°58E 69 A7
Fiji ■ Pac. Oc. 17°20S 179°0E 99 D14
Filby U.K. 52°40N 1°39E 25 A12
Filey U.K. 54°12N 0°18W 22 D8
Filey B. U.K. 54°12N 0°15W 22 D8
Filton U.K. 51°30N 2°34W 24 C3
Fincham U.K. 52°38N 0°30E 25 A9
Findhorn → U.K. 57°38N 3°38W 19 G10
Findlay U.S.A. 41°2N 83°39W 112 E6
Finedon U.K. 52°21N 0°39W 25 B7
Finglas Ireland 53°23N 6°19W 31 B10
Finike Turkey 36°21N 30°10E 86 B2
Finland ■ Europe 63°0N 27°0E 63 E9
Finland, G. of Europe 60°0N 26°0E 63 F9
Finlay → Canada 57°0N 125°10W 108 D7
Finn → Ireland 54°51N 7°28W 28 B7
Firozabad India 27°10N 78°25E 84 F11
Firozpur India 30°55N 74°40E 84 D9
Fish → Namibia 28°7S 17°10E 97 K3
Fishguard U.K. 52°0N 4°58W 26 D4
Fishtoft U.K. 52°58N 0°1E 23 G9
Fisterra, C. Spain 42°50N 9°19W 69 A1
Fitchburg U.S.A. 42°35N 71°48W 113 D12
Flagstaff U.S.A. 35°12N 111°39W 110 C4
Flamborough U.K. 54°7N 0°7W 22 D8
Flamborough Hd. U.K. 54°7N 0°5W 22 D8
Flandre Europe 50°50N 2°30E 65 D2
Flathead L. U.S.A. 47°51N 114°8W 110 A4
Flattery, C. U.S.A. 48°23N 124°29W 110 A2
Fleet U.K. 51°17N 0°50W 25 D7
Fleetwood U.K. 53°55N 3°1W 23 E2
Flensburg Germany 54°47N 9°27E 66 A5
Flers France 48°47N 0°33W 68 B3
Flevoland ☐ Neths. 52°30N 5°30E 65 B5
Flimby U.K. 54°42N 3°30W 22 C2
Flin Flon Canada 54°46N 101°53W 108 D9
Flinders → Australia 17°36S 140°36E 98 D7
Flinders I. Australia 40°0S 148°0E 98 H8
Flinders Ranges Australia 31°30S 138°30E 98 G6
Flint U.K. 53°15N 3°8W 26 A7
Flint U.S.A. 43°1N 83°41W 112 D6
Flint → U.S.A. 30°57N 84°34W 111 D10
Flint I. Kiribati 11°26S 151°48W 103 J12
Flintshire ☐ U.K. 53°17N 3°17W 26 A7
Flitwick U.K. 52°0N 0°30W 25 C8
Flodden U.K. 55°37N 2°8W 22 A4
Flora U.S.A. 38°40N 88°29W 112 F3
Florence Italy 43°46N 11°15E 70 C4
Florence U.S.A. 34°12N 79°46W 111 D11
Florencia Colombia 1°36N 75°36W 120 B2
Flores Indonesia 8°35S 121°0E 83 D4
Flores Sea Indonesia 6°30S 120°0E 83 D4
Florianópolis Brazil 27°30S 48°30W 121 E5
Florida Uruguay 34°7S 56°10W 121 F4
Florida ☐ U.S.A. 28°0N 82°0W 111 E10
Florida, Straits of U.S.A. 25°0N 80°0W 115 C9
Florida Keys U.S.A. 24°40N 81°0W 111 F10
Florø Norway 61°35N 5°1E 63 E5
Fly → Papua N. G. 8°25S 143°0E 98 B7
Fochabers U.K. 57°37N 3°6W 19 G11
Focşani Romania 45°41N 27°15E 67 F14
Fóggia Italy 41°27N 15°34E 70 D6
Foix France 42°58N 1°38E 68 E4
Foligno Italy 42°57N 12°42E 70 C5
Folkestone U.K. 51°5N 1°12E 25 D11
Fond-du-Lac Canada 59°19N 107°12W 108 D9
Fond du Lac U.S.A. 43°47N 88°27W 112 D3
Fongafale Tuvalu 8°31S 179°13E 99 B14
Fontainebleau France 48°24N 2°40E 68 B5
Fontenay-le-Comte France 46°28N 0°48W 68 C3
Fordham U.K. 52°19N 0°23E 25 B9
Fordingbridge U.K. 50°56N 1°47W 24 E5
Forel, Mt. Greenland 66°52N 36°55W 54 C6
Forest Row U.K. 51°5N 0°3E 25 D9
Forfar U.K. 56°39N 2°53W 19 J12
Forlì Italy 44°13N 12°3E 70 B5
Formartine U.K. 57°20N 2°15W 19 H13
Formby U.K. 53°34N 3°4W 23 E2
Formby Pt. U.K. 53°33N 3°6W 23 E2
Formentera Spain 38°43N 1°27E 69 C6
Formiga Brazil 20°27S 45°25W 122 D1
Formosa = Taiwan ■ Asia 23°30N 121°0E 81 D7
Formosa Argentina 26°15S 58°10W 121 E4
Formosa Brazil 15°32S 47°20W 122 C1
Forres U.K. 57°37N 3°37W 19 G10
Forsayth Australia 18°33S 143°34E 98 D7
Fort Albany Canada 52°15N 81°35W 109 D11
Fort Augustus U.K. 57°9N 4°42W 19 H8
Fort Chipewyan Canada 58°42N 111°8W 108 D8
Fort Collins U.S.A. 40°35N 105°5W 110 B5
Fort-Coulonge Canada 45°50N 76°45W 112 C9
Fort-de-France Martinique 14°36N 61°2W 114 c
Fort Dodge U.S.A. 42°30N 94°11W 111 B8
Fort Good Hope Canada 66°14N 128°40W 108 C7
Fort Kent U.S.A. 47°15N 68°36W 113 B13
Fort Lauderdale U.S.A. 26°7N 80°8W 111 E10
Fort Liard Canada 60°14N 123°30W 108 C7
Fort MacKay Canada 57°12N 111°41W 108 D8
Fort Macleod Canada 49°45N 113°30W 108 E8
Fort McMurray Canada 56°44N 111°7W 108 D8
Fort McPherson Canada 67°30N 134°55W 108 C6
Fort Morgan U.S.A. 40°15N 103°48W 110 B6
Fort Myers U.S.A. 26°39N 81°52W 111 E10
Fort Nelson Canada 58°50N 122°44W 108 D7
Fort Nelson → Canada 59°32N 124°0W 108 D7
Fort Peck L. U.S.A. 48°0N 106°26W 110 A5
Fort Providence Canada 61°3N 117°40W 108 C8
Fort Resolution Canada 61°10N 113°40W 108 C8
Fort St. John Canada 56°15N 120°50W 108 D7
Fort Scott U.S.A. 37°50N 94°42W 111 C8
Fort Shevchenko Kazakhstan 44°35N 50°23E 73 F9
Fort Simpson Canada 61°45N 121°15W 108 C7
Fort Smith Canada 60°0N 111°51W 108 B8
Fort Smith U.S.A. 35°23N 94°25W 111 C8
Fort Stockton U.S.A. 30°53N 102°53W 110 D6
Fort Wayne U.S.A. 41°4N 85°9W 112 E5
Fort William U.K. 56°49N 5°7W 18 J7
Fort Worth U.S.A. 32°43N 97°19W 111 D7
Fort Yukon U.S.A. 66°34N 145°16W 108 C5
Fortaleza Brazil 3°45S 38°35W 120 C6
Forth → U.K. 56°9N 3°50W 21 B8
Forth, Firth of U.K. 56°5N 2°55W 21 B10
Fortrose U.K. 57°35N 4°9W 19 G9
Foshan China 23°4N 113°5E 81 D6
Fostoria U.S.A. 41°10N 83°25W 112 E6
Fotherby U.K. 53°23N 0°3W 23 F9
Fotheringhay U.K. 52°32N 0°27W 25 A8
Fougères France 48°21N 1°14W 68 B3
Foula U.K. 60°10N 2°5W 64 A5
Foulness I. U.K. 51°36N 0°55E 25 C10
Foulness Pt. U.K. 51°37N 0°58E 25 C10
Foulsham U.K. 52°48N 0°59E 25 A10
Fountainhall U.K. 55°44N 2°53W 21 C10
Fouta Djallon Guinea 11°20N 12°10W 94 F3
Fovant U.K. 51°4N 2°0W 24 D5
Fowey U.K. 50°20N 4°39W 27 G4
Fownhope U.K. 52°0N 2°36W 24 B3
Foxe Basin Canada 66°0N 77°0W 109 C12
Foxe Chan. Canada 65°0N 80°0W 109 C12
Foxe Pen. Canada 65°0N 76°0W 109 C12
Foyle → U.K. 55°3N 7°15W 29 A7
Foyle, Lough U.K. 55°7N 7°4W 29 A7
Foynes Ireland 52°37N 9°7W 30 C4
Foz do Iguaçu Brazil 25°30S 54°30W 121 E4
Fraddon U.K. 50°23N 4°58W 27 G4

Framlingham

Greenville

Framlingham U.K. 52°14N 1°21E 25 B11
Franca Brazil 20°33S 47°30W 122 D1
France ■ Europe 47°0N 3°0E 68 C5
Franceville Gabon 1°40S 13°32E 96 E2
Franche-Comté □ France 46°50N 5°55E 68 C6
Francis Case, L. U.S.A. 43°4N 98°34W 110 B7
Francistown Botswana 21°7S 27°33E 97 J5
François L. Canada 54°0N 125°30W 108 D7
Frankfort Ind., U.S.A. 40°17N 86°31W 112 E4
Frankfort Ky., U.S.A. 38°12N 84°52W 112 F5
Frankfurt Brandenburg, Germany 52°20N 14°32E 66 B8
Frankfurt Hessen, Germany 50°7N 8°41E 66 C5
Fränkische Alb Germany 49°10N 11°23E 66 D6
Franklin N.H., U.S.A. 43°27N 71°39W 113 D12
Franklin Pa., U.S.A. 41°24N 79°50W 112 E8
Franklin B. Canada 69°45N 126°0W 108 C7
Franklin D. Roosevelt L. U.S.A. 48°18N 118°9W 110 A3
Franklin L. U.S.A. 40°25N 115°22W 110 B3
Franklin Mts. Canada 65°0N 125°0W 108 C7
Franklin Str. Canada 72°0N 96°0W 108 B10
Frant U.K. 51°5N 0°16E 25 D9
Franz Josef Land Russia 82°0N 55°0E 54 A10
Fraser → Canada 49°7N 123°11W 108 E7
Fraserburgh U.K. 57°42N 2°1W 19 G13
Frederick U.S.A. 39°25N 77°25W 112 F9
Fredericksburg U.S.A. 38°18N 77°28W 112 F9
Fredericktown U.S.A. 37°34N 90°18W 112 G2
Fredericton Canada 45°57N 66°40W 113 C14
Frederikshavn Denmark 57°28N 10°31E 63 F6
Fredonia U.S.A. 42°26N 79°20W 112 D8
Fredrikstad Norway 59°13N 10°57E 63 F6
Free State □ S. Africa 28°30S 27°0E 97 K5
Freeport Bahamas 26°30N 78°47W 115 B9
Freeport Ill., U.S.A. 42°17N 89°36W 112 D3
Freeport Tex., U.S.A. 28°57N 95°21W 111 E7
Freetown S. Leone 8°30N 13°17W 94 G3
Freiburg Germany 47°59N 7°51E 66 E4
Fréjus France 43°25N 6°44E 68 E7
Fremont U.S.A. 41°21N 83°7W 112 E6
French Creek → U.S.A. 41°24N 79°50W 112 E8
French Guiana ☑ S. Amer. 4°0N 53°0W 120 B4
French Polynesia ☑ Pac. Oc. 20°0S 145°0W 103 K13
Frenchman Cr. → N. Amer. 48°31N 107°10W 110 A5
Freshwater U.K. 50°41N 1°31W 24 E5
Fresnillo Mexico 23°10N 102°53W 114 C4
Fresno U.S.A. 36°44N 119°47W 110 C3
Fria, C. Namibia 18°0S 12°0E 90 H5
Fridaythorpe U.K. 54°2N 0°39W 23 D7
Friedrichshafen Germany 47°39N 9°30E 66 E5
Friesland □ Neths. 53°5N 5°50E 65 A5
Frimley U.K. 51°19N 0°44W 25 D7
Frinton-on-Sea U.K. 51°49N 1°15E 25 C11
Frio, C. Brazil 22°50S 41°50W 116 F6
Frizington U.K. 54°33N 3°28W 22 C2
Frobisher B. Canada 62°30N 66°0W 109 C13
Frobisher L. Canada 56°20N 108°15W 108 D9
Frodsham U.K. 53°18N 2°43W 23 F3
Frome U.K. 51°14N 2°19W 24 D4
Frome → U.K. 50°41N 2°6W 24 E4
Front Range U.S.A. 40°25N 105°45W 110 B5
Front Royal U.S.A. 38°55N 78°12W 112 F8
Frutal Brazil 20°0S 49°0W 122 C1
Frýdek-Místek Czech Rep. 49°40N 18°20E 67 D10
Fuchū Japan 34°34N 133°14E 82 F3
Fuengirola Spain 36°32N 4°41W 69 D3
Fuerte → Mexico 25°54N 109°22W 114 B3
Fuerteventura Canary Is. 28°30N 14°0W 94 C3
Fuhai China 47°2N 87°25E 80 B3
Fuji Japan 35°9N 138°39E 82 F6
Fuji-San Japan 35°22N 138°44E 82 F6
Fujian □ China 26°0N 118°0E 81 D6
Fukui Japan 36°5N 136°10E 82 E5
Fukuoka Japan 33°39N 130°21E 82 G2
Fukushima Japan 37°44N 140°28E 82 E7
Fukuyama Japan 34°35N 133°20E 82 F3
Fulda Germany 50°32N 9°40E 66 C5
Fulda → Germany 51°25N 9°39E 66 C5
Fulton U.S.A. 43°19N 76°25W 112 D9
Fulwood U.K. 53°47N 2°40W 23 E3
Funabashi Japan 35°45N 140°0E 82 F7
Funchal Madeira 32°38N 16°54W 94 B2
Fundy, B. of Canada 45°0N 66°0W 113 C15
Furnas, Reprêsa de Brazil 20°50S 45°30W 122 D1
Furneaux Group Australia 40°10S 147°50E 98 J8
Fürth Germany 49°28N 10°59E 66 D6
Fury and Hecla Str. Canada 69°56N 84°0W 109 C11
Fushun China 41°50N 123°56E 81 B7
Fustic Barbados 13°16N 59°38W 115 g
Fuxin China 42°5N 121°48E 81 B7
Fuyang China 33°0N 115°48E 81 C6
Fuyu Heilongjiang, China 47°49N 124°27E 81 B7
Fuyu Jilin, China 45°12N 124°43E 81 B7
Fuyun China 47°0N 89°28E 80 B3
Fuzhou China 26°5N 119°16E 81 D6
Fylingdales Moor U.K. 54°25N 0°41W 22 D7
Fyn Denmark 55°20N 10°30E 63 F6
Fyne, L. U.K. 55°59N 5°23W 20 C5

G
Gabès Tunisia 33°53N 10°2E 95 B8
Gabès, G. de Tunisia 34°0N 10°30E 95 B8
Gabon ■ Africa 0°10S 10°0E 96 E2
Gaborone Botswana 24°45S 25°57E 97 J5
Gabrovo Bulgaria 42°52N 25°19E 71 C11
Gachsārān Iran 30°15N 50°45E 87 D7
Gadarwara India 22°50N 78°50E 84 H11
Gadsden U.S.A. 34°1N 86°1W 111 D9
Gafsa Tunisia 34°24N 8°43E 95 B7
Gagnoa Ivory C. 6°56N 5°16W 94 G4
Gagnon Canada 51°50N 68°5W 109 D13
Gainesville Fla., U.S.A. 29°40N 82°20W 111 E10
Gainesville Ga., U.S.A. 34°18N 83°50W 111 D10
Gainford U.K. 54°34N 1°44W 22 C5
Gainsborough U.K. 53°24N 0°46W 23 F7

Gairdner, L. Australia 31°30S 136°0E 98 G6
Gairloch U.K. 57°43N 5°41W 18 G6
Gairloch, L. U.K. 57°43N 5°45W 18 G6
Galapagos Ecuador 0°0 91°0W 116 D1
Galashiels U.K. 55°37N 2°49W 21 C10
Galați Romania 45°27N 28°2E 67 F15
Galax U.S.A. 36°40N 80°56W 112 G7
Galcaio Somali Rep. 6°30N 47°30E 88 F4
Galdhøpiggen Norway 61°38N 8°18E 63 E5
Galena U.S.A. 64°44N 156°56W 108 C4
Galesburg U.S.A. 40°57N 90°22W 112 E2
Galgate U.K. 53°59N 2°46W 23 E3
Galicia □ Spain 42°43N 7°45W 69 A2
Galilee, Sea of Israel 32°45N 35°35E 86 C3
Galina Pt. Jamaica 18°24N 76°58W 114 a
Gallan Hd. U.K. 58°15N 7°2W 18 F3
Galle Sri Lanka 6°5N 80°10E 84 R12
Galley Hd. Ireland 51°32N 8°55W 30 E5
Gallinas, Pta. Colombia 12°28N 71°40W 120 A2
Gallipolis U.S.A. 38°49N 82°12W 112 F6
Gällivare Sweden 67°9N 20°40E 63 D8
Galloway U.K. 55°1N 4°29W 20 D7
Galloway, Mull of U.K. 54°39N 4°52W 20 E6
Gallup U.S.A. 35°32N 108°45W 110 C5
Galmpton U.K. 50°23N 3°35W 27 G6
Galston U.K. 55°36N 4°24W 20 C7
Galty Mts. Ireland 52°22N 8°10W 30 D6
Galtymore Ireland 52°21N 8°11W 30 D6
Galveston U.S.A. 29°18N 94°48W 111 E8
Galway Ireland 53°17N 9°3W 30 B4
Galway □ Ireland 53°22N 9°1W 30 B4
Galway B. Ireland 53°13N 9°10W 30 B4
Gambia ■ W. Afr. 13°25N 16°0W 94 F2
Gambia → W. Afr. 13°28N 16°34W 94 F2
Gamlingay U.K. 52°10N 0°11W 25 B8
Gan Jiang → China 29°15N 116°0E 81 D6
Gananoque Canada 44°20N 76°10W 113 C9
Gäncä Azerbaijan 40°45N 46°20E 73 F8
Gand = Gent Belgium 51°2N 3°42E 65 C3
Gandak → India 25°39N 85°13E 85 G14
Gander Canada 48°58N 54°35W 109 E14
Gandhi Sagar India 24°40N 75°40E 84 G9
Gandia Spain 38°58N 0°9W 69 C5
Ganga → India 23°20N 90°30E 85 H17
Gangneung S. Korea 37°45N 128°54E 81 C7
Gangtok India 27°20N 88°37E 85 F16
Gannett Peak U.S.A. 43°11N 109°39W 110 B5
Gansu □ China 36°0N 104°0E 80 C5
Ganzhou China 25°51N 114°56E 81 D6
Gao Mali 16°15N 0°5W 94 E5
Gar China 32°10N 79°58E 80 C2
Garanhuns Brazil 8°50S 36°30W 122 A3
Garboldisham U.K. 52°23N 0°57E 25 B10
Garden City U.S.A. 37°58N 100°53W 110 C6
Gardēz Afghan. 33°37N 69°9E 87 C12
Gare L. U.K. 56°1N 4°50W 20 B6
Garforth U.K. 53°47N 1°24W 23 E6
Gargrave U.K. 53°59N 2°7W 23 E4
Garioch U.K. 57°18N 2°40W 19 H12
Garissa Kenya 0°25S 39°40E 96 E7
Garoe Somali Rep. 8°25N 48°33E 88 F4
Garonne → France 45°2N 0°36W 68 D3
Garoua Cameroon 9°19N 13°21E 95 G8
Garron Pt. U.K. 55°3N 5°59W 29 A10
Garry → U.K. 56°44N 3°47W 19 J10
Garry, L. Canada 65°58N 100°18W 108 C9
Garsdale Head U.K. 54°20N 2°20W 22 D4
Garstang U.K. 53°55N 2°46W 23 E3
Gary U.S.A. 41°36N 87°20W 112 E4
Garzê China 31°38N 100°1E 80 C5
Gascogne France 43°45N 0°20E 68 E4
Gascogne, G. de Europe 44°0N 2°0W 68 D2
Gashua Nigeria 12°54N 11°0E 95 F8
Gaspé Canada 48°52N 64°30W 109 E13
Gaspé, C. Canada 48°48N 64°7W 113 A15
Gaspésie, Pén. de la Canada 48°45N 65°40W 113 A15
Gata, Sierra de Spain 40°20N 6°45W 69 B2
Gatehouse of Fleet U.K. 54°53N 4°12W 20 E7
Gateshead U.K. 54°57N 1°35W 22 C5
Gatineau Canada 45°29N 75°39W 113 C10
Gatineau → Canada 45°27N 75°42W 113 C10
Gatley U.K. 53°24N 2°15W 23 F4
Gatwick, London ✈ (LGW) U.K. 51°10N 0°11W 25 D8
Gävle Sweden 60°40N 17°9E 63 E7
Gawilgarh Hills India 21°15N 76°45E 84 J10
Gawthwaite U.K. 54°16N 3°8W 22 D2
Gaxun Nur China 42°22N 100°30E 80 B5
Gaya India 24°47N 85°4E 85 G14
Gaylord U.S.A. 45°2N 84°41W 112 C5
Gayton U.K. 52°45N 0°36E 25 A10
Gaywood U.K. 52°46N 0°26E 25 A9
Gaza Gaza Strip 31°30N 34°28E 86 D3
Gaza Strip ■ Asia 31°29N 34°25E 86 D3
Gaziantep Turkey 37°6N 37°23E 73 G6
Gdańsk Poland 54°22N 18°40E 67 A10
Gdynia Poland 54°35N 18°33E 67 A10
Gebze Turkey 40°47N 29°25E 73 F4
Gedaref Sudan 14°2N 35°28E 95 F13
Gedney U.K. 52°48N 0°4E 23 G9
Gedser Denmark 54°35N 11°55E 63 G6
Geelong Australia 38°10S 144°22E 98 H7
Gejiu China 23°20N 103°10E 80 D5
Gela Italy 37°4N 14°15E 70 F6
Gelderland □ Neths. 52°5N 6°10E 65 B6
Gelibolu Turkey 40°28N 26°43E 73 F4
Gelsenkirchen Germany 51°32N 7°6E 66 C4
General Acha Argentina 37°20S 64°38W 121 F3
General Alvear Argentina 35°0S 67°40W 121 F3
General Pico Argentina 35°45S 63°50W 121 F3
General Santos Phil. 6°5N 125°14E 83 C4
Geneva Switz. 46°12N 6°9E 66 E4
Geneva U.S.A. 42°52N 76°59W 112 D9
Geneva, L. = Léman, L. Europe 46°26N 6°30E 66 E4

Genk Belgium 50°58N 5°32E 65 D5
Gennargentu, Mti. del Italy 40°1N 9°19E 70 D3
Genoa Italy 44°25N 8°57E 70 B3
Génova, G. di Italy 44°0N 9°0E 70 C3
Gent Belgium 51°2N 3°42E 65 C3
George S. Africa 33°58S 22°29E 97 L4
George → Canada 58°49N 66°10W 109 D13
George, L. U.S.A. 29°17N 81°36W 111 E10
George Town Cayman Is. 19°20N 81°24W 115 D8
George Town Malaysia 5°25N 100°20E 83 C2
George V Land Antarctica 69°0S 148°0E 55 C10
Georgetown Guyana 6°50N 58°12W 120 B4
Georgetown Ky., U.S.A. 38°13N 84°33W 112 F5
Georgetown S.C., U.S.A. 33°23N 79°17W 111 D11
Georgia □ U.S.A. 32°50N 83°15W 111 D10
Georgia ■ Asia 42°0N 43°0E 73 F7
Georgian B. Canada 45°15N 81°0W 112 C7
Georgiyevsk Russia 44°12N 43°28E 73 F7
Gera Germany 50°53N 12°4E 66 C7
Geraldton Australia 28°48S 114°32E 98 F1
Germany ■ Europe 51°0N 10°0E 66 C6
Germiston S. Africa 26°13S 28°10E 97 K5
Gerrans B. U.K. 50°12N 4°57W 27 G4
Gerrards Cross U.K. 51°35N 0°33W 25 C7
Getafe Spain 40°18N 3°43W 69 B4
Ghadāmis Libya 30°11N 9°29E 95 B7
Ghaghara → India 25°45N 84°40E 85 G14
Ghana ■ W. Afr. 8°0N 1°0W 94 G5
Ghardaïa Algeria 32°20N 3°37E 94 B6
Gharyān Libya 32°10N 13°0E 95 B8
Ghats, Eastern India 14°0N 78°50E 84 N11
Ghats, Western India 14°0N 75°0E 84 N9
Ghazal, Bahr el → Chad 13°0N 15°47E 95 F9
Ghazâl, Bahr el → Sudan 9°31N 30°25E 95 G12
Ghaziabad India 28°42N 77°26E 84 E10
Ghazipur India 25°38N 83°35E 85 G13
Ghazni Afghan. 33°30N 68°28E 87 C12
Ghent = Gent Belgium 51°2N 3°42E 65 C3
Ghowr □ Afghan. 34°0N 64°20E 87 C11
Giamama Somali Rep. 0°4N 42°44E 88 G3
Giants Causeway U.K. 55°16N 6°29W 29 A9
Gibraltar ☑ Europe 36°7N 5°22W 69 D3
Gibraltar, Str. of Medit. S. 35°55N 5°40W 69 E3
Gibraltar Pt. U.K. 53°6N 0°19E 23 F9
Gibson Desert Australia 24°0S 126°0E 98 E4
Gifu Japan 35°30N 136°45E 82 F5
Giggleswick U.K. 54°5N 2°17W 22 D4
Gigha U.K. 55°42N 5°44W 20 C4
Gijón Spain 43°32N 5°42W 69 A3
Gila → U.S.A. 32°43N 114°33W 110 D4
Gīlān □ Iran 37°0N 50°0E 86 B7
Gilbert Is. Kiribati 1°0N 172°0E 102 G9
Gilgit India 35°50N 74°15E 84 B9
Gillam Canada 56°20N 94°40W 108 D10
Gillette U.S.A. 44°18N 105°30W 110 B5
Gillingham Dorset, U.K. 51°2N 2°18W 24 D4
Gillingham Medway, U.K. 51°23N 0°33E 25 D10
Gilsland U.K. 55°0N 2°34W 22 C3
Gimie, Mt St. Lucia 13°54N 61°0W 115 f
Giohar Somali Rep. 2°48N 45°30E 88 G4
Girdle Ness U.K. 57°9N 2°3W 19 H13
Giresun Turkey 40°55N 38°30E 73 F6
Girga Egypt 26°17N 31°55E 95 C12
Girona Spain 41°58N 2°46E 69 B7
Gironde → France 45°32N 1°7W 68 D3
Girvan U.K. 55°14N 4°51W 20 D6
Gisborne N.Z. 38°39S 178°5E 99 H14
Gisburn U.K. 53°56N 2°16W 23 E4
Gitega Burundi 3°26S 29°56E 96 E5
Gizhiga Russia 62°3N 160°30E 79 C18
Gjoa Haven Canada 68°38N 95°53W 108 C10
Glace Bay Canada 46°11N 59°58W 113 B18
Glacier Nat. Park △ U.S.A. 48°42N 113°48W 110 A4
Gladstone Australia 23°52S 151°16E 98 E9
Gladstone U.S.A. 45°51N 87°1W 112 C4
Gladwin U.S.A. 43°59N 84°29W 112 D5
Glamorgan, Vale of □ U.K. 51°28N 3°25W 27 E7
Glanaruddery Mts. Ireland 52°20N 9°27W 30 D4
Glanton U.K. 55°26N 1°54W 22 B5
Glasgow U.K. 55°51N 4°15W 20 C7
Glasgow Ky., U.S.A. 37°0N 85°55W 112 G5
Glasgow Mont., U.S.A. 48°12N 106°38W 110 A5
Glasgow Int. ✈ (GLA) U.K. 55°51N 4°21W 20 C7
Glasnevin Ireland 53°22N 6°15W 31 B10
Glastonbury U.K. 51°9N 2°43W 24 D3
Glazov Russia 58°9N 52°40E 72 C9
Glemsford U.K. 52°6N 0°40E 25 C10
Glen U.K. 52°51N 0°7W 23 G8
Glen Affric U.K. 57°17N 5°1W 18 H7
Glen Almond U.K. 56°28N 3°50W 21 B8
Glen Coe U.K. 56°40N 5°0W 18 J7
Glen Etive U.K. 56°37N 5°0W 20 A5
Glen Garry Highl., U.K. 57°3N 5°7W 18 H7
Glen Garry Perth & Kinr., U.K. 56°47N 4°5W 19 J9
Glen Mor U.K. 57°9N 4°37W 19 H8
Glen Moriston U.K. 57°11N 4°52W 18 H8
Glen Orchy U.K. 56°27N 4°52W 20 B6
Glen Orrin U.K. 57°31N 4°45W 19 H8
Glen Oykel U.K. 58°5N 4°50W 19 F8
Glen Roy U.K. 56°56N 4°50W 18 J8
Glen Shee U.K. 56°50N 3°28W 19 J11
Glen Shiel U.K. 57°9N 5°18W 18 H7
Glen Spean U.K. 56°53N 4°40W 18 J8
Glendale Ariz., U.S.A. 33°32N 112°11W 110 D4
Glendale Calif., U.S.A. 34°9N 118°15W 110 D3
Glendive U.S.A. 47°7N 104°43W 110 A6
Gleneagles U.K. 56°17N 3°43W 21 B8
Glenfinnan U.K. 56°53N 5°27W 18 J6
Glengarriff Ireland 51°45N 9°34W 30 E3
Glenkens, The U.K. 55°12N 4°12W 20 D7
Glenluce U.K. 54°52N 4°48W 20 E6
Glennallen U.S.A. 62°7N 145°33W 108 C5
Glenrothes U.K. 56°12N 3°10W 21 B9
Glens Falls U.S.A. 43°19N 73°39W 113 D11
Glenties Ireland 54°49N 8°16W 28 B5
Glenveagh △ Ireland 55°3N 8°1W 28 A5
Gliwice Poland 50°22N 18°41E 67 C10

Globe U.S.A. 33°24N 110°47W 110 D4
Głogów Poland 51°37N 16°5E 66 C9
Glomma → Norway 59°12N 10°57E 63 F6
Glossop U.K. 53°27N 1°56W 23 F5
Gloucester U.K. 51°53N 2°15W 24 C4
Gloucestershire □ U.K. 51°46N 2°15W 24 C4
Gloversville U.S.A. 43°3N 74°21W 113 D10
Gniezno Poland 52°30N 17°35E 67 B9
Gnosall U.K. 52°48N 2°14W 23 G4
Goa India 15°33N 73°59E 84 M8
Goa □ India 15°33N 73°59E 84 M8
Goat Fell U.K. 55°38N 5°11W 20 C5
Gobi Asia 44°0N 110°0E 81 B5
Godalming U.K. 51°11N 0°36W 25 D7
Godavari → India 16°25N 82°18E 85 L13
Goderich Canada 43°45N 81°41W 112 D7
Godhra India 22°49N 73°40E 84 H8
Godmanchester U.K. 52°20N 0°11W 25 B8
Godoy Cruz Argentina 32°56S 68°52W 121 F3
Gods → Canada 56°22N 92°51W 108 D10
Gods L. Canada 54°40N 94°15W 108 D10
Godshill U.K. 50°38N 1°15W 24 E6
Godstone U.K. 51°14N 0°3W 25 D8
Gogama Canada 47°35N 81°43W 112 C7
Goiânia Brazil 16°43S 49°20W 122 C1
Goiás Brazil 15°55S 50°10W 120 D4
Goiás □ Brazil 12°10S 48°0W 122 C1
Goio-Erê Brazil 24°12S 53°1W 121 E4
Gold Coast Australia 28°0S 153°25E 98 F9
Gold Coast W. Afr. 4°0N 1°40W 94 H5
Golden Vale Ireland 52°33N 8°17W 30 D6
Goldsboro U.S.A. 35°23N 77°59W 111 C11
Golspie U.K. 57°58N 3°59W 19 G10
Goma Dem. Rep. of the Congo 1°37S 29°10E 96 E5
Gomel Belarus 52°28N 31°0E 67 B16
Gomera Canary Is. 28°7N 17°14W 94 C2
Gómez Palacio Mexico 25°34N 103°30W 114 B4
Gonābād Iran 34°15N 58°45E 87 C9
Gonaïves Haiti 19°20N 72°42W 115 D10
Gonbad-e Kāvūs Iran 37°20N 55°25E 87 B8
Gonda India 27°9N 81°58E 85 F12
Gonder Ethiopia 12°39N 37°30E 88 E2
Gonghe China 36°18N 100°32E 80 C5
Good Hope, C. of S. Africa 34°24S 18°30E 97 L3
Goodrich U.K. 51°52N 2°37W 24 C3
Goodwood U.K. 50°53N 0°44W 25 E7
Goole U.K. 53°42N 0°53W 23 E7
Goose L. U.S.A. 41°56N 120°26W 110 B2
Gorakhpur India 26°47N 83°23E 85 F13
Gordon U.K. 55°41N 2°34W 21 C10
Gore Ethiopia 8°12N 35°32E 88 F2
Gorebridge U.K. 55°50N 3°2W 21 C9
Gorey Ireland 52°41N 6°18W 31 C10
Gorgān Iran 36°55N 54°30E 87 B8
Goring U.K. 51°31N 1°7W 24 C6
Goring-by-Sea U.K. 50°49N 0°24W 25 E8
Gorleston U.K. 52°35N 1°44E 25 A12
Görlitz Germany 51°9N 14°58E 66 C8
Gorontalo Indonesia 0°35N 123°5E 83 C4
Gort Ireland 53°3N 8°49W 30 B5
Gorzów Wielkopolski Poland 52°43N 15°15E 66 B8
Gosford U.K. 55°26N 3°27W 22 D2
Gosforth U.K. 54°26N 3°27W 22 D2
Gosport U.K. 50°48N 1°9W 24 E6
Göta kanal Sweden 58°30N 15°58E 63 F7
Götaland Sweden 57°30N 14°30E 63 F6
Göteborg Sweden 57°43N 11°59E 63 F6
Gotha Germany 50°56N 10°42E 66 C6
Gothenburg = Göteborg Sweden 57°43N 11°59E 63 F6
Gotland Sweden 57°30N 18°33E 63 F7
Gotō-Rettō Japan 32°55N 129°5E 82 G1
Göttingen Germany 51°31N 9°55E 66 C5
Gouda Neths. 52°1N 4°42E 65 B4
Goudhurst U.K. 51°6N 0°29E 25 D9
Gouin, Rés. Canada 48°35N 74°40W 113 A10
Goulburn Australia 34°44S 149°44E 98 G8
Goulimine Morocco 28°56N 10°0W 94 C3
Goundam Mali 16°27N 3°40W 94 E5
Gourock U.K. 55°57N 4°49W 20 C6
Governador Valadares Brazil 18°15S 41°57W 122 C2
Gower U.K. 51°35N 4°10W 27 D5
Gowna, L. Ireland 53°51N 7°34W 28 D6
Goya Argentina 29°10S 59°10W 121 E4
Gozo Malta 36°3N 14°15E 70 a
Graaff-Reinet S. Africa 32°13S 24°32E 97 L4
Gracias a Dios, C. Honduras 15°0N 83°10W 115 E8
Grafham Water U.K. 52°19N 0°18W 25 B8
Grafton Australia 29°38S 152°58E 98 F9
Grafton U.S.A. 48°25N 97°25W 111 A7
Graham Land Antarctica 65°0S 64°0W 55 C17
Grahamstown S. Africa 33°19S 26°31E 97 L5
Grain Coast W. Afr. 4°20N 10°0W 94 H3
Grainthorpe U.K. 53°27N 0°5E 23 F9
Grampian Mts. U.K. 56°50N 4°0W 19 J9
Gran Canaria Canary Is. 27°55N 15°35W 94 C2
Gran Chaco S. Amer. 25°0S 61°0W 121 E3
Gran Sasso d'Italia Italy 42°27N 13°42E 70 C5
Granada Nic. 11°58N 86°0W 114 E7
Granada Spain 37°10N 3°35W 69 D4
Granard Ireland 53°47N 7°30W 28 D6
Granby Canada 45°25N 72°45W 113 C11
Grand → U.S.A. 45°40N 100°45W 110 A6
Grand Bahama I. Bahamas 26°40N 78°30W 115 B9
Grand-Bourg Guadeloupe 15°53N 61°19W 114 b
Grand Canyon U.S.A. 36°3N 112°9W 110 C4
Grand Canyon Nat. Park △ U.S.A. 36°15N 112°30W 110 C4
Grand Cayman Cayman Is. 19°20N 81°20W 115 D8
Grand Erg de Bilma Niger 18°30N 14°0E 95 E8
Grand Falls Canada 47°3N 67°44W 109 E13
Grand Falls-Windsor Canada 48°56N 55°40W 109 E14
Grand Forks U.S.A. 47°55N 97°3W 111 A7
Grand Haven U.S.A. 43°4N 86°13W 112 D4
Grand Island U.S.A. 40°55N 98°21W 110 B7
Grand Junction U.S.A. 39°4N 108°33W 110 C5

Grand L. Canada 45°57N 66°7W 113 C14
Grand Manan I. Canada 44°45N 66°52W 113 C14
Grand-Mère Canada 46°36N 72°40W 113 B11
Grand Rapids Canada 53°12N 99°19W 108 D10
Grand Rapids U.S.A. 42°58N 85°40W 112 D4
Grand St-Bernard, Col du Europe 45°50N 7°10E 66 F4
Grand Teton U.S.A. 43°54N 110°50W 110 B4
Grande → Bolivia 15°51S 64°39W 120 D3
Grande → Brazil 11°30S 44°30W 122 B2
Grande, B. Argentina 50°30S 68°20W 121 H3
Grande, Rio → N. Amer. 25°58N 97°9W 111 E7
Grande Baleine, R. de la → Canada 55°16N 77°47W 109 D12
Grande Prairie Canada 55°10N 118°50W 108 D8
Grande-Terre Guadeloupe 16°20N 61°25W 114 b
Grande Vigie, Pte. de la Guadeloupe 16°32N 61°27W 114 b
Grange-over-Sands U.K. 54°12N 2°54W 22 D3
Grangemouth U.K. 56°1N 3°42W 21 B8
Grangeville U.S.A. 45°56N 116°7W 110 A3
Grantham U.K. 52°55N 0°38W 23 G7
Grantown-on-Spey U.K. 57°20N 3°36W 19 H11
Grants Pass U.S.A. 42°26N 123°19W 110 B2
Granville U.S.A. 43°24N 73°16W 113 D11
Grasmere U.K. 54°28N 3°1W 22 D2
Grasse France 43°38N 6°56E 68 E7
Grassington U.K. 54°5N 1°59W 22 D5
Graulhet France 43°45N 1°59E 68 E4
Gravatá Brazil 8°10S 35°29W 122 A3
Gravesend U.K. 51°26N 0°22E 25 D9
Grayling U.S.A. 44°40N 84°43W 112 C5
Grayrigg U.K. 54°23N 2°39W 22 D3
Grays U.K. 51°28N 0°21E 25 D9
Graz Austria 47°4N 15°27E 66 E8
Great Australian Bight Australia 33°30S 130°0E 98 G5
Great Ayton U.K. 54°30N 1°8W 22 D6
Great Baddow U.K. 51°43N 0°31E 25 C10
Great Barrier Reef Australia 18°0S 146°50E 98 D8
Great Basin U.S.A. 40°0N 117°0W 110 B3
Great Bear → Canada 65°0N 124°0W 108 C7
Great Bear L. Canada 65°30N 120°0W 108 B7
Great Bend U.S.A. 38°22N 98°46W 110 C7
Great Bentley U.K. 51°51N 1°4E 25 C11
Great Bernera U.K. 58°14N 6°50W 18 F4
Great Blasket I. Ireland 52°6N 10°32W 30 D1
Great Britain Europe 54°0N 2°15W 56 E5
Great Broughton U.K. 54°26N 1°9W 22 D6
Great Camanoe Br. Virgin Is. 18°30N 64°35W 115 e
Great Chesterford U.K. 52°4N 0°13E 25 B9
Great Clifton U.K. 54°39N 3°29W 22 C2
Great Dividing Ra. Australia 23°0S 146°0E 98 E8
Great Dunmow U.K. 51°52N 0°23E 25 C9
Great Exuma I. Bahamas 23°30N 75°50W 115 C9
Great Falls U.S.A. 47°30N 111°17W 110 A4
Great Harwood U.K. 53°47N 2°24W 23 E4
Great Inagua I. Bahamas 21°0N 73°20W 115 C10
Great Karoo S. Africa 31°55S 21°0E 97 L4
Great Khingan Mts. China 48°0N 121°0E 81 B7
Great Malvern U.K. 52°7N 2°18W 24 B4
Great Massingham U.K. 52°47N 0°40E 25 A10
Great Missenden U.K. 51°42N 0°41W 25 C7
Great Ormes Head U.K. 53°20N 3°52W 26 A6
Great Ouse → U.K. 52°48N 0°21E 25 A9
Great Pedro Bluff Jamaica 17°51N 77°44W 114 a
Great Plains N. Amer. 47°0N 105°0W 110 A6
Great Salt Desert Iran 34°30N 55°0E 87 C8
Great Salt L. U.S.A. 41°15N 112°40W 110 B4
Great Salt Lake Desert U.S.A. 40°50N 113°30W 110 B4
Great Sandy Desert Australia 21°0S 124°0E 98 E3
Great Sandy Desert U.S.A. 43°35N 120°15W 110 B2
Great Shefford U.K. 51°28N 1°28W 24 D6
Great Shelford U.K. 52°9N 0°8E 25 B9
Great Shunner Fell U.K. 54°22N 2°14W 22 D4
Great Skellig Ireland 51°47N 10°33W 30 E1
Great Slave L. Canada 61°23N 115°38W 108 C8
Great Snow Mt. Canada 57°26N 124°0W 108 D7
Great Torrington U.K. 50°57N 4°9W 27 F5
Great Victoria Desert Australia 29°30S 126°30E 98 F4
Great Wall China 38°30N 109°30E 81 C5
Great Waltham U.K. 51°47N 0°28E 25 C9
Great Whernside U.K. 54°10N 1°58W 22 D5
Great Yarmouth U.K. 52°37N 1°44E 25 A12
Greater Antilles W. Indies 17°40N 74°0W 115 D10
Greater London □ U.K. 51°31N 0°6W 25 C8
Greater Manchester □ U.K. 53°30N 2°15W 23 E4
Greater Sunda Is. Indonesia 7°0S 112°0E 83 D3
Greece ■ Europe 40°0N 23°0E 71 E9
Greeley U.S.A. 40°25N 104°42W 110 B6
Greely Fd. Canada 80°30N 85°0W 109 A11
Green → Ky., U.S.A. 37°54N 87°30W 112 G4
Green → Utah, U.S.A. 38°11N 109°53W 110 C5
Green B. U.S.A. 45°0N 87°30W 112 C4
Green Bay U.S.A. 44°31N 88°0W 112 C4
Green Hammerton U.K. 54°1N 1°18W 23 D6
Green River U.S.A. 41°32N 109°28W 110 B5
Greencastle U.K. 54°2N 5°55W 29 C10
Greenfield Ind., U.S.A. 39°47N 85°46W 112 F5
Greenfield Mass., U.S.A. 42°35N 72°36W 113 D11
Greenhead U.K. 54°59N 2°30W 22 C3
Greenland ☑ N. Amer. 66°0N 45°0W 54 C5
Greenland Sea Arctic 73°0N 10°0W 54 B7
Greenlaw U.K. 55°43N 2°27W 21 C10
Greenock U.K. 55°57N 4°46W 20 C6
Greenodd U.K. 54°14N 3°4W 22 D2
Greenore Ireland 54°1N 6°9W 29 B9
Greenore Pt. Ireland 52°14N 6°19W 31 D10
Greensboro U.S.A. 36°4N 79°48W 111 C11
Greensburg Ind., U.S.A. 39°20N 85°29W 112 F5
Greensburg Pa., U.S.A. 40°18N 79°33W 112 E8
Greenstone Pt. U.K. 57°55N 5°37W 18 G6
Greenville Ala., U.S.A. 31°50N 86°38W 111 D9
Greenville Maine, U.S.A. 45°28N 69°35W 113 C13
Greenville Mich., U.S.A. 43°11N 85°15W 112 D5

Greenville *Miss., U.S.A.* 33°24N 91°4W **111** D8
Greenville *Ohio, U.S.A.* 40°6N 84°38W **112** E5
Greenville *S.C., U.S.A.* 34°51N 82°24W **111** D10
Greenwich □ *U.K.* 51°29N 0°1E **25** D9
Greenwood *U.S.A.* 33°31N 90°11W **111** D8
Gremikha *Russia* 67°59N 39°47E **72** A6
Grenada ■ *W. Indies* 12°10N 61°40W **115** E12
Grenoble *France* 45°12N 5°42E **68** D6
Greta → *U.K.* 54°9N 2°37W **22** D3
Gretna *U.K.* 55°0N 3°3W **21** E9
Gretna Green *U.K.* 55°1N 3°3W **21** D9
Gretton *U.K.* 52°33N 0°40W **25** A7
Grey Ra. *Australia* 27°0S 143°30E **98** F7
Greymouth *N.Z.* 42°29S 171°13E **99** J13
Greystoke *U.K.* 54°41N 2°51W **22** C3
Greystones *Ireland* 53°9N 6°5W **31** B10
Griffith *Australia* 34°18S 146°2E **98** G8
Grimsay *U.K.* 57°29N 7°14W **18** H3
Grimsby *U.K.* 53°34N 0°5W **23** E8
Gris-Nez, C. *France* 50°52N 1°35E **68** A4
Grise Fiord *Canada* 76°25N 82°57W **109** B11
Grizebeck *U.K.* 54°16N 3°10W **22** D2
Groningen *Neths.* 53°15N 6°35E **65** A6
Groote Eylandt *Australia* 14°0S 136°40E **98** C6
Gros Islet *St. Lucia* 14°5N 60°58W **115** f
Gros Piton *St. Lucia* 13°49N 61°5W **115** f
Gros Piton Pt. *St. Lucia* 13°49N 61°5W **115** f
Grosseto *Italy* 42°46N 11°8E **70** C4
Grossglockner *Austria* 47°5N 12°40E **66** E7
Groundhog → *Canada* 48°45N 82°58W **112** A6
Groznyy *Russia* 43°20N 45°45E **73** F8
Grudziądz *Poland* 53°30N 18°47E **67** B10
Gruinard B. *U.K.* 57°56N 5°35W **18** G6
Guadalajara *Mexico* 20°40N 103°20W **114** C4
Guadalajara *Spain* 40°37N 3°12W **69** B4
Guadalcanal *Solomon Is.* 9°32S 160°12E **99** B11
Guadalete → *Spain* 36°35N 6°13W **69** D2
Guadalquivir → *Spain* 36°47N 6°22W **69** D2
Guadarrama, Sierra de *Spain* 41°0N 4°0W **69** B4
Guadeloupe ⊠ *W. Indies* 16°20N 61°40W **114** b
Guadiana → *Portugal* 37°14N 7°22W **69** D2
Guadix *Spain* 37°18N 3°11W **69** D4
Guafo, Boca del *Chile* 43°35S 74°0W **121** G2
Guajará-Mirim *Brazil* 10°50S 65°20W **120** D3
Guajira, Pen. de la *Colombia* 12°0N 72°0W **120** A2
Gualeguaychú *Argentina* 33°3S 59°31W **121** F4
Guam ⊠ *Pac. Oc.* 13°27N 144°45E **102** F6
Guamúchil *Mexico* 25°28N 108°6W **114** B3
Guana I. *Br. Virgin Is.* 18°30N 64°30W **115** e
Guanajuato *Mexico* 21°1N 101°15W **114** C4
Guane *Cuba* 22°10N 84°7W **115** C8
Guangdong □ *China* 23°0N 113°0E **81** D6
Guangxi Zhuang □ *China* 24°0N 109°0E **81** D5
Guangzhou *China* 23°6N 113°13E **81** D6
Guanica *Puerto Rico* 17°58N 66°55W **115** d
Guantánamo *Cuba* 20°10N 75°14W **115** C9
Guantánamo B. *Cuba* 19°59N 75°10W **115** D9
Guaporé → *Brazil* 11°55S 65°4W **120** D3
Guaqui *Bolivia* 16°41S 68°54W **120** D3
Guarapuava *Brazil* 25°20S 51°30W **121** E4
Guaratinguetá *Brazil* 22°49S 45°9W **122** D1
Guarulhos *Brazil* 23°29S 46°33W **122** D1
Guarus *Brazil* 21°44S 41°20W **122** D2
Guatemala *Guatemala* 14°40N 90°22W **114** E6
Guatemala ■ *Cent. Amer.* 15°40N 90°30W **114** D6
Guaviare → *Colombia* 4°3N 67°44W **120** B3
Guaxupé *Brazil* 21°10S 47°5W **122** D1
Guayama *Puerto Rico* 17°59N 66°7W **115** d
Guayaquil *Ecuador* 2°15S 79°52W **120** C2
Guayaquil, G. de *Ecuador* 3°10S 81°0W **120** C1
Guaymas *Mexico* 27°56N 110°54W **114** B2
Gubkin *Russia* 51°17N 37°32E **73** D6
Guelph *Canada* 43°35N 80°20W **112** D7
Guéret *France* 46°11N 1°51E **68** C4
Guernsey *U.K.* 49°26N 2°35W **27** J8
Guestling Green *U.K.* 50°53N 0°39E **25** E10
Guiana Highlands *S. Amer.* 5°10N 60°40W **116** C4
Guidónia-Montecélio *Italy* 42°1N 12°45E **70** C5
Guildford *U.K.* 51°14N 0°34W **25** D7
Guilin *China* 25°18N 110°15E **81** D6
Guinea *Africa* 8°0N 8°0E **90** F4
Guinea ■ *W. Afr.* 10°20N 11°30W **94** F3
Guinea, Gulf of *Atl. Oc.* 3°0N 2°30E **90** F4
Guinea-Bissau ■ *Africa* 12°0N 15°0W **94** F3
Güines *Cuba* 22°50N 82°0W **115** C8
Guingamp *France* 48°34N 3°10W **68** B2
Guisborough *U.K.* 54°33N 1°4W **22** C6
Guiyang *China* 26°32N 106°40E **80** D5
Guizhou □ *China* 27°0N 107°0E **80** D5
Gujarat □ *India* 23°20N 71°0E **84** H7
Gujranwala *Pakistan* 32°10N 74°12E **84** C9
Gujrat *Pakistan* 32°40N 74°2E **84** C9
Gulbarga *India* 17°20N 76°50E **84** L10
Gulf, The = Persian Gulf *Asia* 27°0N 50°0E **87** E7
Gulfport *U.S.A.* 30°22N 89°6W **111** D9
Gulu *Uganda* 2°48N 32°17E **96** D6
Guna *India* 24°40N 77°19E **84** G10
Gunnison → *U.S.A.* 39°4N 108°35W **110** C5
Gunsan *S. Korea* 35°59N 126°45E **81** C7
Guntur *India* 16°23N 80°30E **85** L12
Gurgueia → *Brazil* 6°50S 43°24W **120** C5
Guri, Embalse de *Venezuela* 7°50N 62°52W **120** B3
Gurkha *Nepal* 28°5N 84°40E **85** E14
Gurnard's Hd. *U.K.* 50°11N 5°37W **27** G2
Gürün *Turkey* 38°43N 37°15E **73** G6
Gurupi *Brazil* 11°43S 49°4W **122** B1
Gurupi → *Brazil* 1°13S 46°6W **120** C5
Gurvan Sayhan Uul *Mongolia* 43°50N 104°0E **80** B5
Gusau *Nigeria* 12°12N 6°40E **94** F7
Guwahati *India* 26°10N 91°45E **85** F17
Guyana ■ *S. Amer.* 5°0N 59°0W **120** B4
Guyenne *France* 44°30N 0°40E **68** D4
Gwādar *Pakistan* 25°10N 62°18E **84** G3
Gwalchmai *U.K.* 53°16N 4°25W **26** A5
Gwalior *India* 26°12N 78°10E **84** F11
Gwanda *Zimbabwe* 20°55S 29°0E **97** J5
Gwangju *S. Korea* 35°9N 126°54E **81** C7
Gweebarra B. *Ireland* 54°51N 8°23W **28** B5
Gweedore *Ireland* 55°3N 8°13W **28** A5
Gweek *U.K.* 50°5N 5°13W **27** G3
Gwennap *U.K.* 50°12N 5°11W **27** G3
Gweru *Zimbabwe* 19°28S 29°45E **97** H5
Gwynedd □ *U.K.* 52°52N 4°10W **26** B6
Gyaring Hu *China* 34°50N 97°40E **80** C4
Gympie *Australia* 26°11S 152°38E **98** F9
Győr *Hungary* 47°41N 17°40E **67** E9
Gyumri *Armenia* 40°47N 43°50E **73** F7

H

Ha Tinh *Vietnam* 18°20N 105°54E **83** B2
Ha'apai Group *Tonga* 19°47S 174°27W **99** D16
Haarlem *Neths.* 52°23N 4°39E **65** B4
Habahe *China* 48°3N 86°23E **80** B3
Hachinohe *Japan* 40°30N 141°29E **82** C7
Hackney □ *U.K.* 51°33N 0°3W **25** C8
Hackthorpe *U.K.* 54°34N 2°42W **22** C3
Ḥadd, Ra's al *Oman* 22°35N 59°50E **87** F9
Haddenham *U.K.* 51°46N 0°55W **25** C7
Haddington *U.K.* 55°57N 2°47W **21** C10
Hadejia *Nigeria* 12°30N 10°5E **94** F7
Hadleigh *U.K.* 52°3N 0°58E **25** B10
Hadlow *U.K.* 51°13N 0°22E **25** D9
Haḍramawt *Yemen* 15°30N 49°30E **88** D4
Haeju *N. Korea* 38°3N 125°45E **81** C7
Hafizabad *Pakistan* 32°5N 73°40E **84** C8
Hagen *Germany* 51°21N 7°27E **66** C4
Hagerstown *U.S.A.* 39°39N 77°43W **112** F9
Hags Hd. *Ireland* 52°57N 9°28W **30** C4
Hague, C. de la *France* 49°44N 1°56W **68** B3
Hague, The *Neths.* 52°7N 4°17E **65** B4
Haguenau *France* 48°49N 7°47E **68** B7
Haifa *Israel* 32°46N 35°0E **86** C3
Haikou *China* 20°1N 110°16E **81** D6
Ḥā'il *Si. Arabia* 27°28N 41°45E **86** E5
Hailar *China* 49°10N 119°38E **81** B6
Hailey *U.S.A.* 43°31N 114°19W **110** B4
Haileybury *Canada* 47°30N 79°38W **112** B8
Hailsham *U.K.* 50°52N 0°16E **25** E9
Hainan □ *China* 19°0N 109°30E **81** E5
Haines Junction *Canada* 60°45N 137°30W **108** C6
Hainton *U.K.* 53°21N 0°14W **23** F8
Haiphong *Vietnam* 20°47N 106°41E **80** D5
Haiti ■ *W. Indies* 19°0N 72°30W **115** D10
Ḥajjah *Yemen* 15°42N 43°36E **88** D3
Hakodate *Japan* 41°45N 140°44E **82** C7
Halaib Triangle *Africa* 22°30N 35°20E **95** D13
Halberstadt *Germany* 51°54N 11°3E **66** C6
Halberton *U.K.* 50°54N 3°25W **27** F7
Halden *Norway* 59°9N 11°23E **63** F6
Haldia *India* 22°5N 88°3E **85** H16
Haldwani *India* 29°31N 79°30E **84** E11
Halesowen *U.K.* 52°27N 2°3W **23** H4
Halesworth *U.K.* 52°20N 1°31E **25** B12
Halifax *Canada* 44°38N 63°35W **113** C16
Halifax *U.K.* 53°43N 1°52W **23** E5
Halkirk *U.K.* 58°30N 3°29W **19** E11
Hall Pen. *Canada* 63°30N 66°0W **109** C13
Halle *Germany* 51°30N 11°56E **66** C6
Hallow *U.K.* 52°14N 2°15W **24** B4
Halls Creek *Australia* 18°16S 127°38E **98** D4
Hallworthy *U.K.* 50°39N 4°35W **27** F4
Halmahera *Indonesia* 0°40N 128°0E **83** C4
Halmstad *Sweden* 56°41N 12°52E **63** F6
Halstead *U.K.* 51°57N 0°40E **25** C10
Haltwhistle *U.K.* 54°58N 2°26W **22** C4
Hamadān *Iran* 34°52N 48°32E **86** C7
Ḥamāh *Syria* 35°5N 36°40E **86** C4
Hamamatsu *Japan* 34°45N 137°45E **82** F5
Hamar *Norway* 60°48N 11°7E **63** E6
Hambantota *Sri Lanka* 6°10N 81°10E **84** R12
Hambledon *U.K.* 50°55N 1°5W **24** E6
Hambleton Hills *U.K.* 54°17N 1°12W **22** D6
Hamburg *Germany* 53°33N 9°59E **66** B5
Hämeenlinna *Finland* 61°0N 24°28E **63** E8
Hameln *Germany* 52°6N 9°21E **66** B5
Hamersley Ra. *Australia* 22°0S 117°45E **98** E2
Hamhŭng *N. Korea* 39°54N 127°30E **81** C7
Hami *China* 42°55N 93°25E **80** B4
Hamilton *Canada* 43°15N 79°50W **109** E12
Hamilton *N.Z.* 37°47S 175°19E **99** H14
Hamilton *U.K.* 55°46N 4°2W **20** C7
Hamilton *U.S.A.* 39°24N 84°34W **112** F5
Hamm *Germany* 51°40N 7°50E **66** C4
Hammerfest *Norway* 70°39N 23°41E **63** C8
Hammersmith and Fulham □ *U.K.* 51°30N 0°14W **25** D8
Hammond *U.S.A.* 41°38N 87°30W **112** E4
Hammonton *U.S.A.* 39°39N 74°48W **113** F10
Hampshire □ *U.K.* 51°7N 1°23W **24** D6
Hampshire Downs *U.K.* 51°15N 1°10W **24** D6
Hampton in Arden *U.K.* 52°26N 1°41W **23** H5
Hancock *U.S.A.* 47°8N 88°35W **112** B31
Handan *China* 36°35N 114°28E **81** C6
Hanford *U.S.A.* 36°20N 119°39W **110** C3
Hangayn Nuruu *Mongolia* 47°30N 99°0E **80** B4
Hangzhou *China* 30°18N 120°11E **81** C7
Hangzhou Wan *China* 30°15N 120°45E **81** C7
Hankö *Finland* 59°50N 22°57E **63** F8
Hanna *Canada* 51°40N 111°54W **108** D8
Hannibal *U.S.A.* 39°42N 91°22W **111** C81
Hanningfield Res. *U.K.* 51°40N 0°31E **25** C10
Hannover *Germany* 52°22N 9°46E **66** B5
Hanoi *Vietnam* 21°5N 105°55E **80** D5
Hanover *U.S.A.* 39°48N 76°59W **112** F9
Hanover, I. *Chile* 51°0S 74°50W **121** H2
Hans Lollik I. *U.S. Virgin Is.* 18°24N 64°53W **115** e
Hanzhong *China* 33°10N 107°1E **80** C5
Haora *India* 22°34N 88°18E **85** H16
Haparanda *Sweden* 65°52N 24°8E **63** D8
Happy Valley-Goose Bay *Canada* 53°15N 60°20W **109** D13
Har Hu *China* 38°20N 97°38E **80** C4
Har Us Nuur *Mongolia* 48°0N 92°0E **80** B4
Ḥaraḍ *Si. Arabia* 24°22N 49°0E **86** E7
Harare *Zimbabwe* 17°43S 31°2E **97** H6
Harbin *China* 45°48N 126°40E **81** B7
Harbor Beach *U.S.A.* 43°51N 82°39W **112** D6
Hardangerfjorden *Norway* 60°5N 6°0E **63** E5
Hardy, Pte. *St. Lucia* 14°6N 60°56W **115** f
Harer *Ethiopia* 9°20N 42°8E **88** F3
Harewood *U.K.* 53°54N 1°30W **23** E6
Hargeisa *Somali Rep.* 9°30N 44°2E **88** F3
Haridwar *India* 29°58N 78°9E **84** E11
Haringey □ *U.K.* 51°34N 0°5W **25** C8
Haringhata → *Bangla.* 22°0N 89°58E **85** J16
Harīrūd → *Asia* 37°24N 60°38E **87** B10
Harlech *U.K.* 52°52N 4°6W **26** B5
Harleston *U.K.* 52°24N 1°18E **25** B11
Harlingen *Neths.* 53°11N 5°25E **65** A5
Harlingen *U.S.A.* 26°12N 97°42W **110** E7
Harlow *U.K.* 51°46N 0°8E **25** C9
Harney L. *U.S.A.* 43°14N 119°8W **110** B3
Härnösand *Sweden* 62°38N 17°55E **63** E7
Haroldswick *U.K.* 60°48N 0°50W **18** A16
Harpenden *U.K.* 51°49N 0°21W **25** C8
Harricana → *Canada* 50°56N 79°32W **109** D12
Harrietsham *U.K.* 51°14N 0°41E **25** D10
Harrington *U.K.* 54°37N 3°33W **22** C1
Harris *U.K.* 57°50N 6°55W **18** G4
Harris, Sd. of *U.K.* 57°44N 7°6W **18** G3
Harrisburg *U.S.A.* 40°16N 76°53W **112** E9
Harrison, C. *Canada* 54°55N 57°55W **109** D14
Harrisonburg *U.S.A.* 38°27N 78°52W **112** F8
Harrisville *U.S.A.* 44°39N 83°17W **112** C6
Harrogate *U.K.* 54°0N 1°33W **23** D5
Harrow □ *U.K.* 51°35N 0°21W **25** C8
Hart *U.S.A.* 43°42N 86°22W **112** D4
Hartest *U.K.* 52°8N 0°40E **25** B10
Hartford *Conn., U.S.A.* 41°46N 72°41W **113** E11
Hartford *Ky., U.S.A.* 37°27N 86°55W **112** G4
Hartford *Wis., U.S.A.* 43°19N 88°22W **112** D3
Hartland *U.K.* 50°59N 4°29W **27** F5
Hartland Pt. *U.K.* 51°1N 4°32W **27** E4
Hartlebury *U.K.* 52°20N 2°14W **24** B4
Hartlepool *U.K.* 54°42N 1°13W **22** C6
Hartley *U.K.* 55°5N 1°28W **22** B6
Hartpury *U.K.* 51°55N 2°17W **24** C4
Harvey *U.S.A.* 41°36N 87°50W **112** E4
Harwell *U.K.* 51°36N 1°17W **24** C6
Harwich *U.K.* 51°56N 1°17E **25** C11
Haryana □ *India* 29°0N 76°10E **84** E10
Harz *Germany* 51°38N 10°44E **66** C6
Hasa *Si. Arabia* 25°50N 49°0E **86** E7
Haslemere *U.K.* 51°5N 0°43W **25** D7
Haslingden *U.K.* 53°42N 2°19W **23** E4
Hasselt *Belgium* 50°56N 5°21E **65** D5
Hastings *U.K.* 50°51N 0°35E **25** E10
Hastings *U.S.A.* 40°35N 98°23W **110** B7
Hat Yai *Thailand* 7°1N 100°27E **83** C2
Hatfield *U.K.* 51°46N 0°13W **25** C8
Hatgal *Mongolia* 50°26N 100°9E **80** A5
Hatherleigh *U.K.* 50°49N 4°5W **27** F5
Hathersage *U.K.* 53°20N 1°39W **23** F5
Hathras *India* 27°36N 78°6E **84** F11
Hatia *Bangla.* 22°30N 91°5E **85** H17
Hatteras, C. *U.S.A.* 35°14N 75°32W **111** C11
Hattiesburg *U.S.A.* 31°20N 89°17W **111** D9
Haugesund *Norway* 59°23N 5°13E **63** F5
Haughley *U.K.* 52°14N 0°57E **25** B10
Havana = La Habana *Cuba* 23°8N 82°22W **115** C8
Havant *U.K.* 50°51N 0°58W **25** E7
Havasu, L. *U.S.A.* 34°18N 114°28W **110** D4
Havel → *Germany* 52°50N 12°3E **66** B7
Haverfordwest *U.K.* 51°48N 4°58W **26** D4
Haverhill *U.K.* 52°5N 0°28E **25** B9
Haverhill *U.S.A.* 42°47N 71°5W **113** D12
Haverigg *U.K.* 54°13N 3°17W **22** D2
Havering □ *U.K.* 51°34N 0°13E **25** C9
Havre *U.S.A.* 48°33N 109°41W **110** A5
Havre-St.-Pierre *Canada* 50°18N 63°33W **109** D13
Hawai'i *U.S.A.* 19°30N 155°30W **110** J17
Hawai'i □ *U.S.A.* 19°30N 156°30W **110** H16
Hawaiian Is. *Pac. Oc.* 20°30N 156°0W **103** E12
Hawaiian Ridge *Pac. Oc.* 24°0N 165°0W **103** E11
Hawes *U.K.* 54°19N 2°12W **22** D4
Haweswater *U.K.* 54°31N 2°47W **22** C3
Hawick *U.K.* 55°26N 2°47W **21** D10
Hawkchurch *U.K.* 50°48N 2°56W **24** E3
Hawkesbury *Canada* 45°37N 74°37W **113** C10
Hawkesbury Upton *U.K.* 51°35N 2°19W **24** C4
Hawkhurst *U.K.* 51°2N 0°32E **25** D10
Hawkshead *U.K.* 54°23N 2°59W **22** D3
Haworth *U.K.* 53°50N 1°58W **23** E5
Hawsker *U.K.* 54°27N 0°34W **22** D7
Haxby *U.K.* 54°1N 1°4W **23** D6
Hay *Australia* 34°30S 144°51E **98** G8
Hay → *Canada* 60°50N 116°26W **108** C8
Hay-on-Wye *U.K.* 52°5N 3°8W **26** C7
Hay River *Canada* 60°51N 115°44W **108** C8
Haydon Bridge *U.K.* 54°58N 2°14W **22** C4
Hayes → *Canada* 57°3N 92°12W **108** D10
Hayle *U.K.* 50°11N 5°26W **27** G3
Hays *U.S.A.* 38°53N 99°20W **110** C7
Hayton *U.K.* 54°55N 2°45W **22** C3
Hayward *U.S.A.* 46°1N 91°29W **112** B2
Haywards Heath *U.K.* 51°0N 0°5W **25** E8
Hazar *Turkmenistan* 39°34N 53°16E **73** G9
Hazard *U.S.A.* 37°15N 83°12W **112** G6
Hazaribag *India* 23°58N 85°26E **85** H14
Heacham *U.K.* 52°54N 0°29E **25** A9
Headcorn *U.K.* 51°10N 0°38E **25** D10
Heanor *U.K.* 53°1N 1°21W **23** F6
Heard I. *Ind. Oc.* 53°0S 74°0E **53** G13
Hearst *Canada* 49°40N 83°41W **109** E11
Heathfield *U.K.* 50°58N 0°16E **25** E9
Heathrow, London ✈ (LHR) *U.K.* 51°28N 0°27W **25** D8
Hebburn *U.K.* 54°59N 1°32W **22** C5
Hebden Bridge *U.K.* 53°45N 2°0W **23** E5
Hebei □ *China* 39°0N 116°0E **81** C6
Hebrides *U.K.* 57°30N 7°0W **56** D4
Hebrides, Sea of the *U.K.* 57°5N 7°0W **18** H4
Hebron *Canada* 58°5N 62°30W **109** D13
Hecate Str. *Canada* 53°10N 130°30W **108** D6
Hechi *China* 24°40N 108°2E **80** D5
Hechuan *China* 30°2N 106°12E **80** C5
Heckington *U.K.* 52°59N 0°17W **23** G8
Hednesford *U.K.* 52°43N 1°59W **23** G5
Hedon *U.K.* 53°44N 0°12W **23** E8
Heerlen *Neths.* 50°55N 5°58E **65** D5
Hefei *China* 31°52N 117°18E **81** C6
Hegang *China* 47°20N 130°19E **81** B8
Heidelberg *Germany* 49°24N 8°42E **66** D5
Heilbronn *Germany* 49°9N 9°13E **66** D5
Heilongjiang □ *China* 48°0N 126°0E **81** B7
Heimaey *Iceland* 63°26N 20°17W **63** B1
Hejaz *Si. Arabia* 24°0N 40°0E **86** E4
Hekou *China* 22°30N 103°59E **80** D5
Helena *U.S.A.* 46°36N 112°2W **110** A4
Helensburgh *U.K.* 56°1N 4°43W **20** B6
Helgoland *Germany* 54°10N 7°53E **66** A4
Hellfield *U.K.* 54°1N 2°12W **23** D4
Helmand → *Afghan.* 31°12N 61°34E **87** D10
Helmond *Neths.* 51°29N 5°41E **65** C5
Helmsdale *U.K.* 58°7N 3°39W **19** F10
Helmsley *U.K.* 54°15N 1°3W **22** D6
Helperby *U.K.* 54°8N 1°19W **22** D6
Helsby *U.K.* 53°17N 2°46W **23** F3
Helsingborg *Sweden* 56°3N 12°42E **63** F6
Helsinki *Finland* 60°10N 24°55E **63** E9
Helston *U.K.* 50°6N 5°17W **27** G3
Helvellyn *U.K.* 54°32N 3°1W **22** C2
Helwân *Egypt* 29°50N 31°20E **95** C12
Hemel Hempstead *U.K.* 51°44N 0°28W **25** C8
Hempton *U.K.* 52°50N 0°50E **25** A10
Hemsworth *U.K.* 53°37N 1°21W **23** E6
Hemyock *U.K.* 50°54N 3°15W **27** F7
Henan □ *China* 34°0N 114°0E **81** C6
Henderson *Ky., U.S.A.* 37°50N 87°35W **112** G4
Henderson *Nev., U.S.A.* 36°2N 114°58W **110** C4
Henfield *U.K.* 50°56N 0°16W **25** E8
Hengelo *Neths.* 52°16N 6°48E **65** B6
Hengyang *China* 26°59N 112°22E **81** D6
Henley-in-Arden *U.K.* 52°18N 1°46W **24** B5
Henley-on-Thames *U.K.* 51°32N 0°54W **25** C7
Henlopen, C. *U.S.A.* 38°48N 75°6W **113** F10
Henlow *U.K.* 52°2N 0°17W **25** B8
Henrietta Maria, C. *Canada* 55°9N 82°20W **109** D11
Henstridge *U.K.* 50°58N 2°24W **24** E4
Hentiyn Nuruu *Mongolia* 48°30N 108°30E **81** B5
Herāt *Afghan.* 34°20N 62°7E **87** C10
Hereford *U.K.* 52°4N 2°43W **24** B3
Herefordshire □ *U.K.* 52°8N 2°40W **24** B3
Herford *Germany* 52°7N 8°39E **66** B5
Herm *U.K.* 49°30N 2°28W **27** J9
Herma Ness *U.K.* 60°50N 0°54W **18** A16
Hermosillo *Mexico* 29°10N 111°0W **114** B2
Hernád → *Hungary* 47°56N 21°8E **67** D11
Herne *Germany* 51°32N 7°14E **65** C7
Herne Bay *U.K.* 51°21N 1°8E **25** D11
Herstmonceux *U.K.* 50°53N 0°20E **25** E9
Hertford *U.K.* 51°48N 0°4W **25** C8
Hertfordshire □ *U.K.* 51°51N 0°5W **25** C8
's-Hertogenbosch *Neths.* 51°42N 5°17E **65** C5
Hessen □ *Germany* 50°30N 9°0E **66** C5
Hessle *U.K.* 53°44N 0°24W **23** E8
Hethersett *U.K.* 52°36N 1°10E **25** A11
Hetton-le-Hole *U.K.* 54°50N 1°26W **22** C6
Hexham *U.K.* 54°58N 2°4W **22** C4
Heybridge *U.K.* 51°45N 0°42E **25** C10
Heysham *U.K.* 54°3N 2°53W **22** D3
Heytesbury *U.K.* 51°11N 2°6W **24** D4
Heywood *U.K.* 53°35N 2°12W **23** E4
Heze *China* 35°14N 115°20E **81** C6
Hibbing *U.S.A.* 47°25N 92°56W **111** A81
Hickman *U.S.A.* 36°34N 89°11W **112** G3
Hidalgo del Parral *Mexico* 26°56N 105°40W **114** B3
Hierro *Canary Is.* 27°44N 18°0W **94** C2
Higashiōsaka *Japan* 34°39N 135°37E **82** F4
High Atlas *Morocco* 32°30N 5°0W **94** B4
High Bentham *U.K.* 54°7N 2°28W **22** D4
High Ercall *U.K.* 52°45N 2°35W **23** G3
High Hesket *U.K.* 54°48N 2°49W **22** C3
High Level *Canada* 58°31N 117°8W **108** D8
High Pike *U.K.* 54°42N 3°4W **22** C2
High Plateaux *Algeria* 35°0N 1°0E **94** B6
High Prairie *Canada* 55°30N 116°30W **108** D8
High River *Canada* 50°30N 113°50W **108** D8
High Veld *Africa* 27°0S 27°0E **90** J6
High Willhays *U.K.* 50°40N 4°0W **27** F5
High Wycombe *U.K.* 51°37N 0°45W **25** C7
Higham Ferrers *U.K.* 52°19N 0°35W **25** B7
Highbridge *U.K.* 51°13N 2°58W **24** D3
Highclere *U.K.* 51°20N 1°21W **24** D6
Highland □ *U.K.* 57°17N 4°21W **18** H7
Highley *U.K.* 52°27N 2°23W **23** H4
Hightae *U.K.* 55°6N 3°26W **21** D9
Highworth *U.K.* 51°37N 1°43W **24** C5
Hiiumaa *Estonia* 58°50N 22°45E **63** F8
Hildesheim *Germany* 52°9N 9°56E **66** B5
Hilgay *U.K.* 52°34N 0°24E **25** A9
Hillaby, Mt. *Barbados* 13°12N 59°35W **115** g
Hillcrest *Barbados* 13°13N 59°31W **115** g
Hillingdon □ *U.K.* 51°32N 0°27W **25** C8
Hillsborough *U.K.* 54°28N 6°5W **29** C9
Hillsdale *U.S.A.* 41°56N 84°38W **112** E5
Hilo *U.S.A.* 19°44N 155°5W **110** J17
Hilpsford Pt. *U.K.* 54°3N 3°12W **22** D2
Hilversum *Neths.* 52°14N 5°10E **65** B5
Himachal Pradesh □ *India* 31°30N 77°0E **84** D10
Himalaya *Asia* 29°0N 84°0E **85** E14
Himeji *Japan* 34°50N 134°40E **82** F4
Hinckley *U.K.* 52°33N 1°22W **23** G6
Hinderwell *U.K.* 54°32N 0°45W **22** C7
Hindhead *U.K.* 51°7N 0°43W **25** D7
Hindley *U.K.* 53°33N 2°35W **23** E3
Hindu Kush *Asia* 36°0N 71°0E **87** C12
Hingham *U.K.* 52°35N 1°0E **25** A10
Hingoli *India* 19°41N 77°15E **84** K10
Hinkley Pt. *U.K.* 51°12N 3°8W **24** D2
Hinstock *U.K.* 52°50N 2°27W **23** G4
Hinton *U.S.A.* 37°40N 80°54W **112** G7
Hirosaki *Japan* 40°34N 140°28E **82** C7
Hiroshima *Japan* 34°24N 132°30E **82** F3
Hisar *India* 29°12N 75°45E **84** E9
Hispaniola *W. Indies* 19°0N 71°0W **115** D10
Histon *U.K.* 52°16N 0°7E **25** B9
Hitachi *Japan* 36°36N 140°39E **82** E7
Hitchin *U.K.* 51°58N 0°16W **25** C8
Hjälmaren *Sweden* 59°18N 15°40E **63** F7
Hkakabo Razi *Burma* 28°25N 97°23E **85** E20
Ho Chi Minh City *Vietnam* 10°58N 106°40E **83** B2
Hoare B. *Canada* 65°17N 62°30W **109** C13
Hobart *Australia* 42°50S 147°21E **98** J8
Hobbs *U.S.A.* 32°42N 103°8W **110** D6
Hodder → *U.K.* 53°57N 2°27W **23** E4
Hoddesdon *U.K.* 51°45N 0°1W **25** C8
Hodge → *U.K.* 54°16N 0°56W **22** D7
Hodgson *Canada* 51°13N 97°36W **108** D10
Hódmezővásárhely *Hungary* 46°28N 20°22E **67** E11
Hodna, Chott el *Algeria* 35°26N 4°43E **94** A6
Hoff *U.K.* 54°34N 2°31W **22** C3
Hōfu *Japan* 34°3N 131°34E **82** F2
Hog's Back *U.K.* 51°13N 0°38W **25** D7
Hoh Xil Shan *China* 35°0N 89°0E **80** C3
Hoher Rhön *Germany* 50°24N 9°58E **66** C5
Hohhot *China* 40°52N 111°40E **81** B6
Hokkaidō □ *Japan* 43°30N 143°0E **82** B8
Holbeach *U.K.* 52°48N 0°1E **23** G9
Holbeach Marsh *U.K.* 52°52N 0°5E **23** G9
Holderness *U.K.* 53°45N 0°5W **23** E8
Holetown *Barbados* 13°11N 59°38W **115** g
Holguín *Cuba* 20°50N 76°20W **115** C9
Holkham *U.K.* 52°57N 0°48E **25** A10
Holland *U.S.A.* 42°47N 86°7W **112** D4
Holland Fen *U.K.* 53°0N 0°8W **23** G8
Holland on Sea *U.K.* 51°48N 1°13E **25** C11
Holman *Canada* 70°44N 117°44W **108** B8
Holme *U.K.* 53°50N 0°46W **23** E7
Holmes Chapel *U.K.* 53°12N 2°21W **23** F4
Holmfirth *U.K.* 53°35N 1°46W **23** E5
Holstebro *Denmark* 56°22N 8°37E **63** F5
Holsworthy *U.K.* 50°48N 4°22W **27** F5
Holt *U.K.* 52°55N 1°6E **25** A11
Holy I. *Anglesey, U.K.* 53°17N 4°37W **26** A4
Holy I. *Northumberland, U.K.* 55°40N 1°47W **22** A5
Holyhead *U.K.* 53°18N 4°38W **26** A4
Holywell *U.K.* 53°16N 3°14W **26** A7
Home B. *Canada* 68°40N 67°10W **109** C13
Homer *U.S.A.* 59°39N 151°33W **108** D4
Homs *Syria* 34°40N 36°45E **86** C4
Honduras ■ *Cent. Amer.* 14°40N 86°30W **114** E7
Honduras, G. of *Caribbean* 16°50N 87°0W **114** D7
Hønefoss *Norway* 60°10N 10°18E **63** E6
Honey L. *U.S.A.* 40°15N 120°19W **110** B2
Hong Gai *Vietnam* 20°57N 107°5E **80** D5
Hong Kong □ *China* 22°11N 114°14E **81** D6
Hongjiang *China* 27°7N 109°59E **81** D5
Hongshui He → *China* 23°48N 109°30E **81** D5
Hongze Hu *China* 33°15N 118°35E **81** C6
Honiara *Solomon Is.* 9°27S 159°57E **99** B10
Honington *U.K.* 52°59N 0°35W **23** G7
Honiton *U.K.* 50°47N 3°11W **27** F7
Honolulu *U.S.A.* 21°19N 157°52W **103** E12
Honshū *Japan* 36°0N 138°0E **82** F6
Hoo *U.K.* 51°25N 0°35E **25** D10
Hood, Mt. *U.S.A.* 45°23N 121°42W **110** A2
Hoogeveen *Neths.* 52°44N 6°28E **65** B6
Hook *U.K.* 51°17N 0°57W **25** D7
Hook Hd. *Ireland* 52°7N 6°56W **31** D9
Hooper Bay *U.S.A.* 61°32N 166°6W **108** C3
Hoopeston *U.S.A.* 40°28N 87°40W **112** E4
Hoorn *Neths.* 52°38N 5°4E **65** B5
Hoover Dam *U.S.A.* 36°1N 114°44W **110** C4
Hope *U.S.A.* 33°40N 93°36W **111** D8
Hopedale *Canada* 55°28N 60°13W **109** D13
Horden *U.K.* 54°46N 1°19W **22** C6
Horley *U.K.* 51°10N 0°10W **25** D8
Horlivka *Ukraine* 48°19N 38°5E **73** E6
Hormozgān □ *Iran* 27°30N 56°0E **87** E9
Hormuz, Str. of *The Gulf* 26°30N 56°30E **87** E9
Horn, C. = Hornos, C. de *Chile* 55°50S 67°30W **121** H3
Horn, Is. *Wall. & F. Is.* 14°16S 178°6W **99** C15
Horn Head *Ireland* 55°14N 8°0W **28** A6
Hornavan *Sweden* 66°15N 17°30E **63** D7
Horncastle *U.K.* 53°13N 0°7W **23** F8
Horndean *U.K.* 50°55N 1°1W **24** E6
Hornell *U.S.A.* 42°20N 77°40W **112** D9
Hornepayne *Canada* 49°14N 84°48W **112** A5
Horningsham *U.K.* 51°10N 2°15W **24** D4
Hornos, C. de *Chile* 55°50S 67°30W **121** H3
Hornsea *U.K.* 53°55N 0°11W **23** E8
Horqin Youyi Qianqi *China* 46°5N 122°3E **81** B7
Horsforth *U.K.* 53°50N 1°39W **23** E5
Horsham *Australia* 36°44S 142°13E **98** H7
Horsham *U.K.* 51°4N 0°20W **25** D8
Horsham St. Faith *U.K.* 52°43N 1°14E **25** A11
Horsted Keynes *U.K.* 51°2N 0°1W **25** D8
Horton → *Canada* 69°56N 126°52W **108** C7
Horton in Ribblesdale *U.K.* 54°9N 2°17W **22** D4
Horwich *U.K.* 53°36N 2°33W **23** E3
Hoste, I. *Chile* 55°0S 69°0W **121** H3
Hot Springs *Ark., U.S.A.* 34°31N 93°3W **111** D8
Hot Springs *S. Dak., U.S.A.* 43°26N 103°29W **110** B6
Hotan *China* 37°25N 79°55E **80** C2
Houghton *U.S.A.* 47°7N 88°34W **112** B31
Houghton L. *U.S.A.* 44°21N 84°44W **112** C5
Houghton-le-Spring *U.K.* 54°51N 1°28W **22** C6
Houghton Regis *U.K.* 51°54N 0°32W **25** C7
Houlton *U.S.A.* 46°8N 67°51W **113** B14
Houma *U.S.A.* 29°36N 90°43W **111** E8
Hounslow □ *U.K.* 51°28N 0°21W **25** D8
Hourn, L. *U.K.* 57°7N 5°35W **18** H6
Houston *U.S.A.* 29°45N 95°21W **111** E7
Hove *U.K.* 50°50N 0°10W **25** E8
Hoveton *U.K.* 52°43N 1°25E **25** A11
Hovingham *U.K.* 54°11N 0°58W **22** D7
Hövsgöl Nuur *Mongolia* 51°0N 100°30E **80** A5

Howden U.K. 53°45N 0°52W 23 E7
Howe, C. Australia 37°30S 150°0E 98 H9
Howell U.S.A. 42°36N 83°56W 112 D6
Howland I. Pac. Oc. 0°48N 176°38W 102 G10
Howth Ireland 53°23N 6°6W 31 B10
Howth Hd. Ireland 53°22N 6°3W 31 B10
Hoxne U.K. 52°21N 1°12E 25 B11
Hoy U.K. 58°50N 3°15W 19 E11
Høyanger Norway 61°13N 6°4E 63 E5
Hoylake U.K. 53°24N 3°10W 23 F2
Hradec Králové Czech Rep. 50°15N 15°50E 66 C8
Hrodna Belarus 53°42N 23°52E 67 B12
Hron → Slovak Rep. 47°49N 18°45E 67 D10
Hsinchu Taiwan 24°48N 120°58E 81 D7
Huacho Peru 11°10S 77°35W 120 D2
Huai He → China 33°0N 118°30E 81 C6
Huaibei China 34°0N 116°48E 81 C6
Huaihua China 27°32N 109°57E 81 D5
Huainan China 32°38N 116°58E 81 C6
Huallaga → Peru 5°15S 75°30W 120 C2
Huambo Angola 12°42S 15°54E 97 G3
Huancavelica Peru 12°50S 75°5W 120 D2
Huancayo Peru 12°5S 75°12W 120 D2
Huangshan China 29°42N 118°25E 81 D6
Huangshi China 30°10N 115°3E 81 C6
Huánuco Peru 9°55S 76°15W 120 C2
Huaraz Peru 9°30S 77°32W 120 C2
Huascarán, Nevado Peru 9°7S 77°37W 120 C2
Huasco Chile 28°30S 71°15W 121 E2
Huatabampo Mexico 26°50N 109°38W 114 B3
Hubei □ China 31°0N 112°0E 81 C6
Hubli India 15°22N 75°15E 84 M9
Hucknall U.K. 53°3N 1°13W 23 F6
Huddersfield U.K. 53°39N 1°47W 23 E5
Hudiksvall Sweden 61°43N 17°10E 63 E7
Hudson → U.S.A. 40°42N 74°2W 113 E10
Hudson Bay Canada 60°0N 86°0W 109 D11
Hudson Falls U.S.A. 43°18N 73°35W 113 D11
Hudson Str. Canada 62°0N 70°0W 109 C13
Hue Vietnam 16°30N 107°35E 83 B2
Huelva Spain 37°18N 6°57W 69 D2
Huesca Spain 42°8N 0°25W 69 A5
Hugh Town U.K. 49°55N 6°19W 27 H1
Hughenden Australia 20°52S 144°10E 98 E7
Hugli → India 21°56N 88°4E 85 J16
Huila, Nevado del Colombia 3°0N 76°0W 120 B2
Huize China 26°24N 103°15E 80 D5
Hull = Kingston upon Hull U.K. 53°45N 0°21W 23 E8
Hull Canada 45°26N 75°43W 113 C10
Hull → U.K. 53°44N 0°20W 23 E8
Hullavington U.K. 51°32N 2°8W 24 C4
Hulme End U.K. 53°8N 1°50W 23 F5
Hulun Nur China 49°0N 117°30E 81 B6
Humacao Puerto Rico 18°9N 65°50W 115 d
Humaitá Brazil 7°35S 63°1W 120 C3
Humber → U.K. 53°42N 0°27W 23 E8
Humber, Mouth of the U.K. 53°32N 0°8E 23 E9
Humboldt Canada 52°15N 105°9W 108 D9
Humboldt → U.S.A. 39°59N 118°36W 110 B3
Humphreys Peak U.S.A. 35°21N 111°41W 110 C4
Humshaugh U.K. 55°3N 2°8W 22 B4
Húnaflói Iceland 65°50N 20°50W 63 A1
Hunan □ China 27°30N 112°0E 81 D6
Hungary ■ Europe 47°20N 19°20E 67 E10
Hungary, Plain of Europe 47°0N 20°0E 56 F10
Hungerford U.K. 51°25N 1°31W 24 D5
Hŭngnam N. Korea 39°49N 127°45E 81 C7
Hunmanby U.K. 54°10N 0°20W 22 D8
Hunsrück Germany 49°56N 7°27E 66 D4
Hunstanton U.K. 52°56N 0°29E 25 A9
Huntingdon U.K. 52°20N 0°11W 25 B8
Huntington Ind., U.S.A. 40°53N 85°30W 112 E5
Huntington W. Va., U.S.A. 38°25N 82°27W 112 F6
Huntly U.K. 57°27N 2°47W 19 H12
Huntsville Canada 45°20N 79°14W 109 E12
Huntsville Ala., U.S.A. 34°44N 86°35W 111 D9
Huntsville Tex., U.S.A. 30°43N 95°33W 111 D7
Hurghada Egypt 27°15N 33°50E 95 C12
Hurley U.S.A. 46°27N 90°11W 112 B2
Huron U.S.A. 44°22N 98°13W 110 B7
Huron, L. U.S.A. 44°30N 82°40W 112 C6
Hursley U.K. 51°2N 1°23W 24 D6
Hurstbourne Tarrant U.K. 51°17N 1°26W 24 D6
Hurstpierpoint U.K. 50°56N 0°11W 25 E8
Húsavík Iceland 66°3N 17°21W 63 A2
Husband's Bosworth U.K. 52°28N 1°4W 23 H6
Hutchinson U.S.A. 38°5N 97°56W 110 C7
Huyton U.K. 53°25N 2°51W 23 F3
Hvar Croatia 43°11N 16°28E 70 C7
Hwang Ho → China 37°55N 118°50E 81 C6
Hwange Zimbabwe 18°18S 26°30E 97 H5
Hyargas Nuur Mongolia 49°0N 93°0E 80 B4
Hyde U.K. 53°27N 2°4W 23 F4
Hyderabad India 17°22N 78°29E 84 L11
Hyderabad Pakistan 25°23N 68°24E 84 G6
Hyères France 43°8N 6°9E 68 E7
Hyères, Îs. d' France 43°0N 6°20E 68 E7
Hyndman Peak U.S.A. 43°45N 114°8W 110 B4
Hythe U.K. 51°4N 1°5E 25 D11

I

Ialomiţa → Romania 44°42N 27°51E 67 F14
Iaşi Romania 47°10N 27°40E 67 E14
Ibadan Nigeria 7°22N 3°58E 94 G6
Ibagué Colombia 4°20N 75°20W 120 B2
Ibarra Ecuador 0°21N 78°7W 120 B2
Ibb Yemen 14°2N 44°10E 88 E3
Iberian Peninsula Europe 40°0N 5°0W 56 H5
Ibiá Brazil 19°30S 46°30W 122 C1
Ibiapaba, Sa. da Brazil 4°0S 41°30W 120 C5
Ibicaraí Brazil 14°51S 39°36W 122 B3
Ibiza = Eivissa Spain 38°54N 1°26E 69 C6
Ibotirama Brazil 12°13S 43°12W 122 B2
Ibstock U.K. 52°42N 1°24W 23 G6
Ica Peru 14°0S 75°48W 120 D2
Içá → Brazil 2°55S 67°58W 120 C3
İçel Turkey 36°51N 34°36E 73 G5
Iceland ■ Europe 64°45N 19°0W 63 B2
Ichihara Japan 35°28N 140°5E 82 F7
Ichinomiya Japan 35°18N 136°48E 82 F5
Idaho □ U.S.A. 45°0N 115°0W 110 B4
Idaho Falls U.S.A. 43°30N 112°2W 110 B4
Idar-Oberstein Germany 49°43N 7°16E 66 D4
Idfû Egypt 24°55N 32°49E 95 D12
Idle → U.K. 53°27N 0°49W 23 F7
Idlib Syria 35°55N 36°36E 86 C4
Idmiston U.K. 51°9N 1°42W 24 D5
Ieper Belgium 50°51N 2°53E 65 D2
Ife Nigeria 7°30N 4°31E 94 G6
Iforas, Adrar des Africa 19°40N 1°40E 94 C5
Igarapava Brazil 20°3S 47°47W 122 D1
Igarka Russia 67°30N 86°33E 79 C10
Iglésias Italy 39°19N 8°32E 70 E3
Igloolik Canada 69°20N 81°49W 109 C11
Ignace Canada 49°30N 91°40W 112 A2
Igoumenitsa Greece 39°32N 20°18E 71 E9
Iguaçu → Brazil 25°36S 54°36W 121 E4
Iguaçu, Cat. del Brazil 25°41S 54°26W 121 E4
Iguala Mexico 18°21N 99°32W 114 D5
Iguatu Brazil 6°20S 39°18W 120 C6
Iguidi, Erg Africa 27°0N 7°0W 94 C4
Iisalmi Finland 63°32N 27°10E 63 E9
Ijebu-Ode Nigeria 6°47N 3°58E 94 G6
IJmuiden Neths. 52°28N 4°35E 65 B4
IJsselmeer Neths. 52°45N 5°20E 65 B5
Ikare Nigeria 7°32N 5°40E 94 G7
Ikaria Greece 37°35N 26°10E 71 F12
Ikeda Japan 34°1N 133°48E 82 F3
Ilagan Phil. 17°7N 121°53E 83 B4
Īlām Iran 33°36N 46°36E 86 C6
Ilchester U.K. 51°0N 2°41W 24 D3
Île-de-France □ France 49°0N 2°20E 68 B5
Ilebo Dem. Rep. of the Congo 4°17S 20°55E 96 E4
Ilesha Nigeria 7°37N 4°40E 94 G6
Ilfracombe U.K. 51°12N 4°8W 27 E5
Ilhéus Brazil 14°49S 39°2W 122 B3
Ili → Kazakhstan 45°53N 77°10E 79 E9
Iliamna L. U.S.A. 59°30N 155°0W 108 D4
Iligan Phil. 8°12N 124°13E 83 C4
Ilkeston U.K. 52°58N 1°19W 23 G6
Ilkley U.K. 53°56N 1°48W 23 E5
Illapel Chile 32°0S 71°10W 121 F2
Iller → Germany 48°23N 9°58E 66 D6
Illimani Bolivia 16°30S 67°50W 120 D3
Illinois □ U.S.A. 40°15N 89°30W 111 B92
Illinois → U.S.A. 38°58N 90°28W 111 C81
Ilmen, L. Russia 58°15N 31°10E 72 C5
Ilminster U.K. 50°55N 2°55W 24 E3
Iloilo Phil. 10°45N 122°33E 83 B4
Ilorin Nigeria 8°30N 4°35E 94 G6
Imabari Japan 34°4N 133°0E 82 F3
Imandra, L. Russia 67°30N 33°0E 72 A5
Imatra Finland 61°12N 28°48E 63 E9
Immingham U.K. 53°37N 0°13W 23 E8
Ímola Italy 44°20N 11°42E 70 B4
Imperatriz Brazil 5°30S 47°29W 120 C5
Impéria Italy 43°53N 8°3E 70 C3
Imphal India 24°48N 93°56E 85 G18
In Salah Algeria 27°10N 2°32E 94 C6
Inari Finland 68°54N 27°1E 63 D9
Inarijärvi Finland 69°0N 28°0E 63 D9
İnce Burun Turkey 42°7N 34°56E 73 F5
Incheon S. Korea 37°27N 126°40E 81 C7
Incomáti → Mozam. 25°46S 32°43E 97 K6
Indalsälven → Sweden 62°36N 17°30E 63 E7
India ■ Asia 20°0N 78°0E 84 K11
Indian Ocean 5°0S 75°0E 53 E13
Indiana U.S.A. 40°37N 79°9W 112 E8
Indiana □ U.S.A. 40°0N 86°0W 112 E4
Indianapolis U.S.A. 39°46N 86°9W 112 F4
Indigirka → Russia 70°48N 148°54E 79 B16
Indira Gandhi Canal India 28°0N 72°0E 84 F8
Indo-China Asia 15°0N 102°0E 74 G12
Indonesia ■ Asia 5°0S 115°0E 83 D3
Indore India 22°42N 75°53E 84 H9
Indre → France 47°16N 0°11E 68 C4
Indus → Pakistan 24°20N 67°47E 84 G5
İnebolu Turkey 41°55N 33°40E 73 F5
Ingatestone U.K. 51°40N 0°24E 25 C9
Ingleborough U.K. 54°10N 2°22W 22 D4
Ingleton U.K. 54°10N 2°27W 22 D4
Ingolstadt Germany 48°46N 11°26E 66 D6
Ingraj Bazar India 24°58N 88°10E 85 G16
Ingushetia □ Russia 43°20N 44°50E 73 F8
Inishbofin Ireland 53°37N 10°13W 28 D1
Inisheer Ireland 53°3N 9°32W 30 B3
Inishfree B. Ireland 55°4N 8°23W 28 A5
Inishkea North Ireland 54°9N 10°11W 28 C1
Inishkea South Ireland 54°7N 10°12W 28 C1
Inishmaan Ireland 53°5N 9°35W 30 B3
Inishmore Ireland 53°8N 9°45W 30 B3
Inishowen Pen. Ireland 55°14N 7°15W 29 A7
Inishshark Ireland 53°37N 10°16W 28 D1
Inishtrahull Ireland 55°26N 7°13W 29 A7
Inishturk Ireland 53°42N 10°7W 28 D1
Inishvickillane Ireland 52°3N 10°37W 30 D1
Inkberrow U.K. 52°13N 1°58W 24 B5
Inland Sea Japan 34°20N 133°30E 82 F3
Inn → Austria 48°35N 13°28E 66 D7
Inner Hebrides U.K. 57°0N 6°30W 18 J4
Inner Mongolia □ China 42°0N 112°0E 81 B6
Inner Sound U.K. 57°30N 5°55W 18 H6
Innerleithen U.K. 55°37N 3°4W 21 C9
Innsbruck Austria 47°16N 11°23E 66 E6
Inowrocław Poland 52°50N 18°12E 67 B10
Insein Burma 16°50N 96°5E 85 L20
Inta Russia 66°5N 60°8E 72 A11
Interlaken Switz. 46°41N 7°50E 66 E4
Inukjuak Canada 58°25N 78°15W 109 D12
Inuvik Canada 68°16N 133°40W 108 C6
Inveraray U.K. 56°14N 5°5W 20 B5
Inverbervie U.K. 56°51N 2°17W 19 J13
Invercargill N.Z. 46°24S 168°24E 99 K12
Invergordon U.K. 57°41N 4°10W 19 G9
Inverkeithing U.K. 56°2N 3°24W 21 B9
Inverness U.K. 57°29N 4°13W 19 H9
Inverurie U.K. 57°17N 2°23W 19 H13
Ioannina Greece 39°42N 20°47E 71 E9
Iona U.K. 56°20N 6°25W 20 B3
Ionia U.S.A. 42°59N 85°4W 112 D5
Ionian Is. Greece 38°40N 20°0E 71 E9
Ionian Sea Medit. S. 37°30N 17°30E 71 E7
Ios Greece 36°41N 25°20E 71 F11
Iowa □ U.S.A. 42°18N 93°30W 111 B8
Iowa City U.S.A. 41°40N 91°32W 111 B81
Ipameri Brazil 17°44S 48°9W 122 C1
Ipatinga Brazil 19°32S 42°30W 122 C2
Ipiales Colombia 0°50N 77°37W 120 B2
Ipoh Malaysia 4°35N 101°5E 83 C2
Ipswich Australia 27°35S 152°40E 98 F9
Ipswich U.K. 52°4N 1°10E 25 B11
Iqaluit Canada 63°44N 68°31W 109 C13
Iquique Chile 20°19S 70°5W 120 E2
Iquitos Peru 3°45S 73°10W 120 C2
Iraklio Greece 35°20N 25°12E 71 G11
Iran ■ Asia 33°0N 53°0E 87 C8
Irapuato Mexico 20°41N 101°28W 114 C4
Iraq ■ Asia 33°0N 44°0E 86 C5
Irazú, Vol. Costa Rica 10°10N 84°20W 115 E8
Irbil Iraq 36°15N 44°5E 86 B6
Irchester U.K. 52°18N 0°39W 25 B7
Ireland ■ Europe 53°50N 7°52W 64 E2
Ireland's Eye Ireland 53°24N 6°4W 31 B10
Iringa Tanzania 7°48S 35°43E 96 F7
Irish Republic ■ Europe 53°50N 7°52W 64 E2
Irish Sea Europe 53°38N 4°48W 64 E4
Irkutsk Russia 52°18N 104°20E 79 D12
Irlam U.K. 53°26N 2°26W 23 F4
Iron Gate Europe 44°44N 22°30E 67 F12
Iron Mountain U.S.A. 45°49N 88°4W 112 C3
Ironbridge U.K. 52°38N 2°30W 23 G3
Ironton U.S.A. 38°32N 82°41W 112 F6
Ironwood U.S.A. 46°27N 90°9W 112 B2
Irrawaddy → Burma 15°50N 95°6E 85 M19
Irt → U.K. 54°23N 3°26W 22 D2
Irthlingborough U.K. 52°20N 0°37W 25 B7
Irtysh → Russia 61°4N 68°52E 79 C8
Irún Spain 43°20N 1°52W 69 A5
Irvine U.K. 55°37N 4°41W 20 C6
Irvinestown U.K. 54°28N 7°39W 28 C6
Isabela Puerto Rico 18°30N 67°2W 115 d
Ísafjörður Iceland 66°5N 23°9W 63 A1
Isar → Germany 48°48N 12°57E 66 D7
Íschia Italy 40°44N 13°57E 70 D5
Isère → France 44°59N 4°51E 68 D6
Ishinomaki Japan 38°32N 141°20E 82 D7
Ishpeming U.S.A. 46°29N 87°40W 112 B4
Isiro Dem. Rep. of the Congo 2°53N 27°40E 96 D5
İskenderun Turkey 36°32N 36°10E 73 G6
Isla → U.K. 56°32N 3°20W 21 A9
Islamabad Pakistan 33°40N 73°10E 84 C8
Island L. Canada 53°47N 94°25W 108 D10
Island Pond U.S.A. 44°49N 71°53W 113 C12
Islay U.K. 55°46N 6°10W 20 C3
Isleham U.K. 52°21N 0°25E 25 B9
Islington □ U.K. 51°33N 0°5W 25 C8
Islip U.K. 51°50N 1°12W 24 C6
Ismâ'ilîya Egypt 30°37N 32°18E 95 B12
Isna Egypt 25°17N 32°30E 95 C12
Isparta Turkey 37°47N 30°30E 73 G5
Israel ■ Asia 32°0N 34°50E 86 C3
Issoire France 45°32N 3°15E 68 D5
Issyk Kul Kyrgyzstan 42°25N 77°15E 79 E9
İstanbul Turkey 41°0N 28°58E 73 F4
Istra Croatia 45°10N 14°0E 70 B5
Istres France 43°31N 4°59E 68 E6
Itaberaba Brazil 12°32S 40°18W 122 B2
Itabira Brazil 19°37S 43°13W 122 C2
Itabuna Brazil 14°48S 39°16W 122 B3
Itacoatiara Brazil 3°8S 58°25W 120 C4
Itajaí Brazil 27°50S 48°39W 121 E5
Itajubá Brazil 22°24S 45°30W 122 D1
Italy ■ Europe 42°0N 13°0E 70 C5
Itaperuna Brazil 21°10S 41°54W 122 D2
Itapetinga Brazil 15°15S 40°15W 122 C2
Itapetininga Brazil 23°36S 48°7W 122 D1
Itapicuru → Brazil 11°47S 37°32W 122 B3
Itaquari Brazil 20°20S 40°25W 122 D2
Itararé Brazil 24°6S 49°23W 122 D1
Itaúna Brazil 20°4S 44°34W 122 D2
Itchen → U.K. 50°55N 1°22W 24 E6
Ithaca U.S.A. 42°27N 76°30W 112 D9
Ittoqqortoormiit Greenland 70°20N 23°0W 54 B6
Itu Brazil 23°17S 47°15W 122 D1
Ivanava Belarus 52°7N 25°29E 67 B13
Ivano-Frankivsk Ukraine 48°40N 24°40E 67 D13
Ivanovo Russia 57°5N 41°0E 72 C7
Ivinghoe U.K. 51°50N 0°37W 25 C7
Ivory Coast ■ Africa 7°30N 5°0W 94 G4
Ivujivik Canada 62°24N 77°55W 109 C12
Ivybridge U.K. 50°23N 3°56W 27 G6
Iwaki Japan 37°3N 140°55E 82 E7
Iwakuni Japan 34°15N 132°8E 82 F3
Iwo Nigeria 7°39N 4°9E 94 G6
Ixworth U.K. 52°18N 0°51E 25 B10
Izhevsk Russia 56°51N 53°14E 72 C9
Izmayil Ukraine 45°22N 28°46E 73 E4
İzmir Turkey 38°25N 27°8E 73 G4
İznik Gölü Turkey 40°27N 29°30E 73 F4
Izumi-Sano Japan 34°23N 135°18E 82 F4

J

Jabalpur India 23°9N 79°58E 84 H11
Jaboatão Brazil 8°7S 35°1W 120 C6
Jaboticabal Brazil 21°15S 48°17W 122 D1
Jacareí Brazil 23°20S 46°0W 122 D1
Jackson Barbados 13°7N 59°36W 115 g
Jackson Ky., U.S.A. 37°33N 83°23W 112 G6
Jackson Mich., U.S.A. 42°15N 84°24W 112 D5
Jackson Miss., U.S.A. 32°18N 90°12W 111 D8
Jackson Mo., U.S.A. 37°23N 89°40W 112 G3
Jackson Tenn., U.S.A. 35°37N 88°49W 111 C9
Jacksonville Fla., U.S.A. 30°20N 81°39W 111 D10
Jacksonville Ill., U.S.A. 39°44N 90°14W 112 F2
Jacmel Haiti 18°14N 72°32W 115 D10
Jacobabad Pakistan 28°20N 68°29E 84 E6
Jacobina Brazil 11°11S 40°30W 122 B2
Jaén Spain 37°44N 3°43W 69 D4
Jaffna Sri Lanka 9°45N 80°2E 84 Q12
Jahrom Iran 28°30N 53°31E 87 D8
Jaipur India 27°0N 75°50E 84 F9
Jakarta Indonesia 6°9S 106°52E 83 D2
Jalālābād Afghan. 34°30N 70°29E 87 C12
Jalgaon India 21°0N 75°42E 84 J9
Jalna India 19°48N 75°38E 84 K9
Jalpaiguri India 26°32N 88°46E 85 F16
Jaluit I. Marshall Is. 6°0N 169°30E 102 G8
Jamaica ■ W. Indies 18°10N 77°30W 114 a
Jamalpur Bangla. 24°52N 89°56E 85 G16
Jamalpur India 25°18N 86°28E 85 G15
Jambi Indonesia 1°38S 103°30E 83 D2
James → U.S.A. 42°52N 97°18W 111 B7
James B. Canada 54°0N 80°0W 109 D12
Jamestown N. Dak., U.S.A. 46°54N 98°42W 110 A7
Jamestown N.Y., U.S.A. 42°6N 79°14W 112 D8
Jammu India 32°43N 74°54E 84 C9
Jammu & Kashmir □ India 34°25N 77°0E 84 B10
Jamnagar India 22°30N 70°6E 84 H7
Jamshedpur India 22°44N 86°12E 85 H15
Jan Mayen Arctic 71°0N 9°0W 54 B7
Janaúba Brazil 15°48S 43°19W 122 C2
Janesville U.S.A. 42°41N 89°1W 112 D3
Januária Brazil 15°25S 44°25W 122 C2
Jaora India 23°40N 75°10E 84 H9
Japan ■ Asia 36°0N 136°0E 82 F5
Japan, Sea of Asia 40°0N 135°0E 82 D4
Japan Trench Pac. Oc. 32°0N 142°0E 102 D6
Japurá → Brazil 3°8S 65°46W 120 C3
Jari → Brazil 1°9S 51°54W 120 C4
Jarrow U.K. 54°59N 1°28W 22 C6
Jarvis I. Pac. Oc. 0°15S 160°5W 103 H12
Jāsk Iran 25°38N 57°45E 87 E9
Jasper Canada 52°55N 118°5W 108 D8
Jaú Brazil 22°10S 48°30W 122 D1
Jauja Peru 11°45S 75°15W 120 D2
Jaunpur India 25°46N 82°44E 85 G13
Java Indonesia 7°0S 110°0E 83 D3
Java Sea Indonesia 4°35S 107°15E 83 D2
Java Trench Ind. Oc. 9°0S 105°0E 83 D2
Jaya, Puncak Indonesia 3°57S 137°17E 83 D5
Jebel, Bahr el → Sudan 9°30N 30°25E 95 G12
Jedburgh U.K. 55°29N 2°33W 21 D10
Jedda Si. Arabia 21°29N 39°10E 86 F4
Jeffersonville U.S.A. 38°17N 85°44W 112 F5
Jeju-do S. Korea 33°29N 126°34E 81 C7
Jelenia Góra Poland 50°50N 15°45E 66 C8
Jelgava Latvia 56°41N 23°49E 63 F8
Jena Germany 50°54N 11°35E 66 C6
Jeonju S. Korea 35°50N 127°4E 81 C7
Jequié Brazil 13°51S 40°5W 122 B2
Jequitinhonha Brazil 16°30S 41°0W 122 C2
Jequitinhonha → Brazil 15°51S 38°53W 122 C3
Jérémie Haiti 18°40N 74°10W 115 D10
Jerez de la Frontera Spain 36°41N 6°7W 69 D2
Jersey U.K. 49°11N 2°7W 27 J9
Jersey City U.S.A. 40°42N 74°4W 113 E10
Jerseyville U.S.A. 39°7N 90°20W 112 F2
Jerusalem Israel/West Bank 31°47N 35°10E 86 D3
Jervaulx U.K. 54°16N 1°43W 22 D5
Jessore Bangla. 23°10N 89°10E 85 H16
Jhang Maghiana Pakistan 31°15N 72°22E 84 D8
Jhansi India 25°30N 78°36E 84 G11
Jharkhand □ India 24°0N 85°50E 85 H14
Jhelum Pakistan 33°0N 73°45E 84 C8
Jhelum → Pakistan 31°20N 72°10E 84 D8
Jiamusi China 46°40N 130°26E 81 B8
Ji'an China 27°6N 114°59E 81 D6
Jiangmen China 22°32N 113°0E 81 D6
Jiangsu □ China 33°0N 120°0E 81 C7
Jiangxi □ China 27°30N 116°0E 81 D6
Jiaxing China 30°49N 120°45E 81 C7
Jihlava → Czech Rep. 48°55N 16°36E 67 D9
Jijiga Ethiopia 9°20N 42°50E 88 F3
Jilin China 43°44N 126°30E 81 B7
Jilin □ China 44°0N 127°0E 81 B7
Jima Ethiopia 7°40N 36°47E 88 F2
Jiménez Mexico 27°8N 104°54W 114 B4
Jinan China 36°38N 117°1E 81 C6
Jinchang China 38°30N 102°10E 80 C5
Jincheng China 35°29N 112°50E 81 C6
Jingdezhen China 29°20N 117°11E 81 D6
Jinggu China 23°35N 100°41E 80 D5
Jingmen China 31°0N 112°10E 81 C6
Jinhua China 29°8N 119°38E 81 D6
Jining Nei Monggol Zizhiqu, China 41°5N 113°0E 81 B6
Jining Shandong, China 35°22N 116°34E 81 C6
Jinja Uganda 0°25N 33°12E 96 D6
Jinxi China 40°52N 120°50E 81 B7
Jinzhou China 41°5N 121°3E 81 B7
Jipijapa Ecuador 1°0S 80°40W 120 C1
Jishou China 28°21N 109°43E 81 D5
Jiujiang China 29°42N 115°58E 81 D6
Jiwani Pakistan 25°1N 61°44E 87 E10
Jixi China 45°20N 130°50E 81 B8
Jīzān Si. Arabia 17°0N 42°20E 88 D3
Jizzakh Uzbekistan 40°6N 67°50E 87 A11
João Pessoa Brazil 7°10S 34°52W 120 C6
Jodhpur India 26°23N 73°8E 84 F8
Joensuu Finland 62°37N 29°49E 63 E9
Johannesburg S. Africa 26°11S 28°2E 97 K5
John Crow Mts. Jamaica 18°5N 76°25W 114 a
John Day → U.S.A. 45°44N 120°39W 110 A2
John o' Groats U.K. 58°38N 3°4W 19 E11
Johnson City U.S.A. 36°19N 82°21W 111 C10
Johnston I. Pac. Oc. 17°10N 169°8W 103 F11
Johnstone U.K. 55°49N 4°31W 20 C6
Johnstown U.S.A. 40°20N 78°55W 112 E8
Johor Bahru Malaysia 1°28N 103°46E 83 C2
Joinville Brazil 26°15S 48°55W 121 E5
Joliet U.S.A. 41°32N 88°5W 112 E3
Joliette Canada 46°3N 73°24W 109 E12
Jolo Phil. 6°0N 121°0E 83 C4
Jones Sound Canada 76°0N 85°0W 109 B11
Jonesboro U.S.A. 35°50N 90°42W 111 C8
Jönköping Sweden 57°45N 14°8E 63 F6
Jonquière Canada 48°27N 71°14W 113 A12
Joplin U.S.A. 37°6N 94°31W 111 C8
Jordan ■ Asia 31°0N 36°0E 86 D4
Jordan → Asia 31°48N 35°32E 86 D3
Jos Nigeria 9°53N 8°51E 94 G7
Joseph Bonaparte G. Australia 14°35S 128°50E 98 C4
Jost Van Dyke I. Br. Virgin Is. 18°29N 64°47W 115 e
Jotunheimen Norway 61°35N 8°25E 63 E5
Jowzjān □ Afghan. 36°10N 66°0E 87 B11
Juan de Fuca, Str of. Canada 48°15N 124°0W 110 A2
Juan Fernández, Arch. de Pac. Oc. 33°50S 80°0W 103 L20
Juàzeiro Brazil 9°30S 40°30W 122 A2
Juàzeiro do Norte Brazil 7°10S 39°18W 120 C6
Jūbā Sudan 4°50N 31°35E 95 H12
Juba → Somali Rep. 1°30N 42°35E 88 G3
Juchitán de Zaragoza Mexico 16°26N 95°1W 114 D5
Juiz de Fora Brazil 21°43S 43°19W 122 D2
Juliaca Peru 15°25S 70°10W 120 D2
Julianatop Suriname 3°40N 56°30W 120 B4
Jullundur India 31°20N 75°40E 84 D9
Junagadh India 21°30N 70°30E 84 J7
Jundiaí Brazil 24°30S 47°0W 122 D1
Juneau U.S.A. 58°18N 134°25W 108 D6
Junín Argentina 34°33S 60°57W 121 F3
Jur, Nahr el → Sudan 8°45N 29°15E 95 G11
Jura Europe 46°40N 6°5E 68 C6
Jura U.K. 56°0N 5°50W 20 C4
Jura, Sd. of U.K. 55°57N 5°45W 20 C4
Juruá → Brazil 2°37S 65°44W 120 C3
Juruena → Brazil 7°20S 58°3W 120 C4
Juticalpa Honduras 14°40N 86°12W 114 E7
Jutland Denmark 56°25N 9°30E 63 F5
Juventud, I. de la Cuba 21°40N 82°40W 115 C8
Jyväskylä Finland 62°14N 25°50E 63 E9

K

K2 Pakistan 35°58N 76°32E 84 B10
Kabardino-Balkaria □ Russia 43°30N 43°30E 73 F7
Kābul Afghan. 34°28N 69°11E 87 C12
Kabwe Zambia 14°30S 28°29E 97 G5
Kachchh, Gulf of India 22°50N 69°15E 84 H6
Kachchh, Rann of India 24°0N 70°0E 84 H7
Kachin □ Burma 26°0N 97°30E 85 G20
Kaçkar Turkey 40°45N 41°10E 73 F7
Kadavu Fiji 19°0S 178°15E 99 E14
Kade Ghana 6°7N 0°56W 94 G5
Kadoma Zimbabwe 18°20S 29°52E 97 H5
Kaduna Nigeria 10°30N 7°21E 94 F7
Kaesŏng N. Korea 37°58N 126°35E 81 C7
Kafue → Zambia 15°30S 29°0E 97 H5
Kaga Bandoro C.A.R. 7°0N 19°10E 96 C3
Kagera → Uganda 0°57S 31°47E 96 E6
Kagoshima Japan 31°35N 130°33E 82 H2
Kaho'olawe U.S.A. 20°33N 156°37W 110 H16
Kahramanmaraş Turkey 37°37N 36°53E 73 G6
Kai, Kepulauan Indonesia 5°55S 132°45E 83 D5
Kaieteur Falls Guyana 5°1N 59°10W 120 B4
Kaifeng China 34°48N 114°21E 81 C6
Kailua U.S.A. 19°39N 155°59W 110 J17
Kainji Res. Nigeria 10°1N 4°40E 94 F6
Kairouan Tunisia 35°45N 10°5E 95 A8
Kaiserslautern Germany 49°26N 7°45E 66 D4
Kaitaia N.Z. 35°8S 173°17E 99 H13
Kaiyuan China 23°40N 103°12E 80 D5
Kajaani Finland 64°17N 27°46E 63 E9
Kajabbi Australia 20°0S 140°1E 98 E7
Kakamega Kenya 0°20N 34°46E 96 D6
Kakhovka Res. Ukraine 47°5N 34°0E 73 E5
Kakinada India 16°57N 82°11E 85 L13
Kalaallit Nunaat = Greenland ☒ N. Amer. 66°0N 45°0W 54 C5
Kalahari Africa 24°0S 21°30E 97 J4
Kalamata Greece 37°3N 22°10E 71 F10
Kalamazoo U.S.A. 42°17N 85°35W 112 D5
Kalamazoo → U.S.A. 42°40N 86°10W 112 D4
Kalemie Dem. Rep. of the Congo 5°55S 29°9E 96 F5
Kalgoorlie-Boulder Australia 30°40S 121°22E 98 G3
Kalimantan Indonesia 0°0 114°0E 83 D3
Kálimnos Greece 37°0N 27°0E 71 F12
Kaliningrad Russia 54°42N 20°32E 63 G8
Kalispell U.S.A. 48°12N 114°19W 110 A4
Kalisz Poland 51°45N 18°8E 67 C10
Kalkaska U.S.A. 44°44N 85°11W 112 C5
Kallsjön Sweden 63°38N 13°0E 63 E6
Kalmar Sweden 56°40N 16°20E 63 F7
Kalmykia □ Russia 46°5N 46°1E 73 E8
Kaluga Russia 54°35N 36°10E 72 D6
Kalutara Sri Lanka 6°35N 80°0E 84 R12
Kalyan India 19°15N 73°9E 84 K8
Kama → Russia 55°45N 52°0E 72 C9
Kamchatka Pen. Russia 57°0N 160°0E 79 D18
Kamina Dem. Rep. of the Congo 8°45S 25°0E 96 F5
Kamloops Canada 50°40N 120°20W 108 D7
Kampala Uganda 0°20N 32°30E 96 D6
Kampong Saom Cambodia 10°38N 103°30E 83 B2
Kamyanets-Podilskyy Ukraine 48°45N 26°40E 67 D14
Kamyshin Russia 50°10N 45°24E 73 D8
Kananga Dem. Rep. of the Congo 5°55S 22°18E 96 F4
Kanash Russia 55°30N 47°32E 72 C8
Kanawha → U.S.A. 38°50N 82°9W 112 F6
Kanazawa Japan 36°30N 136°38E 82 E5
Kanchenjunga Nepal 27°50N 88°10E 85 F16
Kanchipuram India 12°52N 79°45E 84 N11
Kandalaksha Russia 67°9N 32°30E 72 A5
Kandalaksha, G. of Russia 66°0N 35°0E 72 A6
Kandanghaur Indonesia 6°21S 108°6E 83 D2
Kandi Benin 11°7N 2°55E 94 F6
Kandy Sri Lanka 7°18N 80°43E 84 R12

Kane

La Junta

Kane U.S.A. 41°40N 78°49W 112 E8
Kāne'ohe U.S.A. 21°25N 157°48W 110 H16
Kangaroo I. Australia 35°45S 137°0E 98 H6
Kangiqsualujjuaq Canada 58°30N 65°59W 109 D13
Kangiqsujuaq Canada 61°30N 72°0W 109 C12
Kangirsuk Canada 60°0N 70°0W 109 D13
Kanin Pen. Russia 68°0N 45°0E 72 A8
Kankakee U.S.A. 41°7N 87°52W 112 E4
Kankakee → U.S.A. 41°23N 88°15W 112 E3
Kankan Guinea 10°23N 9°15W 94 F4
Kano Nigeria 12°2N 8°30E 94 F7
Kanpur India 26°28N 80°20E 84 F12
Kansas □ U.S.A. 38°30N 99°0W 110 C7
Kansas → U.S.A. 39°7N 94°37W 111 C8
Kansas City U.S.A. 39°6N 94°35W 111 C8
Kanturk Ireland 52°11N 8°54W 30 D5
Kanye Botswana 24°55S 25°28E 97 J5
Kaohsiung Taiwan 22°35N 120°16E 81 D7
Kaolack Senegal 14°5N 16°8W 94 F2
Kapaa U.S.A. 22°5N 159°19W 110 G15
Kapiri Mposhi Zambia 13°59S 28°43E 97 G5
Kāpisā □ Afghan. 35°0N 69°20E 87 C12
Kaposvár Hungary 46°25N 17°47E 67 E9
Kaptai L. Bangla. 22°40N 92°20E 85 H18
Kapuas → Indonesia 0°25S 109°20E 83 D2
Kapuskasing Canada 49°25N 82°30W 112 A6
Kara Bogaz Gol Turkmenistan 41°0N 53°30E 87 A8
Kara Kum Turkmenistan 39°30N 60°0E 87 B9
Kara Sea Russia 75°0N 70°0E 79 B8
Karabük Turkey 41°12N 32°37E 73 F5
Karachey-Cherkessia □
  Russia 43°40N 41°30E 73 F7
Karachi Pakistan 24°50N 67°0E 84 G5
Karaganda Kazakhstan 49°50N 73°10E 79 E9
Karagiye Depression
  Kazakhstan 43°27N 51°45E 73 F9
Karakalpakstan □ Uzbekistan 43°0N 58°0E 87 A9
Karakoram Pakistan 35°30N 77°0E 84 B10
Karaman Turkey 37°14N 33°13E 73 G5
Karamay China 45°30N 84°58E 80 B3
Karatax Shan China 35°57N 81°0E 80 C3
Karawang Indonesia 6°30S 107°15E 83 D2
Karayazı Turkey 39°41N 42°9E 73 G7
Karbalā' Iraq 32°36N 44°3E 86 C6
Karelia □ Russia 65°30N 32°30E 72 A5
Kariba, L. Zimbabwe 16°40S 28°25E 97 H5
Kariba Dam Zimbabwe 16°30S 28°35E 97 H5
Karimata, Str. of Indonesia 2°0S 108°40E 83 D2
Karlovac Croatia 45°31N 15°36E 70 B6
Karlskrona Sweden 56°10N 15°35E 63 F7
Karlsruhe Germany 49°0N 8°23E 66 D5
Karlstad Sweden 59°23N 13°30E 63 F6
Karnak Egypt 25°43N 32°39E 95 C12
Karnal India 29°42N 77°2E 84 E10
Karnataka □ India 13°15N 77°0E 84 N10
Kärnten □ Austria 46°52N 13°30E 66 E8
Karpathos Greece 35°37N 27°10E 71 G12
Kars Turkey 40°40N 43°5E 73 F7
Karwar India 14°55N 74°13E 84 M9
Kasai → Dem. Rep. of the Congo 3°30S 16°10E 96 E3
Kasaragod India 12°30N 74°58E 84 N9
Kashân Iran 34°5N 51°30E 87 C7
Kashi China 39°30N 76°2E 80 C2
Kasongo Dem. Rep. of the Congo 4°30S 26°33E 96 E5
Kassalâ Sudan 15°30N 36°0E 95 E13
Kassel Germany 51°18N 9°26E 66 C5
Kastamonu Turkey 41°25N 33°43E 73 F5
Kasur Pakistan 31°5N 74°25E 84 D9
Katanga □ Dem. Rep. of the Congo 8°0S 25°0E 96 F4
Kathiawar India 22°20N 71°0E 84 H7
Katihar India 25°34N 87°36E 85 G15
Katima Mulilo Zambia 17°28S 24°13E 97 H4
Katiola Ivory C. 8°10N 5°10W 94 G4
Katmandu Nepal 27°45N 85°20E 85 F14
Katowice Poland 50°17N 19°5E 67 C10
Katrine, L. U.K. 56°15N 4°30W 20 B7
Katsina Nigeria 13°0N 7°32E 94 F7
Kattegat Denmark 56°40N 11°0E 63 F6
Kaua'i U.S.A. 22°3N 159°30W 110 H15
Kauai Channel U.S.A. 21°45N 158°50W 110 H15
Kaukauna U.S.A. 44°17N 88°17W 112 C3
Kaunakakai U.S.A. 21°6N 157°1W 110 H16
Kaunas Lithuania 54°54N 23°54E 63 G8
Kavala Greece 40°57N 24°28E 71 D11
Kavieng Papua N. G. 2°36S 150°51E 98 A9
Kawagoe Japan 35°55N 139°29E 82 F6
Kawaguchi Japan 35°52N 139°45E 82 F6
Kawardha India 22°0N 81°17E 85 J12
Kawasaki Japan 35°31N 139°43E 82 F6
Kawawachikamach
  Canada 54°48N 66°50W 109 D13
Kayah □ Burma 19°15N 97°15E 85 K20
Kayes Mali 14°25N 11°30W 94 F3
Kayin □ Burma 18°0N 97°30E 85 L20
Kayseri Turkey 38°45N 35°30E 73 G6
Kazakhstan ■ Asia 50°0N 70°0E 79 E9
Kazan Russia 55°50N 49°10E 72 C8
Kazan-Rettō Pac. Oc. 25°0N 141°0E 102 E6
Kazanlük Bulgaria 42°38N 25°20E 71 C11
Kea Greece 37°35N 24°22E 71 F11
Kea U.K. 50°14N 5°6W 27 G3
Keady U.K. 54°15N 6°42W 29 C8
Kearney U.S.A. 40°42N 99°5W 110 B7
Keban Turkey 38°50N 38°50E 73 G6
Keban Baraji Turkey 38°41N 38°33E 73 G6
Kebnekaise Sweden 67°53N 18°33E 63 D7
Kebri Dehar Ethiopia 6°45N 44°17E 88 F3
Kebumen Indonesia 7°42S 109°40E 83 D2
Kecskemét Hungary 46°57N 19°42E 67 E10
Kediri Indonesia 7°51S 112°1E 83 D3
Keelby U.K. 53°35N 0°16W 23 E8
Keele U.K. 53°0N 2°17W 23 F4
Keene U.S.A. 42°56N 72°17W 113 D11
Keeper Hill Ireland 52°45N 8°16W 30 C6
Keetmanshoop Namibia 26°35S 18°8E 97 K3
Kefalonia Greece 38°15N 20°30E 71 E9
Keflavík Iceland 64°2N 22°35W 63 B1

Kegworth U.K. 52°50N 1°17W 23 G6
Keighley U.K. 53°52N 1°54W 23 E5
Keith U.K. 57°32N 2°57W 19 G12
Keld U.K. 54°24N 2°10W 22 D4
Kelkit → Turkey 40°45N 36°32E 73 F6
Kellett, C. Canada 72°0N 126°0W 109 B7
Kellogg U.S.A. 47°32N 116°7W 110 A3
Kelowna Canada 49°50N 119°25W 108 E8
Kelsale U.K. 52°14N 1°31E 25 B12
Kelsall U.K. 53°13N 2°43W 23 F3
Kelso U.K. 55°36N 2°26W 21 C11
Kelvedon U.K. 51°50N 0°43E 25 C10
Kem Russia 65°0N 34°38E 72 B5
Kemble U.K. 51°40N 1°59W 24 C5
Kemerovo Russia 55°20N 86°5E 79 D10
Kemi Finland 65°44N 24°34E 63 D8
Kemijoki → Finland 65°47N 24°32E 63 D8
Kemp Land Antarctica 69°0S 55°0E 55 C5
Kempsey U.K. 52°8N 2°12W 24 B4
Kempston U.K. 52°7N 0°30W 25 B7
Kempten Germany 47°45N 10°17E 66 E6
Kenai U.S.A. 60°33N 151°16W 108 C4
Kendari Indonesia 3°50S 122°30E 83 D4
Kendal U.K. 54°20N 2°44W 22 D3
Kenema S. Leone 7°50N 11°14W 94 G3
Kenilworth U.K. 52°21N 1°34W 24 B5
Kenitra Morocco 34°15N 6°40W 94 B4
Kenmare Ireland 51°53N 9°36W 30 E3
Kenmare River Ireland 51°48N 9°51W 30 E2
Kennet → U.K. 51°27N 0°57W 25 D7
Kennewick U.S.A. 46°12N 119°7W 110 A3
Kenninghall U.K. 52°26N 1°0E 25 B11
Kenninghall U.K. 52°26N 1°0E 25 B11
Kenogami → Canada 51°6N 84°28W 109 D11
Kenora Canada 49°47N 94°29W 108 E10
Kenosha U.S.A. 42°35N 87°49W 112 E4
Kent U.S.A. 41°9N 81°22W 112 E7
Kent □ U.K. 51°12N 0°40E 25 D10
Kent Pen. Canada 68°30N 107°0W 108 C9
Kentisbeare U.K. 50°51N 3°20W 27 F7
Kenton U.S.A. 40°39N 83°37W 112 E6
Kentucky □ U.S.A. 37°0N 84°0W 112 G5
Kentucky → U.S.A. 38°41N 85°11W 112 F5
Kentville Canada 45°6N 64°29W 109 E13
Kenya ■ Africa 1°0N 38°0E 96 D7
Kenya, Mt. Kenya 0°10S 37°18E 96 E7
Kerala □ India 11°0N 76°15E 84 P10
Kerch Ukraine 45°20N 36°20E 73 E6
Kerguelen Ind. Oc. 49°15S 69°10E 53 G13
Kericho Kenya 0°22S 35°15E 96 E7
Kerinci Indonesia 1°40S 101°15E 83 D2
Kermadec Is. Pac. Oc. 30°0S 178°15W 99 G15
Kermadec Trench Pac. Oc. 30°30S 176°0W 99 G15
Kermān Iran 30°15N 57°1E 87 D9
Kermānshāh Iran 34°23N 47°0E 86 C6
Kerrera Canada 56°24N 5°33W 20 B4
Kerrobert Canada 51°56N 109°8W 108 D9
Kerry □ Ireland 52°7N 9°35W 30 D3
Kerry Hd. Ireland 52°25N 9°56W 30 D3
Kerulen → Asia 48°48N 117°0E 81 B6
Kessingland U.K. 52°26N 1°43E 25 B12
Keswick U.K. 54°36N 3°8W 22 C2
Ketchikan U.S.A. 55°21N 131°39W 108 D6
Kettering U.S.A. 52°24N 0°43W 25 B7
Kettle Ness U.K. 54°33N 0°42W 22 C7
Kettlewell U.K. 54°9N 2°3W 22 D4
Kewaunee U.S.A. 44°27N 87°31W 112 C4
Keweenaw B. U.S.A. 47°0N 88°15W 112 B3
Keweenaw Pen. U.S.A. 47°15N 88°15W 112 B3
Keweenaw Pt. U.S.A. 47°25N 87°43W 112 B4
Kexby U.K. 53°22N 0°42W 23 F7
Key West U.S.A. 24°33N 81°48W 111 F10
Keyingham U.K. 53°43N 0°7W 23 E8
Keymer U.K. 50°55N 0°7W 25 E8
Keynsham U.K. 51°24N 2°29W 24 D4
Keyser U.S.A. 39°26N 78°59W 112 F8
Keyworth U.K. 52°52N 1°5W 23 G6
Khabarovsk Russia 48°30N 135°5E 79 E15
Khairpur Pakistan 27°32N 68°49E 84 F6
Khambhat India 22°23N 72°33E 84 H8
Khambhat, G. of India 20°45N 72°30E 84 J8
Khamis Mushayt S. Arabia 18°18N 42°44E 88 D3
Khandyga Russia 62°42N 135°35E 79 C15
Khanewal Pakistan 30°20N 71°55E 84 D7
Kharagpur India 22°20N 87°25E 85 H15
Kharg Iran 29°15N 50°28E 86 D7
Khârga, El Wâhât-el Egypt 25°10N 30°35E 95 C12
Kharkov Ukraine 49°58N 36°20E 73 E6
Khartoum Sudan 15°31N 32°35E 95 E12
Khaskovo Bulgaria 41°56N 25°30E 71 D11
Khatanga Russia 72°0N 102°20E 79 B12
Khemisset Morocco 33°50N 6°1W 94 B4
Khenchela Algeria 35°28N 7°11E 94 A7
Kherson Ukraine 46°35N 32°35E 73 E5
Khmelnytskyy Ukraine 49°23N 27°0E 67 D14
Khojak Pass Afghan. 30°51N 66°34E 87 D11
Kholm Afghan. 36°45N 67°40E 87 B11
Khon Kaen Thailand 16°30N 102°47E 83 B2
Khorrāmābād Iran 33°30N 48°25E 86 C7
Khorrāmshahr Iran 30°29N 48°15E 86 D7
Khouribga Morocco 32°58N 6°57W 94 B4
Khudzhand Tajikistan 40°17N 69°37E 87 B12
Khulna Bangla. 22°45N 89°34E 85 H16
Khulna □ Bangla. 22°25N 89°35E 85 H16
Khunjerab Pass Asia 36°40N 75°25E 84 A9
Khushab Pakistan 32°20N 72°20E 84 C8
Khuzdar Pakistan 27°52N 66°30E 84 F5
Khvoy Iran 38°35N 45°0E 86 B6
Khyber Pass Afghan. 34°10N 71°8E 84 B7
Kibworth Beauchamp U.K. 52°33N 0°59W 23 G7
Kicking Horse Pass Canada 51°28N 116°16W 108 D8
Kidderminster U.K. 52°24N 2°15W 24 B4
Kidlington U.K. 51°50N 1°15W 24 C6
Kidsgrove U.K. 53°5N 2°14W 23 F4
Kidstones U.K. 54°13N 2°2W 22 D4
Kidwelly U.K. 51°44N 4°18W 26 D5
Kiel Germany 54°19N 10°8E 66 A6
Kiel Canal = Nord-Ostsee-Kanal
  Germany 54°12N 9°32E 66 A5

Kielce Poland 50°52N 20°42E 67 C11
Kielder U.K. 55°14N 2°35W 22 B3
Kieler Bucht Germany 54°35N 10°25E 66 A6
Kiev Ukraine 50°30N 30°28E 67 C16
Kigali Rwanda 1°59S 30°4E 96 E6
Kigoma-Ujiji Tanzania 4°55S 29°36E 96 E5
Kikwit Dem. Rep. of the Congo 5°0S 18°45E 96 E3
Kīlauea U.S.A. 19°25N 155°17W 110 J17
Kilbirnie U.K. 55°46N 4°41W 20 C6
Kilbrannan Sd. U.K. 55°37N 5°26W 20 C5
Kildare Ireland 53°9N 6°55W 31 B9
Kildare □ Ireland 53°10N 6°50W 31 B9
Kilfinnane Ireland 52°21N 8°28W 30 D6
Kilham U.K. 54°4N 0°23W 22 D8
Kilifi Kenya 3°40S 39°48E 96 E7
Kilimanjaro Tanzania 3°7S 37°20E 96 E7
Kilindini Kenya 4°4S 39°40E 96 E7
Kilkee Ireland 52°41N 9°39W 30 C3
Kilkeel U.K. 54°4N 6°0W 29 C10
Kilkenny Ireland 52°39N 7°15W 31 C8
Kilkenny □ Ireland 52°35N 7°15W 31 C8
Kilkhampton U.K. 50°52N 4°31W 27 F4
Kilkieran B. Ireland 53°20N 9°41W 30 B3
Killala Ireland 54°13N 9°12W 28 B3
Killala B. Ireland 54°16N 9°8W 28 B3
Killaloe Ireland 52°48N 8°28W 30 C6
Killarney Ireland 52°4N 9°30W 30 D4
Killarney □ Ireland 52°0N 9°33W 31 C8
Killary Harbour Ireland 53°38N 9°52W 28 D2
Killeen U.S.A. 31°7N 97°44W 110 D7
Killin U.K. 56°28N 4°19W 20 B7
Killiney Ireland 53°15N 6°7W 31 B10
Killinghall U.K. 54°2N 1°33W 22 D5
Killorglin Ireland 52°6N 9°47W 30 D3
Killybegs Ireland 54°38N 8°26W 28 B5
Kilmarnock U.K. 55°37N 4°29W 20 C6
Kilrush Ireland 52°38N 9°29W 30 C4
Kilsby U.K. 52°20N 1°10W 24 B6
Kilsyth U.K. 55°59N 4°3W 20 C7
Kilwa Kivinje Tanzania 8°45S 39°25E 96 F7
Kilwinning U.K. 55°39N 4°43W 20 C6
Kimberley Australia 16°20S 127°0E 98 D4
Kimberley S. Africa 28°43S 24°46E 97 K4
Kimbolton U.K. 52°18N 0°24W 25 B8
Kimch'aek N. Korea 40°40N 129°10E 81 B7
Kimmirut Canada 62°50N 69°50W 109 C13
Kimry Russia 56°55N 37°15E 72 C6
Kinabalu, Gunung Malaysia 6°3N 116°14E 83 C3
Kincardine Canada 44°10N 81°40W 112 C7
Kincardine Aberds., U.K. 56°57N 2°25W 19 J13
Kinder Scout U.K. 53°24N 1°52W 23 F5
Kindersley Canada 51°30N 109°10W 108 D9
Kindia Guinea 10°0N 12°52W 94 F3
Kindu Dem. Rep. of the Congo 2°55S 25°50E 96 E5
Kineshma Russia 57°30N 42°5E 72 C7
Kineton U.K. 52°10N 1°31W 24 B5
King George I. Antarctica 60°0S 60°0W 55 C18
King George Is. Canada 57°20N 80°30W 109 D11
King I. Australia 39°50S 144°0E 98 H7
King William I. Canada 69°10N 97°25W 108 C10
Kingman U.S.A. 35°12N 114°4W 110 C4
King's Lynn U.K. 52°45N 0°24E 25 A9
King's Sutton U.K. 52°2N 1°15W 24 B6
King's Worthy U.K. 51°6N 1°17W 24 D6
Kingsbridge U.K. 50°17N 3°47W 27 G6
Kingsbury U.K. 52°34N 1°40W 23 G5
Kingscourt Ireland 53°55N 6°48W 29 D8
Kingskerswell U.K. 50°29N 3°35W 27 G6
Kingsland U.K. 52°15N 2°49W 24 B3
Kingsteignton U.K. 50°33N 3°36W 27 F6
Kingston Canada 44°14N 76°30W 112 C9
Kingston Jamaica 18°0N 76°50W 114 a
Kingston N.Y., U.S.A. 41°56N 73°59W 113 E10
Kingston Pa., U.S.A. 41°16N 75°54W 113 E10
Kingston upon Hull U.K. 53°45N 0°21W 23 E8
Kingston-upon-Thames □
  U.K. 51°24N 0°17W 25 D8
Kingstown St. Vincent 13°10N 61°10W 115 E12
Kingsville U.S.A. 27°31N 97°52W 110 E7
Kingswear U.K. 50°21N 3°35W 27 G6
Kingswood U.K. 51°27N 2°31W 24 D3
Kingussie U.K. 57°6N 4°2W 19 H9
Kinki □ Japan 35°0N 135°45E 82 F4
Kinloch Rannoch U.K. 56°43N 4°2W 20 B6
Kinlochleven U.K. 56°43N 5°0W 18 J7
Kinnairds Hd. U.K. 57°43N 2°1W 19 G13
Kinross U.K. 56°13N 3°25W 21 B9
Kinsale Ireland 51°42N 8°31W 30 E5
Kinsale, Old Hd. of Ireland 51°37N 8°33W 30 E5
Kinshasa Dem. Rep. of the Congo 4°20S 15°15E 96 E3
Kintore U.K. 57°14N 2°20W 19 H13
Kintyre U.K. 55°30N 5°35W 20 D4
Kintyre, Mull of U.K. 55°17N 5°47W 20 D4
Kippure Ireland 53°11N 6°21W 31 B10
Kirensk Russia 57°50N 107°55E 79 D12
Kirgiz Steppe Eurasia 50°0N 55°0E 73 D10
Kiribati ■ Pac. Oc. 3°0S 180°0E 102 H10
Kırıkkale Turkey 39°51N 33°32E 73 G5
Kiritimati Kiribati 1°58N 157°27W 103 G12
Kirkbean U.K. 54°55N 3°36W 21 E9
Kirkburton U.K. 53°37N 1°42W 23 E5
Kirkby U.K. 53°30N 2°54W 23 F3
Kirkby-in-Ashfield U.K. 53°6N 1°14W 23 F6
Kirkby Lonsdale U.K. 54°12N 2°36W 22 D3
Kirkby Malzeard U.K. 54°10N 1°37W 22 D5
Kirkby Stephen U.K. 54°29N 2°21W 22 D4
Kirkby Thore U.K. 54°38N 2°32W 22 C4
Kirkbymoorside U.K. 54°17N 0°56W 22 D7
Kirkcaldy U.K. 56°7N 3°9W 21 B9
Kirkcudbright U.K. 54°50N 4°2W 21 E8
Kirkham U.K. 53°47N 2°53W 23 E3
Kirkintilloch U.K. 55°56N 4°8W 20 C7
Kirkland Lake Canada 48°9N 80°2W 109 E11
Kırklareli Turkey 41°44N 27°15E 86 A1
Kirkoswald U.K. 54°46N 2°41W 22 C3
Kirksville U.S.A. 40°12N 92°35W 111 B81
Kirkūk Iraq 35°30N 44°21E 86 C6

Kirkwall U.K. 58°59N 2°58W 19 E12
Kirkwhelpington U.K. 55°9N 1°59W 22 B5
Kirov Russia 58°35N 49°40E 72 C8
Kirovohrad Ukraine 48°35N 32°20E 73 E5
Kirriemuir U.K. 56°41N 3°1W 19 J11
Kırşehir Turkey 39°14N 34°5E 73 G5
Kirthar Range Pakistan 27°0N 67°0E 84 F5
Kirtling U.K. 52°12N 0°28E 25 B9
Kirtlington U.K. 51°53N 1°15W 24 C6
Kirton U.K. 52°56N 0°3W 23 G8
Kirton in Lindsey U.K. 53°29N 0°34W 23 F7
Kiruna Sweden 67°52N 20°15E 63 D8
Kiryū Japan 36°24N 139°20E 82 E6
Kisangani
  Dem. Rep. of the Congo 0°35N 25°15E 96 D5
Kishanganj India 26°3N 88°14E 85 F16
Kishinev Moldova 47°2N 28°50E 67 E15
Kisii Kenya 0°40S 34°45E 96 E6
Kislovodsk Russia 43°50N 42°45E 73 F7
Kismayu Somali Rep. 0°22S 42°32E 88 H3
Kisumu Kenya 0°3S 34°45E 96 E6
Kitakyūshū Japan 33°50N 130°50E 82 G2
Kitale Kenya 1°0N 35°0E 96 D7
Kitami Japan 43°48N 143°54E 82 B8
Kitchener Canada 43°27N 80°29W 112 D7
Kithnos Greece 37°26N 24°27E 71 F11
Kitimat Canada 54°3N 128°38W 108 D7
Kittanning U.S.A. 40°49N 79°31W 112 E8
Kitwe Zambia 12°54S 28°13E 97 G5
Kivu, L. Dem. Rep. of the Congo 1°48S 29°0E 96 E5
Kızıl Irmak → Turkey 41°44N 35°58E 73 F6
Kizlyar Russia 43°51N 46°40E 73 F8
Kladno Czech Rep. 50°10N 14°7E 66 C8
Klagenfurt Austria 46°38N 14°20E 66 E8
Klaipėda Lithuania 55°43N 21°10E 63 F8
Klamath → U.S.A. 41°33N 124°5W 110 B2
Klamath Falls U.S.A. 42°13N 121°46W 110 B2
Klang Malaysia 3°2N 101°26E 83 D2
Klarälven → Sweden 59°23N 13°32E 63 F6
Klerksdorp S. Africa 26°53S 26°38E 97 K5
Kluane L. Canada 61°15N 138°40W 108 C6
Kluczbork Poland 50°58N 18°12E 67 C10
Klyuchevskaya, Gora
  Russia 55°50N 160°30E 79 D18
Knaresborough U.K. 54°1N 1°28W 23 D6
Knebworth U.K. 51°52N 0°11W 25 C8
Knighton U.K. 52°21N 3°3W 26 C7
Knock Ireland 53°48N 8°55W 28 D4
Knockmealdown Mts. Ireland 52°14N 7°56W 30 D7
Knossos Greece 35°16N 25°10E 71 G11
Knottingley U.K. 53°43N 1°16W 23 E6
Knowle U.K. 52°24N 1°44W 23 H5
Knoxville U.S.A. 35°58N 83°55W 111 C10
Knoydart U.K. 57°3N 5°33W 18 H6
Knutsford U.K. 53°18N 2°21W 23 F4
Kōbe Japan 34°41N 135°13E 82 F4
Koblenz Germany 50°21N 7°36E 66 C4
Kocaeli Turkey 40°45N 29°50E 73 F4
Koch Bihar India 26°22N 89°29E 85 F16
Kochi Japan 33°30N 133°35E 82 G3
Kodiak U.S.A. 57°47N 152°24W 108 D4
Kodiak I. U.S.A. 57°30N 152°45W 108 D4
Koforidua Ghana 6°3N 0°17W 94 G5
Kōfu Japan 35°40N 138°30E 82 F6
Kohat Pakistan 33°40N 71°29E 84 C7
Kohima India 25°35N 94°10E 85 G19
Kohtla-Järve Estonia 59°20N 27°20E 63 F9
Kokkola Finland 63°50N 23°8E 63 E8
Koko Kyunzu Burma 14°10N 93°25E 85 M18
Kokomo U.S.A. 40°29N 86°8W 112 E4
Kokshetaü Kazakhstan 53°20N 69°25E 79 D8
Koksoak → Canada 58°30N 68°10W 109 D13
Kola Pen. Russia 67°30N 38°0E 72 A6
Kolar Gold Fields India 12°58N 78°16E 84 N11
Kolguyev Russia 69°20N 48°30E 72 A8
Kolhapur India 16°43N 74°15E 84 L9
Kolkata India 22°34N 88°21E 85 H16
Kolomna Russia 55°8N 38°45E 72 C6
Kolomyya Ukraine 48°31N 25°2E 73 E4
Kolpino Russia 59°44N 30°39E 72 C5
Kolwezi Dem. Rep. of the Congo 10°40S 25°25E 96 G5
Kolyma → Russia 69°30N 161°0E 79 C18
Kolyma Ra. Russia 63°0N 157°0E 79 C17
Komandorskiye Is. Russia 55°0N 167°0E 79 D18
Komatsu Japan 36°25N 136°30E 82 E5
Komi □ Russia 64°0N 55°0E 72 B10
Kompong Cham Cambodia 12°0N 105°30E 83 B2
Komsomolsk Russia 50°30N 137°0E 79 D15
Konarhâ □ Afghan. 34°30N 71°3E 87 C12
Kongur Shan China 38°34N 75°18E 80 C2
Konin Poland 52°12N 18°15E 67 B10
Konosha Russia 61°0N 40°5E 72 B7
Konotop Ukraine 51°12N 33°7E 73 D5
Końqi He → China 41°0N 86°0E 80 B3
Konya Turkey 37°52N 32°35E 73 G5
Kootenay L. Canada 49°45N 116°50W 108 E8
Kopet Dagh Asia 38°0N 58°0E 87 B9
Korçë Albania 40°37N 20°50E 71 D9
Korčula Croatia 42°56N 16°57E 70 C7
Kordestān □ Iran 36°0N 47°0E 86 C6
Kordofân Sudan 13°0N 29°0E 95 F11
Korea, North ■ Asia 40°0N 127°0E 81 C7
Korea, South ■ Asia 36°0N 128°0E 81 C7
Korea Bay Korea 39°0N 124°0E 81 C7
Korea Strait Asia 34°0N 129°30E 81 C7
Korhogo Ivory C. 9°29N 5°28W 94 G4
Kōriyama Japan 37°24N 140°23E 82 E7
Korla China 41°45N 86°4E 80 B3
Koror Palau 7°20N 134°28E 102 G5
Körös → Hungary 46°43N 20°12E 67 E11
Korosten Ukraine 50°54N 28°36E 73 D4
Kortrijk Belgium 50°50N 3°17E 65 D3
Koryak Ra. Russia 61°0N 171°0E 79 C19
Kos Greece 36°50N 27°15E 71 F12
Kosciuszko, Mt. Australia 36°27S 148°16E 98 H8
Košice Slovak Rep. 48°42N 21°15E 67 D11
Kosovo □ Serbia 42°30N 21°0E 71 C9
Kosovska Mitrovica Serbia 42°54N 20°52E 71 C9

Kôstî Sudan 13°8N 32°43E 95 F12
Kostroma Russia 57°50N 40°58E 72 C7
Koszalin Poland 54°11N 16°8E 66 A9
Kota India 25°14N 75°49E 84 G9
Kota Bharu Malaysia 6°7N 102°14E 83 C2
Kota Kinabalu Malaysia 6°0N 116°4E 83 C3
Kotabumi Indonesia 4°49S 104°54E 83 D2
Kotelnich Russia 58°22N 48°24E 72 C8
Kotka Finland 60°28N 26°58E 63 E9
Kotlas Russia 61°17N 46°43E 72 B8
Kotor Montenegro 42°25N 18°47E 71 C8
Kotri Pakistan 25°22N 68°22E 84 G6
Kotuy → Russia 71°54N 102°6E 79 B12
Kotzebue U.S.A. 66°53N 162°39W 108 C3
Koudougou Burkina Faso 12°10N 2°20W 94 F5
Koumra Chad 8°50N 17°35E 95 G9
Kovel Ukraine 51°11N 24°38E 72 D3
Kovrov Russia 56°25N 41°25E 72 C7
Kpalimé Togo 6°57N 0°44E 94 G6
Kra, Isthmus of Thailand 10°15N 99°30E 83 B1
Kragujevac Serbia 44°2N 20°56E 71 B9
Krakatoa Indonesia 6°10S 105°20E 83 D2
Kraków Poland 50°4N 19°57E 67 C10
Kraljevo Serbia 43°44N 20°41E 71 C9
Kramatorsk Ukraine 48°50N 37°30E 73 E6
Krasnodar Russia 45°5N 39°0E 73 E6
Krasnokamsk Russia 58°4N 55°48E 72 C10
Krasnoturinsk Russia 59°46N 60°12E 72 C11
Krasnoyarsk Russia 56°8N 93°0E 79 D11
Krasnyy Luch Ukraine 48°13N 39°0E 73 E6
Krefeld Germany 51°20N 6°33E 66 C4
Kremenchuk Ukraine 49°5N 33°25E 73 E5
Kribi Cameroon 2°57N 9°56E 96 D1
Krishna → India 15°57N 80°59E 85 M12
Kristiansand Norway 58°8N 8°1E 63 F5
Kristiansund Norway 63°7N 7°45E 63 E5
Krivoy Rog Ukraine 47°51N 33°20E 73 E5
Krk Croatia 45°8N 14°40E 70 B6
Kronshtadt Russia 59°57N 29°51E 72 B4
Kroonstad S. Africa 27°43S 27°19E 97 K5
Kropotkin Russia 45°28N 40°28E 73 E7
Krosno Poland 49°42N 21°46E 67 D11
Krugersdorp S. Africa 26°5S 27°46E 97 K5
Kruševac Serbia 43°35N 21°28E 71 C9
Ksar el Kebir Morocco 35°0N 6°0W 94 B4
Kuala Belait Malaysia 4°35N 114°11E 83 C3
Kuala Lumpur Malaysia 3°9N 101°41E 83 C2
Kuala Terengganu Malaysia 5°20N 103°8E 83 C2
Kuantan Malaysia 3°49N 103°20E 83 C2
Kuching Malaysia 1°33N 110°25E 83 C3
Kudymkar Russia 59°1N 54°39E 72 C9
Kugluktuk Canada 67°50N 115°5W 108 C7
Kuito Angola 12°22S 16°55E 97 G3
Kūlob Tajikistan 37°55N 69°50E 87 B12
Kulsary Kazakhstan 46°59N 54°1E 73 E9
Kuma → Russia 44°55N 47°0E 73 F8
Kumagaya Japan 36°9N 139°22E 82 E6
Kumamoto Japan 32°45N 130°45E 82 G2
Kumanovo Macedonia 42°9N 21°42E 71 C9
Kumasi Ghana 6°41N 1°38W 94 G5
Kumba Cameroon 4°36N 9°24E 96 D1
Kumbakonam India 10°58N 79°25E 84 P11
Kumertau Russia 52°45N 55°57E 72 D10
Kungur Russia 57°25N 56°57E 72 C10
Kunlun Shan Asia 36°0N 86°30E 80 C3
Kunming China 25°1N 102°41E 80 D5
Kuopio Finland 62°53N 27°35E 63 E9
Kupang Indonesia 10°19S 123°39E 83 E4
Kuqa China 41°35N 82°30E 80 B3
Kür → Azerbaijan 39°29N 49°15E 73 G8
Kurdistan Asia 37°20N 43°30E 86 B5
Kure Japan 34°14N 132°32E 82 F3
Kurgan Russia 55°26N 65°18E 79 D8
Kuril Is. Russia 45°0N 150°0E 79 E17
Kuril-Kamchatka Trench
  Pac. Oc. 44°0N 153°0E 102 C7
Kurnool India 15°45N 78°0E 84 M11
Kursk Russia 51°42N 36°11E 72 D6
Kuruktag China 41°0N 89°0E 80 B3
Kurume Japan 33°15N 130°30E 82 G2
Kushiro Japan 43°0N 144°25E 82 B9
Kushtia Bangla. 23°55N 89°5E 85 H16
Kuskokwim B. U.S.A. 59°45N 162°25W 108 D3
Kütahya Turkey 39°30N 30°2E 73 G5
Kutaisi Georgia 42°19N 42°40E 73 F7
Kuujjuaq Canada 58°6N 68°15W 109 D13
Kuujjuarapik Canada 55°20N 77°35W 109 D12
Kuwait Kuwait 29°30N 48°0E 86 D7
Kuwait ■ Asia 29°30N 47°30E 86 D6
Kuybyshev Res. Russia 55°2N 49°30E 72 C8
Kuznetsk Russia 53°12N 46°40E 72 D8
Kuzomen Russia 66°22N 36°50E 72 A6
KwaMashu S. Africa 29°45S 30°58E 97 K6
KwaZulu Natal □ S. Africa 29°0S 30°0E 97 K6
Kwekwe Zimbabwe 18°58S 29°48E 97 H5
Kyle of Lochalsh U.K. 57°17N 5°44W 18 H6
Kyoga, L. Uganda 1°35N 33°0E 96 D6
Kyōto Japan 35°0N 135°45E 82 F4
Kyrenia Cyprus 35°20N 33°20E 86 C3
Kyrgyzstan ■ Asia 42°0N 75°0E 79 E9
Kythira Greece 36°8N 23°0E 71 F10
Kyūshū Japan 33°0N 131°0E 82 G2
Kyustendil Bulgaria 42°16N 22°41E 71 C10
Kyzyl Kum Uzbekistan 42°30N 65°0E 87 A10
Kyzyl-Orda Kazakhstan 44°48N 65°28E 79 E8

L

La Alcarria Spain 40°31N 2°45W 69 B4
La Ceiba Honduras 15°40N 86°50W 114 D7
La Coruña Spain 43°20N 8°25W 69 A1
La Crosse U.S.A. 43°48N 91°15W 112 D2
La Désirade Guadeloupe 16°18N 61°3W 114 b
La Grande U.S.A. 45°20N 118°5W 110 A3
La Grande → Canada 53°50N 79°0W 109 D12
La Grange U.S.A. 33°2N 85°2W 111 D10
La Habana Cuba 23°8N 82°22W 115 C8
La Junta U.S.A. 37°59N 103°33W 110 C6

La Línea de la Concepción   Lucania, Mt.

La Línea de la Concepción
Spain 36°15N 5°23W **69** D3
La Loche Canada 56°29N 109°26W **108** D9
La Louvière Belgium 50°27N 4°10E **65** D4
La Mancha Spain 39°10N 2°54W **69** C4
La Oroya Peru 11°32S 75°54W **120** D2
La Palma Canary Is. 28°40N 17°50W **94** C2
La Paz Bolivia 16°20S 68°10W **120** D3
La Paz Mexico 24°10N 110°18W **114** C2
La Perouse Str. Asia 45°40N 142°0E **102** C6
La Plata Argentina 35°0S 57°55W **121** F4
La Quiaca Argentina 22°5S 65°35W **121** E3
La Rioja Argentina 29°20S 67°0W **121** E3
La Rioja □ Spain 42°20N 2°20W **69** A4
La Roche-sur-Yon France 46°40N 1°25W **68** C3
La Rochelle France 46°10N 1°9W **68** C3
La Romana Dom. Rep. 18°27N 68°57W **115** D11
La Ronge Canada 55°5N 105°20W **108** D9
La Sarre Canada 48°45N 79°15W **112** A8
La Serena Chile 29°55S 71°10W **121** E2
La Seyne-sur-Mer France 43°7N 5°52E **68** E6
La Spézia Italy 44°7N 9°50E **70** B3
La Tortuga Venezuela 11°0N 65°22W **120** A3
La Trinité Martinique 14°43N 60°58W **114** c
La Tuque Canada 47°30N 72°50W **109** E12
La Vega Dom. Rep. 19°20N 70°30W **115** D10
Labé Guinea 11°24N 12°16W **94** F3
Labinsk Russia 44°40N 40°48E **73** F7
Laborie St. Lucia 13°45N 61°2W **115** f
Labrador Canada 53°20N 61°0W **109** D13
Labrador City Canada 52°57N 66°55W **109** D13
Labrador Sea Atl. Oc. 57°0N 54°0W **109** D14
Labuan Malaysia 5°21N 115°13E **83** C3
Lac La Biche Canada 54°45N 111°58W **108** D8
Lac-Mégantic Canada 45°35N 70°53W **113** C12
Laccadive Is. = Lakshadweep Is.
India 10°0N 72°30E **74** G9
Laceby U.K. 53°33N 0°10W **23** E8
Lacock U.K. 51°24N 2°7W **24** D4
Lacombe Canada 52°30N 113°44W **108** D8
Laconia U.S.A. 43°32N 71°28W **113** D12
Ladakh Ra. India 34°0N 78°0E **84** C11
Ladder Hills U.K. 57°13N 3°16W **19** H11
Ladock U.K. 50°19N 4°58W **27** G4
Ladoga, L. Russia 61°15N 30°30E **72** B5
Ladysmith S. Africa 28°32S 29°46E **97** K5
Ladysmith U.S.A. 45°28N 91°12W **112** C2
Lae Papua N. G. 6°40S 147°2E **98** B8
Lafayette Ind., U.S.A. 40°25N 86°54W **112** E4
Lafayette La., U.S.A. 30°14N 92°1W **111** D8
Lafia Nigeria 8°30N 8°34E **94** G7
Lagan → U.K. 54°36N 5°55W **29** B10
Lagarto Brazil 10°54S 37°41W **122** B3
Lagdo, Rés. de Cameroon 8°40N 14°0E **95** G8
Laghouat Algeria 33°50N 2°59E **94** B6
Lagos Nigeria 6°25N 3°27E **94** G6
Lagos Portugal 37°5N 8°41W **69** D1
Lahn → Germany 50°19N 7°37E **66** C4
Lahore Pakistan 31°32N 74°22E **84** D9
Lahti Finland 60°58N 25°40E **63** E9
Lairg U.K. 58°2N 4°24W **19** F9
Laizhou China 37°8N 119°57E **81** C6
Lake Charles U.S.A. 30°14N 93°13W **111** D8
Lake City U.S.A. 30°11N 82°38W **111** D10
Lake District △ U.K. 54°30N 3°21W **22** C2
Lake Havasu City U.S.A. 34°27N 114°22W **110** D4
Lakeland U.S.A. 28°3N 81°57W **111** E10
Lakenheath U.K. 52°25N 0°32E **25** B10
Lakewood U.S.A. 41°28N 81°47W **112** E7
Lakshadweep Is. India 10°0N 72°30E **74** G9
Lamar U.S.A. 38°5N 102°37W **110** C6
Lambaréné Gabon 0°41S 10°12E **96** E2
Lambay I. Ireland 53°29N 6°1W **31** B10
Lamberhurst U.K. 51°5N 0°24E **25** D9
Lambeth □ U.K. 51°28N 0°6W **25** D8
Lambley U.K. 54°56N 2°30W **22** C4
Lambourn U.K. 51°30N 1°32W **24** C5
Lamesa U.S.A. 32°44N 101°58W **110** D6
Lammermuir U.K. 55°50N 2°25W **21** C11
Lammermuir Hills U.K. 55°50N 2°40W **21** C10
Lamon B. Phil. 14°30N 122°20E **83** B4
Lampedusa Medit. S. 35°36N 12°40E **70** G5
Lampeter U.K. 52°7N 4°4W **26** C5
Lamu Kenya 2°16S 40°55E **96** E8
Lanark U.K. 55°40N 3°47W **21** C8
Lancashire □ U.K. 53°50N 2°48W **23** E3
Lancaster U.K. 54°3N 2°48W **22** D3
Lancaster N.H., U.S.A. 44°29N 71°34W **113** C12
Lancaster Pa., U.S.A. 40°2N 76°19W **112** E9
Lancaster Wis., U.S.A. 42°51N 90°43W **112** D2
Lancaster Sd. Canada 74°13N 84°0W **109** B11
Lanchester U.K. 54°50N 1°44W **22** C5
Lancing U.K. 50°49N 0°19W **25** E8
Landes France 44°0N 1°0W **68** D3
Landkey U.K. 51°3N 4°0W **27** E6
Land's End U.K. 50°4N 5°44W **27** G2
Langholm U.K. 55°9N 3°0W **21** D10
Langport U.K. 51°2N 2°50W **24** D3
Langreo Spain 43°18N 5°40W **69** A3
Langres France 47°52N 5°20E **68** C6
Langres, Plateau de France 47°45N 5°3E **68** C6
Langsa Indonesia 4°30N 97°57E **83** C1
Langstrothdale Chase U.K. 54°14N 2°13W **22** D4
Langtoft U.K. 52°42N 0°20W **23** G8
Langtree U.K. 50°55N 4°13W **27** F5
Languedoc France 43°58N 3°55E **68** E5
Lannion France 48°46N 3°29W **68** B2
L'Annonciation Canada 46°25N 74°55W **113** C12
L'Anse U.S.A. 46°45N 88°27W **112** B31
L'Anse la Raye St. Lucia 13°55N 61°3W **115** f
Lansing U.S.A. 42°44N 84°33W **112** D5
Lanzarote Canary Is. 29°0N 13°40W **94** C3
Lanzhou China 36°1N 103°52E **80** C5
Laoag Phil. 18°7N 120°34E **83** B4
Laois □ Ireland 52°57N 7°36E **31** C7
Laon France 49°33N 3°35E **68** B5
Laos ■ Asia 17°45N 105°0E **83** B2
Lapeer U.S.A. 43°3N 83°19W **112** D6

Lapford U.K. 50°51N 3°48W **27** F6
Lapland Europe 68°7N 24°0E **63** D8
LaPorte U.S.A. 41°36N 86°43W **112** E4
Laptev Sea Russia 76°0N 125°0E **79** B14
L'Áquila Italy 42°22N 13°22E **70** C5
Laramie U.S.A. 41°19N 105°35W **110** B5
Laramie Mts. U.S.A. 42°0N 105°30W **110** B5
Laredo U.S.A. 27°30N 99°30W **110** E7
Largs U.K. 55°47N 4°52W **20** C6
Larisa Greece 39°36N 22°27E **71** E10
Larnaca Cyprus 34°55N 33°38E **86** C3
Larne U.K. 54°51N 5°51W **29** B10
Larne L. U.K. 54°50N 5°48W **29** B10
Larrimah Australia 15°35S 133°12E **98** D5
Larsen Ice Shelf Antarctica 67°0S 62°0W **55** C17
Larvik Norway 59°4N 10°2E **63** F6
Las Cruces U.S.A. 32°19N 106°47W **110** D5
Las Palmas Canary Is. 28°7N 15°26W **94** C2
Las Tunas Cuba 20°58N 76°59W **115** C9
Las Vegas N. Mex., U.S.A. 35°36N 105°13W **110** C5
Las Vegas Nev., U.S.A. 36°10N 115°8W **110** D3
Lashio Burma 22°56N 97°45E **85** H20
Lassen Pk. U.S.A. 40°29N 121°30W **110** B2
Lastoursville Gabon 0°55S 12°38E **96** E2
Latacunga Ecuador 0°50S 78°35W **120** C2
Latakia Syria 35°30N 35°45E **86** C3
Latina Italy 41°28N 12°52E **70** D5
Latvia ■ Europe 56°50N 24°0E **63** F8
Lauder U.K. 55°43N 2°43W **21** C10
Lauderdale U.K. 55°44N 2°41W **21** C10
Launceston Australia 41°24S 147°8E **98** J8
Launceston U.K. 50°38N 4°22W **27** F5
Laune → Ireland 52°7N 9°47W **30** D3
Laurel U.S.A. 31°41N 89°8W **111** D9
Laurencekirk U.K. 56°50N 2°28W **19** J13
Lausanne Switz. 46°32N 6°38E **66** E4
Lavagh More Ireland 54°46N 8°6W **28** B5
Laval Canada 45°33N 73°42W **113** C11
Laval France 48°4N 0°48W **68** B3
Lavendon U.K. 52°11N 0°39W **25** B7
Lavenham U.K. 52°6N 0°48E **25** B10
Lavras Brazil 21°20S 45°0W **122** D2
Lawrence Kans., U.S.A. 38°58N 95°14W **111** C7
Lawrence Mass., U.S.A. 42°43N 71°10W **113** D12
Lawton U.S.A. 34°37N 98°25W **110** D7
Laxey U.K. 54°14N 4°23W **29** C13
Laxfield U.K. 52°18N 1°22E **25** B11
Laxford, L. U.K. 58°24N 5°6W **18** F7
Leysdown on Sea U.K. 51°24N 0°56E **25** D10
Leyte □ Phil. 11°0N 125°0E **83** B4
Lhasa China 29°25N 90°58E **80** D4
Lhazê China 29°5N 87°38E **80** D3
L'Hospitalet de Llobregat Spain 41°21N 2°6E **69** B7
Lianyungang China 34°40N 119°11E **81** C6
Liaodong Pen. China 40°0N 122°30E **81** C7
Liaoning □ China 41°40N 122°30E **81** B7
Liaoyang China 41°15N 122°58E **81** B7
Liaoyuan China 42°58N 125°2E **81** B7
Liard → Canada 61°51N 121°18W **108** C7
Liberal U.S.A. 37°3N 100°55W **110** C6
Liberec Czech Rep. 50°47N 15°7E **66** C8
Liberia ■ W. Afr. 6°30N 9°30W **94** G4
Libourne France 44°55N 0°14W **68** D3
Libreville Gabon 0°25N 9°26E **96** D1
Libya ■ N. Afr. 27°0N 17°0E **95** C9
Libyan Desert Africa 25°0N 25°0E **95** C10
Libyan Plateau Egypt 30°40N 26°30E **95** B11
Lichfield U.K. 52°41N 1°49W **23** G5
Liddesdale U.K. 55°14N 2°50W **21** D10
Lidköping Sweden 58°31N 13°7E **63** F6
Liechtenstein ■ Europe 47°8N 9°35E **66** E5
Liège Belgium 50°38N 5°35E **65** D5
Liepaja Latvia 56°30N 21°0E **63** F8
Liffey → Ireland 53°21N 6°13W **31** B10
Lifford Ireland 54°51N 7°29W **28** B7
Liguria □ Italy 44°30N 8°50E **70** B3
Ligurian Sea Medit. S. 43°20N 9°0E **70** C3
Lihue U.S.A. 21°59N 159°23W **110** H15
Lijiang China 26°55N 100°20E **80** D5
Likasi Dem. Rep. of the Congo 10°55S 26°48E **96** G5
Lille France 50°38N 3°3E **68** A5
Lillehammer Norway 61°8N 10°30E **63** E6
Lilleshall U.K. 52°44N 2°23W **23** G4
Lilongwe Malawi 14°0S 33°48E **97** G6
Lima Peru 12°3S 77°2W **120** D2
Lima U.S.A. 40°44N 84°6W **112** E5
Limassol Cyprus 34°42N 33°1E **86** C3
Limavady U.K. 55°3N 6°56W **29** A8
Limay → Argentina 39°0S 68°0W **121** F3
Limbe Cameroon 4°1N 9°10E **96** D1
Limburg □ Neths. 51°20N 5°55E **65** C5
Limeira Brazil 22°35S 47°28W **122** D1
Limerick Ireland 52°40N 8°37W **30** D5
Limerick □ Ireland 52°30N 8°50W **30** D5
Limfjorden Denmark 56°55N 9°0E **63** F5
Limnos Greece 39°50N 25°5E **71** E11
Limoges France 45°50N 1°15E **68** D4
Limón Costa Rica 10°0N 83°2W **115** F8
Limousin France 45°30N 1°30E **68** D4
Limoux France 43°4N 2°12E **68** E5
Limpopo → Africa 25°5S 33°30E **97** K6
Linares Chile 35°50S 71°40W **121** F2
Linares Mexico 24°52N 99°34W **114** C5
Linares Spain 38°10N 3°40W **69** C4
Linchuan China 27°57N 116°15E **81** D6
Lincoln U.K. 53°14N 0°32W **23** F7
Lincoln Ill., U.S.A. 40°9N 89°22W **112** E3
Lincoln Maine, U.S.A. 45°22N 68°30W **113** C13
Lincoln Nebr., U.S.A. 40°49N 96°41W **111** B7
Lincoln Sea Arctic 84°0N 55°0W **54** A5
Lincolnshire □ U.K. 53°14N 0°32W **23** F7
Lincolnshire Wolds U.K. 53°26N 0°13W **23** F8
Lindale U.K. 54°14N 2°53W **22** D3
Lindesnes Norway 57°58N 7°3E **63** G5
Lindsay Canada 44°22N 78°43W **112** C8
Linfen China 36°3N 111°30E **81** C6
Lingfield U.K. 51°11N 0°0 **25** D8
Lingga, Kepulauan Indonesia 0°10S 104°30E **83** D2
Linhai China 28°50N 121°8E **81** D7
Linhares Brazil 19°25S 40°4W **122** C2
Linhe China 40°48N 107°20E **80** B5
Linkinhorne U.K. 50°32N 4°24W **27** F5

Leominster U.K. 52°14N 2°43W **24** B3
Leominster U.S.A. 42°32N 71°46W **113** D12
León Mexico 21°6N 101°41W **114** C4
León Nic. 12°20N 86°51W **114** E7
León Spain 42°38N 5°34W **69** A3
Leonora Australia 28°49S 121°19E **98** F3
Leopoldina Brazil 21°28S 42°40W **122** D2
Lerwick U.K. 60°9N 1°9W **18** B15
Les Cayes Haiti 18°15N 73°46W **115** D10
Les Sables-d'Olonne France 46°30N 1°45W **68** C3
Lesbos Greece 39°10N 26°20E **71** E12
Lesbury U.K. 55°25N 1°36W **22** B5
Leshan China 29°33N 103°41E **80** D5
Leskovac Serbia 43°0N 21°58E **71** C9
Lesotho ■ Africa 29°40S 28°0E **97** K5
Lesser Antilles W. Indies 15°0N 61°0W **115** E12
Lesser Slave L. Canada 55°30N 115°25W **108** D8
Lesser Sunda Is. Indonesia 8°0S 120°0E **83** D4
Leszno Poland 51°50N 16°30E **67** C9
Letchworth U.K. 51°59N 0°13W **25** C8
Lethbridge Canada 49°45N 112°45W **108** E8
Leti, Kepulauan Indonesia 8°10S 128°0E **83** D4
Leticia Colombia 4°9S 70°0W **120** C2
Letterkenny Ireland 54°57N 7°45W **28** B6
Leuchars U.K. 56°24N 2°53W **21** B10
Leuven Belgium 50°52N 4°42E **65** D4
Leven E. Riding, U.K. 53°53N 0°18W **23** E8
Leven Fife, U.K. 56°12N 3°0W **21** B10
Leven → U.K. 54°31N 1°19W **22** C6
Leven, L. Highl., U.K. 56°42N 5°6W **18** J7
Leven, L. Perth & Kinr., U.K. 56°12N 3°22W **21** B9
Lévis Canada 46°48N 71°9W **113** B12
Lewes U.K. 50°52N 0°1E **25** E9
Lewis U.K. 58°9N 6°40W **18** F4
Lewis, Butt of U.K. 58°31N 6°16W **18** E5
Lewisham □ U.K. 51°27N 0°1W **25** D8
Lewisporte Canada 49°15N 55°3W **109** E14
Lewiston Idaho, U.S.A. 46°25N 117°1W **110** A3
Lewiston Maine, U.S.A. 44°6N 70°13W **113** C12
Lewistown Mont., U.S.A. 47°4N 109°26W **110** A5
Lewistown Pa., U.S.A. 40°36N 77°34W **112** E9
Lexington U.S.A. 38°3N 84°30W **112** F5
Lexington Park U.S.A. 38°16N 76°27W **112** F9
Leyburn U.K. 54°19N 1°48W **22** D5
Leyland U.K. 53°42N 2°43W **23** E3

Linköping Sweden 58°28N 15°36E **63** F7
Linnhe, L. U.K. 56°36N 5°25W **20** A5
Linqing China 36°50N 115°42E **81** C6
Linslade U.K. 51°54N 0°41W **25** C7
Linstead Jamaica 18°8N 77°2W **114** a
Linton U.K. 52°6N 0°17E **25** B9
Linton U.S.A. 39°2N 87°10W **112** F4
Linxia China 35°36N 103°10E **80** C5
Linyi China 35°5N 118°21E **81** C6
Linz Austria 48°18N 14°18E **66** D8
Lion, G. du France 43°10N 4°0E **68** E6
Lipa Phil. 13°57N 121°10E **83** B4
Lipari Italy 38°26N 14°58E **70** E6
Lipetsk Russia 52°37N 39°35E **72** D6
Lippe → Germany 51°39N 6°36E **66** C4
Liquillo, Sierra de Puerto Rico 18°20N 65°47W **115** d
Lisbon Portugal 38°42N 9°8W **69** C1
Lisburn U.K. 54°31N 6°3W **29** B9
Liscannor B. Ireland 52°55N 9°24W **30** C4
Lisianski I. U.S.A. 26°2N 174°0W **102** E10
Lisieux France 49°10N 0°12E **68** B4
Liskeard U.K. 50°27N 4°29W **27** G5
Liski Russia 51°3N 39°30E **73** D6
Lismore Australia 28°44S 153°21E **98** F9
Lismore Ireland 52°8N 7°55W **30** D7
Liss U.K. 51°3N 0°54W **25** D7
Listowel Canada 43°44N 80°58W **112** D7
Listowel Ireland 52°27N 9°29W **30** D4
Litani → Lebanon 33°20N 35°15E **86** C3
Litcham U.K. 52°44N 0°47E **25** A10
Litchfield U.S.A. 39°11N 89°39W **112** F3
Litherland U.K. 53°29N 2°59W **23** F3
Lithuania ■ Europe 55°30N 24°0E **63** F8
Little Current Canada 45°55N 82°0W **112** C7
Little Khingan Mts. China 49°0N 127°0E **81** B7
Little Minch U.K. 57°35N 6°45W **18** G4
Little Missouri → U.S.A. 47°36N 102°25W **110** A6
Little Ouse → U.K. 52°22N 1°12E **25** B11
Little Rock U.S.A. 34°45N 92°17W **111** D8
Little Walsingham U.K. 52°54N 0°52E **25** A10
Littlehampton U.K. 50°49N 0°32W **25** E7
Littleport U.K. 52°27N 0°19E **25** B9
Littlestone-on-Sea U.K. 50°58N 0°58E **25** E10
Liupanshui China 26°38N 104°48E **80** D5
Liuzhou China 24°22N 109°22E **81** D5
Liverpool Canada 44°5N 64°41W **109** E13
Liverpool U.K. 53°25N 3°0W **23** F3
Liverpool Bay U.K. 53°30N 3°20W **23** F2
Livingston U.K. 55°54N 3°30W **21** C9
Livingston U.S.A. 45°40N 110°34W **110** A4
Livingstone Zambia 17°46S 25°52E **97** H5
Livonia U.S.A. 42°23N 83°23W **112** D6
Livorno Italy 43°33N 10°19E **70** C4
Lizard U.K. 49°58N 5°13W **27** H3
Lizard Pt. U.K. 49°57N 5°13W **27** H3
Ljubljana Slovenia 46°4N 14°33E **66** E8
Llandeilo U.K. 51°53N 3°59W **26** D6
Llandovery U.K. 51°59N 3°48W **26** D6
Llandrindod Wells U.K. 52°14N 3°22W **26** C7
Llandudno U.K. 53°19N 3°50W **26** A6
Llanelli U.K. 51°41N 4°10W **26** D5
Llanerchymedd U.K. 53°20N 4°23W **26** A5
Llanfair Caereinion U.K. 52°39N 3°20W **26** B7
Llanfair Talhaiarn U.K. 53°13N 3°37W **26** A6
Llanfairfechan U.K. 53°15N 3°58W **26** A6
Llangefni U.K. 53°15N 4°18W **26** A5
Llangollen U.K. 52°58N 3°11W **26** B7
Llanidloes U.K. 52°27N 3°31W **26** C6
Llanllyfni U.K. 53°2N 4°17W **26** A5
Llano Estacado U.S.A. 33°30N 103°0W **110** D6
Llanos S. Amer. 5°0N 71°35W **120** B2
Llanquihue, L. Chile 41°10S 72°50W **121** G2
Llanrhystyd U.K. 52°19N 4°7E **26** C5
Llantrisant U.K. 51°32N 3°22W **27** D7
Llantwit-Major U.K. 51°24N 3°29W **27** E7
Llanwrtyd Wells U.K. 52°7N 3°38W **26** C6
Llanybydwel U.K. 52°48N 3°8W **26** B7
Llanymynech U.K. 52°47N 3°8W **26** B7
Lleida Spain 41°37N 0°39E **69** B6
Lleyn Peninsula U.K. 52°51N 4°36W **26** B4
Llobregat → Spain 41°19N 2°5E **69** B7
Lloret de Mar Spain 41°41N 2°53E **69** B7
Lloydminster Canada 53°17N 110°0W **108** D9
Llullaillaco, Volcán S. Amer. 24°43S 68°30W **121** E3
Lobatse Botswana 25°12S 25°40E **97** K5
Lobito Angola 12°18S 13°35E **97** G2
Loch Lomond and the Trossachs △
U.K. 56°59N 5°1W **18** J7
Locharbriggs U.K. 55°7N 3°35W **21** D8
Lochboisdale U.K. 57°9N 7°20W **18** H3
Loches France 47°7N 1°0E **68** C4
Lochgelly U.K. 56°7N 3°19W **21** B9
Lochgilphead U.K. 56°2N 5°26W **20** B5
Lochinver U.K. 58°9N 5°14W **18** F7
Lochmaben U.K. 55°8N 3°27W **21** D9
Lochmaddy U.K. 57°36N 7°10W **18** G3
Lochnagar U.K. 56°57N 3°15W **19** J11
Lochy, L. U.K. 57°0N 4°53W **18** J8
Lock Haven U.S.A. 41°8N 77°28W **112** E9
Lockerbie U.K. 55°7N 3°21W **21** D9
Loddon U.K. 52°32N 1°31E **25** A12
Lodwar Kenya 3°7N 35°36E **96** D7
Łódź Poland 51°45N 19°27E **67** C10
Lofoten Norway 68°30N 14°0E **63** D6
Loftus U.K. 54°34N 0°53W **22** C7
Logan Ohio, U.S.A. 39°32N 82°25W **112** F6
Logan Utah, U.S.A. 41°44N 111°50W **110** B4
Logan W. Va., U.S.A. 37°51N 81°59W **112** G7
Logan, Mt. Canada 60°34N 140°23W **108** C5
Logansport U.S.A. 40°45N 86°22W **112** E4
Logroño Spain 42°28N 2°27W **69** A4
Lohardaga India 23°27N 84°45E **85** H14
Loir → France 47°33N 0°32W **68** C3
Loire → France 47°16N 2°10W **68** C2
Loja Ecuador 3°59S 79°16W **120** C2

Lombárdia □ Italy 45°40N 9°30E **70** B3
Lomblen Indonesia 8°30S 123°32E **83** D4
Lombok Indonesia 8°45S 116°30E **83** D3
Lomé Togo 6°9N 1°20E **94** G6
Lomela →
Dem. Rep. of the Congo 0°15S 20°40E **96** E4
Lomond, L. U.K. 56°8N 4°38W **20** B6
Lomza Poland 53°10N 22°2E **67** B12
London Canada 42°59N 81°15W **112** D7
London U.K. 51°30N 0°3W **25** D8
London Gatwick ✕ (LGW)
U.K. 51°10N 0°11W **25** D8
London Heathrow ✕ (LHR)
U.K. 51°28N 0°27W **25** D8
London Stansted ✕ (STN) U.K. 51°54N 0°14E **25** C9
Londonderry U.K. 55°0N 7°20W **28** A7
Londonderry □ U.K. 55°0N 7°20W **29** B7
Londonderry, C. Australia 13°45S 126°55E **98** C4
Londrina Brazil 23°18S 51°10W **121** E4
Long, L. U.K. 56°4N 4°50W **20** B6
Long Beach U.S.A. 33°46N 118°11W **110** D3
Long Bennington U.K. 52°59N 0°44W **23** G7
Long Branch U.S.A. 40°18N 74°0W **113** E11
Long Clawson U.K. 52°51N 0°55W **23** G7
Long Crendon U.K. 51°46N 0°59W **25** C7
Long Eaton U.K. 52°53N 1°15W **23** G6
Long I. Bahamas 23°20N 75°10W **115** C9
Long I. Ireland 51°30N 9°34W **30** F3
Long I. U.S.A. 40°45N 73°30W **113** E11
Long Itchington U.K. 52°16N 1°22W **24** B6
Long Melford U.K. 52°4N 0°45E **25** B10
Long Mynd, The U.K. 52°35N 2°50W **23** G3
Long Preston U.K. 54°2N 2°14W **23** D4
Long Sutton U.K. 52°48N 0°7E **23** G9
Long Xuyen Vietnam 10°19N 105°28E **83** B2
Longford Ireland 53°43N 7°49W **28** D6
Longford □ Ireland 53°42N 7°45W **28** D6
Longframlington U.K. 55°18N 1°47W **22** B5
Longhoughton U.K. 55°26N 1°37W **22** B5
Longlac Canada 49°45N 86°25W **112** A4
Longridge U.K. 53°50N 2°35W **23** E3
Longton U.K. 53°44N 2°48W **23** E3
Longtown Cumb., U.K. 55°1N 2°58W **22** B3
Longtown Hereford, U.K. 51°58N 2°59W **24** C3
Longueuil Canada 45°31N 73°29W **113** C11
Longview Tex., U.S.A. 32°30N 94°44W **111** D8
Longview Wash., U.S.A. 46°8N 122°57W **110** A2
Longyan China 25°10N 117°0E **81** D6
Lons-le-Saunier France 46°40N 5°31E **68** C6
Looe U.K. 50°22N 4°28W **27** G5
Loop Hd. Ireland 52°34N 9°56W **30** C3
Lop China 37°3N 80°11E **80** C3
Lop Nur China 40°20N 90°10E **80** B4
Lopez, C. Gabon 0°47S 8°40E **90** G4
Lorain U.S.A. 41°28N 82°11W **112** E6
Loralai Pakistan 30°20N 68°41E **84** D6
Lorca Spain 37°41N 1°42W **69** D5
Lord Howe I. Pac. Oc. 31°33S 159°6E **99** G10
Lord Howe Rise Pac. Oc. 30°0S 162°30E **99** H12
Lordsburg U.S.A. 32°21N 108°43W **110** D5
Lorestán □ Iran 33°30N 48°40E **86** C6
Lorient France 47°45N 3°23W **68** C2
Lorn U.K. 56°26N 5°10W **20** B5
Lorn, Firth of U.K. 56°20N 5°40W **20** B5
Lorraine □ France 48°53N 6°0E **68** B7
Los Alamos U.S.A. 35°53N 106°19W **110** C5
Los Andes Chile 32°50S 70°40W **121** F2
Los Angeles Chile 37°28S 72°23W **121** F2
Los Angeles U.S.A. 34°4N 118°15W **110** D3
Los Mochis Mexico 25°45N 108°57W **114** B3
Los Roques Is. Venezuela 11°50N 66°45W **120** A3
Losíni Croatia 44°30N 14°30E **70** B6
Lossiemouth U.K. 57°42N 3°17W **19** G11
Lostwithiel U.K. 50°24N 4°41W **27** G4
Lot → France 44°18N 0°20E **68** D4
Lota Chile 37°5S 73°10W **121** F2
Loubomo Congo 4°9S 12°47E **96** E2
Loughborough U.K. 52°47N 1°11W **23** G6
Lougheed I. Canada 77°26N 105°6W **109** B9
Loughrea Ireland 53°12N 8°33W **30** B5
Loughros More B. Ireland 54°48N 8°32W **28** B4
Louis XIV, Pte. Canada 54°37N 79°45W **109** D12
Louisa U.S.A. 38°7N 82°36W **112** F6
Louisiade Arch. Papua N. G. 11°10S 153°0E **98** C9
Louisiana □ U.S.A. 30°50N 92°0W **111** D8
Louisville U.S.A. 38°15N 85°46W **112** F5
Lourdes France 43°6N 0°3W **68** E3
Louth Ireland 53°58N 6°32W **29** D8
Louth U.K. 53°22N 0°1W **23** F8
Louth □ Ireland 53°56N 6°34W **29** D8
Lovech Bulgaria 43°8N 24°42E **71** C11
Lowell U.S.A. 42°38N 71°19W **113** D12
Lower Beeding U.K. 51°2N 0°15S **25** D8
Lower Saxony = Niedersachsen □
Germany 52°50N 9°0E **66** B5
Lower Tunguska → Russia 65°48N 88°4E **79** C10
Lowestoft U.K. 52°29N 1°45E **25** B12
Lowick U.K. 55°39N 1°57W **22** A5
Lowther Hills U.K. 55°20N 3°40W **21** D8
Lowville U.S.A. 43°47N 75°29W **113** D10
Loyauté, Îs. N. Cal. 20°50S 166°30E **99** E12
Lualaba →
Dem. Rep. of the Congo 0°26N 25°20E **96** D5
Luanda Angola 8°50S 13°15E **96** F2
Luang Prabang Laos 19°52N 102°10E **83** B2
Luangwa → Zambia 14°25S 30°25E **97** G6
Luanshya Zambia 13°3S 28°28E **97** G5
Luapula → Africa 14°55S 13°30E **97** G2
Lubango Angola 14°55S 13°30E **97** G2
Lubbock U.S.A. 33°35N 101°51W **110** D6
Lübeck Germany 53°52N 10°40E **66** B6
Lublin Poland 51°12N 22°38E **67** C12
Lubumbashi
Dem. Rep. of the Congo 11°40S 27°28E **97** G5
Lucania, Mt. Canada 61°1N 140°27W **108** C5

Lucca   Melbourn

Lucca Italy 43°50N 10°29E 70 C4
Luce Bay U.K. 54°45N 4°48W 20 E6
Lucea Jamaica 18°27N 78°10W 114 a
Lucena Phil. 13°56N 121°37E 83 B4
Lucknow India 26°50N 81°0E 85 F12
Lüda = Dalian China 38°50N 121°40E 81 C7
Lüderitz Namibia 26°41S 15°8E 97 K3
Ludgershall U.K. 51°15N 1°37W 24 D5
Ludgvan U.K. 50°9N 5°30W 27 G2
Ludhiana India 30°57N 75°56E 84 D9
Ludington U.S.A. 43°57N 86°27W 112 D4
Ludlow U.K. 52°22N 2°42W 23 H3
Ludwigsburg Germany 48°53N 9°11E 66 D5
Ludwigshafen Germany 49°29N 8°26E 66 D5
Lufkin U.S.A. 31°21N 94°44W 111 D8
Luga Russia 58°40N 29°55E 72 C4
Lugano Switz. 46°1N 8°57E 66 E5
Lugansk Ukraine 48°38N 39°15E 73 E6
Lugnaquillia Ireland 52°58N 6°28W 31 C10
Lugo Spain 43°2N 7°35W 69 A2
Lugwardine U.K. 52°4N 2°39W 23 H3
Luing U.K. 56°14N 5°39W 20 B4
Luleå Sweden 65°35N 22°10E 63 D8
Luleälven → Sweden 65°35N 22°10E 63 D8
Lundy U.K. 51°10N 4°41W 27 E4
Lune → U.K. 54°0N 2°51W 23 D3
Lüneburger Heide Germany 53°10N 10°12E 66 B6
Lunéville France 48°36N 6°30E 68 B7
Luni → India 24°41N 71°14E 84 G7
Luofu Dem. Rep. of the Congo 0°10S 29°15E 96 E5
Luoyang China 34°40N 112°26E 81 C6
Luray U.S.A. 38°40N 78°28W 112 F8
Lurgan U.K. 54°28N 6°19W 29 C9
Lusaka Zambia 15°28S 28°16E 97 H5
Lut, Dasht-e Iran 31°30N 58°0E 87 D9
Lutherstadt Wittenberg Germany 51°53N 12°39E 66 C7
Luton U.K. 51°53N 0°24W 25 C8
Lutselk'e Canada 62°24N 110°44W 108 C8
Lutsk Ukraine 50°50N 25°15E 67 C13
Lutterworth U.K. 52°28N 1°12W 24 H6
Luvua → Dem. Rep. of the Congo 6°50S 27°30W 90 G6
Luxembourg Lux. 49°37N 6°9E 65 E6
Luxembourg ■ Europe 49°45N 6°0E 65 E5
Luzern Switz. 47°3N 8°18E 66 E5
Luzhou China 28°52N 105°20E 80 D5
Luziânia Brazil 16°20S 48°0W 122 C1
Luzon Phil. 16°0N 121°0E 83 B4
Lvov Ukraine 49°50N 24°0E 67 D13
Lyakhov Is. Russia 73°40N 141°0E 79 B16
Lybster U.K. 58°18N 3°15W 19 F11
Lydd U.K. 50°57N 0°55E 25 E10
Lydford U.K. 50°38N 4°8W 27 F5
Lydham U.K. 52°31N 2°58W 23 G3
Lyme B. U.K. 50°42N 2°53W 24 E3
Lyme Regis U.K. 50°43N 2°57W 24 E3
Lyminge U.K. 51°7N 1°6E 25 D11
Lymington U.K. 50°45N 1°32W 24 E5
Lymm U.K. 53°23N 2°29W 23 F4
Lympne U.K. 51°4N 1°2E 25 D11
Lynchburg U.S.A. 37°25N 79°9W 112 G8
Lyndhurst U.K. 50°52N 1°35W 24 E5
Lyneham U.K. 51°30N 1°58W 24 C5
Lynmouth U.K. 51°13N 3°49W 27 E6
Lynn Lake Canada 56°51N 101°3W 108 D9
Lynton U.K. 51°13N 3°50W 27 E6
Lyonnais France 45°45N 4°15E 68 D6
Lyons France 45°46N 4°50E 68 D6
Lysva Russia 58°7N 57°49E 72 C10
Lysychansk Ukraine 48°55N 38°30E 73 E6
Lytchett Minster U.K. 50°44N 2°4W 24 E4
Lytham St. Anne's U.K. 53°45N 3°0W 23 E2
Lythe U.K. 54°31N 0°41W 22 C7
Lyubertsy Russia 55°40N 37°51E 72 C6

M

Ma-ubin Burma 16°44N 95°39E 85 L19
Ma'ān Jordan 30°12N 35°44E 86 D3
Ma'anshan China 31°44N 118°29E 81 C6
Maas → Neths. 51°45N 4°32E 65 C4
Maastricht Neths. 50°50N 5°40E 65 D5
Mablethorpe U.K. 53°20N 0°15E 23 F9
Macaé Brazil 22°20S 41°43W 122 D2
McAlester U.S.A. 34°56N 95°46W 111 D7
McAllen U.S.A. 26°12N 98°14W 111 E7
MacAlpine L. Canada 66°32N 102°45W 108 C9
Macapá Brazil 0°5S 51°4W 120 B4
Macau Brazil 5°15S 36°40W 120 C6
Macau China 22°12N 113°33E 81 D6
Macclesfield U.K. 53°15N 2°8W 23 F4
M'Clintock Chan. Canada 72°0N 102°0W 108 B9
M'Clure Str. Canada 75°0N 119°0W 109 B8
McComb U.S.A. 31°15N 90°27W 111 D8
McCook U.S.A. 40°12N 100°38W 110 B6
McDonald Is. Ind. Oc. 53°0S 73°0E 53 G13
MacDonnell Ranges Australia 23°40S 133°0E 98 E5
Macduff U.K. 57°40N 2°31W 19 G12
Macedonia □ Greece 40°39N 22°0E 71 D10
Macedonia ■ Europe 41°53N 21°40E 71 D9
Maceió Brazil 9°40S 35°41W 122 A3
Macgillicuddy's Reeks Ireland 51°58N 9°45W 30 E3
Mach Pakistan 29°50N 67°20E 84 E5
Machakos Kenya 1°30S 37°15E 96 E7
Machala Ecuador 3°20S 79°57W 120 B2
Machars, The U.K. 54°46N 4°30W 20 E6
Machias U.S.A. 44°43N 67°28W 113 C14
Machilipatnam India 16°12N 81°8E 85 L12
Machrihanish U.K. 55°25N 5°43W 20 D4
Machupicchu Peru 13°8S 72°30W 120 D2
Machynlleth U.K. 52°35N 3°50W 26 B5
Mackay Australia 21°8S 149°11E 98 E8
Mackay, L. Australia 22°30S 129°0E 98 E4
McKeesport U.S.A. 40°20N 79°51W 112 E8
Mackenzie Canada 55°20N 123°5W 108 D7
Mackenzie → Canada 69°10N 134°20W 108 C6
Mackenzie King I. Canada 77°45N 111°0W 109 B8

Mackenzie Mts. Canada 64°0N 130°0W 108 B6
Mackinaw City U.S.A. 45°47N 84°44W 112 C5
McKinley, Mt. U.S.A. 63°4N 151°0W 108 C4
McKinley Sea Arctic 82°0N 0°0 54 A7
McMinnville U.S.A. 45°13N 123°12W 110 A2
McMurdo Sd. Antarctica 77°0S 170°0E 55 D11
Macomb U.S.A. 40°27N 90°40W 112 E2
Mâcon France 46°19N 4°50E 68 C6
Macon U.S.A. 32°51N 83°38W 111 D10
McPherson U.S.A. 38°22N 97°40W 110 C7
Macquarie Is. Pac. Oc. 54°36S 158°55E 102 N7
Macroom Ireland 51°54N 8°57W 30 E5
Madagascar ■ Africa 20°0S 47°0E 97 J9
Madang Papua N. G. 5°12S 145°49E 98 B8
Madeira Atl. Oc. 32°50N 17°0W 94 B2
Madeira → Brazil 3°22S 58°45W 120 C4
Madeleine, Îs. de la Canada 47°30N 61°40W 113 B17
Madeley U.K. 53°0N 2°20W 23 F4
Madhya Pradesh □ India 22°50N 78°0E 84 H11
Madison Ind., U.S.A. 38°44N 85°23W 112 F5
Madison S. Dak., U.S.A. 44°0N 97°7W 111 B7
Madison Wis., U.S.A. 43°4N 89°24W 112 D2
Madisonville U.S.A. 37°20N 87°30W 112 G4
Madiun Indonesia 7°38S 111°32E 83 D3
Madley U.K. 52°2N 2°51W 24 B3
Madras = Chennai India 13°8N 80°19E 84 N12
Madre de Dios → Bolivia 10°59S 66°8W 120 D3
Madre de Dios, I. Chile 50°20S 75°10W 121 H2
Madre Occidental, Sierra Mexico 27°0N 107°0W 114 B3
Madre Oriental, Sierra Mexico 25°0N 100°0W 114 C5
Madrid Spain 40°24N 3°42W 69 B4
Madura Indonesia 7°30S 114°0E 83 D3
Madurai India 9°55N 78°10E 84 Q11
Maebashi Japan 36°24N 139°4E 82 E6
Maesteg U.K. 51°36N 3°40W 27 D6
Mafeking S. Africa 25°50S 25°38E 97 K5
Mafia I. Tanzania 7°45S 39°50E 96 F7
Magadan Russia 59°38N 150°50E 79 D17
Magallanes, Estrecho de Chile 52°30S 75°0W 121 H2
Magangué Colombia 9°14N 74°45W 120 B2
Magdalena → Colombia 11°6N 74°51W 120 A2
Magdeburg Germany 52°7N 11°38E 66 B6
Magee, I. U.K. 54°48N 5°43W 29 B10
Magelang Indonesia 7°29S 110°13E 83 D3
Magellan's Str. = Magallanes, Estrecho de Chile 52°30S 75°0W 121 H2
Maggiore, Lago Italy 45°57N 8°39E 70 B3
Maggotty Jamaica 18°9N 77°46W 114 a
Maghâgha Egypt 28°38N 30°50E 95 C12
Magherafelt U.K. 54°45N 6°37W 29 B8
Maghreb N. Afr. 32°0N 4°0W 90 C3
Maghull U.K. 53°31N 2°57W 23 E3
Magnetic Pole (North) Canada 82°42N 114°24W 54 A2
Magnetic Pole (South) Antarctica 64°8S 138°8E 55 C9
Magnitogorsk Russia 53°27N 59°4E 72 D10
Magog Canada 45°18N 72°9W 113 C11
Magwe Burma 20°10N 95°0E 85 J19
Mahābād Iran 36°50N 45°45E 86 B6
Mahajanga Madag. 15°40S 46°25E 97 H9
Mahakam → Indonesia 0°35S 117°17E 83 D3
Mahalapye Botswana 23°1S 26°51E 97 J5
Mahallāt Iran 33°55N 50°30E 87 C7
Mahanadi → India 20°20N 86°25E 85 J15
Maharashtra □ India 20°30N 75°30E 84 J9
Mahdia Tunisia 35°28N 11°0E 95 A8
Mahesana India 23°39N 72°26E 84 H8
Mahilyow Belarus 53°55N 30°18E 67 B16
Mai-Ndombe, L. Dem. Rep. of the Congo 2°0S 18°20E 96 E3
Maiden Bradley U.K. 51°9N 2°17W 24 D4
Maiden Newton U.K. 50°46N 2°34W 24 E3
Maidenhead U.K. 51°31N 0°42W 25 C7
Maidstone U.K. 51°16N 0°32E 25 D10
Maiduguri Nigeria 12°0N 13°20E 95 F8
Maijdi Bangla. 22°48N 91°10E 85 H17
Main → Germany 50°0N 8°18E 66 C5
Main → U.K. 54°48N 6°18W 29 B9
Maine France 48°20N 0°15W 68 C3
Maine □ U.S.A. 45°20N 69°0W 113 C13
Maine → Ireland 52°9N 9°45W 30 D3
Mainland Orkney, U.K. 58°59N 3°8W 19 E11
Mainland Shet., U.K. 60°15N 1°22W 18 B15
Mainz Germany 50°1N 8°14E 66 C5
Maiquetía Venezuela 10°36N 66°57W 120 A3
Majorca = Mallorca Spain 39°30N 3°0E 69 C7
Makale Indonesia 3°6S 119°51E 83 D3
Makasar, Str. of Indonesia 1°0S 118°20E 83 D3
Makgadikgadi Salt Pans Botswana 20°40S 25°45E 97 J5
Makhachkala Russia 43°0N 47°30E 73 F8
Makhado S. Africa 23°1S 29°43E 97 J5
Makran Coast Range Pakistan 25°40N 64°0E 84 G4
Makurdi Nigeria 7°43N 8°35E 94 G7
Mal B. Ireland 52°50N 9°30W 30 C4
Malabar Coast India 11°0N 75°0E 84 P9
Malacca, Straits of Indonesia 3°0N 101°0E 83 C2
Málaga Spain 36°43N 4°23W 69 D3
Malahide Ireland 53°26N 6°9W 31 B10
Malaita Solomon Is. 9°0S 161°0E 99 B11
Malakâl Sudan 9°33N 31°40E 95 G12
Malakula Vanuatu 16°15S 167°30E 99 D12
Malang Indonesia 7°59S 112°45E 83 D3
Malanje Angola 9°36S 16°17E 96 F3
Mälaren Sweden 59°30N 17°10E 63 F7
Malatya Turkey 38°25N 38°20E 73 G6
Malawi ■ Africa 11°55S 34°0E 97 G6
Malawi, L. Africa 12°30S 34°30E 97 G6
Malay Pen. Asia 7°25N 100°0E 74 H2
Malāyer Iran 34°19N 48°51E 86 C7
Malaysia ■ Asia 5°0N 110°0E 83 C4
Malden U.S.A. 36°34N 89°57W 112 G3
Malden I. Kiribati 4°3S 155°1W 103 H12
Maldives ■ Ind. Oc. 5°0N 73°0E 75 H9

Maldon U.K. 51°44N 0°42E 25 C10
Maldonado Uruguay 34°59S 55°0W 121 F4
Malegaon India 20°30N 74°38E 84 J9
Malham Tarn U.K. 54°6N 2°10W 22 D4
Malheur L., U.S.A. 43°20N 118°48W 110 B3
Mali ■ Africa 17°0N 3°0W 94 E5
Malin Hd. Ireland 55°23N 7°23W 28 A7
Malin Pen. Ireland 55°20N 7°17W 29 A7
Malindi Kenya 3°12S 40°5E 96 E8
Mallaig U.K. 57°0N 5°50W 18 H6
Mallawi Egypt 27°44N 30°44E 95 C12
Mallorca Spain 39°30N 3°0E 69 C7
Mallow Ireland 52°8N 8°39W 30 D5
Malmesbury U.K. 51°35N 2°5W 24 C4
Malmö Sweden 55°36N 12°59E 63 F6
Malone U.S.A. 44°51N 74°18W 113 C10
Malpas U.K. 53°1N 2°45W 23 F3
Malpelo, I. de Colombia 4°3N 81°35W 103 G19
Malta ■ Europe 35°55N 14°26E 70 a
Maltby U.K. 53°25N 1°12W 23 F6
Malton U.K. 54°8N 0°49W 22 D7
Malvinas, Is. = Falkland Is. ☑ Atl. Oc. 51°30S 59°0W 121 H4
Mamoré → Bolivia 10°23S 65°53W 120 D3
Mamoudzou Mayotte 12°48S 45°14E 91 H8
Man Ivory C. 7°30N 7°40W 94 G4
Man, I. of U.K. 54°15N 4°30W 29 C12
Manacles, The U.K. 50°2N 5°4W 27 G3
Manado Indonesia 1°29N 124°51E 83 C4
Managua Nic. 12°6N 86°20W 114 E7
Manas China 44°17N 85°56E 80 B3
Manati Puerto Rico 18°26N 66°29W 115 d
Manby U.K. 53°21N 0°6E 23 F9
Manchester U.K. 53°29N 2°12W 23 F4
Manchester U.S.A. 42°59N 71°28W 113 D12
Manchester Int. ✈ (MAN) U.K. 53°21N 2°17W 23 F4
Manchuria China 45°0N 125°0E 81 B7
Manchurian Plain China 47°0N 124°0E 74 D14
Mandal Norway 58°2N 7°25E 63 F5
Mandalay Burma 22°0N 96°4E 85 J20
Mandalgovĭ Mongolia 45°45N 106°10E 80 B5
Mandan U.S.A. 46°50N 100°54W 110 A6
Mandeville Jamaica 18°2N 77°31W 114 a
Mandla India 22°39N 80°30E 85 H12
Mandsaur India 24°3N 75°8E 84 G9
Mandvi India 22°51N 69°22E 84 H6
Manea U.K. 52°29N 0°10E 25 B9
Manfalût Egypt 27°30N 30°52E 95 C12
Manfredónia Italy 41°38N 15°55E 70 D6
Mangabeiras, Chapada das Brazil 10°0S 46°30W 122 B1
Mangalore India 12°55N 74°47E 84 N9
Mangnai China 37°52N 91°43E 80 C4
Mangole Indonesia 1°50S 125°55E 83 D4
Mangotsfield U.K. 51°29N 2°30W 24 C4
Manhattan U.S.A. 39°11N 96°35W 111 C7
Manhuaçu Brazil 20°15S 42°2W 122 D2
Manica Mozam. 18°58S 32°59E 97 H6
Manicoré Brazil 5°48S 61°16W 120 C3
Manicouagan → Canada 49°30N 68°30W 109 E13
Manicouagan, Rés. Canada 51°5N 68°40W 109 D13
Manihiki Cook Is. 10°24S 161°1W 103 J11
Manila Phil. 14°35N 120°58E 83 B4
Manipur □ India 25°0N 94°0E 85 G19
Manisa Turkey 38°38N 27°30E 73 G4
Manistee U.S.A. 44°15N 86°19W 112 C4
Manistee → U.S.A. 44°15N 86°21W 112 C4
Manistique U.S.A. 45°57N 86°15W 112 C4
Manitoba □ Canada 53°30N 97°0W 108 D10
Manitoba, L. Canada 51°0N 98°45W 108 D10
Manitou Is. U.S.A. 45°8N 86°0W 112 C4
Manitoulin I. Canada 45°40N 82°30W 112 C6
Manitowoc U.S.A. 44°5N 87°40W 112 C4
Manizales Colombia 5°5N 75°32W 120 B2
Mankato U.S.A. 44°10N 94°0W 111 B8
Mannar Sri Lanka 9°1N 79°54E 84 Q11
Mannar, G. of Asia 8°30N 79°0E 84 Q11
Mannheim Germany 49°29N 8°29E 66 D5
Manning Canada 56°53N 117°39W 108 D8
Manningtree U.K. 51°56N 1°5E 25 C11
Manokwari Indonesia 0°54S 134°0E 83 D5
Manosque France 43°49N 5°47E 68 E6
Manresa Spain 41°48N 1°50E 69 B6
Mansel I. Canada 62°0N 80°0W 109 C12
Mansfield U.K. 53°9N 1°11W 23 F6
Mansfield U.S.A. 40°45N 82°31W 112 E6
Mansfield Woodhouse U.K. 53°11N 1°12W 23 F6
Manta Ecuador 1°0S 80°40W 120 C1
Mantes-la-Jolie France 48°58N 1°41E 68 B4
Mantiqueira, Serra da Brazil 22°0S 44°0W 116 F6
Manton U.K. 52°38N 0°41W 23 G7
Mántova Italy 45°9N 10°48E 70 B4
Manuel Alves → Brazil 11°19S 48°28W 122 B1
Manzai Pakistan 32°12N 70°15E 84 C7
Manzanillo Cuba 20°20N 77°31W 115 C9
Manzanillo Mexico 19°3N 104°20W 114 D4
Manzhouli China 49°35N 117°25E 81 B6
Maó Spain 39°53N 4°16E 69 C8
Maoming China 21°50N 110°54E 81 D6
Mapam Yumco China 30°45N 81°28E 80 C3
Maputo Mozam. 25°58S 32°32E 97 K6
Maputo B. Mozam. 25°50S 32°45E 97 K6
Maquinchao Argentina 41°15S 68°50W 121 G3
Maquoketa U.S.A. 42°4N 90°40W 112 D2
Mar U.K. 57°11N 2°53W 19 H13
Mar, Serra do Brazil 25°30S 49°0W 116 F6
Mar Chiquita, L. Argentina 30°40S 62°50W 121 F3
Mar del Plata Argentina 38°0S 57°30W 121 F4
Marabá Brazil 5°20S 49°5W 120 C5
Maracá, I. de Brazil 2°10N 50°30W 120 B4
Maracaibo Venezuela 10°40N 71°37W 120 A2
Maracaibo, L. Venezuela 9°40N 71°30W 120 B2
Maracay Venezuela 10°15N 67°28W 120 A3
Maradi Niger 13°29N 7°20E 94 F7
Maragogipe Brazil 12°46S 38°55W 122 B3

Marajó, I. de Brazil 1°0S 49°30W 120 C5
Maranguape Brazil 3°55S 38°50W 120 C6
Maranhão □ Brazil 5°0S 46°0W 120 C5
Marañón → Peru 4°30S 73°35W 120 C2
Marazion U.K. 50°7N 5°29W 27 G3
Marbella Spain 36°30N 4°57W 69 D3
March U.K. 52°33N 0°5E 25 A9
Marche France 46°5N 1°20E 68 C4
Marcus I. Pac. Oc. 24°20N 153°58E 102 E7
Mardan Pakistan 34°20N 72°0E 84 B8
Marden U.K. 52°7N 2°42W 24 B3
Mardin Turkey 37°20N 40°43E 73 G7
Maree, L. U.K. 57°40N 5°26W 18 G7
Mareham le Fen U.K. 53°8N 0°4W 23 F8
Marfleet U.K. 53°45N 0°17W 23 E8
Margarita, I. de Venezuela 11°0N 64°0W 120 A3
Margate U.K. 51°23N 1°23E 25 D11
Marghilon Uzbekistan 40°27N 71°42E 87 A12
Märgow, Dasht-e Afghan. 30°40N 62°30E 87 D10
Mari El □ Russia 56°30N 48°0E 72 C8
Mariana Trench Pac. Oc. 13°0N 145°0E 102 F6
Marias, Is. Mexico 21°25N 106°28W 114 C3
Maribor Slovenia 46°36N 15°40E 66 E8
Marie Byrd Land Antarctica 79°30S 125°0W 55 D14
Marie-Galante Guadeloupe 15°56N 61°16W 114 b
Mariental Namibia 24°36S 18°0E 97 J3
Marietta U.S.A. 39°25N 81°27W 112 F7
Marília Brazil 22°13S 50°0W 120 E4
Marinette U.S.A. 45°6N 87°38W 112 C4
Marion Ill., U.S.A. 37°44N 88°56W 112 G3
Marion Ind., U.S.A. 40°32N 85°40W 112 E5
Marion Ohio, U.S.A. 40°35N 83°8W 112 E6
Mariupol Ukraine 47°5N 37°31E 73 E6
Markam China 29°42N 98°38E 80 D4
Market Bosworth U.K. 52°38N 1°24W 23 G6
Market Deeping U.K. 52°41N 0°19W 23 G8
Market Drayton U.K. 52°54N 2°29W 23 G4
Market Harborough U.K. 52°29N 0°55W 23 H7
Market Lavington U.K. 51°17N 1°58W 24 D5
Market Rasen U.K. 53°24N 0°20W 23 F8
Market Weighton U.K. 53°52N 0°40W 23 E7
Markfield U.K. 52°42N 1°17W 23 G6
Markham, Mt. Antarctica 83°0S 164°0E 55 E11
Marks Tey U.K. 51°52N 0°49E 25 C10
Marlborough U.K. 51°25N 1°43W 24 D5
Marlborough Downs U.K. 51°27N 1°53W 24 D5
Marlow U.K. 51°34N 0°46W 25 C7
Marmara, Sea of Turkey 40°45N 28°15E 73 F4
Marmaris Turkey 36°50N 28°14E 86 b2
Marmora Canada 44°28N 77°41W 112 C9
Marne → France 48°47N 2°29E 68 B5
Marnhull U.K. 50°57N 2°19W 24 E4
Maroua Cameroon 10°40N 14°20E 95 F8
Marple U.K. 53°24N 2°4W 23 F4
Marquette U.S.A. 46°33N 87°24W 112 B4
Marquis St. Lucia 14°2N 60°54W 115 f
Marquises, Îs. French Polynesia 9°30S 140°0W 103 H14
Marrakesh Morocco 31°9N 8°0W 94 B4
Marree Australia 29°39S 138°1E 98 F6
Marsá Matrûh Egypt 31°19N 27°9E 95 B11
Marsabit Kenya 2°18N 38°0E 96 D7
Marsala Italy 37°48N 12°26E 70 F5
Marseilles France 43°18N 5°23E 68 E6
Marsh I. U.S.A. 29°34N 91°53W 111 E8
Marshall U.S.A. 32°33N 94°23W 111 D8
Marshall Is. ■ Pac. Oc. 9°0N 171°0E 102 G9
Marshfield U.K. 51°28N 2°19W 24 D4
Marshfield U.S.A. 44°40N 90°10W 112 C2
Marske by the Sea U.K. 54°36N 1°0W 22 C7
Marston Moor U.K. 53°58N 1°17W 23 E6
Martaban Burma 16°30N 97°35E 85 L20
Martaban, G. of Burma 16°5N 96°30E 85 L20
Martapura Indonesia 3°22S 114°47E 83 D3
Martham U.K. 52°42N 1°37E 25 A12
Martha's Vineyard U.S.A. 41°25N 70°38W 113 E12
Martigues France 43°24N 5°4E 68 E6
Martinique ☑ W. Indies 14°40N 61°0W 114 c
Martin's Bay Barbados 13°12N 59°29W 115 g
Martinsburg U.S.A. 39°27N 77°58W 112 F9
Martinsville U.S.A. 39°26N 86°25W 112 F4
Martley U.K. 52°15N 2°21W 24 B4
Martock U.K. 50°58N 2°46W 24 E3
Marwar India 25°43N 73°45E 84 G8
Mary Turkmenistan 37°40N 61°50E 87 B10
Maryborough Australia 25°31S 152°37E 98 F9
Maryland □ U.S.A. 39°0N 76°30W 112 F9
Maryport U.K. 54°44N 3°28W 22 C2
Marystown Canada 47°10N 55°10W 109 E14
Marytavy U.K. 50°36N 4°7W 27 F5
Marzûq Libya 25°53N 13°57E 95 C8
Masai Steppe Tanzania 4°30S 36°30E 96 E7
Masan S. Korea 35°11N 128°32E 81 C7
Masandam, Ra's Oman 26°30N 56°30E 88 B6
Masaya Nic. 12°0N 86°7W 114 E7
Masbate Phil. 12°21N 123°36E 83 B4
Mascara Algeria 35°26N 0°6E 94 A6
Maseru Lesotho 29°18S 27°30E 97 K5
Masham U.K. 54°14N 1°39W 22 D5
Mashhad Iran 36°20N 59°35E 87 B9
Mashonaland Zimbabwe 16°30S 31°0E 97 H6
Maşirah Oman 21°0N 58°50E 88 C6
Masjed Soleyman Iran 31°55N 49°18E 86 D7
Mask, L. Ireland 53°36N 9°22W 28 D2
Mason City U.S.A. 43°9N 93°12W 111 B8
Massa Italy 44°1N 10°9E 70 B4
Massachusetts □ U.S.A. 42°30N 72°0W 113 D11
Massawa Eritrea 15°35N 39°25E 89 D2
Massena U.S.A. 44°56N 74°54W 113 C10
Massif Central France 44°55N 3°0E 68 D5
Massillon U.S.A. 40°48N 81°32W 112 E7
Masurian Lakes Poland 53°50N 21°0E 67 B11
Masvingo Zimbabwe 20°8S 30°49E 97 J6
Mata-Utu Wall. & F. Is. 13°17S 176°8W 99 C15
Matabeleland Zimbabwe 18°0S 27°0E 97 H5
Matadi Dem. Rep. of the Congo 5°52S 13°31E 96 F2
Matagalpa Nic. 13°0N 85°58W 114 E7

Matagami Canada 49°45N 77°34W 109 E12
Matagami, L. Canada 49°50N 77°40W 109 E12
Matagorda I. U.S.A. 28°15N 96°30W 111 E7
Matamoros Mexico 25°32N 103°15W 114 B5
Matane Canada 48°50N 67°33W 109 E13
Matanzas Cuba 23°0N 81°40W 115 C8
Matara Sri Lanka 5°58N 80°30E 84 S12
Mataró Spain 41°32N 2°29E 69 B7
Matehuala Mexico 23°39N 100°39W 114 C4
Mateke Hills Zimbabwe 21°48S 31°0E 97 J6
Matera Italy 40°40N 16°36E 70 D7
Mathura India 27°30N 77°40E 84 F10
Mati Phil. 6°55N 126°15E 83 C4
Matlock U.K. 53°9N 1°33W 23 F5
Mato Grosso □ Brazil 14°0S 55°0W 120 D4
Mato Grosso, Planalto do Brazil 15°0S 55°0W 120 D4
Mato Grosso do Sul □ Brazil 18°0S 55°0W 120 D4
Matopo Hills Zimbabwe 20°36S 28°20E 97 J5
Maţraḥ Oman 23°37N 58°30E 87 F9
Matsue Japan 35°25N 133°10E 82 F3
Matsumoto Japan 36°15N 138°0E 82 E6
Matsusaka Japan 34°34N 136°32E 82 F5
Matsuyama Japan 33°45N 132°45E 82 G3
Mattagami → Canada 50°43N 81°29W 109 D11
Mattancheri India 9°50N 76°15E 84 Q10
Mattawa Canada 46°20N 78°45W 112 B8
Matterhorn Switz. 45°58N 7°39E 66 F4
Matthew, Î. N. Cal. 22°29S 171°15E 99 E13
Mattoon U.S.A. 39°29N 88°23W 112 F3
Maturín Venezuela 9°45N 63°11W 120 B3
Maubeuge France 50°17N 3°57E 68 A6
Maudin Sun Burma 16°0N 94°30E 85 M19
Maui U.S.A. 20°48N 156°20W 110 H16
Maumee → U.S.A. 41°42N 83°28W 112 E6
Maumturk Mts. Ireland 53°32N 9°42W 28 D2
Maun Botswana 20°0S 23°26E 97 H4
Mauna Kea U.S.A. 19°50N 155°28W 110 J17
Mauna Loa U.S.A. 19°30N 155°35W 110 J17
Mauritania ■ Africa 20°50N 10°0W 94 E3
Mauritius ■ Ind. Oc. 20°0S 57°0E 91 J9
Mawgan U.K. 50°4N 5°13W 27 G3
Maxwellheugh U.K. 55°35N 2°26W 21 C11
May, I. of U.K. 56°11N 2°32W 21 B10
May Pen Jamaica 17°58N 77°15W 114 a
Mayaguana Bahamas 22°30N 72°44W 115 C10
Mayagüez Puerto Rico 18°12N 67°9W 115 d
Maybole U.K. 55°21N 4°42W 20 D6
Mayfield E. Sussex, U.K. 51°1N 0°17E 25 D9
Mayfield Staffs., U.K. 53°1N 1°47W 23 F5
Mayfield U.S.A. 36°44N 88°38W 112 G3
Maykop Russia 44°35N 40°10E 73 F7
Maynooth Ireland 53°23N 6°34W 31 B9
Mayo Canada 63°38N 135°57W 108 C6
Mayo □ Ireland 53°53N 9°3W 28 D3
Mayon Volcano Phil. 13°15N 123°41E 83 B4
Mayotte ☑ Ind. Oc. 12°50S 45°10E 97 G9
Maysville U.S.A. 38°39N 83°46W 112 F6
Māzandarān □ Iran 36°30N 52°0E 87 B8
Mazar China 36°32N 77°1E 80 C2
Mazār-e Sharīf Afghan. 36°41N 67°0E 87 B11
Mazaruni → Guyana 6°25N 58°35W 120 B4
Mazatlán Mexico 23°13N 106°25W 114 C3
Mazyr Belarus 51°59N 29°15E 72 D4
Mbabane Swaziland 26°18S 31°6E 97 K6
Mbaïki C.A.R. 3°53N 18°1E 96 D3
Mbala Zambia 8°46S 31°24E 96 F6
Mbale Uganda 1°8N 34°12E 96 D6
Mbandaka Dem. Rep. of the Congo 0°1N 18°18E 96 D3
Mbanza Ngungu Dem. Rep. of the Congo 5°12S 14°53E 96 F2
Mbeya Tanzania 8°54S 33°29E 96 F6
Mbour Senegal 14°22N 16°54W 94 F2
Mbuji-Mayi Dem. Rep. of the Congo 6°9S 23°40E 96 F4
Mdantsane S. Africa 32°56S 27°46E 97 L5
Mead, L. U.S.A. 36°0N 114°44W 110 C4
Meadow Lake Canada 54°10N 108°26W 108 D9
Meadville U.S.A. 41°39N 80°9W 112 E7
Meaford Canada 44°36N 80°35W 112 C7
Mealsgate U.K. 54°47N 3°13W 22 C2
Mearns, Howe of the U.K. 56°52N 2°26W 19 J13
Measham U.K. 52°43N 1°31W 23 G5
Meath □ Ireland 53°40N 6°57W 29 D8
Meaux France 48°58N 2°50E 68 B5
Mecca Si. Arabia 21°30N 39°54E 86 F4
Mechelen Belgium 51°2N 4°29E 65 C4
Mecklenburg Germany 53°33N 11°40E 66 B6
Mecklenburger Bucht Germany 54°20N 11°40E 66 A6
Medan Indonesia 3°40N 98°38E 83 C1
Médéa Algeria 36°12N 2°50E 94 A6
Medellín Colombia 6°15N 75°35W 120 B2
Medford Oreg. U.S.A. 42°19N 122°52W 110 B2
Medford Wis., U.S.A. 45°9N 90°20W 112 C2
Medicine Hat Canada 50°0N 110°45W 108 E8
Medina Si. Arabia 24°35N 39°52E 86 E4
Mediterranean Sea Europe 35°0N 15°0E 90 C5
Médoc France 45°10N 0°50W 68 D3
Medstead U.K. 51°8N 1°3W 24 D6
Medvezhyegorsk Russia 63°0N 34°25E 72 B5
Medway □ U.K. 51°27N 0°46E 25 D10
Medway → U.K. 51°27N 0°46E 25 D10
Meekatharra Australia 26°32S 118°29E 98 F2
Meerut India 29°1N 77°42E 84 E10
Meghalaya □ India 25°50N 91°0E 85 G17
Meghna → Bangla. 22°50N 90°50E 85 H17
Megisti Greece 36°8N 29°34E 86 b2
Meighen I. Canada 80°0N 99°30W 109 B10
Meiktila Burma 20°53N 95°54E 85 J19
Meizhou China 24°16N 116°6E 81 D6
Mejillones Chile 23°10S 70°30W 121 E2
Mekele Ethiopia 13°33N 39°30E 89 E2
Mekhtar Pakistan 30°30N 69°15E 84 D6
Meknès Morocco 33°57N 5°33W 94 B4
Mekong → Asia 9°30N 106°15E 83 C2
Melaka Malaysia 2°15N 102°15E 83 C2
Melanesia Pac. Oc. 4°0S 155°0E 102 H7
Melbourn U.K. 52°4N 0°0 25 B9

Melbourne   **Nangarhār**

Melbourne Australia 37°48S 144°58E 98 H8
Melbourne U.K. 52°50N 1°25W 23 G6
Mèlèzes → Canada 57°40N 69°29W 109 D13
Melfort Canada 52°50N 104°37W 108 D9
Melilla N. Afr. 35°21N 2°57W 69 E4
Melitopol Ukraine 46°50N 35°22E 73 E6
Melksham U.K. 51°23N 2°8W 24 D4
Melmerby U.K. 54°45N 2°35W 22 C3
Melrhir, Chott Algeria 34°13N 6°30E 94 B7
Melrose U.K. 55°36N 2°43W 21 C10
Melsonby U.K. 54°29N 1°42W 22 D5
Melton Constable U.K. 52°52N 1°2E 25 A11
Melton Mowbray U.K. 52°47N 0°54W 23 G7
Melun France 48°32N 2°39E 68 B5
Melville Canada 50°55N 102°50W 108 D9
Melville I. Australia 11°30S 131°0E 98 C5
Melville I. Canada 75°30N 112°0W 109 B8
Melville Pen. Canada 68°0N 84°0W 109 C11
Memphis U.S.A. 35°8N 90°2W 111 C9
Menai Bridge U.K. 53°14N 4°10W 26 A5
Menai Strait U.K. 53°11N 4°13W 26 A5
Mende France 44°31N 3°30E 68 D5
Mendip Hills U.K. 51°17N 2°40W 24 D3
Mendlesham U.K. 52°16N 1°6E 25 B11
Mendocino, C. U.S.A. 40°26N 124°25W 110 B2
Mendota U.S.A. 41°33N 89°7W 112 E3
Mendoza Argentina 32°50S 68°52W 121 F3
Mengzi China 23°20N 103°22E 80 D5
Menominee U.S.A. 45°6N 87°37W 112 C4
Menominee → U.S.A. 45°6N 87°35W 112 C4
Menomonie U.S.A. 44°53N 91°55W 112 C2
Menorca Spain 40°0N 4°0E 69 C8
Mentawai, Kepulauan Indonesia 2°0S 99°0E 83 D1
Merca Somali Rep. 1°48N 44°50E 88 G3
Merced U.S.A. 37°18N 120°29W 110 C2
Mercedes Corrientes, Argentina 29°10S 58°5W 121 E4
Mercedes San Luis, Argentina 33°40S 65°21W 121 F3
Mercedes Uruguay 33°12S 58°0W 121 F4
Mercy, C. Canada 65°0N 63°30W 109 C13
Mere U.K. 51°6N 2°16W 24 D4
Mergui Burma 12°26N 98°34E 83 B1
Mérida Mexico 20°58N 89°37W 114 C7
Mérida Spain 38°55N 6°25W 69 C2
Mérida Venezuela 8°24N 71°8W 120 B2
Mérida, Cord. de Venezuela 9°0N 71°0W 116 C3
Meriden U.K. 52°26N 1°38W 23 H5
Meriden U.S.A. 41°32N 72°48W 113 E11
Meridian U.S.A. 32°22N 88°42W 111 D9
Merrick U.K. 55°8N 4°28W 20 D7
Merrill U.S.A. 45°11N 89°41W 112 C3
Merritt Canada 50°10N 120°45W 108 D7
Merse U.K. 55°43N 2°16W 21 C11
Mersea I. U.K. 51°47N 0°58E 25 C10
Mersey → U.K. 53°25N 3°1W 23 F2
Merseyside □ U.K. 53°31N 3°2W 23 E2
Merthyr Tydfil U.K. 51°45N 3°22W 26 D7
Merton □ U.K. 51°25N 0°11W 25 D8
Meru Kenya 0°3N 37°40E 96 D7
Meru Tanzania 3°15S 36°46E 96 E7
Mesa U.S.A. 33°25N 111°50W 110 D4
Mesopotamia Iraq 33°30N 44°0E 86 C5
Messina Italy 38°11N 15°34E 70 E6
Messina, Str. di Italy 38°15N 15°35E 70 F6
Mestre, Espigão Brazil 12°30S 46°10W 122 B1
Meta → S. Amer. 6°12N 67°28W 120 B3
Meta Incognita Pen. Canada 62°45N 68°30W 109 C13
Metheringham U.K. 53°9N 0°23W 23 F8
Methwold U.K. 52°32N 0°33E 25 A10
Metlakatla U.S.A. 55°8N 131°35W 108 D6
Metropolis U.S.A. 37°9N 88°44W 112 G3
Metz France 49°8N 6°10E 68 B7
Meuse → Europe 50°45N 5°41E 65 D5
Mevagissey U.K. 50°16N 4°48W 27 G4
Mevagissey B. U.K. 50°17N 4°47W 27 G4
Mexborough U.K. 53°30N 1°15W 23 E6
Mexiana, I. Brazil 0°0 49°30W 120 B5
Mexicali Mexico 32°40N 115°30W 114 A1
México Mexico 19°24N 99°9W 114 D5
Mexico ■ Cent. Amer. 25°0N 105°0W 114 C4
Mexico, G. of Cent. Amer. 25°0N 90°0W 114 C7
Meymaneh Afghan. 35°53N 64°38E 87 C11
Mezen → Russia 65°44N 44°22E 72 A7
Miami U.S.A. 25°46N 80°11W 111 E10
Miändowāb Iran 37°0N 46°5E 86 B6
Miäneh Iran 37°30N 47°40E 86 B6
Mianwali Pakistan 32°38N 71°28E 84 C7
Mianyang China 31°22N 104°47E 80 C5
Miass Russia 54°59N 60°6E 72 D11
Micheldever U.K. 51°9N 1°14W 24 D6
Michigan □ U.S.A. 44°0N 85°0W 112 B4
Michigan, L. U.S.A. 44°0N 87°0W 112 B4
Michipicoten I. Canada 47°40N 85°40W 112 B5
Michurinsk Russia 52°58N 40°27E 72 D7
Mickle Fell U.K. 54°37N 2°18W 22 C4
Mickleover U.K. 52°55N 1°33W 23 G5
Mickleton U.K. 54°36N 2°2W 22 C4
Micoud St. Lucia 13°49N 60°54W 115 f
Micronesia Pac. Oc. 11°0N 160°0E 102 G7
Micronesia, Federated States of ■ Pac. Oc. 9°0N 150°0E 102 G7
Middelburg Neths. 51°30N 3°36E 65 C3
Middelburg S. Africa 31°30S 25°0E 97 L5
Middle Atlas Morocco 33°0N 5°0W 94 B4
Middle East Asia 35°0N 40°0E 74 E5
Middleham U.K. 54°17N 1°48W 22 C5
Middlemarsh U.K. 50°51N 2°28W 24 E4
Middlesbrough U.K. 54°35N 1°13W 22 C6
Middleton Gt. Man., U.K. 53°33N 2°12W 23 E4
Middleton Norfolk, U.K. 52°43N 0°29E 25 A9
Middleton Cheney U.K. 52°5N 1°16W 24 B6
Middleton in Teesdale U.K. 54°38N 2°4W 22 C4
Middleton on the Wolds U.K. 53°56N 0°35W 23 E7
Middletown U.K. 54°17N 6°51W 29 C8
Middletown N.Y., U.S.A. 41°27N 74°25W 113 E10
Middletown Ohio, U.S.A. 39°31N 84°24W 112 F5
Middlewich U.K. 53°12N 2°28W 23 F4
Middlezoy U.K. 51°5N 2°54W 24 D3

Midhurst U.K. 50°59N 0°44W 25 E7
Midi, Canal du → France 43°45N 1°21E 68 E4
Midland Canada 44°45N 79°50W 112 C8
Midland Mich., U.S.A. 43°37N 84°14W 112 D5
Midland Tex., U.S.A. 32°0N 102°3W 110 D6
Midleton Ireland 51°55N 8°10W 30 E6
Midsomer Norton U.K. 51°17N 2°28W 24 D4
Midway Is. Pac. Oc. 28°13N 177°22W 102 E10
Mieres Spain 43°18N 5°48W 69 A3
Mikhaylovka Russia 50°3N 43°5E 73 D7
Milan Italy 45°28N 9°10E 70 B3
Milborne Port U.K. 50°58N 2°28W 24 E4
Mildenhall U.K. 52°21N 0°32E 25 B10
Mildura Australia 34°13S 142°9E 98 G7
Miles City U.S.A. 46°25N 105°51W 110 A5
Milford U.S.A. 38°55N 75°26W 113 F10
Milford Haven U.K. 51°42N 5°7W 26 D3
Milford on Sea U.K. 50°43N 1°35W 24 E5
Milh, Bahr al Iraq 32°40N 43°35E 86 C5
Milk → U.S.A. 48°4N 106°19W 110 A5
Millau France 44°8N 3°4E 68 D5
Millbrook U.K. 50°20N 4°14W 27 G5
Millet St. Lucia 13°55N 60°59W 115 f
Millinocket U.S.A. 45°39N 68°43W 113 C13
Millom U.K. 54°13N 3°16W 22 C2
Milltown Malbay Ireland 52°52N 9°24W 30 C4
Millville U.S.A. 39°24N 75°2W 113 F10
Milngavie U.K. 55°56N 4°19W 20 C7
Milnthorpe U.K. 54°14N 2°45W 22 C3
Milos Greece 36°44N 24°25E 71 F11
Milton Abbot U.K. 50°35N 4°16W 27 F5
Milton Keynes U.K. 52°1N 0°44W 25 B7
Milverton U.K. 51°1N 3°16W 24 D2
Milwaukee U.S.A. 43°2N 87°54W 112 D4
Min Jiang → Fujian, China 26°0N 119°35E 81 D6
Min Jiang → Sichuan, China 28°45N 104°40E 80 D5
Minas Uruguay 34°20S 55°10W 121 F4
Minas Gerais □ Brazil 18°50S 46°0W 122 C1
Minatitlán Mexico 17°59N 94°31W 114 D6
Minchinhampton U.K. 51°42N 2°11W 24 C4
Mindanao Phil. 8°0N 125°0E 83 C4
Mindoro Phil. 13°0N 121°0E 83 B4
Mindoro Str. Phil. 12°30N 120°30E 83 B4
Minehead U.K. 51°12N 3°29W 24 D2
Mineral Wells U.S.A. 32°48N 98°7W 110 D7
Minfeng China 37°4N 82°46E 80 C3
Minginish U.K. 57°14N 6°15W 18 H5
Mingulay U.K. 56°49N 7°39W 18 J2
Minna Nigeria 9°37N 6°30E 94 G7
Minneapolis U.S.A. 44°57N 93°16W 111 B8
Minnesota □ U.S.A. 46°0N 94°15W 111 A8
Minorca = Menorca Spain 40°0N 4°0E 69 C8
Minot U.S.A. 48°14N 101°18W 110 A6
Minsk Belarus 53°52N 27°30E 67 B14
Minster Kent, U.K. 51°20N 1°20E 25 D11
Minster Kent, U.K. 51°25N 0°50E 25 D10
Minsterley U.K. 52°39N 2°54W 23 G3
Minto, L. Canada 57°13N 75°0W 109 D12
Miramichi B. Canada 47°15N 65°0W 113 B15
Mirim, L. S. Amer. 32°45S 52°50W 121 F4
Mirnyy Russia 62°33N 113°53E 79 C13
Mirpur Khas Pakistan 25°30N 69°0E 84 G6
Mirtoo Sea Greece 37°0N 23°20E 71 F10
Mirzapur India 25°10N 82°34E 85 G13
Mishan China 45°37N 131°48E 81 B8
Mishawaka U.S.A. 41°40N 86°11W 112 E4
Miskolc Hungary 48°7N 20°50E 67 D11
Misool Indonesia 1°52S 130°10E 83 D5
Mişrātah Libya 32°24N 15°3E 95 B9
Missinaibi → Canada 50°43N 81°29W 109 D11
Mississippi □ U.S.A. 33°0N 90°0W 111 D9
Mississippi → U.S.A. 29°9N 89°15W 111 E9
Mississippi River Delta U.S.A. 29°10N 89°15W 111 E9
Missoula U.S.A. 46°52N 114°1W 110 A4
Missouri □ U.S.A. 38°25N 92°30W 111 C8
Missouri → U.S.A. 38°49N 90°7W 111 C8
Mistassini, L. Canada 51°0N 73°30W 109 D12
Misterton Notts., U.K. 53°27N 0°50W 23 F7
Misterton Somst., U.K. 50°52N 2°47W 24 E3
Mitcheldean U.K. 51°51N 2°28W 24 C4
Mitchell U.S.A. 43°43N 98°2W 110 B7
Mitchell → Australia 15°12S 141°35E 98 D7
Mitchelstown Ireland 52°15N 8°16W 30 D6
Mito Japan 36°20N 140°30E 82 E7
Mitú Colombia 1°15N 70°13W 120 B2
Mitumba, Mts. Dem. Rep. of the Congo 7°0S 27°30E 96 F5
Miyakonojō Japan 31°40N 131°5E 82 H2
Miyazaki Japan 31°56N 131°30E 82 H2
Mizen Hd. Cork, Ireland 51°27N 9°50W 30 F3
Mizen Hd. Wicklow, Ireland 52°51N 6°4W 31 C10
Mizoram □ India 23°30N 92°40E 85 H18
Mjøsa Norway 60°40N 11°0E 63 E6
Mljet Croatia 42°43N 17°30E 70 C7
Mo i Rana Norway 66°20N 14°7E 63 D6
Moab U.S.A. 38°35N 109°33W 110 C5
Moate Ireland 53°24N 7°44W 28 E6
Mobaye C.A.R. 4°25N 21°5E 96 D4
Moberly U.S.A. 39°25N 92°26W 111 C8
Mobile U.S.A. 30°41N 88°3W 111 D9
Mobridge U.S.A. 45°32N 100°26W 110 A6
Moçambique Mozam. 15°3S 40°42E 97 H8
Mochudi Botswana 24°27S 26°7E 97 J5
Mocoa Colombia 1°7N 76°35W 120 C2
Mococa Brazil 21°28S 47°0W 122 D1
Mocuba Mozam. 16°54S 36°57E 97 H7
Modbury U.K. 50°21N 3°55W 27 G6
Módena Italy 44°40N 10°55E 70 B4
Modesto U.S.A. 37°39N 121°0W 110 C2
Moffat U.K. 55°21N 3°27W 21 D9
Mogadishu Somali Rep. 2°2N 45°25E 88 G4
Mogi das Cruzes Brazil 23°31S 46°11W 122 D1
Mogi-Mirim Brazil 22°29S 47°0W 122 D1
Mohammedia Morocco 33°44N 7°21W 94 B4
Moher, Cliffs of Ireland 52°58N 9°27W 30 C4
Moidart U.K. 56°49N 5°41W 18 J6

Moidart, L. U.K. 56°47N 5°52W 18 J6
Moisie → Canada 50°14N 66°5W 109 D13
Mojave Desert U.S.A. 35°0N 116°30W 110 D3
Mold U.K. 53°9N 3°8W 26 A7
Molde Norway 62°45N 7°9E 63 E5
Moldova ■ Europe 47°0N 28°0E 67 E15
Mole → U.K. 51°24N 0°21W 25 D8
Molepolole Botswana 24°28S 25°28E 97 J5
Mollendo Peru 17°0S 72°0W 120 D2
Moloka'i U.S.A. 21°8N 157°0W 110 H16
Molopo → Africa 28°30S 20°12E 97 K4
Molucca Sea Indonesia 0°0 125°0E 83 D4
Moluccas Indonesia 1°0S 127°0E 83 D4
Mombasa Kenya 4°3S 39°40E 96 E7
Mompós Colombia 9°14N 74°26W 120 B2
Mon □ Burma 16°0N 97°30E 85 L20
Mona Passage W. Indies 18°30N 67°45W 115 D11
Monach Is. U.K. 57°32N 7°40W 18 G2
Monaco ■ Europe 43°46N 7°23E 68 E7
Monadhliath Mts. U.K. 57°10N 4°4W 19 H9
Monaghan Ireland 54°15N 6°57W 29 C8
Monaghan □ Ireland 54°11N 6°56W 29 C8
Monar, L. U.K. 57°26N 5°8W 18 H7
Monar Forest U.K. 57°27N 5°10W 18 H7
Monasterevin Ireland 53°8N 7°4W 31 B8
Monavullagh Mts. Ireland 52°14N 7°35W 31 D7
Mönchengladbach Germany 51°11N 6°27E 66 C4
Monclova Mexico 26°54N 101°25W 114 B4
Moncton Canada 46°7N 64°51W 113 B15
Moneague Jamaica 18°16N 77°7W 114 a
Moneymore U.K. 54°41N 6°40W 29 B8
Mongolia ■ Asia 47°0N 103°0E 80 B5
Mongolia, Plateau of Asia 45°0N 105°0E 74 D12
Mongu Zambia 15°16S 23°12E 97 H4
Monifieth U.K. 56°30N 2°48W 21 B10
Monmouth U.K. 51°48N 2°42W 26 D8
Monmouth U.S.A. 40°55N 90°39W 112 E2
Monmouthshire □ U.K. 51°48N 2°54W 26 D8
Monnow → U.K. 51°49N 2°24W 24 C3
Monroe La., U.S.A. 32°30N 92°7W 111 D8
Monroe Mich., U.S.A. 41°55N 83°24W 112 E6
Monroe Wis., U.S.A. 42°36N 89°38W 112 D3
Monrovia Liberia 6°18N 10°47W 94 G3
Mons Belgium 50°27N 3°58E 65 D3
Mont-de-Marsan France 43°54N 0°31W 68 E3
Mont-Laurier Canada 46°35N 75°30W 109 E12
Montana Bulgaria 43°27N 23°16E 71 C10
Montaña Peru 6°0S 73°0W 120 C2
Montana □ U.S.A. 47°0N 110°0W 110 A5
Montargis France 47°59N 2°43E 68 C5
Montauban France 44°2N 1°21E 68 D4
Montbéliard France 47°31N 6°48E 68 C7
Montceau-les-Mines France 46°40N 4°23E 68 C6
Monte Azul Brazil 15°9S 42°53W 122 C2
Monte-Carlo Monaco 43°44N 7°25E 68 E7
Monte Caseros Argentina 30°10S 57°50W 121 F4
Monte Cristi Dom. Rep. 19°52N 71°39W 115 D10
Montego Bay Jamaica 18°28N 77°55W 114 a
Montélimar France 44°33N 4°45E 68 D6
Montemorelos Mexico 25°12N 99°49W 114 B5
Montenegro ■ Europe 42°40N 19°20E 71 C8
Monteria Colombia 8°46N 75°53W 120 B2
Monterrey Mexico 25°40N 100°19W 114 B4
Montes Claros Brazil 16°30S 43°50W 122 C2
Montevideo Uruguay 34°50S 56°11W 121 F4
Montgomery U.K. 52°34N 3°8W 26 B7
Montgomery U.S.A. 32°23N 86°19W 111 D9
Monticello U.S.A. 40°45N 86°46W 112 E4
Montluçon France 46°22N 2°36E 68 C5
Montmagny Canada 46°58N 70°34W 113 B12
Montpelier Idaho, U.S.A. 42°19N 111°18W 110 B4
Montpelier Vt., U.S.A. 44°16N 72°35W 113 C11
Montpellier France 43°37N 3°52E 68 E5
Montréal Canada 45°30N 73°33W 113 C11
Montreux Switz. 46°26N 6°55E 66 E4
Montrose U.K. 56°44N 2°27W 19 J13
Montrose U.S.A. 38°29N 107°53W 110 C5
Montserrat ☑ W. Indies 16°40N 62°10W 115 D12
Monywa Burma 22°7N 95°11E 85 H19
Monza Italy 45°35N 9°16E 70 B3
Monze, C. Pakistan 24°47N 66°37E 84 G5
Moorfoot Hills U.K. 55°44N 3°8W 21 C9
Moorhead U.S.A. 46°53N 96°45W 111 A7
Moose Jaw Canada 50°24N 105°30W 108 D9
Moosehead L. U.S.A. 45°38N 69°40W 113 C13
Moosomin Canada 50°9N 101°40W 108 D9
Moosonee Canada 51°17N 80°39W 109 D11
Mopti Mali 14°30N 4°0W 94 F5
Mora Sweden 61°2N 14°38E 63 E6
Moradabad India 28°50N 78°50E 84 E11
Morant Bay Jamaica 17°53N 76°25W 114 a
Morant Pt. Jamaica 17°55N 76°12W 114 a
Morar, L. U.K. 56°57N 5°40W 18 J6
Moratuwa Sri Lanka 6°45N 79°55E 84 R11
Morava → Serbia 44°36N 21°4E 71 B9
Morava → Slovak Rep. 48°10N 16°59E 67 D9
Moravian Hts. Czech Rep. 49°30N 15°40E 56 F9
Moray □ U.K. 57°31N 3°18W 19 G11
Moray Firth U.K. 57°40N 3°52W 19 G9
Morden Canada 49°15N 98°10W 108 E10
Mordvinia □ Russia 54°20N 44°30E 72 D8
Moreau → U.S.A. 45°18N 100°43W 110 A6
Morebattle U.K. 55°31N 2°22W 21 C11
Morecambe U.K. 54°5N 2°52W 22 C3
Morecambe B. U.K. 54°7N 3°0W 22 C3
Moree Australia 29°28S 149°54E 98 F9
Morehead City U.S.A. 38°11N 83°26W 112 F6
Morelia Mexico 19°42N 101°7W 114 D4
Morena, Sierra Spain 38°20N 4°0W 69 C3
Moresby I. Canada 52°30N 131°40W 108 D6
Moreton-in-Marsh U.K. 51°59N 1°41W 24 C5
Moretonhampstead U.K. 50°39N 3°46W 27 F6
Morgan City U.S.A. 29°42N 91°11W 111 E8
Morgantown U.S.A. 39°38N 79°57W 112 F8
Morioka Japan 39°45N 141°8E 82 D7
Morlaix France 48°36N 3°52W 68 B2

Morley U.K. 53°45N 1°36W 23 E5
Morocco ■ N. Afr. 32°0N 5°50W 94 B4
Morogoro Tanzania 6°50S 37°40E 96 F7
Morón Cuba 22°8N 78°39W 115 C9
Morondava Madag. 20°17S 44°17E 97 J8
Moroni Comoros Is. 11°40S 43°16E 91 H8
Morotai Indonesia 2°10N 128°30E 83 C4
Morpeth U.K. 55°10N 1°41W 22 B5
Morphou Cyprus 35°12N 32°59E 86 C3
Morrinhos Brazil 17°45S 49°10W 122 C1
Morris U.S.A. 41°22N 88°26W 112 E3
Morte Bay U.K. 51°9N 4°14W 27 E5
Morte Pt. U.K. 51°11N 4°14W 27 E5
Mortehoe U.K. 51°11N 4°12W 27 E5
Morton Fen U.K. 52°49N 0°20W 23 G8
Morvan France 47°5N 4°3E 68 C6
Morwenstow U.K. 50°54N 4°33W 27 F4
Moscos Is. Burma 14°0N 97°30E 85 N20
Moscow Russia 55°45N 37°37E 72 C6
Moscow U.S.A. 46°44N 117°0W 110 A3
Mosel → Europe 50°22N 7°36E 66 C4
Moses Lake U.S.A. 47°8N 119°17W 110 A3
Moshi Tanzania 3°22S 37°18E 96 E7
Mosjøen Norway 65°51N 13°12E 63 D6
Mosselbaai S. Africa 34°11S 22°8E 97 L4
Mossley U.K. 53°31N 2°1W 23 E4
Mossoró Brazil 5°10S 37°15W 120 C6
Most Czech Rep. 50°31N 13°38E 66 C7
Mostaganem Algeria 35°54N 0°5E 94 A6
Mostar Bos.-H. 43°22N 17°50E 71 C7
Mosul Iraq 36°15N 43°5E 86 B5
Motcombe U.K. 51°1N 2°13W 24 D4
Motherwell U.K. 55°47N 3°58W 21 C8
Motihari India 26°30N 84°55E 85 F14
Motril Spain 36°31N 3°37W 69 D4
Mottisfont U.K. 51°2N 1°32W 24 D5
Mouila Gabon 1°50S 11°0E 96 E2
Moule à Chique, C. St. Lucia 13°43N 60°57W 115 f
Moulins France 46°35N 3°19E 68 C5
Moulmein Burma 16°30N 97°40E 85 L20
Moulouya, O. → Morocco 35°5N 2°25W 94 B5
Moulton U.K. 52°17N 0°52W 25 B7
Moundou Chad 8°40N 16°10E 95 G9
Moundsville U.S.A. 39°55N 80°44W 112 F7
Mount Carmel U.S.A. 38°25N 87°46W 112 F4
Mount Desert I. U.S.A. 44°21N 68°20W 113 C13
Mount Gambier Australia 37°50S 140°46E 98 H7
Mount Hagen Papua N. G. 5°52S 144°16E 98 B7
Mount Isa Australia 20°42S 139°26E 98 E6
Mount Magnet Australia 28°2S 117°47E 98 F2
Mount Pleasant U.S.A. 43°36N 84°46W 112 D5
Mount Sterling U.S.A. 38°4N 83°56W 112 F6
Mount Vernon Ind., U.S.A. 37°56N 87°54W 112 F3
Mount Vernon Ohio, U.S.A. 40°23N 82°29W 112 E6
Mountain Ash U.K. 51°40N 3°23W 26 D7
Mountain Home U.S.A. 43°8N 115°41W 110 B3
Mountain View U.S.A. 19°33N 155°7W 110 J17
Mountmellick Ireland 53°7N 7°20W 31 B8
Mountrath Ireland 53°0N 7°28W 31 B8
Mount's Bay U.K. 50°5N 5°31W 27 G2
Mountsorrel U.K. 52°44N 1°8W 23 G6
Mourne → U.K. 54°52N 7°26W 28 B7
Mourne Mts. U.K. 54°10N 6°0W 29 C9
Mouscron Belgium 50°45N 3°12E 65 D3
Moville Ireland 55°11N 7°3W 28 A7
Moy → Ireland 54°8N 9°8W 28 C3
Mozambique ■ Africa 19°0S 35°0E 97 H7
Mozambique Chan. Africa 17°30S 42°30E 91 H8
Mozdok Russia 43°45N 44°48E 73 F7
Mpanda Tanzania 6°23S 31°1E 96 F6
Mpumalanga S. Africa 29°50S 30°33E 97 K6
Msaken Tunisia 35°49N 10°33E 95 A8
Mthatha S. Africa 31°36S 28°49E 97 L5
Mtwara-Mikindani Tanzania 10°20S 40°20E 96 G8
Muar Malaysia 2°3N 102°34E 83 C2
Mubi Nigeria 10°18N 13°16E 95 F8
Much Dewchurch U.K. 51°58N 2°45W 24 C4
Much Marcle U.K. 51°59N 2°29W 24 C4
Much Wenlock U.K. 52°35N 2°33W 23 G3
Muchinga Mts. Zambia 11°30S 31°30E 97 G6
Muck U.K. 56°50N 6°15W 18 J5
Muckle Flugga U.K. 60°51N 0°54W 18 A16
Muckle Roe U.K. 60°23N 1°27W 18 B15
Mucuri Brazil 18°0S 39°36E 122 C3
Mudanjiang China 44°38N 129°30E 81 B7
Mufulira Zambia 12°32S 28°15E 97 G5
Muğla Turkey 37°15N 28°22E 73 G4
Muine Bheag Ireland 52°42N 6°58W 31 C9
Muir of Ord U.K. 57°32N 4°28W 19 G9
Muktsar India 30°30N 74°30E 84 D9
Mulde → Germany 51°53N 12°15E 66 C7
Mulhacén Spain 37°4N 3°20W 69 D4
Mulhouse France 47°40N 7°20E 68 C7
Mull U.K. 56°25N 5°56W 20 B4
Mull, Sound of U.K. 56°30N 5°50W 20 A4
Mullaghareirk Mts. Ireland 52°20N 9°10W 30 D4
Mullet Pen. Ireland 54°13N 10°2W 28 B1
Mullingar Ireland 53°31N 7°21W 28 D7
Mullion U.K. 51°5N 1°16W 27 G3
Mulroy B. Ireland 55°15N 7°46W 28 A6
Multan Pakistan 30°15N 71°36E 84 D7
Mumbai India 18°56N 72°50E 84 K8
Mumbles Hd. U.K. 51°34N 3°59W 27 D6
Muna Indonesia 5°0S 122°30E 83 D4
Muncie U.S.A. 40°12N 85°23W 112 E5
Mundesley U.K. 52°53N 1°25E 25 A11
Mundo Novo Brazil 11°50S 40°29W 122 B2
Munger India 25°23N 86°30E 85 G15
Munich Germany 48°8N 11°34E 66 D6
Munising U.S.A. 46°25N 86°40W 112 B4
Münster Germany 51°58N 7°37E 66 C4
Munster □ Ireland 52°18N 8°44W 30 D5
Murashi Russia 59°30N 49°0E 72 C8
Murat → Turkey 38°46N 40°0E 73 G7
Murchison → Australia 27°45S 114°0E 98 F1
Murcia Spain 38°5N 1°10W 69 D5
Murcia □ Spain 37°50N 1°30W 69 D5

Mureş → Romania 46°15N 20°13E 67 E11
Murfreesboro U.S.A. 35°51N 86°24W 111 C9
Muriaé Brazil 21°8S 42°23W 122 D2
Müritz Germany 53°25N 12°42E 66 B7
Murmansk Russia 68°57N 33°10E 72 A5
Murom Russia 55°35N 42°3E 72 C7
Muroran Japan 42°25N 141°0E 82 B7
Murray U.S.A. 36°37N 88°19W 112 G3
Murray → Australia 35°20S 139°22E 98 H6
Murton U.K. 54°50N 1°22W 22 C6
Mururoa French Polynesia 21°52S 138°55W 103 K14
Murwara India 23°46N 80°28E 85 H12
Muş Turkey 38°45N 41°30E 73 G7
Mûsa, Gebel Egypt 28°33N 33°59E 86 D3
Muscat Oman 23°37N 58°36E 87 F9
Musgrave Ranges Australia 26°0S 132°0E 98 F5
Musina S. Africa 22°20S 30°5E 97 J6
Muskegon U.S.A. 43°14N 86°16W 112 D4
Muskegon → U.S.A. 43°14N 86°21W 112 D4
Muskogee U.S.A. 35°45N 95°22W 111 C7
Musselburgh U.K. 55°57N 3°2W 21 C9
Musselshell → U.S.A. 47°21N 107°57W 110 A5
Mutare Zimbabwe 18°58S 32°38E 97 H6
Mutton I. Ireland 52°49N 9°32W 30 C3
Muynak Uzbekistan 43°44N 59°10E 87 A9
Muz Tag China 36°25N 87°25E 80 C3
Muzaffarabad Pakistan 34°25N 73°30E 84 B8
Muzaffarnagar India 29°26N 77°40E 84 E10
Muztagh-Ata China 38°17N 75°7E 80 C2
Mwanza Tanzania 2°30S 32°58E 96 E6
Mweelrea Ireland 53°39N 9°49W 28 D2
Mwene-Ditu Dem. Rep. of the Congo 6°35S 22°27E 96 F4
Mweru, L. Zambia 9°0S 28°40E 96 F5
My Tho Vietnam 10°29N 106°23E 83 B2
Myanmar = Burma ■ Asia 21°0N 96°30E 85 J20
Mycenæ Greece 37°43N 22°46E 71 F10
Myddle U.K. 52°49N 2°47W 23 G3
Myingyan Burma 21°30N 95°20E 85 J19
Myitkyina Burma 25°24N 97°26E 85 G20
Mymensingh Bangla. 24°45N 90°24E 85 G17
Mynydd Du U.K. 51°52N 3°50W 26 D6
Mynydd Preseli U.K. 51°57N 4°48W 26 D4
Mysore India 12°17N 76°41E 84 N10
Mytishchi Russia 55°50N 37°50E 72 C6

N

Naab → Germany 49°1N 12°2E 66 D6
Naas Ireland 53°12N 6°40W 31 B9
Naberezhnyye Chelny Russia 55°42N 52°19E 72 C9
Nabeul Tunisia 36°30N 10°44E 95 A8
Nābulus West Bank 32°14N 35°15E 86 C3
Nacala Mozam. 14°31S 40°34E 97 G8
Nacogdoches U.S.A. 31°36N 94°39W 111 D8
Nacozari de García Mexico 30°25N 109°38W 114 A3
Nadiad India 22°41N 72°56E 84 H8
Nador Morocco 35°14N 2°58W 94 B5
Nafferton U.K. 54°1N 0°23W 23 D8
Nafud Desert Si. Arabia 28°15N 41°0E 86 D5
Naga Phil. 13°38N 123°15E 83 B4
Nagaland □ India 26°0N 94°30E 85 G19
Nagano Japan 36°40N 138°10E 82 E6
Nagaoka Japan 37°27N 138°51E 82 E6
Nagappattinam India 10°46N 79°51E 84 P11
Nagasaki Japan 32°47N 129°50E 82 G1
Nagaur India 27°15N 73°45E 84 F8
Nagercoil India 8°12N 77°26E 84 Q10
Nagles Mts. Ireland 52°8N 8°30W 30 D6
Nagorno-Karabakh □ Azerbaijan 39°55N 46°45E 73 F8
Nagoya Japan 35°10N 136°50E 82 F5
Nagpur India 21°8N 79°10E 84 J11
Naguabo Puerto Rico 18°13N 65°44W 115 d
Naha Japan 26°13N 127°42E 81 D7
Nailsea U.K. 51°26N 2°44W 24 D3
Nailsworth U.K. 51°41N 2°14W 24 C4
Nain Canada 56°34N 61°40W 109 D13
Nairn U.K. 57°35N 3°53W 19 G10
Nairobi Kenya 1°17S 36°48E 96 E7
Naivasha Kenya 0°40S 36°30E 96 E7
Najafābād Iran 32°40N 51°15E 87 C7
Najd Si. Arabia 26°30N 42°0E 86 E5
Najibabad India 29°40N 78°20E 84 E11
Najrān Si. Arabia 17°34N 44°18E 88 D3
Nakhon Ratchasima Thailand 14°59N 102°12E 83 B2
Nakhon Sawan Thailand 15°35N 100°10E 83 B2
Nakhon Si Thammarat Thailand 8°29N 100°0E 83 C2
Nakina Canada 50°10N 86°40W 109 D11
Nakuru Kenya 0°15S 36°4E 96 E7
Nalchik Russia 43°30N 43°33E 73 F7
Nallamalai Hills India 15°30N 78°50E 84 M11
Nam Co China 30°30N 90°45E 80 C4
Nam Dinh Vietnam 20°25N 106°5E 83 A2
Namak, Daryācheh-ye Iran 34°30N 52°0E 87 C8
Namaland Namibia 26°0S 17°0E 97 K3
Namangan Uzbekistan 41°0N 71°40E 87 A12
Namcha Barwa China 29°40N 95°10E 80 D4
Namib Desert Namibia 22°30S 15°0E 97 J3
Namibe Angola 15°7S 12°11E 97 H2
Namibia ■ Africa 22°0S 18°9E 97 J3
Nampa U.S.A. 43°34N 116°34W 110 B3
Namp'o N. Korea 38°52N 125°10E 81 C7
Nampula Mozam. 15°6S 39°15E 97 H7
Namumea Tuvalu 5°41S 176°9E 99 B14
Nan Ling China 25°0N 112°30E 81 D6
Nan-ch'ang China 28°42N 115°55E 81 D6
Nanaimo Canada 49°10N 124°0W 108 E7
Nanchong China 30°43N 106°2E 80 C5
Nancy France 48°42N 6°12E 68 B7
Nanda Devi India 30°23N 79°59E 84 D11
Nanded India 19°10N 77°20E 84 K10
Nandurbar India 21°20N 74°15E 84 J9
Nanga Parbat Pakistan 35°10N 74°35E 84 B9
Nangarhār □ Afghan. 34°20N 70°0E 87 C12

Nanjing *China* 32°2N 118°47E 81 C6
Nanning *China* 22°48N 108°20E 80 D5
Nanping *China* 26°38N 118°10E 81 D6
Nansen Sd. *Canada* 81°0N 91°0W 109 A10
Nantes *France* 47°12N 1°33W 68 C3
Nantong *China* 32°1N 120°52E 81 C7
Nantucket I. *U.S.A.* 41°16N 70°5W 113 E12
Nantwich *U.K.* 53°4N 2°31W 23 F3
Nanuque *Brazil* 17°50S 40°21W 122 C2
Nanyang *China* 33°11N 112°30E 81 C6
Nanyuki *Kenya* 0°2N 37°4E 96 D7
Napa *U.S.A.* 38°18N 122°17W 110 C2
Napier *N.Z.* 39°30S 176°56E 99 H14
Naples *Italy* 40°50N 14°15E 70 D6
Napo → *Peru* 3°20S 72°40W 120 C2
Nappa *U.K.* 53°58N 2°13W 23 D3
Narayanganj *Bangla.* 23°40N 90°33E 85 H17
Narberth *U.K.* 51°47N 4°44W 26 D4
Narbonne *France* 43°11N 3°0E 68 E5
Narborough *U.K.* 52°34N 1°13W 23 G6
Nares Str. *Arctic* 80°0N 70°0W 109 A13
Narmada → *India* 21°38N 72°36E 84 J8
Narodnaya *Russia* 65°5N 59°58E 72 A10
Narva *Estonia* 59°23N 28°12E 63 F9
Narvik *Norway* 68°28N 17°26E 63 D7
Naryan-Mar *Russia* 67°42N 53°12E 72 A9
Naseby *U.K.* 52°24N 0°59W 25 B7
Nashua *U.S.A.* 42°45N 71°28W 113 D12
Nashville *U.S.A.* 36°10N 86°47W 111 C9
Nasik *India* 19°58N 73°50E 84 K8
Nasirabad *India* 26°15N 74°45E 84 F9
Nasiriyah *Iraq* 31°0N 46°15E 86 D6
Nassau *Bahamas* 25°5N 77°20W 115 B9
Nasser, L. *Egypt* 23°0N 32°30E 95 D12
Natal *Brazil* 5°47S 35°13W 120 C6
Natashquan *Canada* 50°14N 61°46W 109 D13
Natashquan → *Canada* 50°7N 61°50W 109 D13
Natchez *U.S.A.* 31°34N 91°24W 111 D8
Natchitoches *U.S.A.* 31°46N 93°5W 111 D8
Nathdwara *India* 24°55N 73°50E 84 G8
Natitingou *Benin* 10°20N 1°26E 94 F6
Natron, L. *Tanzania* 2°20S 36°0E 96 E7
Natuna Besar, Kepulauan
  Indonesia 4°0N 108°15E 83 C2
Nauru ■ *Pac. Oc.* 1°0S 166°0E 102 H8
Navarino, I. *Chile* 55°0S 67°40W 121 H3
Navarra □ *Spain* 42°40N 1°40W 69 A5
Navenby *U.K.* 53°6N 0°31W 23 F7
Naver → *U.K.* 58°32N 4°14W 19 E9
Navojoa *Mexico* 27°6N 109°26W 114 B3
Navsari *India* 20°57N 72°59E 84 J8
Nawabshah *Pakistan* 26°15N 68°25E 84 F6
Naxçıvan ☐ *Azerbaijan* 39°25N 45°26E 73 G8
Naxos *Greece* 37°8N 25°25E 71 F11
Nazaré *Brazil* 13°2S 39°0W 122 B3
Nazas → *Mexico* 25°12N 104°12W 114 B4
Nazca *Peru* 14°50S 74°57W 120 D2
Naze, The *U.K.* 51°53N 1°18E 25 C11
Nazret *Ethiopia* 8°32N 39°22E 88 F2
Ndjamena *Chad* 12°10N 14°59E 95 F8
Ndola *Zambia* 13°0S 28°34E 97 G5
Neagh, Lough *U.K.* 54°37N 6°25W 29 B9
Near Is. *U.S.A.* 52°30N 174°0E 108 C1
Neath *U.K.* 51°39N 3°48W 26 D6
Nebraska □ *U.S.A.* 41°30N 99°30W 110 B7
Nébrodi, Monti *Italy* 37°54N 14°35E 70 F6
Neckar → *Germany* 49°27N 8°29E 66 D5
Necochea *Argentina* 38°30S 58°50W 121 F4
Needham Market *U.K.* 52°9N 1°4E 25 B11
Needles, The *U.K.* 50°39N 1°35W 24 E5
Neenah *U.S.A.* 44°11N 88°28W 112 C3
Neepawa *Canada* 50°15N 99°30W 108 D10
Neftekumsk *Russia* 44°46N 44°50E 73 F7
Negaunee *U.S.A.* 46°30N 87°36W 112 B4
Negele *Ethiopia* 5°20N 39°36E 88 F2
Negombo *Sri Lanka* 7°12N 79°50E 84 R11
Negra, Pta. *Peru* 6°6S 81°10W 116 D2
Negril *Jamaica* 18°22N 78°20W 114 a
Negro → *Argentina* 41°2S 62°47W 121 G3
Negro → *Brazil* 3°0S 60°0W 120 C3
Negros *Phil.* 9°30N 122°40E 83 C4
Neijiang *China* 29°35N 104°55E 80 D5
Neisse → *Europe* 52°4N 14°46E 66 B8
Neiva *Colombia* 2°56N 75°18W 120 B2
Nellore *India* 14°27N 79°59E 84 M11
Nelson *Canada* 49°30N 117°20W 108 E8
Nelson *N.Z.* 41°18S 173°16E 99 J13
Nelson *U.K.* 53°50N 2°13W 23 E4
Nelson → *Canada* 54°33N 98°2W 108 D10
Neman → *Lithuania* 55°25N 21°10E 63 F8
Nenagh *Ireland* 52°52N 8°11W 30 C6
Nene → *U.K.* 52°49N 0°11E 25 A9
Nenjiang *China* 49°10N 125°10E 81 B7
Neosho → *U.S.A.* 36°48N 95°18W 111 C7
Nepal ■ *Asia* 28°0N 84°30E 85 F14
Nephi *U.S.A.* 39°43N 111°50W 110 C4
Nephin *Ireland* 54°1N 9°22W 28 C3
Nephin Beg Range *Ireland* 54°0N 9°40W 28 C2
Nerastro, Sarīr *Libya* 24°20N 20°37E 95 D10
Neryungri *Russia* 57°38N 124°28E 79 D14
Ness, L. *U.K.* 57°15N 4°32W 19 H8
Neston *U.K.* 53°17N 3°4W 23 F2
Netherbury *U.K.* 50°46N 2°45E 24 E3
Netherlands ■ *Europe* 52°0N 5°30E 65 C5
Netherlands Antilles ☐
  W. Indies 12°15N 69°0W 115 E11
Netley *U.K.* 50°52N 1°20W 24 E6
Nettilling L. *Canada* 66°30N 71°0W 109 C12
Nettlebed *U.K.* 51°34N 0°59W 25 C7
Nettleham *U.K.* 53°16N 0°29W 23 F8
Neuchâtel *Switz.* 47°0N 6°55E 66 E4
Neuchâtel, Lac de *Switz.* 46°53N 6°50E 66 E4
Neuquén *Argentina* 38°55S 68°0W 121 F3
Neusiedler See *Austria* 47°50N 16°47E 67 E9
Neva → *Russia* 59°56N 30°20E 72 C5
Nevada □ *U.S.A.* 39°0N 117°0W 110 C3
Nevers *France* 47°0N 3°9E 68 C5
Nevinnomyssk *Russia* 44°40N 42°0E 73 F7

New Abbey *U.K.* 54°59N 3°37W 21 E9
New Alresford *U.K.* 51°5N 1°8W 24 D6
New Amsterdam *Guyana* 6°15N 57°36W 120 B4
New Bedford *U.S.A.* 41°38N 70°56W 113 E12
New Britain *Papua N. G.* 5°50S 150°20E 98 B9
New Britain *U.S.A.* 41°40N 72°47W 113 E11
New Brunswick *U.S.A.* 40°30N 74°27W 113 E10
New Brunswick □ *Canada* 46°50N 66°30W 113 B14
New Caledonia ☑ *Pac. Oc.* 21°0S 165°0E 99 E12
New Castle *Ind., U.S.A.* 39°55N 85°22W 112 F5
New Castle *Pa., U.S.A.* 41°0N 80°21W 112 E7
New Delhi *India* 28°36N 77°11E 84 E10
New England *U.S.A.* 43°0N 71°0W 111 B12
New Forest △ *U.K.* 50°53N 1°34W 24 E5
New Galloway *U.K.* 55°5N 4°9W 20 D7
New Georgia Is. *Solomon Is.* 8°15S 157°30E 99 B10
New Glasgow *Canada* 45°35N 62°36W 109 E13
New Guinea *Oceania* 4°0S 136°0E 98 B7
New Hampshire □ *U.S.A.* 44°0N 71°30W 113 D12
New Haven *U.S.A.* 41°18N 72°55W 113 E11
New Hebrides = Vanuatu ■
  Pac. Oc. 15°0S 168°0E 99 D12
New Holland *U.K.* 53°42N 0°21W 23 E8
New Iberia *U.S.A.* 30°1N 91°49W 111 D8
New Ireland *Papua N. G.* 3°20S 151°50E 98 A9
New Jersey □ *U.S.A.* 40°0N 74°30W 113 E10
New Lexington *U.S.A.* 39°43N 82°13W 112 F6
New Liskeard *Canada* 47°31N 79°41W 109 E12
New London *U.S.A.* 41°22N 72°6W 113 E11
New Madrid *U.S.A.* 36°36N 89°32W 112 G3
New Mexico □ *U.S.A.* 34°30N 106°0W 110 D5
New Mills *U.K.* 53°23N 2°0W 23 F5
New Milton *U.K.* 50°45N 1°40W 24 E5
New Orleans *U.S.A.* 29°57N 90°4W 111 E8
New Philadelphia *U.S.A.* 40°30N 81°27W 112 E7
New Plymouth *N.Z.* 39°4S 174°5E 99 H13
New Providence *Bahamas* 25°25N 78°35W 115 B9
New Quay *U.K.* 52°13N 4°21W 26 C5
New Radnor *U.K.* 52°15N 3°9W 26 C7
New Romney *U.K.* 50°59N 0°57E 25 E10
New Ross *Ireland* 52°23N 6°57W 31 D9
New Rossington *U.K.* 53°29N 1°4W 23 F6
New Siberian Is. *Russia* 75°0N 142°0E 79 B15
New South Wales □ *Australia* 33°0S 146°0E 98 G8
New York *U.S.A.* 40°43N 74°0W 113 E11
New York □ *U.S.A.* 43°0N 75°0W 113 D10
New Zealand ■ *Oceania* 40°0S 176°0E 99 J14
Newark *Del., U.S.A.* 39°41N 75°46W 113 F10
Newark *N.J., U.S.A.* 40°44N 74°10W 113 E10
Newark *N.Y., U.S.A.* 43°3N 77°6W 112 D9
Newark *Ohio, U.S.A.* 40°3N 82°24W 112 E6
Newark-on-Trent *U.K.* 53°5N 0°48W 23 F7
Newberry *U.S.A.* 46°21N 85°30W 112 B5
Newbiggin-by-the-Sea *U.K.* 55°11N 1°31W 22 B5
Newbigging *U.K.* 55°42N 3°34W 21 C8
Newburgh *U.K.* 56°21N 3°15W 21 B9
Newburgh *U.S.A.* 41°30N 74°1W 113 E10
Newburn *U.K.* 54°59N 1°43W 22 C5
Newbury *U.K.* 51°24N 1°20W 24 D6
Newburyport *U.S.A.* 42°49N 70°53W 113 D12
Newby Bridge *U.K.* 54°17N 2°57W 22 D3
Newcastle *Australia* 33°0S 151°46E 98 G9
Newcastle *Canada* 47°1N 65°38W 113 B15
Newcastle *S. Africa* 27°45S 29°58E 97 K5
Newcastle Emlyn *U.K.* 52°2N 4°28W 26 C5
Newcastle-under-Lyme *U.K.* 53°1N 2°14W 23 F4
Newcastle West *Ireland* 52°27N 9°3W 30 D4
Newcastleton *U.K.* 55°11N 2°49W 21 D10
Newent *U.K.* 51°56N 2°24W 24 C4
Newfoundland & Labrador □
  Canada 53°0N 58°0W 109 D14
Newham □ *U.K.* 51°31N 0°3E 25 C9
Newhaven *U.K.* 50°47N 0°3E 25 E9
Newington *Kent, U.K.* 51°6N 1°7E 25 D11
Newington *Kent, U.K.* 51°21N 0°41E 25 D10
Newlyn *U.K.* 50°6N 5°34W 27 G2
Newlyn East *U.K.* 50°22N 5°5W 27 G3
Newman *Australia* 23°18S 119°45E 98 E2
Newmarket *Ireland* 52°13N 9°0W 30 D5
Newmarket *U.K.* 52°15N 0°25E 25 B9
Newnham *U.K.* 51°48N 2°27W 24 C4
Newport *Ireland* 53°53N 9°33W 28 D2
Newport *Essex, U.K.* 51°59N 0°14E 25 C9
Newport *I. of W., U.K.* 50°42N 1°17W 24 E6
Newport *Newport, U.K.* 51°35N 3°0W 27 D8
Newport *Pembs., U.K.* 52°1N 4°51W 26 C4
Newport *Telford & Wrekin, U.K.* 52°46N 2°22W 23 G4
Newport *Ark., U.S.A.* 35°37N 91°16W 111 C8
Newport *Ky., U.S.A.* 39°5N 84°29W 112 F5
Newport *R.I., U.S.A.* 41°29N 71°19W 113 E12
Newport *Vt., U.S.A.* 44°56N 72°13W 113 C11
Newport News *U.S.A.* 36°58N 76°25W 111 C11
Newport Pagnell *U.K.* 52°5N 0°43W 25 B7
Newquay *U.K.* 50°25N 5°6W 27 G3
Newry *U.K.* 54°11N 6°21W 29 C9
Newton Abbot *U.K.* 50°32N 3°37W 27 F6
Newton Arlosh *U.K.* 54°53N 3°14W 22 C2
Newton Aycliffe *U.K.* 54°37N 1°34W 22 C5
Newton Ferrers *U.K.* 50°19N 4°3W 27 G5
Newton le Willows *U.K.* 53°28N 2°38W 23 F3
Newton St. Cyres *U.K.* 50°46N 3°36W 27 F6
Newton Stewart *U.K.* 54°57N 4°30W 20 E6
Newtonmore *U.K.* 57°4N 4°8W 19 H9
Newtown *U.K.* 52°31N 3°19W 26 B7
Newtown St. Boswells *U.K.* 55°34N 2°40W 21 C10
Newtownabbey *U.K.* 54°40N 5°56W 29 B10
Newtownards *U.K.* 54°36N 5°42W 29 B10
Newtownstewart *U.K.* 54°43N 7°23W 28 B7
Neyshābūr *Iran* 36°10N 58°50E 87 B9
Nganglong Kangri *China* 33°0N 81°0E 80 C3
Ngaoundéré *Cameroon* 7°15N 13°35E 96 C2
Ngoring Hu *China* 34°55N 97°5E 80 C4
Ngorongoro *Tanzania* 3°11S 35°32E 96 E7
Nguru *Nigeria* 12°56N 10°29E 95 F8
Nha Trang *Vietnam* 12°16N 109°10E 83 B2
Nhamundá → *Brazil* 2°12S 56°41W 120 C4
Niagara Falls *Canada* 43°7N 79°5W 109 E12

Niagara Falls *U.S.A.* 43°5N 79°4W 112 D8
Niamey *Niger* 13°27N 2°6E 94 F6
Nias *Indonesia* 1°0N 97°30E 83 C1
Nicaragua ■ *Cent. Amer.* 11°40N 85°30W 114 E7
Nicaragua, L. de *Nic.* 12°0N 85°30W 114 E7
Nice *France* 43°42N 7°14E 68 E7
Nicholasville *U.S.A.* 37°53N 84°34W 112 G5
Nicobar Is. *Ind. Oc.* 8°0N 93°30E 83 C1
Nicosia *Cyprus* 35°10N 33°25E 86 C3
Nicoya, Pen. de *Costa Rica* 9°45N 85°40W 114 F7
Nidd → *U.K.* 53°59N 1°23W 23 E6
Nidderdale *U.K.* 54°5N 1°46W 22 D5
Niedersachsen □ *Germany* 52°50N 9°0E 66 B5
Nieuw Nickerie *Suriname* 6°0N 56°59W 120 B4
Niğde *Turkey* 37°58N 34°40E 86 B3
Niger ■ *W. Afr.* 17°30N 10°0E 94 E7
Niger → *W. Afr.* 5°33N 6°33E 94 G7
Nigeria ■ *W. Afr.* 8°30N 8°0E 94 G7
Niigata *Japan* 37°58N 139°0E 82 E6
Ni'ihau *U.S.A.* 21°54N 160°9W 110 H14
Nijmegen *Neths.* 51°50N 5°52E 65 C5
Nikolayev *Ukraine* 46°58N 32°0E 73 E5
Nikolayevsk-na-Amur
  Russia 53°8N 140°44E 79 D16
Nikopol *Ukraine* 47°35N 34°25E 73 E5
Nikšić *Montenegro* 42°50N 18°57E 71 C8
Nile → *Africa* 30°10N 31°6E 95 B12
Nimach *India* 24°30N 74°56E 84 G9
Nîmes *France* 43°50N 4°23E 68 E6
Nimrūz □ *Afghan.* 30°0N 62°0E 87 D10
Ninawá *Iraq* 36°25N 43°10E 86 B5
Ninfield *U.K.* 50°53N 0°26E 25 E9
Ningbo *China* 29°51N 121°28E 81 D7
Ningjing Shan *China* 30°0N 98°20E 80 C4
Ningxia Hui □ *China* 38°0N 106°0E 80 C5
Niobrara → *U.S.A.* 42°46N 98°3W 110 B7
Niort *France* 46°19N 0°29W 68 C3
Nipawin *Canada* 53°20N 104°0W 108 D9
Nipigon *Canada* 49°0N 88°17W 112 A3
Nipigon, L. *Canada* 49°50N 88°30W 109 E11
Nipissing, L. *Canada* 46°20N 80°0W 109 E12
Niquelândia *Brazil* 14°33S 48°23W 122 B1
Niterói *Brazil* 22°53S 43°7W 122 D2
Nith → *U.K.* 55°14N 3°33W 21 D8
Nith → *U.K.* 55°1N 1°42W 21 D9
Nitra *Slovak Rep.* 48°19N 18°4E 67 D10
Nitra → *Slovak Rep.* 47°46N 18°10E 67 E10
Niuafo'ou *Tonga* 15°30S 175°58W 99 D17
Niue *Cook Is.* 19°2S 169°54W 99 D17
Nivernais *France* 47°15N 3°30E 68 C5
Nizamabad *India* 18°45N 78°7E 84 K11
Nizhnekamsk *Russia* 55°38N 51°49E 72 C9
Nizhnevartovsk *Russia* 60°56N 76°38E 79 C9
Nizhniy Novgorod *Russia* 56°20N 44°0E 72 C7
Nizhniy Tagil *Russia* 57°55N 59°57E 72 C10
Nizhyn *Ukraine* 51°5N 31°55E 73 D5
Nizwá *Oman* 22°56N 57°32E 88 C6
Nkawkaw *Ghana* 6°36N 0°49W 94 G5
Nkongsamba *Cameroon* 4°55N 9°55E 96 D1
Nobeoka *Japan* 32°36N 131°41E 82 G2
Noblesville *U.S.A.* 40°3N 86°1W 112 E4
Nogales *Mexico* 31°19N 110°56W 114 A2
Nogales *U.S.A.* 31°21N 110°56W 110 D4
Noirmoutier, Î. de *France* 46°58N 2°10W 68 C2
Nola *C.A.R.* 3°35N 16°4E 96 D3
Nome *U.S.A.* 64°30N 165°25W 108 C3
Nord-Ostsee-Kanal *Germany* 54°12N 9°32E 66 A5
Nordelph *U.K.* 52°35N 0°17E 25 A9
Norderstedt *Germany* 53°42N 10°1E 66 B5
Nordfriesische Inseln *Germany* 54°40N 8°20E 66 A5
Nordkapp *Norway* 71°10N 25°50E 63 C9
Nordrhein-Westfalen □
  Germany 51°45N 7°30E 66 C4
Nordvik *Russia* 74°2N 111°32E 79 B13
Nore → *Ireland* 52°25N 6°58W 31 D9
Norfolk *Nebr., U.S.A.* 42°2N 97°25W 111 B7
Norfolk *Va., U.S.A.* 36°50N 76°17W 111 C11
Norfolk □ *U.K.* 52°39N 0°54E 25 A10
Norfolk Broads △ *U.K.* 52°45N 1°30E 25 A11
Norfolk I. *Pac. Oc.* 28°58S 168°3E 99 F12
Norham *U.K.* 55°43N 2°9W 22 A4
Norilsk *Russia* 69°20N 88°6E 79 C10
Normal *U.S.A.* 40°31N 88°59W 112 E3
Norman *U.S.A.* 35°13N 97°26W 110 C7
Norman Wells *Canada* 65°17N 126°51W 108 C7
Normandie *France* 48°45N 0°10E 68 B4
Normanton *Australia* 17°40S 141°10E 98 D7
Normanton *U.K.* 53°42N 1°24W 23 E6
Norristown *U.S.A.* 40°7N 75°21W 113 E10
Norrköping *Sweden* 58°37N 16°11E 63 F7
Norrland *Sweden* 62°15N 15°45E 63 E7
Norseman *Australia* 32°8S 121°43E 98 G3
Norte, Serra do *Brazil* 11°20S 59°0W 120 D4
North, C. *Canada* 47°2N 60°20W 113 B17
North Ayrshire □ *U.K.* 55°45N 4°44W 20 C6
North Battleford *Canada* 52°50N 108°17W 108 D9
North Bay *Canada* 46°20N 79°30W 109 E12
North Berwick *U.K.* 56°4N 2°42W 21 B10
North C. *Canada* 47°5N 64°0W 113 B15
North C. *N.Z.* 34°23S 173°4E 99 G13
North Canadian → *U.S.A.* 35°22N 95°37W 110 C7
North Carolina □ *U.S.A.* 35°30N 80°0W 111 C11
North Cerney *U.K.* 51°45N 1°57W 24 C5
North Channel *Canada* 46°0N 83°0W 112 B6
North Channel *U.K.* 55°13N 5°52W 20 D4
North Dakota □ *U.S.A.* 47°30N 100°15W 110 A7
North Dorset Downs *U.K.* 50°45N 2°25W 24 E4
North Downs *U.K.* 51°19N 0°21E 25 D9
North Esk → *U.K.* 56°46N 2°24W 19 J13
North European Plain *Europe* 55°0N 25°0E 56 E10
North Foreland *U.K.* 51°22N 1°28E 25 D11
North Harris *U.K.* 58°0N 6°55W 18 F4
North Hill *U.K.* 50°33N 4°27W 27 F5
North Hykeham *U.K.* 53°11N 0°35W 23 F7
North I. *N.Z.* 38°0S 175°0E 99 H14
North Korea ■ *Asia* 40°0N 127°0E 81 C7
North Magnetic Pole *Canada* 82°42N 114°24W 54 A2

North Minch *U.K.* 58°5N 5°55W 18 F6
North Molton *U.K.* 51°3N 3°49W 27 E6
North Ossetia □ *Russia* 43°30N 44°30E 73 F7
North Petherton *U.K.* 51°5N 3°1W 24 D2
North Platte *U.S.A.* 41°8N 100°46W 110 B6
North Platte → *U.S.A.* 41°7N 100°42W 110 B6
North Pole *Arctic* 90°0N 0°0 54 A
North Pt. *Barbados* 13°20N 59°37W 115 g
North Ronaldsay *U.K.* 59°22N 2°26W 19 D13
North Saskatchewan →
  Canada 53°15N 105°5W 108 D9
North Sea *Europe* 56°0N 4°0E 64 C7
North Sea Canal = Nord-Ostsee-Kanal
  Germany 54°12N 9°32E 66 A5
North Somercotes *U.K.* 53°27N 0°8E 23 F9
North Sunderland *U.K.* 55°34N 1°40W 22 A5
North Tawton *U.K.* 50°48N 3°54W 27 F6
North Thompson →
  Canada 50°40N 120°20W 108 D7
North Thoresby *U.K.* 53°28N 0°4W 23 F8
North Tidworth *U.K.* 51°15N 1°40W 24 D5
North Tyne → *U.K.* 55°0N 2°8W 22 C4
North Uist *U.K.* 57°40N 7°15W 18 G3
North Vernon *U.S.A.* 39°0N 85°38W 112 F5
North Walsham *U.K.* 52°50N 1°22E 25 A11
North West C. *Australia* 21°45S 114°9E 98 E1
North West Frontier □ *Pakistan* 34°0N 72°0E 84 C7
North West Highlands *U.K.* 57°33N 4°58W 19 G8
North West River *Canada* 53°30N 60°10W 109 D13
North York Moors *U.K.* 54°23N 0°53W 22 D7
North York Moors △ *U.K.* 54°27N 0°51W 22 D7
North Yorkshire □ *U.K.* 54°15N 1°25W 22 D6
Northallerton *U.K.* 54°20N 1°26W 22 D6
Northam *Australia* 31°35S 116°42E 98 G2
Northam *U.K.* 51°2N 4°13W 27 E5
Northampton *U.K.* 52°15N 0°53W 25 B7
Northampton *U.S.A.* 42°19N 72°38W 113 D11
Northamptonshire □ *U.K.* 52°16N 0°55W 25 B7
Northern Areas □ *Pakistan* 36°30N 73°0E 84 B9
Northern Circars *India* 17°30N 82°30E 85 L13
Northern Ireland □ *U.K.* 54°45N 7°0W 29 B8
Northern Marianas ■ *Pac. Oc.* 17°0N 145°0E 102 F6
Northern Sporades *Greece* 39°15N 23°30E 71 E10
Northern Territory □ *Australia* 20°0S 133°0E 98 E5
Northfleet *U.K.* 51°26N 0°20E 25 D9
Northiam *U.K.* 50°59N 0°36E 25 E10
Northleach *U.K.* 51°49N 1°50W 24 C5
Northrepps *U.K.* 52°54N 1°21E 25 A11
Northumberland □ *U.K.* 55°12N 2°0W 22 B4
Northumberland △ *Northumberland,*
  U.K. 55°15N 2°20W 22 B4
Northumberland Str.
  Canada 46°20N 64°0W 109 E13
Northwest Territories □
  Canada 63°0N 118°0W 108 C9
Northwich *U.K.* 53°15N 2°31W 23 F3
Northwold *U.K.* 52°33N 0°36E 25 A10
Norton *N. Yorks., U.K.* 54°8N 0°47W 22 D7
Norton *Suffolk, U.K.* 52°16N 0°52E 25 B10
Norton Fitzwarren *U.K.* 51°1N 3°8W 24 D2
Norton Sd. *U.S.A.* 63°50N 164°0W 108 C3
Norwalk *U.S.A.* 41°15N 82°37W 112 E6
Norway ■ *Europe* 63°0N 11°0E 63 E6
Norway House *Canada* 53°59N 97°50W 108 D10
Norwegian B. *Canada* 77°30N 90°0W 109 B11
Norwegian Sea *Atl. Oc.* 66°0N 1°0E 54 C8
Norwich *U.K.* 52°38N 1°18E 25 A11
Norwich *U.S.A.* 42°32N 75°32W 113 D10
Noss Hd. *U.K.* 58°28N 3°3W 19 E11
Nossob → *S. Africa* 26°55S 20°45E 97 K4
Notre Dame B. *Canada* 49°45N 55°30W 109 E14
Nottaway → *Canada* 51°22N 78°55W 109 D12
Nottingham *U.K.* 52°58N 1°10W 23 G6
Nottingham *U.S.A.* 63°20N 77°55W 109 C12
Nottinghamshire □ *U.K.* 53°10N 1°3W 23 F6
Nouâdhibou *Mauritania* 20°54N 17°0W 94 D2
Nouâdhibou, Ras *Mauritania* 20°50N 17°0W 94 D2
Nouakchott *Mauritania* 18°9N 15°58W 94 E2
Nouméa *N. Cal.* 22°17S 166°30E 99 E12
Nova Casa Nova *Brazil* 9°25S 41°5W 122 A2
Nova Friburgo *Brazil* 22°16S 42°30W 122 D2
Nova Iguaçu *Brazil* 22°45S 43°28W 122 D2
Nova Lima *Brazil* 19°59S 43°51W 122 D2
Nova Scotia □ *Canada* 45°10N 63°0W 113 C16
Nova Venécia *Brazil* 18°45S 40°24W 122 C2
Novara *Italy* 45°28N 8°38E 70 B3
Novaya Zemlya *Russia* 75°0N 56°0E 79 B7
Novgorod *Russia* 58°30N 31°25E 72 C5
Novi Pazar *Serbia* 43°12N 20°28E 71 C9
Novi Sad *Serbia* 45°18N 19°52E 71 B8
Novo Remanso *Brazil* 9°41S 42°4W 122 A2
Novocherkassk *Russia* 47°27N 40°15E 73 E7
Novokuybyshevsk *Russia* 53°7N 49°58E 72 D8
Novokuznetsk *Russia* 53°45N 87°10E 79 D10
Novomoskovsk *Russia* 54°5N 38°15E 72 D6
Novorossiysk *Russia* 44°43N 37°46E 73 F6
Novoshakhtinsk *Russia* 47°46N 39°58E 73 E6
Novosibirsk *Russia* 55°0N 83°5E 79 D10
Novotroitsk *Russia* 51°10N 58°15E 72 D10
Nowy Sącz *Poland* 49°40N 20°41E 67 D11
Nubia *Africa* 21°0N 32°0E 90 D7
Nubian Desert *Sudan* 21°30N 33°30E 95 D12
Nueces → *U.S.A.* 27°51N 97°30W 110 E7
Nueltin L. *Canada* 60°30N 99°30W 108 C10
Nueva Rosita *Mexico* 27°57N 101°13W 114 B4
Nuevitas *Cuba* 21°30N 77°20W 115 C9
Nuevo Laredo *Mexico* 27°30N 99°31W 114 B5
Nuku'alofa *Tonga* 21°10S 174°0W 99 E16
Nukus *Uzbekistan* 42°27N 59°41E 87 A9
Nullarbor Plain *Australia* 31°10S 129°0E 98 G4
Numan *Nigeria* 9°29N 12°3E 95 G8
Numazu *Japan* 35°7N 138°51E 82 F6
Nunavut □ *Canada* 66°0N 85°0W 109 C11
Nuneaton *U.K.* 52°32N 1°27W 23 G6
Nunivak I. *U.S.A.* 60°10N 166°30W 108 C3
Nunney *U.K.* 51°12N 2°22W 24 D4
Nuoro *Italy* 40°20N 9°20E 70 D3

Nuremberg *Germany* 49°27N 11°3E 66 D6
Nusaybin *Turkey* 37°3N 41°10E 73 G7
Nuuk *Greenland* 64°10N 51°35W 54 C5
Nuweveldberge *S. Africa* 32°10S 21°45E 97 L4
Nyahururu *Kenya* 0°2N 36°27E 96 D7
Nyainqentanglha Shan *China* 30°0N 90°0E 80 D3
Nyâlâ *Sudan* 12°2N 24°58E 95 F10
Nyíregyháza *Hungary* 47°58N 21°47E 67 E11
Nysa *Poland* 50°30N 17°22E 67 C9
Nzérékoré *Guinea* 7°49N 8°48W 94 G4

O

Oa, Mull of *U.K.* 55°35N 6°20W 20 C3
Oadby *U.K.* 52°36N 1°5W 23 G6
Oahe, L. *U.S.A.* 44°27N 100°24W 110 A6
O'ahu *U.S.A.* 21°28N 157°58W 110 H16
Oak Hill *U.S.A.* 37°59N 81°9W 112 G7
Oak Ridge *U.S.A.* 36°1N 84°16W 111 C10
Oakengates *U.K.* 52°41N 2°26W 23 G4
Oakham *U.K.* 52°40N 0°43W 23 G7
Oakland *U.S.A.* 37°48N 122°18W 110 C2
Oates Land *Antarctica* 69°0S 160°0E 55 C11
Oaxaca *Mexico* 17°3N 96°43W 114 D5
Ob → *Russia* 66°45N 69°30E 79 C8
Ob, G. of *Russia* 69°0N 73°0E 79 C9
Oba *Canada* 49°4N 84°7W 109 E11
Oban *U.K.* 56°25N 5°29W 20 B5
Oberhausen *Germany* 51°28N 6°51E 66 C4
Obi, Kepulauan *Indonesia* 1°23S 127°45E 83 D4
Óbidos *Brazil* 1°50S 55°30W 120 C4
Obihiro *Japan* 42°56N 143°12E 82 B8
Obozerskiy *Russia* 63°34N 40°21E 72 B7
Obshchi Syrt *Russia* 52°0N 53°0E 56 E16
Ocala *U.S.A.* 29°11N 82°8W 111 E10
Occidental, Cordillera *Colombia* 5°0N 76°0W 116 C3
Occidental, Grand Erg *Algeria* 30°20N 1°0E 94 B6
Ocean City *U.S.A.* 39°17N 74°35W 113 F10
Oceanside *U.S.A.* 33°12N 117°23W 110 D3
Ochil Hills *U.K.* 56°14N 3°40W 21 B8
Ocho Rios *Jamaica* 18°24N 77°6W 114 a
Oconto *U.S.A.* 44°53N 87°52W 112 C4
Odawara *Japan* 35°20N 139°6E 82 F6
Odense *Denmark* 55°22N 10°23E 63 F6
Oder → *Europe* 53°33N 14°38E 66 B8
Odessa *Ukraine* 46°30N 30°45E 73 E5
Odessa *U.S.A.* 31°52N 102°23W 110 D6
Odiham *U.K.* 51°15N 0°55W 25 D7
Odintsovo *Russia* 55°40N 37°16E 72 C6
Odzi *Zimbabwe* 19°0S 32°20E 97 H6
Offa *Nigeria* 8°13N 4°42E 94 G6
Offaly □ *Ireland* 53°15N 7°30W 31 B8
Offenbach *Germany* 50°6N 8°44E 66 C5
Ogaden *Ethiopia* 7°30N 45°30E 88 F3
Ōgaki *Japan* 35°21N 136°37E 82 F5
Ogasawara Gunto *Pac. Oc.* 27°0N 142°0E 102 E6
Ogbomosho *Nigeria* 8°1N 4°11E 94 G6
Ogden *U.S.A.* 41°13N 111°58W 110 B4
Ogdensburg *U.S.A.* 44°42N 75°30W 113 C10
Ogooué → *Gabon* 1°0S 9°0E 96 E1
Ohio □ *U.S.A.* 40°15N 82°45W 112 E5
Ohio → *U.S.A.* 36°59N 89°8W 111 C9
Ohře → *Czech Rep.* 50°30N 14°10E 66 C8
Ohrid, L. *Macedonia* 41°8N 20°52E 71 D9
Oil City *U.S.A.* 41°26N 79°42W 112 E8
Oise → *France* 49°0N 2°4E 68 B5
Oistins *Barbados* 13°4N 59°33W 115 g
Oistins B. *Barbados* 13°4N 59°33W 115 g
Ōita *Japan* 33°14N 131°36E 82 G2
Ojos del Salado, Cerro
  Argentina 27°0S 68°40W 121 E3
Oka → *Russia* 56°20N 43°59E 72 C7
Okara *Pakistan* 30°50N 73°31E 84 D8
Okavango Delta *Botswana* 18°45S 22°45E 97 H4
Okayama *Japan* 34°40N 133°54E 82 F3
Okazaki *Japan* 34°57N 137°10E 82 F5
Okeechobee, L. *U.S.A.* 27°0N 80°50W 111 E10
Okehampton *U.K.* 50°44N 4°0W 27 F5
Okhotsk *Russia* 59°20N 143°10E 79 D16
Okhotsk, Sea of *Asia* 55°0N 145°0E 79 D16
Oki-Shotō *Japan* 36°5N 133°15E 82 E3
Okinawa-Jima *Japan* 26°32N 128°0E 81 D7
Oklahoma □ *U.S.A.* 35°20N 97°30W 110 C7
Oklahoma City *U.S.A.* 35°30N 97°30W 110 C7
Oktyabrsk *Kazakhstan* 49°28N 57°25E 73 E10
Oktyabrskiy *Russia* 54°28N 53°28E 72 D9
Öland *Sweden* 56°45N 16°38E 63 F7
Olavarría *Argentina* 36°55S 60°20W 121 F3
Ólbia *Italy* 40°55N 9°31E 70 D3
Old Basing *U.K.* 51°16N 1°3W 24 D6
Old Crow *Canada* 67°30N 139°55W 108 C6
Old Fletton *U.K.* 52°33N 0°14W 25 A8
Old Leake *U.K.* 53°2N 0°5E 23 F9
Old Town *U.S.A.* 44°56N 68°39W 113 C13
Oldbury *U.K.* 51°38N 2°33W 24 C3
Oldcastle *Ireland* 53°46N 7°10W 29 D7
Oldenburg *Germany* 53°9N 8°13E 66 B5
Oldham *U.K.* 53°33N 2°7W 23 E4
Oldmeldrum *U.K.* 57°20N 2°19W 19 H13
Olean *U.S.A.* 42°5N 78°26W 112 D8
Olekminsk *Russia* 60°25N 120°30E 79 C14
Olenek → *Russia* 73°0N 120°10E 79 B14
Oléron, Î. d' *France* 45°55N 1°15W 68 D3
Ólgiy *Mongolia* 48°56N 89°57E 80 B3
Olímpia *Brazil* 20°44S 48°54W 122 D1
Oliveira *Brazil* 20°50S 44°50W 122 D2
Ollagüe *Chile* 21°15S 68°10W 120 E3
Ollerton *U.K.* 53°12N 1°1W 23 F6
Olney *U.K.* 52°9N 0°41W 25 B7
Olney *U.S.A.* 38°44N 88°5W 112 F3
Olomouc *Czech Rep.* 49°38N 17°12E 67 D9
Olsztyn *Poland* 53°48N 20°29E 67 B11
Olt → *Romania* 43°43N 24°51E 67 G13
Olympia *Greece* 37°39N 21°39E 71 F9
Olympia *U.S.A.* 47°3N 122°53W 110 A2
Olympus, Mt. *Greece* 40°6N 22°23E 71 D10
Olympus, Mt. *U.S.A.* 47°48N 123°43W 110 A2
Omagh *U.K.* 54°36N 7°19W 28 B7

Omaha   Plauen

Omaha U.S.A. 41°17N 95°58W 111 B7
Oman ■ Asia 23°0N 58°0E 88 C6
Oman, G. of Asia 24°30N 58°30E 87 E9
Ombersley U.K. 52°16N 2°13W 24 B4
Omdurmân Sudan 15°40N 32°28E 95 E12
Ometepec Mexico 16°41N 98°25W 114 D5
Omsk Russia 55°0N 73°12E 79 D9
Ōmuta Japan 33°5N 130°26E 82 G2
Ondangwa Namibia 17°57S 16°4E 97 H3
Onega Russia 63°58N 38°2E 72 B6
Onega, L. Russia 61°44N 35°22E 72 B6
Onega B. Russia 64°24N 36°38E 72 B6
Oneida U.S.A. 43°6N 75°39W 113 D10
O'Neill U.S.A. 42°27N 98°39W 110 B7
Oneonta U.S.A. 42°27N 75°4W 113 D10
Onitsha Nigeria 6°6N 6°42E 94 G7
Onny → U.K. 52°24N 2°47W 23 H3
Onslow B. U.S.A. 34°20N 77°15W 111 D11
Ontario U.S.A. 44°2N 116°58W 110 B3
Ontario □ Canada 48°0N 83°0W 109 E11
Ontario, L. N. Amer. 43°20N 78°0W 112 D8
Ontonagon U.S.A. 46°52N 89°19W 112 B31
Oostende Belgium 51°15N 2°54E 65 C2
Opava Czech Rep. 49°57N 17°58E 67 D9
Opole Poland 50°42N 17°58E 67 C9
Oradea Romania 47°2N 21°58E 67 E11
Öræfajökull Iceland 64°2N 16°39W 63 B2
Oral Kazakhstan 51°20N 51°20E 73 D9
Oran Algeria 35°45N 0°39W 94 A5
Orange Australia 33°15S 149°7E 98 G8
Orange France 44°8N 4°47E 68 D6
Orange U.S.A. 38°15N 78°7W 112 F8
Orange → S. Africa 28°41S 16°28E 97 K3
Orange, C. Brazil 4°20N 51°30W 120 B4
Orangeburg U.S.A. 33°30N 80°52W 111 D10
Orangeville Canada 43°55N 80°5W 112 D7
Ordos Desert China 39°0N 109°0E 81 C5
Ordu Turkey 40°55N 37°53E 73 F6
Örebro Sweden 59°20N 15°18E 63 F7
Oregon □ U.S.A. 44°0N 121°0W 110 B2
Orekhovo-Zuyevo Russia 55°50N 38°55E 72 C6
Orel Russia 52°57N 36°3E 72 D6
Orem U.S.A. 40°19N 111°42W 110 B4
Orenburg Russia 51°45N 55°6E 72 D10
Orford U.K. 52°6N 1°33E 25 B12
Orford Ness U.K. 52°5N 1°35E 25 B12
Orhon Gol → Mongolia 50°21N 106°0E 80 A5
Oriental, Cordillera Colombia 6°0N 73°0W 116 C3
Oriental, Grand Erg Algeria 30°0N 6°30E 94 B7
Orihuela Spain 38°7N 0°55W 69 C5
Orinoco → Venezuela 9°15N 61°30W 120 B3
Orissa □ India 20°0N 84°0E 85 K14
Oristano Italy 39°54N 8°36E 70 E3
Orizaba Mexico 18°51N 97°6W 114 D5
Orizaba, Pico de Mexico 18°58N 97°15W 114 D5
Orkney □ U.K. 59°2N 3°13W 19 D11
Orkney Is. U.K. 59°0N 3°0W 64 B5
Orlando U.S.A. 28°32N 81°22W 111 E10
Orléanais France 48°0N 2°0E 68 C5
Orléans France 47°54N 1°52E 68 C4
Orléans, Î. d' Canada 46°54N 70°58W 113 B12
Ormara Pakistan 25°16N 64°33E 84 G4
Ormesby St. Margaret U.K. 52°41N 1°41E 25 A12
Ormoc Phil. 11°0N 124°37E 83 B4
Ormskirk U.K. 53°35N 2°54W 23 E3
Örnsköldsvik Sweden 63°17N 18°40E 63 E7
Oronsay U.K. 56°1N 6°15W 20 B3
Orsha Belarus 54°30N 30°25E 72 D5
Ortegal, C. Spain 43°43N 7°52W 69 A2
Oruro Bolivia 18°0S 67°9W 120 D3
Oruzgân □ Afghan. 33°0N 66°0E 87 C11
Orwell → U.K. 51°59N 1°18E 25 C11
Ōsaka Japan 34°42N 135°30E 82 F4
Oshakati Namibia 17°45S 15°40E 97 H3
Oshawa Canada 43°50N 78°50W 109 E12
Oshkosh U.S.A. 44°1N 88°33W 112 D3
Oshogbo Nigeria 7°48N 4°37E 94 G6
Osijek Croatia 45°34N 18°41E 71 B8
Osizweni S. Africa 27°49S 30°7E 97 K6
Oskaloosa U.S.A. 41°18N 92°39W 111 B81
Oskarshamn Sweden 57°15N 16°27E 63 F7
Öskemen Kazakhstan 50°0N 82°36E 79 D10
Oslo Norway 59°54N 10°43E 63 F6
Oslofjorden Norway 59°20N 10°35E 63 F6
Osmaniye Turkey 37°5N 36°10E 73 G6
Osmotherley U.K. 54°22N 1°18W 22 D6
Osnabrück Germany 52°17N 8°3E 66 B5
Osorno Chile 40°25S 73°0W 121 G2
Ossa, Mt. Australia 41°52S 146°3E 98 J8
Ossett U.K. 53°41N 1°34W 23 E5
Ostend = Oostende Belgium 51°15N 2°54E 65 C2
Österdalälven Sweden 61°30N 13°45E 63 E6
Östersund Sweden 63°10N 14°38E 63 E6
Ostfriesische Inseln Germany 53°42N 7°0E 66 B4
Ostrava Czech Rep. 49°51N 18°18E 67 D10
Ostrołęka Poland 53°4N 21°32E 67 B11
Ostrów Wielkopolski Poland 51°36N 17°44E 67 C9
Ostrowiec-Świętokrzyski Poland 50°55N 21°22E 67 C11
Oswaldtwistle U.K. 53°43N 2°26W 23 E4
Oswego U.S.A. 43°27N 76°31W 112 D9
Oswestry U.K. 52°52N 3°3W 23 G2
Otaru Japan 43°10N 141°0E 82 B7
Otjiwarongo Namibia 20°30S 16°33E 97 J3
Otley U.K. 53°54N 1°41W 23 E5
Otranto Italy 40°9N 18°28E 71 D8
Otranto, Str. of Italy 40°15N 18°40E 71 D8
Ōtsu Japan 35°0N 135°50E 82 F4
Ottawa Canada 45°26N 75°42W 113 C10
Ottawa U.S.A. 41°21N 88°51W 112 E3
Ottawa Is. Canada 59°35N 80°10W 109 D11
Otter → U.K. 50°38N 3°19W 27 F7
Otterburn U.K. 55°14N 2°11W 22 B5
Ottery St. Mary U.K. 50°44N 3°17W 27 F7
Ottumwa U.S.A. 41°1N 92°25W 111 B81
Ouachita → U.S.A. 31°38N 91°49W 111 D8
Ouachita Mts. U.S.A. 34°30N 94°30W 111 D8
Ouagadougou Burkina Faso 12°25N 1°30W 94 F5

Oubangi → Dem. Rep. of the Congo 0°30S 17°50E 96 E3
Oudtshoorn S. Africa 33°35S 22°14E 97 L4
Ouezzane Morocco 34°51N 5°35W 94 B4
Oughterard Ireland 53°26N 9°18W 30 B4
Oujda Morocco 34°41N 1°55W 94 B5
Oulton U.K. 52°30N 1°43E 25 B12
Oulton Broad U.K. 52°28N 1°42E 25 B12
Oulu Finland 65°1N 25°29E 63 D9
Oulujärvi Finland 64°25N 27°15E 63 E9
Oulujoki → Finland 65°1N 25°30E 63 D9
Oundle U.K. 52°29N 0°28W 25 B8
Ourense Spain 42°19N 7°55W 69 A2
Ouro Fino Brazil 22°16S 46°25W 122 D1
Ouro Prêto Brazil 20°20S 43°30W 122 D2
Ouse → E. Sussex, U.K. 50°47N 0°4E 25 E9
Ouse → N. Yorks., U.K. 53°44N 0°55W 23 E7
Outaouais → Canada 45°27N 74°8W 109 E12
Outer Hebrides U.K. 57°30N 7°40W 18 H2
Outjo Namibia 20°5S 16°7E 97 J3
Outwell U.K. 52°37N 0°14E 25 B9
Ovalle Chile 30°33S 71°18W 121 F2
Ovamboland Namibia 18°30S 16°0E 97 H3
Over Wallop U.K. 51°9N 1°36W 24 D5
Overijssel □ Neths. 52°25N 6°35E 65 B6
Overton U.K. 51°15N 1°15W 24 D6
Oviedo Spain 43°25N 5°50W 69 A3
Owatonna U.S.A. 44°5N 93°14W 111 B8
Owen Sound Canada 44°35N 80°55W 109 E11
Owen Stanley Ra. Papua N. G. 8°30S 147°0E 98 B8
Owens L. U.S.A. 36°26N 117°57W 110 C3
Owensboro U.S.A. 37°46N 87°7W 112 G4
Owo Nigeria 7°10N 5°39E 94 G7
Owosso U.S.A. 43°0N 84°10W 112 D5
Owston Ferry U.K. 53°29N 0°47W 23 F7
Owyhee → U.S.A. 43°49N 117°2W 110 B3
Oxford U.K. 51°46N 1°15W 24 D6
Oxfordshire □ U.K. 51°48N 1°16W 24 C6
Oxnard U.S.A. 34°12N 119°11W 110 D3
Oyama Japan 36°18N 139°48E 82 E6
Oyem Gabon 1°34N 11°31E 96 D2
Oykel → U.K. 57°56N 4°26W 19 G9
Oyo Nigeria 7°46N 3°56E 94 G6
Ozark Plateau U.S.A. 37°20N 91°40W 111 C81
Ozarks, L. of the U.S.A. 38°12N 92°38W 111 C81

P
Paarl S. Africa 33°45S 18°56E 97 L3
Pab Hills Pakistan 26°30N 66°45E 84 F5
Pabbay U.K. 57°46N 7°14W 18 G3
Pabna Bangla. 24°1N 89°18E 85 G16
Pacaraima, Sa. S. Amer. 4°0N 62°30W 120 B3
Pacasmayo Peru 7°20S 79°35W 120 C2
Pachuca Mexico 20°7N 98°44W 114 C5
Pacific Antarctic Ridge Pac. Oc. 43°0S 115°0W 103 M16
Pacific Ocean 10°0N 140°0W 103 G14
Padang Indonesia 1°0S 100°20E 83 D2
Padangsidempuan Indonesia 1°30N 99°15E 83 C1
Paddock Wood U.K. 51°11N 0°24E 25 D9
Paderborn Germany 51°42N 8°45E 66 C5
Padiham U.K. 53°48N 2°18W 23 E4
Padre I. U.S.A. 27°10N 97°25W 111 E7
Padstow U.K. 50°33N 4°58W 27 F4
Padstow B. U.K. 50°34N 4°57W 27 F4
Padua Italy 45°25N 11°53E 70 B4
Paducah U.S.A. 37°5N 88°37W 112 G3
Pag Croatia 44°25N 15°3E 70 B6
Pagadian Phil. 7°55N 123°30E 83 C4
Page U.S.A. 36°57N 111°27W 110 C4
Pāhala U.S.A. 19°12N 155°29W 110 J17
Paignton U.K. 50°26N 3°35W 27 G6
Paine, Cerro Chile 50°59S 73°4W 121 H2
Painesville U.S.A. 41°43N 81°15W 112 E7
Painswick U.K. 51°47N 2°10W 24 C4
Painted Desert U.S.A. 36°0N 111°0W 110 C4
Paintsville U.S.A. 37°49N 82°48W 112 G6
Pais Vasco □ Spain 42°50N 2°45W 69 A4
Paisley U.K. 55°50N 4°25W 20 C7
Paita Peru 5°11S 81°9W 120 C1
Pakistan ■ Asia 30°0N 70°0E 84 E7
Paktīā □ Afghan. 33°0N 69°15E 87 C12
Pakxe Laos 15°5N 105°52E 83 B2
Palagruža Croatia 42°24N 16°15E 70 C7
Palani Hills India 10°14N 77°33E 84 P10
Palanpur India 24°10N 72°25E 84 G8
Palapye Botswana 22°30S 27°7E 97 J5
Palau ■ Palau 7°30N 134°30E 83 C5
Palawan Phil. 9°30N 118°30E 83 C3
Palembang Indonesia 3°0S 104°50E 83 D2
Palencia Spain 42°1N 4°34W 69 A3
Palermo Italy 38°7N 13°22E 70 E5
Palestine U.S.A. 31°46N 95°38W 111 D7
Palghat India 10°46N 76°42E 84 P10
Palgrave U.K. 52°22N 1°6E 25 B11
Pali India 25°50N 73°20E 84 G8
Palikir Micronesia 6°55N 158°9E 102 G7
Palk Strait Asia 10°0N 79°45E 84 Q11
Palma de Mallorca Spain 39°35N 2°39E 69 C7
Palmares Brazil 8°41S 35°28W 122 A3
Palmas, C. Liberia 4°27N 7°46W 94 H4
Palmeira dos Índios Brazil 9°25S 36°37W 122 A3
Palmer U.S.A. 61°36N 149°7W 108 C5
Palmer Land Antarctica 73°0S 63°0W 55 D18
Palmerston North N.Z. 40°21S 175°39W 99 J14
Palmira Colombia 3°32N 76°16W 120 B2
Palmyra Syria 34°36N 38°15E 86 C4
Palmyra Is. Pac. Oc. 5°52N 162°5W 103 G11
Palopo Indonesia 3°0S 120°16E 83 D4
Palu Indonesia 1°0S 119°52E 83 D3
Palu Turkey 38°45N 40°0E 73 G7
Pamiers France 43°7N 1°39E 68 E4
Pamir Tajikistan 37°40N 73°0E 87 B13
Pamlico Sd. U.S.A. 35°20N 76°0W 111 C11
Pampa U.S.A. 35°32N 100°58W 110 C6
Pampas Argentina 35°0S 63°0W 121 F3

Pamplona Spain 42°48N 1°38W 69 A5
Pana U.S.A. 39°23N 89°5W 112 F3
Panaji India 15°25N 73°50E 84 M8
Panamá Panama 9°0N 79°25W 115 F9
Panama ■ Cent. Amer. 8°48N 79°55W 115 F9
Panamá, G. de Panama 8°4N 79°20W 115 F9
Panama Canal Panama 9°10N 79°37W 115 F9
Panama City U.S.A. 30°10N 85°40W 111 D9
Panay Phil. 11°10N 122°30E 83 B4
Pančevo Serbia 44°52N 20°41E 71 B9
Panevėžys Lithuania 55°42N 24°25E 63 F8
Pangani Tanzania 5°25S 38°58E 96 F7
Pangbourne U.K. 51°29N 1°6W 24 D6
Pangkalpinang Indonesia 2°0S 106°0E 83 D2
Pangnirtung Canada 66°8N 65°43W 109 C13
Pantar Indonesia 8°28S 124°10E 83 D4
Pante Macassar E. Timor 9°30S 123°58E 83 D4
Pantelleria Italy 36°50N 11°57E 70 F4
Panzhihua China 26°33N 101°44E 80 D5
Papa Stour U.K. 60°20N 1°42W 18 B14
Papa Westray U.K. 59°20N 2°55W 19 D12
Papantla Mexico 20°27N 97°19W 114 C5
Papeete Tahiti 17°32S 149°34W 103 J13
Paphos Cyprus 34°46N 32°25E 86 C3
Papua □ Indonesia 4°0S 137°0E 83 D5
Papua, G. of Papua N. G. 9°0S 144°50E 98 B7
Papua New Guinea ■ Oceania 8°0S 145°0E 98 B8
Pará □ Brazil 3°20S 52°0W 120 C4
Paracatu Brazil 17°10S 46°50W 122 C1
Paracel Is. S. China Sea 15°50N 112°0E 83 B3
Paragould U.S.A. 36°3N 90°29W 111 C81
Paraguaçu → Brazil 12°45S 38°54W 122 B3
Paraguaná, Pen. de Venezuela 12°0N 70°0W 120 A3
Paraguari Paraguay 25°36S 57°0W 121 E4
Paraguay ■ S. Amer. 23°0S 57°0W 121 E4
Paraguay → Paraguay 27°18S 58°38W 121 E4
Paraíba □ Brazil 7°0S 36°0W 120 C6
Paraíba → Brazil 21°37S 41°3W 122 D2
Parakou Benin 9°25N 2°40E 94 G6
Paramaribo Suriname 5°50N 55°10W 120 B4
Paraná Argentina 31°45S 60°30W 121 F3
Paraná □ Brazil 12°30S 47°48W 122 B1
Paraná → Brazil 24°30S 51°0W 121 E4
Paraná → Argentina 33°43S 59°15W 121 F4
Paranaguá Brazil 25°30S 48°30W 121 E5
Paranaíba → Brazil 20°6S 51°4W 120 E4
Paranapanema → Brazil 22°40S 53°9W 121 E4
Paratinga Brazil 12°40S 43°10W 122 B2
Parbhani India 19°8N 76°52E 84 K10
Pardo → Brazil 15°40S 39°0W 122 C3
Pardubice Czech Rep. 50°3N 15°45E 66 C8
Parecis, Serra dos Brazil 13°0S 60°0W 120 D4
Parepare Indonesia 4°0S 119°40E 83 D3
Parima, Serra Brazil 2°30N 64°0W 120 B3
Pariñas, Pta. S. Amer. 4°30S 82°0W 116 D2
Parintins Brazil 2°40S 56°50W 120 C4
Pariparit Kyun Burma 14°55N 93°45E 85 M18
Paris France 48°53N 2°20E 68 B5
Paris U.S.A. 33°40N 95°33W 111 D7
Park Falls U.S.A. 45°56N 90°27W 112 C2
Parkersburg U.S.A. 39°16N 81°34W 112 F7
Parla Spain 40°14N 3°46W 69 B4
Parma Italy 44°48N 10°20E 70 B4
Parnaguá Brazil 10°10S 44°38W 122 B2
Parnaíba Brazil 2°54S 41°47W 120 C5
Parnaíba → Brazil 3°0S 41°50W 120 C5
Pärnu Estonia 58°28N 24°33E 63 F8
Paros Greece 37°5N 25°12E 71 F11
Parracombe U.K. 51°11N 3°56W 27 E6
Parrett → U.K. 51°12N 3°1W 24 D2
Parry Is. Canada 77°0N 110°0W 109 B9
Parry Sound Canada 45°20N 80°0W 109 E12
Parsons U.S.A. 37°20N 95°16W 111 C7
Partney U.K. 53°12N 0°7E 23 F9
Parton U.K. 54°35N 3°33W 22 C1
Partry Mts. Ireland 53°40N 9°28W 28 D3
Paru → Brazil 1°33S 52°38W 120 C4
Parvān □ Afghan. 35°0N 69°0E 87 C12
Pas, The Canada 53°45N 101°15W 108 D9
Pasadena Calif., U.S.A. 34°9N 118°8W 110 D3
Pasadena Tex., U.S.A. 29°43N 95°13W 111 E7
Pasco, Cerro de Peru 10°45S 76°10W 120 D2
Pascua, I. de Chile 27°7S 109°23W 103 K17
Paso Robles U.S.A. 35°38N 120°41W 110 C2
Passage West Ireland 51°52N 8°21W 30 E6
Passau Germany 48°34N 13°28E 66 D7
Passo Fundo Brazil 28°10S 52°20W 121 E4
Passos Brazil 20°45S 46°37W 122 D1
Pastaza → Peru 4°50S 76°52W 120 C2
Pasto Colombia 1°13N 77°17W 120 B2
Patagonia Argentina 45°0S 69°0W 121 G3
Patan India 23°54N 72°14E 84 H8
Pateley Bridge U.K. 54°5N 1°44W 22 D5
Paterson U.S.A. 40°54N 74°9W 113 E10
Pathankot India 32°18N 75°45E 84 C9
Pathfinder Res. U.S.A. 42°28N 106°51W 110 B5
Patkai Bum India 27°0N 95°30E 85 F19
Patmos Greece 37°21N 26°36E 71 F12
Patna India 25°35N 85°12E 85 G14
Patos Brazil 6°55S 37°16W 120 C6
Patos, L. dos Brazil 31°20S 51°0W 121 F4
Patos de Minas Brazil 18°35S 46°32W 122 C1
Patra Greece 38°14N 21°47E 71 E9
Patrington U.K. 53°41N 0°1W 23 E8
Patrocínio Brazil 18°57S 47°0W 122 C1
Patten U.S.A. 46°0N 68°38W 113 C13
Patterdale U.K. 54°32N 2°56W 22 C3
Pau France 43°19N 0°25W 68 E3
Paulatuk Canada 69°25N 124°0W 108 C7
Paulistana Brazil 8°9S 41°9W 122 A2
Paull U.K. 53°44N 0°14W 23 E8
Paulo Afonso Brazil 9°21S 38°15W 122 A3
Pavia Italy 45°7N 9°8E 70 B3
Pavlodar Kazakhstan 52°33N 77°0E 79 D9
Pavlohrad Ukraine 48°30N 35°52E 73 E6
Pavlovo Russia 55°58N 43°5E 72 C7
Pawtucket U.S.A. 41°53N 71°23W 113 E12
Paxton U.S.A. 40°27N 88°6W 112 E3
Payakumbuh Indonesia 0°20S 100°35E 83 D2
Payette U.S.A. 44°5N 116°56W 110 B3

Payne L. Canada 59°30N 74°30W 109 D12
Paysandú Uruguay 32°19S 58°8W 121 F4
Payson U.S.A. 34°14N 111°20W 110 D4
Paz, B. de la Mexico 24°9N 110°25W 114 C2
Pazardzhik Bulgaria 42°12N 24°20E 71 C11
Peace → Canada 59°0N 111°25W 108 D8
Peace River Canada 56°15N 117°18W 108 D8
Peacehaven U.K. 50°48N 0°0 25 E8
Peak District U.K. 53°24N 1°46W 23 F5
Pearl City U.S.A. 21°24N 157°59W 110 H16
Pearl Harbor U.S.A. 21°21N 157°57W 110 H16
Peasenhall U.K. 52°16N 1°27E 25 B11
Peawanuck Canada 55°15N 85°12W 109 D11
Peć Serbia 42°40N 20°17E 71 C9
Pechora Russia 65°10N 57°11E 72 A10
Pechora → Russia 68°13N 54°15E 72 A9
Pechora B. Russia 68°40N 54°0E 72 A9
Pecos U.S.A. 31°26N 103°30W 110 D6
Pecos → U.S.A. 29°42N 101°22W 110 E6
Pécs Hungary 46°5N 18°15E 67 E10
Pedra Azul Brazil 16°2S 41°17W 122 C2
Pedro Afonso Brazil 9°0S 48°10W 122 A1
Peebles U.K. 55°40N 3°11W 21 C9
Peel I. of Man 54°13N 4°40W 29 C12
Peel → Canada 67°0N 135°0W 108 C6
Peel Fell U.K. 55°18N 2°34W 22 B3
Peel Sd. Canada 73°0N 96°0W 108 B10
Pegswood U.K. 55°11N 1°39W 22 B5
Pegu Burma 17°20N 96°29E 85 L20
Pegu Yoma Burma 19°0N 96°0E 85 K20
Pegwell Bay U.K. 51°18N 1°24E 25 D11
Peixe Brazil 12°0S 48°40W 122 B1
Pekalongan Indonesia 6°53S 109°40E 83 D2
Pekanbaru Indonesia 0°30N 101°15E 83 D2
Pekin U.S.A. 40°35N 89°40W 112 E3
Peking = Beijing China 39°53N 116°21E 81 C6
Pelagie, Is. Italy 35°39N 12°33E 70 G5
Pelée, Mt. Martinique 14°48N 61°10W 114 c
Peleng Indonesia 1°20S 123°30E 83 D4
Peljesac Croatia 42°55N 17°25E 70 C7
Pelly → Canada 62°47N 137°19W 108 C6
Pelly Bay Canada 68°38N 89°50W 109 C11
Peloponnese □ Greece 37°10N 22°0E 71 F10
Pelotas Brazil 31°42S 52°23W 121 F4
Pelvoux, Massif du France 44°52N 6°20E 68 D7
Pematangsiantar Indonesia 2°57N 99°5E 83 C1
Pemba Mozam. 12°58S 40°30E 97 G8
Pemba I. Tanzania 5°0S 39°45E 96 F7
Pembina → U.S.A. 52°13N 2°52W 24 B3
Pembroke Canada 45°50N 77°7W 109 E12
Pembroke U.K. 51°41N 4°55W 26 D4
Pembrokeshire □ U.K. 51°52N 4°56W 26 D3
Pembrokeshire Coast △ U.K. 51°50N 5°2W 26 D3
Pembury U.K. 51°8N 0°20E 25 D9
Pen-y-Ghent U.K. 54°10N 2°14W 22 D4
Penarth U.K. 51°26N 3°11W 27 E7
Peñas, G. de Chile 47°0S 75°0W 121 G2
Pend Oreille, L. U.S.A. 48°10N 116°21W 110 A3
Pendeen U.K. 50°9N 5°41W 27 G2
Pendle Hill U.K. 53°52N 2°19W 23 E4
Pendleton U.S.A. 45°40N 118°47W 110 A3
Penedo Brazil 10°15S 36°36W 122 B3
Penetanguishene Canada 44°50N 79°55W 112 C8
Penicuik U.K. 55°50N 3°13W 21 C9
Peninsular Malaysia □ Malaysia 4°0N 102°0E 83 C2
Penistone U.K. 53°31N 1°37W 23 E5
Penkridge U.K. 52°44N 2°6W 23 G4
Penmarch, Pte. de France 47°48N 4°22W 68 C1
Penn Yan U.S.A. 42°40N 77°3W 112 D9
Pennines U.K. 54°45N 2°27E 22 C4
Pennsylvania □ U.S.A. 40°45N 77°30W 112 E8
Penong Australia 31°56S 133°1E 98 G5
Penrith U.K. 54°40N 2°45W 22 C3
Penryn U.K. 50°9N 5°7W 27 G3
Pensacola U.S.A. 30°25N 87°13W 111 D9
Pensacola Mts. Antarctica 84°0S 40°0W 55 E1
Penshurst U.K. 51°10N 0°12E 25 D9
Penticton Canada 49°30N 119°38W 108 E8
Pentire Pt. U.K. 50°35N 4°56W 27 F4
Pentland Firth U.K. 58°43N 3°10W 19 E11
Pentland Hills U.K. 55°48N 3°25W 21 C9
Penwortham U.K. 53°45N 2°46W 23 E3
Penygroes U.K. 53°3N 4°17W 26 A5
Penza Russia 53°15N 45°5E 72 D8
Penzance U.K. 50°7N 5°33W 27 G2
Peoria U.S.A. 40°42N 89°36W 112 E3
Perabumulih Indonesia 3°27S 104°15E 83 D2
Perdido, Mte. Spain 42°40N 0°5E 69 A6
Pereira Colombia 4°49N 75°43W 120 B2
Pergamino Argentina 33°52S 60°30W 121 F3
Péribonka → Canada 48°45N 72°5W 109 E12
Périgueux France 45°10N 0°42E 68 D4
Perm Russia 58°0N 56°10E 72 C10
Pernambuco □ Brazil 8°0S 37°0W 120 C6
Pernik Bulgaria 42°35N 23°2E 71 C10
Perpignan France 42°42N 2°53E 68 E5
Perranporth U.K. 50°20N 5°11W 27 G3
Perranzabuloe U.K. 50°19N 5°9W 27 G3
Perryton U.S.A. 36°24N 100°48W 110 C6
Perryville U.S.A. 37°43N 89°52W 112 G3
Persepolis Iran 29°55N 52°50E 87 D8
Pershore U.K. 52°7N 2°4W 24 B4
Persian Gulf Asia 27°0N 50°0E 87 E7
Perth Australia 31°57S 115°52E 98 G2
Perth Canada 44°55N 76°15W 112 C9
Perth U.K. 56°24N 3°26W 21 B9
Perth & Kinross □ U.K. 56°45N 3°55W 19 J9
Peru U.S.A. 40°45N 86°4W 112 E4
Peru ■ S. Amer. 4°0S 75°0W 120 C2
Peru-Chile Trench Pac. Oc. 20°0S 72°0W 103 K20
Perúgia Italy 43°7N 12°23E 70 C5
Pervomaysk Ukraine 48°10N 30°46E 73 E5
Pervouralsk Russia 56°59N 59°59E 72 C10
Pésaro Italy 43°54N 12°55E 70 C5
Pescara Italy 42°28N 14°13E 70 C6
Peshawar Pakistan 34°2N 71°37E 84 B7
Pesqueira Brazil 8°20S 36°42W 122 A3

Petah Tiqwa Israel 32°6N 34°53E 86 C3
Peter I. Br. Virgin Is. 18°22N 64°35W 115 e
Peterborough Canada 44°20N 78°20W 109 E12
Peterborough U.K. 52°35N 0°15W 25 A8
Peterchurch U.K. 52°2N 2°56W 24 B3
Peterculter U.K. 57°6N 2°16W 19 H13
Peterhead U.K. 57°31N 1°48W 19 G14
Peterlee U.K. 54°47N 1°20W 22 C6
Petersburg Alaska, U.S.A. 56°48N 132°58W 108 D6
Petersburg Va., U.S.A. 37°14N 77°24W 112 G9
Petersfield U.K. 51°1N 0°56W 25 D7
Petit-Canal Guadeloupe 16°25N 61°31W 114 b
Petit Piton St. Lucia 13°51N 61°5W 115 f
Petite Terre, Îles de la Guadeloupe 16°13N 61°9W 114 b
Petitot → Canada 60°14N 123°29W 108 C7
Petitsikapau L. Canada 54°37N 66°25W 109 D13
Peto Mexico 20°8N 88°55W 114 C7
Petoskey U.S.A. 45°22N 84°57W 112 C5
Petra Jordan 30°20N 35°22E 86 D3
Petrolândia Brazil 9°5S 38°20W 122 A3
Petrolina Brazil 9°24S 40°30W 122 A2
Petropavlovsk-Kamchatskiy Russia 53°3N 158°43E 79 D17
Petrópolis Brazil 22°33S 43°9W 122 D2
Petrozavodsk Russia 61°41N 34°20E 72 B5
Petworth U.K. 51°0N 0°36W 25 E7
Pevensey U.K. 50°49N 0°23E 25 E9
Pevensey Levels U.K. 50°50N 0°20E 25 E9
Pewsey U.K. 51°20N 1°45W 24 D5
Pewsey, Vale of U.K. 51°22N 1°40W 24 D5
Pforzheim Germany 48°52N 8°41E 66 D5
Phalodi India 27°12N 72°24E 84 F8
Phan Rang Vietnam 11°34N 109°0E 83 B2
Phan Thiet Vietnam 11°1N 108°9E 83 B2
Philadelphia U.S.A. 39°57N 75°9W 113 E10
Philippine Sea Pac. Oc. 18°0N 125°0E 74 G14
Philippine Trench Pac. Oc. 12°0N 126°6E 83 B4
Philippines ■ Asia 12°0N 123°0E 83 B4
Phillips U.S.A. 45°42N 90°24W 112 C2
Phitsanulok Thailand 16°50N 100°12E 83 B2
Phnom Penh Cambodia 11°33N 104°55E 83 B2
Phoenix U.S.A. 33°26N 112°4W 110 D4
Phoenix Is. Kiribati 3°30S 172°0W 99 A16
Phra Nakhon Si Ayutthaya Thailand 14°25N 100°30E 83 B2
Phuket Thailand 7°53N 98°24E 83 C1
Piacenza Italy 45°1N 9°40E 70 B3
Piatra Neamț Romania 46°56N 26°21E 67 E14
Piauí □ Brazil 7°0S 43°0W 120 C5
Piauí → Brazil 6°38S 42°42W 120 C5
Piave → Italy 45°32N 12°44E 70 B5
Picardie □ France 49°50N 3°0E 68 B5
Pichilemu Chile 34°22S 72°0W 121 F2
Pickering U.K. 54°15N 0°46W 22 D7
Pickering, Vale of U.K. 54°14N 0°45W 22 D7
Picos Brazil 7°5S 41°28W 120 C5
Picton Canada 44°1N 77°9W 112 C9
Pidley U.K. 52°23N 0°2W 25 B8
Pidurutalagala Sri Lanka 7°10N 80°50E 84 R12
Piedmont U.S.A. 34°42N 82°28W 111 D10
Piedras Negras Mexico 28°42N 100°31W 114 B4
Piemonte □ Italy 45°0N 8°0E 70 B2
Pierre U.S.A. 44°22N 100°21W 110 B6
Pietermaritzburg S. Africa 29°35S 30°25E 97 K6
Pikes Peak U.S.A. 38°50N 105°3W 110 C5
Pikeville U.S.A. 37°29N 82°31W 112 G6
Pilar Paraguay 26°50S 58°20W 121 E4
Pilcomayo → Paraguay 25°21S 57°42W 121 E4
Pilibhit India 28°40N 79°50E 84 E11
Pilica → Poland 51°52N 21°17E 67 C11
Pilling U.K. 53°56N 2°54W 23 E3
Pilton U.K. 51°10N 2°36W 24 D3
Pimentel Peru 6°45S 79°55W 120 C2
Pinar del Río Cuba 22°26N 83°40W 115 C8
Pinatubo, Mt. Phil. 15°8N 120°21E 83 B4
Pinchbeck U.K. 52°50N 0°9W 23 G8
Pinckneyville U.S.A. 38°5N 89°23W 112 F3
Pindus Mts. Greece 40°0N 21°0E 71 E9
Pine Bluff U.S.A. 34°13N 92°1W 111 D8
Pine Point Canada 60°50N 114°28W 108 C8
Pinega → Russia 64°30N 44°19E 72 B8
Pingdingshan China 33°43N 113°27E 81 C6
Pingliang China 35°35N 106°31E 80 C5
P'ingtung Taiwan 22°38N 120°30E 81 D7
Pingxiang China 22°6N 106°46E 80 D5
Pinheiro Brazil 2°31S 45°5W 120 C5
Pinhoe U.K. 50°44N 3°28W 27 F7
Pinsk Belarus 52°10N 26°1E 72 D4
Piombino Italy 42°55N 10°32E 70 C4
Piotrków Trybunalski Poland 51°23N 19°43E 67 C10
Pipmuacan, Rés. Canada 49°45N 70°30W 113 A12
Piracicaba Brazil 22°45S 47°40W 122 D1
Pirapora Brazil 17°20S 44°56W 122 C2
Pireas Greece 37°57N 23°42E 71 F10
Pirmasens Germany 49°12N 7°36E 66 D4
Pisa Italy 43°43N 10°23E 70 C4
Pisagua Chile 19°40S 70°15W 120 D2
Pishan China 37°30N 78°33E 80 C2
Pistóia Italy 43°55N 10°54E 70 C4
Pit → U.S.A. 40°47N 122°6W 110 B2
Pitcairn I. Pac. Oc. 25°5S 130°5W 103 K14
Piteå Sweden 65°20N 21°25E 63 D8
Pitești Romania 44°52N 24°54E 67 F13
Pitlochry U.K. 56°42N 3°44W 19 J10
Pittsburg U.S.A. 37°25N 94°42W 111 C7
Pittsburgh U.S.A. 40°26N 79°58W 112 E8
Pittsfield U.S.A. 42°27N 73°15W 113 D11
Piura Peru 5°15S 80°38W 120 C1
Placentia Canada 47°20N 54°0W 109 E14
Placentia B. Canada 47°0N 54°40W 109 E14
Placetas Cuba 22°15N 79°44W 115 C9
Plainview U.S.A. 34°11N 101°43W 110 D6
Plata, Río de la → S. Amer. 34°45S 57°30W 121 F4
Platte → U.S.A. 39°16N 94°50W 111 F7
Plattsburgh U.S.A. 44°42N 73°28W 113 C11
Plauen Germany 50°30N 12°8E 66 C7

Plenty, B. of   Rhossili B.

Plenty, B. of *N.Z.* 37°45S 177°0E 99 H14
Plessisville *Canada* 46°14N 71°47W 113 B12
Pleven *Bulgaria* 43°26N 24°37E 71 C11
Plock *Poland* 52°32N 19°40E 67 B10
Ploieşti *Romania* 44°57N 26°5E 67 F14
Plovdiv *Bulgaria* 42°8N 24°44E 71 C11
Plymouth *U.K.* 50°22N 4°10W 27 G5
Plymouth *Ind., U.S.A.* 41°21N 86°19W 112 E4
Plymouth *Wis., U.S.A.* 43°45N 87°59W 112 D4
Plympton *U.K.* 50°23N 4°5W 27 G5
Plymstock *U.K.* 50°21N 4°7W 27 G5
Plzeň *Czech Rep.* 49°45N 13°22E 66 D7
Po → *Italy* 44°57N 12°4E 70 B5
Pobedy, Pik *Kyrgyzstan* 42°0N 79°58E 80 B2
Pocatello *U.S.A.* 42°52N 112°27W 110 B4
Pocklington *U.K.* 53°56N 0°46W 23 E7
Poços de Caldas *Brazil* 21°50S 46°33W 122 D1
Podgorica *Montenegro* 42°30N 19°19E 71 C8
Podolsk *Russia* 55°25N 37°30E 72 C6
Pohnpei *Micronesia* 6°55N 158°10E 102 G7
Point Hope *U.S.A.* 68°21N 166°47W 108 C3
Point L. *Canada* 65°15N 113°4W 108 C8
Point Pleasant *U.S.A.* 38°51N 82°8W 112 F6
Pointe-à-Pitre *Guadeloupe* 16°10N 61°32W 114 b
Pointe-Noire *Congo* 4°48S 11°53E 96 E2
Pointe-Noire *Guadeloupe* 16°14N 61°47W 114 b
Poitiers *France* 46°35N 0°20E 68 C4
Poitou *France* 46°40N 0°10W 68 C3
Pokhara *Nepal* 28°14N 83°58E 85 E13
Poland ■ *Europe* 52°0N 20°0E 67 C10
Polatsk *Belarus* 55°30N 28°50E 72 C4
Polden Hills *U.K.* 51°7N 2°50W 24 D3
Polegate *U.K.* 50°49N 0°16E 25 E9
Polesworth *U.K.* 52°37N 1°36W 23 G5
Polevskoy *Russia* 56°26N 60°11E 72 C11
Polokwane *S. Africa* 23°54S 29°25E 97 J5
Polperro *U.K.* 50°20N 4°32W 27 G4
Polruan *U.K.* 50°19N 4°38W 27 G4
Poltava *Ukraine* 49°35N 34°35E 73 E5
Polynesia *Pac. Oc.* 10°0S 162°0W 103 F11
Ponca City *U.S.A.* 36°42N 97°5W 111 C7
Ponce *Puerto Rico* 18°1N 66°37W 115 d
Pond Inlet *Canada* 72°40N 77°0W 109 B12
Pondicherry *India* 11°59N 79°50E 84 P11
Ponferrada *Spain* 42°32N 6°35W 69 A2
Ponta Grossa *Brazil* 25°7S 50°10W 121 E4
Pontardawe *U.K.* 51°43N 3°51W 26 D6
Pontardulais *U.K.* 51°43N 4°3W 26 D5
Pontarlier *France* 46°54N 6°20E 68 C7
Pontchartrain, L. *U.S.A.* 30°5N 90°5W 111 D9
Ponte Nova *Brazil* 20°25S 42°54W 122 D2
Pontefract *U.K.* 53°42N 1°18W 23 E6
Ponteland *U.K.* 55°3N 1°45W 22 B5
Pontevedra *Spain* 42°26N 8°40W 69 A1
Pontiac *Ill., U.S.A.* 40°53N 88°38W 112 E3
Pontiac *Mich., U.S.A.* 42°38N 83°18W 112 D6
Pontianak *Indonesia* 0°3S 109°15E 83 D2
Pontine Mts. *Turkey* 41°0N 36°45E 73 F6
Pontivy *France* 48°5N 2°58W 68 B2
Pontrilas *U.K.* 51°56N 2°52W 24 C5
Pontypool *U.K.* 51°42N 3°2W 26 D7
Pontypridd *U.K.* 51°36N 3°20W 27 D7
Ponziane, Ísole *Italy* 40°55N 12°57E 70 D5
Poole *U.K.* 50°43N 1°59W 24 E5
Poole Harbour *U.K.* 50°41N 2°0W 24 E5
Pooley Bridge *U.K.* 54°37N 2°48W 22 C3
Poopó, L. de *Bolivia* 18°30S 67°35W 120 D3
Popayán *Colombia* 2°27N 76°36W 120 B2
Poplar Bluff *U.S.A.* 36°46N 90°24W 111 C81
Popocatépetl, Volcán *Mexico* 19°2N 98°38W 114 D5
Porbandar *India* 21°44N 69°43E 84 J6
Porcupine → *U.S.A.* 66°34N 145°19W 108 C5
Pori *Finland* 61°29N 21°48E 63 E8
Porlock *U.K.* 51°13N 3°35W 27 E6
Port Alberni *Canada* 49°14N 124°50W 108 E7
Port Antonio *Jamaica* 18°10N 76°26W 114 a
Port Arthur *U.S.A.* 29°54N 93°56W 111 E8
Port-au-Prince *Haiti* 18°40N 72°20W 115 D10
Port Augusta *Australia* 32°30S 137°50E 98 G6
Port Carlisle *U.K.* 54°57N 3°11W 22 C2
Port-Cartier *Canada* 50°2N 66°50W 109 D13
Port-de-Paix *Haiti* 19°50N 72°50W 115 D10
Port Elgin *Canada* 44°25N 81°25W 112 C7
Port Elizabeth *S. Africa* 33°58S 25°40E 97 L5
Port Ellen *U.K.* 55°38N 6°11W 20 D3
Port Erin *I. of Man* 54°5N 4°45W 29 C12
Port-Gentil *Gabon* 0°40S 8°50E 96 E1
Port Glasgow *U.K.* 55°56N 4°41W 20 C6
Port Harcourt *Nigeria* 4°40N 7°10E 94 H7
Port Hawkesbury *Canada* 45°36N 61°22W 109 E13
Port Hedland *Australia* 20°25S 118°35E 98 E2
Port Hope Simpson *Canada* 52°33N 56°18W 109 D14
Port Huron *U.S.A.* 42°58N 82°26W 112 D6
Port Isaac *U.K.* 50°35N 4°50W 27 F4
Port Isaac B. *U.K.* 50°36N 4°50W 27 F4
Port Laoise *Ireland* 53°2N 7°18W 31 B8
Port Lincoln *Australia* 34°42S 135°52E 98 G6
Port-Louis *Guadeloupe* 16°28N 61°32W 114 b
Port Louis *Mauritius* 20°10S 57°30E 91 H9
Port McNeill *Canada* 50°35N 127°6W 108 D7
Port Macquarie *Australia* 31°25S 152°25E 98 G9
Port Maria *Jamaica* 18°22N 76°54W 114 a
Port Morant *Jamaica* 17°54N 76°19W 114 a
Port Moresby *Papua N. G.* 9°24S 147°8E 98 B8
Port Nolloth *S. Africa* 29°17S 16°52E 97 K3
Port of Spain *Trin. & Tob.* 10°40N 61°31W 120 A3
Port Pirie *Australia* 33°10S 138°1E 98 G6
Port Said *Egypt* 31°16N 32°18E 95 B12
Port St. Lucie *U.S.A.* 27°18N 80°21W 111 E10
Port St. Mary *U.K.* 54°5N 4°44W 29 C12
Port Shepstone *S. Africa* 30°44S 30°28E 97 L6
Port Sudan *Sudan* 19°32N 37°9E 95 E13
Port Talbot *U.K.* 51°35N 3°47W 27 D6
Port Vila *Vanuatu* 17°45S 168°18E 99 D12
Port Washington *U.S.A.* 43°23N 87°53W 112 D4
Port William *U.K.* 54°46N 4°35W 20 E6
Portadown *U.K.* 54°25N 6°27W 29 C9
Portaferry *U.K.* 54°23N 5°33W 29 C10

Portage *U.S.A.* 43°33N 89°28W 112 D3
Portage la Prairie *Canada* 49°58N 98°18W 108 E10
Portarlington *Ireland* 53°9N 7°14W 31 B8
Porthcawl *U.K.* 51°29N 3°42W 27 E6
Porthleven *U.K.* 50°4N 5°19W 27 G3
Porthmadog *U.K.* 52°55N 4°8W 26 B5
Portishead *U.K.* 51°29N 2°46W 24 D3
Portknockie *U.K.* 57°42N 2°51W 19 G12
Portland *Maine, U.S.A.* 43°39N 70°16W 113 D12
Portland *Oreg., U.S.A.* 45°32N 122°37W 110 A2
Portland, I. of *U.K.* 50°33N 2°26W 24 E4
Portland Bight *Jamaica* 17°52N 77°5W 114 a
Portland Bill *U.K.* 50°31N 2°28W 24 E4
Portland Pt. *Jamaica* 17°42N 77°11W 114 a
Portmarnock *Ireland* 53°26N 6°8W 31 B10
Portmore *Jamaica* 17°53N 77°53W 114 a
Porto *Portugal* 41°8N 8°40W 69 B1
Pôrto Alegre *Brazil* 30°5S 51°10W 121 F4
Pôrto Esperança *Brazil* 19°37S 57°29W 120 D4
Pôrto Nacional *Brazil* 10°40S 48°30W 122 B1
Porto-Novo *Benin* 6°23N 2°42E 94 G6
Pôrto Seguro *Brazil* 16°26S 39°5W 122 C3
Porto Tórres *Italy* 40°50N 8°24E 70 D3
Porto-Vecchio *France* 41°35N 9°16E 68 F8
Pôrto Velho *Brazil* 8°46S 63°54W 120 C3
Porton *U.K.* 51°8N 1°43W 24 D5
Portpatrick *U.K.* 54°51N 5°7W 20 E5
Portree *U.K.* 57°25N 6°12W 18 H5
Portrush *U.K.* 55°12N 6°40W 29 A8
Portslade *U.K.* 50°50N 0°12W 25 E8
Portsmouth *U.K.* 50°48N 1°6W 24 E6
Portsmouth *N.H., U.S.A.* 43°5N 70°45W 113 D12
Portsmouth *Ohio, U.S.A.* 38°44N 82°57W 112 F6
Portsmouth *Va., U.S.A.* 36°58N 76°23W 111 C11
Portsoy *U.K.* 57°41N 2°41W 19 G12
Portstewart *U.K.* 55°11N 6°43W 29 A8
Porttipahdan tekojärvi *Finland* 68°5N 26°40E 63 D9
Portugal ■ *Europe* 40°0N 8°0W 69 C1
Portumna *Ireland* 53°6N 8°14W 30 B6
Posadas *Argentina* 27°30S 55°50W 121 E4
Posse *Brazil* 14°4S 46°18W 122 B1
Postmasburg *S. Africa* 28°18S 23°5E 97 K4
Potchefstroom *S. Africa* 26°41S 27°7E 97 K5
Potenza *Italy* 40°38N 15°48E 70 D6
Poti *Georgia* 42°10N 41°38E 73 F7
Potiskum *Nigeria* 11°39N 11°2E 95 F8
Potomac → *U.S.A.* 38°0N 76°23W 112 F9
Potosí *Bolivia* 19°38S 65°50W 120 D3
Potsdam *Germany* 52°23N 13°3E 66 B7
Potsdam *U.S.A.* 44°40N 74°59W 113 C10
Potter Heigham *U.K.* 52°42N 1°34E 25 A12
Potterne *U.K.* 51°20N 2°0W 24 D4
Potters Bar *U.K.* 51°42N 0°11W 25 C8
Potterspury *U.K.* 52°5N 0°52W 25 B7
Pottstown *U.S.A.* 40°15N 75°39W 113 E10
Pottsville *U.S.A.* 40°41N 76°12W 113 E9
Pottuvil *Sri Lanka* 6°55N 81°50E 84 R12
Poughkeepsie *U.S.A.* 41°42N 73°56W 113 E11
Poulaphouca Res. *Ireland* 53°8N 6°30W 31 B10
Poulton-le-Fylde *U.K.* 53°51N 2°58W 23 E3
Poundstock *U.K.* 50°44N 4°36W 27 F4
Pouso Alegre *Brazil* 22°14S 45°57W 122 D1
Powder → *U.S.A.* 46°45N 105°26W 110 A5
Powell, L. *U.S.A.* 36°57N 111°29W 110 C4
Powell River *Canada* 49°50N 124°35W 108 E7
Powers *U.S.A.* 45°41N 87°32W 112 C4
Powick *U.K.* 52°10N 2°14W 24 B4
Powys □ *U.K.* 52°20N 3°20W 26 C7
Poyang Hu *China* 29°5N 116°20E 81 D6
Poza Rica *Mexico* 20°33N 97°27W 114 C5
Poznań *Poland* 52°25N 16°55E 67 B9
Pozzuoli *Italy* 40°49N 14°7E 70 D6
Prado *Brazil* 17°20S 39°13W 122 C3
Prague *Czech Rep.* 50°4N 14°25E 66 C8
Praia *C. Verde Is.* 15°2N 23°34W 91 E1
Prairie du Chien *U.S.A.* 43°3N 91°9W 112 D2
Prata *Brazil* 19°25S 48°54W 122 C1
Prato *Italy* 43°53N 11°6E 70 C4
Pratt *U.S.A.* 37°39N 98°44W 111 C7
Prawle Pt. *U.K.* 50°12N 3°44W 27 G6
Praya *Indonesia* 8°39S 116°17E 83 D3
Prees *U.K.* 52°54N 2°40W 23 G3
Preesall *U.K.* 53°55N 2°57W 23 E3
Prescott *Canada* 44°45N 75°30W 113 C10
Prescott *U.S.A.* 34°33N 112°28W 110 D4
Presidencia Roque Saenz Peña *Argentina* 26°45S 60°30W 121 E3
Presidente Prudente *Brazil* 22°5S 51°25W 120 E4
Presidio *U.S.A.* 29°34N 104°22W 110 E6
Prespa, L. *Macedonia* 40°55N 21°0E 71 D9
Presque Isle *U.S.A.* 46°41N 68°1W 113 B13
Prestatyn *U.K.* 53°20N 3°24W 26 A7
Prestbury *U.K.* 51°54N 2°2W 24 C4
Presteigne *U.K.* 52°17N 3°0W 26 D7
Preston *Borders, U.K.* 55°49N 2°19W 21 C11
Preston *Dorset, U.K.* 50°38N 2°26W 24 E4
Preston *Lancs., U.K.* 53°46N 2°42W 23 E3
Preston *U.S.A.* 42°6N 111°53W 110 B4
Prestonpans *U.K.* 55°58N 2°58W 21 C10
Prestwich *U.K.* 53°32N 2°17W 23 E4
Prestwick *U.K.* 55°29N 4°37W 20 D6
Pretoria *S. Africa* 25°44S 28°12E 97 K5
Pribilof Is. *U.S.A.* 57°0N 170°0W 108 D2
Price *U.S.A.* 39°36N 110°49W 110 C4
Prieska *S. Africa* 29°40S 22°42E 97 K4
Prilep *Macedonia* 41°21N 21°32E 71 D9
Prince Albert *Canada* 53°15N 105°50W 108 D9
Prince Albert Pen. *Canada* 72°30N 116°0W 108 B8
Prince Albert Sd. *Canada* 70°25N 115°0W 108 B8
Prince Alfred, C. *Canada* 74°20N 124°40W 109 B7
Prince Charles I. *Canada* 67°47N 76°12W 109 C12
Prince Charles Mts. *Antarctica* 72°0S 67°0E 55 D6
Prince Edward I. □ *Canada* 46°20N 63°20W 113 B16
Prince Edward Is. *Ind. Oc.* 46°35S 38°0E 53 G11
Prince George *Canada* 53°55N 122°50W 108 D7
Prince Gustaf Adolf Sea *Canada* 78°30N 107°0W 109 B9
Prince of Wales I. *Canada* 73°0N 99°0W 108 B10

Prince of Wales I. *U.S.A.* 55°47N 132°50W 108 D6
Prince Patrick I. *Canada* 77°0N 120°0W 109 B8
Prince Rupert *Canada* 54°20N 130°20W 108 D6
Princes Risborough *U.K.* 51°43N 0°49W 25 C7
Princeton *Ill., U.S.A.* 41°23N 89°28W 112 E3
Princeton *Ind., U.S.A.* 38°21N 87°34W 112 F4
Princeton *Ky., U.S.A.* 37°7N 87°53W 112 G4
Princeton *W. Va., U.S.A.* 37°22N 81°6W 112 G7
Principe, I. de *Atl. Oc.* 1°37N 7°27E 90 F4
Pripet → *Europe* 51°20N 30°15E 67 C16
Pripet Marshes *Europe* 52°10N 28°10E 67 B15
Priština *Serbia* 42°40N 21°13E 71 C9
Privas *France* 44°45N 4°37E 68 D6
Prizren *Serbia* 42°13N 20°45E 71 C9
Probolinggo *Indonesia* 7°46S 113°13E 83 D3
Probus *U.K.* 50°17N 4°58W 27 G4
Progreso *Mexico* 21°20N 89°40W 114 C7
Prome *Burma* 18°49N 95°13E 85 K19
Propriá *Brazil* 10°13S 36°51W 122 B3
Provence *France* 43°40N 5°46E 68 E6
Providence *U.S.A.* 41°49N 71°24W 113 E12
Providencia, I. de *Colombia* 13°25N 81°26W 115 E8
Provins *France* 48°33N 3°15E 68 B5
Provo *U.S.A.* 40°14N 111°39W 110 B4
Prudhoe *U.K.* 54°57N 1°52W 22 C5
Prudhoe Bay *U.S.A.* 70°18N 148°22W 108 B5
Pruszków *Poland* 52°9N 20°49E 67 B11
Prut → *Romania* 45°28N 28°10E 67 F15
Pryluky *Ukraine* 50°30N 32°24E 73 D5
Przemyśl *Poland* 49°50N 22°45E 67 D12
Pskov *Russia* 57°50N 28°25E 72 C4
Puddletown *U.K.* 50°44N 2°20W 24 E4
Pudsey *U.K.* 53°47N 1°40W 23 E5
Puebla *Mexico* 19°3N 98°12W 114 D5
Pueblo *U.S.A.* 38°16N 104°37W 110 C6
Puerca, Pta. *Puerto Rico* 18°13N 65°36W 115 d
Puerto Aisén *Chile* 45°27S 73°0W 121 G2
Puerto Barrios *Guatemala* 15°40N 88°32W 114 D7
Puerto Cabello *Venezuela* 10°28N 68°1W 120 A3
Puerto Cabezas *Nic.* 14°0N 83°30W 115 E8
Puerto Carreño *Colombia* 6°12N 67°22W 120 B3
Puerto Cortés *Honduras* 15°51N 88°0W 114 D7
Puerto Deseado *Argentina* 47°55S 66°0W 121 G3
Puerto La Cruz *Venezuela* 10°13N 64°38W 120 A3
Puerto Madryn *Argentina* 42°48S 65°4W 121 G3
Puerto Maldonado *Peru* 12°30S 69°10W 120 D3
Puerto Montt *Chile* 41°28S 73°0W 121 G2
Puerto Plata *Dom. Rep.* 19°48N 70°45W 115 D10
Puerto Princesa *Phil.* 9°46N 118°45E 83 C3
Puerto Rico ☑ *W. Indies* 18°15N 66°45W 115 d
Puerto San Julián *Argentina* 49°18S 67°43W 121 G3
Puerto Suárez *Bolivia* 18°58S 57°52W 120 D4
Puerto Wilches *Colombia* 7°21N 73°54W 120 B2
Puertollano *Spain* 38°43N 4°7W 69 C3
Puffin I. *Ireland* 51°50N 10°24W 30 E2
Puget Sound *U.S.A.* 47°50N 122°30W 110 A2
Pukapuka *Cook Is.* 10°53S 165°49W 103 J11
Pula *Croatia* 44°54N 13°57E 70 B5
Pulacayo *Bolivia* 20°25S 66°41W 120 E3
Pulaski *U.S.A.* 37°3N 80°47W 111 C10
Pulborough *U.K.* 50°58N 0°30W 25 E8
Pulham Market *U.K.* 52°26N 1°13E 25 B11
Pulham St. Mary *U.K.* 52°26N 1°16E 25 B11
Pullman *U.S.A.* 46°44N 117°10W 110 A3
Pumlumon Fawr *U.K.* 52°28N 3°46W 26 C6
Pune *India* 18°29N 73°57E 84 K8
Punjab □ *India* 31°0N 76°0E 84 D10
Punjab □ *Pakistan* 32°0N 72°30E 84 E9
Puno *Peru* 15°55S 70°3W 120 D2
Punta, Cerro de *Puerto Rico* 18°10N 66°37W 115 d
Punta Arenas *Chile* 53°10S 71°0W 121 H2
Punxsatawney *U.S.A.* 40°57N 78°59W 112 E8
Purbeck, Isle of *U.K.* 50°39N 1°59W 24 E5
Purfleet *U.K.* 51°29N 0°16E 25 D9
Puri *India* 19°50N 85°58E 85 K14
Purley on Thames *U.K.* 51°29N 1°3W 24 D6
Purnia *India* 25°45N 87°31E 85 G15
Puruliya *India* 23°17N 86°24E 85 H15
Purus → *Brazil* 3°42S 61°28W 120 C3
Putian *China* 25°23N 119°0E 81 D6
Putorana *Russia* 69°0N 95°0E 79 C11
Puttalam *Sri Lanka* 8°1N 79°55E 84 Q11
Putumayo → *S. Amer.* 3°7S 67°58W 120 C3
Puy-de-Dôme *France* 45°46N 2°57E 68 D5
Pwllheli *U.K.* 52°53N 4°25W 26 B5
Pyatigorsk *Russia* 44°2N 43°6E 73 F7
Pyinmana *Burma* 19°45N 96°12E 85 K20
P'yŏngyang *N. Korea* 39°0N 125°30E 81 C7
Pyramid L. *U.S.A.* 40°1N 119°35W 110 C3
Pyrénées *Europe* 42°45N 0°18E 68 E4

Q

Qaanaaq *Greenland* 77°40N 69°0W 54 B4
Qā'emshahr *Iran* 36°30N 52°53E 87 B8
Qaidam Basin *China* 37°0N 95°0E 80 C4
Qandahār *Afghan.* 31°32N 65°43E 87 D11
Qaqortoq *Greenland* 60°43N 46°0W 54 C5
Qarqan He → *China* 39°30N 88°30E 80 C3
Qarshi *Uzbekistan* 38°53N 65°48E 87 B11
Qatar ■ *Asia* 25°30N 51°15E 87 E7
Qattâra Depression *Egypt* 29°30N 27°30E 95 C11
Qazvin *Iran* 36°15N 50°0E 86 B7
Qena *Egypt* 26°10N 32°43E 95 C12
Qeqertarsuaq *Greenland* 69°15N 53°38W 54 C5
Qeshm *Iran* 26°55N 56°10E 87 E9
Qiemo *China* 38°8N 85°32E 80 C3
Qijiaojing *China* 43°28N 91°36E 80 B4
Qikiqtarjuaq *Canada* 67°33N 63°0W 109 C13
Qilian Shan *China* 38°30N 96°0E 80 C4
Qingdao *China* 36°5N 120°20E 81 C7
Qinghai □ *China* 36°0N 98°0E 80 C4
Qinghai Hu *China* 36°40N 100°10E 80 C5
Qinhuangdao *China* 39°56N 119°30E 81 C6
Qinzhou *China* 21°58N 108°38E 80 D5
Qiqihar *China* 47°26N 124°0E 81 B7

Qira *China* 37°0N 80°48E 80 C3
Qitai *China* 44°2N 89°35E 80 B3
Qom *Iran* 34°40N 51°0E 87 C7
Qondūz *Afghan.* 36°50N 68°50E 87 B12
Quadring *U.K.* 52°54N 0°10W 23 G8
Quang Ngai *Vietnam* 15°13N 108°58E 83 B2
Quantock Hills *U.K.* 51°8N 3°10W 24 D2
Quanzhou *China* 24°55N 118°34E 81 D6
Quaqtaq *Canada* 60°55N 69°40W 109 C13
Quartu Sant'Elena *Italy* 39°15N 9°10E 70 E3
Québec *Canada* 46°52N 71°13W 113 B12
Québec □ *Canada* 48°0N 74°0W 109 E12
Queen Charlotte Is. *Canada* 53°20N 132°10W 108 D6
Queen Charlotte Sd. *Canada* 51°0N 128°0W 108 D7
Queen Elizabeth Is. *Canada* 76°0N 95°0W 109 B10
Queen Maud G. *Canada* 68°15N 102°30W 108 C9
Queenborough *U.K.* 51°25N 0°46E 25 D10
Queensbury *U.K.* 53°46N 1°50W 23 E5
Queensland □ *Australia* 22°0S 142°0E 98 E7
Queenstown *N.Z.* 45°1S 168°40E 99 K12
Queenstown *S. Africa* 31°52S 26°52E 97 L5
Queimadas *Brazil* 11°0S 39°38W 122 B3
Quelimane *Mozam.* 17°53S 36°58E 97 H7
Quendale, B. of *U.K.* 59°53N 1°20W 18 C15
Querétaro *Mexico* 20°36N 100°23W 114 C4
Quesnel *Canada* 53°0N 122°30W 108 D7
Quesnel L. *Canada* 52°30N 121°20W 108 D7
Quetta *Pakistan* 30°15N 66°55E 84 D5
Quezaltenango *Guatemala* 14°50N 91°30W 114 E6
Quezon City *Phil.* 14°37N 121°2E 83 B4
Qui Nhon *Vietnam* 13°40N 109°13E 83 B2
Quibdo *Colombia* 5°42N 76°40W 120 B2
Quiberon *France* 47°29N 3°9W 68 C2
Quilán, C. *Chile* 43°15S 74°30W 121 G2
Quilon *India* 8°50N 76°38E 84 Q10
Quilpie *Australia* 26°35S 144°11E 98 F7
Quimper *France* 48°0N 4°9W 68 B1
Quincy *Ill., U.S.A.* 39°56N 91°23W 111 C81
Quincy *Mass., U.S.A.* 42°14N 71°0W 113 D12
Quinte West *Canada* 44°10N 77°34W 112 C9
Quito *Ecuador* 0°15S 78°35W 120 C2
Qûnghirot *Uzbekistan* 43°2N 58°50E 87 A9
Quorndon *U.K.* 52°46N 1°10W 23 G6
Qŭqon *Uzbekistan* 40°31N 70°56E 87 A12
Quseir *Egypt* 26°7N 34°16E 95 C12
Quzhou *China* 28°57N 118°54E 81 D6

R

Raahe *Finland* 64°40N 24°28E 63 E8
Raasay *U.K.* 57°25N 6°4W 18 H5
Raasay, Sd. of *U.K.* 57°30N 6°8W 18 H5
Raba *Indonesia* 8°36S 118°55E 83 D3
Rabat *Morocco* 34°2N 6°48W 94 B4
Rabaul *Papua N. G.* 4°24S 152°18E 98 A9
Rābigh *Si. Arabia* 22°50N 39°5E 88 C2
Race, C. *Canada* 46°40N 53°5W 109 E14
Rach Gia *Vietnam* 10°5N 105°5E 83 B2
Racine *U.S.A.* 42°44N 87°47W 112 D4
Rackheath *U.K.* 52°40N 1°22E 25 A11
Radcliffe *U.K.* 53°34N 2°18W 23 E4
Radcliffe-on-Trent *U.K.* 52°57N 1°2W 23 G6
Radford *U.S.A.* 37°8N 80°34W 112 G7
Radley *U.K.* 51°41N 1°14W 24 C6
Radnor Forest *U.K.* 52°17N 3°10W 26 C7
Radom *Poland* 51°23N 21°12E 67 C11
Radstock *U.K.* 51°17N 2°26W 24 D4
Rae *Canada* 62°50N 116°3W 108 C8
Rae Bareli *India* 26°18N 81°20E 85 F12
Rae Isthmus *Canada* 66°40N 87°30W 109 C11
Rafaela *Argentina* 31°10S 61°30W 121 F3
Rafsanjān *Iran* 30°30N 56°5E 87 D9
Ragusa *Italy* 36°55N 14°44E 70 F6
Rahimyar Khan *Pakistan* 28°30N 70°25E 84 E7
Raichur *India* 16°10N 77°20E 84 L10
Raigarh *India* 21°56N 83°25E 85 J12
Rainbow Lake *Canada* 58°30N 119°23W 108 D8
Rainham *U.K.* 51°22N 0°37E 25 D10
Rainier, Mt. *U.S.A.* 46°52N 121°46W 110 A2
Rainworth *U.K.* 53°7N 1°7W 23 F6
Rainy L. *Canada* 48°42N 93°10W 108 E10
Raipur *India* 21°17N 81°45E 85 J12
Raj Nandgaon *India* 21°5N 81°5E 85 J12
Rajahmundry *India* 17°1N 81°48E 85 L12
Rajapalaiyam *India* 9°25N 77°35E 84 Q10
Rajasthan □ *India* 26°45N 73°30E 84 F8
Rajkot *India* 22°15N 70°56E 84 H7
Rajshahi *Bangla.* 24°22N 88°39E 85 G16
Rajshahi □ *Bangla.* 25°0N 89°0E 85 G16
Raleigh *U.S.A.* 35°47N 78°39W 111 C11
Rame Head *U.K.* 50°19N 4°13W 27 G5
Ramgarh *India* 23°40N 85°35E 85 H14
Ramna Stacks *U.K.* 60°35N 1°24W 18 A15
Râmnicu Vâlcea *Romania* 45°9N 24°21E 67 F13
Rampside *U.K.* 54°6N 3°9W 22 D2
Rampur *India* 28°50N 79°5E 84 E11
Ramree I. *Burma* 19°0N 93°40E 85 K19
Ramsbottom *U.K.* 53°38N 2°19W 23 E4
Ramsbury *U.K.* 51°26N 1°36W 24 D5
Ramsey *I. of Man* 54°20N 4°22W 29 C12
Ramsey *Cambs., U.K.* 52°27N 0°7E 25 B9
Ramsey *Essex, U.K.* 51°55N 1°13E 25 C11
Ramsgate *U.K.* 51°20N 1°25E 25 D11
Rancagua *Chile* 34°10S 70°50W 121 F2
Ranchi *India* 23°19N 85°27E 85 H14
Randalstown *U.K.* 54°45N 6°19W 29 B9
Randers *Denmark* 56°29N 10°1E 63 F6
Rangoon *Burma* 16°45N 96°20E 85 L20
Rangpur *Bangla.* 25°42N 89°22E 85 G16
Rankin Inlet *Canada* 62°30N 93°0W 108 C10
Rannoch *U.K.* 56°40N 4°20W 19 J9
Rannoch, L. *U.K.* 56°41N 4°20W 19 J9
Rannoch Moor *U.K.* 56°38N 4°48W 19 J8
Rantoul *U.S.A.* 40°19N 88°9W 112 E3
Rapa *French Polynesia* 27°35S 144°20W 103 K13
Rapallo *Italy* 44°21N 9°14E 70 B3
Raper, C. *Canada* 69°44N 67°6W 109 C13
Rapid City *U.S.A.* 44°5N 103°14W 110 B6
Rarotonga *Cook Is.* 21°30S 160°0W 103 K12

Ra's al Khaymah *U.A.E.* 25°50N 55°59E 87 E9
Rasht *Iran* 37°20N 49°40E 86 B7
Rat Islands *U.S.A.* 52°0N 178°0E 108 D1
Ratangarh *India* 28°5N 74°35E 84 E9
Rath Luirc *Ireland* 52°21N 8°40W 30 D5
Rathcoole *Ireland* 53°17N 6°29W 31 B10
Rathdrum *Ireland* 52°56N 6°14W 31 C10
Rathkeale *Ireland* 52°32N 8°56W 30 C5
Rathlin I. *U.K.* 55°18N 6°14W 29 A9
Rathmelton *Ireland* 55°2N 7°38W 28 A6
Ratlam *India* 23°20N 75°0E 84 H9
Ratnagiri *India* 16°57N 73°18E 84 L8
Raton *U.S.A.* 36°54N 104°24W 110 C6
Rattray Hd. *U.K.* 57°38N 1°50W 19 G14
Rauma *Finland* 61°10N 21°30E 63 E8
Raunds *U.K.* 52°21N 0°32W 25 B7
Raurkela *India* 22°14N 84°50E 85 H14
Ravenglass *U.K.* 54°22N 3°24W 22 D2
Ravenna *Italy* 44°25N 12°12E 70 B5
Ravenstonedale *U.K.* 54°26N 2°25W 22 D4
Ravi → *Pakistan* 30°35N 71°49E 84 D7
Rawalpindi *Pakistan* 33°38N 73°8E 84 C8
Rawāndūz *Iraq* 36°40N 44°30E 86 B6
Rawlins *U.S.A.* 41°47N 107°14W 110 B5
Rawmarsh *U.K.* 53°27N 1°21W 23 F6
Rawson *Argentina* 43°15S 65°5W 121 G3
Rawtenstall *U.K.* 53°42N 2°17W 23 E4
Ray, C. *Canada* 47°33N 59°15W 109 E14
Rayleigh *U.K.* 51°36N 0°37E 25 C10
Rayong *Thailand* 12°40N 101°20E 83 B2
Raz, Pte. du *France* 48°2N 4°47W 68 C1
Ré, Î. de *France* 46°12N 1°30W 68 C3
Reading *U.K.* 51°27N 0°58W 25 D7
Reading *U.S.A.* 40°20N 75°56W 113 E10
Reay Forest *U.K.* 58°22N 4°55W 19 F8
Rebiana Desert *Libya* 24°30N 21°0E 95 D10
Recife *Brazil* 8°0S 35°0W 122 A3
Reconquista *Argentina* 29°10S 59°45W 121 E4
Red → *U.S.A.* 31°1N 91°45W 111 D8
Red Bluff *U.S.A.* 40°11N 122°15W 110 B2
Red Deer *Canada* 52°20N 113°50W 108 D8
Red Dial *U.K.* 54°49N 3°10W 22 C2
Red L. *U.S.A.* 48°8N 94°45W 111 A8
Red Lake *Canada* 51°3N 93°49W 108 D10
Red Oak *U.S.A.* 41°1N 95°14W 111 B7
Red River of the North → *N. Amer.* 49°0N 97°15W 108 D10
Red Sea *Asia* 25°0N 36°0E 88 C2
Red Wing *U.S.A.* 44°34N 92°31W 111 B81
Redbridge □ *U.K.* 51°35N 0°7E 25 C9
Redcar *U.K.* 54°37N 1°4W 22 C6
Redding *U.S.A.* 40°35N 122°24W 110 B2
Redditch *U.K.* 52°18N 1°55W 24 B5
Rede → *U.K.* 55°9N 2°13W 22 B4
Redesmouth *U.K.* 55°8N 2°13W 22 B4
Redhill *U.K.* 51°14N 0°9W 25 D8
Redlynch *U.K.* 50°59N 1°41W 24 E5
Redmile *U.K.* 52°55N 0°48W 23 G7
Redmire *U.K.* 54°19N 1°55W 22 D5
Redon *France* 47°40N 2°6W 68 C2
Redruth *U.K.* 50°14N 5°14W 27 G3
Ree, L. *Ireland* 53°35N 8°0W 28 D6
Reedham *U.K.* 52°34N 1°34E 25 A12
Reepham *U.K.* 52°46N 1°6E 25 A11
Reese → *U.S.A.* 40°48N 117°4W 110 B3
Reeth *U.K.* 54°23N 1°56W 22 D5
Regensburg *Germany* 49°1N 12°6E 66 D7
Réggio di Calábria *Italy* 38°6N 15°39E 70 E6
Réggio nell'Emília *Italy* 44°43N 10°36E 70 B4
Regina *Canada* 50°27N 104°35W 108 D9
Reichenbach *Germany* 50°37N 12°17E 66 C7
Reigate *U.K.* 51°14N 0°12W 25 D8
Reims *France* 49°15N 4°1E 68 B6
Reina Adelaida, Arch. *Chile* 52°20S 74°0W 121 H2
Reindeer L. *Canada* 57°15N 102°15W 108 D9
Remscheid *Germany* 51°11N 7°12E 65 C7
Renfrew *Canada* 45°30N 76°40W 112 C9
Renfrew *U.K.* 55°52N 4°24W 20 C7
Rennell *Solomon Is.* 11°40S 160°10E 99 C11
Rennes *France* 48°7N 1°41W 68 B3
Reno *U.S.A.* 39°31N 119°48W 110 C3
Repton *U.K.* 52°50N 1°33W 23 G5
Republican → *U.S.A.* 39°4N 96°48W 111 C7
Repulse Bay *Canada* 66°30N 86°30W 109 C11
Resistencia *Argentina* 27°30S 59°0W 121 E4
Resolute *Canada* 74°42N 94°54W 109 B10
Resolution I. *Canada* 61°30N 65°0W 109 C13
Reston *U.K.* 55°51N 2°10W 21 C11
Retford *U.K.* 53°19N 0°56W 23 F7
Rethimno *Greece* 35°18N 24°30E 71 G11
Réunion ☑ *Ind. Oc.* 21°0S 56°0E 91 J9
Reus *Spain* 41°10N 1°5E 69 B6
Reutlingen *Germany* 48°29N 9°12E 66 D5
Revda *Russia* 56°48N 59°57E 72 C10
Revelstoke *Canada* 51°0N 118°10W 108 D8
Revillagigedo, Is. de *Pac. Oc.* 18°40N 112°0W 114 D2
Rewa *India* 24°33N 81°25E 85 G12
Rexburg *U.S.A.* 43°49N 111°47W 110 B4
Rey Malabo *Eq. Guin.* 3°45N 8°50E 96 D1
Reykjavík *Iceland* 64°10N 21°57E 63 B1
Reynosa *Mexico* 26°7N 98°18W 114 B5
Rēzekne *Latvia* 56°30N 27°17E 63 F9
Rhayader *U.K.* 52°18N 3°29W 26 C7
Rheidol → *U.K.* 52°25N 4°5W 26 C5
Rheine *Germany* 52°17N 7°26E 66 B4
Rheinland-Pfalz □ *Germany* 50°0N 7°0E 66 C4
Rhine → *Europe* 51°52N 6°2E 65 C6
Rhinelander *U.S.A.* 45°38N 89°25W 112 C3
Rhinns Pt. *U.K.* 55°40N 6°29W 20 C3
Rhins, The *U.K.* 54°52N 5°3W 20 E5
Rhode Island □ *U.S.A.* 41°40N 71°30W 113 E12
Rhodes *Greece* 36°15N 28°10E 71 F13
Rhodope Mts. *Bulgaria* 41°40N 24°20E 71 D11
Rhondda *U.K.* 51°39N 3°31W 26 D6
Rhône → *France* 43°28N 4°42E 68 E6
Rhosllanerchrugog *U.K.* 53°1N 3°3W 26 A7
Rhossili *U.K.* 51°34N 4°17W 27 D5
Rhossili B. *U.K.* 51°32N 4°14W 27 D5

Rhum

San Miguel

Rhum *U.K.* 57°0N 6°20W **18** J5
Rhum, Sound of *U.K.* 56°55N 6°14W **18** J5
Rhyl *U.K.* 53°20N 3°29W **26** A7
Rhymney *U.K.* 51°46N 3°17W **26** D7
Riau, Kepulauan *Indonesia* 0°30N 104°20E **83** C2
Ribble → *U.K.* 53°52N 2°25W **23** E4
Ribeirão Prêto *Brazil* 21°10S 47°50W **122** D1
Riberalta *Bolivia* 11°0S 66°0W **120** D3
Riccall *U.K.* 53°50N 1°3W **23** E6
Rice Lake *U.S.A.* 45°30N 91°44W **112** C2
Richards Bay *S. Africa* 28°48S 32°6E **97** K6
Richfield *U.S.A.* 38°46N 112°5W **110** C4
Richland *U.S.A.* 46°17N 119°18W **110** A3
Richland Center *U.S.A.* 43°21N 90°23W **112** D2
Richlands *U.S.A.* 37°6N 81°48W **112** G7
Richmond *U.K.* 54°25N 1°43W **22** D5
Richmond *Ind., U.S.A.* 39°50N 84°53W **112** F5
Richmond *Ky., U.S.A.* 37°45N 84°18W **112** G5
Richmond *Va., U.S.A.* 37°33N 77°27W **112** G9
Richmond-upon-Thames □ *U.K.* 51°27N 0°17W **25** D8
Rickmansworth *U.K.* 51°38N 0°29W **25** C8
Ridgecrest *U.S.A.* 35°38N 117°40W **110** C3
Ridgway *U.S.A.* 41°25N 78°44W **112** E8
Ridsdale *U.K.* 55°9N 2°9W **22** B4
Rievaulx *U.K.* 54°16N 1°7W **22** D6
Rift Valley *Africa* 7°0N 30°0E **90** G7
Riga *Latvia* 56°53N 24°8E **63** F8
Riga, G. of *Latvia* 57°40N 23°45E **63** F8
Rīgestān *Afghan.* 30°15N 65°0E **87** D11
Rigolet *Canada* 54°10N 58°23W **109** D14
Rijeka *Croatia* 45°20N 14°21E **70** B6
Rillington *U.K.* 54°9N 0°42W **22** D7
Rimini *Italy* 44°3N 12°33E **70** B5
Rimouski *Canada* 48°27N 68°30W **109** E13
Ringmer *U.K.* 50°53N 0°5E **25** E9
Ringwood *U.K.* 50°50N 1°47W **24** E5
Rio Branco *Brazil* 9°58S 67°49W **120** C3
Rio Claro *Brazil* 22°19S 47°35W **122** D1
Rio Cuarto *Argentina* 33°10S 64°25W **121** F3
Rio de Janeiro *Brazil* 22°54S 43°12W **122** D2
Rio de Janeiro □ *Brazil* 22°50S 43°0W **122** D2
Rio Gallegos *Argentina* 51°35S 69°15W **121** H3
Rio Grande *Brazil* 32°0S 52°20W **121** F4
Rio Grande *Nic.* 12°54N 83°33W **115** E8
Rio Grande *Puerto Rico* 18°23N 65°50W **115** d
Rio Grande → *N. Amer.* 25°58N 97°9W **111** E7
Rio Grande de Santiago → *Mexico* 21°36N 105°26W **114** C3
Rio Grande do Norte □ *Brazil* 5°40S 36°0W **120** C6
Rio Grande do Sul □ *Brazil* 30°0S 53°0W **121** E4
Rio Largo *Brazil* 9°28S 35°50W **122** A3
Río Muni □ *Eq. Guin.* 1°30N 10°0E **96** D2
Riohacha *Colombia* 11°33N 72°55W **120** A2
Ripley *Derby, U.K.* 53°3N 1°24W **23** F6
Ripley *N. Yorks., U.K.* 54°3N 1°34W **22** D5
Ripon *U.K.* 54°9N 1°31W **22** D5
Ripon *U.S.A.* 43°51N 88°50W **112** D3
Risca *U.K.* 51°37N 3°5W **27** D7
Rishton *U.K.* 53°46N 2°26W **23** E4
Rivera *Uruguay* 31°0S 55°50W **121** F4
Riverhead *U.S.A.* 40°55N 72°40W **113** E11
Riverside *U.S.A.* 33°59N 117°22W **110** D3
Riverton *U.S.A.* 43°2N 108°23W **110** B5
Rivière-du-Loup *Canada* 47°50N 69°30W **109** E13
Rivière-Pilote *Martinique* 14°26N 60°53W **114** c
Rivière-Salée *Martinique* 14°31N 61°0W **114** c
Rivne *Ukraine* 50°40N 26°10E **67** C14
Riyadh *Si. Arabia* 24°41N 46°42E **86** E6
Rize *Turkey* 41°0N 40°30E **73** F7
Rizhao *China* 35°25N 119°30E **81** C6
Road Town *Br. Virgin Is.* 18°27N 64°37W **115** e
Roade *U.K.* 52°9N 0°53W **25** B7
Roanne *France* 46°3N 4°4E **68** C6
Roanoke *U.S.A.* 37°16N 79°56W **112** G8
Roanoke → *U.S.A.* 35°57N 76°42W **111** C11
Roberton *U.K.* 55°25N 2°54W **21** D10
Robertval *Canada* 48°32N 72°15W **109** E12
Robin Hood's Bay *U.K.* 54°27N 0°32W **22** D7
Robson, Mt. *Canada* 53°10N 119°10W **108** D8
Roca, C. da *Portugal* 38°40N 9°31W **69** C1
Rocester *U.K.* 52°57N 1°50W **23** G5
Rocha *Uruguay* 34°30S 54°25W **121** F4
Rochdale *U.K.* 53°38N 2°9W **23** E4
Roche *U.K.* 50°24N 4°50W **27** G4
Rochefort *France* 45°56N 0°57W **68** D3
Rochester *Northumberland, U.K.* 55°17N 2°17W **22** B4
Rochester *U.K.* 41°4N 86°13W **112** E4
Rochester *Minn., U.S.A.* 44°1N 92°28W **111** B8
Rochester *N.H., U.S.A.* 43°18N 70°59W **113** D12
Rochester *N.Y., U.S.A.* 43°10N 77°37W **112** D9
Rochford *U.K.* 51°34N 0°43E **25** C10
Rock Hill *U.S.A.* 34°56N 81°1W **111** D10
Rock Island *U.S.A.* 41°30N 90°34W **112** E2
Rock Springs *U.S.A.* 41°35N 109°14W **110** B5
Rockall *Atl. Oc.* 57°37N 13°42W **56** D3
Rockcliffe *U.K.* 54°57N 3°0W **22** C2
Rockford *U.S.A.* 42°16N 89°6W **112** D3
Rockhampton *Australia* 23°22S 150°32E **98** E9
Rockingham *Australia* 32°27S 115°27E **98** G2
Rockingham Forest *U.K.* 52°29N 0°42W **25** B7
Rockland *U.S.A.* 44°6N 69°7W **113** C13
Rocky Mount *U.S.A.* 35°57N 77°48W **111** C11
Rocky Mts. *N. Amer.* 49°0N 115°0W **108** D7
Rodez *France* 44°21N 2°33E **68** D5
Roding → *U.K.* 51°31N 0°6E **25** C9
Rodriguez *Ind. Oc.* 19°45S 63°20E **53** E13
Roe → *U.K.* 55°6N 6°59W **29** A8
Roermond *Neths.* 51°12N 6°0E **65** C6
Roes Welcome Sd. *Canada* 65°0N 87°0W **109** C11
Roeselare *Belgium* 50°57N 3°7E **65** D3
Rogans Seat *U.K.* 54°26N 2°7W **22** D4
Rogate *U.K.* 51°0N 0°50W **25** D7
Rogers City *U.S.A.* 45°25N 83°49W **112** C6
Rohri *Pakistan* 27°45N 68°51E **84** F6
Rojo, C. *Mexico* 21°33N 97°20W **114** C5

Rolla *U.S.A.* 37°57N 91°46W **111** C81
Roma *Australia* 26°32S 148°49E **98** F8
Romaine → *Canada* 50°18N 63°47W **109** D13
Romania ■ *Europe* 46°0N 25°0E **67** F12
Romans-sur-Isère *France* 45°3N 5°3E **68** D6
Rome *Italy* 41°54N 12°28E **70** D5
Rome *Ga., U.S.A.* 34°15N 85°10W **111** D9
Rome *N.Y., U.S.A.* 43°13N 75°27W **113** D10
Romney *U.S.A.* 39°21N 78°45W **112** F8
Romney Marsh *U.K.* 51°2N 0°54E **25** D10
Romorantin-Lanthenay *France* 47°21N 1°45E **68** C4
Romsey *U.K.* 51°0N 1°29W **24** E6
Rona *U.K.* 57°34N 5°59W **18** G6
Roncador, Serra do *Brazil* 12°30S 52°30W **120** D4
Rondônia □ *Brazil* 11°0S 63°0W **120** D3
Rondonópolis *Brazil* 16°28S 54°38W **120** D4
Ronge, L. la *Canada* 55°6N 105°17W **108** D9
Ronne Ice Shelf *Antarctica* 77°30S 60°0W **55** D18
Ronse *Belgium* 50°45N 3°35E **65** D3
Roosendaal *Neths.* 51°32N 4°29E **65** C4
Roosevelt → *Brazil* 7°35S 60°20W **120** C3
Roosevelt I. *Antarctica* 79°30S 162°0W **55** D12
Ropsley *U.K.* 52°54N 0°30W **23** G8
Roquetas de Mar *Spain* 36°46N 2°36W **69** D4
Roraima □ *Brazil* 2°0N 61°30W **120** B3
Roraima, Mt. *Venezuela* 5°10N 60°40W **120** B3
Rosario *Argentina* 33°0S 60°40W **121** F3
Rosario *Mexico* 22°58N 105°53W **114** C3
Rosario de la Frontera *Argentina* 25°50S 65°0W **121** E3
Roscommon *Ireland* 53°38N 8°11W **28** D5
Roscommon □ *Ireland* 53°49N 8°23W **28** D5
Roscrea *Ireland* 52°57N 7°49W **30** C7
Roseau *Dominica* 15°17N 61°24W **115** D12
Roseburg *U.S.A.* 43°13N 123°20W **110** B2
Rosedale Abbey *U.K.* 54°21N 0°52W **22** D7
Rosehearty *U.K.* 57°42N 2°7W **19** G13
Rosenheim *Germany* 47°51N 12°7E **66** E7
Rosetown *Canada* 51°35N 107°59W **108** D9
Roseville *U.S.A.* 38°45N 121°17W **110** C2
Roslavl *Russia* 53°57N 32°55E **72** D5
Ross Ice Shelf *Antarctica* 80°0S 180°0E **55** E12
Ross-on-Wye *U.K.* 51°54N 2°34W **24** C3
Ross River *Canada* 62°30N 131°30W **108** C6
Ross Sea *Antarctica* 74°0S 178°0E **55** D11
Rossall Pt. *U.K.* 53°55N 3°3W **23** E2
Rossan Pt. *Ireland* 54°42N 8°47W **28** B4
Rosses, The *Ireland* 55°2N 8°20W **28** A5
Rossignol L. *Canada* 44°12N 65°10W **113** C15
Rosslare *Ireland* 52°17N 6°24W **31** D10
Rosslare Harbour *Ireland* 52°15N 6°20W **31** D10
Rossosh *Russia* 50°15N 39°28E **73** D6
Rostock *Germany* 54°5N 12°8E **66** A7
Rostov *Russia* 47°15N 39°45E **73** E6
Roswell *Ga., U.S.A.* 34°2N 84°22W **111** D10
Roswell *N. Mex., U.S.A.* 33°24N 104°32W **110** D6
Rothbury *U.K.* 55°19N 1°58W **22** B5
Rothbury Forest *U.K.* 55°19N 1°50W **22** B5
Rother → *U.K.* 50°59N 0°45E **25** E10
Rotherham *U.K.* 53°26N 1°20W **23** F6
Rothes *U.K.* 57°32N 3°13W **19** G11
Rothesay *U.K.* 55°50N 5°3W **20** D5
Rothwell *Northants., U.K.* 52°25N 0°48W **25** B7
Rothwell *W. Yorks., U.K.* 53°45N 1°28W **23** E6
Roti *Indonesia* 10°50S 123°0E **83** E4
Rotorua *N.Z.* 38°9S 176°16E **99** H14
Rottingdean *U.K.* 50°48N 0°4W **25** E8
Rotuma *Fiji* 12°25S 177°5E **99** C14
Roubaix *France* 50°40N 3°10E **68** A5
Rouen *France* 49°27N 1°4E **68** B4
Round Mt. *Australia* 30°26S 152°16E **98** G9
Rousay *U.K.* 59°10N 3°2W **19** D11
Roussillon *France* 42°30N 2°35E **68** E5
Rouyn-Noranda *Canada* 48°20N 79°0W **109** E12
Rovaniemi *Finland* 66°29N 25°41E **63** D9
Rovigo *Italy* 45°4N 11°47E **70** B4
Rowanburn *U.K.* 55°5N 2°55W **21** D10
Roxas *Phil.* 11°36N 122°49E **83** B4
Roxburgh *U.K.* 55°35N 2°28W **21** C11
Roxby *U.K.* 53°38N 0°38W **23** E7
Royal Canal *Ireland* 53°30N 7°13W **31** B8
Royal Leamington Spa *U.K.* 52°18N 1°31W **24** B5
Royal Tunbridge Wells *U.K.* 51°7N 0°16E **25** D9
Royale, Isle *U.S.A.* 48°0N 88°54W **112** B3
Royan *France* 45°37N 1°2W **68** D3
Royston *U.K.* 52°3N 0°0 **25** B8
Royton *U.K.* 53°34N 2°8W **23** E4
Rub' al Khālī *Si. Arabia* 19°0N 48°0E **88** D4
Rubery *U.K.* 52°24N 2°1W **24** B4
Rubh a' Mhail *U.K.* 55°56N 6°8W **20** C3
Rubha Hunish *U.K.* 57°42N 6°20W **18** G5
Ruby L. *U.S.A.* 40°10N 115°28W **110** B3
Rudston *U.K.* 54°6N 0°20W **22** D8
Ruffling Pt. *Br. Virgin Is.* 18°44N 64°27W **115** e
Rufford *U.K.* 53°38N 2°50W **23** E3
Rufiji → *Tanzania* 7°50S 39°15E **96** F7
Rugby *U.K.* 52°23N 1°16W **24** B6
Rugeley *U.K.* 52°46N 1°55W **23** G5
Rügen *Germany* 54°22N 13°24E **66** A7
Ruhr → *Germany* 51°27N 6°43E **64** C4
Ruki → *Dem. Rep. of the Congo* 0°5N 18°17E **96** E3
Rukwa, L. *Tanzania* 8°0S 32°20E **96** F6
Rumania = Romania ■ *Europe* 46°0N 25°0E **67** F12
Rumford *U.S.A.* 44°33N 70°33W **113** C12
Runaway Bay *Jamaica* 18°27N 77°20W **114** a
Runcorn *U.K.* 53°21N 2°44W **23** F3
Rundu *Namibia* 17°52S 19°43E **97** H3
Rungwe *Tanzania* 9°11S 33°32E **90** G7
Ruoqiang *China* 38°55N 88°10E **80** C3
Rupert → *Canada* 51°29N 78°45W **109** D12
Rupert *Canada* 51°29N 78°45W **109** D12
Ruse *Bulgaria* 43°48N 25°59E **71** C12
Rush *Ireland* 53°31N 6°6W **31** A10
Rushden *U.K.* 52°18N 0°35W **25** B7
Rushville *Ill., U.S.A.* 40°7N 90°34W **112** E2
Rushville *Ind., U.S.A.* 39°37N 85°27W **112** F5
Ruskington *U.K.* 53°3N 0°22W **23** F8

Russellville *U.S.A.* 35°17N 93°8W **111** C81
Russia ■ *Eurasia* 62°0N 105°0E **79** C12
Rustavi *Georgia* 41°30N 45°0E **73** F8
Rustenburg *S. Africa* 25°41S 27°14E **97** K5
Rutherglen *U.K.* 55°49N 4°13W **20** C7
Ruthin *U.K.* 53°6N 3°19W **26** A7
Ruthwell *U.K.* 55°0N 3°25W **21** E9
Rutog *China* 33°27N 79°42E **80** C2
Ruvuma → *Tanzania* 10°29S 40°28E **96** G8
Ruwenzori *Africa* 0°30N 29°55E **96** D5
Rwanda ■ *Africa* 2°0S 30°0E **96** E5
Ryan, L. *U.K.* 55°0N 5°2W **20** E5
Ryazan *Russia* 54°40N 39°40E **72** D6
Rybachy Pen. *Russia* 69°43N 32°0E **72** A5
Rybinsk *Russia* 58°5N 38°50E **72** C6
Rybinsk Res. *Russia* 58°30N 38°25E **72** C6
Rydal *U.K.* 54°27N 2°59W **22** D3
Ryde *U.K.* 50°43N 1°9W **24** E6
Rye *U.K.* 50°57N 0°45E **25** E10
Rye → *U.K.* 54°11N 0°44W **22** D7
Rye Bay *U.K.* 50°52N 0°49E **25** E10
Ryhope *U.K.* 54°53N 1°21W **22** C6
Ryton *U.K.* 52°22N 1°25W **24** B6
Ryukyu Is. *Japan* 26°0N 126°0E **81** D7
Rzeszów *Poland* 50°5N 21°58E **67** C11
Rzhev *Russia* 56°20N 34°20E **72** C5

S

Saale → *Germany* 51°56N 11°54E **66** C6
Saar → *Europe* 49°41N 6°32E **65** E6
Saarbrücken *Germany* 49°14N 6°59E **66** D4
Saaremaa *Estonia* 58°30N 22°30E **63** F8
Sabadell *Spain* 41°28N 2°7E **69** B7
Sabah □ *Malaysia* 6°0N 117°0E **83** C3
Sabará *Brazil* 19°55S 43°46W **122** C2
Sabhā *Libya* 27°9N 14°29E **95** C8
Sabinas *Mexico* 27°51N 101°7W **114** B4
Sabinas Hidalgo *Mexico* 26°30N 100°10W **114** B4
Sabine → *U.S.A.* 29°59N 93°47W **111** E8
Sable, C. *Canada* 43°29N 65°38W **113** D15
Sable, C. *U.S.A.* 25°9N 81°8W **111** E10
Sable I. *Canada* 44°0N 60°0W **109** E14
Sachsen □ *Germany* 50°55N 13°10E **66** C7
Sachsen-Anhalt □ *Germany* 52°0N 12°0E **66** C7
Saco *U.S.A.* 43°30N 70°27W **113** D12
Sacramento *U.S.A.* 38°35N 121°29W **110** C2
Sacramento → *U.S.A.* 38°3N 121°56W **110** C2
Sacramento Mts. *U.S.A.* 32°30N 105°30W **110** D5
Sado *Japan* 38°0N 138°25E **82** D6
Safford *U.S.A.* 32°50N 109°43W **110** D5
Saffron Walden *U.K.* 52°1N 0°16E **25** B9
Safi *Morocco* 32°18N 9°20W **94** B4
Saga *Japan* 33°15N 130°16E **82** G2
Sagaing *Burma* 21°52N 95°59E **85** J19
Sagar *India* 23°50N 78°44E **84** H11
Saginaw *U.S.A.* 43°26N 83°56W **112** D6
Saginaw B. *U.S.A.* 43°50N 83°40W **112** D6
Sagua la Grande *Cuba* 22°50N 80°10W **115** C8
Saguenay → *Canada* 48°22N 71°0W **113** A12
Sagunt *Spain* 39°42N 0°18W **69** C5
Sahara *Africa* 23°0N 5°0E **94** D6
Saharan Atlas *Algeria* 33°30N 1°0E **94** B6
Saharanpur *India* 29°58N 77°33E **84** E10
Sahel *Africa* 16°0N 5°0E **94** E5
Sahiwal *Pakistan* 30°45N 73°8E **84** D8
Saidpur *Bangla.* 25°48N 89°0E **85** G16
St. Abb's Head *U.K.* 55°55N 2°8W **21** C11
St. Agnes *U.K.* 50°19N 5°13W **27** G3
St. Agnes *Corn., U.K.* 49°54N 6°21W **27** H1
St. Agnes Hd. *U.K.* 51°45N 0°19W **25** C8
St. Albans *U.K.* 51°45N 0°19W **25** C8
St. Albans *Vt., U.S.A.* 44°49N 73°5W **113** C11
St. Albans *W. Va., U.S.A.* 38°23N 81°50W **112** F7
St. Alban's Head *U.K.* 50°34N 2°4W **24** E4
St. Andrews *U.K.* 56°20N 2°47W **21** B10
St. Ann's *U.K.* 55°14N 3°28W **21** D9
St. Ann's Bay *Jamaica* 18°26N 77°12W **114** a
St. Anthony *Canada* 51°22N 55°35W **109** D14
St. Asaph *U.K.* 53°15N 3°27W **26** A7
St-Augustin *Canada* 51°13N 58°38W **109** D14
St. Augustine *U.S.A.* 29°54N 81°19W **111** E10
St. Austell *U.K.* 50°20N 4°47W **27** G4
St. Bees *U.K.* 54°30N 3°35W **22** C1
St. Bees Hd. *U.K.* 54°31N 3°38W **22** C1
St. Blazey *U.K.* 50°22N 4°43W **27** G4
St. Brides B. *U.K.* 51°49N 5°9W **26** D3
St-Brieuc *France* 48°30N 2°46W **68** B2
St. Buryan *U.K.* 50°4N 5°37W **27** G2
St. Catharines *Canada* 43°10N 79°15W **112** D8
St. Catherine's Pt. *U.K.* 50°34N 1°18W **24** E6
St. Charles *U.S.A.* 38°47N 90°29W **112** F2
St. Clair, L. *N. Amer.* 42°27N 82°39W **112** D6
St. Clears *U.K.* 51°49N 4°31W **26** D4
St. Cloud *U.S.A.* 45°34N 94°10W **111** A8
St. Columb Major *U.K.* 50°26N 4°58W **27** G4
St. Croix *U.S. Virgin Is.* 17°45N 64°45W **115** D12
St. David's *U.K.* 51°53N 5°16W **26** D3
St. David's Head *U.K.* 51°54N 5°19W **26** D3
St-Denis *France* 48°56N 2°20E **68** B5
St. Dennis *U.K.* 50°23N 4°53W **27** G4
St-Dizier *France* 48°38N 4°56E **68** B6
St. Dominick *U.K.* 50°29N 4°14W **27** G5
St. Elias, Mt. *U.S.A.* 60°18N 140°56W **108** C5
St. Elias Mts. *N. Amer.* 60°33N 139°28W **108** D6
St. Enoder *U.K.* 50°22N 4°58W **27** G4
St. Erth *U.K.* 50°9N 5°26W **27** G2
St-Étienne *France* 45°27N 4°22E **68** D6
St-Félicien *Canada* 48°40N 72°25W **113** A11
St-Flour *France* 45°2N 3°6E **68** D5
St. Gallen *Switz.* 47°26N 9°22E **66** E5
St-Gaudens *France* 43°6N 0°44E **68** E4
St. George *U.S.A.* 37°6N 113°35W **110** C4
St-Georges *Canada* 46°8N 70°40W **113** B12
St. George's *Grenada* 12°5N 61°43W **115** E12
St. George's Channel *Europe* 52°0N 6°0W **31** E11
St. Germans *U.K.* 50°24N 4°19W **27** G5
St. Helena *Atl. Oc.* 15°58S 5°42W **52** E9

St. Helens *U.K.* 53°27N 2°44W **23** F3
St. Helens, Mt. *U.S.A.* 46°12N 122°12W **110** A2
St. Helier *U.K.* 49°10N 2°7W **27** J9
St-Hyacinthe *Canada* 45°40N 72°58W **109** E12
St. Ignace *U.S.A.* 45°52N 84°44W **112** C5
St. Issey *U.K.* 50°30N 4°57W **27** G4
St. Ives *Cambs., U.K.* 52°20N 0°4W **25** B8
St. Ives *Corn., U.K.* 50°12N 5°30W **27** G3
St. Ives B. *U.K.* 50°13N 5°27W **27** G3
St-Jean, L. *Canada* 48°40N 72°0W **113** A12
St-Jérôme *Canada* 45°47N 74°0W **113** C11
St. John *Canada* 45°20N 66°8W **109** E13
St. John I. *U.S. Virgin Is.* 18°20N 64°42W **115** e
St. John's *Antigua & B.* 17°6N 61°51W **115** D12
St. John's *Canada* 47°35N 52°40W **109** E14
St. Johns → *U.S.A.* 30°24N 81°24W **111** D10
St. Johns *Mich., U.S.A.* 42°59N 84°33W **112** D5
St. Johns Chapel *U.K.* 54°44N 2°10W **22** C4
St. John's Pt. *Ireland* 54°34N 8°27W **28** B5
St. Johnsbury *U.S.A.* 44°25N 72°1W **113** C11
St-Joseph *Martinique* 14°39N 61°4W **114** c
St. Joseph *Mich., U.S.A.* 42°6N 86°29W **112** D4
St. Joseph *Mo., U.S.A.* 39°46N 94°50W **111** C8
St. Joseph, L. *Canada* 51°10N 90°35W **109** D10
St. Just *U.K.* 50°7N 5°42W **27** G2
St. Keverne *U.K.* 50°3N 5°6W **27** G3
St. Kilda *U.K.* 57°49N 8°34W **64** C2
St. Kitts & Nevis ■ *W. Indies* 17°20N 62°40W **115** D12
St. Lawrence → *Canada* 49°30N 66°0W **109** E13
St. Lawrence, Gulf of *Canada* 48°25N 62°0W **109** E13
St. Lawrence I. *U.S.A.* 63°30N 170°30W **108** C3
St. Levan *U.K.* 50°2N 5°41W **27** G2
St-Lô *France* 49°7N 1°5W **68** B3
St-Louis *Guadeloupe* 15°56N 61°19W **114** b
St. Louis *Senegal* 16°8N 16°27W **94** E2
St. Louis *U.S.A.* 38°37N 90°11W **112** F2
St. Lucia ■ *W. Indies* 14°0N 60°57W **115** f
St. Mabyn *U.K.* 50°30N 4°47W **27** F4
St. Magnus B. *U.K.* 60°25N 1°35W **18** B14
St-Malo *France* 48°39N 2°1W **68** B2
St-Marc *Haiti* 19°10N 72°41W **115** D10
St. Margaret's-at-Cliffe *U.K.* 51°9N 1°23E **25** D11
St-Martin ☑ *W. Indies* 18°0N 63°0W **115** D12
St-Martin, C. *Martinique* 14°52N 61°14W **114** c
St. Martins *Barbados* 13°5N 59°28W **115** g
St. Martin's *U.K.* 49°58N 6°17W **27** H1
St. Mary Bourne *U.K.* 51°15N 1°24W **24** D6
St. Mary's *Corn., U.K.* 49°55N 6°18W **27** H1
St. Mary's *Orkney, U.K.* 58°54N 2°54W **19** E12
St. Marys *U.S.A.* 41°26N 78°34W **112** E8
St. Mary's Sd. *U.K.* 49°54N 6°20W **27** H1
St. Matthew I. *U.S.A.* 60°24N 172°42W **108** C2
St. Mawes *U.K.* 50°10N 5°2W **27** G3
St. Merryn *U.K.* 50°32N 5°1W **27** F3
St. Michael's Mount *U.K.* 50°7N 5°29W **27** G3
St. Minver *U.K.* 50°33N 4°53W **27** F4
St. Moritz *Switz.* 46°30N 9°51E **66** E5
St-Nazaire *France* 47°17N 2°12W **68** C2
St. Neots *U.K.* 52°14N 0°15W **25** B8
St-Niklaas *Belgium* 51°10N 4°8E **65** C4
St-Omer *France* 50°45N 2°15E **68** A5
St. Osyth *U.K.* 51°47N 1°5E **25** C11
St. Paul *U.S.A.* 44°56N 93°5W **111** B8
St. Paul, I. *Ind. Oc.* 38°55S 77°34E **53** F13
St. Peter Port *U.K.* 49°26N 2°33W **27** J8
St. Petersburg *Russia* 59°55N 30°20E **72** C5
St. Petersburg *U.S.A.* 27°46N 82°40W **111** E10
St-Pierre *Martinique* 14°45N 61°10W **114** c
St-Pierre-et-Miquelon ☑ *N. Amer.* 46°55N 56°10W **109** E14
St-Quentin *France* 49°50N 3°16E **68** B5
St. Stephen *Canada* 45°16N 67°17W **113** C14
St. Stephen *U.K.* 50°21N 4°53W **27** G4
St. Teath *U.K.* 50°35N 4°45W **27** F4
St. Thomas *Canada* 42°45N 81°10W **112** D7
St. Thomas I. *U.S. Virgin Is.* 18°20N 64°55W **115** e
St-Tropez *France* 43°17N 6°38E **68** E7
St. Tudy *U.K.* 50°33N 4°45W **27** F4
St. Vincent, G. *Australia* 35°0S 138°0E **98** G6
St. Vincent & the Grenadines ■ *W. Indies* 13°0N 61°10W **115** E12
Ste-Anne *Guadeloupe* 16°13N 61°24W **114** b
Ste. Genevieve *U.S.A.* 37°59N 90°2W **112** G2
Ste-Marie *Canada* 46°26N 71°0W **113** B12
Ste-Marie *Martinique* 14°48N 61°1W **114** c
Ste-Rose *Guadeloupe* 16°20N 61°45W **114** b
Saintes *France* 45°45N 0°37W **68** D3
Saintes, Îs. des *Guadeloupe* 15°50N 61°35W **114** b
Saintfield *U.K.* 54°28N 5°49W **29** C10
Saintonge *France* 45°40N 0°50W **68** D3
Saipan *N. Marianas* 15°12N 145°45E **102** F6
Sajama *Bolivia* 18°7S 69°0W **120** D3
Sakakawea, L. *U.S.A.* 47°30N 101°25W **110** A6
Sakarya *Turkey* 40°48N 30°25E **73** F5
Sakata *Japan* 38°55N 139°50E **82** D6
Sakhalin *Russia* 51°0N 143°0E **79** D16
Sala *Sweden* 59°58N 16°35E **63** F7
Sala-y-Gómez *Pac. Oc.* 26°28S 105°28W **103** K17
Salado → *La Pampa, Argentina* 37°30S 67°0W **121** F3
Salado → *Santa Fe, Argentina* 31°40S 60°41W **121** F3
Salālah *Oman* 16°56N 53°59E **88** D5
Salamanca *Spain* 40°58N 5°39W **69** B3
Salamanca *U.S.A.* 42°10N 78°43W **112** D8
Salar de Uyuni *Bolivia* 20°30S 67°45W **120** E3
Salavat *Russia* 53°21N 55°55E **72** D10
Salaverry *Peru* 8°15S 79°0W **120** C2
Salaya *Indonesia* 6°7S 120°30E **83** F6
Salcombe *U.K.* 50°14N 3°47W **27** H5
Saldanha *S. Africa* 33°0S 17°58E **97** L3
Sale *Australia* 38°6S 147°6E **98** H8
Salé *Morocco* 34°3N 6°48W **94** B4
Sale *U.K.* 53°26N 2°19W **23** F4
Salekhard *Russia* 66°30N 66°35E **79** C8
Salem *India* 11°40N 78°11E **84** P11
Salem *Ind., U.S.A.* 38°36N 86°6W **112** F4
Salem *Mass., U.S.A.* 42°31N 70°53W **113** D12
Salem *Ohio, U.S.A.* 40°54N 80°52W **112** E7

Salem *Oreg., U.S.A.* 44°56N 123°2W **110** B2
Salem *Va., U.S.A.* 37°18N 80°3W **112** G7
Salerno *Italy* 40°41N 14°47E **70** D6
Salford *U.K.* 53°30N 2°18W **23** F4
Salford Priors *U.K.* 52°10N 1°53W **24** B5
Salida *U.S.A.* 38°32N 106°0W **110** C5
Salina *U.S.A.* 38°50N 97°37W **111** C7
Salina Cruz *Mexico* 16°10N 95°12W **114** D5
Salinas *Ecuador* 2°10S 80°58W **120** C1
Salinas *U.S.A.* 36°40N 121°39W **110** C2
Salinas → *U.S.A.* 36°45N 121°48W **110** C2
Salinas Grandes *Argentina* 30°0S 65°0W **121** E3
Salisbury *U.K.* 51°4N 1°47W **24** D5
Salisbury *U.S.A.* 38°22N 75°36W **113** F10
Salisbury I. *Canada* 63°30N 77°0W **109** C12
Salisbury Plain *U.K.* 51°14N 1°55W **24** D5
Salmon *U.S.A.* 45°11N 113°54W **110** A4
Salmon → *U.S.A.* 45°51N 116°47W **110** A3
Salmon Arm *Canada* 50°40N 119°15W **108** D8
Salmon River Mts. *U.S.A.* 44°50N 115°30W **110** B4
Salon-de-Provence *France* 43°39N 5°6E **68** E6
Salsk *Russia* 46°28N 41°30E **73** E7
Salt → *U.S.A.* 33°23N 112°19W **110** D4
Salt Lake City *U.S.A.* 40°45N 111°53W **110** B4
Salta *Argentina* 24°57S 65°25W **121** E3
Saltash *U.K.* 50°24N 4°14W **27** G5
Saltburn by the Sea *U.K.* 54°35N 0°58W **22** C7
Saltcoats *U.K.* 55°38N 4°47W **20** C6
Saltee Is. *Ireland* 52°7N 6°37W **31** D9
Saltfleet *U.K.* 53°25N 0°11E **23** F9
Saltfleetby *U.K.* 53°23N 0°10E **23** F9
Saltillo *Mexico* 25°25N 101°0W **114** B4
Salton Sea *U.S.A.* 33°15N 115°45W **110** D3
Saltwood *U.K.* 51°4N 1°2E **25** D11
Salvador *Brazil* 13°0S 38°30W **122** B3
Salvador, El ■ *Cent. Amer.* 13°50N 89°0W **114** E7
Salween → *Burma* 16°31N 97°37E **85** L20
Salyan *Azerbaijan* 39°33N 48°59E **73** G8
Salzburg *Austria* 47°48N 13°2E **66** E7
Salzgitter *Germany* 52°9N 10°19E **66** B6
Samangān □ *Afghan.* 36°15N 68°3E **87** B12
Samar *Phil.* 12°0N 125°0E **83** B4
Samara *Russia* 53°8N 50°6E **72** D9
Samarinda *Indonesia* 0°30S 117°9E **83** D3
Samarkand *Uzbekistan* 39°40N 66°55E **87** B11
Sambalpur *India* 21°28N 84°4E **85** J14
Sambhal *India* 28°35N 78°37E **84** E11
Sambhar *India* 26°52N 75°6E **84** F9
Samoa ■ *Pac. Oc.* 14°0S 172°0W **99** C16
Samos *Greece* 37°45N 26°50E **71** F12
Samothraki *Greece* 40°28N 25°28E **71** D11
Sampford Courtenay *U.K.* 50°47N 3°58W **27** F6
Samsun *Turkey* 41°15N 36°22E **73** F6
Samui, Ko *Thailand* 9°30N 100°0E **83** C2
San → *Poland* 50°45N 21°51E **67** C11
San Ambrosio *Pac. Oc.* 26°28S 79°53W **103** K20
San Andrés, I. de *Caribbean* 12°42N 81°46W **115** E8
San Andres Mts. *U.S.A.* 33°0N 106°30W **110** D5
San Andrés Tuxtla *Mexico* 18°27N 95°13W **114** D5
San Angelo *U.S.A.* 31°28N 100°26W **110** D6
San Antonio *Chile* 33°40S 71°40W **121** F2
San Antonio *U.S.A.* 29°25N 98°29W **110** E7
San Antonio → *U.S.A.* 28°30N 96°54W **111** E7
San Antonio Oeste *Argentina* 40°40S 65°0W **121** G3
San Bernardino *U.S.A.* 34°7N 117°19W **110** D3
San Bernardino Str. *Phil.* 13°0N 125°0E **83** B4
San Bernardo *Chile* 33°40S 70°50W **121** F2
San Blas, C. *U.S.A.* 29°40N 85°21W **111** E9
San Carlos *Phil.* 10°29N 123°25E **83** B4
San Carlos de Bariloche *Argentina* 41°10S 71°25W **121** G2
San Carlos de Bolívar *Argentina* 36°15S 61°6W **121** F3
San Cristóbal *Argentina* 30°20S 61°10W **121** F3
San Cristóbal *Solomon Is.* 10°30S 161°0E **99** C11
San Cristóbal *Venezuela* 7°46N 72°14W **120** B2
San Cristóbal de las Casas *Mexico* 16°45N 92°38W **114** D6
San Diego *U.S.A.* 32°42N 117°9W **110** D3
San Felipe *Venezuela* 10°20N 68°44W **120** A3
San Félix *Pac. Oc.* 26°23S 80°0W **103** K20
San Fernando *Chile* 34°30S 71°0W **121** F2
San Fernando *Spain* 36°28N 6°17W **69** D2
San Fernando de Apure *Venezuela* 7°54N 67°15W **120** B3
San Francisco *U.S.A.* 37°46N 122°23W **110** C2
San Francisco, C. de *Colombia* 6°18N 77°29W **116** C3
San Francisco de Macorís *Dom. Rep.* 19°19N 70°15W **115** D10
San Germán *Puerto Rico* 18°4N 67°4W **115** d
San Gottardo, P. del *Switz.* 46°33N 8°33E **66** E5
San Ignacio *Bolivia* 16°20S 60°55W **120** D3
San Joaquin → *U.S.A.* 38°4N 121°51W **110** C2
San Jorge, G. *Argentina* 46°0S 66°0W **121** G3
San Jose *Costa Rica* 9°55N 84°2W **115** F8
San Jose *Phil.* 12°27N 121°4E **83** B4
San Jose → *U.S.A.* 37°20N 121°53W **110** C2
San José *U.S.A.* 34°25N 106°45W **110** D5
San José de Chiquitos *Bolivia* 17°53S 60°50W **120** D3
San José de Jáchal *Argentina* 30°15S 68°46W **121** F3
San José de Mayo *Uruguay* 34°27S 56°40W **121** F4
San Juan *Argentina* 31°30S 68°30W **121** F3
San Juan *Puerto Rico* 18°28N 66°7W **115** d
San Juan → *Nic.* 10°56N 83°42W **115** E8
San Juan → *U.S.A.* 37°16N 110°26W **110** C4
San Juan de los Morros *Venezuela* 9°55N 67°21W **120** B3
San Juan Mts. *U.S.A.* 37°30N 107°0W **110** C5
San Lorenzo, Mte. *Argentina* 47°40S 72°20W **121** G2
San Lucas, C. *Mexico* 22°52N 109°53W **114** C3
San Luis *Argentina* 33°20S 66°20W **121** F3
San Luis Obispo *U.S.A.* 35°17N 120°40W **110** C2
San Luis Potosí *Mexico* 22°9N 100°59W **114** C4
San Marcos *U.S.A.* 29°53N 97°56W **110** E7
San Marino ■ *Europe* 43°56N 12°25E **70** C5
San Matías, G. *Argentina* 41°30S 64°0W **121** G3
San Miguel *El Salv.* 13°30N 88°12W **114** E7

San Miguel de Tucumán   Skelmorlie

San Miguel de Tucumán
  Argentina 26°50S 65°20W 121 E3
San Nicolás Argentina 33°25S 60°10W 121 F3
San Pédro Ivory C. 4°50N 6°33W 94 H4
San Pedro de las Colonias
  Mexico 25°45N 102°59W 114 B4
San Pedro de Macorís
  Dom. Rep. 18°30N 69°18W 115 D11
San Pedro Sula Honduras 15°30N 88°0W 114 D7
San Pietro Italy 39°8N 8°17E 70 E3
San Rafael Argentina 34°40S 68°21W 121 F3
San Remo Italy 43°49N 7°46E 70 C2
San Salvador El Salv. 13°40N 89°10W 114 E7
San Salvador de Jujuy
  Argentina 24°10S 64°48W 121 E3
San Salvador I. Bahamas 24°0N 74°40W 115 C10
San Sebastián Puerto Rico 18°20N 66°59W 115 d
San Severo Italy 41°41N 15°23E 70 D6
San Valentín, Mte. Chile 46°30S 73°30W 121 G2
Sana' Yemen 15°27N 44°12E 88 D3
Sanaga → Cameroon 3°35N 9°38E 96 D1
Sanandaj Iran 35°18N 47°1E 86 C6
Sancti Spíritus Cuba 21°52N 79°33W 115 C9
Sancy, Puy de France 45°32N 2°50E 68 D5
Sandakan Malaysia 5°53N 118°4E 83 C3
Sanday U.K. 59°16N 2°31W 19 D12
Sandbach U.K. 53°9N 2°21W 23 F4
Sandgate U.K. 51°4N 1°10E 25 D11
Sandhurst U.K. 51°21N 0°48W 25 D7
Sandown U.K. 50°40N 1°10W 24 E6
Sandpoint U.S.A. 48°17N 116°33W 110 A3
Sandray U.K. 56°53N 7°31W 18 J2
Sandringham U.K. 52°51N 0°31E 25 A10
Sandusky U.S.A. 41°27N 82°42W 112 E6
Sandwich U.K. 51°16N 1°21E 25 D11
Sandy U.K. 52°8N 0°17W 25 B8
Sandy L. Canada 40°32N 111°50W 110 B4
Sanford, Mt. U.S.A. 62°13N 144°8W 108 C5
Sangihe, Pulau Indonesia 3°35N 125°30E 83 C4
Sangli India 16°55N 74°33E 84 L9
Sangre de Cristo Mts.
  U.S.A. 37°30N 105°20W 110 C5
Sanikiluaq Canada 56°32N 79°14W 109 D12
Sanirajak Canada 68°46N 81°12W 109 C11
Sankt Pölten Austria 48°12N 15°38E 66 D8
Sankuru →
  Dem. Rep. of the Congo 4°17S 20°25E 96 E4
Sanliurfa Turkey 37°12N 38°50E 73 G6
Sanlúcar de Barrameda Spain 36°46N 6°21W 69 D2
Sanmenxia China 34°47N 111°12E 81 C6
Sanming China 26°15N 117°40E 81 D6
Sanquhar U.K. 55°22N 3°54W 21 D8
Sant Feliu de Guíxols Spain 41°45N 3°1E 69 B7
Santa Ana El Salv. 14°0N 89°31W 114 E7
Santa Ana U.S.A. 33°46N 117°52W 110 D3
Sant' Antioco Italy 39°4N 8°27E 70 E3
Santa Barbara U.S.A. 34°25N 119°42W 110 D3
Santa Catarina □ Brazil 27°25S 48°30W 121 E5
Santa Clara Cuba 22°20N 80°0W 115 C9
Santa Clarita U.S.A. 34°24N 118°33W 110 D3
Santa Coloma de Gramenet
  Spain 41°27N 2°13E 69 B7
Santa Cruz Bolivia 17°43S 63°10W 120 D3
Santa Cruz U.S.A. 36°58N 122°1W 110 C2
Santa Cruz de Tenerife
  Canary Is. 28°28N 16°15W 94 C2
Santa Cruz Is. Solomon Is. 10°30S 166°0E 99 C12
Santa Cruz Mts. Jamaica 17°58N 77°43W 114 a
Santa Fé Argentina 31°35S 60°41W 121 F3
Santa Fe U.S.A. 35°41N 105°57W 110 C5
Santa Inés, I. Chile 54°0S 73°0W 121 H2
Santa Isabel Solomon Is. 8°0S 159°0E 99 B10
Santa Maria Brazil 29°40S 53°48W 121 E4
Santa Maria U.S.A. 34°57N 120°26W 110 D2
Santa María → Mexico 31°0N 107°14W 114 A3
Santa Marta Colombia 11°15N 74°13W 120 A2
Santa Marta, Sierra Nevada de
  Colombia 10°55N 73°50W 120 A2
Santa Rosa Argentina 36°40S 64°17W 121 F3
Santa Rosa U.S.A. 38°26N 122°43W 110 C2
Santai China 31°5N 104°58E 80 C5
Santana do Livramento
  Brazil 30°55S 55°30W 121 F4
Santander Spain 43°27N 3°51W 69 A4
Santarém Brazil 2°25S 54°42W 120 C4
Santarém Portugal 39°12N 8°42W 69 C1
Santiago Chile 33°26S 70°40W 121 F2
Santiago de Compostela Spain 42°52N 8°37W 69 A1
Santiago de Cuba Cuba 20°0N 75°49W 115 D9
Santiago de los Caballeros
  Dom. Rep. 19°30N 70°40W 115 D10
Santiago del Estero
  Argentina 27°50S 64°15W 121 E3
Santo Amaro Brazil 12°30S 38°43W 122 E3
Santo André Brazil 23°39S 46°29W 122 D1
Santo Antônio de Jesus
  Brazil 12°58S 39°16W 122 B3
Santo Domingo Dom. Rep. 18°30N 69°59W 115 D11
Santo Domingo de los Colorados
  Ecuador 0°15S 79°9W 120 C2
Santorini Greece 36°23N 25°27E 71 F11
Santos Brazil 24°0S 46°20W 122 D1
Santos Dumont Brazil 22°55S 43°10W 122 D2
Sanya China 18°14N 109°29E 81 E5
São Bernardo do Campo
  Brazil 23°45S 46°34W 122 D1
São Borja Brazil 28°39S 56°0W 121 E4
São Caitano Brazil 8°21S 36°6W 122 B3
São Carlos Brazil 22°0S 47°50W 122 D1
São Francisco → Brazil 10°30S 36°24W 122 B3
São Gonçalo Brazil 22°48S 43°5W 122 D2
São João da Boa Vista Brazil 22°0S 46°52W 122 D1
São João del Rei Brazil 21°8S 44°15W 122 D2
São João do Piauí Brazil 8°21S 42°15W 122 A2
São José do Rio Prêto Brazil 20°50S 49°20W 122 D1
São José dos Campos Brazil 23°7S 45°52W 122 D1
São Lourenço Brazil 22°7S 45°3W 122 D1

São Luís Brazil 2°39S 44°15W 120 C5
São Marcos → Brazil 18°15S 47°37W 122 C1
São Marcos, B. de Brazil 2°0S 44°0W 120 C5
São Mateus Brazil 18°44S 39°50W 122 C3
São Paulo Brazil 23°32S 46°38W 122 D1
São Paulo □ Brazil 22°0S 49°0W 120 E5
São Roque, C. de Brazil 5°30S 35°16W 120 C6
São Sebastião do Paraíso
  Brazil 20°54S 46°59W 122 D1
São Tomé São Tomé & Príncipe 0°10N 6°39E 90 F4
São Tomé & Príncipe ■ Africa 0°12N 6°39E 91 F4
São Vicente Brazil 23°57S 46°23W 122 D1
São Vicente, C. de Portugal 37°0N 9°0W 69 D1
Saône → France 45°44N 4°50E 68 D6
Sapele Nigeria 5°50N 5°40E 94 G7
Sapporo Japan 43°0N 141°21E 82 B7
Saqqez Iran 36°15N 46°20E 86 B6
Sar-e-Pol Afghan. 36°10N 66°0E 87 B11
Saraburi Thailand 14°30N 100°55E 83 B2
Sarajevo Bos.-H. 43°52N 18°26E 71 C8
Saranac Lakes U.S.A. 44°20N 74°28W 113 C10
Saransk Russia 54°10N 45°10E 72 D8
Sarapul Russia 56°28N 53°48E 72 C9
Sarasota U.S.A. 27°20N 82°32W 111 E10
Saratoga Springs U.S.A. 43°5N 73°47W 113 D11
Saratov Russia 51°30N 46°2E 73 D8
Sarawak □ Malaysia 2°0N 113°0E 83 C3
Sarda → India 27°21N 81°23E 85 F12
Sardinia □ Italy 40°0N 9°0E 70 D3
Sargasso Sea Atl. Oc. 27°0N 72°0W 103 D20
Sargodha Pakistan 32°10N 72°40E 84 C8
Sark Chad 9°5N 18°23E 95 G9
Sārī Iran 36°30N 53°4E 87 B8
Sark U.K. 49°25N 2°22W 27 J9
Sarlat-la-Canéda France 44°54N 1°13E 68 D4
Sarmiento Argentina 45°35S 69°5W 121 G3
Sarnia Canada 42°58N 82°23W 109 E11
Sarreguemines France 49°5N 7°4E 68 B7
Sarthe → France 47°33N 0°31W 68 C3
Sasebo Japan 33°10N 129°43E 82 G1
Saskatchewan □ Canada 54°40N 106°0W 108 D9
Saskatchewan → Canada 53°37N 100°40W 108 D9
Saskatoon Canada 52°10N 106°38W 108 D9
Sássari Italy 40°43N 8°34E 70 D3
Sassnitz Germany 54°29N 13°39E 66 A7
Satmala Hills Andhra Pradesh,
  India 19°45N 78°45E 84 K11
Satmala Hills Maharashtra,
  India 20°15N 74°40E 84 J9
Satna India 24°35N 80°50E 85 G12
Satpura Ra. India 21°25N 76°10E 84 J10
Satu Mare Romania 47°46N 22°55E 67 E12
Saudi Arabia ■ Asia 26°0N 44°0E 88 C3
Sault Ste. Marie Canada 46°30N 84°20W 112 B5
Saumur France 47°15N 0°5W 68 C3
Saundersfoot U.K. 51°43N 4°42W 26 D4
Saurimo Angola 9°40S 20°12E 96 F4
Sava → Serbia 44°50N 20°26E 71 B9
Savai'i Samoa 13°28S 172°24W 99 C16
Savanna-la-Mar Jamaica 18°10N 78°10W 114 a
Savannah U.S.A. 32°5N 81°6W 111 D10
Savannah → U.S.A. 32°2N 80°53W 111 D10
Savannakhet Laos 16°30N 104°49E 83 B2
Savoie □ France 45°26N 6°25E 68 D7
Savona Italy 44°17N 8°30E 70 B3
Sawatch Range U.S.A. 39°0N 106°30W 110 C5
Sawbridgeworth U.K. 51°48N 0°9E 25 C9
Sawel Mt. U.K. 54°50N 7°2W 29 B7
Sawston U.K. 52°8N 0°10E 25 B9
Sawtry U.K. 52°27N 0°17W 25 B8
Sawu Indonesia 10°35S 121°50E 83 D4
Sawu Sea Indonesia 9°30S 121°50E 83 D4
Saxilby U.K. 53°16N 0°38W 23 F7
Saxlingham Nethergate U.K. 52°32N 1°18E 25 A11
Saxmundham U.K. 52°13N 1°30E 25 B12
Sayan Mts. Russia 54°0N 96°0E 79 D11
Saydā Lebanon 33°35N 35°25E 86 C3
Sayre U.S.A. 41°59N 76°32W 112 D9
Sázava → Czech Rep. 49°53N 14°24E 66 D8
Scafell Pike U.K. 54°27N 3°14W 22 D2
Scalby U.K. 54°18N 0°26W 22 D8
Scalloway U.K. 60°9N 1°17W 18 B15
Scalpay Highl., U.K. 57°18N 6°0W 18 H6
Scalpay W. Isles, U.K. 57°52N 6°40W 18 G4
Scamblesby U.K. 53°17N 0°5W 23 F8
Scandicci Italy 43°45N 11°11E 70 C4
Scandinavia Europe 64°0N 12°0E 56 B8
Scapa Flow U.K. 58°53N 3°3W 19 E11
Scarba U.K. 56°11N 5°43W 20 B4
Scarborough U.K. 54°17N 0°24W 22 D8
Scariff I. Ireland 51°44N 10°15W 30 E2
Scarning U.K. 52°41N 0°54E 25 A10
Scarp U.K. 58°1N 7°8W 18 F3
Scebeli, Wabi → Somali Rep. 2°0N 44°0E 88 G3
Schaffhausen Switz. 47°42N 8°39E 66 E5
Schelde → Belgium 51°15N 4°16E 65 C4
Schenectady U.S.A. 42°49N 73°57W 113 D11
Schiedam Neths. 51°55N 4°25E 65 C4
Schiehallion U.K. 56°40N 4°6W 20 A7
Schiphol, Amsterdam ✈ (AMS)
  Neths. 52°18N 4°45E 65 B4
Schleswig Germany 54°31N 9°34E 66 A5
Schleswig-Holstein □ Germany 54°30N 9°30E 66 A5
Schœlcher Martinique 14°36N 61°7W 114 c
Schreiber Canada 48°45N 87°20W 112 A4
Schwäbische Alb Germany 48°20N 9°30E 66 D5
Schwarzwald Germany 48°30N 8°20E 66 D5
Schwerin Germany 53°36N 11°22E 66 B6
Schwyz Switz. 47°2N 8°39E 66 E5
Scilly, Isles of U.K. 49°56N 6°22W 27 H1
Scioto → U.S.A. 38°44N 83°1W 112 F6
Scole U.K. 52°22N 1°10E 25 B11
Scone U.K. 56°25N 3°24W 21 B9
Scopwick U.K. 53°8N 0°24W 23 F8
Scotia Sea Antarctica 56°5S 56°0W 55 B18
Scotland □ U.K. 57°0N 4°0W 64 C5
Scott I. Antarctica 67°0S 179°0E 55 C11
Scottish Borders □ U.K. 55°35N 2°50W 21 C10

Scottsbluff U.S.A. 41°52N 103°40W 110 B6
Scottsburg U.S.A. 38°41N 85°47W 112 F5
Scrabster U.K. 58°36N 3°33W 19 E10
Scranton U.S.A. 41°25N 75°40W 113 E10
Scremerston U.K. 55°44N 2°0W 22 A5
Scunthorpe U.K. 53°36N 0°39W 23 E7
Scutari Albania 42°4N 19°32E 71 C8
Scutari Turkey 41°1N 29°0E 86 A2
Seaford U.K. 50°47N 0°7E 25 E9
Seaford U.S.A. 38°39N 75°37W 113 F10
Seaforth, L. U.K. 57°52N 6°36W 18 G4
Seaham U.K. 54°50N 1°20W 22 C6
Seahouses U.K. 55°34N 1°39W 22 A5
Seal → Canada 59°4N 94°48W 108 D10
Seamer U.K. 54°15N 0°26W 22 D8
Seascale U.K. 54°24N 3°29W 22 D2
Seaton Cumb., U.K. 54°40N 3°31W 22 C1
Seaton Devon, U.K. 50°42N 3°5W 27 F7
Seaton Delaval U.K. 55°5N 1°33W 22 B5
Seattle U.S.A. 47°36N 122°19W 110 A2
Sebastián Vizcaíno, B.
  Mexico 28°0N 114°30W 114 B2
Şebinkarahisar Turkey 40°22N 38°28E 73 F6
Sedalia U.S.A. 38°42N 93°14W 111 C8
Sedan France 49°43N 4°57E 68 B6
Sedbergh U.K. 54°20N 2°31W 22 D3
Sedgefield U.K. 54°40N 1°26W 22 C6
Seend U.K. 51°21N 2°4W 24 D4
Segesta Italy 37°56N 12°50E 70 F5
Ségou Mali 13°30N 6°16W 94 F4
Segovia Spain 40°57N 4°10W 69 B3
Séguéla Ivory C. 7°55N 6°40W 94 G4
Sehore India 23°10N 77°5E 84 H10
Seil U.K. 56°18N 5°38W 20 B4
Seine → France 49°26N 0°26E 68 B4
Sekondi-Takoradi Ghana 4°58N 1°45W 94 H5
Selborne U.K. 51°6N 0°56W 25 D7
Selby U.K. 53°47N 1°5W 23 E6
Selebi-Pikwe Botswana 21°58S 27°48E 97 J5
Selenge Mörön → Asia 52°16N 106°16E 80 A5
Sélestat France 48°16N 7°26E 68 B7
Selkirk Canada 50°10N 96°55W 108 D10
Selkirk U.K. 55°33N 2°50W 21 C10
Selkirk Mts. Canada 51°15N 117°40W 108 D8
Selma U.S.A. 32°25N 87°1W 111 D9
Selsey U.S.A. 50°44N 0°47W 25 E7
Selsey Bill U.K. 50°43N 0°47W 25 E7
Selvas Brazil 6°30S 67°0W 120 C3
Selwyn L. Canada 60°0N 104°30W 108 C9
Selwyn Mts. Canada 63°0N 130°0W 108 C6
Semarang Indonesia 7°0S 110°26E 83 D3
Semey Kazakhstan 50°30N 80°10E 78 D9
Semnān Iran 35°40N 53°23E 87 C8
Sena Madureira Brazil 9°5S 68°45W 120 C3
Sendai Japan 38°15N 140°53E 82 D7
Seneca L. U.S.A. 42°40N 76°54W 112 D9
Senegal ■ W. Afr. 14°30N 14°30W 94 F3
Sénégal → W. Afr. 15°48N 16°32W 94 E2
Senegambia Africa 12°45N 12°0W 90 E2
Senhor-do-Bonfim Brazil 10°30S 40°10W 122 B2
Senja Norway 69°25N 17°30E 63 D7
Senlis France 49°13N 2°35E 68 B5
Sennen U.K. 50°4N 5°42W 27 G2
Sens France 48°11N 3°15E 68 B5
Seoul S. Korea 37°31N 126°58E 81 C7
Seph → U.K. 54°18N 1°9W 22 D6
Sept-Îles Canada 50°13N 66°22W 109 D13
Seram Indonesia 3°10S 129°0E 83 D4
Seram Sea Indonesia 2°30S 128°30E 83 D4
Serang Indonesia 6°8S 106°10E 83 D2
Serbia ■ Europe 43°20N 20°0E 71 B9
Serdar Turkmenistan 39°4N 56°23E 87 B9
Seremban Malaysia 2°43N 101°53E 83 C2
Serengeti Plain Tanzania 2°40S 35°0E 96 E7
Sergipe □ Brazil 10°30S 37°30W 122 B3
Sergiyev Posad Russia 56°20N 38°10E 72 C6
Serhetabat Turkmenistan 35°20N 62°18E 87 D10
Serifos Greece 37°9N 24°30E 71 F11
Serov Russia 59°29N 60°35E 72 C11
Serowe Botswana 22°25S 26°43E 97 J5
Serpukhov Russia 54°55N 37°28E 72 D6
Serra de Mesa, Barragem de
  Brazil 14°30S 49°10W 122 B1
Serrinha Brazil 11°39S 39°0W 122 B3
Sète France 43°25N 3°42E 68 E5
Sete Lagôas Brazil 19°27S 44°16W 122 C2
Sétif Algeria 36°9N 5°26E 94 A7
Settat Morocco 33°0N 7°40W 94 B4
Settle U.K. 54°5N 2°16W 22 D4
Settlement, The Br. Virgin Is. 18°43N 64°22W 115 e
Setúbal Portugal 38°30N 8°58W 69 C1
Setúbal, B. de Portugal 38°40N 8°56W 69 C1
Seul, Lac Canada 50°20N 92°30W 108 D10
Sevan, L. Armenia 40°30N 45°20E 73 F8
Sevastopol Ukraine 44°35N 33°30E 73 F5
Seven → U.K. 54°12N 0°52W 22 D7
Sevenoaks U.K. 51°16N 0°11E 25 D9
Severn → Canada 56°2N 87°36W 109 D11
Severn → U.K. 51°35N 2°40W 24 C3
Severn Beach U.K. 51°33N 2°39W 24 C3
Severn Stoke U.K. 52°6N 2°12W 24 B4
Severnaya Zemlya Russia 79°0N 100°0E 79 B11
Severodvinsk Russia 64°27N 39°58E 72 B6
Severomorsk Russia 69°5N 33°27E 72 A5
Sevier → U.S.A. 39°4N 113°6W 110 C4
Sevier L. U.S.A. 38°54N 113°9W 110 C4
Seville Spain 37°23N 5°58W 69 D2
Seward U.S.A. 60°7N 149°27W 108 C5
Seward Peninsula U.S.A. 65°30N 166°0W 108 C3
Seychelles ■ Ind. Oc. 5°0S 56°0E 91 G9
Seyðisfjörður Iceland 65°16N 13°57E 63 A3
Seydişehir Turkey 37°25N 31°51E 73 G5
Seymour U.S.A. 38°58N 85°53W 112 F5
Sfântu Gheorghe Romania 45°52N 25°48E 67 F13
Sfax Tunisia 34°49N 10°48E 95 B8
Shaanxi □ China 35°0N 109°0E 81 C5
Shache China 38°20N 77°10E 80 C2
Shaftesbury U.K. 51°0N 2°11W 24 D4
Shahjahanpur India 27°54N 79°57E 84 F11

Shakhty Russia 47°40N 40°16E 73 E7
Shaki Nigeria 8°41N 3°21E 94 G6
Shaldon U.K. 50°32N 3°31W 27 F6
Shaluli Shan China 30°40N 99°55E 80 C4
Shamo, L. Ethiopia 5°45N 37°30E 88 F2
Shan □ Burma 21°30N 98°30E 85 J21
Shandong □ China 36°0N 118°0E 81 C6
Shandong Pen. China 37°0N 121°0E 81 C7
Shanghai China 31°15N 121°26E 81 C7
Shangqiu China 34°26N 115°36E 81 C6
Shangrao China 28°25N 117°59E 81 D6
Shangshui China 33°42N 114°35E 81 C6
Shanklin U.K. 50°38N 1°11W 24 E6
Shannon → Ireland 52°35N 9°30W 30 C5
Shannon ✈ (SNN) Ireland 52°42N 8°57W 30 C5
Shannon, Mouth of the
  Ireland 52°30N 9°55W 30 D3
Shantou China 23°18N 116°40E 81 D6
Shanxi □ China 37°0N 112°0E 81 C6
Shaoguan China 24°48N 113°35E 81 D6
Shaoxing China 30°0N 120°35E 81 C7
Shaoyang China 27°14N 111°25E 81 D6
Shap U.K. 54°32N 2°40W 22 C3
Shapinsay U.K. 59°3N 2°51W 19 D12
Shaqra' Si. Arabia 25°15N 45°16E 86 E6
Shaqrā' Yemen 13°22N 45°44E 88 E4
Sharjah U.A.E. 25°23N 55°26E 87 E8
Shark B. Australia 25°30S 113°32E 98 F1
Sharm el Sheikh Egypt 27°53N 34°18E 86 E3
Sharon U.S.A. 41°14N 80°31W 112 E7
Sharpness U.K. 51°43N 2°28W 24 C4
Sharya Russia 58°22N 45°20E 72 C8
Shashi China 30°25N 112°14E 81 C6
Shasta, Mt. U.S.A. 41°25N 122°12W 110 B2
Shatt al Arab Asia 29°57N 48°34E 86 D7
Shawano U.S.A. 44°47N 88°36W 112 C3
Shawbury U.K. 52°48N 2°39W 23 G3
Shawinigan Canada 46°35N 72°50W 109 E12
Shawnee U.S.A. 35°20N 96°55W 111 C7
Shebbear U.K. 50°51N 4°15W 27 F5
Sheboygan U.S.A. 43°46N 87°45W 112 D4
Sheelin, L. Ireland 53°48N 7°20W 28 D7
Sheep Haven Ireland 55°11N 7°52W 28 A6
Sheerness U.K. 51°26N 0°47E 25 D10
Sheffield U.K. 53°23N 1°28W 23 F6
Shefford U.K. 52°2N 0°20W 25 B8
Shehy Mts. Ireland 51°47N 9°15W 30 E4
Shelburne Canada 43°47N 65°20W 113 D15
Shelby U.S.A. 48°30N 111°51W 110 A4
Shelbyville Ill., U.S.A. 39°24N 88°48W 112 F3
Shelbyville Ind., U.S.A. 39°31N 85°47W 112 F5
Shelekhov G. Russia 59°30N 157°0E 79 D17
Shenandoah U.S.A. 40°49N 76°12W 113 E9
Shenandoah → U.S.A. 39°19N 77°44W 112 F9
Shendī Sudan 16°46N 33°22E 95 E12
Shenfield U.K. 51°38N 0°22E 25 C9
Shenyang China 41°48N 123°27E 81 B7
Shenzhen China 22°32N 114°5E 81 D6
Shepparton Australia 36°23S 145°26E 98 H8
Sheppey, I. of U.K. 51°25N 0°48E 25 D10
Shepshed U.K. 52°47N 1°18W 23 G6
Shepton Mallet U.K. 51°11N 2°33W 24 D3
Sherborne U.K. 50°57N 2°31W 24 E3
Sherborne St. John U.K. 51°17N 1°7W 24 D6
Sherbrooke Canada 45°28N 71°57W 113 C12
Sherburn N. Yorks., U.K. 54°11N 0°32W 22 D7
Sherburn N. Yorks., U.K. 53°48N 1°15W 23 E6
Shere U.K. 51°13N 0°27W 25 D8
Sherfield English U.K. 51°1N 1°34W 24 D5
Sheridan U.S.A. 44°48N 106°58W 110 B5
Sheriff Hutton U.K. 54°5N 1°0W 22 D7
Sheringham U.K. 52°56N 1°13E 25 A11
Sherkin I. Ireland 51°28N 9°26W 30 E4
Sherman U.S.A. 33°38N 96°36W 111 D7
Sherston U.K. 51°34N 2°14W 24 C4
Sherwood Forest U.K. 53°6N 1°7W 23 F6
Shetland □ U.K. 60°30N 1°30W 18 B15
Shetland Is. U.K. 60°30N 1°30W 64 A6
Sheyenne → U.S.A. 47°2N 96°50W 111 A7
Shibām Yemen 15°59N 48°36E 88 D4
Shiel, L. U.K. 56°48N 5°34W 18 J6
Shihezi China 44°15N 86°2E 80 B3
Shijiazhuang China 38°2N 114°28E 81 C6
Shikarpur Pakistan 27°57N 68°39E 84 F6
Shikoku □ Japan 33°30N 133°30E 82 G3
Shilbottle U.K. 55°22N 1°40W 22 B5
Shildon U.K. 54°38N 1°38W 22 C5
Shiliguri India 26°45N 88°25E 85 F16
Shillelagh Ireland 52°45N 6°32W 31 D9
Shillingstone U.K. 50°53N 2°15W 24 E4
Shillong India 25°35N 91°53E 85 G17
Shimla India 31°2N 77°9E 84 D10
Shimoga India 13°57N 75°32E 84 N9
Shimonoseki Japan 33°58N 130°55E 82 G2
Shin, L. U.K. 58°5N 4°30W 19 F8
Shinyanga Tanzania 3°45S 33°27E 96 E6
Shipdham U.K. 52°38N 0°54E 25 A10
Shipley U.K. 53°50N 1°47W 23 E5
Shipston-on-Stour U.K. 52°3N 1°37W 24 B5
Shipton under Wychwood
  U.K. 51°51N 1°36W 24 C5
Shīrāz Iran 29°42N 52°30E 87 D8
Shire → Africa 17°42S 35°19E 97 H7
Shirebrook U.K. 53°12N 1°13E 23 F6
Shivpuri India 25°26N 77°42E 84 G10
Shizuishan China 39°15N 106°50E 80 C5
Shizuoka Japan 34°57N 138°24E 82 F6
Shoeburyness U.K. 51°32N 0°49E 25 C10
Shoreham by Sea U.K. 50°50N 0°16W 25 E8
Shreveport U.S.A. 32°31N 93°45W 111 D8
Shrewsbury U.K. 52°43N 2°45W 23 G3
Shrewton U.K. 51°12N 1°54W 24 D5
Shrirampur India 22°44N 88°21E 85 H16
Shrivenham U.K. 51°36N 1°38W 24 C5
Shropshire □ U.K. 52°36N 2°45W 23 G3

Shuangliao China 43°29N 123°30E 81 B7
Shuangyashan China 46°28N 131°5E 81 B8
Shule China 39°25N 76°3E 80 C2
Shumagin Is. U.S.A. 55°7N 160°30W 108 D4
Shumen Bulgaria 43°18N 26°55E 71 C12
Shwebo Burma 22°30N 95°45E 85 H19
Si Kiang → China 22°5N 113°20E 81 D6
Siahan Range Pakistan 27°30N 64°40E 84 F4
Sialkot Pakistan 32°32N 74°30E 84 C9
Šiauliai Lithuania 55°56N 23°15E 63 F8
Šibenik Croatia 43°48N 15°54E 70 C6
Siberia Russia 60°0N 100°0E 79 C11
Siberut Indonesia 1°30S 99°0E 83 D1
Sibi Pakistan 29°30N 67°54E 84 E5
Sibiu Romania 45°45N 24°9E 67 F13
Sible Hedingham U.K. 51°59N 0°37E 25 C10
Sibolga Indonesia 1°42N 98°45E 83 C1
Sibsey U.K. 53°2N 0°1E 23 F9
Sibu Malaysia 2°18N 111°49E 83 C3
Sibuyan Sea Phil. 12°30N 122°20E 83 B4
Sichuan □ China 30°30N 103°0E 80 C5
Sicily Italy 37°30N 14°30E 70 F6
Sicuani Peru 14°21S 71°10W 120 D2
Sidbury U.K. 50°42N 3°14W 27 F7
Sidi-bel-Abbès Algeria 35°13N 0°39W 94 A5
Sidlaw Hills U.K. 56°32N 3°2W 21 A9
Sidlesham U.K. 50°47N 0°47W 25 E7
Sidmouth U.K. 50°40N 3°15W 27 F7
Sidney Nebr., U.S.A. 41°8N 102°59W 110 B6
Sidney Ohio, U.S.A. 40°17N 84°9W 112 E5
Sidra, G. of Libya 31°40N 18°30E 95 B9
Siedlce Poland 52°10N 22°20E 67 B12
Siegen Germany 50°51N 8°0E 66 C5
Siena Italy 43°19N 11°21E 70 C4
Sierra Blanca Peak U.S.A. 33°23N 105°49W 110 D5
Sierra Leone ■ W. Afr. 9°0N 12°0W 94 G3
Sierra Madre Occidental
  Mexico 27°0N 107°0W 114 B3
Sierra Madre Oriental Mexico 25°0N 100°0W 114 C5
Sierra Nevada Spain 37°3N 3°15W 69 D4
Sierra Nevada U.S.A. 39°0N 120°30W 110 C2
Sierra Vista U.S.A. 31°33N 110°18W 110 D4
Sifnos Greece 37°0N 24°45E 71 F11
Sighty Crag U.K. 55°7N 2°38W 22 B3
Sikar India 27°33N 75°10E 84 F9
Sikasso Mali 11°18N 5°35W 94 F4
Sikeston U.S.A. 36°53N 89°35W 112 G3
Sikhote Alin Ra. Russia 45°0N 136°0E 79 E15
Sikkim □ India 27°50N 88°30E 85 F16
Silesia Poland 51°0N 16°30E 66 C9
Silifke Turkey 36°22N 33°58E 73 G5
Siling Co China 31°50N 89°20E 80 C3
Silloth U.K. 54°52N 3°23W 22 C2
Silsden U.K. 53°55N 1°55W 23 E5
Silver City U.S.A. 32°46N 108°17W 110 D5
Silvermine Mts. Ireland 52°47N 8°15W 30 C6
Silverstone U.K. 52°5N 1°2W 24 B6
Silverton U.K. 50°49N 3°29W 27 F7
Simbirsk Russia 54°20N 48°25E 72 D8
Simcoe, L. Canada 44°25N 79°20W 112 C8
Simeulue Indonesia 2°45N 95°45E 83 C1
Simferopol Ukraine 44°55N 34°3E 73 F5
Simi Greece 36°35N 27°50E 71 F12
Simonsbath U.K. 51°8N 3°46W 27 E6
Simonside U.K. 55°17N 1°59W 22 B5
Simplonpass Switz. 46°15N 8°3E 66 E5
Simpson Desert Australia 25°0S 137°0E 98 F6
Simpson Pen. Canada 68°34N 88°45W 109 C11
Sinai Egypt 29°0N 34°0E 95 C12
Sincelejo Colombia 9°18N 75°24W 120 B2
Sinclair's B. U.K. 58°31N 3°5W 19 E11
Sind Sagar Doab Pakistan 32°0N 71°30E 84 D7
Sindh □ Pakistan 26°0N 69°0E 84 G6
Sines Portugal 37°56N 8°51W 69 D1
Singapore ■ Asia 1°17N 103°51E 83 C2
Singaraja Indonesia 8°7S 115°6E 83 D3
Singida Tanzania 4°49S 34°48E 96 E6
Singkawang Indonesia 1°0N 108°57E 83 C2
Singleton U.K. 50°55N 0°46W 25 E7
Sinkiang □ China 42°0N 86°0E 80 C3
Sinop Turkey 42°1N 35°11E 73 F6
Sintra Portugal 38°47N 9°25W 69 C1
Sion Switz. 46°14N 7°20E 66 E4
Sion Mills U.K. 54°48N 7°29W 28 B7
Sioux City U.S.A. 42°30N 96°24W 111 B7
Sioux Falls U.S.A. 43°33N 96°44W 111 B7
Sioux Lookout Canada 50°10N 91°50W 108 D10
Siping China 43°8N 124°21E 81 B7
Sir James MacBrien, Mt.
  Canada 62°7N 127°41W 108 C7
Siracusa Italy 37°4N 15°17E 70 F6
Sirajganj Bangla. 24°25N 89°47E 85 G16
Sirsa India 29°33N 75°4E 84 E9
Sīstān Asia 30°50N 61°0E 87 D10
Sitapur India 27°38N 80°45E 85 F12
Sitges Spain 41°17N 1°47E 69 B6
Sitka U.S.A. 57°3N 135°20W 108 D6
Sittingbourne U.K. 51°21N 0°45E 25 D10
Sittwe Burma 20°18N 92°45E 85 J18
Sivas Turkey 39°43N 36°58E 73 G6
Sivrihisar Turkey 39°30N 31°35E 73 G5
Sīwa Egypt 29°11N 25°31E 95 C11
Siwalik Range Nepal 28°0N 83°0E 85 F13
Siwan India 26°13N 84°21E 85 F14
Six Cross Roads Barbados 13°7N 59°28W 115 g
Sixmilebridge Ireland 52°44N 8°46W 30 C5
Sizewell U.K. 52°12N 1°37E 25 B12
Sjælland Denmark 55°30N 11°30E 63 F6
Skagerrak Denmark 57°30N 9°0E 63 F5
Skagway U.S.A. 59°28N 135°19W 108 D6
Skeena → Canada 54°9N 130°5W 108 D6
Skegness U.K. 53°9N 0°20E 23 F9
Skeleton Coast Namibia 20°0S 13°0E 97 J2
Skellefteå Sweden 64°45N 20°50E 63 E8
Skellefteälv → Sweden 64°45N 21°10E 63 E8
Skellingthorpe U.K. 53°15N 0°37W 23 F7
Skelmersdale U.K. 53°33N 2°48W 23 E3
Skelmorlie U.K. 55°52N 4°53W 20 C6

Skelton

Talgarth

Skelton Cleve., U.K. 54°34N 0°58W 22 C7
Skelton Cumb., U.K. 54°43N 2°51W 22 C3
Skerries, The U.K. 53°25N 4°36W 26 A4
Skiathos Greece 39°12N 23°30E 71 E10
Skibbereen Ireland 51°33N 9°16W 30 E4
Skiddaw U.K. 54°39N 3°9W 22 C2
Skien Norway 59°12N 9°35E 63 F5
Skikda Algeria 36°50N 6°58E 94 A7
Skipsea U.K. 53°58N 0°13W 23 E8
Skipton U.K. 53°58N 2°3W 23 E4
Skopelos Greece 39°9N 23°47E 71 E10
Skopje Macedonia 42°1N 21°26E 71 C9
Skovorodino Russia 54°0N 124°0E 79 D14
Skowhegan U.S.A. 44°46N 69°43W 113 C13
Skull Ireland 51°32N 9°34W 30 E3
Skye U.K. 57°15N 6°10W 18 H5
Skyros Greece 38°55N 24°34E 71 E11
Slaidburn U.K. 53°58N 2°26W 23 E4
Slaney → Ireland 52°26N 6°33W 31 D9
Slatina Romania 44°28N 24°22E 67 F13
Slave → 61°18N 113°39W 108 C8
Slave Coast W. Afr. 6°0N 2°30E 94 G6
Slave Lake Canada 55°17N 114°43W 108 D8
Sleaford U.K. 53°0N 0°24W 23 F8
Sleat, Sd. of U.K. 57°5N 5°47W 18 H6
Sledmere U.K. 54°4N 0°35W 22 D7
Sleeper Is. Canada 58°30N 81°0W 109 D11
Sleights U.K. 54°27N 0°40W 22 D7
Slieve Aughty Ireland 53°4N 8°30W 30 B5
Slieve Bloom Ireland 53°4N 7°40W 31 B7
Slieve Donard U.K. 54°11N 5°55W 29 C10
Slieve Gamph Ireland 54°6N 9°0W 28 C4
Slieve Gullion U.K. 54°7N 6°26W 29 C9
Slieve League Ireland 54°40N 8°42W 28 B4
Slieve Mish Ireland 52°12N 9°50W 30 D3
Slievenamon Ireland 52°25N 7°34W 31 D7
Sligo Ireland 54°16N 8°28W 28 C5
Sligo □ Ireland 54°8N 8°42W 28 C4
Sligo B. Ireland 54°18N 8°40W 28 C4
Sliven Bulgaria 42°42N 26°19E 71 C12
Slough U.K. 51°30N 0°36W 25 C7
Slovak Rep. ■ Europe 48°30N 20°0E 67 D10
Slovenia ■ Europe 45°58N 14°30E 66 F8
Slovyansk Ukraine 48°55N 37°36E 73 E6
Slupsk Poland 54°30N 17°3E 67 A9
Slutsk Belarus 53°2N 27°31E 72 D4
Slyne Hd. Ireland 53°25N 10°10W 28 E1
Smallwood Res. Canada 54°5N 64°30W 109 D13
Smederevo Serbia 44°40N 20°57E 71 B9
Smerwick Harbour Ireland 52°12N 10°23W 30 D2
Smethwick U.K. 52°30N 1°57W 23 G5
Smithfield U.K. 54°59N 2°51W 22 C3
Smiths Falls Canada 44°55N 76°0W 113 C9
Smoky → Canada 56°10N 117°21W 108 D8
Smoky Hill → U.S.A. 39°4N 96°48W 111 C7
Smolensk Russia 54°45N 32°5E 72 D5
Snaefell I. of Man 54°16N 4°27W 29 C13
Snainton U.K. 54°14N 0°35W 22 D7
Snaith U.K. 53°42N 1°1W 23 E6
Snake → U.S.A. 46°12N 119°2W 110 A3
Snape U.K. 52°10N 1°30E 25 B12
Snettisham U.K. 52°53N 0°31E 25 A10
Snizort, L. U.K. 57°33N 6°28W 18 G5
Snøhetta Norway 62°19N 9°16E 63 E5
Snow Hill U.K. 38°11N 75°24W 113 F10
Snowdon U.K. 53°4N 4°5W 26 A5
Snowdonia △ U.K. 53°7N 3°59W 26 A6
Snowy Mts. Australia 36°30S 148°20E 98 H8
Sobat, Nahr → Sudan 9°22N 31°33E 95 G12
Sobradinho, Reprêsa de Brazil 9°30S 42°0W 122 A2
Sobral Brazil 3°50S 40°20W 120 C5
Soc Trang Vietnam 9°37N 105°50E 83 C2
Sochi Russia 43°35N 39°40E 73 F6
Société, Îs. de la French Polynesia 17°0S 151°0W 103 J12
Socorro U.S.A. 34°4N 106°54W 110 D5
Socotra Yemen 12°30N 54°0E 88 E5
Söderhamn Sweden 61°18N 17°10E 63 E7
Sofia Bulgaria 42°45N 23°20E 71 C10
Sognefjorden Norway 61°10N 5°50E 63 E5
Sohâg Egypt 26°33N 31°43E 95 C12
Soham U.K. 52°21N 0°21E 25 B9
Soissons France 49°25N 3°19E 68 B5
Sokhumi Georgia 43°0N 41°0E 73 F7
Sokodé Togo 9°0N 1°11E 94 G6
Sokoto Nigeria 13°2N 5°16E 94 F7
Solapur India 17°43N 75°56E 84 L9
Soldotna U.S.A. 60°29N 151°3W 108 C4
Soledad Colombia 10°55N 74°46W 120 A2
Solent, The U.K. 50°45N 1°25W 24 E6
Solihull U.K. 52°26N 1°47W 23 H5
Solikamsk Russia 59°38N 56°50E 72 C10
Solingen Germany 51°10N 7°5E 66 C4
Sóller Spain 39°46N 2°43E 69 C7
Sologne France 47°40N 1°45E 68 C4
Solomon Is. ■ Pac. Oc. 6°0S 155°0E 99 B10
Solomon Sea Papua N. G. 7°0S 150°0E 98 B9
Solon China 46°32N 121°10E 81 B7
Solothurn Switz. 47°13N 7°32E 66 E4
Solway Firth U.K. 54°49N 3°35W 22 C1
Somali Pen. Africa 7°0N 46°0E 90 F8
Somali Rep. ■ Africa 7°0N 47°0E 88 F4
Somaliland □ Somali Rep. 9°0N 46°0E 88 F4
Sombrerete Mexico 23°38N 103°39W 114 C4
Somerby U.K. 52°42N 0°50W 23 G7
Somerset U.K. 51°9N 3°0W 24 D2
Somerset □ U.K. 51°9N 3°0W 24 D2
Somerset I. Canada 73°30N 93°0W 108 A10
Somersham U.K. 52°24N 0°1W 25 B8
Somerton U.K. 51°2N 2°43W 24 D3
Somme → France 50°11N 1°38E 68 A4
Songhua Hu China 43°35N 126°50E 81 B7
Songhua Jiang → China 47°45N 132°30E 81 B8
Songkhla Thailand 7°13N 100°37E 83 C2
Songpan China 32°40N 103°30E 80 C5
Sonning U.K. 51°28N 0°54W 25 D7
Sonora → Mexico 29°5N 110°55W 114 B2
Sonoran Desert U.S.A. 33°40N 113°30W 110 D4

Sonoyta Mexico 31°51N 112°50W 114 A2
Sonsonate El Salv. 13°43N 89°44W 114 E7
Sopot Poland 54°27N 18°31E 67 A10
Sorel-Tracy Canada 46°0N 73°10W 113 C11
Soria Spain 41°43N 2°32W 69 B4
Sorocaba Brazil 23°31S 47°27W 122 D1
Søroya Norway 70°40N 22°30E 63 C8
Sosnowiec Poland 50°20N 19°10E 67 C10
Soufrière Guadeloupe 16°5N 61°40W 114 b
Soufrière St. Lucia 13°51N 61°3W 115 f
Soufrière Bay St. Lucia 11°50N 61°21W 115 f
Sound, The U.K. 50°20N 4°10W 27 G5
Souris → Canada 49°40N 99°34W 108 E9
Sousse Tunisia 35°50N 10°38E 95 A8
South Africa ■ Africa 32°0S 23°0E 97 L4
South America 10°0S 60°0W 116 E5
South Atlantic Ocean 20°0S 10°0W 50 F9
South Australia □ Australia 32°0S 139°0E 98 G6
South Ayrshire □ U.K. 55°18N 4°41W 20 D6
South Bend U.S.A. 41°41N 86°15W 112 E4
South Benfleet U.K. 51°33N 0°36E 25 C10
South Brent U.K. 50°25N 3°51W 27 G6
South Carolina □ U.S.A. 34°0N 81°0W 111 D10
South Cave U.K. 53°47N 0°37W 23 E7
South Charleston U.S.A. 38°22N 81°44W 112 F7
South China Sea Asia 10°0N 113°0E 83 C3
South Dakota □ U.S.A. 44°15N 100°0W 110 B7
South Dorset Downs U.K. 50°40N 2°26W 24 E4
South Downs U.K. 50°52N 0°25W 25 E8
South East C. Australia 43°40S 146°50E 98 J8
South Elkington U.K. 53°23N 0°4W 23 F8
South Esk → U.K. 56°43N 2°31W 19 J12
South Foreland U.K. 51°8N 1°24E 25 D11
South Georgia Antarctica 54°30S 37°0W 55 B1
South Harris U.K. 57°50N 7°0W 18 G4
South Hayling U.K. 50°47N 0°58W 25 E7
South Honshu Ridge Pac. Oc. 23°0N 143°0E 102 E6
South I. N.Z. 44°0S 170°0E 99 J13
South Korea ■ Asia 36°0N 128°0E 81 C7
South Lanarkshire □ U.K. 55°37N 3°53W 21 C8
South Magnetic Pole Antarctica 64°8S 138°8E 55 C9
South Molton U.K. 51°1N 3°51W 27 E6
South Nahanni → Canada 61°3N 123°21W 108 C7
South Negril Pt. Jamaica 18°16N 78°22W 114 a
South Orkney Is. Antarctica 63°0S 45°0W 55 C18
South Ossetia □ Georgia 42°21N 44°2E 73 F7
South Petherton U.K. 50°57N 2°46W 24 E3
South Petherwin U.K. 50°36N 4°24W 27 F5
South Platte → U.S.A. 41°7N 100°42W 110 B6
South Pole Antarctica 90°0S 0°0E 55 E
South Pt. Barbados 13°2N 59°32W 115 g
South Queensferry U.K. 56°0N 3°23W 21 C9
South Ronaldsay U.K. 58°48N 2°58W 19 E12
South Sandwich Is. Antarctica 57°0S 27°0W 55 B1
South Saskatchewan → Canada 53°15N 105°5W 108 D9
South Shetland Is. Antarctica 62°0S 59°0W 55 C18
South Shields U.K. 55°0N 1°25W 22 C6
South Tawton U.K. 50°44N 3°55W 27 F6
South Tyne → U.K. 54°59N 2°8W 22 C4
South Uist U.K. 57°20N 7°15W 18 H3
South Woodham Ferrers U.K. 51°39N 0°37E 25 C10
South Yorkshire □ U.K. 53°27N 1°36W 23 F5
Southam U.K. 52°15N 1°23W 24 B6
Southampton U.K. 50°54N 1°23W 24 E6
Southampton I. Canada 64°30N 84°0W 109 C11
Southborough U.K. 51°9N 0°16E 25 D9
Southend-on-Sea U.K. 51°32N 0°44E 25 C10
Southern Alps N.Z. 43°41S 170°11E 99 J13
Southern Indian L. Canada 57°10N 98°30W 108 D10
Southern Ocean Antarctica 62°0S 60°0E 53 H13
Southern Uplands U.K. 55°28N 3°52W 21 D8
Southery U.K. 52°31N 0°24E 25 A9
Southminster U.K. 51°40N 0°51E 25 C10
Southport U.K. 53°39N 3°0W 23 E2
Southwark □ U.K. 51°29N 0°6W 25 D8
Southwell U.K. 53°4N 0°57W 23 F7
Southwick U.K. 50°50N 0°13W 25 E8
Southwold U.K. 52°20N 1°41E 25 B12
Sovetsk Russia 55°6N 21°50E 63 F8
Sowerby U.K. 54°14N 1°21W 22 D6
Soweto S. Africa 26°14S 27°52E 97 K5
Spain ■ Europe 39°0N 4°0W 69 B4
Spalding U.K. 52°48N 0°9W 23 G8
Spanish Canada 46°12N 82°20W 112 B6
Spanish Town Br. Virgin Is. 17°43N 64°26W 115 e
Spanish Town Jamaica 18°0N 76°57W 114 a
Sparkford U.K. 51°2N 2°33W 24 D3
Sparks U.S.A. 39°32N 119°45W 110 C3
Sparta Greece 37°5N 22°25E 71 F10
Sparta U.S.A. 43°56N 90°49W 112 D2
Spartanburg U.S.A. 34°56N 81°57W 111 D10
Spartivento, C. Italy 37°55N 16°4E 70 F7
Speightstown Barbados 13°15N 59°39W 115 g
Speke U.K. 53°21N 2°52W 23 F3
Spencer U.S.A. 43°9N 95°9W 111 B7
Spencer G. Australia 34°0S 137°20E 98 G6
Spennymoor U.K. 54°42N 1°36W 22 C5
Sperrin Mts. U.K. 54°50N 7°0W 29 B7
Spey → U.K. 57°40N 3°6W 19 G11
Spilsby U.K. 53°10N 0°6E 23 F9
Spithead U.K. 50°45N 1°10W 24 E6
Split Croatia 43°31N 16°26E 70 C7
Spofforth U.K. 53°57N 1°27W 23 E6
Spokane U.S.A. 47°40N 117°24W 110 A3
Spooner U.S.A. 45°50N 91°53W 112 C2
Spratly Is. S. China Sea 8°20N 112°0E 83 C3
Spree → Germany 52°32N 13°12E 66 B7
Spring Hall Barbados 13°18N 59°36W 115 g
Springbok S. Africa 29°42S 17°54E 97 K3
Springfield Ill., U.S.A. 39°48N 89°39W 112 F3
Springfield Mass., U.S.A. 42°6N 72°35W 113 D11
Springfield Mo., U.S.A. 37°13N 93°17W 111 C8
Springfield Ohio, U.S.A. 39°55N 83°49W 112 F6
Springhill Canada 45°40N 64°4W 113 C15
Springs S. Africa 26°13S 28°25E 97 K5
Sproatley U.K. 53°47N 0°11W 23 E8

Spurn Hd. U.K. 53°35N 0°8E 23 E9
Srebrenica Bos.-H. 44°6N 19°18E 71 B8
Sredinny Ra. Russia 57°0N 160°0E 79 D18
Sri Lanka ■ Asia 7°30N 80°50E 84 R12
Srikakulam India 18°14N 83°58E 85 K13
Srinagar India 34°5N 74°50E 84 B9
Staffa U.K. 56°27N 6°21W 20 B3
Stafford U.K. 52°49N 2°7W 23 G4
Staffordshire □ U.K. 52°53N 2°10W 23 G4
Staindrop U.K. 54°36N 1°47W 22 C5
Staines U.K. 51°26N 0°29W 25 D8
Stainforth U.K. 53°37N 1°0W 23 E7
Stainmore Forest U.K. 54°29N 2°3W 22 C4
Stainton U.K. 53°18N 0°24W 23 F8
Staithes U.K. 54°34N 0°46W 22 C7
Stakhanov Ukraine 48°35N 38°40E 73 E6
Stalbridge U.K. 50°57N 2°23W 24 E4
Stalham U.K. 52°47N 1°31E 25 A12
Stallingborough U.K. 53°36N 0°12W 23 E8
Stalybridge U.K. 53°28N 2°3W 23 F4
Stamford U.K. 52°39N 0°29W 23 G8
Stamford U.S.A. 41°3N 73°32W 113 E11
Stamford Bridge U.K. 54°0N 0°54W 23 E7
Stamfordham U.K. 55°3N 1°53W 22 B5
Standish U.K. 53°35N 2°41W 23 E3
Standish U.S.A. 43°59N 83°57W 112 D6
Stanford on Teme U.K. 52°18N 2°25W 24 B4
Stanhope U.K. 54°45N 2°1W 22 C4
Stanley Falk. Is. 51°40S 59°51W 121 H4
Stanley U.K. 54°53N 1°41W 22 C5
Stannington U.K. 55°7N 1°40W 22 B5
Stanovoy Ra. Russia 55°0N 130°0E 79 D14
Stansted, London ✈ (STN) U.K. 51°54N 0°14E 25 C9
Stansted Mountfitchet U.K. 51°52N 0°11E 25 C9
Stanwix U.K. 54°55N 2°56W 22 C3
Stapleford U.K. 52°57N 1°16W 23 G6
Staplehurst U.K. 51°9N 0°34E 25 D10
Stara Zagora Bulgaria 42°26N 25°39E 71 C11
Staraya Russa Russia 57°58N 31°23E 72 C5
Starbuck I. Kiribati 5°37S 155°55W 103 H12
Start B. U.K. 50°13N 3°39W 27 G6
Start Pt. U.K. 50°13N 3°39W 27 G6
Staryy Oskol Russia 51°19N 37°55E 73 D6
State College U.S.A. 40°48N 77°52W 112 E9
Staten, I. = Estados, I. de Los Argentina 54°40S 64°30W 121 H3
Staunton U.K. 51°57N 2°17W 24 C4
Staunton U.S.A. 38°9N 79°4W 112 F8
Stavanger Norway 58°57N 5°40E 63 F5
Staveley Cumb., U.K. 54°23N 2°48W 22 D3
Staveley Derby., U.K. 53°16N 1°21W 23 F6
Stavropol Russia 45°5N 42°0E 73 E7
Steiermark □ Austria 47°26N 15°0E 66 E8
Steinkjer Norway 64°1N 11°31E 63 E6
Stellarton Canada 45°32N 62°30W 113 C16
Stellenbosch S. Africa 33°58S 18°50E 97 L3
Stenhousemuir U.K. 56°2N 3°48W 21 B8
Stephenville Canada 48°31N 58°30W 109 E14
Steppe Asia 50°0N 50°0E 74 C7
Sterling Colo., U.S.A. 40°37N 103°13W 110 B6
Sterling Ill., U.S.A. 41°48N 89°42W 112 E3
Sterlitamak Russia 53°40N 56°0E 72 D10
Stettiner Haff Germany 53°47N 14°15E 66 B8
Stettler Canada 52°19N 112°40W 108 D8
Steubenville U.S.A. 40°22N 80°37W 112 E7
Stevenage U.K. 51°55N 0°13W 25 C8
Stevens Point U.S.A. 44°31N 89°34W 112 C3
Stevenston U.K. 55°39N 4°45W 20 C6
Stewart Canada 55°56N 129°57W 108 D7
Stewart → Canada 63°19N 139°26W 108 C6
Stewart I. N.Z. 46°58S 167°54E 99 K12
Stewarton U.K. 55°40N 4°32W 20 C6
Steyning U.K. 50°53N 0°18W 25 E8
Steyr Austria 48°3N 14°25E 66 D8
Stikine → Canada 56°40N 132°30W 108 D6
Stillington U.K. 54°6N 1°6W 22 D6
Stillwater U.S.A. 36°7N 94°4W 111 A8
Stiperstones U.K. 52°36N 2°55W 23 G3
Stirling U.K. 56°8N 3°57W 21 B8
Stirling □ U.K. 56°12N 4°18W 20 B7
Stobo U.K. 55°38N 3°17W 21 C9
Stockbridge U.K. 51°7N 1°29W 24 D6
Stockholm Sweden 59°19N 18°4E 63 F7
Stockport U.K. 53°25N 2°9W 23 F4
Stocksbridge U.K. 53°29N 1°35W 23 F5
Stockton U.S.A. 37°58N 121°17W 110 C2
Stockton-on-Tees U.K. 54°35N 1°19W 22 C6
Stoer, Pt. of U.K. 58°16N 5°23W 18 F7
Stoke U.K. 51°26N 0°41E 25 D10
Stoke Ferry U.K. 52°34N 0°31E 25 A10
Stoke Fleming U.K. 50°19N 3°37W 27 G6
Stoke Mandeville U.K. 51°47N 0°47W 25 C7
Stoke-on-Trent U.K. 53°1N 2°11W 23 F4
Stoke Prior U.K. 52°19N 2°4W 24 B4
Stokesley U.K. 54°28N 1°12W 22 D6
Stone Bucks., U.K. 51°48N 0°52W 25 C7
Stone Staffs., U.K. 52°55N 2°9W 23 G4
Stonehaven U.K. 56°59N 2°12W 19 J13
Stonehouse U.K. 51°45N 2°16W 24 C4
Stonham Aspal U.K. 52°12N 1°8E 25 B11
Stony Stratford U.K. 52°3N 0°50W 25 B7
Stony Tunguska → Russia 61°50N 90°13E 79 C11
Stora Lulevatten Sweden 67°10N 19°30E 63 D7
Storavan Sweden 65°45N 18°10E 63 D7
Store Bælt Denmark 55°20N 11°0E 63 F6
Stormberge S. Africa 31°16S 26°17E 97 L5
Stornoway U.K. 58°13N 6°23W 18 F5
Storsjön Sweden 63°9N 14°30E 63 E6
Stort → U.K. 51°46N 0°2E 25 C9
Storuman Sweden 65°5N 17°10E 63 D7
Stotfold U.K. 52°1N 0°13W 25 B8
Stour → Dorset, U.K. 50°43N 1°47W 24 E6
Stour → Kent, U.K. 51°18N 1°22E 25 D11
Stour → Suffolk, U.K. 51°57N 1°4E 25 C11
Stour → Worcs., U.K. 52°21N 2°17W 24 B4
Stourbridge U.K. 52°28N 2°8W 23 H4

Stourport-on-Severn U.K. 52°21N 2°17W 24 B4
Stow U.K. 55°42N 2°50W 21 C10
Stow Bardolph U.K. 52°38N 0°24E 25 A9
Stow-on-the-Wold U.K. 51°56N 1°42W 24 C5
Stowmarket U.K. 52°12N 1°0E 25 B10
Strabane U.K. 54°50N 7°27W 28 B7
Stradbroke U.K. 52°19N 1°16E 25 B11
Stralsund Germany 54°18N 13°4E 66 A7
Strangford L. U.K. 54°30N 5°37W 29 C10
Stranraer U.K. 54°54N 5°1W 20 D5
Strasbourg France 48°35N 7°42E 68 B7
Stratford Canada 43°23N 81°0W 112 D7
Stratford St. Mary U.K. 51°58N 1°0E 25 C10
Stratford-upon-Avon U.K. 52°12N 1°42W 24 B5
Strath Avon → U.K. 57°18N 3°23W 19 H11
Strath Dearn U.K. 57°20N 4°0W 19 H9
Strath Glass U.K. 57°22N 4°42W 19 H8
Strath Halladale U.K. 58°30N 3°51W 19 F10
Strath Naver U.K. 58°24N 4°12W 19 F9
Strath of Kildonan U.K. 58°14N 3°56W 19 F10
Strath Spey U.K. 57°9N 3°49W 19 H10
Strath Tay U.K. 56°40N 3°48W 21 A8
Strathaven U.K. 55°40N 4°5W 20 C7
Strathbogie U.K. 57°25N 2°45W 19 H12
Strathmore Angus, U.K. 56°37N 3°7W 19 J11
Strathmore Highl., U.K. 58°22N 4°40W 19 F8
Strathpeffer U.K. 57°35N 4°32W 19 G8
Strathroy Canada 42°58N 81°38W 112 D7
Strathy Pt. U.K. 58°36N 4°1W 19 E9
Stratton U.K. 50°49N 4°32W 27 F4
Stratton St. Margaret U.K. 51°35N 1°44W 24 C5
Streatley U.K. 51°31N 1°8W 24 C6
Street U.K. 51°8N 2°44W 24 D3
Strensall U.K. 54°3N 1°4W 22 D6
Stretford U.K. 53°28N 2°17W 23 F4
Stroma U.K. 58°41N 3°7W 19 E11
Strómboli Italy 38°47N 15°13E 70 E6
Stromeferry U.K. 57°21N 5°33W 18 H6
Stromness U.K. 58°58N 3°17W 19 E11
Stronsay U.K. 59°7N 2°35W 19 D12
Stroud U.K. 51°45N 2°13W 24 C4
Stuart L. Canada 54°30N 124°30W 108 D7
Studland U.K. 50°39N 1°58W 24 E5
Studley U.K. 52°16N 1°54W 24 B5
Sturgeon Bay U.S.A. 44°50N 87°23W 112 C4
Sturgeon Falls Canada 46°25N 79°57W 112 B8
Sturminster Marshall U.K. 50°47N 2°5W 24 E4
Sturminster Newton U.K. 50°55N 2°18W 24 E4
Sturt Stony Desert Australia 28°30S 141°0E 98 F6
Sturton U.K. 53°19N 0°39W 23 F7
Stuttgart Germany 48°48N 9°11E 66 D5
Stuttgart U.S.A. 34°30N 91°33W 111 D8
Suakin Sudan 19°8N 37°20E 95 E13
Subotica Serbia 46°6N 19°39E 71 A8
Suceava Romania 47°38N 26°16E 67 E14
Suck → Ireland 53°17N 8°3W 30 B6
Sucre Bolivia 19°0S 65°15W 120 D3
Sudan ■ Africa 15°0N 30°0E 95 E11
Sudbury Canada 46°30N 81°0W 112 B7
Sudbury Derby., U.K. 52°54N 1°45E 23 G5
Sudbury Suffolk, U.K. 52°2N 0°45E 25 B10
Sûdd Sudan 8°20N 30°0E 95 G12
Sudeten Europe 50°20N 16°45E 67 C9
Suez Egypt 29°58N 32°31E 95 C12
Suez, G. of Egypt 28°40N 33°0E 95 C12
Suez Canal Egypt 31°0N 32°20E 95 B12
Suffolk □ U.K. 52°16N 1°0E 25 B11
Sugluk Canada 62°14N 75°38W 109 C12
Şuḩār Oman 24°20N 56°40E 87 E9
Suihua China 46°32N 126°55E 81 B7
Suining China 30°26N 105°35E 80 C5
Suir → Ireland 52°16N 7°9W 31 D8
Sukabumi Indonesia 6°56S 106°50E 83 D2
Sukhona → Russia 61°15N 46°39E 72 C8
Sukkur Pakistan 27°42N 68°54E 84 F6
Sulaiman Range Pakistan 30°30N 69°50E 84 D6
Sulawesi Indonesia 2°0S 120°0E 83 D4
Sullana Peru 4°52S 80°39W 120 C1
Sullom Voe U.K. 60°27N 1°20W 18 B15
Sulu Arch. Phil. 6°0N 121°0E 83 C4
Sulu Sea E. Indies 8°0N 120°0E 83 C4
Sumatra Indonesia 0°40N 100°20E 83 C2
Sumba Indonesia 9°45S 119°35E 83 D3
Sumbawa Indonesia 8°26S 117°30E 83 D3
Sumburgh Hd. U.K. 59°52N 1°17E 18 C15
Sumenep Indonesia 7°1S 113°52E 83 D3
Summer L. U.S.A. 42°50N 120°45W 110 B2
Summerside Canada 46°24N 63°47W 109 E13
Sumqayıt Azerbaijan 40°34N 49°38E 73 F8
Sumter U.S.A. 33°55N 80°21W 111 D10
Sumy Ukraine 50°57N 34°50E 73 D5
Sun Valley U.S.A. 43°42N 114°21W 110 B4
Sunart, L. U.K. 56°43N 5°42W 18 J6
Sunart, L. U.K. 56°42N 5°43W 18 J6
Sunbury U.S.A. 40°52N 76°48W 112 E9
Sunda, Selat Indonesia 6°20S 105°30E 83 D2
Sunda Is. Indonesia 5°0S 105°0E 102 H2
Sundarbans Asia 22°0N 89°0E 85 J16
Sunderland U.K. 54°55N 1°23W 22 C6
Sundsvall Sweden 62°23N 17°17E 63 E7
Sungaipenuh Indonesia 2°1S 101°20E 83 D2
Sunk Island U.K. 53°39N 0°6W 23 E8
Sunninghill U.K. 51°25N 0°39W 25 D7
Sunshine Coast Australia 26°30S 153°0E 98 F9
Superior U.S.A. 46°44N 92°6W 112 B1
Superior, L. N. Amer. 47°0N 87°0W 112 B4
Sûr Lebanon 33°19N 35°16E 86 C3
Sura → Russia 56°6N 46°0E 72 C8
Surabaya Indonesia 7°17S 112°45E 83 D3
Surakarta Indonesia 7°35S 110°48E 83 D3
Surat India 21°12N 72°55E 84 J8
Surgut Russia 61°14N 73°20E 79 C9
Surigao Phil. 9°47N 125°29E 83 C4
Suriname ■ S. Amer. 4°0N 56°0W 120 B4
Surrey □ U.K. 51°15N 0°31W 25 D7
Surt Libya 31°11N 16°39E 95 B9
Surtsey Iceland 63°20N 20°30W 63 B1
Susquehanna → U.S.A. 39°33N 76°5W 112 F9

Sussex Canada 45°45N 65°37W 113 C15
Sutherland U.K. 58°12N 4°50W 19 F8
Sutlej → Pakistan 29°23N 71°3E 84 E7
Sutterton U.K. 52°55N 0°6W 23 G8
Sutton □ U.K. 51°21N 0°11W 25 D8
Sutton Bridge U.K. 52°47N 0°10E 23 G9
Sutton Coldfield U.K. 52°35N 1°49W 23 G5
Sutton Courtenay U.K. 51°39N 1°16W 24 C6
Sutton in Ashfield U.K. 53°8N 1°16W 23 F6
Sutton-on-Sea U.K. 53°18N 0°16E 23 F9
Sutton Scotney U.K. 51°9N 1°20W 24 D6
Suva Fiji 18°6S 178°30E 99 D14
Suvorov Is. Cook Is. 13°15S 163°5W 103 J11
Suwałki Poland 54°8N 22°59E 67 A12
Suzhou China 31°19N 120°38E 81 C7
Svalbard Arctic 78°0N 17°0E 54 B8
Svealand □ Sweden 60°20N 15°0E 63 E7
Sverdrup Chan. Canada 79°56N 96°25W 109 B10
Sverdrup Is. Canada 79°0N 97°0W 109 B10
Svir → Russia 60°30N 32°48E 72 B5
Swadlincote U.K. 52°47N 1°33W 23 G5
Swaffham U.K. 52°39N 0°42E 25 A10
Swakopmund Namibia 22°37S 14°30E 97 J2
Swale → U.K. 54°5N 1°20W 25 D11
Swan Hill Australia 35°20S 143°33E 98 H7
Swan River Canada 52°10N 101°16W 108 D9
Swanage U.K. 50°36N 1°58W 24 E5
Swansea U.K. 51°37N 3°57W 27 D6
Swansea B. U.K. 51°32N 3°57W 27 D6
Swartberge S. Africa 33°20S 22°0E 90 K6
Swaziland ■ Africa 26°30S 31°30E 97 K6
Sweden ■ Europe 57°0N 15°0E 63 F7
Sweetwater U.S.A. 32°28N 100°25W 110 D6
Swellendam S. Africa 34°1S 20°26E 97 L4
Swift Current Canada 50°20N 107°45W 108 D9
Swilly, L. Ireland 55°12N 7°33W 28 A6
Swindon U.K. 51°34N 1°46W 24 C5
Swineshead U.K. 52°57N 0°10W 23 G8
Swinford Ireland 53°57N 8°58W 28 D4
Swinton Borders, U.K. 55°43N 2°15W 21 C11
Swinton Gt. Man., U.K. 53°31N 2°20W 23 E4
Swinton S. Yorks., U.K. 53°29N 1°20W 23 F6
Switzerland ■ Europe 46°30N 8°0E 66 E5
Swords Ireland 53°28N 6°13W 31 B10
Sydney Australia 33°52S 151°12E 98 G9
Sydney Canada 46°7N 60°7W 113 C17
Syktyvkar Russia 61°45N 50°40E 72 B9
Sylhet Bangla. 24°54N 91°52E 85 G17
Sylhet □ Bangla. 24°50N 91°50E 85 G17
Symington U.K. 55°36N 3°36W 21 C8
Symonds Yat U.K. 51°51N 2°38W 24 C3
Syracuse U.S.A. 43°3N 76°9W 113 D9
Syrdarya → Kazakhstan 46°3N 61°0E 78 E8
Syria ■ Asia 35°0N 38°0E 86 C4
Syrian Desert Asia 32°0N 40°0E 86 C4
Syros Greece 37°28N 24°57E 71 F11
Syston U.K. 52°42N 1°3W 23 G6
Syzran Russia 53°12N 48°30E 72 D8
Szczecin Poland 53°27N 14°27E 66 B8
Szechwan = Sichuan □ China 30°30N 103°0E 80 C5
Szeged Hungary 46°16N 20°10E 67 E11
Székesfehérvár Hungary 47°15N 18°25E 67 E10
Szekszárd Hungary 46°22N 18°42E 67 E10
Szolnok Hungary 47°10N 20°15E 67 E11
Szombathely Hungary 47°14N 16°38E 67 E9

T

Ṭabas Iran 33°35N 56°55E 87 C9
Tablas Phil. 12°25N 122°2E 83 B4
Table B. S. Africa 33°35S 18°25E 97 L3
Table Mt. S. Africa 34°0S 18°22E 97 L3
Tabora Tanzania 5°2S 32°50E 96 F6
Tabrīz Iran 38°7N 46°20E 86 B6
Tabuaeran Kiribati 3°51N 159°22W 103 G12
Tacheng China 46°40N 82°58E 80 B3
Tacloban Phil. 11°15N 124°58E 83 B4
Tacna Peru 18°0S 70°20W 120 D2
Tacoma U.S.A. 47°14N 122°26W 110 A2
Tacuarembó Uruguay 31°45S 56°0W 121 F4
Tadcaster U.K. 53°53N 1°16W 23 E6
Tademaït, Plateau du Algeria 28°30N 2°30E 94 C6
Tadley U.K. 51°21N 1°7W 24 D6
Taganrog Russia 47°12N 38°50E 73 E6
Taguatinga Brazil 12°27S 46°22W 122 B1
Tagus → Europe 38°40N 9°24W 69 C1
Tahiti French Polynesia 17°37S 149°27W 103 J13
Tahoe, L. U.S.A. 39°6N 120°2W 110 C2
Tahoua Niger 14°57N 5°16E 94 F7
Tahta Egypt 26°44N 31°32E 95 C12
Taichung Taiwan 24°9N 120°37E 81 D7
Taimyr, L. Russia 74°20N 102°0E 79 B12
Taimyr Peninsula Russia 75°0N 100°0E 79 B11
Tain U.K. 57°49N 4°4W 19 G9
T'ainan Taiwan 23°0N 120°10E 81 D7
Taipei Taiwan 25°4N 121°29E 81 D7
Taiping Malaysia 4°51N 100°44E 83 C2
Taitao, Pen. de Chile 46°30S 75°0W 121 G2
T'aitung Taiwan 22°43N 121°4E 81 D7
Taiwan ■ Asia 23°30N 121°0E 81 D7
Taiyuan China 37°52N 112°33E 81 C6
Ta'izz Yemen 13°35N 44°2E 88 E3
Tajikistan ■ Asia 38°30N 70°0E 87 B12
Tak Thailand 16°52N 99°8E 83 B1
Takamatsu Japan 34°20N 134°5E 82 F4
Takaoka Japan 36°47N 137°0E 82 E5
Takasaki Japan 36°20N 139°0E 82 E6
Takeshima = Tokdo Asia 37°15N 131°52E 82 E2
Takhār □ Afghan. 36°40N 70°0E 87 B12
Takla Makan China 38°0N 83°0E 80 C3
Talara Peru 4°38S 81°18W 120 C1
Talaud, Kepulauan Indonesia 4°30N 126°50E 83 C4
Talavera de la Reina Spain 39°55N 4°46W 69 C3
Talca Chile 35°28S 71°40W 121 F2
Talcahuano Chile 36°40S 73°10W 121 F2
Taldyqorghan Kazakhstan 45°10N 78°45E 79 E9
Talgarth U.K. 52°0N 3°14W 26 D7

Taliabu   Tuticorin

Taliabu *Indonesia* 1°50S 125°0E **83 D4**
Tallaght *Ireland* 53°17N 6°22W **31 B10**
Tallahassee *U.S.A.* 30°27N 84°17W **111 D10**
Tallinn *Estonia* 59°22N 24°48E **63 F8**
Taloyoak *Canada* 69°32N 93°32W **108 C10**
Taltal *Chile* 25°23S 70°33W **121 E2**
Tamale *Ghana* 9°22N 0°50W **94 G5**
Tamana *Kiribati* 2°30S 175°59E **99 A13**
Tamanrasset *Algeria* 22°50N 5°30E **94 D7**
Tamar → *U.K.* 50°27N 4°15W **27 G5**
Tambov *Russia* 52°45N 41°28E **72 D7**
Tame → *U.K.* 52°44N 1°43W **23 G5**
Tamerton Foliot *U.K.* 50°25N 4°11W **27 G5**
Tamil Nadu □ *India* 11°0N 77°0E **84 P10**
Tampa *U.S.A.* 27°56N 82°27W **111 E10**
Tampa B. *U.S.A.* 27°50N 82°30W **111 E10**
Tampere *Finland* 61°30N 23°50E **63 E8**
Tampico *Mexico* 22°13N 97°51W **114 C5**
Tamworth *Australia* 31°7S 150°58E **98 G9**
Tamworth *U.K.* 52°39N 1°41W **23 G5**
Tana → *Kenya* 2°32S 40°31E **96 E8**
Tana → *Norway* 70°30N 28°14E **63 D9**
Tana, L. *Ethiopia* 13°5N 37°30E **88 E2**
Tanami Desert *Australia* 18°50S 132°0E **98 D5**
Tanana → *U.S.A.* 65°10N 151°58W **108 C4**
Tandil *Argentina* 37°15S 59°6W **121 F4**
Tandragee *U.K.* 54°21N 6°24W **29 C9**
Tanezrouft *Algeria* 23°9N 0°11E **94 D6**
Tanga *Tanzania* 5°5S 39°2E **96 F7**
Tanganyika, L. *Africa* 6°40S 30°0E **96 F6**
Tanggula Shan *China* 32°40N 92°10E **80 C4**
Tangier *Morocco* 35°50N 5°49W **94 A4**
Tangshan *China* 39°38N 118°10E **81 C6**
Tanimbar, Kepulauan *Indonesia* 7°30S 131°30E **83 D5**
Tanjungbalai *Indonesia* 2°55N 99°44E **83 C1**
Tanjungpandan *Indonesia* 2°43S 107°38E **83 D2**
Tanjungredeb *Indonesia* 2°9N 117°29E **83 C3**
Tanna *Vanuatu* 19°30S 169°20E **99 D12**
Tanta *Egypt* 30°45N 30°57E **95 B12**
Tanworth *U.K.* 52°20N 1°50W **24 B5**
Tanzania ■ *Africa* 6°0S 34°0E **96 F6**
Taolanaro *Madag.* 25°2S 47°0E **97 K9**
Taos *U.S.A.* 36°24N 105°35W **110 C5**
Tapachula *Mexico* 14°54N 92°17W **114 E6**
Tapajós → *Brazil* 2°24S 54°41W **120 C4**
Tapti → *India* 21°8N 72°41E **84 J8**
Taquaritinga *Brazil* 21°24S 48°30W **122 D1**
Tarakan *Indonesia* 3°20N 117°35E **83 C3**
Taransay *U.K.* 57°54N 7°0W **18 G3**
Táranto *Italy* 40°28N 17°14E **70 D7**
Táranto, G. di *Italy* 40°8N 17°20E **70 D7**
Tarawa *Kiribati* 1°30N 173°0E **102 G9**
Taraz *Kazakhstan* 42°54N 71°22E **87 A12**
Tarbagatai Ra. *Kazakhstan* 48°0N 83°0E **79 E10**
Tarbat Ness *U.K.* 57°52N 3°47W **19 G10**
Tarbert *Argyll & Bute, U.K.* 55°52N 5°25W **20 C5**
Tarbert *W. Isles, U.K.* 57°54N 6°49W **18 G4**
Tarbes *France* 43°15N 0°3E **68 E4**
Tarcoola *Australia* 30°44S 134°36E **98 G5**
Taree *Australia* 31°50S 152°30E **98 G9**
Tarfaya *Morocco* 27°55N 12°55W **94 C3**
Târgoviște *Romania* 44°55N 25°27E **67 F13**
Târgu-Jiu *Romania* 45°5N 23°19E **67 F12**
Târgu Mureş *Romania* 46°31N 24°38E **67 E13**
Tarija *Bolivia* 21°30S 64°40W **120 E3**
Tarim Basin *China* 40°0N 84°0E **80 B3**
Tarim He → *China* 39°30N 88°30E **80 C3**
Tarleton *U.K.* 53°41N 2°50W **23 E3**
Tarn → *France* 44°5N 1°6E **68 E4**
Tarnów *Poland* 50°3N 21°0E **67 C11**
Taroudannt *Morocco* 30°30N 8°52W **94 B4**
Tarporley *U.K.* 53°10N 2°40W **23 F4**
Tarragona *Spain* 41°5N 1°17E **69 B6**
Tarsus *Turkey* 36°58N 34°55E **73 G5**
Tartu *Estonia* 58°20N 26°44E **63 F9**
Ţarţūs *Syria* 34°55N 35°55E **86 C3**
Tashkent *Uzbekistan* 41°20N 69°10E **87 A12**
Tasiilaq *Greenland* 65°40N 37°20W **54 C6**
Tasikmalaya *Indonesia* 7°18S 108°12E **83 D2**
Tasman Sea *Pac. Oc.* 36°0S 160°0E **99 H10**
Tasmania □ *Australia* 42°0S 146°30E **98 J8**
Tassili n' Ajjer *Algeria* 25°47N 8°1E **94 C7**
Tatarstan □ *Russia* 55°30N 51°30E **72 C9**
Tatnam, C. *Canada* 57°16N 91°0W **109 D10**
Tatra *Slovak Rep.* 49°20N 20°0E **67 D11**
Tatta *Pakistan* 24°42N 67°55E **84 G5**
Tattenhall *U.K.* 53°7N 2°46W **23 F3**
Tatuí *Brazil* 23°25S 47°53W **122 D1**
Tatvan *Turkey* 38°31N 42°15E **73 G7**
Taubaté *Brazil* 23°0S 45°36W **122 D1**
Tauern *Austria* 47°15N 12°40E **66 E7**
Taunggyi *Burma* 20°50N 97°0E **85 J20**
Taunton *U.K.* 51°1N 3°5W **24 D2**
Taunton *U.S.A.* 41°54N 71°6W **113 E12**
Taunus *Germany* 50°13N 8°34E **66 C5**
Taurus Mts. *Turkey* 37°0N 32°30E **73 G5**
Tavan Bogd Uul *Mongolia* 49°10N 87°49E **80 B4**
Tavistock *U.K.* 50°33N 4°9W **27 F5**
Taw → *U.K.* 51°4N 4°4W **27 F5**
Tawas City *U.S.A.* 44°16N 83°31W **112 C6**
Tawau *Malaysia* 4°20N 117°55E **83 C3**
Taxkorgan Tajik Zizhixian *China* 37°49N 75°14E **80 C2**
Tay → *U.K.* 56°37N 3°38W **21 A8**
Tay, Firth of *U.K.* 56°25N 3°8W **21 B9**
Tay, L. *U.K.* 56°32N 4°8W **20 A7**
Taylor, Mt. *U.S.A.* 35°14N 107°37W **110 C5**
Taylorville *U.S.A.* 39°33N 89°18W **112 F3**
Tayport *U.K.* 56°27N 2°52W **21 B10**
Taz → *Russia* 67°32N 78°40E **79 C9**
Taza *Morocco* 34°16N 4°6W **94 B5**
Tbilisi *Georgia* 41°43N 44°50E **73 F7**
Tebay *U.K.* 54°26N 2°35W **22 D3**
Tébessa *Algeria* 35°22N 8°8E **94 A7**
Tees → *U.K.* 54°37N 1°10W **22 C6**
Teesdale *U.K.* 54°37N 2°10W **22 C4**
Teesside *U.K.* 54°36N 1°15W **22 C6**
Tegal *Indonesia* 6°52S 109°8E **83 D2**

Tegucigalpa *Honduras* 14°5N 87°14W **114 E7**
Tehrān *Iran* 35°41N 51°25E **87 C7**
Tehuantepec *Mexico* 16°21N 95°13W **114 D5**
Tehuantepec, G. de *Mexico* 15°50N 95°12W **114 D5**
Tehuantepec, Istmo de *Mexico* 17°15N 94°30W **114 D6**
Teifi → *U.K.* 52°5N 4°41W **26 C4**
Teign → *U.K.* 50°32N 3°32W **27 F6**
Teignmouth *U.K.* 50°33N 3°31W **27 F6**
Tejen *Turkmenistan* 37°23N 60°31E **87 B10**
Tekirdağ *Turkey* 40°58N 27°30E **73 F4**
Tel Aviv-Jaffa *Israel* 32°4N 34°48E **86 C3**
Tela *Honduras* 15°40N 87°28W **114 D7**
Telegraph Creek *Canada* 58°0N 131°10W **108 D6**
Teles Pires → *Brazil* 7°21S 58°3W **120 C4**
Telford *U.K.* 52°40N 2°27W **23 G4**
Tell City *U.S.A.* 37°57N 86°46W **112 G4**
Tellicherry *India* 11°45N 75°30E **84 P9**
Telpos Iz *Russia* 63°16N 59°13E **72 B10**
Teluk Intan *Malaysia* 4°3N 101°0E **83 C2**
Tema *Ghana* 5°41N 0°0 **94 G5**
Teme → *U.K.* 52°11N 2°13W **24 B4**
Témiscaming *Canada* 46°44N 79°5W **112 B8**
Temple *U.S.A.* 31°6N 97°21W **111 D7**
Temple Combe *U.K.* 51°0N 2°24W **24 D4**
Temple Ewell *U.K.* 51°8N 1°17E **25 D11**
Temple Sowerby *U.K.* 54°38N 2°36W **22 C3**
Templemore *Ireland* 52°47N 7°51W **30 C7**
Temuco *Chile* 38°45S 72°40W **121 F2**
Tenali *India* 16°15N 80°35E **85 L12**
Tenbury Wells *U.K.* 52°19N 2°35W **24 B3**
Tenby *U.K.* 51°40N 4°42W **26 D4**
Tenerife *Canary Is.* 28°15N 16°35W **94 C2**
Tengchong *China* 25°0N 98°28E **80 D4**
Tengger Desert *China* 38°0N 104°0E **80 C5**
Tennant Creek *Australia* 19°30S 134°15E **98 D5**
Tennessee □ *U.S.A.* 36°0N 86°30W **111 C9**
Tennessee → *U.S.A.* 37°4N 88°34W **111 C9**
Tenterden *U.K.* 51°4N 0°42E **25 D10**
Teófilo Otoni *Brazil* 17°50S 41°30W **122 C2**
Tepic *Mexico* 21°30N 104°54W **114 C4**
Teraina *Kiribati* 4°43N 160°25W **103 G11**
Téramo *Italy* 42°39N 13°42E **70 C5**
Teresina *Brazil* 5°9S 42°45W **120 C5**
Termiz *Uzbekistan* 37°15N 67°15E **87 B11**
Ternate *Indonesia* 0°45N 127°25E **83 C4**
Terni *Italy* 42°34N 12°37E **70 C5**
Ternopil *Ukraine* 49°30N 25°40E **67 C13**
Terrace *Canada* 54°30N 128°35W **108 D7**
Terrassa *Spain* 41°34N 2°1E **69 B7**
Terre Haute *U.S.A.* 39°28N 87°25W **112 F4**
Teruel *Spain* 40°22N 1°8W **69 B5**
Tesiyn Gol → *Mongolia* 50°40N 93°20E **80 A4**
Teslin *Canada* 60°10N 132°43W **108 C6**
Test → *U.K.* 50°56N 1°29W **24 E6**
Tetbury *U.K.* 51°38N 2°10W **24 C4**
Tete *Mozam.* 16°13S 33°33E **97 H6**
Tetney *U.K.* 53°29N 0°1W **23 F8**
Tétouan *Morocco* 35°35N 5°21W **94 A4**
Tetovo *Macedonia* 42°1N 20°59E **71 C9**
Teuco → *Argentina* 25°35S 60°11W **121 E3**
Teutoburger Wald *Germany* 52°5N 8°22E **66 B5**
Teviot → *U.K.* 55°29N 2°38W **21 D10**
Teviotdale *U.K.* 55°25N 2°50W **21 D10**
Teviothead *U.K.* 55°20N 2°56W **21 D10**
Tewkesbury *U.K.* 51°59N 2°9W **24 C4**
Texarkana *U.S.A.* 33°26N 94°3W **111 D8**
Texas □ *U.S.A.* 31°40N 98°30W **110 D7**
Texel *Neths.* 53°5N 4°50E **65 A4**
Teynham *U.K.* 51°20N 0°50E **25 D10**
Tezpur *India* 26°40N 92°45E **85 F18**
Thabana Ntlenyana *Lesotho* 29°30S 29°16E **97 K5**
Thabazimbi *S. Africa* 24°40S 27°21E **97 J5**
Thailand ■ *Asia* 16°0N 102°0E **83 B2**
Thailand, G. of *Asia* 11°30N 101°0E **83 B2**
Thal Desert *Pakistan* 31°10N 71°30E **84 D7**
Thame *U.K.* 51°45N 0°58W **25 C7**
Thame → *U.K.* 51°39N 1°9W **24 C6**
Thames → *Canada* 42°20N 82°25W **112 D6**
Thames → *U.K.* 51°29N 0°34E **25 D10**
Thane *India* 19°12N 72°59E **84 K8**
Thanet, I. of *U.K.* 51°21N 1°20E **25 D11**
Thanh Hoa *Vietnam* 19°48N 105°46E **83 B2**
Thanjavur *India* 10°48N 79°12E **84 P11**
Thar Desert *India* 28°0N 72°0E **84 F8**
Thargomindah *Australia* 27°58S 143°46E **98 F7**
Thasos *Greece* 40°40N 24°40E **71 D11**
Thatcham *U.K.* 51°24N 1°15W **24 D6**
Thaxted *U.K.* 51°57N 0°22E **25 C9**
The Everglades *U.S.A.* 25°50N 81°0W **111 E10**
The Pas *Canada* 53°45N 101°15W **108 D9**
The Wash *U.K.* 52°58N 0°20E **25 A9**
The Weald *U.K.* 51°4N 0°20E **25 D9**
Theale *U.K.* 51°26N 1°5W **24 D6**
Thebes *Egypt* 25°40N 32°35E **95 C12**
Thelon → *Canada* 64°16N 96°4W **108 C9**
Thermopolis *U.S.A.* 43°39N 108°13W **110 B5**
Thessalon *Canada* 46°20N 83°30W **112 B6**
Thessaloniki *Greece* 40°38N 22°58E **71 D10**
Thetford *U.K.* 52°25N 0°45E **25 B10**
Thetford Mines *Canada* 46°8N 71°18W **109 E12**
Thiers *France* 45°52N 3°33E **68 D5**
Thiès *Senegal* 14°50N 16°51W **94 F2**
Thika *Kenya* 1°1S 37°5E **96 E7**
Thimphu *Bhutan* 27°31N 89°45E **85 F16**
Thionville *France* 49°20N 6°10E **68 B7**
Thira = Santorini *Greece* 36°23N 25°27E **71 F11**
Thirlmere *U.K.* 54°32N 3°4W **22 C2**
Thirsk *U.K.* 54°14N 1°19W **22 D6**
Thlewiaza → *Canada* 60°29N 94°40W **108 D9**
Thomasville *U.S.A.* 30°50N 83°59W **111 D10**
Thompson *Canada* 55°45N 97°52W **108 D10**
Thornaby on Tees *U.K.* 54°33N 1°18W **22 C6**
Thornbury *U.K.* 51°36N 2°31W **24 C4**
Thorndon *U.K.* 52°17N 1°9E **25 B11**
Thorne *U.K.* 53°37N 0°57W **23 E7**
Thorney *U.K.* 52°37N 0°6W **25 A8**
Thornham *U.K.* 52°58N 0°35E **25 A10**
Thornthwaite *U.K.* 54°37N 3°13W **22 C2**

Thornton *U.K.* 53°52N 2°59W **23 E3**
Thornton Dale *U.K.* 54°15N 0°42W **22 D7**
Thorpe *U.K.* 52°38N 1°22E **25 A11**
Thorpe le Soken *U.K.* 51°51N 1°11E **25 C11**
Thrace *Turkey* 41°0N 27°0E **71 D12**
Thrapston *U.K.* 52°24N 0°32W **25 B7**
Three Gorges Dam *China* 30°45N 111°15E **81 C6**
Threlkeld *U.K.* 54°37N 3°3W **22 C2**
Threshfield *U.K.* 54°4N 2°1W **22 D4**
Thunder B. *U.S.A.* 45°0N 83°20W **112 C6**
Thunder Bay *Canada* 48°20N 89°15W **112 A3**
Thüringer Wald *Germany* 50°35N 11°0E **66 C6**
Thurlby *U.K.* 52°45N 0°22W **23 G8**
Thurles *Ireland* 52°41N 7°49W **30 C7**
Thurmaston *U.K.* 52°40N 1°5W **23 G6**
Thursby *U.K.* 54°51N 3°2W **22 C2**
Thurso *U.K.* 58°36N 3°32W **19 E10**
Thurso → *U.K.* 58°36N 3°32W **19 E10**
Thurston I. *Antarctica* 72°0S 100°0W **55 D16**
Tian Shan *Asia* 40°30N 76°0E **80 B3**
Tianjin *China* 39°7N 117°12E **81 C6**
Tianmen *China* 30°39N 113°9E **81 C6**
Tianshui *China* 34°32N 105°40E **80 C5**
Tiaret *Algeria* 35°20N 1°21E **94 A6**
Tibasti, Sarīr *Libya* 22°50N 18°30E **95 D9**
Tiber → *Italy* 41°44N 12°14E **70 D5**
Tiberias, L. = Galilee, Sea of *Israel* 32°45N 35°35E **86 C3**
Tibesti *Chad* 21°0N 17°30E **95 D9**
Tibet □ *China* 32°0N 88°0E **80 C3**
Tibet, Plateau of *Asia* 32°0N 86°0E **74 E10**
Tiburón, I. *Mexico* 29°0N 112°25W **114 B2**
Ticehurst *U.K.* 51°3N 0°25E **25 D9**
Ticino → *Italy* 45°9N 9°14E **70 B3**
Tickhill *U.K.* 53°26N 1°6W **23 F6**
Ticonderoga *U.S.A.* 43°51N 73°26W **113 D11**
Tideswell *U.K.* 53°17N 1°47W **23 F5**
Tieling *China* 42°20N 123°55E **81 B7**
Tierra de Campos *Spain* 42°10N 4°50W **69 A3**
Tierra del Fuego, I. Gr. de *Argentina* 54°0S 69°0W **121 H3**
Tiffin *U.S.A.* 41°7N 83°11W **112 E6**
Tighina *Moldova* 46°50N 29°30E **67 E15**
Tignish *Canada* 46°58N 64°2W **113 B15**
Tigris → *Asia* 31°0N 47°25E **86 D6**
Tijuana *Mexico* 32°32N 117°1W **114 A1**
Tikhoretsk *Russia* 45°56N 40°5E **73 E7**
Tikhvin *Russia* 59°35N 33°30E **72 C5**
Tikrīt *Iraq* 34°35N 43°37E **86 C5**
Tiksi *Russia* 71°40N 128°45E **79 B14**
Tilburg *Neths.* 51°31N 5°6E **65 C5**
Tilbury *U.K.* 51°27N 0°22E **25 D9**
Till → *U.K.* 55°41N 2°13W **22 A4**
Tillicoultry *U.K.* 56°9N 3°45W **21 B8**
Tilmanstone *U.K.* 51°12N 1°18E **25 D11**
Tilt → *U.K.* 56°46N 3°51W **19 J10**
Timaru *N.Z.* 44°23S 171°14E **99 J13**
Timișoara *Romania* 45°43N 21°15E **67 F11**
Timmins *Canada* 48°28N 81°25W **109 E11**
Timor *Asia* 9°0S 125°0E **83 D4**
Timor Leste = East Timor ■ *Asia* 8°50S 126°0E **83 D4**
Timor Sea *Ind. Oc.* 12°0S 127°0E **83 E4**
Tingewick *U.K.* 51°59N 1°2W **24 E6**
Tinogasta *Argentina* 28°5S 67°32W **121 E3**
Tinos *Greece* 37°33N 25°8E **71 F11**
Tintagel *U.K.* 50°39N 4°46W **27 F4**
Tintagel Hd. *U.K.* 50°40N 4°47W **27 F4**
Tipperary *Ireland* 52°28N 8°10W **30 D6**
Tipperary □ *Ireland* 52°37N 7°55W **30 C7**
Tipton *U.K.* 52°32N 2°4W **23 G4**
Tipton *U.S.A.* 41°46N 91°8W **112 E2**
Tiptree *U.K.* 51°48N 0°46E **25 C10**
Tiranë *Albania* 41°18N 19°49E **71 D8**
Tiraspol *Moldova* 46°55N 29°35E **67 E15**
Tirebolu *Turkey* 40°58N 38°45E **73 F6**
Tiree *U.K.* 56°31N 6°55W **20 A2**
Tiree, Passage of *U.K.* 56°30N 6°30W **20 B2**
Tirich Mir *Pakistan* 36°15N 71°55E **84 A7**
Tirol □ *Austria* 47°3N 10°43E **66 E6**
Tiruchchirappalli *India* 10°45N 78°45E **84 P11**
Tirunelveli *India* 8°45N 77°45E **84 Q10**
Tiruppur *India* 11°5N 77°22E **84 P10**
Tisa → *Serbia* 45°15N 20°17E **71 B9**
Tisbury *U.K.* 51°4N 2°5W **24 D4**
Tisdale *Canada* 52°50N 104°0W **108 D9**
Titchfield *U.K.* 50°50N 1°15W **24 E6**
Titicaca, L. *S. Amer.* 15°30S 69°30W **120 D3**
Titusville *U.S.A.* 41°38N 79°41W **112 E8**
Tiverton *U.K.* 50°54N 3°29W **27 F7**
Tivoli *Italy* 41°58N 12°45E **70 D5**
Tizi-Ouzou *Algeria* 36°42N 4°3E **94 A6**
Tlaxiaco *Mexico* 17°25N 97°35W **114 D5**
Tlemcen *Algeria* 34°52N 1°21W **94 B5**
Toamasina *Madag.* 18°10S 49°25E **97 H9**
Toba, Danau *Indonesia* 2°30N 97°30E **83 C1**
Toba Kakar *Pakistan* 31°30N 69°0E **84 D6**
Tobago *Trin. & Tob.* 11°10N 60°30W **120 A3**
Tobermory *Canada* 45°12N 81°40W **112 C7**
Tobermory *U.K.* 56°38N 6°5W **20 A3**
Tocantins → *Brazil* 1°45S 49°10W **120 C5**
Toddington *U.K.* 51°57N 0°32W **25 C7**
Todmorden *U.K.* 53°43N 2°6W **23 E4**
Todos os Santos, B. de *Brazil* 12°48S 38°38W **122 B3**
Toe Hd. *U.K.* 57°50N 7°8W **18 G3**
Togliatti *Russia* 53°32N 49°24E **72 D8**
Togo ■ *W. Afr.* 8°30N 1°35E **94 G6**
Tok *U.K.* 63°20N 142°59W **108 C5**
Tokat *Turkey* 40°22N 36°35E **73 F6**
Tokdo *Asia* 37°15N 131°52E **82 E2**
Tokelau Is. ■ *Pac. Oc.* 9°0S 171°45W **99 B16**
Tokushima *Japan* 34°4N 134°34E **82 F4**
Tokuyama *Japan* 34°3N 131°50E **82 F2**
Tōkyō *Japan* 35°43N 139°45E **82 F6**
Toledo *Spain* 39°50N 4°2W **69 C3**
Toledo *U.S.A.* 41°39N 83°33W **112 E6**
Toledo, Montes de *Spain* 39°33N 4°20W **69 C3**
Toliara *Madag.* 23°21S 43°40E **97 J8**
Tolima *Colombia* 4°40N 75°19W **120 B2**

Tollesbury *U.K.* 51°45N 0°51E **25 C10**
Toluca *Mexico* 19°17N 99°40W **114 D5**
Tomah *U.S.A.* 43°59N 90°30W **112 D2**
Tomakomai *Japan* 42°38N 141°36E **82 B7**
Tomaszów Mazowiecki *Poland* 51°30N 20°2E **67 C10**
Tombador, Serra do *Brazil* 12°0S 58°0W **120 D4**
Tombigbee → *U.S.A.* 31°8N 87°57W **111 D9**
Tombouctou *Mali* 16°50N 3°0W **94 E5**
Tomini, Teluk *Indonesia* 0°10S 121°0E **83 D4**
Tomintoul *U.K.* 57°15N 3°23W **19 H11**
Tomsk *Russia* 56°30N 85°5E **79 D10**
Tonbridge *U.K.* 51°11N 0°17E **25 D9**
Tone → *U.K.* 50°58N 3°20W **27 F7**
Tong *U.K.* 52°40N 2°17W **23 G4**
Tonga ■ *Pac. Oc.* 19°50S 174°30W **99 D16**
Tonga Trench *Pac. Oc.* 18°0S 173°0W **99 D16**
Tongareva *Cook Is.* 9°0S 158°0W **103 H12**
Tongatapu Group *Tonga* 21°0S 175°0W **99 E16**
Tongchuan *China* 35°6N 109°3E **81 C5**
Tonghua *China* 41°42N 125°58E **81 B7**
Tongliao *China* 43°38N 122°18E **81 B7**
Tongling *China* 30°55N 117°48E **81 C6**
Tongue *U.K.* 58°29N 4°25W **19 F9**
Tongue → *U.S.A.* 46°25N 105°52W **110 A5**
Tonk *India* 26°6N 75°54E **84 F9**
Tonkin, G. of *Asia* 20°0N 108°0E **80 E5**
Tonle Sap *Cambodia* 13°0N 104°0E **83 B2**
Tonopah *U.S.A.* 38°4N 117°14W **110 C3**
Toowoomba *Australia* 27°32S 151°56E **98 F9**
Topeka *U.S.A.* 39°3N 95°40W **111 C7**
Topolobampo *Mexico* 25°36N 109°3W **114 B3**
Tor B. *U.K.* 50°25N 3°33W **27 G6**
Torbay *U.K.* 50°26N 3°31W **27 G6**
Torne älv → *Europe* 65°50N 24°12E **63 D8**
Torneträsk *Sweden* 68°24N 19°15E **63 D7**
Tornio *Finland* 65°50N 24°12E **63 D8**
Toro, Cerro del *Chile* 29°10S 69°50W **121 E3**
Toronto *Canada* 43°39N 79°20W **112 D8**
Torpoint *U.K.* 50°23N 4°13W **27 G5**
Torquay *U.K.* 50°27N 3°32W **27 G6**
Torre del Greco *Italy* 40°47N 14°22E **70 D6**
Torrejón de Ardoz *Spain* 40°27N 3°29W **69 B4**
Torrelavega *Spain* 43°20N 4°5W **69 A3**
Torremolinos *Spain* 36°38N 4°30W **69 D3**
Torrens, L. *Australia* 31°0S 137°50E **98 G6**
Torrent *Spain* 39°27N 0°28W **69 C5**
Torreón *Mexico* 25°33N 103°26W **114 B4**
Torres Strait *Australia* 9°50S 142°20E **98 C7**
Torridge → *U.K.* 51°0N 4°13W **27 E5**
Torridon, L. *U.K.* 57°35N 5°50W **18 G6**
Torthorwald *U.K.* 55°6N 3°32W **21 D8**
Tortola *Br. Virgin Is.* 18°19N 64°45W **115 e**
Tortosa *Spain* 40°49N 0°31E **69 B6**
Toruń *Poland* 53°2N 18°39E **67 B10**
Torver *U.K.* 54°20N 3°6W **22 D2**
Tory I. *Ireland* 55°16N 8°14W **28 A5**
Toscana □ *Italy* 43°25N 11°0E **70 C4**
Toshka Lakes *Egypt* 22°50N 31°0E **95 D12**
Totland *U.K.* 50°41N 1°32W **24 E5**
Totley *U.K.* 53°20N 1°32W **23 F5**
Totnes *U.K.* 50°26N 3°42W **27 G6**
Totton *U.K.* 50°55N 1°29W **24 E6**
Tottori *Japan* 35°30N 134°15E **82 F4**
Toubkal, Djebel *Morocco* 31°0N 8°0W **94 B4**
Touggourt *Algeria* 33°6N 6°4E **94 B7**
Toul *France* 48°40N 5°53E **68 B6**
Toulon *France* 43°10N 5°55E **68 E6**
Toulouse *France* 43°37N 1°27E **68 E4**
Touraine *France* 47°20N 0°30E **68 C4**
Tournai *Belgium* 50°35N 3°25E **65 D3**
Tournon-sur-Rhône *France* 45°4N 4°50E **68 D6**
Tours *France* 47°22N 0°40E **68 C4**
Towanda *U.S.A.* 41°46N 76°27W **112 E9**
Towcester *U.K.* 52°8N 0°59W **25 C7**
Town Yetholm *U.K.* 55°33N 2°17W **21 C11**
Townsville *Australia* 19°15S 146°45E **98 D8**
Towson *U.S.A.* 39°24N 76°36W **112 F9**
Toyama *Japan* 36°40N 137°15E **82 E5**
Toyohashi *Japan* 34°45N 137°25E **82 F5**
Toyota *Japan* 35°3N 137°7E **82 F5**
Trabzon *Turkey* 41°0N 39°45E **73 F6**
Trafalgar, C. *Spain* 36°10N 6°2W **69 D2**
Trail *Canada* 49°5N 117°40W **108 E8**
Tralee *Ireland* 52°16N 9°42W **30 D3**
Tralee B. *Ireland* 52°17N 9°55W **30 D3**
Tramore *Ireland* 52°10N 7°10W **31 D8**
Tramore B. *Ireland* 52°9N 7°10W **31 D8**
Tranent *U.K.* 55°57N 2°57W **21 C10**
Trang *Thailand* 7°33N 99°38E **83 C1**
Transantarctic Mts. *Antarctica* 85°0S 170°0W **55 E12**
Transylvania *Romania* 46°30N 24°0E **67 E12**
Transylvanian Alps *Romania* 45°30N 25°0E **67 F13**
Trápani *Italy* 38°1N 12°29E **70 E5**
Trasimeno, L. *Italy* 43°8N 12°6E **70 C5**
Traverse City *U.S.A.* 44°46N 85°38W **112 C5**
Trawbreaga B. *Ireland* 55°20N 7°25W **28 A7**
Trawsfynydd *U.K.* 52°54N 3°55W **26 B6**
Tredegar *U.K.* 51°47N 3°14W **26 D7**
Tregaron *U.K.* 52°14N 3°56W **26 C6**
Treinta y Tres *Uruguay* 33°16S 54°17W **121 F4**
Trelew *Argentina* 43°10S 65°20W **121 G3**
Trent → *U.K.* 53°41N 0°42W **23 E7**
Trentham *U.K.* 52°58N 2°11W **23 G4**
Trento *Italy* 46°4N 11°8E **70 A4**
Trenton *U.S.A.* 40°14N 74°46W **113 E10**
Três Arroyos *Argentina* 38°26S 60°20W **121 F3**
Três Corações *Brazil* 21°44S 45°15W **122 D1**
Três Lagoas *Brazil* 20°50S 51°43W **120 E4**
Três Pontas *Brazil* 21°23S 45°29W **122 D1**
Três Rios *Brazil* 22°6S 43°15W **122 D2**
Tresco *U.K.* 49°57N 6°20W **27 H1**
Treviso *Italy* 45°40N 12°15E **70 B5**
Trevose Hd. *U.K.* 50°32N 5°3W **27 F3**
Tribal Areas □ *Pakistan* 33°0N 70°0E **84 C7**

Trichur *India* 10°30N 76°18E **84 P10**
Trier *Germany* 49°45N 6°38E **66 D4**
Trieste *Italy* 45°40N 13°46E **70 B5**
Trim *Ireland* 53°33N 6°48W **29 D8**
Trimdon *U.K.* 54°42N 1°24W **22 C6**
Trincomalee *Sri Lanka* 8°38N 81°15E **84 Q12**
Trindade, I. *Atl. Oc.* 20°20S 29°50W **52 F8**
Trinidad *Bolivia* 14°46S 64°50W **120 D3**
Trinidad *Cuba* 21°48N 80°0W **115 C9**
Trinidad *U.S.A.* 37°10N 104°31W **110 C6**
Trinidad & Tobago ■ *W. Indies* 10°30N 61°20W **115 E12**
Trinity → *U.S.A.* 29°45N 94°43W **111 E8**
Trinity B. *Canada* 48°20N 53°10W **109 E14**
Trinity Is. *U.S.A.* 56°33N 154°25W **108 D4**
Tripoli *Lebanon* 34°31N 35°50E **86 C3**
Tripoli *Libya* 32°49N 13°7E **95 B8**
Tripolitania *N. Afr.* 31°0N 13°0E **95 B8**
Tripura □ *India* 24°0N 92°0E **85 H18**
Tristan da Cunha *Atl. Oc.* 37°6S 12°20W **52 F9**
Trivandrum *India* 8°41N 77°0E **84 Q10**
Trnava *Slovak Rep.* 48°23N 17°35E **67 D9**
Trois-Rivières *Canada* 46°25N 72°34W **109 E12**
Trois-Rivières *Guadeloupe* 15°57N 61°40W **114 b**
Trollhättan *Sweden* 58°17N 12°20E **63 F6**
Trombetas → *Brazil* 1°55S 55°35W **120 C4**
Tromsø *Norway* 69°40N 18°56E **63 D7**
Tronador *Argentina* 41°10S 71°50W **121 G2**
Trondheim *Norway* 63°36N 10°25E **63 E6**
Trondheimsfjorden *Norway* 63°35N 10°30E **63 E6**
Troon *U.K.* 55°33N 4°39W **20 C6**
Trossachs, The *U.K.* 56°14N 4°24W **20 B7**
Trostan *U.K.* 55°3N 6°10W **29 A9**
Trotternish *U.K.* 57°32N 6°15W **18 G5**
Trou Gras Pt. *St. Lucia* 13°51N 60°53W **115 f**
Trout L. *N.W.T., Canada* 60°40N 121°14W **108 C7**
Trout L. *Ont., Canada* 51°20N 93°15W **108 D10**
Trowbridge *U.K.* 51°18N 2°12W **24 D4**
Troy *Turkey* 39°57N 26°12E **73 G4**
Troy *Ala., U.S.A.* 31°48N 85°58W **111 D9**
Troy *N.Y., U.S.A.* 42°44N 73°41W **113 D11**
Troy *Ohio, U.S.A.* 40°2N 84°12W **112 E5**
Troyes *France* 48°19N 4°3E **68 B6**
Trujillo *Honduras* 16°0N 86°0W **114 D7**
Trujillo *Peru* 8°6S 79°0W **120 C2**
Trujillo *Venezuela* 9°22N 70°38W **120 B2**
Trull *U.K.* 51°0N 3°6W **24 E2**
Trumpington *U.K.* 52°10N 0°7E **25 B9**
Truro *Canada* 45°21N 63°14W **109 E13**
Truro *U.K.* 50°16N 5°4W **27 G3**
Tsavo *Kenya* 2°59S 38°28E **96 E7**
Tsetserleg *Mongolia* 47°36N 101°32E **80 B5**
Tshikapa *Dem. Rep. of the Congo* 6°28S 20°48E **96 F4**
Tsiigehtchic *Canada* 67°15N 134°0W **108 C6**
Tsimlyansk Res. *Russia* 48°0N 43°0E **73 E7**
Tskhinvali *Georgia* 42°14N 44°1E **73 F7**
Tsuchiura *Japan* 36°5N 140°15E **82 E7**
Tsugaru Str. *Japan* 41°35N 141°0E **82 C7**
Tsumeb *Namibia* 19°9S 17°44E **97 H3**
Tsuruoka *Japan* 38°44N 139°50E **82 D6**
Tsushima *Japan* 34°20N 129°20E **82 F1**
Tuam *Ireland* 53°31N 8°51W **28 D4**
Tuamotu, Is. *French Polynesia* 17°0S 144°0W **103 J13**
Tuamotu Ridge *Pac. Oc.* 20°0S 138°0W **103 K14**
Tuapse *Russia* 44°5N 39°10E **73 F6**
Tubarão *Brazil* 28°30S 49°0W **121 E5**
Tübingen *Germany* 48°31N 9°4E **66 D5**
Tubruq *Libya* 32°7N 23°55E **95 B10**
Tubuai, Is. *French Polynesia* 25°0S 150°0W **103 K13**
Tucson *U.S.A.* 32°13N 110°58W **110 D4**
Tucumcari *U.S.A.* 35°10N 103°44W **110 C6**
Tucupita *Venezuela* 9°2N 62°3W **120 B3**
Tucuruí *Brazil* 3°42S 49°44W **120 C5**
Tucuruí, Reprêsa de *Brazil* 4°0S 49°30W **120 C5**
Tuguegarao *Phil.* 17°35N 121°42E **83 B4**
Tuktoyaktuk *Canada* 69°27N 133°2W **108 C6**
Tula *Russia* 54°13N 37°38E **72 D6**
Tulancingo *Mexico* 20°5N 98°22W **114 C5**
Tulare *U.S.A.* 36°13N 119°21W **110 C3**
Tulcán *Ecuador* 0°48N 77°43W **120 B2**
Tulcea *Romania* 45°13N 28°46E **67 F15**
Tulita *Canada* 64°57N 125°30W **108 C7**
Tulla *Ireland* 52°53N 8°46W **30 C5**
Tullamore *Ireland* 53°16N 7°31W **31 B7**
Tulle *France* 45°16N 1°46E **68 D4**
Tullow *Ireland* 52°49N 6°45W **31 C9**
Tulsa *U.S.A.* 36°10N 95°55W **111 C7**
Tumaco *Colombia* 1°50N 78°45W **120 B2**
Tumbes *Peru* 3°37S 80°27W **120 C1**
Tummel → *U.K.* 56°42N 4°5W **19 J9**
Tummel, L. *U.K.* 56°43N 3°55W **19 J10**
Tumucumaque, Serra *Brazil* 2°0N 55°0W **120 B4**
Tunis *Tunisia* 36°50N 10°11E **95 A8**
Tunisia ■ *Africa* 33°30N 9°10E **95 A8**
Tunja *Colombia* 5°33N 73°25W **120 B2**
Tunstall *U.K.* 52°9N 1°27E **25 B11**
Tupaciguara *Brazil* 18°35S 48°42W **122 C1**
Tupelo *U.S.A.* 34°16N 88°43W **111 D9**
Tupiza *Bolivia* 21°30S 65°40W **120 E3**
Turfan Basin *China* 42°40N 89°25E **80 B3**
Turgutlu *Turkey* 38°30N 27°43E **73 G4**
Turin *Italy* 45°3N 7°40E **70 B2**
Turkana, L. *Africa* 3°30N 36°5E **96 D7**
Turkey ■ *Eurasia* 39°0N 36°0E **73 G6**
Türkmenabat *Turkmenistan* 39°6N 63°34E **87 B10**
Türkmenbashi *Turkmenistan* 40°5N 53°5E **87 A8**
Turkmenistan ■ *Asia* 39°0N 59°0E **87 B9**
Turks & Caicos Is. □ *W. Indies* 21°20N 71°20W **115 C10**
Turku *Finland* 60°30N 22°19E **63 E8**
Turnberry *U.K.* 55°18N 4°49W **20 D6**
Turneffe Is. *Belize* 17°20N 87°50W **114 D7**
Turpan *China* 43°58N 89°10E **80 B3**
Turriff *U.K.* 57°32N 2°27W **19 H13**
Tuscaloosa *U.S.A.* 33°12N 87°34W **111 D9**
Tuscany = Toscana □ *Italy* 43°25N 11°0E **70 C4**
Tutbury *U.K.* 52°51N 1°41W **23 G5**
Tuticorin *India* 8°50N 78°12E **84 Q11**

Tutuila *Amer. Samoa* 14°19S 170°50W **99** C16
Tutume *Botswana* 20°30S 27°5E **97** J5
Tuvalu ■ *Pac. Oc.* 8°0S 178°0E **99** B14
Tuxford *U.K.* 53°14N 0°54W **23** F7
Tuxpan *Mexico* 20°57N 97°24W **114** C5
Tuxtla Gutiérrez *Mexico* 16°45N 93°7W **114** D6
Tuz Gölü *Turkey* 38°42N 33°18E **73** G5
Tuzla *Bos.-H.* 44°34N 18°41E **71** B8
Tver *Russia* 56°55N 35°55E **72** C6
Tweed → *U.K.* 55°45N 2°0W **21** C11
Tweedmouth *U.K.* 55°45N 2°0W **22** A5
Tweedshaws *U.K.* 55°27N 3°29W **21** D9
Twenty *U.K.* 52°47N 0°17W **23** G8
Twin Falls *U.S.A.* 42°34N 114°28W **110** B4
Two Harbors *U.S.A.* 47°2N 91°40W **112** B2
Two Rivers *U.S.A.* 44°9N 87°34W **112** C4
Twyford *Hants., U.K.* 51°1N 1°19W **24** D6
Twyford *Wokingham, U.K.* 51°28N 0°51W **25** D7
Tychy *Poland* 50°9N 18°59E **67** C10
Tydd St. Mary *U.K.* 52°45N 0°7E **23** G9
Tyler *U.S.A.* 32°21N 95°18W **111** D7
Tyndrum *U.K.* 56°26N 4°42W **20** B6
Tyne → *U.K.* 54°59N 1°32W **22** C5
Tyne & Wear □ *U.K.* 55°6N 1°17W **22** B6
Tynemouth *U.K.* 55°1N 1°26W **22** B6
Tyrol = Tirol □ *Austria* 47°3N 10°43E **66** E6
Tyrone □ *U.K.* 54°38N 7°11W **29** B7
Tyrrhenian Sea *Medit. S.* 40°0N 12°30E **70** E5
Tyumen *Russia* 57°11N 65°29E **79** D8
Tywardreath *U.K.* 50°21N 4°42W **27** G4
Tywi → *U.K.* 51°48N 4°21W **26** D5
Tywyn *U.K.* 52°35N 4°5W **26** B5
Tzaneen *S. Africa* 23°47S 30°9E **97** J6

U

U.S.A. = United States of America ■ *N. Amer.* 37°0N 96°0W **110** C7
U.S. Virgin Is. ⧄ *W. Indies* 18°20N 65°0W **115** e
Uanle Uen *Somali Rep.* 2°37N 44°54E **88** G3
Uaupés → *Brazil* 0°2N 67°16W **120** B3
Ubá *Brazil* 21°8S 43°0W **122** D2
Ubaitaba *Brazil* 14°18S 39°20W **122** B3
Ube *Japan* 33°56N 131°15E **82** G2
Uberaba *Brazil* 19°50S 47°55W **122** C1
Uberlândia *Brazil* 19°0S 48°20W **122** C1
Ubon Ratchathani *Thailand* 15°15N 104°50E **83** B2
Ucayali → *Peru* 4°30S 73°30W **120** C2
Uckfield *U.K.* 50°58N 0°7E **25** E9
Udagamandalam *India* 11°30N 76°44E **84** P10
Udaipur *India* 24°36N 73°44E **84** G8
Uddingston *U.K.* 55°49N 4°5W **20** C7
Údine *Italy* 46°3N 13°14E **70** A5
Udmurtia □ *Russia* 57°30N 52°30E **72** C9
Udon Thani *Thailand* 17°29N 102°46E **83** B2
Udupi *India* 13°25N 74°42E **84** N9
Uele → *Dem. Rep. of the Congo* 3°45N 24°45E **96** D4
Ufa *Russia* 54°45N 55°55E **72** D10
Uffculme *U.K.* 50°54N 3°20W **27** F7
Ufford *U.K.* 52°8N 1°23E **25** B11
Uganda ■ *Africa* 2°0N 32°0E **96** D6
Ugborough *U.K.* 50°22N 3°53W **27** G6
Uig *U.K.* 57°35N 6°21W **18** G5
Uinta Mts. *U.S.A.* 40°45N 110°30W **110** B4
Uitenhage *S. Africa* 33°40S 25°28E **97** L5
Ujjain *India* 23°9N 75°43E **84** H9
Ujung Pandang *Indonesia* 5°10S 119°20E **83** D3
Ukhta *Russia* 63°34N 53°41E **72** B9
Ukiah *U.S.A.* 39°9N 123°13W **110** C2
Ukraine ■ *Europe* 49°0N 32°0E **73** E5
Ulaanbaatar *Mongolia* 47°55N 106°53E **80** B5
Ulaangom *Mongolia* 50°5N 92°10E **80** A4
Ulaanjirem *Mongolia* 45°5N 105°30E **80** B5
Ulan Ude *Russia* 51°45N 107°40E **79** D12
Ulceby Cross *U.K.* 53°15N 0°7E **23** F9
Ulhasnagar *India* 19°15N 73°10E **84** K8
Ullapool *U.K.* 57°54N 5°9W **18** G7
Ulleungdo *S. Korea* 37°30N 130°30E **82** E2
Ullswater *U.K.* 54°34N 2°52W **22** C3
Ulm *Germany* 48°23N 9°58E **66** D5
Ulster □ *U.K.* 54°35N 6°30W **29** B9
Ulungur He → *China* 47°1N 87°24E **80** B3
Uluru *Australia* 25°23S 131°5E **98** F5
Ulva *U.K.* 56°29N 6°13W **20** B3
Ulverston *U.K.* 54°13N 3°5W **22** D2
Ulyasutay *Mongolia* 47°56N 97°28E **80** B4
Uman *Ukraine* 48°40N 30°12E **73** E5
Umeå *Sweden* 63°45N 20°20E **63** E8
Umeälven → *Sweden* 63°45N 20°20E **63** E8
Umlazi *S. Africa* 29°59S 30°54E **97** L6
Umm al Qaywayn *U.A.E.* 25°30N 55°35E **87** E8
Umnak I. *U.S.A.* 53°15N 168°20W **108** D3
Umuarama *Brazil* 23°45S 53°20W **121** E4
Unalakleet *U.S.A.* 63°52N 160°47W **108** C3
Unalaska *U.S.A.* 53°53N 166°32W **108** D3
Unalaska I. *U.S.A.* 53°35N 166°50W **108** D3
'Unayzah *Si. Arabia* 26°6N 43°58E **86** E5
Uncía *Bolivia* 18°25S 66°40W **120** D3
Ungava, Pén. d' *Canada* 60°0N 74°0W **109** D12
Ungava B. *Canada* 59°30N 67°30W **109** D13
União dos Palmares *Brazil* 9°10S 36°2W **122** A3
Unimak I. *U.S.A.* 54°45N 164°0W **108** D3
Union City *U.S.A.* 36°26N 89°3W **112** G3
Uniontown *U.S.A.* 39°54N 79°44W **112** F8
United Arab Emirates ■ *Asia* 23°50N 54°0E **87** F8
United Kingdom ■ *Europe* 53°0N 2°0W **64** E6
United States of America ■ *N. Amer.* 37°0N 96°0W **110** C7
Unst *U.K.* 60°44N 0°53W **18** A16
Upavon *U.K.* 51°18N 1°48W **24** D5
Upington *S. Africa* 28°25S 21°15E **97** K4
'Upolu *Samoa* 13°58S 172°0W **99** C16
Upper Heyford *U.K.* 51°56N 1°15W **24** C6
Upper Klamath L. *U.S.A.* 42°25N 121°55W **110** B2
Uppingham *U.K.* 52°36N 0°43W **23** G7
Uppsala *Sweden* 59°53N 17°38E **63** F7
Upton *U.K.* 53°13N 2°53W **23** F3
Upton-upon-Severn *U.K.* 52°3N 2°12W **24** B4
Upwey *U.K.* 50°39N 2°29W **24** E4
Ur *Iraq* 30°55N 46°25E **86** D6
Ural → *Kazakhstan* 47°0N 51°48E **73** E9
Ural Mts. *Eurasia* 60°0N 59°0E **72** C10
Uranium City *Canada* 59°34N 108°37W **108** D9
Uraricoera → *Brazil* 3°2N 60°30W **120** B3
Urbana *Ill., U.S.A.* 40°7N 88°12W **112** E3
Urbana *Ohio, U.S.A.* 40°7N 83°45W **112** E6
Ure → *U.K.* 54°5N 1°20W **22** D5
Urganch *Uzbekistan* 41°40N 60°41E **87** A10
Urmia *Iran* 37°40N 45°0E **86** B6
Urmia, L. *Iran* 37°50N 45°30E **86** B6
Urmston *U.K.* 53°27N 2°21W **23** F4
Uroyan, Mts. de *Puerto Rico* 18°12N 67°0W **115** d
Uruaçu *Brazil* 14°30S 49°10W **122** B1
Uruapan *Mexico* 19°24N 102°3W **114** D4
Urubamba → *Peru* 10°43S 73°48W **120** D2
Uruguai → *Brazil* 26°0S 53°30W **121** E4
Uruguaiana *Brazil* 29°50S 57°0W **121** E4
Uruguay ■ *S. Amer.* 32°30S 56°30W **121** F4
Uruguay → *S. Amer.* 34°12S 58°18W **116** G5
Ürümqi *China* 43°45N 87°45E **80** B3
Usa → *Russia* 66°16N 59°49E **72** A10
Uşak *Turkey* 38°43N 29°28E **73** G4
Usakos *Namibia* 21°54S 15°31E **97** J3
Usedom *Germany* 53°55N 14°2E **66** B8
Ushant *France* 48°28N 5°6W **68** B1
Ushuaia *Argentina* 54°50S 68°23W **121** H3
Usk → *U.K.* 51°33N 2°58W **27** D8
Uspallata, P. de *Argentina* 32°37S 69°22W **121** F3
Usselby *U.K.* 53°26N 0°21W **23** F8
Ussuriysk *Russia* 43°48N 131°59E **82** B2
Ust-Ilimsk *Russia* 58°3N 102°39E **79** D12
Ústí nad Labem *Czech Rep.* 50°41N 14°3E **66** C8
Ústica *Italy* 38°42N 13°11E **70** E5
Ustyurt Plateau *Asia* 44°0N 55°0E **79** E7
Usu *China* 44°27N 84°40E **80** B3
Usumacinta → *Mexico* 18°24N 92°38W **114** D6
Utah □ *U.S.A.* 39°20N 111°30W **110** C4
Utah L. *U.S.A.* 40°12N 111°48W **110** B4
Utica *U.S.A.* 43°6N 75°14W **113** D10
Utrecht *Neths.* 52°5N 5°8E **65** B5
Utsunomiya *Japan* 36°30N 139°50E **82** E6
Uttar Pradesh □ *India* 27°0N 80°0E **84** F12
Uttaradit *Thailand* 17°36N 100°5E **83** B2
Uttaranchal □ *India* 30°0N 79°30E **84** D11
Uttoxeter *U.K.* 52°54N 1°52W **23** G5
Utuado *Puerto Rico* 18°16N 66°42W **115** d
Uusikaupunki *Finland* 60°47N 21°25E **63** E8
Uvalde *U.S.A.* 29°13N 99°47W **110** E7
Uvira *Dem. Rep. of the Congo* 3°22S 29°3E **96** E5
Uvs Nuur *Mongolia* 50°20N 92°30E **80** A4
Uyuni *Bolivia* 20°28S 66°47W **120** E3
Uzbekistan ■ *Asia* 41°30N 65°0E **87** A10
Uzhhorod *Ukraine* 48°36N 22°18E **67** D12

V

Vaal → *S. Africa* 29°4S 23°38E **97** K4
Vaasa *Finland* 63°6N 21°38E **63** E8
Vadodara *India* 22°20N 73°10E **84** H8
Vadsø *Norway* 70°3N 29°50E **63** C9
Vaduz *Liech.* 47°8N 9°31E **66** E5
Váh → *Slovak Rep.* 47°43N 18°7E **67** D9
Vail *U.S.A.* 39°40N 106°20W **110** C5
Vaila *U.K.* 60°12N 1°36W **18** B14
Val-d'Or *Canada* 48°7N 77°47W **109** E12
Valahia *Romania* 44°35N 25°0E **67** F13
Valdai Hills *Russia* 57°0N 33°30E **72** C5
Valdés, Pen. *Argentina* 42°30S 63°45W **121** G3
Valdez *U.S.A.* 61°7N 146°16W **108** C5
Valdivia *Chile* 39°50S 73°14W **121** F2
Valdosta *U.S.A.* 30°50N 83°17W **111** D10
Vale of Glamorgan □ *U.K.* 51°28N 3°25W **27** E7
Valença *Brazil* 13°20S 39°5W **122** B3
Valence *France* 44°57N 4°54E **68** D6
Valencia *Spain* 39°27N 0°23W **69** C5
Valencia *Venezuela* 10°11N 68°0W **120** A3
Valencia □ *Spain* 39°20N 0°40W **69** C5
Valencia, G. de *Spain* 39°30N 0°20E **69** C6
Valencia I. *Ireland* 51°54N 10°22W **30** E2
Valenciennes *France* 50°20N 3°34E **68** A5
Valera *Venezuela* 9°19N 70°37W **120** B2
Valladolid *Mexico* 20°41N 88°12W **114** C7
Valladolid *Spain* 41°38N 4°43W **69** B3
Valledupar *Colombia* 10°29N 73°15W **120** A2
Vallejo *U.S.A.* 38°7N 122°14W **110** C2
Vallenar *Chile* 28°30S 70°50W **121** E2
Valletta *Malta* 35°54N 14°31E **70** G6
Valley *U.K.* 53°16N 4°34W **26** A4
Valley City *U.S.A.* 46°55N 98°0W **110** A7
Valparaíso *Chile* 33°2S 71°40W **121** F2
Van *Turkey* 38°30N 43°20E **73** G7
Van, L. *Turkey* 38°30N 43°0E **73** G7
Van Buren *U.S.A.* 47°10N 67°58W **113** B13
Van Wert *U.S.A.* 40°52N 84°35W **112** E5
Vanadzor *Armenia* 40°48N 44°30E **73** F7
Vancouver *Canada* 49°15N 123°7W **108** E7
Vancouver *U.S.A.* 45°38N 122°40W **110** A2
Vancouver I. *Canada* 49°50N 126°0W **108** E7
Vandalia *U.S.A.* 38°58N 89°6W **112** F3
Vanderhoof *Canada* 54°0N 124°0W **108** D7
Vänern *Sweden* 58°47N 13°30E **63** F6
Vanino *Russia* 48°50N 140°5E **79** E16
Vännäs *Sweden* 63°58N 19°48E **63** E7
Vannes *France* 47°40N 2°47W **68** C2
Vanrhynsdorp *S. Africa* 31°36S 18°44E **97** L3
Vantaa *Finland* 60°18N 24°56E **63** E8
Vanua Levu *Fiji* 16°33S 179°15E **99** D14
Vanuatu ■ *Pac. Oc.* 15°0S 168°0E **99** D12
Varanasi *India* 25°22N 83°0E **85** G13
Varangerfjorden *Norway* 70°3N 29°25E **63** C9
Varberg *Sweden* 57°6N 12°20E **63** F6
Vardak □ *Afghan.* 34°0N 68°0E **87** C12
Vardø *Norway* 70°23N 31°5E **63** C10
Varese *Italy* 45°48N 8°50E **70** B3
Varginha *Brazil* 21°33S 45°25W **122** D1
Varna *Bulgaria* 43°13N 27°56E **71** C12
Vasa Barris → *Brazil* 11°10S 37°10W **122** B3
Västerås *Sweden* 59°37N 16°38E **63** F7
Västervik *Sweden* 57°43N 16°33E **63** F7
Vaté *Vanuatu* 17°40S 168°25E **99** D12
Vatersay *U.K.* 56°55N 7°32W **18** J2
Vatican City ■ *Europe* 41°54N 12°27E **70** D5
Vatnajökull *Iceland* 64°30N 16°48W **63** B2
Vättern *Sweden* 58°25N 14°30E **63** F6
Vaughn *U.S.A.* 34°36N 105°13W **110** D5
Vava'u Group *Tonga* 18°40S 174°0W **99** D16
Vega *Norway* 65°40N 11°55E **63** D6
Vega Baja *Puerto Rico* 18°27N 66°23W **115** d
Vegreville *Canada* 53°30N 112°5W **108** D8
Vélez-Málaga *Spain* 36°48N 4°5W **69** D3
Velhas → *Brazil* 17°13S 44°49W **122** C2
Velikiye Luki *Russia* 56°25N 30°32E **72** C5
Veliko Tŭrnovo *Bulgaria* 43°5N 25°41E **71** C11
Velikonda Range *India* 14°45N 79°10E **84** M11
Vellore *India* 12°57N 79°10E **84** N11
Velsk *Russia* 61°10N 42°5E **72** B7
Vendée □ *France* 46°50N 1°35W **68** C3
Vendôme *France* 47°47N 1°3E **68** C4
Venézia, G. di *Italy* 45°15N 13°0E **70** B5
Venezuela ■ *S. Amer.* 8°0N 66°0W **120** B3
Venezuela, G. de *Venezuela* 11°30N 71°0W **120** A2
Vengurla *India* 15°53N 73°45E **84** M8
Venice *Italy* 45°27N 12°21E **70** B5
Venlo *Neths.* 51°22N 6°11E **65** C6
Ventnor *U.K.* 50°36N 1°12W **24** E6
Ventoux, Mt. *France* 44°10N 5°17E **68** D6
Ventspils *Latvia* 57°25N 21°32E **63** F8
Veracruz *Mexico* 19°11N 96°8W **114** D5
Veraval *India* 20°53N 70°27E **84** J7
Vercelli *Italy* 45°19N 8°25E **70** B3
Verde → *U.S.A.* 33°33N 111°40W **110** D4
Verdun *France* 49°9N 5°24E **68** B6
Vereeniging *S. Africa* 26°38S 27°57E **97** K5
Verkhoyansk *Russia* 67°35N 133°25E **79** C15
Verkhoyansk Ra. *Russia* 66°0N 129°0E **79** C14
Vermont □ *U.S.A.* 44°0N 73°0W **113** D11
Vernal *U.S.A.* 40°27N 109°32W **110** B5
Vernon *Canada* 50°20N 119°15W **108** D8
Vernon *U.S.A.* 34°9N 99°17W **110** D7
Verona *Italy* 45°27N 10°59E **70** B4
Versailles *France* 48°48N 2°7E **68** B5
Vert, C. *Senegal* 14°45N 17°30W **94** F2
Verviers *Belgium* 50°37N 5°52E **65** D5
Verwood *U.K.* 50°52N 1°52W **24** E5
Veryan *U.K.* 50°13N 4°56W **27** G4
Veryan B. *U.K.* 50°13N 4°51W **27** G4
Vesoul *France* 47°40N 6°11E **68** C7
Vesterålen *Norway* 68°45N 15°0E **63** D7
Vestfjorden *Norway* 67°55N 14°0E **63** D6
Vesuvio *Italy* 40°49N 14°26E **70** D6
Veszprém *Hungary* 47°8N 17°57E **67** E9
Vianópolis *Brazil* 16°40S 48°35W **122** C1
Viaréggio *Italy* 43°52N 10°14E **70** C4
Vicenza *Italy* 45°33N 11°33E **70** B4
Vichada → *Colombia* 4°55N 67°50W **120** B3
Vichy *France* 46°9N 3°26E **68** C5
Vickerstown *U.K.* 54°6N 3°15W **22** D2
Vicksburg *U.S.A.* 32°21N 90°53W **111** D8
Victoria *Canada* 48°30N 123°25W **108** E7
Victoria *U.S.A.* 28°48N 97°0W **111** E7
Victoria □ *Australia* 37°0S 144°0E **98** H7
Victoria, L. *Africa* 1°0S 33°0E **96** E6
Victoria Falls *Zimbabwe* 17°58S 25°52E **97** H5
Victoria I. *Canada* 71°0N 111°0W **108** B8
Victoria Ld. *Antarctica* 75°0S 160°0E **55** D11
Victoria Str. *Canada* 69°31N 100°30W **108** C9
Victoriaville *Canada* 46°4N 71°56W **113** B12
Vidin *Bulgaria* 43°59N 22°50E **71** C10
Viedma, L. *Argentina* 49°30S 72°30W **121** G2
Vienna *Austria* 48°12N 16°22E **66** D9
Vienne *France* 45°31N 4°53E **68** D6
Vienne → *France* 47°13N 0°5E **68** C4
Vientiane *Laos* 17°58N 102°36E **83** B2
Vieques *Puerto Rico* 18°8N 65°25W **115** d
Vierge Pt. *St. Lucia* 13°49N 60°53W **115** f
Vierzon *France* 47°13N 2°5E **68** C5
Vietnam ■ *Asia* 19°0N 106°0E **83** B2
Vieux Fort *St. Lucia* 13°46N 60°58W **115** f
Vigévano *Italy* 45°19N 8°51E **70** B3
Vigo *Spain* 42°12N 8°41W **69** A1
Vijayawada *India* 16°31N 80°39E **85** L12
Vikna *Norway* 64°55N 10°58E **63** E6
Vila Nova de Gaia *Portugal* 41°8N 8°37W **69** B1
Vila Velha *Brazil* 20°20S 40°17W **122** D2
Vilaine → *France* 47°30N 2°27W **68** C2
Vilhelmina *Sweden* 64°35N 16°39E **63** E7
Vilhena *Brazil* 12°40S 60°5W **120** D3
Vilkitski Str. *Russia* 78°0N 103°0E **79** B12
Villa Bella *Bolivia* 10°25S 65°22W **120** D3
Villa María *Argentina* 32°20S 63°10W **121** F3
Villach *Austria* 46°37N 13°51E **66** E7
Villahermosa *Mexico* 17°59N 92°55W **114** D6
Villajoyosa *Spain* 38°30N 0°12W **69** C5
Villarrica *Paraguay* 25°40S 56°30W **121** E4
Villavicencio *Colombia* 4°9N 73°37W **120** B2
Ville-Marie *Canada* 47°20N 79°30W **112** B8
Villeneuve-sur-Lot *France* 44°24N 0°42E **68** D4
Vilnius *Lithuania* 54°38N 25°19E **63** G9
Vilyuy → *Russia* 64°24N 126°26E **79** C14
Vilyuysk *Russia* 63°40N 121°35E **79** C14
Viña del Mar *Chile* 33°0S 71°30W **121** F2
Vincennes *U.S.A.* 38°41N 87°32W **112** F4
Vindhya Ra. *India* 22°50N 77°0E **84** H10
Vineland *U.S.A.* 39°29N 75°2W **113** F10
Vinnytsya *Ukraine* 49°15N 28°30E **67** D15
Virden *Canada* 49°50N 100°56W **108** E9
Vire *France* 48°50N 0°53W **68** B3
Vírgenes, C. *Argentina* 52°19S 68°21W **121** H3
Virgin → *U.S.A.* 36°28N 114°21W **110** C4
Virgin Gorda *Br. Virgin Is.* 18°30N 64°26W **115** e
Virgin Is. (British) ⧄ *W. Indies* 18°30N 64°30W **115** e
Virgin Is. (U.S.) ⧄ *W. Indies* 18°20N 65°0W **115** e
Virginia *S. Africa* 28°8S 26°55E **97** K5
Virginia *U.S.A.* 47°31N 92°32W **111** A81
Virginia □ *U.S.A.* 37°30N 78°45W **112** G8
Virginia Beach *U.S.A.* 36°44N 76°0W **111** C11
Viroqua *U.S.A.* 43°34N 90°53W **112** D2
Vis *Croatia* 43°4N 16°10E **70** C7
Visalia *U.S.A.* 36°20N 119°18W **110** C3
Visby *Sweden* 57°37N 18°18E **63** F7
Viscount Melville Sd. *Canada* 74°10N 108°0W **109** B9
Vishakhapatnam *India* 17°45N 83°20E **85** L13
Vistula → *Poland* 54°22N 18°55E **67** A10
Vitebsk *Belarus* 55°10N 30°15E **72** C5
Viterbo *Italy* 42°25N 12°6E **70** C5
Viti Levu *Fiji* 17°30S 177°30E **99** D14
Vitim → *Russia* 59°26N 112°34E **79** D13
Vitória *Brazil* 20°20S 40°22W **122** D2
Vitória da Conquista *Brazil* 14°51S 40°51W **122** B2
Vitoria-Gasteiz *Spain* 42°50N 2°41W **69** A4
Vittória *Italy* 36°57N 14°32E **70** F6
Vizianagaram *India* 18°6N 83°30E **85** K13
Vlaardingen *Neths.* 51°55N 4°21E **65** C4
Vladikavkaz *Russia* 43°0N 44°35E **73** F7
Vladimir *Russia* 56°15N 40°30E **72** C7
Vladivostok *Russia* 43°10N 131°53E **79** E15
Vlissingen *Neths.* 51°26N 3°34E **65** C3
Vlorë *Albania* 40°32N 19°28E **71** D8
Vltava → *Czech Rep.* 50°21N 14°30E **66** D8
Voe *U.K.* 60°21N 1°16W **18** B15
Vogelsberg *Germany* 50°31N 9°12E **66** C5
Vohimena, Tanjon' i *Madag.* 25°36S 45°8E **97** K9
Voi *Kenya* 3°25S 38°32E **96** E7
Vojvodina □ *Serbia* 45°20N 20°0E **71** B9
Volga → *Russia* 46°0N 48°30E **73** E8
Volga Hts. *Russia* 51°0N 46°0E **73** D8
Volgodonsk *Russia* 47°33N 42°5E **73** E7
Volgograd *Russia* 48°40N 44°25E **73** E7
Volgograd Res. *Russia* 50°0N 45°20E **73** D8
Vologda *Russia* 59°10N 39°45E **72** C6
Volos *Greece* 39°24N 22°59E **71** E10
Volsk *Russia* 52°5N 47°22E **72** D8
Volta → *Ghana* 5°46N 0°41E **94** G6
Volta, L. *Ghana* 7°30N 0°0 **94** G6
Volta Redonda *Brazil* 22°31S 44°5W **122** D2
Volzhskiy *Russia* 48°56N 44°46E **73** E7
Vorkuta *Russia* 67°48N 64°20E **72** A11
Voronezh *Russia* 51°40N 39°10E **73** D6
Vosges *France* 48°20N 7°10E **68** B7
Vostok I. *Kiribati* 10°5S 152°23W **103** J12
Votkinsk *Russia* 57°0N 53°55E **72** C9
Vratsa *Bulgaria* 43°15N 23°30E **71** C10
Vryburg *S. Africa* 26°55S 24°45E **97** K4
Vryheid *S. Africa* 27°45S 30°47E **97** K6
Vulcano *Italy* 38°24N 14°58E **70** E6
Vung Tau *Vietnam* 10°21N 107°4E **83** B2
Vyazma *Russia* 55°10N 34°15E **72** C5
Vyborg *Russia* 60°43N 28°47E **72** B4
Vychegda → *Russia* 61°18N 46°36E **72** B8
Vyrnwy, L. *U.K.* 52°48N 3°31W **26** B6
Vyshniy Volochek *Russia* 57°30N 34°30E **72** C5

W

Waal → *Neths.* 51°37N 5°0E **65** C5
Wabasca → *Canada* 58°22N 115°20W **108** D8
Wabash *U.S.A.* 40°48N 85°49W **112** E5
Wabash → *U.S.A.* 37°48N 88°2W **112** G3
Waco *U.S.A.* 31°33N 97°9W **111** D7
Wad Medanî *Sudan* 14°28N 33°30E **95** F12
Waddenzee *Neths.* 53°6N 5°10E **65** A5
Waddesdon *U.K.* 51°51N 0°55W **25** C7
Waddingham *U.K.* 53°27N 0°32W **23** F7
Waddington *U.K.* 53°10N 0°32W **23** F7
Waddington, Mt. *Canada* 51°23N 125°15W **108** D7
Wadebridge *U.K.* 50°31N 4°51W **27** F4
Wadhurst *U.K.* 51°3N 0°20E **25** D9
Wadi Halfa *Sudan* 21°53N 31°19E **95** D12
Wager B. *Canada* 65°26N 88°40W **109** C11
Wagga Wagga *Australia* 35°7S 147°24E **98** H8
Wah *Pakistan* 33°45N 72°40E **84** C8
Wahiawä *U.S.A.* 21°30N 158°2W **110** H15
Waigeo *Indonesia* 0°20S 130°40E **83** D5
Wailuku *U.S.A.* 20°53N 156°30W **110** H16
Wainfleet All Saints *U.K.* 53°7N 0°15E **23** F9
Wakayama *Japan* 34°15N 135°15E **82** F4
Wake I. *Pac. Oc.* 19°18N 166°36E **102** F8
Wakefield *Jamaica* 18°26N 77°42W **114** a
Wakefield *U.K.* 53°41N 1°29W **23** E6
Wakkanai *Japan* 45°28N 141°35E **82** A7
Walberswick *U.K.* 52°19N 1°40E **25** B12
Wałbrzych *Poland* 50°45N 16°18E **66** C9
Walbury Hill *U.K.* 51°21N 1°28W **24** D6
Walcheren *Neths.* 51°30N 3°35E **65** C3
Waldron *U.K.* 50°56N 0°13E **25** E9
Wales □ *U.K.* 52°19N 4°43W **26** C4
Walgett *Australia* 30°0S 148°5E **98** G8
Walker L. *U.S.A.* 38°42N 118°43W **110** C3
Walla Walla *U.S.A.* 46°4N 118°20W **110** A3
Wallaceburg *Canada* 42°34N 82°23W **112** D6
Wallachia = Valahia *Romania* 44°35N 25°0E **67** F13
Wallasey *U.K.* 53°25N 3°2W **23** F2
Wallingford *U.K.* 51°35N 1°8W **24** C6
Wallis & Futuna, Is. *Pac. Oc.* 13°18S 176°10W **99** C15
Walls *U.K.* 60°14N 1°33W **18** B14
Wallsend *U.K.* 54°59N 1°31W **22** C5
Walmer *U.K.* 51°11N 1°25E **25** D11
Walney, I. of *U.K.* 54°6N 3°15W **22** D2
Walpole *U.K.* 52°45N 0°13E **25** A9
Walsall *U.K.* 52°35N 1°58W **23** G5
Walsenburg *U.S.A.* 37°38N 104°47W **110** C6
Walsoken *U.K.* 52°41N 0°11E **25** A9
Waltham *U.K.* 53°31N 0°7W **23** E8
Waltham Abbey *U.K.* 51°41N 0°1E **25** C9
Waltham Forest □ *U.K.* 51°35N 0°0 **25** C9
Waltham on the Wolds *U.K.* 52°50N 0°48W **23** G7
Walton-on-the-Naze *U.K.* 51°51N 1°17E **25** C11
Walvis Bay *Namibia* 23°0S 14°28E **97** J2
Wamba *Dem. Rep. of the Congo* 2°10N 27°57E **96** D5
Wanborough *U.K.* 51°33N 1°42W **24** C5
Wandsworth □ *U.K.* 51°27N 0°11W **25** D8
Wanganui *N.Z.* 39°56S 175°3E **99** H14
Wansbeck → *U.K.* 55°10N 1°32W **22** B5
Wantage *U.K.* 51°35N 1°25W **24** C6
Wanxian *China* 30°42N 108°20E **80** C5
Wapakoneta *U.S.A.* 40°34N 84°12W **112** E5
Warangal *India* 17°58N 79°35E **84** L11
Warboys *U.K.* 52°24N 0°4W **25** B8
Ward *Ireland* 53°26N 6°20W **31** B10
Wardha *India* 20°45N 78°39E **84** J11
Wardington *U.K.* 52°7N 1°17W **24** B6
Wardle *U.K.* 53°7N 2°35W **23** F3
Ward's Stone *U.K.* 54°1N 2°36W **23** D3
Ware *U.K.* 51°49N 0°0 **25** C8
Wareham *U.K.* 50°42N 2°7W **24** E4
Wark *U.K.* 55°6N 2°14W **22** B4
Warkworth *U.K.* 55°21N 1°37W **22** B5
Warley *U.K.* 52°30N 1°59W **23** H5
Warminster *U.K.* 51°12N 2°10W **24** D4
Warrego → *Australia* 30°24S 145°21E **98** G8
Warren *Mich., U.S.A.* 42°28N 83°1W **112** D6
Warren *Ohio, U.S.A.* 41°14N 80°49W **112** E7
Warren *Pa., U.S.A.* 41°51N 79°9W **112** E8
Warrenpoint *U.K.* 54°6N 6°15W **29** C9
Warri *Nigeria* 5°30N 5°41E **94** G7
Warrington *U.K.* 53°24N 2°35W **23** F3
Warrnambool *Australia* 38°25S 142°30E **98** H7
Warsaw *Poland* 52°14N 21°0E **67** B11
Warsaw *U.S.A.* 41°14N 85°51W **112** E5
Warsop *U.K.* 53°12N 1°9W **23** F6
Warta → *Poland* 52°35N 14°39E **66** B8
Warwick *U.K.* 52°18N 1°35W **24** B5
Warwick *U.S.A.* 41°42N 71°28W **113** E12
Warwickshire □ *U.K.* 52°14N 1°38W **24** B5
Wasatch Ra. *U.S.A.* 40°0N 111°30W **110** B4
Wash, The *U.K.* 52°58N 0°20E **25** A9
Washburn *U.S.A.* 46°40N 90°54W **112** B2
Washford *U.K.* 51°9N 3°21W **24** D2
Washington *U.K.* 54°55N 1°30W **22** C6
Washington *D.C., U.S.A.* 38°53N 77°2W **112** F9
Washington *Ind., U.S.A.* 38°40N 87°10W **112** F4
Washington *Pa., U.S.A.* 40°10N 80°15W **112** E7
Washington □ *U.S.A.* 47°30N 120°30W **110** A2
Washington, Mt. *U.S.A.* 44°16N 71°18W **113** C12
Washington I. *U.S.A.* 45°23N 86°54W **112** C4
Wasilla *U.S.A.* 61°35N 149°26W **108** C5
Waskaganish *Canada* 51°30N 78°40W **109** D12
Wast Water *U.K.* 54°26N 3°18W **22** D2
Watampone *Indonesia* 4°29S 120°25E **83** D4
Watchet *U.K.* 51°10N 3°19W **24** D2
Waterbeach *U.K.* 52°16N 0°12E **25** B9
Waterbury *U.S.A.* 41°33N 73°3W **113** E11
Waterford *Ireland* 52°15N 7°8W **31** D8
Waterford □ *Ireland* 52°10N 7°40W **31** D7
Waterford Harbour *Ireland* 52°8N 6°58W **31** D9
Watergate B. *U.K.* 50°26N 5°4W **27** G3
Waterloo *Belgium* 50°43N 4°25E **65** D4
Waterloo *Canada* 43°30N 80°32W **112** D7
Waterloo *Ill., U.S.A.* 38°20N 90°9W **112** F2
Waterloo *Iowa, U.S.A.* 42°30N 92°21W **111** B81
Watersmeet *U.S.A.* 46°16N 89°11W **112** B3
Watertown *N.Y., U.S.A.* 43°59N 75°55W **113** D10
Watertown *S. Dak., U.S.A.* 44°54N 97°7W **111** B7
Watertown *Wis., U.S.A.* 43°12N 88°43W **112** D3
Waterville *U.S.A.* 44°33N 69°38W **113** C13
Watford *U.K.* 51°40N 0°24W **25** C8
Watlington *Norfolk, U.K.* 52°40N 0°24E **25** A9
Watlington *Oxon., U.K.* 51°38N 1°0W **24** C6
Watrous *Canada* 51°40N 105°25W **108** D9
Watsa *Dem. Rep. of the Congo* 3°4N 29°30E **96** D5
Watseka *U.S.A.* 40°47N 87°44W **112** E4
Watson Lake *Canada* 60°6N 128°49W **108** C7
Watton *U.K.* 52°34N 0°51E **25** A10
Waukegan *U.S.A.* 42°22N 87°50W **112** D4
Waukesha *U.S.A.* 43°1N 88°14W **112** D31
Waupaca *U.S.A.* 44°21N 89°5W **112** C3
Waupun *U.S.A.* 43°38N 88°44W **112** D3
Wausau *U.S.A.* 44°58N 89°38W **112** C3
Wautoma *U.S.A.* 44°4N 89°18W **112** C3
Wauwatosa *U.S.A.* 43°2N 88°0W **112** D4
Waveney → *U.K.* 52°35N 1°39E **25** A12
Waver → *U.K.* 54°50N 3°15W **22** C2
Wâw *Sudan* 7°45N 28°1E **95** G11
Wawa *Canada* 47°59N 84°47W **112** B5
Waycross *U.S.A.* 31°13N 82°21W **111** D10
Wayne *U.S.A.* 38°13N 82°27W **112** F6
Waynesboro *U.S.A.* 38°4N 78°53W **112** F8
Waynesburg *U.S.A.* 39°54N 80°11W **112** F7
Wazirabad *Pakistan* 32°30N 74°8E **84** C9
Weald, The *U.K.* 51°4N 0°20E **25** D9
Wear → *U.K.* 54°55N 1°23W **22** C6
Weardale *U.K.* 54°44N 2°5W **22** C4
Wearhead *U.K.* 54°45N 2°13W **22** C4
Weaver → *U.K.* 53°17N 2°35W **23** F3
Weaverham *U.K.* 53°16N 2°35W **23** F3
Webster Springs *U.S.A.* 38°29N 80°25W **112** F7
Weddell Sea *Antarctica* 72°30S 40°0W **55** D1
Wedmore *U.K.* 51°13N 2°48W **24** D3
Wednesbury *U.K.* 52°34N 2°1W **23** G4
Wednesfield *U.K.* 52°37N 2°2W **23** G4
Weedon Bec *U.K.* 52°15N 1°5W **24** B6
Weifang *China* 36°44N 119°7E **81** C6
Weipa *Australia* 12°40S 141°50E **98** C7
Welch *U.S.A.* 37°26N 81°35W **112** G7
Weldon *U.K.* 55°17N 1°45W **22** B5
Welford *Northants., U.K.* 52°25N 1°3W **24** B6
Welford *W. Berkshire, U.K.* 51°27N 1°24W **24** D6
Welkom *S. Africa* 28°0S 26°46E **97** K5
Welland *Canada* 43°0N 79°15W **112** D8
Welland → *U.K.* 52°51N 0°5W **23** G8
Wellesley Is. *Australia* 16°42S 139°30E **98** D6
Wellingborough *U.K.* 52°19N 0°41W **25** B7
Wellington *N.Z.* 41°19S 174°46E **99** J13
Wellington *Somst., U.K.* 50°58N 3°13W **24** E2
Wellington *Telford & Wrekin, U.K.* 52°42N 2°30W **23** G3
Wellington, I. *Chile* 49°30S 75°0W **121** G2
Wellington Chan. *Canada* 75°0N 93°0W **109** B10
Wells *U.K.* 51°13N 2°39W **24** D3
Wells-next-the-Sea *U.K.* 52°57N 0°51E **25** A10
Wellsboro *U.S.A.* 41°45N 77°18W **112** E9
Wellsville *U.S.A.* 42°7N 77°57W **112** D9

Welney   Zwickau

Welney U.K. 52°31N 0°15E 25 A9
Wels Austria 48°9N 14°1E 66 D8
Welshpool U.K. 52°39N 3°8W 26 B7
Welton U.K. 53°18N 0°29W 23 F8
Welwyn Garden City U.K. 51°48N 0°12W 25 C8
Wem U.K. 52°52N 2°44W 23 G3
Wembury U.K. 50°19N 4°6W 27 G5
Wemindji Canada 53°0N 78°49W 109 D12
Wemyss Bay U.K. 55°53N 4°53W 20 C6
Wenatchee U.S.A. 47°25N 120°19W 110 A2
Wendover U.K. 51°45N 0°44W 25 C7
Wenlock Edge U.K. 52°30N 2°43W 23 H3
Wensleydale U.K. 54°17N 2°0W 22 D4
Wensu China 41°15N 80°10E 80 B3
Wensum → U.K. 52°40N 1°15E 25 A11
Wenzhou China 28°0N 120°38E 81 D7
Weobley U.K. 52°11N 2°50W 24 B3
Werrington U.K. 50°39N 4°23W 27 F5
Weser → Germany 53°36N 8°28E 66 B5
West Antarctica Antarctica 80°0S 90°0W 55 D15
West Auckland U.K. 54°38N 1°43W 22 C5
West Bank ■ Asia 32°6N 35°13E 86 C3
West Bend U.S.A. 43°25N 88°11W 112 D3
West Bengal □ India 23°0N 88°0E 85 H16
West Berkshire □ U.K. 51°25N 1°17W 24 D6
West Beskids Europe 49°30N 19°0E 67 D10
West Bridgford U.K. 52°55N 1°8W 23 G6
West Bromwich U.K. 52°32N 1°59W 23 G5
West Burra U.K. 60°5N 1°21W 18 B15
West Calder U.K. 55°51N 3°33W 21 C8
West Coker U.K. 50°55N 2°40W 24 E3
West Falkland Falk. Is. 51°40S 60°0W 121 H3
West Fen U.K. 53°5N 0°5W 23 F8
West Frankfort U.S.A. 37°54N 88°55W 111 C9
West Grinstead U.K. 50°58N 0°19W 25 E8
West Haddon U.K. 52°20N 1°3W 24 B6
West Kirby U.K. 53°23N 3°11W 23 F2
West Linton U.K. 55°46N 3°21W 21 C9
West Lulworth U.K. 50°37N 2°14W 24 E4
West Malling U.K. 51°17N 0°26E 25 D9
West Meon U.K. 51°1N 1°5W 24 D6
West Mersea U.K. 51°46N 0°56E 25 C10
West Midlands □ U.K. 52°26N 2°0W 23 H5
West Moors U.K. 50°49N 1°53W 24 E5
West Palm Beach U.S.A. 26°43N 80°3W 111 E10
West Point U.S.A. 37°32N 76°48W 112 G9
West Rasen U.K. 53°23N 0°24W 23 F8
West Seneca U.S.A. 42°51N 78°48W 112 D8
West Siberian Plain Russia 62°0N 75°0E 78 C9
West Sussex □ U.K. 50°55N 0°30W 25 E8
West Virginia □ U.S.A. 38°45N 80°30W 112 F7
West Yorkshire □ U.K. 53°45N 1°40W 23 E5
Westbourne U.K. 50°52N 0°55W 25 E7
Westbrook U.S.A. 43°41N 70°22W 113 D12
Westbury Shrops., U.K. 52°41N 2°55W 23 G3
Westbury Wilts., U.K. 51°15N 2°11W 24 D4
Westbury-on-Severn U.K. 51°50N 2°25W 24 C4
Wester Ross U.K. 57°37N 4°51W 19 G8
Westerham U.K. 51°16N 0°5E 25 D9
Western Australia □ Australia 25°0S 118°0E 98 F2
Western Ghats India 14°0N 75°0E 84 N9
Western Isles □ U.K. 57°30N 7°10W 18 G3
Western Sahara ■ Africa 25°0N 13°0W 94 D3
Westerschelde → Neths. 51°25N 3°25E 65 C3
Westerwald Germany 50°38N 7°56E 66 C4
Westfield U.K. 50°55N 0°35E 25 E10
Westhill U.K. 57°9N 2°19W 19 H13
Westhoughton U.K. 53°33N 2°31W 23 E3
Westmeath □ Ireland 53°33N 7°34W 28 D6
Westminster U.K. 39°34N 76°59W 112 F9
Westmoreland Barbados 13°13N 59°37W 115 g
Weston U.K. 52°51N 2°1W 23 G4
Weston U.S.A. 39°2N 80°28W 112 F7
Weston-super-Mare U.K. 51°21N 2°58W 24 D3
Westport Ireland 53°48N 9°31W 28 D2
Westray U.K. 59°18N 3°0W 19 D11
Westruther U.K. 55°45N 2°35W 21 C10
Westward Ho! U.K. 51°2N 4°15W 27 E5
Wetar Indonesia 7°48S 126°30E 83 D4
Wetaskiwin Canada 52°55N 113°24W 108 D8
Wetherby U.K. 53°56N 1°23W 23 E6
Wetwang U.K. 54°1N 0°35W 23 D7
Wewak Papua N. G. 3°38S 143°41E 98 A7
Wexford Ireland 52°20N 6°28W 31 D10
Wexford □ Ireland 52°20N 6°25W 31 D10
Wexford Harbour Ireland 52°20N 6°25W 31 D10
Wey → U.K. 51°22N 0°27W 25 D8
Weybourne U.K. 52°57N 1°9E 25 A11
Weybridge U.K. 51°22N 0°27W 25 D8
Weyburn Canada 49°40N 103°50W 108 E9
Weymouth U.K. 50°37N 2°28W 24 E4
Wha Ti Canada 63°8N 117°16W 108 C8
Whale Cove Canada 62°10N 92°34W 108 C10
Whales, B. of Antarctica 78°0S 160°0W 55 D12
Whalley U.K. 53°49N 2°24W 23 E4
Whalsay U.K. 60°22N 0°59W 18 B16
Whalton U.K. 55°8N 1°46W 22 B5
Whangarei N.Z. 35°43S 174°21E 99 H13
Whaplode U.K. 52°42N 0°3W 23 G8
Wharfe → U.K. 53°51N 1°9W 23 E6
Wharfedale U.K. 54°6N 2°1W 22 D4
Wheatley Hill U.K. 54°45N 1°23W 22 C6
Wheeler Pk. U.S.A. 38°57N 114°15W 110 C4
Wheeling U.S.A. 40°4N 80°43W 112 E7
Whernside U.K. 54°14N 2°24W 22 D4
Whicham U.K. 54°15N 3°22W 22 D2
Whimple U.K. 50°46N 3°20W 27 F7
Whipsnade U.K. 51°51N 0°32W 25 C7
Whissendine U.K. 52°43N 0°46W 23 G7
Whitburn U.K. 55°52N 3°40W 21 C8
Whitby U.K. 54°29N 0°37W 22 D7
Whitchurch Devon, U.K. 50°32N 4°9W 27 F5
Whitchurch Hants., U.K. 51°14N 1°20W 24 D6
Whitchurch Hereford, U.K. 51°51N 2°39W 24 C3
Whitchurch Shrops., U.K. 52°58N 2°40W 23 G3
White → Ark., U.S.A. 33°57N 91°5W 111 D8
White → Ind., U.S.A. 38°25N 87°45W 112 F4
White → Utah, U.S.A. 40°4N 109°41W 110 B5

White Esk → U.K. 55°13N 3°11W 21 D9
White Horse, Vale of U.K. 51°37N 1°30W 24 C5
White Horse Hill U.K. 51°34N 1°33W 24 C5
White Mts. Calif., U.S.A. 37°30N 118°15W 110 C3
White Mts. N.H., U.S.A. 44°15N 71°15W 111 B12
White Nile → Sudan 15°38N 32°31E 95 E12
White Sea Russia 66°30N 38°0E 72 A6
Whiteadder Water → U.K. 55°51N 2°25W 21 C11
Whitecourt Canada 54°10N 115°45W 108 D8
Whitefish Point U.S.A. 46°45N 84°59W 112 B5
Whitehall U.K. 44°22N 91°19W 112 C2
Whitehaven U.K. 54°33N 3°35W 22 C1
Whitehorse Canada 60°43N 135°3W 108 C6
Whitesand B. U.K. 50°21N 4°18W 27 G5
Whithorn U.K. 54°44N 4°26W 20 E7
Whitley Bay U.K. 55°3N 1°27W 22 B6
Whitstable U.K. 51°21N 1°3E 25 D11
Whittington Derby, U.K. 53°16N 1°26W 23 F6
Whittington Shrops., U.K. 52°52N 3°0W 23 G3
Whittlesey U.K. 52°33N 0°8W 25 A8
Whittlesford U.K. 52°7N 0°9E 25 B9
Whitwell Derby, U.K. 53°17N 1°12W 23 F6
Whitwell I. of W., U.K. 50°36N 1°15W 24 E6
Whitwick U.K. 52°45N 1°22W 23 G6
Whitworth U.K. 53°39N 2°11W 23 E4
Wholdaia L. Canada 60°43N 104°20W 108 C9
Whyalla Australia 33°2S 137°30E 98 G6
Wiarton Canada 44°40N 81°10W 112 C7
Wiay U.K. 57°24N 7°13W 18 H3
Wichita U.S.A. 37°42N 97°20W 111 C7
Wichita Falls U.S.A. 33°54N 98°30W 110 D7
Wick U.K. 58°26N 3°5W 19 F11
Wickford U.K. 51°36N 0°33E 25 C10
Wickham U.K. 50°54N 1°11W 24 E6
Wickham Market U.K. 52°9N 1°23E 25 B11
Wicklow Ireland 52°59N 6°3W 31 C10
Wicklow □ Ireland 52°57N 6°25W 31 C10
Wicklow Hd. Ireland 52°58N 6°0W 31 C11
Wicklow Mts. Ireland 52°58N 6°26W 31 C10
Wicklow Mts. △ Ireland 53°6N 6°21W 31 B11
Wickwar U.K. 51°36N 2°23W 24 C4
Widecombe U.K. 50°34N 3°49W 27 F6
Widemouth U.K. 50°47N 4°34W 27 F4
Widnes U.K. 53°23N 2°45W 23 F3
Wiener Neustadt Austria 47°49N 16°16E 66 E9
Wiesbaden Germany 50°4N 8°14E 66 C5
Wigan U.K. 53°33N 2°38W 23 E3
Wight, I. of U.K. 50°41N 1°17W 24 E6
Wight, Isle of □ U.K. 50°41N 1°17W 24 E6
Wigmore U.K. 52°19N 2°51W 24 B3
Wigston U.K. 52°35N 1°6W 23 G6
Wigton U.K. 54°50N 3°10W 22 C2
Wigtown U.K. 54°53N 4°27W 20 E7
Wigtown B. U.K. 54°46N 4°15W 20 E7
Wilhelm, Mt. Papua N. G. 5°50S 145°1E 98 B8
Wilhelmshaven Germany 53°31N 8°7E 66 B5
Wilkes-Barre U.S.A. 41°15N 75°53W 113 E10
Wilkes Land Antarctica 69°0S 120°0E 55 D9
Willemstad Neth. Ant. 12°5N 68°55W 115 E11
Willenhall U.K. 52°36N 2°2W 23 G4
Willesborough U.K. 51°8N 0°56E 25 D10
Williams Lake Canada 52°10N 122°10W 108 D7
Williamsburg U.S.A. 37°16N 76°43W 112 G9
Williamson U.S.A. 37°41N 82°17W 112 G6
Williamsport U.S.A. 41°15N 77°1W 112 E9
Willingdon U.K. 50°47N 0°17E 25 E9
Williston S. Africa 31°20S 20°53E 97 L4
Williston L. Canada 56°0N 124°0W 108 D7
Williton U.K. 51°9N 3°19W 24 D2
Willmar U.S.A. 45°7N 95°3W 111 A7
Willoughby U.K. 53°13N 0°12E 23 F9
Willoughton U.K. 50°47N 3°7W 27 F7
Wilmington Del., U.S.A. 39°45N 75°33W 113 F10
Wilmington N.C., U.S.A. 34°14N 77°55W 111 D11
Wilmslow U.K. 53°19N 2°13W 23 F4
Wilnecote U.K. 52°36N 1°39W 23 G5
Wilton U.K. 51°5N 1°51W 24 D5
Wiltshire □ U.K. 51°18N 1°53W 24 D5
Wimblington U.K. 52°31N 0°4E 25 A9
Wimborne Minster U.K. 50°48N 1°59W 24 E5
Wincanton U.K. 51°3N 2°24W 24 D4
Winchelsea U.K. 50°55N 0°43E 25 E10
Winchester U.K. 51°4N 1°18W 24 D6
Winchester Ky., U.S.A. 37°59N 84°11W 112 G6
Winchester Va., U.S.A. 39°11N 78°10W 112 F8
Wind → U.S.A. 43°12N 108°12W 110 B5
Wind River Range U.S.A. 43°0N 109°30W 110 B5
Windermere U.K. 54°23N 2°55W 22 D3
Windhoek Namibia 22°35S 17°4E 97 J3
Windrush → U.K. 51°43N 1°24W 24 C6
Windsor Canada 42°18N 83°0W 109 E11
Windsor U.K. 51°29N 0°36W 25 D7
Windward Is. W. Indies 13°0N 61°0W 115 E12
Windward Passage Caribbean 20°0N 74°0W 115 D10
Wing U.K. 51°53N 0°43W 25 C7
Wingham U.K. 51°16N 1°13E 25 D11
Winisk → Canada 55°17N 85°5W 109 D11
Winkleigh U.K. 50°50N 3°58W 27 F6
Winkler Canada 49°10N 97°56W 108 E10
Winneba Ghana 5°25N 0°36W 94 G5
Winnebago, L. U.S.A. 44°0N 88°26W 112 D3
Winnemucca U.S.A. 40°58N 117°44W 110 B3
Winnipeg Canada 49°54N 97°9W 108 E10
Winnipeg, L. Canada 52°0N 97°0W 108 D10
Winnipegosis L. Canada 52°30N 100°0W 108 C9
Winona U.S.A. 44°3N 91°39W 111 B8
Winooski U.S.A. 44°29N 73°11W 113 C11
Winsford U.K. 53°12N 2°31W 23 F3
Winslow U.K. 51°57N 0°52W 25 C7
Winslow U.S.A. 35°2N 110°42W 110 C4
Winster U.K. 53°9N 1°39W 23 F5
Winston-Salem U.S.A. 36°6N 80°15W 111 C10
Winterborne Abbas U.K. 50°42N 2°33W 24 E3
Winterthur Switz. 47°30N 8°44E 66 E5
Winterton N. Lincs., U.K. 53°39N 0°37W 23 E7

Winterton Norfolk, U.K. 52°43N 1°41E 25 A12
Winton Australia 22°24S 143°3E 98 E7
Wirksworth U.K. 53°6N 1°35W 23 F5
Wirral U.K. 53°25N 3°0W 23 F2
Wisbech U.K. 52°41N 0°9E 25 A9
Wisborough Green U.K. 51°2N 0°30W 25 D7
Wisconsin □ U.S.A. 44°45N 89°30W 111 B9
Wisconsin Rapids U.S.A. 44°23N 89°49W 112 C3
Wishaw U.K. 55°46N 3°54W 21 C8
Wiske → U.K. 54°19N 1°27W 22 D6
Witbank S. Africa 25°51S 29°14E 97 K5
Witham U.K. 51°48N 0°40E 25 C10
Witham → U.K. 52°59N 0°2W 23 G8
Withern U.K. 53°18N 0°8E 23 F9
Withernsea U.K. 53°44N 0°1E 23 E9
Witley U.K. 51°9N 0°39W 25 D7
Witney U.K. 51°48N 1°28W 24 C6
Wittersham U.K. 51°0N 0°43E 25 D10
Wiveliscombe U.K. 51°2N 3°19W 24 D2
Wivenhoe U.K. 51°51N 0°59E 25 C10
Wkra → Poland 52°27N 20°44E 67 B11
Wloclawek Poland 52°40N 19°3E 67 B10
Woburn U.K. 51°59N 0°36W 25 C7
Woburn Sands U.K. 52°1N 0°39W 25 B7
Wodonga Australia 36°5S 146°50E 98 H8
Woking U.K. 51°19N 0°34W 25 D7
Wokingham U.K. 51°24N 0°49W 25 D7
Wolf Rock U.K. 49°57N 5°49W 27 H2
Wolfsburg Germany 52°25N 10°48E 66 B6
Wolin Poland 53°50N 14°37E 66 B8
Wollaston L. Canada 58°7N 103°10W 108 D9
Wollaston Pen. Canada 69°30N 115°0W 108 C8
Wollongong Australia 34°25S 150°54E 98 G9
Wolsingham U.K. 54°44N 1°52W 22 C5
Wolverhampton U.K. 52°35N 2°7W 23 G4
Wolverton U.K. 52°3N 0°47W 25 B7
Wolviston U.K. 54°38N 1°18W 22 C6
Wombwell U.K. 53°32N 1°25W 23 E6
Wŏnsan N. Korea 39°11N 127°27E 81 C7
Wonston U.K. 51°8N 1°18W 24 D6
Woodbridge U.K. 52°6N 1°20E 25 B11
Woodbury U.K. 50°41N 3°24W 27 F7
Woodhall Spa U.K. 53°10N 0°12W 23 F8
Woodhouse U.K. 53°22N 1°21W 23 F6
Woodley U.K. 51°27N 0°53W 25 D7
Woodroffe, Mt. Australia 26°20S 131°45E 98 F5
Woods, L. of the Canada 49°15N 94°45W 108 E10
Woodstock N.B., Canada 46°11N 67°37W 109 E13
Woodstock Ont., Canada 43°10N 80°45W 112 D7
Woodstock U.K. 51°51N 1°20W 24 C6
Woodstock U.S.A. 42°19N 88°27W 112 D3
Wookey U.K. 51°13N 2°41W 24 D3
Wookey Hole U.K. 51°14N 2°40W 24 D3
Wool U.K. 50°40N 2°12W 24 E4
Woolacombe U.K. 51°10N 4°13W 27 E5
Wooler U.K. 55°33N 2°1W 22 A4
Woonsocket U.S.A. 42°0N 71°31W 113 E11
Wootton Bassett U.K. 51°32N 1°54W 24 C5
Wootton Wawen U.K. 52°16N 1°47W 24 B5
Worcester S. Africa 33°39S 19°27E 97 L3
Worcester U.K. 52°11N 2°12W 24 B4
Worcester U.S.A. 42°16N 71°48W 113 D12
Worcestershire □ U.K. 52°13N 2°10W 24 B4
Worfield U.K. 52°34N 2°21W 23 G4
Workington U.K. 54°39N 3°33W 22 C1
Worksop U.K. 53°18N 1°7W 23 F6
Worms Germany 49°37N 8°21E 66 D5
Wortham U.K. 52°21N 1°3E 25 B11
Worthing Barbados 13°5N 59°35W 115 g
Worthing U.K. 50°49N 0°21W 25 E8
Worthington U.S.A. 43°37N 95°36W 111 B7
Wotton under Edge U.K. 51°37N 2°20W 24 C4
Wragby U.K. 53°18N 0°17W 23 F8
Wrangel I. Russia 71°0N 180°0E 79 B19
Wrangell U.S.A. 56°28N 132°23W 108 D6
Wrangell Mts. U.S.A. 61°30N 142°0W 108 C5
Wrangle U.K. 53°3N 0°7E 23 F9
Wrath, C. U.K. 58°38N 5°1W 18 C7
Wrekin, The U.K. 52°41N 2°32W 23 G3
Wrentham U.K. 52°23N 1°40E 25 B12
Wrexham U.K. 53°3N 3°0W 26 A8
Wrexham □ U.K. 53°1N 2°58W 26 D3
Wrigley Canada 63°16N 123°37W 108 C7
Writtle U.K. 51°44N 0°27E 25 C9
Wroclaw Poland 51°5N 17°5E 67 C9
Wroughton U.K. 51°31N 1°47W 24 C5
Wroxham U.K. 52°42N 1°24E 25 A11
Wu Jiang → China 29°40N 107°20E 80 D5
Wuhai China 39°47N 106°52E 80 C5
Wuhan China 30°31N 114°18E 81 C6
Wuhu China 31°22N 118°21E 81 C6
Wukari Nigeria 7°51N 9°42E 94 G7
Würzburg Germany 49°46N 9°55E 66 D5
Wushi China 41°9N 79°13E 80 B2
Wutongqiao China 29°22N 103°50E 80 D5
Wuwei China 37°57N 102°34E 80 C5
Wuxi China 31°33N 120°18E 81 C7
Wuyi Shan China 27°0N 117°0E 81 D6
Wuzhong China 38°2N 106°12E 80 C5
Wuzhou China 23°30N 111°18E 81 D6
Wye U.K. 51°10N 0°57E 25 D10
Wye → U.K. 51°38N 2°40W 24 C3
Wylye → U.K. 51°5N 1°51W 24 D5
Wymondham Leics., U.K. 52°45N 0°43W 23 G7
Wymondham Norfolk, U.K. 52°35N 1°7E 25 A11
Wyndham Australia 15°33S 128°3E 98 D4
Wyoming □ U.S.A. 43°0N 107°30W 110 B5
Wyre → U.K. 53°52N 2°57W 23 E3
Wyre Forest U.K. 52°24N 2°24W 23 H4

X

Xaçmaz Azerbaijan 41°31N 48°42E 73 F8
Xainza China 30°58N 88°35E 80 C3
Xalapa Mexico 19°32N 96°55W 114 D5
Xankāndi Azerbaijan 39°52N 46°49E 73 G8
Xenia U.S.A. 39°41N 83°56W 112 F6

Xiaguan China 25°32N 100°16E 80 D5
Xiamen China 24°25N 118°4E 81 D6
Xi'an China 34°15N 109°0E 81 C5
Xiang Jiang → China 28°55N 112°50E 81 D6
Xiangfan China 32°2N 112°8E 81 C6
Xiangtan China 27°51N 112°54E 81 D6
Xianyang China 34°20N 108°40E 81 C5
Xichang China 27°51N 102°19E 80 D5
Xigazê China 29°5N 88°45E 80 D3
Xing'an China 25°38N 110°40E 81 D6
Xinghua China 32°58N 119°48E 81 C6
Xingu → Brazil 1°30S 51°53W 120 C4
Xining China 36°34N 101°40E 80 C5
Xinxiang China 35°18N 113°50E 81 C6
Xinyang China 32°6N 114°3E 81 C6
Xique-Xique Brazil 10°50S 42°40W 122 B2
Xuanhua China 40°40N 115°2E 81 B6
Xuzhou China 34°18N 117°10E 81 C6

Y

Yablonovyy Ra. Russia 53°0N 114°0E 79 D13
Yabucoa Puerto Rico 18°3N 65°53W 115 d
Yacuiba Bolivia 22°0S 63°43W 120 E3
Yakima U.S.A. 46°36N 120°31W 110 A2
Yakutat U.S.A. 59°33N 139°44W 108 D6
Yakutsk Russia 62°5N 129°50E 79 C14
Yala Thailand 6°33N 101°18E 83 C2
Yalong Jiang → China 26°40N 101°55E 80 D5
Yalta Ukraine 44°30N 34°10E 73 F5
Yalu Jiang → China 39°55N 124°19E 81 C7
Yamagata Japan 38°15N 140°15E 82 D7
Yamaguchi Japan 34°10N 131°32E 82 F2
Yamal Pen. Russia 71°0N 70°0E 78 B8
Yambol Bulgaria 42°30N 26°30E 71 C12
Yamethin Burma 20°29N 96°18E 85 J20
Yamoussoukro Ivory C. 6°49N 5°17W 94 G4
Yampa → U.S.A. 40°32N 108°59W 110 B5
Yamuna → India 25°30N 81°53E 85 G12
Yamzho Yumco China 28°48N 90°35E 80 D4
Yan'an China 36°35N 109°26E 81 C5
Yanbu 'al Baḥr Si. Arabia 24°0N 38°5E 86 E4
Yancheng China 33°35N 120°8E 81 C7
Yangambi Dem. Rep. of the Congo 0°47N 24°24E 96 D4
Yangjiang China 21°50N 111°59E 81 D6
Yangquan China 37°58N 113°31E 81 C6
Yangtze → China 31°48N 121°10E 81 C7
Yangzhou China 32°21N 119°26E 81 C6
Yanji China 42°59N 129°30E 81 B7
Yankton U.S.A. 42°53N 97°23W 111 B7
Yanqi China 42°5N 86°35E 80 B3
Yantai China 37°34N 121°22E 81 C7
Yaoundé Cameroon 3°50N 11°35E 96 D2
Yap Pac. Oc. 9°30N 138°10E 102 G5
Yapen Indonesia 1°50S 136°0E 83 D5
Yaqui → Mexico 27°37N 110°39W 114 B2
Yaraka Australia 24°53S 144°3E 98 E7
Yarcombe U.K. 50°51N 3°5W 27 F7
Yare → U.K. 52°35N 1°38E 25 A12
Yarkant He → China 40°26N 80°59E 80 B3
Yarkhun → Pakistan 36°17N 72°30E 84 A8
Yarm U.K. 54°31N 1°21W 22 C6
Yarmouth Canada 43°50N 66°7W 109 E13
Yarmouth U.K. 50°42N 1°29W 24 E6
Yaroslavl Russia 57°35N 39°55E 72 C6
Yarrow U.K. 55°33N 3°1W 21 C9
Yarumal Colombia 6°58N 75°24W 120 B2
Yate U.K. 51°32N 2°25W 24 C4
Yathkyed L. Canada 62°40N 98°0W 108 C10
Yatsushiro Japan 32°30N 130°40E 82 G2
Yatton U.K. 51°23N 2°49W 24 D3
Yauco Puerto Rico 18°2N 66°51W 115 d
Yavari → Peru 4°21S 70°2W 120 C2
Yaxley U.K. 52°31N 0°16W 25 A8
Yazd Iran 31°55N 54°27E 87 D8
Yazoo → U.S.A. 32°22N 90°54W 111 D8
Yazoo City U.S.A. 32°51N 90°25W 111 D8
Yealmpton U.K. 50°21N 4°1W 27 G5
Yecheng China 37°54N 77°26E 80 C2
Yekaterinburg Russia 56°50N 60°30E 78 D8
Yelets Russia 52°40N 38°30E 72 D6
Yell U.K. 60°35N 1°5W 18 A15
Yell Sd. U.K. 60°33N 1°15W 18 A15
Yellow Sea China 35°0N 123°0E 81 C7
Yellowhead Pass Canada 52°53N 118°25W 108 D8
Yellowknife Canada 62°27N 114°29W 108 C8
Yellowstone → U.S.A. 47°59N 103°59W 110 A6
Yellowstone Nat. Park △ U.S.A. 44°40N 110°30W 110 B5
Yemen ■ Asia 15°0N 44°0E 88 E3
Yenisey → Russia 71°50N 82°40E 78 B10
Yeo → U.K. 51°2N 2°54W 24 D3
Yeola India 20°2N 74°30E 84 J9
Yeovil U.K. 50°57N 2°38W 24 E3
Yerevan Armenia 40°10N 44°31E 73 F7
Yes Tor U.K. 50°41N 4°0W 27 F5
Yeu, Î. d' France 46°42N 2°20W 68 C2
Yevpatoriya Ukraine 45°15N 33°20E 73 E5
Yeysk Russia 46°40N 38°12E 73 E6
Yibin China 28°45N 104°32E 80 D5
Yichang China 30°40N 111°20E 81 C6
Yichun China 47°44N 128°52E 81 B7
Yinchuan China 38°30N 106°15E 80 C5
Yingkou China 40°37N 122°18E 81 B7
Yining China 43°58N 81°10E 80 B3
Yishan China 24°28N 108°38E 80 D5
Yiyang China 28°35N 112°18E 81 D6
Yogyakarta Indonesia 7°49S 110°22E 83 D3
Yokkaichi Japan 34°55N 136°38E 82 F5
Yokohama Japan 35°27N 139°28E 82 F6
Yonago Japan 35°25N 133°19E 82 F3
Yong'an China 25°59N 117°25E 81 D6
Yonkers U.S.A. 40°56N 73°52W 113 E11
Yonne → France 48°23N 2°58E 68 B5
York U.K. 53°58N 1°6W 23 E6

York U.S.A. 39°58N 76°44W 112 F9
York, C. Australia 10°42S 142°31E 98 C7
York, Vale of U.K. 54°15N 1°25W 22 D6
Yorkshire Dales △ U.K. 54°12N 2°10W 22 D4
Yorkshire Wolds U.K. 54°8N 0°31W 22 D7
Yorkton Canada 51°11N 102°28W 108 D9
Yosemite Nat. Park △ U.S.A. 37°45N 119°40W 110 C3
Yoshkar Ola Russia 56°38N 47°55E 72 C8
Youghal Ireland 51°56N 7°52W 30 E7
Youghal B. Ireland 51°55N 7°49W 30 E7
Youlgreave U.K. 53°11N 1°40W 23 F5
Youngstown U.S.A. 41°6N 80°39W 112 E7
Yoxall U.K. 52°46N 1°47W 23 G5
Yoxford U.K. 52°16N 1°31E 25 B12
Yozgat Turkey 39°51N 34°47E 73 G5
Yreka U.S.A. 41°44N 122°38W 110 B2
Ystalyfera U.K. 51°46N 3°48W 26 D6
Ythan → U.K. 57°19N 1°59W 19 H14
Yu Jiang → China 23°22N 110°3E 81 D6
Yuan Jiang → China 28°55N 111°50E 81 D6
Yuba City U.S.A. 39°8N 121°37W 110 C2
Yucatán Mexico 19°30N 89°0W 114 C7
Yucatan Channel Caribbean 22°0N 86°30W 114 C7
Yuci China 37°42N 112°46E 81 C6
Yueyang China 29°21N 113°5E 81 D6
Yugoslavia = Serbia ■ Europe 43°20N 20°0E 71 B9
Yukon → U.S.A. 62°32N 163°54W 108 C3
Yukon Territory □ Canada 63°0N 135°0W 108 C6
Yulin China 38°20N 109°30E 81 C5
Yuma U.S.A. 32°43N 114°37W 110 D4
Yumen China 39°50N 97°30E 80 C4
Yungas Bolivia 17°0S 66°0W 120 D3
Yunnan □ China 25°0N 102°0E 80 D5
Yurimaguas Peru 5°55S 76°7W 120 C2
Yushu China 33°5N 96°55E 80 C4
Yutian China 36°52N 81°42E 80 C3
Yuzhno-Sakhalinsk Russia 46°58N 142°45E 79 E16
Yuzhou China 34°10N 113°28E 81 C6
Yvetot France 49°37N 0°44E 68 B4

Z

Zāb al Kabīr → Iraq 36°1N 43°24E 86 B5
Zābol Afghan. 32°0N 67°0E 87 D11
Zabrze Poland 50°18N 18°50E 67 C10
Zacatecas Mexico 22°47N 102°35W 114 C4
Zadar Croatia 44°8N 15°14E 70 B6
Zagaoua Chad 15°30N 22°24E 95 E10
Zagazig Egypt 30°40N 31°30E 95 B12
Zagreb Croatia 45°50N 15°58E 70 B7
Zagros Mts. Iran 33°45N 48°5E 86 C7
Zāhedān Iran 29°30N 60°50E 87 D10
Zahlah Lebanon 33°52N 35°50E 86 C3
Zakynthos Greece 37°47N 20°54E 71 F9
Zambezi → Africa 18°35S 36°20E 97 H7
Zambia ■ Africa 15°0S 28°0E 97 G5
Zamboanga Phil. 6°59N 122°3E 83 C4
Zamora Mexico 19°59N 102°16W 114 D4
Zamora Spain 41°30N 5°45W 69 B3
Zamość Poland 50°43N 23°15E 67 C12
Zanesville U.S.A. 39°56N 82°1W 112 F6
Zanjān Iran 36°40N 48°35E 86 B7
Zanzibar Tanzania 6°12S 39°12E 96 F7
Zaouiet Reggâne Algeria 26°32N 0°3E 94 C6
Zaoyang China 32°10N 112°45E 81 C6
Zaozhuang China 34°50N 117°35E 81 C6
Zapala Argentina 39°0S 70°5W 121 F2
Zaporozhye Ukraine 47°50N 35°10E 73 E6
Zaragoza Spain 41°39N 0°53W 69 B5
Zaranj Afghan. 30°55N 61°55E 87 D10
Zárate Argentina 34°7S 59°0W 121 F4
Zaria Nigeria 11°0N 7°40E 94 F7
Zarzis Tunisia 33°31N 11°2E 95 B8
Zaskar Mts. India 33°15N 77°30E 84 C10
Zāwiyat al Bayḍā Libya 32°50N 21°44E 95 B10
Zeebrugge Belgium 51°19N 3°12E 65 C3
Zeeland □ Neths. 51°30N 3°50E 65 C3
Zeil, Mt. Australia 23°30S 132°23E 98 E5
Zeist Neths. 52°5N 5°15E 65 B5
Zelenograd Russia 56°1N 37°12E 72 C6
Zenica Bos.-H. 44°10N 17°57E 71 B7
Zhangjiakou China 40°48N 114°55E 81 B6
Zhangye China 38°50N 100°23E 80 C5
Zhangzhou China 24°30N 117°35E 81 D6
Zhanjiang China 21°15N 110°20E 81 D6
Zhanyi China 25°38N 103°48E 80 D5
Zhaoqing China 23°0N 112°20E 81 D6
Zhaotong China 27°20N 103°44E 80 D5
Zhejiang □ China 29°0N 120°0E 81 D7
Zhengzhou China 34°45N 113°34E 81 C6
Zhezqazghan Kazakhstan 47°44N 67°40E 78 E8
Zhigansk Russia 66°48N 123°27E 79 C14
Zhlobin Belarus 52°55N 30°0E 72 D5
Zhob Pakistan 31°20N 69°31E 84 D6
Zhongdian China 27°48N 99°42E 80 D4
Zhumadian China 32°59N 114°2E 81 C6
Zhytomyr Ukraine 50°20N 28°40E 67 C15
Zibo China 36°47N 118°3E 81 C6
Zielona Góra Poland 51°57N 15°31E 66 C8
Zigong China 29°15N 104°48E 80 D5
Ziguinchor Senegal 12°35N 16°20W 94 F2
Žilina Slovak Rep. 49°12N 18°42E 67 D10
Zimbabwe ■ Africa 19°0S 30°0E 97 H5
Zinder Niger 13°48N 8°50E 94 F7
Ziway, L. Ethiopia 8°0N 38°50E 88 F2
Zlatoust Russia 55°10N 59°40E 72 C10
Zlín Czech Rep. 49°14N 17°40E 67 D9
Zonguldak Turkey 41°28N 31°50E 73 F5
Zrenjanin Serbia 45°22N 20°23E 71 B9
Zug Switz. 47°10N 8°31E 66 E5
Zunyi China 27°42N 106°53E 80 D5
Zürich Switz. 47°22N 8°32E 66 E5
Zuwārah Libya 32°58N 12°1E 95 B8
Zvishavane Zimbabwe 20°17S 30°2E 97 J6
Zwelitsha S. Africa 32°55S 27°22E 97 L5
Zwickau Germany 50°44N 12°30E 66 C7

SATELLITE IMAGE OF THE SEVERN ESTUARY

This Landsat false-colour composite image was captured in October. The cities of Bristol and Cardiff are clearly visible, as are the Black Mountains and the Brecon Beacons in Wales. Images such as this are used for recording and monitoring land use. *(EROS)*